HOSPITALITY INDUSTRY MANAGERIAL ACCOUNTING

EDUCATIONAL INSTITUTE BOOKS

HOSPITALITY INDUSTRY MANAGERIAL ACCOUNTING

Ninth Edition

Raymond S. Schmidgall, Ph.D., CPA
Agnes L. DeFranco, Ed.D

LEGAL NOTICE

ISBN 978-0-86612-753-0 (print version)

Printed in the USA

2 3 4 5 6 7 8 9 10 28 27 26 25 24 23

CONTENTS

13 Capital Budgeting 598

14 Lease Accounting 636

We are grateful for the industry support that makes this book possible. Exhibits throughout the book are courtesy of several hospitality companies and companies serving the hospitality industry, including ARAMARK corporation, CBRE, Hilton Hotels, Integrated Hospitality Management Ltd., Marriott International, and Oberoi Holdings (Wendy's).

In addition, many users of this textbook, especially professors in hospitality management programs, have provided helpful suggestions for revision. A special thanks to Michael Flannery from Purdue University-Calumet, Chuck Day of IHG, Edward Bushaw from the Gulf Coast Culinary Institute, Christopher Garland of Four Seasons, Joanna Fee of Plante Moran, Tanner Lucas, Food Service Director of ARAMARK, Rosa Tang, Director of Finance and Accounting of Marriott International, Inc., Ricki Oberoi, President, and Edith Hernandez, Director of Operations of Oberoi Holdings, Michael W. Duffy, SVP, Chief Accounting and Risk Officer of Hilton, Ralph Miller, President and Lisa M. Hubenig, Corporate Controller of Integrated Hospitality Management Ltd., Sean Hennessey from New York University, Robert Mandelbaum, Research Director at CBRE, Dennis Reynolds, Dean of the Conrad N. Hilton College of Global Hospitality Leadership, and Frank Wolfe, CEO of HFTP. Their significant comments and contributions to the recent editions are much appreciated. Rather than try to list additional contributors and err in leaving someone out, we simply say thank you to the entire group of hospitality educators teaching hospitality accounting.

Finally, Ray thanks his wife, Barbara, his daughters, Erica, Monica, Kristina, and Joanna; and his sons-in-law, Jeremy, Bryan, and Jim. Agnes also thanks her husband John, her son GianCarlo, and her daughter-in-law, Elizabeth. They all have been extremely patient during the long time periods it has taken us to write and revise this book.

Dedication

In memory of Raymond Klein Schmidgall, loving father, entrepreneur, and leader of people by example; and K.F. Lee & S.W. Lee, devoted and inspiring parents.

Hospitality Industry Managerial Accounting, Ninth Edition, presents managerial accounting concepts and explains how they apply to specific operations within the hospitality industry. This book is written not only for managers in the hospitality industry, but also for hospitality students at both the two-year and four-year college levels. Readers of this textbook should already be familiar with basic accounting concepts and procedures or have taken an introductory course in basic accounting.

Each chapter begins by posing a number of questions that managers in the hospitality industry may have regarding accounting concepts that will be developed within the chapter. At the close of each chapter, there are a number of review questions and a set of 25 problems, designed to test the reader's understanding of the concepts covered within the chapter. Appendices are also included in the back of this book that present more detailed approaches to concepts mentioned in the text.

The text consists of 15 chapters. It begins with an overview of accounting in Chapter 1. Chapters 2 through 4 cover the three basic financial statements—the balance sheet, the income statement, and the statement of cash flows, respectively. While the presentations of the balance sheet and the statement of cash flows are similar to the coverage found in most financial accounting texts, the presentation of the income statement is based on the various schedules from the Uniform Systems of Accounts for the Lodging Industry. Chapter 3 also looks at income statements for restaurants and clubs.

Chapter 5 focuses on ratio analysis as a means of interpreting information reported on financial statements. For each ratio represented, the chapter outlines its purpose, the source of data needed for the calculation of the ratios, the formulas by which they are calculated, and the interpretation of the ratio results from the varying viewpoints of owners, creditors, and managers. A new section on flow through and flex ratios is also incorporated.

Chapters 6, 7, and 8 cover basic cost concepts, cost-volume-profit analysis, and cost approaches to pricing. Chapter 6 presents the various types of costs and how managers can identify the relevant costs in particular decision-making situations. New sections on Out-of-Pocket costs and Activity-Based Costing (ABC) have been added. The discussion of cost-volume-profit analysis in Chapter 7 is presented in both equation and graphic form. In addition, this chapter discusses and illustrates the determination of each breakeven point. Chapter 8 takes a cost approach to pricing and includes pricing examples for food, beverages, and rooms, as well as dynamic pricing and measuring revenue management yield. An excerpt of an article regarding designing menus for the web is also included.

Forecasting methods and operating budgets are the subject of Chapter 9 and 10 respectively. Chapter 9 focuses on basic mathematical models for forecasting sales. This chapter also presents hospitality industry examples of labor and sales forecasting procedures at Hilton Hotels, Oberoi Holdings (Wendy's), and Aramark. Chapter 10 discusses how budgets are prepared, how budgets are used for control in operations, and how the operations budget process may take different forms at multi-unit and single unit hospitality enterprises. Several exhibits for this chapters have been provided by Marriott International Inc. and Integrated Hospitality Management Ltd.

Chapter 11 covers cash management and includes sections on cash budgeting and managing working capital, gift card accounting, unsecured bank loans, as well as a new section on mobile payment. Chapter 12 presents basic requirements of internal accounting control for various accounting functions, including cash receipts, cash disbursements, accounts receivable, accounts payable, inventories, payroll, fixed assets, marketable securities, and the Sarbanes Oxley act of 2002. A new section covering technology in internal control is included in this chapter. Capital budgeting is the subject of Chapter 13. The capital budgeting models presented include pay back, accounting rate of return, net present value, internal rate of return, and profitability index.

The final two chapters deal with lease accounting and income taxes. Although both of these topics are generally found in financial accounting texts, they are addressed here because managers of hospitality operations should have some knowledge in each of these areas. Due to ASC 842 and IFRS 16, Chapter 14 on lease accounting has been updated and includes illustrations of accounting for various types of leases. Chapter 15 on income taxes does not dwell on tax details. Instead, it provides an overview of the elements of taxes, discuss tax avoidance, and presents the advantages and disadvantages of various forms of business organization from a tax point of view, including the Tax Cut and Jobs Act of 2017.

Students studying *Hospitality Industry Managerial Accounting* may earn an AHLEI certificate, a recognized credential demonstrating acquired knowledge in the course area. Learn more about academic and industry credentials and additional training and resources by visiting www.ahlei.org.

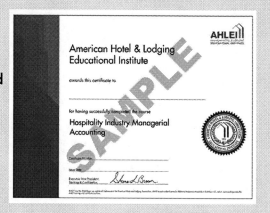

Raymond S. Schmidgall

Raymond S. Schmidgall is the Hilton Hotels Professor Emeritus at The School of Hospitality Business at Michigan State University. He holds a B.B.A. in accounting from Evangel University, and an M.B.A. and a Ph.D. in accounting from Michigan State University. He is also a Certified Public Accountant. He has published numerous articles in *Lodging, Club Management, The Bottomline, The Consultant, Restaurant Business*, and the *Cornell Hospitality Quarterly*. Dr. Schmidgall has written or co-written five accounting textbooks oriented to the hospitality industry, including basic texts on financial management, financial accounting, and managerial accounting. He has conducted workshops and seminars for the Club Managers Association of America, American Hotel and Lodging Association, National Automatic Merchandising Association, and Hospitality Financial and Technology Professionals. Dr. Schmidgall is the Secretary of the International Association of Hospitality Financial Management Educators (iAHFME) and is also on the editorial board of its journal—*Journal of Hospitality Financial Management*. He has served on a number of hospitality organizations and committees over the years including being a member of the AHLA Financial Management Committee and was involved in several revisions of the *Uniform System of Accounts for the Lodging Industry*. Dr. Schmidgall was also a member of the International Council on Hotel, Restaurant, and Institutional Education's Finance Committee and Investment Committee, an editorial board member of *The Journal of Hospitality and Tourism Research*, the Associate Editor of the *Cornell Hospitality Quarterly*, and a member of several professional accounting associations. He currently serves on the Board of Directors of Evangel University, Eagle Vision, University Club of Michigan State University, and New Life Assembly.

Agnes L. DeFranco

Agnes L. DeFranco has served as the Associate Dean and Interim Dean of the Conrad N. Hilton College of Global Hospitality Leadership, and the Associate Vice President for Undergraduate Studies for the University of Houston. She earned her B.S., M.B.A., and Ed.D all from the University of Houston and is currently a full professor and the Conrad N. Hilton Distinguished Chair at the Hilton College. In addition to her refereed articles, Dr. DeFranco has a number of non-refereed publications and authored or co-authored eight textbooks. Her grants include a Department of State USIA research grant on Curriculum Development in International Convention and Conference Management at Meio University in Okinawa, Japan, and three USDA Cochran Programs on Restaurant Management. Her other educational grants include a grant with the Houston Endowment on transfer student success, and over 10 other grants on topics such as on online course development, diversity and curriculum development, empirical analysis of the relationship between financial ratios and profitability, and financial forecasting. Teaching is her passion, and she has won the Teaching Excellence Award of the Hilton College multiple times and also the University of Houston's Teaching Excellence Career Award. Dr. DeFranco is a past global president and Paragon winner of the Hospitality Financial and Technology Professionals, past treasurer of the International Council on Hotel, Restaurant, and Institutional Education, and past presidents for Phi Kappa Phi and Phi Beta Delta at the University of Houston. She has conducted presentations across the United States and internationally. Besides serving on committees for HFTP, she is a member of the Financial Management Committee of the AHLA, and a board member of the University of Houston Alumni Association Foundation.

1

INTRODUCTION TO MANAGERIAL ACCOUNTING

Chapter 1 Outline

Competencies

1. Describe characteristics of the hospitality industry and identify the major function of hospitality accounting. (pp. 5–12)

2. Apply generally accepted accounting principles to hospitality situations. (pp. 12–18)

3. Distinguish between cash basis accounting and accrual basis accounting. (pp. 18–19)

4. Describe the six branches of accounting. (pp. 19–20)

5. Explain the fundamental accounting equation and identify normal account balances for various types of accounts. (pp. 20–21)

6. Explain the nine steps in the accounting cycle. (pp. 21–24)

7. Describe four basic forms of business organization. (pp. 24–26)

account

accounting cycle

accrual basis accounting

adjusting entries

assets

balance

business entity principle

C corporation

cash basis accounting

conservatism principle

consistency principle

continuity of the business
    unit principle

corporation

cost principle

credit

debit

dividends

financial audit

full disclosure principle

fundamental accounting
    equation

general journal

general partner

generally accepted
    accounting principles
    (GAAP)

going concern principle

journals

ledger accounts

liabilities

limited liability company
    (LLC)

limited partner

limited partnership

matching principle

materiality principle

objective evidence principle

owners' equity

partnership

permanent accounts

posting

revenue recognition
    principle

S corporation

sole proprietorship

specialized journal

temporary accounts

trial balance

unit of measurement
    principle

Hospitality is a huge and growing industry. A property manager needs more knowledge today than ever before and will need even more tomorrow. Managerial accounting focuses upon those aspects of accounting that concern hospitality managers most. These aspects include internal financial statements, budgeting, internal control, and costs. This introductory chapter will provide answers to many questions about the hospitality industry and accounting, including the following:

1. How does the hospitality industry differ from many other industries?

2. Why are food and beverage inventories relatively low in hospitality operations?

3. What are three aspects of seasonality in lodging properties?

4. What is the scope of the accounting function in hotels?

5. What are the major principles of accounting?

6. What are the various branches of accounting?

7. Why are rooms, in essence, perishable inventory?

8. What are the four forms of business organization?

This chapter will present an overview of the hospitality industry and then focus on the accounting function within the industry. We will briefly review the principles, branches, and mechanics of accounting; discuss the accounting cycle; and describe the four forms of business organization. The chapter concludes with a brief look at ethical issues and hospitality accounting.

1.1 OVERVIEW OF THE HOSPITALITY INDUSTRY

The hospitality industry consists of several different types of operations providing both products and services to its clients or guests. It includes hotels, motels, motor hotels, inns, quick-service restaurants, fine-dining restaurants, bed and breakfasts, cafeterias, resorts, country clubs, and city clubs, to mention a few. Most of these hospitality operations serve both the traveling public and local residents. While this is particularly true of food and beverage operations, many lodging properties also market their accommodations to local residents by promoting "weekend escape" packages.

Properties in the lodging segment of the hospitality industry range from single-unit operations of fewer than ten rooms to Marriott Hotels, with thirty brand names, 5,493 franchised and licensed properties, and 873,912 rooms.[1] There are also many mega hotels around the world, with the First World Hotel & Plaza in Malaysia having over 7,350 rooms, while the Venetian Resort in Las Vegas, with its complex linking the Venetian Las Vegas and the Palazzo, has almost 7,100 rooms. The differences among lodging operations are vast. At one extreme, there are budget hotels and motels providing only rooms, and, at the other, luxury properties providing nearly every imaginable service a guest might desire.

There are also many different types of foodservice operations. Properties in the food and beverage segment of the hospitality industry range from the single-unit operation with window-only service to the McDonald's Corporation, with over 39,000 restaurants throughout the world. In the club segment of the hospitality industry, there are some operations with fewer than 200 members and others with over 15,000 members. Lodging facilities in the United States added $660 billion to the U.S. gross domestic product in the 2020s, while foodservice industry revenues exceeded $659 billion.

Exhibits 1.1 and 1.2 provide further insights into financial aspects of the hospitality industry. Exhibit 1.1 illustrates what happens to the average revenue dollar in the lodging industry—where it comes from and where it goes. Exhibit 1.2 illustrates this for the average revenue dollar in two segments of the restaurant industry. Notice that in the lodging industry, food sales are the second-largest source of total revenues. Also notice that the largest category of expense for both lodging and restaurant operations involves salaries, wages, and benefits. Finally, note that for foodservice operations, income before income taxes represents a relatively small percentage of total revenues.

Seasonality of Business

Although both manufacturing firms and hospitality operations frequently experience seasonal fluctuations in sales volume, hospitality operations also deal with activity variations throughout the day. Check-in times vary, but many hotels are busiest with check-ins between 3 and 5 p.m. Check-out at many hotels is extremely busy between 7 and 9 a.m. and between 11 a.m. and 1 p.m. Similarly,

Exhibit 1.1	U.S. Lodging Industry Dollar – 2021

Source and Disposition of the Industry Dollar

Revenues	Percent of Total
Rooms	73.0.%
Food and Beverage	17.3
Other Operated Departments	6.7
Miscellaneous Income	3.0
Total	100.0 %
Costs and Expenses	
Labor Costs and Related Expenses	40.5%
Operating Expenses	37.1
Cost of Sales	5.7
Non-Operating Income and Expenses	12.4
Management Fees	4.3
Total	100.0%

Source: Trends in the Hotel Industry – U.S. Edition 2022 (Atlanta: CBRE Hotels Research, 2022)

Exhibit 1.2	The Restaurant Industry Dollar

	Full-Service Restaurants		Limited-Service Restaurants	
	Average Checks			
	Under $18	$18 and over	Under $10	$10 and over
Where It Came From*				
Food and Beverage Sales	100%	100%	100%	100%
Where It Went*				
Cost of Sales – Food	34.5	34.6	34.3	33.3
Cost of Sales – Beverage (Liquor)	**	22.6	**	**
Cost of Sales – Beverage (Beer)	**	27.0	**	**
Cost of Sales – Beverage (Wine)	**	31.0	**	**
Salaries & Wages[1]	32.7	32.5	28.9	25.2
Restaurant Occupancy Costs	5.3	5.9	**	2.9
Other Controllable Costs	10.8	14.6	**	12.3
Other	**	0.3	**	**
Income Before Income Tax	5.6	6.1	8.1	6.2

[1]Includes employee benefits
*All figures are medians, are computed individually for each cost category, and are rounded. All amounts are reflected as a percentage of total sales except Food and Beverage costs which are based on their respective sales.
**Insufficient data
Source: National Restaurant Association and Deloitte & Touche LLP, *Restaurant Operations Report* 2016 Edition.

some foodservice operations may be full from 7:30 to 8:30 a.m., 11:30 a.m. to 1:30 p.m., and 6 to 8 p.m., and nearly empty during other hours of the day. Hospitality business may also vary during the week.

A common measure of activity for lodging operations is paid occupancy percentage. Paid occupancy percentage indicates what percentage of the rooms available for sale are actually sold. It is calculated by dividing the number of rooms sold by the number of rooms available. Transient hotels—that is, hotels catering primarily to businesspeople—may experience very high occupancy, even close to or at 100 percent occupancy—Monday through Thursday and at lows of 30 percent occupancy Friday through Sunday, averaging 70 percent for the week. Weekly seasonality for many resort hotels results in the opposite distribution; their busiest periods are usually weekends rather than weekdays. In addition, their multiple occupancy, determined by dividing the number of rooms with more than one guest by the total number of rooms occupied, is higher than that of transient hotels. Generally, multiple occupancy is highest at resort hotels and lowest at transient hotels.

Seasonality throughout the year is a serious factor for many hotels. Many resorts are open for only one season of the year. Other lodging establishments, although open all year, have much more sales activity during certain times of the year. For example, the occupancy of many Florida hotels is higher during the winter months as vacationers from the north descend on Florida to enjoy its warmth and sunshine. At the same time, ski resorts occupancy percentages are higher in the winter months.

Exhibit 1.3 shows the monthly occupancy rates in selected U.S. cities for 2019. As mentioned earlier, for a city such as Orlando, Florida, the occupancy was 83.1 percent and 88.4 percent for February and March, respectively. Boston hotels registered 84.1 percent occupancy in June and 54.4 percent in January, while hotels in New York City registered a high of 90.5 percent in October and a low of 71.4 percent in January. Thus, Exhibit 1.3 reveals both seasonal fluctuations and large differences among cities.[2]

Short Distribution Chain and Time Span

In a foodservice operation, there is a relatively fast conversion of raw materials into a finished product and of the product into cash. Like manufacturing operations, foodservice operations must offer products that meet the consumer's expectations. However, the distribution chain and time span is considerably shorter for hospitality "products" than for most consumer goods.

For example, a new automobile purchased from a dealer may have been assembled several months before the sale, thousands of miles away, by a different company using finished parts supplied by more than 50 companies. In hospitality operations, inventory is often purchased one day and sold the next. The product is produced, sold, and consumed at the same location, often in less than two hours, sometimes within minutes. The foodservice "manufacturer" purchases the raw ingredients, prepares them to suit the consumer's tastes, and serves the finished product on the premises. The foodservice operator will in many cases receive immediate feedback on the quality of the food and service product, especially if it failed to meet the consumer's expectations.

As a result of this short distribution chain and time span, hospitality operations do little advance production. Thus, they maintain a minimal inventory of the goods they provide. This is reflected in the fact that major operations in the hospitality industry generally have less than 5 percent of their total assets invested in inventory of goods for resale. In contrast, the inventory of many major manufacturing firms equals at least 30 percent of their total assets.

	2019 Average	Jan	Feb	Mar	Apr	May	Jun	Jul	Aug	Sep	Oct	Nov	Dec
Overall US	66.1	54.7	62.0	68.3	67.9	68.6	73.7	73.7	71.3	67.3	69.2	61.7	54.3
Anaheim/Santa Ana, CA	78.0	68.6	76.3	82.3	78.2	75.1	81.6	86.6	81.3	76.2	82.1	75.1	73.1
Atlanta, GA	69.4	65.5	69.9	74.8	73.1	71.0	73.1	73.8	68.6	68.4	71.3	65.4	58.1
Boston, MA	73.8	54.4	61.7	68.5	77.8	81.3	84.1	83.4	82.6	81.4	83.1	69.3	58.3
Chicago, IL	69.6	47.6	56.4	65.4	71.8	77.2	83.2	79.0	78.9	76.2	77.3	65.3	56.5
Dallas, TX	67.6	62.0	67.4	72.4	71.7	69.1	72.8	70.1	65.1	66.5	72.9	64.9	56.1
Denver, CO	73.8	59.5	65.8	71.2	73.7	77.3	86.2	88.4	84.3	81.2	78.3	64.3	55.7
Detroit, MI	65.4	53.4	57.9	63.5	64.4	67.1	72.5	74.5	73.9	70.2	71.7	62.9	53.1
Houston, TX	63.0	55.6	65.8	69.2	66.3	66.5	63.9	65.1	60.6	61.1	67.8	60.6	53.2
Los Angeles/Long Beach, CA	79.7	71.6	79.5	81.7	81.7	78.5	84.1	85.8	84.7	79.2	81.4	76.7	71.2
Miami/Hialeah, FL	75.9	78.3	84.0	85.7	81.0	76.1	72.9	75.3	71.6	60.7	68.5	78.2	78.1
Minneapolis/St Paul, MN-WI	66.6	51.3	59.2	62.9	67.7	68.1	78.9	77.9	81.3	74.5	70.1	56.5	50.4
Nashville, TN	73.4	57.1	68.2	79.1	78.5	78.8	80.6	77.0	75.7	77.3	81.9	69.8	57.4
New Orleans, LA	69.5	64.5	73.0	84.1	76.9	73.4	70.9	60.3	60.6	66.5	73.5	69.1	60.9
New York, NY	86.2	71.4	76.5	84.0	88.0	89.3	90.4	89.0	89.9	89.6	90.5	86.9	88.4
Norfolk/Virginia Beach, VA	63.5	43.3	50.5	61.8	68.9	68.7	77.7	79.6	78.4	63.6	63.9	57.3	48.0
Oahu Island, HI	84.1	82.4	86.5	80.4	79.9	82.9	87.9	88.0	89.0	84.9	82.8	82.0	83.1
Orlando, FL	76.3	74.5	83.1	88.9	80.8	74.8	77.9	78.1	68.9	61.5	75.0	76.5	75.5
Philadelphia, PA-NJ	70.0	51.7	59.5	68.5	73.2	76.5	81.0	76.2	75.4	72.5	75.7	70.6	58.7
Phoenix, AZ	70.7	73.5	83.7	87.5	75.2	68.8	65.6	60.0	63.3	64.0	71.5	72.4	63.3
San Diego, CA	76.7	69.2	75.4	80.1	79.6	74.0	85.2	86.7	82.6	77.7	75.0	71.8	62.7
San Francisco/San Mateo, CA	82.0	73.0	80.0	79.9	83.2	84.0	86.7	84.2	89.4	86.4	86.9	78.2	72.2
Seattle, WA	73.9	61.3	66.6	73.4	71.9	75.8	84.4	84.7	84.7	81.0	75.3	67.0	60.7
St Louis, MO-IL	64.7	46.1	56.0	67.2	67.6	70.0	75.9	71.4	71.1	71.2	68.9	60.5	50.3
Tampa/St Petersburg, FL	72.3	70.7	85.1	87.7	77.2	72.4	73.6	73.2	65.8	60.5	67.1	67.5	67.1
Washington, DC-MD-VA	70.5	50.5	60.3	73.4	79.7	80.4	81.5	77.5	71.6	72.4	77.6	67.1	54.6

Source: STR

A Labor-Intensive Industry

There is another important difference between the hospitality and manufacturing industries. In the manufacturing sector, automation has greatly reduced the need for labor. This is not the case in the hospitality industry. As we have already seen, payroll expense is a major element in the cost of sales for both the lodging and foodservice segments of the hospitality industry. The seasonality of hospitality sales also contributes to the labor intensity of the industry. The busy check-in and check-out times during daily hotel operations require much labor to provide quality service. Similarly, foodservice operations have increased labor needs for spurts of activity throughout the day. Scheduling personnel for busy times is important if a hospitality operation is to generate profits while meeting guests' needs and wants.

Another important dimension of food and beverage operations in lodging facilities is the need to provide service even when it may not be profitable. For example, foodservice must be provided to guests even on low-occupancy days, and room service must always be available in first-class properties.

The short distribution chain and time span characteristic of the delivery and consumption of hospitality products and services also contributes to the industry's labor intensity. Personnel must prepare, produce, sell, and serve the operation's offerings. Labor must be available to prepare food when a guest wants it. Some foodservice operations promise the finished product within minutes after the guest's order is taken. Such prompt guest-oriented service can only be provided by a large and efficient staff. The total labor cost may be as low as 20 percent of the total revenue dollar at a quick-service restaurant or over 50 percent at a private club. Controlling labor costs while satisfying the needs and wants of guests is crucial to the success of any hospitality operation.

Major Investment in Fixed Assets

In addition to being labor-intensive, hospitality properties are, for the most part, fixed-asset-intensive. Lodging facilities provide rooms for guests to relax, rest, entertain, and conduct business in. The room as a product is carried as a fixed asset, and its cost is written off (depreciated) over time. The basic cost of the room is the same whether or not it is occupied. In this sense, a room is the most perishable product a lodging operation has, because the revenue lost from an unsold room can never be regained. The construction cost of lodging facilities, including the furniture and fixtures, may vary between $40,000 and $1 million per room. The cost of rooms represents a major investment by lodging operations, and the fixed assets of major hotels constitute between 55 percent and 85 percent of their total assets. In contrast, the fixed assets of many manufacturing companies approximate only 30 percent of their total assets.

This overview has shown that the hospitality industry is greatly affected by seasonal (daily, weekly, monthly, and yearly) sales fluctuations, by the short distribution chain and quick consumption of its offerings, by the need for a large, efficient work force, and by large investment in fixed assets. These characteristics of hospitality operations give shape to the challenges that the accounting function must face within the industry.

1.2 THE ACCOUNTING FUNCTION IN THE HOSPITALITY INDUSTRY

The accounting function in hospitality industry properties is performed by a group of specialists ranging from bookkeepers to executives with such titles as executive vice president, director of finance and accounting, and controller. Chief accounting executives are responsible for typical accounting functions such as receivables, payables, payroll, and, in some cases, storage and security. Exhibit 1.4 summarizes the results of a survey of 278 hotel *property* (as opposed to *corporate*) controllers and shows a wide range of reported responsibilities.

The size of an accounting staff may vary widely—from a part-time bookkeeper in a 10-room motel to several hundred people in a large hotel or restaurant chain. The size of the accounting staff at an individual property varies with the size and diversity of the hotel's operations. The accounting staff at hotels with more than 1,000 rooms ranges from 30 to 50 people. The accounting staff at one major worldwide hotel company totals approximately 250, while the corporate accounting staff (accounts payable, payroll, internal audit, tax, and so forth) at a major foodservice headquarters totals 150. Exhibit 1.5 is a sample organization chart for the accounting function at a large hotel.

Exhibit 1.4	Responsibilities of Hotel Controllers

Area	Percentage Reporting Responsibility
General Accounting	92%
Accounts Payable	92%
Accounts Receivable	91%
Computer System—Accounting	88%
Payroll	87%
Night Audits	80%
Cash Management	77%
Beverage Controls	67%
Food Controls	65%
Cashiers	64%
Tax Returns	61%
Purchasing	60%
Computer System—Front Office Reservations	58%
Receiving	52%
Storage	52%
Investments	42%
Security	22%

Exhibit 1.5 | Sample Accounting Department Organization Chart, Large Hotel

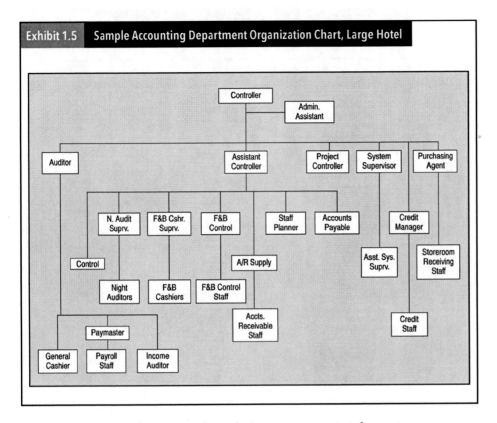

The accounting function within a lodging property is information-oriented—that is, its major role is providing information to users. For external users such as financial institutions, accounting usually communicates through financial statements. Internally, accounting provides a wide variety of financial reports, including operating statements. The operating statements are formatted to reflect revenues and related expenses by areas of responsibility. In addition to the income statement of the property as a whole, departmental statements are prepared for each department generating revenues and incurring expenses, such as rooms, food and beverage, and gift shop. Service centers such as sales and marketing and property operation and maintenance also provide separate statements.

Regardless of the size of an operation's accounting department, the diversity of its responsibilities, or the number and types of reports produced, the accounting staff is responsible for providing *service*. The accounting staff must work closely with the managers within all of the hotel's departments in order for the hospitality property to meet its objectives. Exhibit 1.6, an organization chart of a major hotel, reflects the relative position of the controller and their staff within the hotel's organization.

Uniform Systems of Accounts

For internal purposes (that is, for management use), uniform accounting systems, commonly called *uniform systems of accounts*, have been developed. These systems are popular among hospitality organizations because they provide a turn-key accounting system. Uniform systems have been tested over time and refined to meet the ever-changing needs of management.

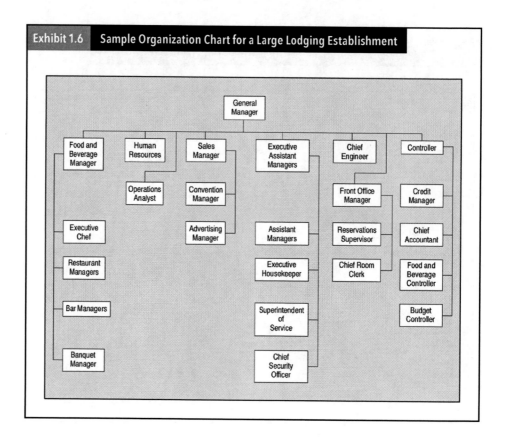

Exhibit 1.6   Sample Organization Chart for a Large Lodging Establishment

1.3 PRINCIPLES OF ACCOUNTING

In order to understand accounting methods, you must understand basic accounting principles. These **generally accepted accounting principles** (often referred to by the acronym *GAAP*) provide a uniform basis for preparing financial statements. Although not etched in stone, accounting principles have become accepted over time through common usage and also through the work of such major accounting bodies as the American Institute of Certified Public Accountants, the American Accounting Association, and the Financial Accounting Standards Board (FASB).

Students of hospitality accounting may often wonder why an accounting transaction is recorded in a particular way at a particular time or why some asset value is not changed at some point. Generally, the reasons relate to accounting principles. The following subsections briefly discuss several generally accepted accounting principles.

Cost

The **cost principle** states that when a transaction is recorded, it is the transaction price or cost that establishes the accounting value for the product or service purchased. For example, if a restaurateur buys a dishwasher, the agreed-upon price between the restaurant and the supplier determines the amount to be recorded. If the agreed-upon price is $10,000, then the dishwasher is initially valued at $10,000 in the restaurant's accounting records. The supplier may have acquired the dishwasher from the manufacturer for $8,000 and the restaurant may receive an offer of $11,000 for it the day it is purchased; however, it is the actual cost that establishes the amount to be recorded. If amounts other than cost (such as estimates or appraisals) were used to record transactions, then accounting records would lose their usefulness. When cost is the basis for recording a transaction, the buyer and seller determine the amount to be recorded. This amount is generally an objective and fair measure of the value of the goods or services purchased.

When the value of *current* assets is clearly less than the cost recorded on the books, this decline in value must be recognized. Thus, the *conservatism principle* (to be discussed in a later subsection) overrides the cost principle. For example, many properties carry inventory at the lower of cost or current market value. On the other hand, property and equipment (frequently called fixed assets) are normally carried at cost less the depreciated amounts and are not reduced to market value as long as management plans to retain them for their useful life. This treatment of property and equipment is based on the *going-concern principle* (also discussed in a later subsection).

Business Entity

The **business entity principle** states that accounting and financial statements are based on the concepts that (1) each business is a business entity that maintains its own set of accounts, and (2) these accounts are separate from the other financial interests of the owners. For example, if a hotel owner decides to take some food home from the hotel for personal use, it should be properly charged to the owner's account. Recording business activity separately from the owner's personal affairs allows a reasonable determination of the property's profitability. Not only does separate recording provide excellent information for managing the business, it is also necessary for properly filing tax returns.

Continuity of the Business Unit (Going Concern)

According to the **continuity of the business unit** or **going concern principle**, in preparing the accounting records and reports it is assumed that the business will continue indefinitely and that liquidation is not in prospect—in other words, the business is a going concern. This assumption is based on the concept that the real value of the hotel or motel is its ability to earn a profit, rather than the value its assets would bring in liquidation. According to this concept, the market value of the property and equipment need not appear on the financial statements, and prepaid expenses are considered assets. If there is a reasonable chance the hospitality property may be unable to continue operations in the near future, allowance for this future event should be reflected in the financial statements. This may be best accomplished by reducing asset values to their market values.

Unit of Measurement

The financial statements are based on transactions expressed in monetary terms. The **unit of measurement principle** states that it is also necessary to use a stable unit of value so that transactions from past periods and the current period can be included on the same statement.

In the late 1970s and early 1980s, annual inflation (as measured by the Consumer Price Index) exceeded 10 percent. The FASB responded by requiring large hospitality firms to show the current replacement cost of their property and equipment in footnotes to their financial statements. For some lodging properties, the current values of property and equipment exceeded twice the amount of the fixed assets carried on the books. Since inflation was relatively low from the mid-1980s through the 2010s, the FASB has rescinded this reporting requirement.

Throughout the 1980s, some hospitality businesses, such as Hilton Hotels Corporation, provided financial information in addition to that required by the FASB. Hilton provided the traditional financial statements based on historical cost, as well as certain figures to reflect current replacement cost. It also provided certain figures based on the present value of income streams from its fixed assets.

Objective Evidence

Accounting transactions and the resulting accounting records should be based as much as possible on the **objective evidence principle**. Generally, this evidence is an invoice and/or a canceled check. However, estimates must be assumed in the absence of such objective evidence. For example, suppose that the owner of a restaurant contributes equipment, purchased several years ago for personal use, to a restaurant corporation in exchange for 100 shares of stock. Further assume that there is no known market value for the restaurant corporation's stock. The owner may believe the equipment is worth $1,200, while the original catalog shows the cost several years ago of $1,400, and an appraiser appraises the equipment at $850. In this example, the most objective estimate of its value today would be the appraiser's estimate of $850.

Full Disclosure

The financial statements must provide information on all the facts pertinent to the interpretation of the financial statements. This **full disclosure principle** is accomplished either by reporting the information in the body of the financial statements or in footnotes to the financial statements. Footnote disclosures might include the accounting methods used, changes in accounting methods, contingent liabilities, events occurring after the financial statement date, and unusual and non-recurring items. An example of each type of disclosure is presented in Exhibit 1.7.

| Exhibit 1.7 | Types of Disclosure |

Type of Disclosure	Example
Accounting methods used	The use of straight-line method of depreciation
Change in the accounting methods	A change from depreciating a fixed asset using the straight-line method to using the double declining balance method
Contingent liability	A lawsuit against the company for alleged failure to provide adequate security for a guest who suffered personal injury
Events occurring after the financial statement date	A fire destroys significant assets of the hotel company one week after the end of the year
Unusual and non-recurring items	A hotel firm in Michigan suffers significant losses due to an earthquake

Consistency

Several accounting methods are often available for reporting a specific kind of activity. Management chooses the method most appropriate under the circumstances. For example, there are several ways to determine inventory values, and there are several methods of depreciating fixed assets. The **consistency principle** requires that, once an accounting method has been adopted, it should be followed from period to period unless a change is warranted and disclosed. The consistency principle allows a user of financial information to make reasonable comparisons between periods. Without consistent accounting, trends indicated by supposedly comparable financial statements might be misleading. When it becomes necessary to change to another method, the change must be disclosed and the dollar effect on earnings and/or the balance sheet must be reported.

The consistency principle does *not* dictate that an operation must or even should use the same accounting methods for preparing tax returns that it uses to prepare financial statements for external users. The principle does not even require that a method selected for one element of a company be used for all similar elements. For example, the straight-line method of depreciation may be used to depreciate one hotel and an accelerated method of depreciation may be used to depreciate another hotel owned by the same company.

Matching

The **matching principle** refers to relating expenses to revenues. For example, suppose that a hotel purchases a computerized reservations system that will benefit the hotel for several years. The cost is therefore recorded as a fixed asset and the cost of the system is written off over the system's life. The result is a partial write-off of the fixed asset each year against the revenues generated in part by using the system. This process is referred to as matching and is the basis for adjusting entries at the end of each accounting period. The matching principle is used when transactions are recorded on an accrual rather than cash basis. The accrual basis and cash basis of accounting are discussed in a later subsection.

Conservatism

The **conservatism principle** calls for recognizing expenses as soon as possible, but delaying the recognition of revenues until they are ensured. The practical result is to be conservative (low) in recognizing net income for the current year. It is not proper to deliberately understate net income; however, many accountants wish to be cautious in recognizing revenues and "generous" in recognizing expenses.

A good example of this is the accounting treatment of lawsuits. If a hotel is a plaintiff in a lawsuit and its legal counsel indicates the case will be won and estimates the amount of settlement, the amount is not recorded as revenue until a judgment is rendered. On the other hand, if the same hotel is a defendant in a lawsuit and its legal counsel indicates the hotel will lose the lawsuit and most likely will pay a stated amount, this "expense" is recognized immediately.

Conservatism is also apparent in the valuation of inventory at the lower of cost or current market value and the recognition of non-refundable deposits for future banquets as a liability until the banquet is catered.

Materiality

According to the **materiality principle**, events or information must be accounted for if they "make a difference" to the user of the financial information. An item is material in comparison to a standard. Some accountants have attempted to establish materiality by rules of thumb; for example, an item may be recognized if it exceeds a certain percentage of total assets or total income. However, this approach fails to address an item's relative importance over time. In addition, several immaterial items may be material when viewed collectively.

The materiality principle is often applied to fixed assets. Tangible items with useful lives beyond one year are commonly recorded as fixed assets. However, when such items cost less than a certain amount (specified by the board of directors of the purchasing organization), they are expensed because the cost is considered immaterial. An example would be a wastebasket. A $59 wastebasket might have a useful life of ten years, but if the company has set a $500 limit for recording expenditures as fixed assets, the cost of the wastebasket would be immaterial and the wastebasket would be expensed.

When a hospitality property provides footnotes to supplement its financial statement, only material or potentially material items are presented.

Revenue Recognition

The **revenue recognition principle** determines when revenues are to be reported. Under the little-used cash accounting system, revenues are recognized when cash is received, regardless of when goods and services are provided. Under the much more commonly used accrual accounting system, it is more complicated. Revenues are recognized when they are realized or realizable (that is, when the related goods or services are provided and payment is reasonably assured), regardless of when the cash related to the sale is received.

Reporting Revenue on a Gross Versus Net Basis. Although it is not actually a timing issue as revenue recognition is, the question of how much revenue should be recognized also needs to be addressed. Consider a hotel that rents videos to its guests for $10 each and pays the provider of the videos $9 each. Should the hotel recognize revenue on each cell as $10 (gross) or simply $1 (net) determined by subtracting the $9 costs from the $10 charged to the guests?

The change in GAAP for Revenue Recognition (ASC 606) was made effective Jan. 1, 2018 for publicly traded companies, and therefore it is worth revisiting this topic in detail. In order to answer this question, it is necessary to establish whether the property is acting as an agent (in which case net revenue is reported) or as a principal (in which case gross revenue is reported), by applying these two steps:

1. Identify the specified goods or services to be provided to the customer.

2. Assess whether it controls the specified goods or services before they are transferred to the customer.

First, a hotel has to determine whether it is a principal or an agent for each specified good or service promised to the customer. For example, when a group stays at a hotel, has meals at the hotel, uses audiovisual services, and also parks at the hotel, the hotel is offering Rooms, Food and Beverage, Audiovisual, and Parking Services to this group. A specified good or service is a separate good or service to be provided to the customer. If this hotel has a contract with this group to provide all four services, the hotel could be a principal for some specified goods or services and an agent for others. Therefore, it is important to identify the specified goods or services to be provided.

Once the specified goods or services are identified, then a hotel must determine whether the nature of its promise is to provide the specified goods or services to the customer or to coordinate with a third party to provide such goods or services. If the hotel is offering its own services, such as the rooms and food and beverage, then the hotel is the principal. As such, a principal controls the specified goods or services before they are transferred to the customer. Thus, the revenue is reported on a gross basis.

If the hotel contracts out its audiovisual and parking services to third parties, it may still be a principal depending on the control it has on the specified goods or services to the customer. If the hotel is still the principal, it recognizes revenue on a gross basis. This means the hotel will bill the entire revenue amount to its customer.

However, if the role of the hotel is simply to coordinate for a third party to provide the goods or services, and has no other controls, then it becomes an agent and should recognize revenue in the net amount it has agreed upon for the arrangement of its agency services. This means the hotel will only record the amount billed to the customer less the amount paid to the supplier or the net commission retained, as revenues.

So, how is control determined? The hotel is regarded as a principal if it:

1. Is primarily responsible for fulfilling the promise to provide the specified good or service;

2. Has inventory risk before the specified good or service has been transferred to a customer, or after the transfer of control to the customer; or

3. Has discretion to establish the prices for the specified good or service.

Although these three indicators of control can be useful in determining whether a hotel is a principal in the transaction, they should note be viewed as a checklist to be met in all scenarios depending on the degree of responsibility, risk, and discretion in establishing the price, as not all indicators have to be present to make the determination either. The best method perhaps is to look at some examples. Exhibit 1.8 presents three sample evaluations regarding audiovisual.

Estimating Gross Revenue as a Principal. Besides determining whether a revenue is to be reported as gross or net, a second question is how much should be recorded. Although this seems to be a straightforward question, it is not for all circumstances. A hotel may not always know the price charged to its customer for its goods or services by a third party due to insufficient transparency in the intermediary's pricing. Thus, for situations where the hotel is a principal and yet the transaction price charged by a third party is not known, the amount which the hotel "expects" to be entitled from the third party should be recorded as revenue.

Reporting Classification. For some revenues, once they are determined to be reported on either gross or net basis, the way they are classified is also important. For Room revenue, be it gross or net, is always recorded in the Rooms department. Audiovisual revenue, whether determined to be reported on a gross or net basis, continues to be recorded in the Food and Beverage department. For limited-service hotels that do not have a Food and Beverage department, any net revenue will be classified as Commissions on Miscellaneous Income. If the revenue is to be reported as gross, it would be reported as a Minor Operated department. For all other revenues, if they are determined to be reported on a gross basis, they will be recorded as revenue and expenses separately within an Other Operated department. If, however, the revenue is determined to be recorded on a net basis, the revenue and expense will be netted and recorded within Miscellaneous Income. Exhibit 1.8 presents three sample evaluations regarding audiovisual.

| Exhibit 1.8 | Audiovisual Revenue: Gross versus Net Reporting |

Scenario One: Property Operation

Structure. Property A operates its audiovisual department, owns or rents the necessary equipment, sets the sales price, invoices the guests, and performs all services for guests requiring the services.

Evaluation. As Property A is primarily responsible for fulfilling the promise to provide audiovisual services, it has inventory risk and has discretion in establishing the prices. As Property A has all three control indicators, the revenue and expenses are recorded on a gross basis. If Property A has a Food and Beverage department, it reports these revenues and expenses as Audiovisual and Audiovisual Cost on Food and Beverage – Schedule 2. If Property A does not have a Food and Beverage department, it reports these revenues and expenses as a Minor Operated department in Other Operated departments.

Scenario Two: Outside Contractor

Structure. Property B contracts with Contractor Z as the exclusive recommended vendor to provide audiovisual services for Property B's guests. Contractor Z employs the personnel to provide the service and is responsible for costs to purchase and maintain the equipment (including liability insurance). Property B employs the sales managers who coordinate the services of Contractor Z with the guests and is responsible for collecting the revenue from the guests. The sales contract between Property B and guests does not explicitly mention Contractor Z, and Property B coordinates and satisfies customer disputes. Property B and Contractor Z agree jointly upon the prices to charge and the standard of service. Contractor Z pays Property B a contracted amount (percent of revenue or fixed amount). Property B is responsible to pay Contractor Z for the services once they are performed regardless of whether the sales price is fully collected.

Evaluation. Property B is primarily responsible for fulfilling the promise to provide the specified good or service and Property B has discretion in establishing the prices for the specified goods or service. Therefore, the two indicators support recording revenue on a gross basis.

Scenario Three: Outside Contractor

Structure. Property C contracts with Contractor Z as the exclusive recommended vendor to provide audiovisual services for Property C's guests. Contractor Z employs the personnel to provide the service and is responsible for costs of purchase and maintenance of the equipment (including liability insurance). Contractor Z determines the prices to charge for services to guests, but Property C has the ability to require Contractor Z to change their prices if it determines that Contractor Z's prices are unreasonable. The sales contract between Property C and guests states that the audiovisual services will be provided by Contractor Z and that Contractor Z is solely responsible for providing such services, or Contractor Z has a contract with guests directly. Contractor Z pays Property C a contracted amount (percent of revenue or fixed amount). Property C is responsible to collect the revenue and remit it to Contractor Z for the services once they are performed; however, if a guest fails to pay, Property C is not liable to Contractor Z.

Evaluation. Contractor Z is primarily responsible for fulfilling the promise to provide the audiovisual services, has inventory risk, and establishes the prices. Although Property C has a right to require Contractor Z to adjust pricing if it determines Contractor Z's prices are unreasonable, pricing control has not been established by Property C. Revenue should be recorded on a net basis in Miscellaneous Income.

Source: *Uniform System of Accounts for the Lodging Industry*, Eleventh Revised Edition (Austin, TX: Hospitality Financial and Technology Professionals, 2018), pp. 364–65.

Cash Versus Accrual Accounting

The cash and accrual bases of accounting are two methods of determining when to record a transaction.

Cash basis accounting recognizes an accounting transaction at the point of cash inflow or outflow. For example, cash received in 20X2 for rooms sold in 20X1 would be treated as 20X2 revenues. Likewise, expenses incurred in 20X1 for which cash was disbursed in 20X2 would be treated as 20X2 expenses. Because of these improper assignments of revenues and expenses, cash basis accounting is generally not a fair reflection of business operations. Cash basis accounting usually violates the generally accepted accounting principles discussed earlier. However, using this method is acceptable if the results do not differ *materially* from those that accrual basis accounting would produce. This method is used only by very small hospitality operations.

The more commonly used **accrual basis accounting** recognizes revenues when earned (regardless of when cash is received) and expenses when incurred (regardless of when cash is disbursed). For example, suppose that a hotel room is sold for the period of Dec. 30, 20X1, through Jan. 2, 20X2, and the hotel guest pays the bill of $400 ($100 per night for four nights) on the morning of Jan. 3, 20X2. Under accrual basis accounting, two days of rooms revenue are recorded in December and two days of rooms revenue are recorded in January.

Expenses must be recognized periodically (because of the matching principle) even when no transaction has occurred. Examples of non-transaction expense recognition include depreciation of property and equipment, reduction of prepaid insurance, accrual of payroll, and provision of an allowance for uncollectible receivables. For example, insurance coverage may be purchased twelve months in advance. Accrual basis accounting would recognize insurance expense over the twelve-month period rather than when the cash is disbursed. The vehicle for this recognition is *adjusting entries*, which are briefly discussed later in Section 1.6.

1.4 BRANCHES OF ACCOUNTING

Accountants classify accounting activities in a variety of ways. However, most agree that there are six distinct (though overlapping) branches. These branches are financial accounting, cost accounting, managerial accounting, tax accounting, auditing, and accounting systems.

Financial accounting refers to accounting for revenues, expenses, assets, and liabilities. It involves the basic accounting processes of recording, classifying, and summarizing transactions. This area is often limited to the accounting necessary to prepare and distribute financial reports. Financial accounting is historical in nature; that is, it deals with past events. Managerial accounting, on the other hand, deals with proposed events.

Cost accounting is the branch of accounting dealing with the recording, classification, allocation, and reporting of current and prospective costs. Cost accountants determine costs by departments, functions, responsibilities, and products and services. The chief purpose of cost accounting is to help operations personnel control operations.

Managerial accounting is the branch of accounting designed to provide information to various management levels for the purpose of enhancing controls. Management accountants prepare performance reports, including comparisons to the budget. One major purpose of these reports is to provide in-depth information as a basis for management decisions. Although managerial accounting may vary among segments of the hospitality industry and certainly among different establishments, many management accountants use various statistical techniques.

Tax accounting is the branch of accounting relating to the preparation and filing of tax forms with governmental agencies. Tax planning to minimize tax payments is a significant part of the tax accountant's work. Tax accounting usually focuses on income tax at the federal, state, and local levels, but may also include sales, excise, payroll, and property taxes. Many hospitality operations employ tax accountants. Some operations contract the services of tax accountants employed by certified public accounting firms.

Auditing is the branch of accounting involved with reviewing and evaluating documents, records, and control systems. Auditing may be either external or internal. It is most often associated with the independent, external audit called a **financial audit**. The external auditor reviews the financial statements of the hospitality operation, its underlying internal control system, and its accounting records (journals, vouchers, invoices, checks, bank statements, and so forth) in order to render an opinion of the financial statements. The auditor usually then provides recommendations for strengthening the operation's internal controls. Financial audits may only be conducted by certified public accounting firms.

Over the past several years, hospitality operations have increasingly employed internal auditors, whose primary purpose is to review and evaluate internal control systems. Many large hospitality firms have a full staff of internal auditors who conduct audits at individual properties to help management maintain the internal control system.

The final branch of accounting is accounting systems. Accounting systems personnel review the information systems of hospitality organizations. Information systems include not only the accounting system but other elements, such as reservations. Because many hospitality operations are now computerized, many accounting systems experts are electronic data processing specialists, such as programmers and systems analysts. The trend toward larger accounting systems staffs in hospitality organizations will continue as the information revolution extends into the twenty-first century.

1.5 REVIEW OF ACCOUNTING MECHANICS

Introductory accounting textbooks use several chapters to cover the mechanics of accounting, from the fundamental accounting equation to the preparation of the financial statements. Let us briefly review these topics.[3]

The **fundamental accounting equation** is simply *assets equal liabilities plus owners' equity*. The equation is a balance to be tested and proven, not a formula to be calculated. This equality is reflected in the balance sheet prepared at the end of each accounting period. **Assets**, simply defined, are things owned by the hospitality operation, including cash, inventory, accounts receivable, land, buildings, and equipment. **Liabilities**, simply stated, are obligations to outside parties and include accounts payable, notes payable, income tax payable, long-term debt payable, and accrued payroll. **Owners' equity** is the residual claims owners have on assets. In other words, assets less liabilities equals owners' equity. After each business transaction is recorded, the total assets must equal the total of liabilities and owners' equity.

There are two major sub-classifications of owners' equity—**permanent accounts** and **temporary accounts**. An **account** is simply a device for showing increases and/or decreases in an individual asset, liability, or owners' equity item. For example, a hospitality operation would have an account for cash in its bank account called "cash in bank." Permanent owners' equity accounts are not closed at the end of an accounting period. They include accounts for recording capital stock and retained earnings. Temporary owners' equity accounts are closed out at the end of each fiscal year and include all revenue and expense accounts. Revenues increase owners' equity, while expenses decrease owners' equity.

The fundamental accounting equation can now be expanded as follows:

Assets (A) = Liabilities (L)

+ Permanent Owners' Equity Accounts (POEA)

+ Temporary Owners' Equity Accounts (TOEA)

Revenues (R) and expenses (E) can be substituted for the TOEA, producing the following equation:

$$A = L + POEA + R - E$$

Debit and Credit

The left side of any account is called the **debit** side and the right side is the **credit** side. To debit an account means to record an amount on the left side, while to credit an account means to record an amount on the right side. The difference between the total debits and total credits of an account is called the **balance**. The normal balance of an account is the kind of balance, either debit or credit, that the account generally shows. The major classes of accounts have normal balances as follows:

Type of Account	Normal Balance
Asset	Debit
Liability	Credit
Owners' Equity:	
Permanent	Credit
Revenue	Credit
Expense	Debit

Each transaction is recorded with equal dollar amounts of debits and credits in **ledger accounts**. This equality of debits and credits in ledger accounts is tested by preparing a **trial balance**, which will be discussed in the next section.

Debits (dr) and credits (cr) increase (+) and decrease (−) the various classes of accounts as follows:

1.6 THE ACCOUNTING CYCLE

In every accounting period (generally one year), an **accounting cycle** begins, starting with recording transactions and ending with a post-closing trial balance. Each step in the cycle will be defined and discussed briefly.

There are five common transactions in a hospitality operation:

1. Sales of products and services

2. Cash receipts

3. Purchases of products and services

4. Payroll

5. Cash disbursements

Exhibit 1.9   Documents and Transactions

Type of Transaction	Documents	
	Prepared by Firm	Prepared Outside of Firm
Sales of products and services	Food guest check Telephone voucher Laundry voucher	—
Cash receipts	Cash register tape	Checks
Purchases of products and services	Purchase order	Suppliers' invoices
Payroll	Time cards Payroll checks	—
Cash disbursements	Check	—

With each transaction, documents are prepared and/or received from which bookkeepers record the transaction. Exhibit 1.9 lists a few key documents for each type of transaction.

Step 1 in the accounting cycle is recording the transactions in journals. **Journals** are simply books used for initially recording individual transactions. There is generally a separate journal (generically called a **specialized journal**) for each type of transaction. In addition, each establishment maintains a **general journal** for recording entries not recorded in specialized journals. The process of recording requires that each transaction be analyzed and that a minimum of two accounts be affected. For example, a cash sales transaction results in increases to the cash account and the sales account.

Step 2 in the accounting cycle is transferring the amounts from the journals to the ledger accounts. This process, called **posting**, tracks individual accounts. For example, assume that cash at the beginning of the period is $1,000, cash receipts for the month total $50,000 (per the cash receipts journal), and cash disbursements equal $45,000 (per the cash disbursements journal). The cash account after these postings would show the following:

Normally, the columns of each specialized journal are totaled and these totals are posted to the proper accounts at the end of the month (EOM). Amounts recorded in the general journal, however, are posted individually. The example shows posting references (P/R) of CR for the cash receipts journal and CD for the cash disbursements journal. The beginning cash balance of $1,000 increased to $6,000 by the end of the month because $50,000 was received and $45,000 disbursed.

CASH

Date	P/R	Debit	Credit	Balance
Bal.		1,000		1,000
EOM	CR	50,000		51,000
EOM	CD		45,000	6,000

Step 3 in the accounting cycle is preparing a trial balance. The trial balance is simply a listing of all account balances, with debit balance accounts and credit balance accounts in separate columns. The totals of each column should be equal and prove the equality of debits and credits. Exhibit 1.10 presents the Mason Motel's trial balance for the month ended Dec. 31, 20X1. Notice that the debit and credit columns both total $488,000.

Step 4 in the accounting cycle is preparing **adjusting entries**. Adjusting entries are required to adjust accounts to reflect the proper account balances. The adjusting entries are recorded in the general journal at the end of the accounting period. The major categories of adjusting entries, along with examples, are shown in Exhibit 1.11.

Step 5 is posting the adjusting entries. All adjusting entries are posted individually from the general journal. All adjustments are different, so there are no common accounts affected by the adjustments (in contrast to the entries recorded in specialized journals).

Step 6 in the accounting cycle is preparing an adjusted trial balance. After the adjusting entries are posted to the accounts, an adjusted trial balance is prepared to once again test the equality of debit and credit accounts. This process may be facilitated by using a worksheet (see Exhibit 1.12).

Exhibit 1.10   Mason Motel Trial Balance

Mason Motel
Trial Balance
December 31, 20X1

	Debits	Credits
Cash	$ 5,000	
Marketable Securities	10,000	
Accounts Receivable	8,000	
Cleaning Supplies	2,500	
Prepaid Insurance	4,500	
Furniture	40,000	
Accumulated Depreciation, Furniture		$ 20,000
Equipment	10,000	
Accumulated Depreciation, Equipment		5,000
Building	300,000	
Accumulated Depreciation, Building		100,000
Land	20,000	
Accounts Payable		5,000
Notes Payable		5,000
Mortgage Payable		100,000
Melvin Mason, Capital		103,000
Room Revenue		150,000
Manager's Salary	15,000	
Assistant Manager's Salary	7,500	
Room Attendants' Wages	15,000	
Payroll Taxes	3,000	
Cleaning Supplies Expense	2,000	
Office Supplies	1,000	
Utilities	5,000	
Advertising	500	
Repairs and Maintenance	9,000	
Property Taxes	22,000	
Interest Expense	8,000	
Total	$ 488,000	$ 488,000

Exhibit 1.11   Major Categories of Adjusting Entries

Category	Examples	Accounts	
		Debited	**Credited**
1. Prepaid expense	a. Reduction of prepaid insurance	Insurance Expense	Prepaid Insurance
	b. Reduction of prepaid rent	Rent Expense	Prepaid Rent
2. Accrued expense	a. Accrual of payroll	Payroll Expense	Accrued Payroll
	b. Accrual of interest expense on a note payable	Interest Expense	Interest Payable
3. Unearned revenue	Reduction of unearned rent	Unearned Rent	Rental Revenue
4. Accrued revenue	Accrual of interest earned on note receivable	Interest Receivable	Interest Income
5. Estimated items	Depreciation expense	Depreciation Expense	Accumulated Depreciation, Fixed Assets
6. Inventory adjustment	Recording of ending inventory from physical inventory. (Note: other account balances such as Purchases are also transferred to the Cost of Goods Sold account.)	Inventory end of month	Cost of Goods Sold

Step 7 is the preparation of the financial statements. Using a worksheet approach, the accountant simply extends all figures from the adjusted trial balance to the proper income statement and balance sheet columns. Exhibit 1.12 reveals that the difference between the debit and credit columns under the "income statement" results in net income. For the Mason Motel, revenues of $150,000 exceeded expenses of $105,350, resulting in net income of $44,650. Net income of $44,650 added to the total credits of $353,150 (balance sheet columns) equals total debits of $397,800 (balance sheet columns).

The accountant then prepares a formal income statement and balance sheet in accordance with generally accepted accounting principles (especially the full disclosure principle). This process may include footnotes to the statements and additional financial statements, such as the statement of cash flows.

In Step 8, after preparation of the financial statements, the revenue and expense accounts are closed. These temporary owners' equity accounts are closed into retained earnings. The closing entries either increase retained earnings (if the hospitality operation earned a profit) or decrease retained earnings (if a loss was suffered). The closing entries result in zero balances in all revenue and expense accounts. The closing entries are recorded in the general journal and posted to the proper accounts.

Step 9, the final step in the accounting cycle, is the preparation of a post-closing trial balance. This balance is prepared to prove once again the equality of debits and credits.

1.7 FORMS OF BUSINESS ORGANIZATION

There are four basic forms of business organization: the sole proprietorship, the partnership, the corporation, and the limited liability company. The business entity principle applies to all businesses. That is, all four forms of business organization are separate from other business entities and separate from their owners for accounting purposes.

Exhibit 1.12 Mason Motel Worksheet

Mason Motel
Worksheet
For the year ended December 31, 20X1

Account Title	Trial Balance Debit	Trial Balance Credit	Adjustments Debit	Adjustments Credit	Adjusted Trial Balance Debit	Adjusted Trial Balance Credit	Income Statement Debit	Income Statement Credit	Balance Sheet Debit	Balance Sheet Credit
Cash	5000				5000				5000	
Marketable Securities	10000				10000				10000	
Accounts Receivable	8000				8000				8000	
Cleaning Supplies	2500			(b) 700	1800				1800	
Prepaid Insurance	4500			(a) 1500	3000				3000	
Furniture	40000				40000				40000	
Accumulated Depreciation, Furniture		20000		(c) 4000		24000				24000
Equipment	10000				10000				10000	
Accumulated Depreciation, Equipment		5000		(d) 1000		6000				6000
Building	300000				300000				300000	
Accumulated Depreciation, Building		100000		(e) 10000		110000				110000
Land	20000				20000				20000	
Accounts Payable		5000				5000				5000
Notes Payable		5000				5000				5000
Mortgage Payable		100000				100000				100000
Melvin Mason, Capital		103000				103000				103000
Room Revenue		150000				150000		150000		
Manager's Salary	15000				15000		15000			
Assistant Manager's Salary	7500				7500		7500			
Maids' Wages	15000		(f) 150		15150		15150			
Payroll Taxes	3000				3000		3000			
Cleaning Supplies Expense	2000		(b) 700		2700		2700			
Office Supplies	1000				1000		1000			
Utilities	5000				5000		5000			
Advertising	500				500		500			
Repairs & Maintenance	9000				9000		9000			
Property Taxes	22000				22000		22000			
Interest Expense	8000				8000		8000			
	488000	488000								
Insurance Expense			(a) 1500		1500		1500			
Depreciation Expense, Furniture			(c) 4000		4000		4000			
Depreciation Expense, Equipment			(d) 1000		1000		1000			
Depreciation Expense, Building			(e) 10000		10000		10000			
Accrued Wages				(f) 150		150				150
			17350	17350	503150	503150	105350	150000	397800	353150
Net Income							44650			44650
							150000	150000	397800	397800

A **sole proprietorship** is a business owned by a single person who generally (but not necessarily) manages the business. Many small lodging and foodservice businesses are organized as sole proprietorships. There are no legal formalities in organizing these businesses; thus, formation is quick and easy. The owner is held legally responsible for all debts of the business. However, the operation is, for accounting purposes, a separate business entity.

A **partnership** is a business owned by two or more people who often manage the business. Partnerships are created by either an oral or written agreement. The written agreement is preferable, as it provides a permanent record of the terms of the partnership. The written agreement includes the duties and initial investment of each partner and the sharing of profits and losses. Each partner is responsible for the debts of the business. As with the sole proprietorship, for accounting purposes, the partnership is a separate business entity.

A **limited partnership** is a form of partnership that offers the protection of limited liability to its **limited partners**. In order to have limited liability, limited partners may not actively participate in managing the business. A limited partnership must have at least one **general partner** who is responsible for the debts of the partnership—that is, the general partner has unlimited liability.

A **corporation** is a business organization incorporated under the laws of one of the United States. The corporation differs from the other forms of business organization because it is a *legal* business entity separate from its owners. Its continued existence depends on its charter from the state, not the lives of its owners. With the exception of the S corporations described below, corporations (known as C corporations) may have any number of owners.

The owners of a **C corporation** are stockholders who buy shares of stock in the corporation. The stockholders are not responsible for the debts of the corporation, and, should the corporation fail, the stockholders lose only the amount they have paid for their shares. In contrast to the personal assets of sole proprietors and partners (or general partners in limited partnerships), the stockholders' personal assets are protected from the corporation's creditors.

The stockholders do not directly manage the lodging corporation, but rather elect a board of directors to represent their interests. The board selects officers (such as president and vice president) who manage the corporation. Payments to the stockholders from the corporation's profits are called **dividends**. Once the board of directors declares dividends, the dividends are legal liabilities of the corporation and must be paid.

A special type of corporation is the **S corporation**. It enjoys favorable tax treatment under the Internal Revenue Code. The S corporation offers limited liability and its owners may participate in management; however, unlike a C corporation, it is not subject to double taxation. The major limitations of a business organized as an S corporation are that it may not have more than 100 stockholders, its stockholders must be U.S. citizens or residents, and its stockholders must generally not include other corporations, partnerships, etc.

A **limited liability company (LLC)** is a relatively new form of business organization now available in a majority of U.S. states. The LLC has been gaining in popularity because it combines the corporate feature of limited liability with the favorable tax treatment of partnerships and sole proprietorships. The LLC, unlike the S corporation, may have an unlimited number of owners (who are referred to as members) and is not restricted to one class of stock.

Exhibit 1.13 reflects major aspects of the types of organizational formats.

| Exhibit 1.13 | Comparative Features of Business Formats | | | |

	Limited Number of Owners	Limited Liability	Double Taxation	Management Participation
Sole Proprietorship	yes	no	no	yes
Partnership				
Limited partners	no	yes	no	no
General partners	no	no	no	yes
Limited Liability Company	no	yes	no	yes
Corporation				
S corporation	yes	yes	no	yes
C corporation	no	yes	yes	yes

1.8 INTERNATIONAL FINANCIAL REPORTING STANDARDS

The accounting standards followed by U.S. businesses are referred to as generally accepted accounting principles (GAAP). As the U.S. economy becomes more globalized, there is a need to communicate financial information in ways that the world understands. The SEC is strongly considering requiring U.S. firms under their authority (companies whose stocks are publicly listed) to follow the International Financial Reporting Standards (IFRS) promulgated by the International Accounting Standards Board (IASB).

The U.S. GAAP is essentially a rules-based system, while the IFRS is a principles-based system. GAAP is constantly being amended or supplemented to enhance accuracy and reduce ambiguity. The major disadvantage of GAAP is the high complexity of preparing financial statements.

The IFRS, on the other hand, sets guidelines but does not dictate every possible case. This approach leaves many things open for interpretation and may lead to inconsistency in reporting from company to company.

Currently, the FASB and IASB are working on a number of projects that should result in some convergence of GAAP and IFRS.

There are some currently accepted accounting methods that most likely will not be accepted under IFRS. For example, last in, first out (LIFO) accounting for inventory is not allowed under IFRS. Very few if any hospitality firms use LIFO accounting today, so there would be minimal impact in this case.

Another area of difference with potentially greater impact on hospitality firms is the revaluation of property and equipment. Under U.S. GAAP, property and equipment is recorded at historical cost and depreciated. These assets are not written up to reflect market values on their books. The IFRS allows a business to choose between the cost model or a revaluation model. Under the revaluation model, property and equipment items whose fair value can be reliably measured are recorded at a revalued amount. Thus, property and equipment may increase in value under IFRS. More details regarding these and other differences between U.S. GAAP and the IFRS are beyond the scope of this book.

1.9 ETHICS AND HOSPITALITY ACCOUNTING

In recent years, considerable attention has been devoted to ethics, both in class-rooms and boardrooms. Many major corporations have a code of ethics, and their managers are required to sign a statement saying that they will abide by the firm's code of ethics. Failure to follow the code often results in termination. Studies of the codes of ethics in America's largest corporations reveal the following common elements: (1) privacy of communication, (2) conflicts of interest, (3) political contributions in the United States, (4) company records, (5) gifts, favors, entertainment, trips, and outings, (6) use of company assets, (7) antitrust laws, (8) relations with competitors, (9) relations with suppliers, and (10) relations with customers.[4]

In the book *Ethics in Hospitality Management* by Stephen S. J. Hall, the role of ethics in accounting is discussed. The topic is divided into two sections: (1) the impact of ethics on accounting and (2) the marriage of theory and practice. The first section includes several ethical conflicts commonly encountered by hospitality accountants. For example:

> A management company president, whose incentive compensation is based on a percentage of income before fixed charges, directs that all repair and maintenance items costing more than $500 be capitalized as capital improvements.

Clearly, this practice will result in greater management fees for the management company when revenue expenditures (expenditures that should be expensed) are accounted for as capital expenditures.

The second section under ethics in accounting states that it is unwise to sepa-rate ethical theories and practices. Theories of ethical behavior that are applied to situations at home and church should also be practiced in business. In accounting, "creativity" is allowed in certain situations if it is clearly explained. For example, different accounting methods can be used for various purposes, such as using an accelerated depreciation method for tax purposes and the straight-line method of depreciation for book purposes. However, this same "creativity" in accounting can lead to unethical practices if it does not reflect reality or is intended to deceive.

When faced with an ethical dilemma, the following questions can be used to make an appropriate decision:

1. Is the decision legal?

2. Is the decision fair?

3. Does the decision hurt anyone?

4. Have I been honest with those affected?

5. Can I live with my decision?

6. Am I willing to publicize my decision?

7. What if everyone did what I did?

If a decision can pass this seven-step test, it will most likely be considered ethical.[5]

The major objectives of this chapter have been to provide a brief overview of the hospitality industry and a review of basic accounting procedures and concepts. Businesses in the hospitality industry, although different in several respects from firms in many other industries, maintain their accounts according to the same basic principles. A hospitality manager should therefore be well versed in general accounting and the special accounting considerations of a hospitality operation.

Hotels and restaurants may experience large fluctuations in demand and often maintain very perishable products. Although a manufacturing firm's inventory may have a shelf life of several years, a restaurant's inventory will perish after a few days and an unsold hotel room night can never be recovered. Hospitality operations do not maintain extensive inventories, so labor must be readily available to prepare and serve food and other products. This labor force must be able to satisfy many ranges of seasonality; different times of the day, days of the week, and seasons of the year will generate different levels of sales.

In order to reflect accurately the operations of these businesses and to ensure consistent recording between periods and properties, hospitality accountants follow generally accepted accounting principles. The cost principle stipulates that items be recorded at the amount for which they are purchased. The continuity of the business unit principle assumes that the organization is a going concern that is not threatened by having to liquidate immediately. The property must be treated as an entity separate from its owners according to the business entity principle. Other requirements are that accountants use objective evidence whenever possible and fully disclose financial items of significance to the users of the financial statements. If these principles are adhered to, the resultant statements will more accurately report the property's operations and financial position.

This chapter also provided a brief overview of basic accounting mechanics. Assets are items owned by the property and have debit balances; liabilities are amounts the property owes and have credit balances. The difference between assets and liabilities is owners' equity—the amount of residual claims owners have on assets. The chapter included a brief description of the four types of business organization (sole proprietorships, partnerships, corporations, and limited liability companies), and concluded with a discussion of ethical issues relating to managerial accounting.

account—A record containing information regarding a particular type of business transaction.

accounting cycle—Sequence of principal accounting procedures of a fiscal period: analyzing transactions, journal entry, posting to ledger, trial balance, adjustments, preparation of periodic financial statements, account closing, post-closing trial balance.

accrual basis accounting—System of reporting revenues and expenses in the period in which they are considered to have been earned or incurred, regardless of the actual time of collection or payment.

adjusting entries—Entries required at the end of an accounting period to record internal transactions.

assets—Resources available for use by the business; that is, anything owned by the business that has monetary value.

balance—The difference between the total debits and total credits of an account.

business entity principle—The generally accepted accounting principle that requires that a business maintain its own set of accounts that are separate from other financial interests of its owners.

C corporation— The owners of the **C corporation** are stockholders who buy shares of stock in the corporation and assume limited liability. They do not directly manage the lodging corporation, but rather elect a board of directors to represent their interests.

cash basis accounting—Reporting of revenues and expenses at the time they are collected or paid.

conservatism principle—The generally accepted accounting principle that requires accounting procedures that recognize expenses as soon as possible, but delay the recognition of revenues until they are ensured. For example, non-refundable deposits for future services should be recognized as a liability until the service is actually performed.

consistency principle—The generally accepted accounting principle that requires that once an accounting method has been adopted, it should be followed from period to period in the future unless a change in accounting methods is warranted and disclosed.

continuity of the business unit principle—The generally accepted accounting principle that requires the assumption in preparing the accounting records and reports that the business will continue indefinitely and that liquidation is not in prospect—in other words, that the business is a going concern. Also called the going concern principle.

corporation—A form of business organization that provides a separate legal entity apart from its owners.

cost principle—The generally accepted accounting principle that requires recording the value of transactions for accounting purposes at the actual transaction price (cost).

credit—Decrease in an asset or increase in a liability or capital—entered on the right side of an account; such amounts are said to be credited to the account.

debit—Increase in an asset or decrease in a liability or capital—entered on the left side of an account; such amounts are said to be debited or charged to the account.

dividends—Distributions of earnings to owners of a corporation's stock.

financial audit—An independent, external audit.

full disclosure principle—The generally accepted accounting principle that requires that financial statements must provide information on all the significant facts that have a bearing on their interpretation. Types of disclosures include the accounting methods used, changes in the accounting methods, contingent liabilities, events occurring subsequent to the financial statement date, and unusual and nonrecurring items.

fundamental accounting equation—Assets equal liabilities plus owners' equity. This equation is a balance to be tested and proven, not a formula to be calculated.

general journal—Record of all accounting transactions.

general partner—A member of a partnership with unlimited liability for the debts of the partnership.

generally accepted accounting principles (GAAP)—Accounting principles that have become accepted over time through common usage and also through the work of major accounting bodies. They provide a uniform basis for preparing financial statements.

going concern principle—The generally accepted accounting principle that requires the preparation of accounting records and reports under the assumption that the business will continue indefinitely and that liquidation is not in prospect; also referred to as the continuity of the business unit principle.

journals—Accounting records of business transactions.

ledger accounts—A group of related accounts that constitute a complete unit.

liabilities—Obligations of a business; largely indebtedness related to the expenses incurred in the process of generating income.

limited liability company (LLC)—A form of business organization that combines the corporate feature of limited liability with the favorable tax treatment of partnerships and sole proprietorships. May have an unlimited number of owners (who are referred to as members) and is not restricted to one class of stock.

limited partner—A member of a limited partnership having limited liability. Limited partners may not actively participate in managing the business.

limited partnership—A form of business organization consisting of a partnership between two or more individuals having at least one general partner and one limited partner in which the latter's liabilities are limited to investments.

matching principle—The generally accepted accounting principle that requires recording expenses in the same period as the revenues to which they relate.

materiality principle—The generally accepted accounting principle that requires that events be recognized and recorded by accounting procedures if they make a difference as determined by some relative standard of comparison. For example, materiality may be established by a rule of thumb that states that an item is recognized if it exceeds x percent or more of total assets or income.

objective evidence principle—The preferred basis of accounting transactions and the resulting accounting records.

owners' equity—Financial interest of the owners of a business; assets minus liabilities.

partnership—A form of business organization involving two or more owners that is not incorporated.

permanent accounts—A classification of owners' equity accounts that are not closed at the end of an accounting period; for example, accounts for recording capital stock and retained earnings.

posting—Transferring data entered in a journal to the appropriate account.

revenue recognition principle—The generally accepted accounting principle for determining the proper timing for recording revenues.

S corporation— A special type of corporation that enjoys favorable tax treatment under the Internal Revenue Code, offering limited liability and its owners may participate in management; unlike the C corporation, however, it is not subject to double taxation.

sole proprietorship—An unincorporated business organized by one person.

specialized journal—A journal used to accelerate the recording of specific kinds of accounting transactions.

temporary accounts—A classification of owners' equity accounts that are closed out at the end of each fiscal year; for example, all revenue and expense accounts.

trial balance—Listing and totaling of all the general ledger accounts on a work-sheet.

unit of measurement principle—The accounting principle that the monetary values stated in financial statements should represent a stable unit of value so that meaningful comparisons of current and past periods are possible.

1. What are some differences between hospitality operations and manufacturing firms?

2. What types of seasonality would a transient hotel most likely experience?

3. Approximately what percentage of total revenues is labor cost in the hospitality industry?

4. What is the matching principle?

5. How does inflation affect the unit of measurement principle?

6. What accounts are included in temporary owners' equity accounts?

7. What is posting?

8. What are the five types of accounts that are included in the general ledger of all hospitality firms?

9. What is the concept of materiality?

10. What are the six branches of accounting and the major responsibilities of each?

Problem 1

Several terms are used in basic financial accounting:

fundamental accounting equation   ledger
assets   journal
liabilities   trial balance
owners' equity   accounting cycle
permanent accounts   posting
account   adjusting entry
debit   income statement
credit   balance sheet

Choose the term above that best completes the following statements:

1. A(n) _____ is a record containing information regarding a particular type of business transaction.

2. A(n) _____ is required at the end of the accounting period to record depreciation expense.

3. The _____ reflects the assets owned by the business organization.

4. The _____ includes all general ledger accounts and the amounts of accounts with _____ balances must equal the amounts of accounts with _____ balances.

5. A = L + E is the _____.

6. Obligations of a business are shown on the balance sheet and are called _____.

7. A(n) _____ is a book of original entry.

8. A(n) _____ is a book of final entry.

9. Transferring amounts from journals to ledgers is referred to as _____.

10. Common stock is an example of a(n) _____.

Problem 2

Ethics continues to be a concern in business organizations. Deb Fields, the general manager (GM) of the 1,000-room Marcus Hotel, needs yard work done each week at her large country home. She quietly approaches the hotel's best maintenance worker and offers to personally pay him the same hourly wage he receives from the hotel for the desired five hours of work each week at her house. The work generally will be on Saturdays when this employee is not required to work at the hotel.

Required:

1. Should the GM have discussed the proposal with the worker's supervisor?

2. If the hotel's best maintenance worker does weekend work at the GM's personal residence, could this cause potential jealousy at the hotel?

3. Evaluate the ethics of this scenario using Hall's seven-step approach.

Problem 3

Fill in the blanks below with the accounting principle that best applies.

A. Cost   F. Continuity of business
B. Business entity   G. Consistency
C. Conservatism   H. Matching
D. Full disclosure   I. Unit of measurement
E. Materiality   J. Objective evidence

1. A hotel describes its inventory valuation method in the footnotes to its financial statement because of _____.

2. A café decides to expense a $40 wastebasket even though it has a five-year, life based on the _____ principle.

3. During 20X3, a club used LIFO to value its inventory. If the club uses the first in, first out (FIFO) method in 20X4 it will violate the _____ principle.

4. The owner of a foodservice operation decides to take some steaks home for dinner. He records the cost of the steaks as a "withdrawal" because of the _____ principle.

5. The _____ principle is the basis for recording the payroll accrual at the end of each month.

6. A new van was purchased for $4,000 below its list price of $25,000. If the purchasing firm records the van at $25,000, it will violate the _____ principle.

7. H. Smith, owner of Smith's Catering, contributes a van to the business. He believes the van is worth $15,000; however, the business records the van at its Blue Book value of $10,000 because of the _____ principle.

8. The Wizard Inn has purchased 100 new water glasses with its "WI" crest on each. The cost per glass is $1.50; however, the resale value is considered to be only $.15 each per glass. The glasses are recorded at cost and will be written off over the next three years rather than written down immediately because of the _____ principle.

Problem 4

Below is a list of 20X3 activities/transactions for the Williamston Inn (WI):

1. The WI paid rent of $9,000 on Oct. 28, 20X3, for the three months of November 20X3–January 20X4.

2. The WI borrowed $60,000 from First National Bank on Aug. 16, 2023. The annual interest rate is 6 percent. No payments have been made and no interest expense has been recognized during 20X3.

3. The physical inventory of food at the end of 20X3 totaled $15,800. The food inventory at the end of 20X3 per the books equaled $15,200.

4. The Inn purchased a new car for $55,000 on July 1, 20X3. The car is expected to have a useful life of five years and a salvage value of $3,000. The Inn uses the straight-line method of depreciation; however, no depreciation for the car has been recorded.

5. The WI invested $10,000 in a 24-month certificate of deposit at Fairly's Bank on Oct. 1, 20X2. The annual interest rate is 10 percent. No income has been recorded for 20X3.

Required:

Prepare an adjusting entry for each situation for the year ended Dec. 31, 20X3.

Problem 5

Multiple choice: Select the best response in each item below.

1. An entry to increase the depreciation account is recorded with a _____ entry.
   a. debit
   b. credit
   c. either debit or credit

2. Food inventory is reduced on the books to its market value when it is lower than cost due to the _____ principle.
   a. cost
   b. going concern
   c. business entity
   d. none of the above

3. Which of the following items is *not* recorded at the end of the accounting period because of the matching principle?
   a. accrual of unpaid wages
   b. recognition of expired insurance coverage
   c. increase in the allowance for doubtful accounts
   d. recording of the dividend declared by the board of directors

4. The branch of accounting involved with reviewing and evaluating documents, records, and control systems is:
   a. cost
   b. managerial
   c. auditing
   d. accounting systems

5. Which of the following business formats has a limited number of owners?
   a. C corporation
   b. S corporation
   c. limited partnership
   d. limited liability company

6. The Triple-Z Ranch purchased a three-year insurance policy on June 1, 20X1, for $36,000. The coverage was for the period of July 1, 20X1, through June 30, 20X4. The amount of prepaid insurance that should be shown on the ranch's balance sheet as a current asset as of Dec. 31, 20X1, is:
   a. $0.
   b. $6,000.
   c. $12,000.
   d. $24,000.

7. The Zebra Inn sold 10,000 shares of its common stock for $20 per share. Its common stock has a par value of $1 per share. Which of the following statements is *false*?
   a. Cash of $200,000 was received.
   b. The common stock account increased by $200,000.
   c. The additional paid-in capital account increased by $190,000.
   d. Retained earnings is not affected by this transaction.

Problem 6

Fill in the blanks below with the accounting principle that best applies.

A. Cost

B. Business entity

C. Conservatism

D. Full disclosure

E. Materiality

F. Continuity of the business unit

G. Consistency

H. Matching

I. Unit of measurement

J. Objective evidence

1. A restaurant records accrued wages at the end of the fiscal year because of the _____ principle.

2. A hotel reduces its inventory values to reflect the market value of its food stocks, which are lower than the original cost, because of the _____ principle.

3. A motel does not reduce the value of its glassware to liquidation value because of the _____ principle.

4. The cost of a few small kitchen utensils is expensed rather than recorded as equipment due to the _____ principle.

5. The method of inventory cost flow used is reflected in the financial report because of the _____ principle.

6. When one method of inventory valuation is used at the end of 20X3 and another method is used at the end of 20X4, this violates the _____ principle.

7. The cost of steaks taken home by the owner for personal use is recorded as a "withdrawal" because of the _____ principle.

8. A tilt frying pan is recorded at $50,500 (the amount paid) rather than the original contract price of $25,000 because of the _____ principle.

Problem 7

Which branch of accounting is described by each statement below?

1. This branch of accounting prepares the independent review of a firm's financial statements.

2. The chief purpose of this branch of accounting is to assist operations personnel in controlling operations.

3. The nature of this branch of accounting is historical.

4. This branch of accounting deals with proposed events.

5. Reports prepared by this branch of accounting should greatly assist management in making future decisions.

6. The focus of this branch of accounting is to minimize taxes paid.

7. This branch of accounting focuses on the review and evaluation of internal control systems.

8. In this branch of accounting, some members are likely to be systems analysts.

Problem 8

Mr. Gregory Vain is a successful businessperson who does not fully understand the fundamental accounting equation and how various transactions affect it. You have been hired to share your knowledge with him.

Required:

1. State the basic equation and briefly explain each element of it.

2. Explain how each type of account could be increased and illustrate with examples. Be sure to describe all the effects of your examples.
   Example: Asset accounts would increase when a new hotel is purchased. However, in order to remain in equilibrium, another asset account, "cash," would decrease if the hotel is purchased with cash.

3. State how temporary accounts relate to the fundamental accounting equation.

Problem 9

January Jones opened JJ's Diner as a sole proprietorship, and recorded the following transactions during its initial month of operations:

1. Rented facilities for $3,000 per month and paid the lessor $9,000 for the first three months.

2. Purchased equipment costing $30,000 on the first of the month. The diner put 20 percent down and borrowed the remainder from Second Bank. (Equipment will be depreciated over sixty months using the straight-line method. Assume a $3,000 salvage value.)

3. Sold 2,000 meals during the month at an average sales price of $20. Twenty percent of the meals were sold on account, while the remainder were cash sales. None of the charge sales were collected by the end of the first month.

4. Cost of food sold percentage is 35 percent. Food purchases totaled $10,000 during the first month, of which 60 percent were paid for during the month.

5. Paid labor costs of 30 percent of sales during the month.

6. Paid all other expenses, which totaled $6,000, with cash.

7. Jones opened the business on the first of the month by investing $50,000.

8. Jones' tax rate is 30 percent. Taxes will be paid subsequent to the first month.

Required:

1. Determine the net income for the first month of business.

2. Determine the total sources and use of cash for the first month.

Problem 10

The Browny B&B, a 50-room lodging facility, has operated for the past three years. Browny's night auditor has kept accurate records over the past year but has not analyzed any of these data. The following is a summary of the rooms sold by month:

Rooms sold:

January	400	May	960	September	800
February	600	June	980	October	705
March	700	July	992	November	650
April	840	August	973	December	500

Assume that the motel is open 365 days per year for business purposes, and that the motel considers its "summer months" to be May, June, July, and August. The off-season comprises all other months.

Required:

Determine the paid occupancy percentage for the summer months, the off-season, and the entire year.

Problem 11

June Bickley desires to organize her lodging business to minimize her taxes, minimize her legal liability, and maintain control. She is willing to include additional investors.

Required:

1. Discuss the organizational format you recommend and state the reasoning behind your recommendation.

2. If she is highly successful and decides to expand into several adjoining states or provinces, would you recommend a change? Explain why or why not.

Problem 12

Tempting Treats is a small frozen yogurt retail store. Its first month's operations resulted in the following activity:

Sales: Sales totaled $6,500, but only $5,500 was received during the month as $1,000 was sold to two businesses for employee socials. These businesses plan to pay next month.

Food purchases: $1,000 worth of frozen yogurt was purchased using cash, and another $300 was purchased on account during the first month and will be paid next month. The food inventory at the end of the first month totaled $100.

Wages: The sole employee was paid $1,500 for the month and is still owed $100 at the end of the month.

Payroll taxes: Payroll taxes of 8 percent are owed to the government on paid wages for the first month and wages payable at the end of the first month. They will be paid the following month.

Electricity:	The electric bill through the 20th day of the first month of $120 was received on the 24th and paid on the 30th day of the month. The estimated electric expense for the remainder of the first month was $30 and will be paid in the second month.
Water:	The water bill for the first month of $40 was received on the first day of the second month.
Supplies:	$300 worth of supplies was purchased and paid for during the first month. At the end of the month, $150 of supplies were still on hand.
Rent:	Rent of $1,500 was paid on the first day of the first month. This payment covers the first three months of operations for both space and equipment.

Note: The business started the first month with $3,000 cash.

Required:

1. Based on the information provided, prepare a simple income statement based on cash activity (cash accounting).

2. Based on the information provided, prepare a simple income statement based on revenue earned and actual expenses incurred (accrual accounting).

3. What is the amount of cash on hand at the end of the first month?

Problem 13

Below is a list of the activities/transactions for Fee's Fountain:

1. A fire insurance policy for January 1, 20X3, through December 31, 20X4 was purchased on December 15, 20X2. The premium paid totaled $36,000 and was recorded as pre-paid insurance.

2. The operation purchased a used cash register costing $10,000 on December 18, 20X2 and recorded it in the equipment account. The cash register is expected to have a useful life of five years and a salvage value of $0. No depreciation has been recorded. Fee's uses the straight-line method of depreciation.

3. The employees were paid for their work through Dec. 28. They worked 100 hours for the period of Dec. 29–31, 20X3, and will be paid on Jan. 10, 20X4. The average hourly wage is $8.00. The related payroll taxes are 10 percent of the wages.

4. Sales for the year totaled $1 million. The allowance for doubtful accounts has a Dec. 31 balance of $1,500 prior to write-off of two accounts totaling $300. The allowance should be adjusted at year-end to ¾ percent of sales for the year.

5. The electric bill for the period of Dec. 15, 20X3, through Jan. 10, 20X4 totaled $320. It has not been recorded and will be paid on Jan. 15, 20X4.

Required:

For each situation, prepare the adjusting entry to record the proper expense for 20X3. In addition, prepare the journal entry to write off the two uncollectible accounts.

Problem 14

Below is a list of the 20X3 activities/transactions for April's Bakery:

1. A business insurance policy for July 1, 20X3, through June 30, 20X4, was purchased on May 15, 20X3. The premium paid totaled $48,000 and was recorded as prepaid insurance.

2. The operation purchased a new cash register costing $12,000 on Sept. 1, 20X3, and recorded it in the equipment account. The cash register is expected to have a useful life of seven years and a salvage value of $1,000. No depreciation has been recorded. Emily's uses the straight-line method of depreciation.

3. The employees were paid for their work through Dec. 26. They worked 300 hours for the period of Dec. 27–31, 20X3, and will be paid on Jan. 10, 20X4. The average hourly wage is $6.00.

4. Sales for the year totaled $800,000. The allowance for doubtful accounts has a Dec. 31 balance of $1,000. The allowance should be adjusted at year-end to ½ percent of sales for the year.

5. The electric bill for the period of Dec. 5, 20X3, through Jan. 4, 20X4, totaled $920. It has not been recorded and will be paid on Jan. 10, 20X4.

Required:

For each situation, prepare the adjusting entry to record the proper expense for 20X3.

Problem 15

The following balance sheet for The Sunflower Suites has several accounts that require adjusting before preparation of the Dec. 31, 20X3, financial statements.

Balance Sheet
The Sunflower Suites
Nov. 30, 20X3

Assets

Current Assets:

Cash	$ 15,000
Accounts Receivable	108,000
Allowance for Doubtful Accounts	(6,000)
Food Inventory	4,000
Prepaid Insurance	3,000
Total Current Assets	124,000

Property and Equipment:

Land	50,000
Building	1,440,000
Equipment	400,000
Accumulated Depreciation	(490,000)
Total Property and Equipment	1,400,000
Total Assets	$ 1,524,000

Liabilities and Owners' Equity

Current Liabilities:

Notes Payable	$ 5,000
Accounts Payable	10,000

	Wages Payable	12,000
	Taxes Payable	17,000
	Total Current Liabilities	44,000
Long-term Liabilities:		
	Mortgage Payable	600,000
Owners' Equity:		
	James Sun, Capital	880,000
	Total Liabilities and Owners' Equity	$ 1,524,000

Additional information:

1. The allowance for doubtful accounts is calculated as 6.5 percent of the total accounts receivable and then rounded to the next $100. The accounts receivable at Dec. 31, 20X3, totaled $123,200.

2. The annual insurance premium of $6,000 was paid on May 15 for the period of June 1, 20X3, through May 31, 20X4.

3. The physical food inventory on Dec. 31, 20X3, totaled $3,800.

4. The building is depreciated over thirty years using the straight-line (SL) method (assume a salvage value of $100,000). The equipment is depreciated over five years using the SL method (assume a salvage value of zero). For purposes of depreciation calculation, assume that the equipment was purchased on Jan. 1, 20X1. Calculate depreciation expense for the month of December only.

Required:

Prepare the adjusting entries for The Sunflower Suites.

Problem 16

Robbie Hanson owns a resort on an excellent fishing lake. Her busy season begins May 15 and extends through mid-fall. During the winter, she engaged a contractor to build a boat house and dock for a total price of $25,000. The contract called for completion by May 15 because the resort was completely booked for the week of May 15 to 22, the opening week of the fishing season. Because the completion date was so important to Hanson, she specified in the contract that if the construction was not completed by May 15, the price would be reduced by $100 per day until completion.

The construction was not completed until June 9, at which time Hanson paid the contract price of $22,500, deducting $100 for each day's delay. Hanson is convinced that she lost goodwill because the resort's facilities were inadequate and that several of her guests shortened their stays because the facilities were still under construction.

Hanson included the boat house and dock as assets valued at $25,000 on the balance sheet prepared on Sept. 30, the end of her fiscal year. Included in her revenues was an item "Penalty payments received in lieu of lost revenue—$2,500."

The auditor who examined Hanson's report objected to this treatment and insisted that the facilities be recorded at their actual cost, $22,500. Hanson stated that she could not understand the logic of this position. "Accounting principles are out of tune with reality," she complained. "What if the contract had been 250 days late and the boat house and dock had cost me nothing; would you record on my balance sheet that I had no asset? I lost at least $100 per day in revenues because of the construction delay."

Required:

At what amount should these facilities be reported on the balance sheet of Sept. 30? (You may ignore depreciation from June 9 to Sept. 30.) Explain your position in terms of accounting principles.

Problem 17

The Greenhill Hotel's total revenue for 20X1 totaled $5 million, while total expenses totaled $4.6 million. Assume the sources of its revenue and the distribution of its expenses were exactly like the lodging industry averages shown in Exhibit 1.1 of the chapter.

Required:

1. What was the hotel's net income for 20X1?

2. What were the hotel's room sales for 20X1?

3. What were the hotel's rentals and other income for 20X1?

4. What were the hotel's salaries, wages, and benefits for 20X1?

Problem 18

The Hornet Catering Company's trial balance prior to making adjusting entries at the end of 20X3 is as follows:

Hornet Catering Company
Trial Balance
Dec. 21, 2023

	DR	CR
Cash	$10,500	
Food Inventory	1,000	
Prepaid Insurance	500	
Equipment	25,000	
Accumulated Depr., Equipment		$5,000
Accounts Payable		1,000
W. H. Hornet, Capital		13,100
Catering Revenue		160,000
Wages	60,000	
Food Expense	60,000	
Supplies Expense	10,000	
Utilities	3,000	
Insurance Expense	1,100	
Advertising	8,000	
Total	$179,100	$179,100

The following adjusting entries must be prepared:

1. The actual food inventory, according to the physical count, is only $500.

2. The paid insurance coverage at the end of 20X3 extends through April 20X4. The average insurance cost per month is $100.

3. Unpaid wages at the end of December 20X3 total $1,000.

4. The unrecorded depreciation expense for the entire year equals $2,000.

Required:

Prepare a worksheet for the year ending Dec. 31, 20X3.

Problem 19

The Café Fountain is a small coffee drink retail store. Its first month's operations resulted in the following activity:

Sales: Sales totaled $5,500, but only $4,800 was received, because the owner of an adjoining shop purchased $200 worth of drinks during the month and plans to pay his bill next month.

Beverage purchases: $1,000 worth of beverages were purchased and paid for during the month. At the end of the month, $200 worth of beverages are on hand for future sales. The beverage inventory was $0 at the beginning of the first month.

Wages: The sole employee was paid $1,500 during the month. The employee is still owed $800 for wages during the month, which will be paid in the following month.

Utilities: No utility bill was received in the month. On the first day of the following month, a utility bill for the first month of $85 was received.

Supplies: $300 worth of supplies was purchased and paid for during the first month. At the end of the month, $100 worth of supplies is still on hand.

Rent: Rent of $800 is paid during the first month for the first two months. Rent covers both space and equipment.

Required:

1. Based on the information just given, prepare a simple income statement based on cash activity (cash accounting).

2. Based on the information just given, prepare a simple income statement based on revenue earned and actual expenses incurred (accrual accounting).

Problem 20

Jill Spartan started a mobile ice cream service on Jan. 2, 20X3, depositing $10,000 of her funds in a bank account in the name of Spartan Mobile Ice Cream. She purchased a fully equipped truck and operated the business on a cash accounting basis for the first year. She provided you with the following information:

1. She purchased a $30,000 fully equipped truck in early January that is depreciable at 25 percent per year. She paid $5,000 cash and financed $25,000 on a note at 6 percent interest.

2. She has $8,000 cash in the bank at the end of the year.

3. Her receipts for cash purchases of ice cream total $20,000.

4. The value of her ice cream inventory at the end of the year is $500.

5. She paid $1,500 cash for all truck operating costs. In addition, she has an unpaid invoice for a recent equipment repair in the amount of $400.

6. She paid $1,500 of interest on the loan and $2,000 to reduce the loan balance.

7. She took $1,500 a month from the business for 12 months to live on. For simplicity purposes treat this as wages expense.

8. She purchased $500 of supplies with cash during the year and has $100 on hand at the end of the year.

9. On Oct. 30, she invested $5,000 in a 90-day certificate of deposit (an investment). Jill admitted she kept no record of the cash sales made during the year.

Required:

1. Determine the cash sales for 20X3.

2. Prepare a simple income statement for 20X3 based on accrual accounting.

Problem 21

For each scenario, indicate whether revenue should be recorded on a gross or net basis and your reasons for your decision.

Scenario One:

Hotel San Jose operates the parking lot and performs all services for guests using the facility. The hotel sets the prices, collects the revenue, employs the parking employees, and is responsible for the costs of operating the facility.

Scenario Two:

Hotel Fountaine contracts with Contractor Parkall to provide parking administration and valet parking services for Hotel Fountaine's guests. The hotel owns the parking structure, employs the personnel, is responsible for costs of maintenance of the facility (including liability insurance), and has approval rights over the price to be charged to guests. The contractor charges the hotel a contracted amount (percent of revenue or fixed amount) to provide the parking services. The hotel is responsible for collecting the amounts charged to guests' folios.

Scenario Three:

Best Resort contracts with Parking Company to provide parking facilities in a preferred provider relationship with the hotel. Parking Company owns and operates the parking lot. The hotel passes the charge set by the Parking Company along to its guests without a mark-up and is responsible for the collection from the guests. The amounts collected on behalf of the Parking Company are remitted back to them on a periodic basis net of a contracted commission.

Problem 22

Below is a list of 20X2 activities/transactions for the Bradford Inn (BI):

1. The BI purchased a new van on July 1, 20X2 for $40,000. The expected life is five years and its expected salvage value is zero. The BI chooses to depreciate the van using the straight-line method. No depreciation has been recorded for 20X2.

2. The BI borrowed $10,000 from the GR Bank on July 1, 20X2. The annual interest rate is 6 percent and the loan is to be repaid with annual payments over a three-year period starting on June 30, 20X3. No interest expense has been recorded for 20X2.

3. The BI invested $25,000 in an 18-month certificate of deposit at GR Bank on December 1, 20X2. The annual interest rate is 4 percent. No income has been recorded in 20X2.

4. The BI paid advanced rent of $12,000 for offsite storage for one year on Oct. 1, 20X2. No rent expense has been recognized for 20X2.

Required

Prepare the adjusting entry to recognize expense or revenue for each situation for the year ending Dec. 31, 20X2.

Problem 23

Indicate whether revenue under the following scenarios at Sunset Resort and Spa should be recorded on a gross or net basis and your reasons for your decision.

Scenario One:

Sunset contracts with an online travel agent (OTA) to sell it room inventory. Sunset sets the price and pays the OTA 18 percent commission on room inventory sold. The guest pays Sunset, which then remits the commission to the OTA.

Scenario Two:

Sunset contracts with Wonderful Video to provide pay-per-view movies and other electronic services to guests on a per-usage basis. Wonderful Video sets the pricing for all services; Sunset bills the guests. Wonderful Video invoices Sunset monthly and Sunset deducts a commission from its remittance to Wonderful Video at 40 percent. Wonderful Video provides staff training in the use of in-room electronic services, manages guest issues and complaints, and oversees programming content, among other services.

Scenario Three:

Sunset operates a tennis center for its resort guests, hires all tennis center staff, purchases all equipment, and pays operating expenses and insurance coverage.

Problem 24

Indicate whether revenue from the following scenarios over the last month at the El Rey, a luxury resort, should be recorded on a gross or net basis and your reasons for your decision.

Scenario One:

El Rey contracts with an OTA to market and sell room inventory online. The OTA will pay El Rey $150 per room net any commission and sets the price offered to the guest, but does not guarantee minimum room-nights sold. It collects payment from the guest and remits the agreed-upon price to El Rey, which has no knowledge of the total amount paid by the guest to the OTA.

Scenario Two:

El Rey operates its own audiovisual department. Commerce Company owns all the necessary equipment, sets the price for and performs all audiovisual services, and invoices the guests.

Scenario Three:

El Rey contracts with ProTennis to operate its tennis facilities. ProTennis pays El Rey 30 percent of retail sales and guest payments for tennis services. El Rey collects the payments, which are charged to guest rooms, and remits 30 percent to ProTennis.

Problem 25

Below is a list of 20X1 transactions for Inn on the Ballpark:

1. Food valued at $4,800 was in the storeroom on Dec. 1. During the month, $35,876 of food was purchased. An inventory taken Dec. 31 showed $3,230 of food remained in the storeroom.

2. Insurance was purchased on Jan. 1 at $24,000 for the entire year.

3. The guest van purchased a year ago has a cost of $60,000, an estimated useful life of five years, and no salvage value. Inn on the Ballpark uses the straight-line depreciation method.

4. The amount owed in wages expense for December is $8,000.

Required: Prepare the adjusting entry to recognize expense or revenue for each situation for the month ending Dec. 31, 20X1.

2

THE BALANCE SHEET

THE BALANCE SHEET FORMULA

Assets
cash, inventory, property

=

Liabilities
*rent, wages, utilities
taxes, loans*

+

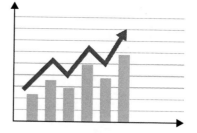

**Shareholders'
Equity**
retained earnings

Chapter 2 Outline

Competencies

1. Explain the purposes of the balance sheet. (pp. 50–51)

2. Identify the limitations of the balance sheet. (pp. 51–52)

3. Define the various elements of assets, liabilities, and owners' equity as presented on the balance sheet. (pp. 52–59)

4. Explain the use of footnotes in balance sheets. (pp. 59–63)

5. Interpret balance sheets using horizontal and vertical analysis as well as base-year comparisons. (pp. 63–67)

KEY TERMS

account format

additional paid-in capital

balance sheet

base-year comparisons

capital stock

common stock

common-size balance sheets

comparative balance sheets

consolidated financial statements

current assets

current liabilities

current ratio

fluctuation explanation

goodwill

horizontal analysis (comparative statement)

liquidity

long-term liabilities

noncurrent receivables

operating equipment

owners' equity

preferred stock

report format

restricted cash

retained earnings

treasury stock

vertical analysis (common-size analysis)

working capital

THE BALANCE SHEET IS A MAJOR financial statement prepared at the end of each accounting period. It reflects a balance between an organization's assets and claims to its assets, called liabilities and owners' equity. This statement is also referred to as a statement of financial position. It contains answers to many questions that managers, owners (investors), and creditors may have, such as the following:

1. How much cash was on hand at the end of the period?
2. What was the total debt of the hospitality operation?
3. What was the mix of internal and external financing at the end of the period?
4. How much was owed to the hotel by guests?
5. What amount of taxes was owed to the various governmental tax agencies?
6. What was the operation's ability to pay its current debt?
7. What was the financial strength of the operation?
8. How much interest do stockholders have in the operation's assets?

This chapter addresses the purposes and limitations of the balance sheet. We will also consider the formats and contents of balance sheets, with special attention to the suggested balance sheet from the *Uniform System of Accounts for the Lodging Industry (USALI)*.[1] In addition, we will discuss the kinds and purposes of footnotes attached to balance sheets. Finally, we will consider techniques for analyzing the financial information contained in a balance sheet. Appendix A at the end of the book includes the financial statements for Hilton Hotels from 2020 and 2021.[2]

2.1 PURPOSES OF THE BALANCE SHEET

Other major financial statements—the income statement, the statement of owners' equity, and the statement of cash flows—pertain to a period of time. The **balance sheet** reflects the financial position of the hospitality operation—its assets, liabilities, and owners' equity—at a given date. It is the financial statement that reflects, or tests and proves, the fundamental accounting equation (assets equal liabilities plus owners' equity).

Management, although generally more interested in the income statement and related department operations statements, will find balance sheets useful for conveying financial information to creditors and investors. In addition, management must determine if the balance sheet reflects to the best extent possible the financial position of the hospitality operation. For example, many long-term loans specify a required **current ratio** (which is current assets divided by current liabilities). Failure to meet the requirement may result in all long-term debt being reclassified as current and thus due immediately. Since few operations could raise large sums of cash quickly, bankruptcy could result. Therefore, management must carefully review the balance sheet to determine that the operation is in compliance. For example, assume that on December 31, 20X1 (year-end), a hotel has $500,000 of current assets and $260,000 of current liabilities. Further assume that the current ratio requirement in a bank's loan agreement with the hotel is 2 to 1. The required current ratio can be attained simply by taking the appropriate action. In this case, the payment of $20,000 of current liabilities with cash of $20,000 results in current assets of $480,000 and current liabilities of $240,000, resulting in a current ratio of 2 to 1.

Creditors are interested in the hospitality operation's ability to pay its current and future obligations. The ability to pay its current obligations is shown, in part, by a comparison of current assets and current liabilities. The ability to pay its future obligations depends, in part, on the relative amounts of long-term financing by owners and creditors. Everything else being the same, the greater the financing from investors, the higher the probability that long-term creditors will be paid and the lower the risk that these creditors take in "investing" in the enterprise.

Investors are most often interested in earnings that lead to dividends. To maximize earnings, an organization should have financial flexibility, which is the operation's ability to change its cash flows to meet unexpected needs and take advantage of opportunities. Everything else being the same, the greater the financial flexibility of the hospitality operation, the greater its opportunities to take advantage of new profitable investments, thus increasing net income and, ultimately, cash dividends for investors.

In addition, the balance sheet reveals the liquidity of the hospitality operation. **Liquidity** measures the operation's ability to convert assets to cash. Even when a property's past earnings have been substantial, this does not in itself guarantee that the operation will be able to meet its obligations as they become due. The hospitality operation should have sufficient liquidity not only to pay its bills, but also to provide its owners with adequate dividends.

Analysis of several balance sheets for several periods will yield trend information that is more valuable than single-period figures. In addition, comparison of balance sheet information with projected balance sheet numbers (when available) will reveal management's ability to meet various financial goals.

2.2 LIMITATIONS OF THE BALANCE SHEET

As useful as the balance sheet is, it is generally considered less useful than the income statement to investors, long-term creditors, and especially to management. Since the balance sheet is based on the cost principle, it often does not reflect current values of some assets, such as property and equipment. For hospitality operations whose assets are appreciating rather than depreciating, this difference may be significant.

Another limitation of balance sheets is that they fail to reflect many elements of value to hospitality operations. Most important to hotels, motels, restaurants, clubs, and other sectors of the hospitality industry are people. Nowhere in the balance sheet is there a reflection of the human resource investment. Millions of dollars are spent in recruiting and training to achieve an efficient and highly motivated workforce, yet this essential ingredient for successful hospitality operations is not shown as an asset.

Balance sheets are limited by their static nature; that is, they reflect the financial position for only a moment. Thereafter, they are less useful because they become outdated. Thus, the user of the balance sheet must be aware that the financial position reflected at year-end may be quite different one month later. For example, a hospitality operation with $1 million of cash may seem financially strong at year-end, but if it invests most of this cash in fixed assets two weeks later, its financial flexibility and liquidity are greatly reduced. This situation would generally be known to the user of financial documents only if a balance sheet and/or other financial statements were available for a date after this investment had occurred.

Finally, the balance sheet, like much of accounting, is based on judgments; that is, it is *not* exact. Certainly, assets equal liabilities plus owners' equity. However, several balance sheet items are based on estimates. The amounts shown as accounts receivable (net) reflect the estimated amounts to be collected. The amounts shown as inventory reflect the lower of the cost or market (i.e., the lower of original cost and current replacement cost) of the items expected to be sold, and the amount shown as property and equipment reflects the cost less estimated depreciation. In each case, accountants use estimates to arrive at values. To the degree that these estimates are in error, the balance sheet items will be wrong.

2.3 BALANCE SHEET FORMATS

The balance sheet can be arranged in either the account or report format. The **account format** lists the asset accounts on the left side of the page and the liability and owners' equity accounts on the right side. Exhibit 2.1 illustrates this arrangement. The **report format** shows assets first, followed by liabilities and owners' equity. The group totals on the report form can show either that assets equal liabilities and owners' equity or that assets minus liabilities equal owners' equity. Exhibit 2.2 illustrates the report format.

2.4 CONTENT OF THE BALANCE SHEET

The balance sheet consists of assets, liabilities, and owners' equity. Simply stated, assets are things owned by the firm, liabilities are claims of outsiders to assets, and **owners' equity** is claims of owners to assets. Thus, assets must equal (balance) liabilities and owners' equity. Assets include various accounts, such as cash, inventory for resale, buildings, and accounts receivable. Liabilities include accounts such as accounts payable, wages payable, and mortgage payable. Owners' equity includes capital stock and retained earnings. These major elements are generally divided into various classes, as shown in Exhibit 2.3. While balance sheets may be organized differently, most hospitality operations follow the order shown in Exhibit 2.3.

Exhibit 2.1	Balance Sheet Account Format

Mason Hotel
Balance Sheet
Dec. 31, 20X1

ASSETS		LIABILITIES AND OWNER'S EQUITY	
Current Assets		Current Liabilities	
Cash	$ 458,714	Accounts Payable	$ 332,581
Accounts Receivable	655,317	Notes Payable	141,588
Inventories	247,618	Payroll Payable	164,721
Prepaid Expenses	145,782	Short-Term Lease Liability	233,672
Other Current Assets	23,588	Other Current Liabilities	128,954
Total Current Assets	1,531,019	Total Current Liabilities	1,001,516
Property & Equipment:		Long-Term Liabilities	
Land	3,000,000	Mortgage Payable	100,589
Building	450,000	Long-Term Lease Liability	1,836,155
Furnishing & Equipment	700,000	Total Long-Term Liabilities	1,936,744
Less: Accumulated Depreciation	(400,000)		
Net Property & Equipment	3,750,000	Equity	
Operating ROU Asset	2,046,217	Melvin Mason, Capital at Jan 1, 20X1	3,130,504
Total Long-Term Assets	5,796,217	Add: Net Income	1,258,472
		Melvin Mason, Capital at Dec 31, 20X1	4,388,976
Total Assets	**$ 7,327,236**		
		Total Liabilities and Owner's Equity	**$ 7,327,236**

Exhibit 2.2 | Balance Sheet Report Format

Mason Hotel
Balance Sheet
Dec. 31, 20X1

ASSETS

Current Assets

Cash	$ 458,714
Accounts Receivable	655,317
Inventories	247,618
Prepaid Expenses	145,782
Other Current Assets	23,588
Total Current Assets	1,531,019

Property & Equipment:

Land	3,000,000
Building	450,000
Furnishing & Equipment	700,000
Less: Accumulated Depreciation	(400,000)
Net Property & Equipment	3,750,000
Operating ROU Asset	2,046,217
Total Long-Term Assets	5,796,217

Total Assets	**$ 7,327,236**

LIABILITIES AND OWNER'S EQUITY

Current Liabilities

Accounts Payable	$ 332,581
Notes Payable	141,588
Payroll Payable	164,721
Short-Term Lease Liability	233,672
Other Current Liabilities	128,954
Total Current Liabilities	1,001,516

Long-Term Liabilities

Mortgage Payable	100,589
Long-Term Lease Liability	1,836,155
Total Long-Term Liabilities	1,936,744

Equity

Melvin Mason, Capital at Jan 1, 20X1	3,130,504
Add: Net Income	1,258,472
Melvin Mason, Capital at Dec 31, 20X1	4,388,976

Total Liabilities and Owner's Equity	**$ 7,327,236**

Current Accounts

Under both "assets" and "liabilities and owners' equity" is a "current" classification. **Current assets** normally refer to items to be converted to cash or used in operations within one year or in a normal operating cycle. **Current liabilities** are obligations that are expected to be satisfied either by using current assets or by creating other current liabilities within one year or in a normal operating cycle.

Exhibit 2.4 reflects a normal operating cycle, which includes (1) the purchase of inventory for resale and labor to produce goods and services, (2) the sale of goods and services, and (3) the collection of accounts receivable from the sale of goods and services.

Exhibit 2.3   Major Elements of the Balance Sheet

Assets

Current Assets
Noncurrent Assets:
      Noncurrent Receivables
      Investments
      Property and Equipment
      Other Assets

Liabilities and Owners' Equity

Current Liabilities
Long-Term Liabilities
Owners' Equity

Exhibit 2.4   Normal Operation Cycle

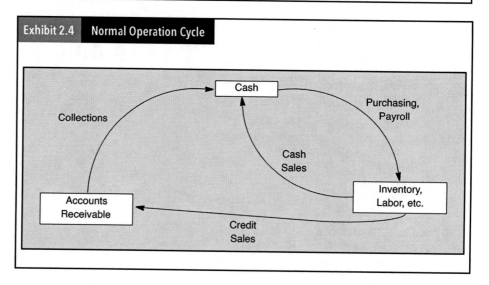

A normal operating cycle may be as short as a few days, as is common for many quick-service restaurants, or it may extend over several months for some hospitality operations. It is common in the hospitality industry to classify assets as current/noncurrent on the basis of one year rather than on the basis of the normal operating cycle.

Current Assets. Current assets, listed in the order of liquidity, generally consist of cash, short-term investments, receivables, inventories, operating equipment, and prepaid expenses. Cash consists of cash in house banks, cash in checking and savings accounts, and certificates of deposit. The exception is cash restricted for retiring long-term debt, which should be shown under other assets. Cash is shown on the balance sheet at its face value.

Short-term investments (also known as marketable securities) are shown as current assets when they are available for conversion to cash. Investments that are not available for conversion to cash are considered investments (noncurrent). Generally, the critical factor in making this current/noncurrent decision is management's intent. Short-term investments should be shown on the balance sheet at market value.

The current asset category of receivables consists of accounts receivable—trade and notes receivable. Accounts receivable—trade are open accounts carried by a hotel or motel on the guest, city, or rent ledgers. Notes receivable due within one year are also listed, except for notes from affiliated companies, which should be shown under "due from owner, management company, or related party." Receivables should be stated at the amount estimated to be collectible. An allowance for doubtful accounts, the amount of receivables estimated to be uncollectible, should be subtracted from receivables to provide a net receivables amount.

Inventories of a hospitality operation consist primarily of merchandise held for resale, such as food and beverage inventory. The cost of unused supplies to be used in operating the property, if significant, should also be reported as part of the inventories. Examples of supplies include cleaning and guest supplies. Inventories are generally an insignificant percentage of the total assets of a hospitality operation and may be valued at cost. If the amount of inventory is material and the difference between cost and market is significant, then the inventory should be stated at the lower of cost or market.

Operating equipment is equipment used in the daily operation of a hotel and includes linen, china, glassware, silver, and uniforms. When the estimated usage of these items is less than one year, the item is considered a current asset and expensed over its useful life not to exceed 12 months. Operating equipment items with useful lives greater than one year are shown as other assets (noncurrent) on the balance sheet.

Another current asset category is prepaid expenses. Prepaid expenses represent purchased goods and services to be used by the hospitality operation within one year. For example, assume that a fire insurance premium of $24,000 affords insurance protection for one year after the transaction. At the date of the expenditure, the $24,000 is classified as prepaid insurance and, thereafter, is amortized by a monthly reduction of $2,000 (1/12 of $24,000), which is shown on the income statement as insurance expense. Other prepaid expenses include prepaid rent, prepaid property taxes, prepaid interest, and prepaid maintenance and service contracts.

Prepaid expenses that will benefit the operation beyond one year from the balance sheet date should be classified as other assets. For example, assume that a three-year fire insurance policy costs $72,000. The entry to record the cash disbursement would be to debit prepaid insurance for $24,000 (the cost of coverage for the next 12 months) and to debit deferred charges—insurance for $48,000 (the cost of insurance coverage paid that benefits the operation for periods beyond 12 months from the balance sheet date).

Other current assets listed on the balance sheet per the *USALI* are restricted cash and items not shown elsewhere that are reasonably expected to be realized in cash or otherwise in the next 12 months. The latest edition of the *USALI* should be viewed for more detailed information.

Current Liabilities. Current liabilities are obligations at the balance sheet date that are expected to be paid by converting current assets or by creating other current liabilities within one year. They generally consist of one of the four following types:

1. Payables resulting from the purchase of goods, services, and labor and from the applicable payroll taxes.

2. Amounts received in advance of the delivery of goods and services, such as advance deposits on rooms and banquet deposits.

3. Obligations to be paid in the current period relating to fixed-asset purchases, operating and finance leases, or to reclassification of long-term debt as current.

4. Dividends payable and income taxes payable.

The major classifications of current liabilities according to the *USALI* are notes payable; current maturities of long-term debt; income taxes payable; accrued expenses; advance deposits; accounts payable; and due to owner, management company, or related party. Notes payable include short-term notes that are due within 12 months. Current maturities of long-term debt include the principal payments of long-term debt such as notes and similar liabilities, sinking fund obligations, and the principal portion of capitalized leases due within 12 months. Accounts payable include amounts due to creditors for merchandise, services, equipment, or other purchases. Current portions of operating lease liability and finance lease liability are also found here. Accrued expenses are expenses incurred before the balance sheet date that are not due until after the balance sheet date. Advance deposits include amounts received for services that have not been provided as of the balance sheet date. Due to owner, management company, or related party includes amounts due the owner, a management company, and/or other related entities for loans, advances for capital improvements, management fees, and other expenses or advances provided to a property. These accounts are classified as either current or long-term based on their payment terms.

Obligations to be paid with **restricted cash** (i.e., cash that has been deposited in separate accounts, often for the purpose of retiring long-term debt) within 12 months of the balance sheet date should be classified as current.

Current liabilities are often compared to current assets. The difference between current assets and current liabilities is commonly called **working capital** (or net working capital). The current ratio results from dividing current assets by current liabilities. Many hospitality properties operate successfully with a current ratio approximating 1 to 1, compared with a reasonable current ratio for many other industries of 2 to 1. The major reason for this difference lies with the relatively low amount of inventories required and relatively high turnover of receivables by hospitality operations as compared to many other industries.

Noncurrent Receivables

Noncurrent receivables include both accounts and notes receivable that are not expected to be collected within one year from the balance sheet date. If any collectibility is uncertain regarding noncurrent receivables, an allowance for doubtful noncurrent receivables should be used (similar to the allowance account for current receivables) and subtracted from total noncurrent receivables to provide net noncurrent receivables.

Investments

Investments generally include debt or equity securities and ownership interests that are expected to be held on a long-term basis. Investments in marketable equity securities and debt securities, where there is no intent and ability to hold such securities to maturity, should be considered "available for sale" and reflected at market value with unrealized gains and losses being shown, net of tax effects, as a separate component of equity. Investment in debt securities where there is the intent and ability to hold such securities to maturity should be considered "held to maturity" and reflected at amortized cost. Investments in affiliated entities should be shown separately, unless insignificant. Investments in property for future development generally should also be accounted for as investments. The method of accounting for and the basis for valuing investments should be disclosed in notes to the financial statements.

Property and Equipment

Property and equipment consists of fixed assets, including land, buildings, furnishings and equipment, construction in progress, and leasehold improvements.[3] With the exception of land, the cost of all property and equipment is written off to expense (depreciation expense) over time due to the matching principal. Depreciation methods used should be disclosed in a footnote to the balance sheet. The depreciation method used for financial reporting to outsiders and that used for tax purposes may differ, resulting in deferred income taxes.

On the balance sheet, property and equipment and right-of-use (ROU) assets are also shown. A right-of-use asset represents the hotel's right to use an underlying asset for the lease term for both operating leases and finance leases; ROU assets for operating leases should be presented separately from ROU assets for finance leases on the balance sheet. Property and equipment are shown at cost and are reduced by the related accumulated depreciation and amortization.

Other Assets

Other assets consist of all noncurrent assets not included in the aforementioned categories. Other assets include the following items.

Intangible assets. These assets lack physical substance and include trademarks, customer lists, and goodwill. **Goodwill** is the excess of a hospitality operation's purchase price over the dollars assigned to its individual assets. The value is evaluated periodically for impairment and when impairment occurs, it is recognized. The other intangible assets are amortized over their expected lives.

Deferred financing costs. Deferred financing costs represent the incremental, direct costs of obtaining financing, such as loan fees and bond issuance costs. Such costs should be reported as a direct reduction from the face amount of the related debt and are usually amortized over the life of the related financing, and all amortization is presented within interest expense. The method and period of amortization should be disclosed in notes to the financial statements.

Operating equipment. Operating equipment includes linen, china, glassware, silver, and uniforms. When a property purchases operating equipment items, it must establish the period of consumption. If the period of consumption of the operating equipment items is expected to be less than one year, the items are classified as current assets. Whether the items are categorized as current or long-term assets, operating equipment items are not depreciated, but instead are expensed to the appropriate department expense account. Most purchases of operating equipment are expected to be consumed within a period of one year or less. However, if a property makes a bulk purchase of china, for example, and the expected usage period is greater than one year, the usage period is appropriately stated at the longer time period.

Restricted cash. Cash that is restricted should be separately classified as current or noncurrent based on the nature of the restriction. If the restriction is to pay for capital improvements and similar items or portions of long-term debt, the cash should be classified as long-term. If the debt is due within 12 months of the balance sheet, the related restricted cash should be classified as current.

Other assets also include the costs to organize the hospitality operation (organization costs), security deposits, and unamortized franchise costs. The initial franchise fee paid by the franchisee should be recorded under other assets and amortized against revenue over the life of the franchise agreement.

Long-Term Liabilities

Long-term liabilities are obligations at the balance sheet date that are expected to be paid beyond the next 12 months. Common long-term liabilities consist of notes payable, mortgages payable, bonds payable, capitalized lease obligations, and deferred income taxes. Any long-term debt to be paid with current assets within the next year is reclassified as current liabilities. Still, long-term debt per the *USALI* is reported on the balance sheet in total, with the amount due within 12 months subtracted as "less current maturities."

Finance lease obligations reported as long-term liabilities generally cover several years, while short-term leases are usually expensed when paid. Deferred income taxes result from timing differences in reporting for financial and income tax purposes—that is, the accounting treatment of an item for financial reporting purposes results in a different amount of expense (or revenue) than that used for tax purposes. Generally, the most significant timing difference for hotels and motels relates to depreciation, since many operations use the straight-line method for financial reporting purposes and an accelerated method for income tax purposes. For example, suppose a hotel decides to depreciate a fixed asset on a straight-line basis at $15,000 a year for reporting purposes, and depreciate the same asset $25,000 for the year using an accelerated method for tax purposes. If the firm's marginal tax rate is 25 percent, then the difference in depreciation expense of $10,000 ($25,000 − $15,000) times 25 percent results in $2,500 cash saved and is reported as a noncurrent liability. The book entry to record this savings is as follows:

Income Tax Expense	$2,500	
Deferred Income Taxes		$2,500

Owners' Equity

The **owners' equity** section of the balance sheet reflects the owners' interest in the operation's assets. The detail of the owners' equity section is a function of the organization of the business. The four major types of business organization are sole proprietorships, partnerships, limited liability companies, and corporations. The owners' equity section of a corporation includes capital stock, additional paid-in capital, retained earnings, and treasury stock. **Capital stock** consists of the shares of ownership of a corporation that generally allow its holders to have voting rights. For most hospitality operations, this is known as **common stock**. In addition, a few operations have also issued **preferred stock**, which provides preferential treatment on dividends but may not give the shareholder voting rights. When more than one type of stock has been issued, each should be reported separately. Capital stock is the product of the number of shares outstanding and the par value of the shares.

The **additional paid-in capital** category consists of payments for capital stock in excess of the stated and/or par value of the capital stock. For example, cash of $50 received from the sale of common stock with a par value of $10 would be recorded as $10 to the common stock account and the remainder ($40) as "additional paid-in capital" or "paid-in capital in excess of par."

Retained earnings reflect earnings generated but not distributed as dividends. Changes in this account during the year are commonly shown on a statement of owners' equity.

Treasury stock represents the property's own capital stock that has been repurchased for future issuance but not retired. The cost of the treasury shares is shown as a reduction of owners' equity.

Exhibit 2.5 shows the prescribed formats of the assets section and the liabilities and owners' equity section of the balance sheet from the *USALI*. Note that the owners' equity section of the balance sheet pertains to a lodging operation organized as a corporation.

When a lodging operation is organized as a sole proprietorship, all of the owner's equity is reflected in one account, as illustrated in Exhibit 2.1 (Melvin Mason, Capital). The $4,388,976 of capital held by Melvin Mason would have been spread across at least two accounts, capital stock and retained earnings, if the Mason Hotel had been incorporated.

Finally, many lodging businesses are organized as partnerships. The owners' equity section of a partnership should reflect each partner's equity. The balance sheet for a partnership with many partners simply will refer to a supplementary schedule showing each partner's share. The owners' equity section of a business organized as a partnership by its three owners is illustrated as follows:

M. Kass, Capital	$ 50,000
J. Ninety, Capital	25,000
R. Chicklets, Capital	25,000
Total Owners' Equity	$ 100,000

A separate statement of owners' equity is presented if there is significant activity in the accounts during the period. If net income or loss is the only change to the equity accounts in the period, it is permissible to reconcile the change in retained earnings at the bottom of the statement of income and exclude presentation of the separate owners' equity statement. The format of the owners' equity statement will depend on the type of entity. Exhibit 2.6 shows an example of the presentation for a corporation.

Footnotes

The balance sheets of hospitality operations, although packed with financial information, are not complete without the other financial statements (income statement and statement of cash flows) and footnotes. Footnotes are discussed below.

The full disclosure principle requires that financial information be sufficient to inform the users—creditors, owners, and others. This can only be accomplished by providing footnote disclosure in addition to the financial statements. Thus, footnotes are an integral part of the financial statements of a hospitality operation. They should contain additional information not presented in the body of the financial statements. They should not contradict or soften the disclosure of the financial statements, but rather provide needed explanations. The financial statements of publicly held companies generally include the following footnotes to describe all significant accounting policies followed by the hospitality firm:

- Description of business
- Earnings per share
- Stock-based compensation
- Basis of consolidation
- Use of estimates
- Cash and temporary cash investments
- Inventory methods and valuation

Exhibit 2.5   Balance Sheet

BALANCE SHEET
Assets

	Current Year	Prior Year
CURRENT ASSETS		
Cash and Cash Equivalents		
House Banks	$	$
Demand Deposits		
Temporary Cash Investments		
Total Cash		
Restricted Cash		
Short-Term Investments		
Receivables		
Accounts Receivable		
Notes Receivable		
Current Maturities of Noncurrent Receivables		
Other		
Total Receivables		
Less Allowance for Doubtful Accounts		
Net Receivables		
Due To/From Owner, Management Company, or Related Party		
Inventories		
Operating Equipment		
Prepaid Expenses		
Deferred Income Taxes—Current		
Other		
Total Current Assets		
NONCURRENT RECEIVABLES, Net of Current Maturities		
INVESTMENTS		
PROPERTY AND EQUIPMENT		
Land		
Buildings		
Leaseholds and Leasehold Improvements		
Furnishings and Equipment		
Construction in Progress		
Total Property and Equipment		
Less Accumulated Depreciation and Amortization		
Net Property and Equipment		
OTHER ASSETS		
Intangible Assets		
Cash Surrender Value of Life Insurance		
Deferred Charges		
Deferred Income Taxes—Noncurrent		
Operating Equipment		
Restricted Cash		
Preopening Expenses		
Other		
Total Other Assets		
TOTAL ASSETS	$	$

BALANCE SHEET
Liabilities and Owners' Equity

	Current Year	Prior Year
CURRENT LIABILITIES		
Notes Payable		
Banks	$	$
Others		
Total Notes Payable		
Due To/From Owner, Management Company, or Related Party		
Accounts Payable		
Accrued Expenses		
Advance Deposits		
Income Taxes Payable		
Deferred Income Taxes—Current		
Maturities of Long-Term Debt		
Gift Certificates and Cards		
Other		
Total Current Liabilities		
LONG-TERM DEBT, Net of Current Maturities		
Mortgage Notes, Other Notes, and Similar Liabilities		
Obligations Under Capital Leases		
Total Long-Term Debt		
OTHER LONG-TERM LIABILITIES		
DEFERRED INCOME TAXES—Noncurrent		
COMMITMENTS AND CONTINGENCIES		
OWNERS' EQUITY—one of the formats found on the next page		
TOTAL LIABILITIES AND OWNERS' EQUITY	$	$

Source: *Uniform System of Accounts for the Lodging Industry,* 11th Revised Edition (Austin, TX: Hospitality Financial and Technology Professionals, 2018).

CORPORATION
Stockholders' Equity

	Current Year	Prior Year
____% Cumulative Preferred Stock, $ ____ par value, authorized ____ shares; issued and outstanding ____ shares	$	$
Common Stock, $ ____ par value, authorized ____ shares; issued and outstanding ____ shares		
Additional Paid-In Capital		
Retained Earnings		
Accumulated Other Comprehensive Income (Loss), Net of Income Tax		
Less: Treasury Stock, ____ shares of Common Stock, at cost		
Total Stockholders' Equity	$	$

Source: *Uniform System of Accounts for the Lodging Industry,* 11th Revised Edition (Austin: Hospitality Financial and Technology Professionals, 2018).

- Accounting for investments, including the valuation of marketable securities
- Property, plant, and equipment
- Depreciation and amortization policies
- Intangibles—Goodwill
- Accounting for deferred charges
- Advertising costs
- Accounting for pensions
- Revenue recognition
- Accounting for income taxes
- Fair value of financial instruments
- Capitalization
- Lease disclosure
- Computation of net income (loss) per share (public companies only)
- Foreign currency translation
- Concentration of credit risk

Disclosure of accounting policy-related footnotes should be followed by such additional notes as are necessary to provide for full disclosure of all significant events or conditions reflected in the financial statements, or as otherwise required by the rules of professional accounting or regulatory organizations. Typical events and conditions which are disclosed in the notes accompanying financial statements include the following:

- Changes in accounting methods
- Long-term debt agreements
- Pension and/or profit-sharing plans
- Other post-retirement and post-employment benefits
- Income taxes
- Long-term contracts
- Extraordinary items of income or expense
- Significant long-term commitments, including leases
- Foreign operations
- Related-party transactions
- Contingent liabilities, including pending litigation
- Subsequent events
- Stockholders' equity transactions
- Financial instruments (including derivatives)
- Impairment or disposal of long-lived assets
- Restructuring costs
- Extinguishment of debt
- Discontinued operations

- Business combinations
- Accumulated other comprehensive income (loss)
- Business segment information (public companies only)
- Quarterly financial information (public companies only)
- Organization (geographic and nature of business)
- Major customers

Consolidated Financial Statements

Many major hospitality companies consist of several corporations. For example, the hypothetical XYZ Hotel Company consists of a parent corporation, XYZ Hotel Company, and three separately incorporated hotels—Hotel X, Hotel Y, and Hotel Z. The XYZ Hotel Company owns 100 percent of the capital stock of each of the three hotels. Each hotel has its own set of financial statements, but for purposes of financial reporting, they are combined with the parent's financial statements. The combined statements are referred to as **consolidated financial statements**. Generally, the first footnote includes a brief description of the principles of consolidation used to combine the statements of a parent corporation and its subsidiary corporations.

In effect, consolidated financial statements reflect a single economic unit rather than the legal separate entities resulting from separate corporations. In general, more than 50 percent of the voting stock of a subsidiary should be owned by the holding company or by the same interests if the associated companies' financial statements are to be combined. Accounting procedures related to financial statement consolidations are covered in advanced accounting textbooks.

2.5 BALANCE SHEET ANALYSIS

The information shown on the balance sheet is most useful when it is properly analyzed. The analysis of a balance sheet may include the following:

1. Horizontal analysis (comparative statements)
2. Vertical analysis (common-size statements)
3. Base-year comparisons
4. Ratio analysis

In the remainder of this chapter, the first three techniques will be discussed.

Horizontal Analysis

Horizontal analysis (comparative statements) compares two balance sheets—the current balance sheet and the balance sheet of the previous period. In this analysis, the two balance sheets are often referred to as **comparative balance sheets**. This represents the simplest approach to analysis and is essential to the fair reporting of the financial information. Often included for management's analysis are the two sets of figures with the changes from one period to the next expressed both in absolute and relative terms. Absolute changes show the change in dollars between two periods. For example, assume that cash was $10,000 at the end of year 20X1 and $15,000 at the end of year 20X2. The absolute change is the difference of $5,000.

The relative change (also called the percentage change) is found by dividing the absolute change by the amount for the previous period. The relative change, using the cash example above, is 50 percent ($5,000 ÷ $10,000). The $5,000 absolute change may not seem significant by itself, but viewed as a relative change, it is a 50 percent increase over the previous year.

Examine the comparative balance sheets for the Stratford Hotel found in Exhibit 2.7. Comparative analysis shows that marketable securities increased by $629,222 in absolute terms and 404.7 percent in relative terms. The increase is substantial. In light of these figures, a manager would desire answers to several questions, including the following:

1. Are the marketable securities readily convertible to cash?

2. Is the amount invested in marketable securities adequate for cash needs in the next few months?

3. Should some of the dollars invested in marketable securities be moved to less liquid but higher rate-of-return investments?

Exhibit 2.7   Comparative Balance Sheets

Comparative Balance Sheets
Stratford Hotel

| | Dec. 31 | | Change from 20X1 to 20X2 | |
	20X2	20X1	Amount	Percentage
ASSETS				
Current Assets:				
Cash	$ 104,625	$ 85,600	$ 19,025	22.2%
Marketable Securities	784,687	155,465	629,222	404.7
Accounts Receivable (net)	1,615,488	1,336,750	278,738	20.9
Inventories	98,350	92,540	5,810	6.3
Other	12,475	11,300	1,175	10.4
Total	2,615,625	1,681,655	933,970	55.5
Property and Equipment:				
Land	905,700	905,700	0	0
Buildings	5,434,200	5,434,200	0	0
Furnishings and Equipment	2,617,125	2,650,500	(33,375)	(1.3)
Less: Accumulated Depreciation	1,221,490	749,915	471,575	62.9
Total	7,735,535	8,240,485	(504,950)	(6.1)
Other Assets	58,350	65,360	(7,010)	(10.7)
Total Assets	$ 10,409,510	$ 9,987,500	$ 422,010	4.2%
LIABILITIES				
Current Liabilities:				
Accounts Payable	$ 1,145,000	$ 838,000	$ 307,000	36.6%
Current Maturities of Long-Term Debt	275,000	275,000	0	0
Income Taxes Payable	273,750	356,000	(82,250)	(23.1)
Total	1,693,750	1,469,000	224,750	15.3
Long-Term Debt:				
Notes Payable	50,000	0	50,000	N.M.
Mortgage Payable	1,500,000	1,775,000	(275,000)	(15.5)
Less: Current Maturities	275,000	275,000	0	0
Total	1,275,000	1,500,000	(225,000)	(15.0)
Total Liabilities	2,968,750	2,969,000	(250)	0
OWNERS' EQUITY				
Common Stock	1,750,000	1,750,000	0	0
Additional Paid-In Capital	250,000	250,000	0	0
Retained Earnings	5,440,760	5,018,500	422,260	8.4
Total	7,440,760	7,018,500	422,260	6.0
Total Liabilities and Owners' Equity	$ 10,409,510	$ 9,987,500	$ 422,010	4.2%

N.M. = not meaningful

Exhibit 2.8	Fluctuation Explanation

Fluctuation Explanation—Marketable Securities
Stratford Hotel

	Balance at Dec. 31		Increase
	20X2	**20X1**	**(Decrease)**
Marketable Securities			
Commercial Paper	$ 240,000	$ 90,000	$ 150,000
Bank Repurchase Agreements	44,687	15,465	29,222
Treasury Bills	150,000	25,000	125,000
Treasury Bonds	150,000	25,000	125,000
Corporate Stocks & Bonds	200,000	–0–	200,000
	$ 784,687	$ 155,465	$ 629,222

Significant changes in other accounts should be similarly investigated.

To explain the drastic change in some balance sheet items, a **fluctuation explanation** may be prepared. This explanation provides detail not available on the balance sheet. Exhibit 2.8 illustrates a fluctuation explanation for the Stratford Hotel's marketable securities.

Vertical Analysis

Another approach to analyzing balance sheets is to reduce them to percentages. This **vertical analysis**, often referred to as **common-size statement** analysis, is accomplished by having total assets equal 100 percent and individual asset categories equal percentages of the total 100 percent. Likewise, total liabilities and owners' equity equal 100 percent and individual categories equal percentages of 100 percent.

Common-size balance sheets permit a comparison of amounts relative to a base within each period. For example, assume that cash at the end of year 20X1 is $10,000 and total assets are $100,000. At the end of year 20X2, assume that cash is $15,000 and total assets are $150,000. Horizontal analysis shows a $5,000/50 percent increase. But cash at the end of each year is 10 percent of the total assets ($10,000 divided by $100,000 equals 10 percent; $15,000 divided by $150,000 equals 10 percent). What first appears to be excessive cash at the end of year 20X2 ($5,000) may not be excessive since cash is 10 percent of total assets in both cases. However, only a detailed investigation would resolve whether cash equal to 10 percent of total assets is required in each case.

Examine the Stratford Hotel's common-size balance sheets (Exhibit 2.9). Notable changes include marketable securities (1.6 percent to 7.5 percent), total current assets (16.9 percent to 25.1 percent), accumulated depreciation (−7.5 percent to −11.7 percent), and accounts payable (8.4 percent to 11.0 percent). Management should investigate significant changes such as these to determine if they are reasonable. If the changes are found to be unreasonable, management should attempt to remedy the situation.

Common-size statement comparisons are not limited strictly to internal use. Comparisons may also be made against other operations' financial statements and against industry averages. Common-size figures are helpful in comparing hospitality operations that differ materially in size. For example, assume that a large hospitality operation has current assets of $500,000, while a much smaller operation's current assets are $50,000 and that both figures are for the same period. If total assets equal $1.5 million for the large operation and $150,000

Exhibit 2.9   Common-Size Balance Sheets

Common-Size Balance Sheets
Stratford Hotel

	Dec. 31		Common Size	
ASSETS	20X2	20X1	20X2	20X1
Current Assets:				
Cash	$ 104,625	$ 85,600	1.0%	0.9%
Marketable Securities	784,687	155,465	7.5	1.6
Accounts Receivable (net)	1,615,488	1,336,750	15.5	13.4
Inventories	98,350	92,540	1.0	0.9
Other	12,475	11,300	0.1	0.1
Total	2,615,625	1,681,655	25.1	16.9
Property and Equipment:				
Land	905,700	905,700	8.7	9.1
Buildings	5,434,200	5,434,200	52.2	54.4
Furnishings and Equipment	2,617,125	2,650,500	25.1	26.5
Less: Accumulated Depreciation	1,221,490	749,915	(11.7)	(7.5)
Total	7,735,535	8,240,485	74.3	82.5
Other Assets	58,350	65,360	0.6	0.6
Total Assets	$ 10,409,510	$ 9,987,500	100.0%	100.0%
LIABILITIES				
Current Liabilities:				
Accounts Payable	$ 1,145,000	$ 838,000	11.0%	8.4%
Current Maturities of Long-Term Debt	275,000	275,000	2.6	2.8
Income Taxes Payable	273,750	356,000	2.6	3.6
Total	1,693,750	1,469,000	16.2	14.8
Long-Term Debt:				
Notes Payable	50,000	0	0.5	0
Mortgage Payable	1,500,000	1,775,000	14.4	17.8
Less: Current Maturities	275,000	275,000	(2.6)	(2.8)
Total	1,275,000	1,500,000	12.3	15.0
Total Liabilities	$ 2,968,750	$ 2,969,000	28.5%	29.8%
OWNERS' EQUITY				
Common Stock	$ 1,750,000	$ 1,750,000	16.8%	17.5%
Additional Paid-In Capital	250,000	250,000	2.4	2.5
Retained Earnings	5,440,760	5,018,500	52.3	50.2
Total	7,440,760	7,018,500	71.5	70.2
Total Liabilities and Owners' Equity	$ 10,409,510	$ 9,987,500	100.0%	100.0%

for the small enterprise, then both operations have current assets equaling 33.3 percent of total assets. These percentages provide a more meaningful comparison than the dollar amount of the current assets when comparing financial statements of the two companies.

Base-Year Comparisons

A third approach to analyzing balance sheets is **base-year comparisons**. This approach allows a meaningful comparison of the balance sheets for several periods. A base period is selected as a starting point, and all subsequent periods are compared with the base. Exhibit 2.10 illustrates the base-year comparisons of the Stratford Hotel's current assets for the years 20X0–20X2.

The base-year comparisons of the Stratford Hotel use 20X0 as the base. Total current assets for 20X2 are 152.71 percent of the total current assets for 20X0. The user of this analysis is quickly able to determine the changes of current assets over a period of time. For example, cash increased only 26.30 percent from the end of 20X0 to the end of 20X2, while marketable securities increased 239.32 percent.

Exhibit 2.10 Base-Year Comparisons

Base-Year Comparisons
Current Assets Stratford Hotel

	20X2	20X1	20X0
Cash	126.30%	103.33%	100.00%
Marketable Securities	339.32%	67.23%	100.00%
Accounts Receivable (net)	124.39%	102.92%	100.00%
Inventories	110.55%	104.02%	100.00%
Other	114.11%	103.37%	100.00%
Total Current Assets	152.71%	98.18%	100.00%

Although the balance sheet may not play the vital role in management decision-making that other financial statements play, it is still an important tool. By examining it, managers, investors, and creditors may determine the financial position of the hospitality operation at a given moment in time. It is used to help determine an operation's ability to pay its debts, offer dividends, and purchase fixed assets.

The balance sheet is divided into three major categories: assets, liabilities, and owners' equity. Assets are the items owned by the operation, while liabilities and owners' equity represent claims to the operation's assets. Liabilities are amounts owed to creditors. Owners' equity represents the residual interest in assets for investors. Both assets and liabilities are divided into current and noncurrent sections. Current assets are cash and other assets that will be converted to cash or used in the property's operations within the next year. Current liabilities represent present obligations that will be paid within one year. The major categories of noncurrent assets include noncurrent receivables, investments, property and equipment, and other assets. Long-term liabilities are present obligations expected to be paid beyond the next 12 months from the date of the balance sheet.

Owners' equity generally includes common stock, paid-in capital in excess of par, and retained earnings. Common stock is the product of the number of shares outstanding and the par value of the shares. Paid-in capital in excess of par is the amount over the par value paid by investors when they purchased the stock from the hospitality property. Retained earnings are the past earnings generated by the operation but not distributed to the stockholders in the form of dividends.

As assets are the items owned by the property, and liabilities and owners' equity are claims to the assets, the relationship involving the three is stated as follows: Assets = Liabilities + Owners' Equity. The balance sheet is prepared either with assets on one side of the page and liabilities and owners' equity on the other (account format) or with the three sections in one column (report format).

In order to gain more information from the balance sheet, it is frequently compared to the balance sheet prepared at the end of the previous period. One tool used is horizontal analysis, which calculates absolute and relative differences between the current year's data and the data from the prior period. Significant differences are generally analyzed. Another type of analysis is vertical analysis, which states all accounts as percentages of either total assets or total liabilities and owners' equity. Differences between the end results of two periods can then be examined. Alternatively, the balance sheet figures for the particular hospitality operation may be compared with data from other properties or with averages for the hospitality industry as a whole. These comparisons can highlight differences and help management identify areas of concern. A third type of analysis is called base-year comparisons. This approach expresses changes over two or more years as percentages of a base year.

account format—A possible arrangement of a balance sheet that lists the asset accounts on the left side of the page and the liability and owners' equity accounts on the right side.

additional paid-in capital—Payments for capital stock in excess of the stated and/or par value of the capital stock. Also called paid-in capital in excess of par.

balance sheet—Statement of the financial position of the hospitality establishment at a given date, giving the account balances for assets, liabilities, and owners' equity.

base-year comparison—An analytical tool that allows a meaningful comparison of financial statements for several periods by using a base period as a starting point (set at 100 percent) and comparing all subsequent periods with the base.

capital stock—Shares of ownership of a corporation.

common stock—Capital stock of a corporation that generally allows its holders to have voting rights.

common-size balance sheets—Balance sheets used in vertical analysis whose information has been reduced to percentages to facilitate comparisons.

comparative balance sheets—Balance sheets from two or more successive periods used in horizontal analysis.

consolidated financial statements—The combined financial statements of a parent corporation and its subsidiary corporations.

current assets—Resources of cash and items that will be converted to cash or used in generating income within one year through normal business operations.

current liabilities—Obligations that are due within one year.

current ratio—Ratio of total current assets to total current liabilities expressed as a coverage of so many times; calculated by dividing current assets by current liabilities.

fluctuation explanation—A document providing detail not available on the balance sheet that explains drastic changes in balance sheet items.

goodwill—The excess of a hospitality operation's purchase price over the dollars assigned to its individual assets.

horizontal analysis (comparative statements)—The analysis of financial statements from the current and previous periods in terms of both absolute and relative variances for each line item. Comparing financial statements for two or more accounting periods in terms of both absolute and relative variances for each line item.

liquidity—The ability of an operation to meet its short-term (current) obligations by maintaining sufficient cash and/or investments easily convertible to cash.

long-term liabilities—Obligations at the balance sheet date that are expected to be paid beyond the next 12 months, or if paid in the next year, will be paid from restricted funds; also called noncurrent liabilities.

noncurrent receivables—Accounts and notes receivable that are not expected to be collected within one year from the balance sheet date.

operating equipment—Equipment used in the daily operation of a hotel, including linen, china, glassware, silver, and uniforms.

owners' equity—Financial interest of the owners of a business; assets minus liabilities.

preferred stock—Stock issued by a corporation that provides preferential treatment on dividends but may not give the stockholder voting rights.

report format—A possible arrangement of a balance sheet that lists assets first, followed by liabilities and owners' equity.

restricted cash—Cash that has been deposited in separate accounts, often for the purpose of retiring long-term debt.

retained earnings—An account for recording undistributed earnings of a corporation.

treasury stock—Capital stock of a corporation that the corporation has repurchased for future issuance.

vertical analysis (common-size analysis)—Analyzing individual financial statements by reducing financial information to percentages of a whole; that is, income statement line items are expressed as percentages of total revenue; balance sheet assets are expressed as percentages of total assets; and so forth.

working capital—Current assets minus current liabilities.

1. How do creditors and investors use the balance sheet?

2. What are some of the limitations of the balance sheet?

3. What are the differences and similarities between the account and report formats of the balance sheet?

4. What are assets, liabilities, and owners' equity? What is the relationship among the three?

5. What is meant by the phrase "the lower of cost or market"? When is it used?

6. What are deferred income taxes? Where are they recorded on the balance sheet?

7. What are the differences between a comparative balance sheet and a common-size balance sheet?

8. What is the order of liquidity for the following accounts (most liquid first): marketable securities, prepaid expenses, cash, inventories, and receivables?

9. How do the terms "current" and "long-term" relate to the balance sheet?

10. How is the current ratio determined? What does it reflect?

Problem 1

The Canyon Café's balance sheet contains several assets, as listed below. Identify the major classification of each based on the *USALI* balance sheet (see Exhibit 2.5).

        Construction in progress
        Cash advance to affiliated company
        Petty cash
        Trade receivables
        Operating equipment
        Notes receivable—long-term
        Office supplies
        Land
        Unamortized franchise costs
        Marketable securities
        Food inventory
        Prepaid insurance
        Leasehold improvements
        Right-of-use assets
        Deferred financing costs

Problem 2

Haley Day is the sole owner of the Daytime Café. The balance sheet accounts for her café are shown below as of the end of December 20X6.

Cash	$ 16,000
Prepaid insurance	9,000
Land	650,000
Accounts payable	16,000
Accounts receivable	7,000
Taxes payable	7,000
Mortgage payable—long-term	800,000
Equipment	300,000
Buildings	550,000
Mortgage payable—current	50,000
Inventories	29,000
Wages payable	11,000
H. Day, Capital	??
Accumulated depreciation	100,000

Required:

Prepare a classified balance sheet for the Daytime Café. Note: the amount of H. Day, Capital is the difference between total assets and total liabilities.

Problem 3

The Shanghai Restaurant Inc. (SRI) has had several activities occur during December 20X2. Explain how each selected activity directly affects balance sheet accounts.

Example	Impact
1,000 shares of common stock are sold at par value of $10 per share	Increases cash by $10,000 and increases common stock by $10,000

Selected Activities:

1. The board of directors declares a cash dividend of $2.00 per share payable in January 20X3 (100,000 shares are outstanding).

2. Accounts receivables of $50,000 are collected.

3. A delivery truck costing $130,000 is purchased. Cash of $10,000 is paid and a note payable for the remainder is signed.

4. Cash sales total $120,000 for the month.

5. Beverage for resale costing $5,000 is purchased on account.

6. Employees are paid $10,000 of wages due for the month.

7. A vendor who supplies produce to SRI is paid $5,000 on account.

8. One thousand shares of SRI's common stock are repurchased at $20.00 per share for reissue at some future date.

9. Long-term debt of $40,000 is reclassified as current at the end of December.

10. The utility bill of $1,000 is paid for December.

Problem 4

Emily Wolfenship has incorporated her foodservice business and sold stock to raise funds in the first year of operations as follows:

1. She sold 30,000 shares of common stock for $25 per share. The stock has a $1 par value. Two hundred thousand shares have been authorized for sale.

2. She sold 10,000 shares of 5 percent cumulative preferred stock for $60 per share. The stock has a par value of $1 per share. Fifty thousand shares have been authorized for sale.

3. Operations for the first year resulted in net income of $300,000.

4. Preferred stockholders were paid their 5 percent dividend for the first year.

Required:

Prepare the owners' equity section of the firm's balance sheet. Refer to Exhibit 2.5 for specific language.

Problem 5

The balance sheet account balances of the J.D. Inn at the end of 20X3 are as follows:

Cash	$ 60,000
Accounts receivable	80,000
Allowance for doubtful accounts	10,000
Food inventory	40,000
Prepaid insurance	22,000
Investments (long-term)	800,000
Land	400,000
Building	13,000,000
Equipment	950,000
Accumulated depreciation—building	2,500,000
Accumulated depreciation—equipment	200,000
Organization costs (unamortized)	100,000
Accounts payable	35,000
Wages payable	29,000
Income taxes payable	45,000
Current maturities of long-term debt	120,000
Long-term debt	9,120,000
Deferred income taxes (long-term liability)	159,000
Common stock	500,000
Paid-in capital in excess of par	1,000,000
Retained earnings	1,064,000

Required:

Prepare the balance sheet in accordance with the USALI.

Problem 6

The Ruby Mountain Motel's balance sheet at December 31, 20X4, is as follows:

Balance Sheet
Dec. 31, 20X4

Assets

Current Assets:	
Cash	$ 14,000
Accounts Receivable	15,000
Cleaning Supplies	4,500
Total Current Assets	33,500
Property and Equipment:	
Land	150,000
Building	800,000
Furnishings and Equipment	50,000
Less: Accumulated Depreciation	125,000

Balance Sheet
Dec. 31, 20X4

Net Property and Equipment	875,000
Total Assets	$ 908,500
LIABILITIES AND OWNER'S EQUITY	
Current Liabilities:	
Notes Payable	$ 22,960
Accounts Payable	9,440
Wages Payable	2,000
Total Current Liabilities	34,400
Long-Term Liabilities:	
Mortgage Payable	430,000
Total Liabilities	464,400
Owner's Equity:	
R. Mountain, Capital at Jan. 1, 20X4	384,100
Net Income for 20X1	60,000
R. Mountain, Capital at Dec. 31, 20X4	444,100
Total Liabilities and Owner's Equity	$ 908,500

Required:

Prepare a common-size balance sheet for the Red Mountain Motel.

Problem 7

The Phoenix Sunrise Hotel's (PSH) list of current accounts and its March 31, 20X7, balances are as follows:

Accounts Receivable	$ 150,000
Accounts Payable	30,000
Accrued Expenses	19,000
Advance Deposits	25,000
Allowance for Doubtful Accounts	3,000
Beverage Inventory	20,000
Cash	35,000
Current Maturities—LTD	50,000
Food Inventory	25,000
Income Taxes Payable	4,000
Prepaid Insurance	5,000
Notes Payable	8,000
Notes Receivable	19,850
Short-Term Investments	18,000

Required:

1. What is the total of the current assets for PSH?

2. What is the sum of PSH's current liabilities?

3. What is the net working capital of PSH?

4. What is the current ratio of PSH?

Problem 8

The Wendall Corporation had several activities during 20X5 that impacted its capital accounts. For each activity, indicate all the balance sheet accounts affected during 20X5, the direction of the impact (increase or decrease), and the amount of the impact.

1. On February 1, 20X5, 100,000 shares of common stock were sold for $25 per share. The par value per share of common stock is $1.

2. On April 15, 10,000 shares of Winchester common stock were repurchased and held for possible reissue. The amount paid per share was $20.

3. Dividends per share of $1 were declared on June 15. One million of common shares were authorized and 350,000 were outstanding on June 15.

4. The dividends declared on June 15 were paid on July 15, 20X5.

5. Preferred stock (5 percent) was sold September 15, 20X5. Ten thousand shares of no-par stock were sold for $55 per share.

6. On December 15, 20X5, a cash dividend for preferred stock was declared equal to 2.5 percent of the book value of the preferred stock. This dividend is to be paid on January 15, 20X6.

Problem 9

Big Montana Hotel, a new lodging operation, will attempt to maximize its cash flow whenever possible. It has $4 million of equipment, which it will depreciate over the next five years as follows:

1. For book purposes, it will use the straight-line method. Assume a salvage value of $0.

2. For tax purposes, it will use the double declining balance method.

Assume Big Montana's marginal tax rate is 30 percent.

Required:

1. Determine the depreciation expense for book purposes for its first year.

2. Determine the depreciation expense for tax purposes for the first year. (Base your calculation on the double declining balance method.)

3. Prepare the journal entry to record deferred taxes based on the above information.

Problem 10

Amelia Café
Unclassified Balance Sheets
Dec. 31, 20X1 and 20X2

Current Assets:	20X1	20X2
Cash	$ 25,000	$ 30,000
Marketable Securities	25,000	35,000
Accounts Receivable	24,000	28,000

Amelia Café
Unclassified Balance Sheets
Dec. 31, 20X1 and 20X2

Inventory	28,000	24,000
Prepaid Expenses	10,000	25,000
Equipment	420,000	567,000
Accumulated Depreciation	(180,000)	(200,000)
Total Assets	$ 352,000	$ 509,000
Current Liabilities:		
Accounts Payable	$ 15,000	$ 29,000
Accrued Expenses	24,000	30,000
Dividends Payable	25,000	30,000
Mortgage Payable (current)	22,000	25,000
Mortgage Payable (long-term)	150,000	215,000
Common Stock	120,000	120,000
Treasury Stock	(20,000)	(40,000)
Retained Earnings	16,000	100,000
Total Liabilities and Owners' Equity	$ 352,000	$ 509,000

Required:

1. Determine the amount of current assets on December 31, 20X1.

2. Determine the amount of current liabilities on December 31, 20X1.

3. Determine the net working capital on December 31, 20X1.

4. Determine the net working capital on December 31, 20X2.

5. Determine the dollar and percentage change in net working capital from December 31, 20X1 to December 31, 20X2.

Problem 11

The Spartan Inn, a sole proprietorship, has several accounts, as follows:

Room sales	$ 1,000,000
Land	80,000
Cash	5,000
Accounts payable	20,000
Inventories	15,000
Accounts receivable	80,000
Bonds payable (long-term)	300,000
Jerry Spartan, Capital (1/1/20X4)	300,000
Accrued expenses	10,000
Prepaid expenses	8,000
Temporary investments	25,000
Building	500,000
Equipment and furnishings	200,000
Franchise fees (deferred)	15,000
Accumulated depreciation	150,000

Income tax payable	10,000
Deferred income taxes (noncurrent/ credit balance)	20,000
Interest expense	25,000

Other information is as follows:

The Spartan Inn's net income for 20X4 was $145,000, and Jerry Spartan withdrew $27,000 for personal use during 20X4.

Required:

Prepare a balance sheet for the Spartan Inn as of December 31, 20X4, in accordance with the USALI (see Exhibit 2.5).

Problem 12

The Singh Park Hotel's activities impacting retained earnings and other equity accounts during 20X2 were as follows:

1. Five thousand shares of common stock with a par value of $5 were sold for $15 per share.

2. Dividends declared in 20X1 of $80,000 were paid in 20X2.

3. Dividends declared in 20X2 and paid in 20X2 totaled $190,000.

4. Dividends declared in 20X2 to be paid during 20X3 totaled $40,000.

5. Net earnings for 20X2 equaled $280,000.

The balance of the retained earnings account was $300,000 at the beginning of 20X2.

Required:

Prepare the Statement of Retained Earnings for 20X2 for the Singh Park Hotel. (Assume the Singh Park Hotel's fiscal year ends on December 31, 20X2.)

Problem 13

The following information is KRS Inc.'s balance sheet account balances as of December 31, 20X1 and 20X2. You have been hired by Kermit Smith, the owner, to prepare a financial package for a bank loan, including comparative balance sheets.

Assets	20X1	20X2
Cash	$ 16,634	$ 20,768
Accounts receivable	16,105	11,618
Marketable securities	10,396	10,496
Inventories	14,554	18,554
Operating equipment (current)	69,255	84,934
Prepaid expenses	4,158	3,874
Land	116,435	116,435
Building	1,007,090	1,007,090
Accumulated depreciation	453,263	537,849

Liabilities and Owners' Equity

Accounts payable	13,265	12,945
Accrued expenses	2,047	1,039
Deferred income taxes (noncurrent)	8,163	7,927
Current portion of long-term debt	20,407	20,060
Long-term debt	553,429	533,369
Retained earnings	192,853	149,380
Common stock	211,200	211,200

Required:

Prepare comparative balance sheets for December 31, 20X1 and 20X2, in accordance with the *USALI*. Note: the comparative approach is shown in Exhibit 2.7.

Problem 14

Mrs. Wolf, the owner of The Foxtail, a small lodging operation, has asked for your help in understanding the balance sheets for 20X1 and 20X2. She is able to present you with the condensed balance sheets as follows:

The Foxtail
Condensed Balance Sheets
Dec. 31, 20X1 and 20X2

	20X1	20X2
Cash	$ 10,000	$ 12,000
Accounts receivable	26,500	18,500
Investments	10,000	20,000
Equipment	200,000	325,000
Accumulated depreciation	(20,000)	(64,000)
Total Assets	$ 226,500	$ 311,500
Current Liabilities:		
Accounts payable	$ 18,000	$ 21,000
Mortgage payable (current)	5,000	22,000
Dividends payable	5,000	8,000
Noncurrent Liabilities:		
Mortgage payable	75,000	110,000
Notes payable	20,000	–0–
Common stock	70,000	100,000
Treasury stock	(20,000)	(30,000)
Retained earnings	53,500	80,500
Total Liabilities and Owners' Equity	$ 226,500	$ 311,500

Required:

Answer the following questions.

1. What amount of existing debt must be paid during 20X3?

2. What is the total of current assets at the end of 20X2?

3. What is the amount of net working capital at the end of 20X2?

4. How has the change in accounts receivable during 20X2 affected cash at the end of 20X2?

5. How much does The Foxtail owe its stockholders at the end of 20X2?

6. What is the net book value of The Foxtail's fixed assets at the end of 20X2?

7. What amount of past earnings are available for distribution to The Foxtail's owners at the end of 20X2?

Problem 15

Below are the modified balance sheets for Melton Corporation for the years ended December 31, 20X1 and 20X2.

Assets	20X1	20X2
Cash	$ 433	$ 388
Marketable securities	101	50
Accounts receivable, net	348	430
Inventory	218	283
Investments	595	373
Property and equipment	2,696	5,998
Accumulated Depreciation	(1,000)	(1,300)
Other assets	52	1,355
Total Assets	$ 3,443	$ 7,577
Liabilities and Stockholders' Equity		
Liabilities:		
Accounts payable	517	648
Income taxes payable	100	150
Dividends payable	300	200
Current portion—LTD	150	200
Long-term debt	920	2,406
Deferred income taxes	202	762
Total Liabilities	2,189	4,366
Stockholders' Equity:		
Common stock, 193 and 249 shares outstanding, respectively	494	642
Additional paid-in capital	–0–	1,745
Retained earnings	902	935
Treasury shares, at cost	(142)	(111)
Total Stockholders' Equity	1,254	3,211
Total Liabilities and Stockholders' Equity	$ 3,443	$ 7,577

Additional Information:

1. During 20X2, marketable securities, which cost $X, were sold for $200, resulting in a gain from the sale of $150.

2. Assume $50 of treasury stock was purchased during 20X2.

3. Assume Melton did <u>not</u> retire any of its common stock, but instead sold stock reflected by the increase in the appropriate accounts.

4. Assume $450 of dividends was declared during 20X2.

Based on the above balance sheets and additional information, answer the questions below:

1. What were the total current assets at the beginning of 20X1?

2. The total net book value of property and equipment at the end of 20X2 was_____.

3. What is meant by "net" after accounts receivable?

4. How much treasury stock was sold during 20X2?

5. What was the amount of money raised by selling common stock during 20X2?

6. What was the amount of long-term debt borrowed during 20X2?

7. Assume the increases in common stock and additional paid-in capital relate solely to the sale of common stock during 20X2. What was the average selling price per share of common stock?

8. What was the net working capital at the end of 20X2?

9. What amount of dividends was paid during 20X2?

10. What was the net income for 20X2?

Problem 16

Ms. Bush, the owner of The Texan, a small hospitality operation, has asked for your help in understanding the balance sheets for 20X1 and 20X2. She is able to present you with the condensed balance sheet as follows:

The Texan
Condensed Balance Sheets
Dec. 31, 20X1 and 20X2

	20X1	20X2
Cash	$ 10,000	$ 5,000
Accounts receivable	126,500	118,500
Investments (long-term)	10,000	25,000
Equipment	800,000	925,000
Accumulated depreciation	(20,000)	(64,000)
Total Assets	$ 926,500	$ 1,009,500
Current Liabilities:		
Accounts payable	$ 18,000	$ 21,000
Notes payable (current)	25,000	42,000
Dividends payable	5,000	6,000
Noncurrent Liabilities:		
Notes payable	675,000	690,000
Common stock	100,000	105,000
Paid-in capital in excess of par	70,000	95,000

The Texan
Condensed Balance Sheets
Dec. 31, 20X1 and 20X2

Treasury stock	(20,000)	(30,000)
Retained earnings	53,500	80,500
Total Liabilities and Owner's Equity	$ 926,500	$ 1,009,500

Additional Information:

a. Assume equipment costing $25,000 and depreciated down to $10,000 was sold for $12,000 during 20X2.

b. Assume all current liabilities at the end of the year are paid during the following year.

c. Assume retained earnings is impacted only by declaration of dividends during the year and net earnings for the year.

Required:

Answer the following questions.

1. What is the amount of cash at the beginning of 20X1?

2. What are the current assets at the beginning of 20X2?

3. What is the amount of net working capital at the end of 20X1?

4. How has the change in accounts payable during 20X2 affected cash at the end of 20X2?

5. What is the net book value of The Texan's equipment at the end of 20X2?

6. Based on the above, what were the net earnings for The Texan for 20X2?

7. If the changes in the common stock and paid-in capital in excess of par from 20X1 to 20X2 are from the sale of additional shares, what was the selling price per share? (Assume 10,000 shares were sold.)

8. How much long-term debt was borrowed during 20X2?

9. What was the total gain or loss on equipment sales?

10. What were the purchases of equipment during 20X2?

11. What was the depreciation expense for 20X2?

Problem 17

James Strat, the owner of The Molehill, a small lodging operation, has asked for your help in answering a few selected questions. He is able to present you with the condensed balance sheets and some additional information, as follows:

The Molehill
Condensed Balance Sheets
Dec. 31, 20X1 and 20X2

	20X1	20X2
Cash	$ 10,000	$ 8,000
Accounts receivable	26,500	22,500

The Molehill
Condensed Balance Sheets
Dec. 31, 20X1 and 20X2

Investments	10,000	20,000
Equipment	200,000	320,000
Accumulated depreciation	(20,000)	(59,000)
Total Assets	$ 226,500	$ 311,500
Current Liabilities:		
Accounts payable	$ 18,000	$ 21,000
Mortgage payable (current)	5,000	22,000
Dividends payable	5,000	8,000
Noncurrent Liabilities:		
Mortgage payable	75,000	110,000
Common stock	50,000	70,000
Retained earnings	73,500	80,500
Total Liabilities and Owner's Equity	$ 226,500	$ 311,500

Additional information regarding activities for 20X2:

a. Equipment costing $20,000 and fully depreciated (to $0) was sold for $5,000.

b. Long-term investments costing $10,000 were sold for $12,000.

c. Common stock was sold and long-term debt was borrowed during 20X2. There were no noncash financing or investing activities during 20X2.

d. Income before gain on the sale of equipment and investments for 20X2 totaled $15,000. The firm's average and marginal tax rates are 15 percent and 20 percent, respectively.

e. Assume all current liabilities are paid on a timely basis.

f. Assume retained earnings is affected only by net earnings and dividends declared.

Required:

Answer the following questions.

1. What was the change in cash during 20X2?

2. What amount of investments were purchased during 20X2?

3. What was the total cost of equipment purchases during 20X2?

4. What was the net book value of fixed assets at the beginning of 20X2?

5. What was the amount of the mortgage payment, excluding interest expense, during 20X2?

6. What were the net earnings for 20X2?

7. What were the amount of dividends declared during 20X2?

8. What were the amount of dividends paid during 20X2?

Problem 18

The trial balance of balance sheet accounts of Lancer's, a popular casual dining spot, as of December 31, 20X3, is as follows:

	Debits	Credits
Cash	$ 5,000	
Marketable securities	10,000	
Accounts receivable	100,000	
Allowance for doubtful accounts		$ 5,000
Food inventory	15,000	
Prepaid rent	5,000	
Prepaid insurance	8,000	
Investments	50,000	
Land	80,000	
Building	420,000	
Equipment	100,000	
Accumulated depreciation		100,000
Accounts payable		15,000
Income taxes payable		–0–
Accrued expenses		25,000
Dividends payable		–0–
Long-term debt		300,000
Capital stock		89,000
Paid-in capital in excess of par		68,000
Retained earnings (1/1/20X3)		61,000

Additional Information:

a. Dividends declared during 20X3 totaled $30,000. Only $20,000 of the dividends declared in 20X3 have been paid as of Dec. 31, 20X3. The unpaid dividends have not been recorded.

b. Operations generated $800,000 of revenue for 20X3. Expenses recorded totaled $650,000. Additional adjustments required are as follows:
   1. The allowance for doubtful accounts should be adjusted to 10 percent of accounts receivable.
   2. Prepaid insurance of $8,000 is the premium paid for insurance coverage for July 1, 20X3, through June 30, 20X4.
   3. Unrecorded depreciation expense for 20X3 totals $41,000.
   4. Income taxes have not been recorded. Lancer's average rate is 20 percent.

c. The long-term debt account includes $50,000 which must be paid on June 30, 20X4.

Required:

Prepare a balance sheet according to the USALI (see Exhibit 2.5).

Problem 19

Below is selected information from the comparative and common-size asset portion of balance sheets for Martin's Motel.

	Dec. 31		Dollar	Common-Size
	20X1	20X2	Difference	(Dec. 31, 20X2)
Current Assets:				
Cash				
House bank	$ _____	$ _____	$ (10)	_____ %
Demand deposit	_____	60	_____	0.6
Total Cash	_____	_____	(10)	1.0
Accounts receivable	1,241	_____	_____	14.0
Inventories	_____	_____	_____	_____
Total Current Assets	_____	1,620	201	_____
Investments	_____	_____	25	2.0
Property & Equipment (net):				
Land	957	1,030	_____	_____
Building	4,350	_____	_____	_____
Furniture	_____	_____	(75)	25.0
Other assets	49	_____	_____	0.5
Total Assets	$ _____	$ _____	$ _____	_____ %

Required:

Fill in the blanks above. Round all amounts to the nearest dollar.

Problem 20

What follows is selected information from the comparative and common-size asset sections of the balance sheets of December 31, 20X1 and 20X2 for the Gordon Lodge:

	December 31		Dollar	Common-Size
	20X1	20X2	Difference	(Dec. 31, 20X1)
Current Liabilities:				
Notes payable	$ 5,000	$ _____	$ _____	1.0 %
Accounts payable	_____	8,000	1,000	_____
Taxes payable	_____	_____	500	0.6
Wages payable	_____	_____	1,000	_____
Total	20,000	18,000	_____	_____
LTD:				
Mortgage payable	$ _____	$ _____	$ (20,000)	40.0 %
Deferred taxes	_____	80,000	_____	_____
Total	280,000	_____	(20,000)	_____
Owners' Equity:				
Common stock	$ _____	$ _____	$ 10,000	30.0 %

	December 31		Dollar	Common-Size
Retained earnings	____	80,000	20,000	____
Treasury stock	____	____	–0–	____
Total				
Total Liabilities and Owners' Equity	$ 500,000	$ ____	$ ____	____ %

Required:

Fill in the blanks above. Round all amounts to the nearest dollar.

Problem 21

The current asset section of the Westwood Inn's balance sheet for 20X1 through 20X3 is as follows:

	20X1	20X2	20X3
Cash	$ 100,000	$ 126,000	$ 143,000
Marketable securities	80,000	70,000	55,000
Accounts receivable	350,000	330,000	360,000
Allowance for doubtful accounts	(30,000)	(33,000)	(42,000)
Food inventory	60,000	63,000	68,000
Prepaid insurance	20,000	28,000	25,000
Total Current Assets	$ 580,000	$ 584,000	$ 609,000

Required:

Prepare base-year comparisons for the current assets section for the three-year period.

Problem 22

You have been hired by Jung Hee Yu, a successful entrepreneur, to assist in analyzing the balance sheet for her two-year-old hotel, the Seiko Inn. The following are the condensed balance sheets of the Seiko Inn.

Seiko Inn
Condensed Balance Sheets
Dec. 31, 20X1 and 20X2

	20X1	20X2
Cash	$ 30,000	$ 40,000
Accounts receivable	190,000	225,000
Inventory	30,000	35,000
Building (net)	10,000,000	9,500,000
Property and equipment (net)	1,400,000	1,500,000
Other assets	200,000	100,000
Total Assets	$ 11,850,000	$ 11,400,000

Seiko Inn
Condensed Balance Sheets
Dec. 31, 20X1 and 20X2

Accounts payable	$ 140,000	$ 135,000
Wages payable	60,000	15,000
Current maturities—LTD	500,000	500,000
Long-term debt	8,500,000	8,000,000
Total Liabilities	9,200,000	8,650,000
Owner's equity	2,650,000	2,750,000
Total Liabilities and Owner's Equity	$ 11,850,000	$ 11,400,000

Required:

1. What was the change in cash during 20X2?

2. What were the total current assets at the beginning of 20X1?

3. What were the total current liabilities at the end of 20X1?

4. What was the amount of net working capital at the end of 20X2?

5. If equipment costing $230,000 was purchased during 20X2 and there were no equipment disposals, what was the depreciation expense related to equipment for 20X2?

6. How did the change in accounts receivable from the two balance sheets affect cash flows for 20X2?

7. Based solely on the two balance sheets, how much long-term debt was paid in 20X2?

8. Assuming $50,000 of cash was "withdrawn" by J. Yu during 20X2 and that owner's equity is affected only by net income and withdrawals, what was the net income of the Seiko Inn during 20X2?

Problem 23

As the new controller of Matteo Ristorante, your owner gives you a list of their accounts and balance as of December 31, 20X9, and would like you to tell him how liquid his restaurant is. The accounts are in alphabetical order, and it also appears that the list included both income statement and balance sheet accounts.

Current Asset Accounts Receivable	$ 90,000
Current Liability Accounts Payable	33,000
Current Liability Accrued Expenses	12,000
Current Liability Advance Deposits	18,000
Current Contra Asset Allowance for Doubtful Accounts	(2,000)
Current Asset Beverage Inventory	18,000
Retained Earnings Beverage Revenue	48,000
Noncurrent Asset Building	1,000,000
Current Asset Cash	25,000

Current Liability Current Maturities of Long-Term Debt	34,000
Current Asset Food Inventory	29,000
Retained Earnings Food Revenue	267,000
Current Liability Income Taxes Payable	4,800
Long-Term Liability Mortgage Payable	50,000
Current Liability Notes Payable	25,750
Noncurrent Asset Notes Receivable (due within a year)	31,500
Noncurrent Asset Operating Equipment (noncurrent)	14,500
Noncurrent Liability Other Long-Term Debt	38,000
Current Asset Prepaid Insurance	9,000
Current Asset Prepaid Rent	8,000
Current Asset Short-Term Investments	55,000

Required:

1. What are the total current assets for Matteo Ristorante?

2. What are the total current liabilities for Matteo Ristorante?

3. What is the net working capital for Matteo Ristorante?

4. What is the current ratio for Matteo Ristorante?

5. If the quick ratio is defined as the total of cash, short-term investments, notes receivable, and accounts receivable divided by current liabilities, what is the quick ratio for Matteo Ristorante?

6. After calculating these five ratios, what is your opinion of Matteo's liquidity?

Problem 24

The retained earnings statement is often embedded within the balance sheet when a corporation presents its set of year-end financial statements and other equity accounts. The McMillan Restaurant Group ends its fiscal year on December 31, 20X8, and below are some additional pieces of information:

1. A total of 2,500 shares of common stock with a par value of $1 were sold for $18 per share.

2. Dividends declared in 20X7 of $60,000 were paid in 20X8.

3. Dividends declared in 20X8 and paid in 20X8 totaled $95,000.

4. Dividends declared in 20X8 to be paid during 20X9 totaled $39,000.

5. Net earnings for 20X8 equaled $330,000.

The balance of the retained earnings account was $433,545 at the beginning of 20X8.

Required:

Prepare the statement of retained earnings for 20X8 for the McMillan Restaurant Group for the end of the year.

Problem 25

Serene is a lovely 50-room resort by the Atlantic Ocean and enjoys strong occupancy year-round. June Atkins bought the resort a few months ago and, unfortunately, a hurricane landed just 20 miles north of Serene last week. While Ms. Atkins has insurance on the property and the resort only has minor damage, the windows of the accounting office were broken and the office has quite a bit of water damage: the computers are beyond repair and the accounting files were scattered and soaked. As Ms. Atkins has been concentrating on building a few new bungalows to add to the property, she had not thought of backing up the accounting information off-site or in the cloud. Due to this hurricane, many of the records as of December 31, 20X8, were destroyed. You are able to find bits and pieces of paper with the following information. Please help her determine the answers to the following questions:

1. One piece of paper shows Serene had a current ratio of 1.4 as of December 31, 20X8. Ms. Atkins also found the figures for current liabilities, at $25,876, and long-term liabilities, at $123,000. What is the amount of current assets for Serene?

2. When looking at her bank records, Ms. Atkins noted that as of December 31, 20X8, she had in her two bank accounts for Serene a total of $13,098 in cash. She also found her inventory book, which showed her total inventory on December 31, 20X8, was $19,499. Assuming the only current assets are cash, inventory, and accounts receivable, and the allowance of doubtful account is found to be $2,500 at the end of the year, what was the total accounts receivable owed to Ms. Atkins on December 31?

3. Ms. Atkins also found a vertical analysis of her balance sheet for December 31, 20X8, but only the percentage column and the accounts are visible. It states that Serene's current assets were 15 percent of the total assets. If so, what are the total assets as of December 31, 20X8?

4. Based on the information in the previous three questions, is there enough information for you to reconstruct the owner's equity as of December 31, 20X8? If so, calculate the owner's equity for Ms. Atkins.

3

THE INCOME STATEMENT

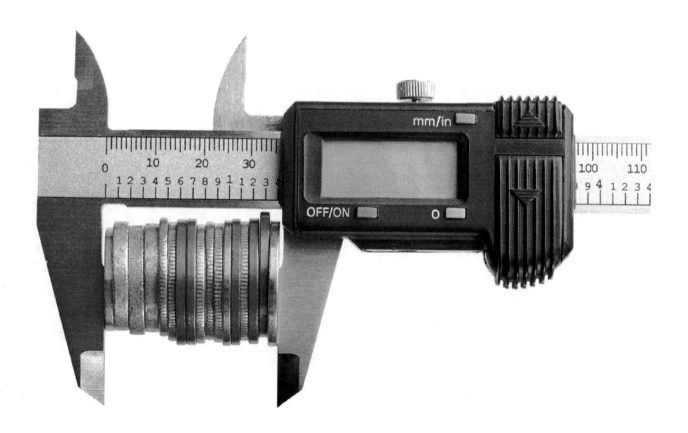

Chapter 3 Outline

Competencies

1. Describe revenues, expenses, gains, and losses as presented on the income statement. (pp. 92–94)

2. Distinguish between income statements prepared for internal users and those prepared for external users. (pp. 94–96)

3. Describe the contents of an income statement and summary operating statement based on the *Uniform System of Accounts for the Lodging Industry (USALI)*. (pp. 96–104)

4. Identify the differences between departmental income statements prepared for profit centers and those prepared for service centers in a hospitality operation. (pp. 104–106)

5. Interpret income statements using horizontal and vertical analysis as well as base-year comparisons. (pp. 110–113)

6. Distinguish the similarities and differences between the *USALI, USAR,* and *USFRC*. (pp. 113–116)

KEY TERMS

capacity costs

common-size income statements

comparative income statement

daily report of operations

departmental statements

expenses

gains

income statements

losses

ratio analysis

responsibility accounting

revenue

schedules

summary income statements

uniform systems of accounts

The income statement, also called the statement of earnings, the profit and loss (or P & L) statement, the statement of operations, and various other titles, reports the success of the hospitality property's operations for a period of time. This statement may be prepared on a weekly or monthly basis for management's use, and quarterly or annually for outsiders such as owners, creditors, and government agencies.

Users of financial statements examine an operation's income statements for answers to many questions, such as the following:

1. How profitable was the hospitality operation during the period?

2. What were the total sales for the period?

3. How much was paid for labor?

4. What is the relationship between sales and cost of sales?

5. How much have sales increased over last year?

6. What is the energy, water, and waste expense for the year, and how does it compare with the expense of a year ago?

7. How much was spent to market the hospitality operation's services?

8. How does net income compare with total sales for the period?

These and many more questions can be answered by reviewing the income statements that cover several periods of time. As mentioned, the **income statements** summarize the profits and losses of an operation and report the success of the hospitality property's operations for a period of time. The income statement, including statements by individual departments called **departmental statements,** are generally considered to be the most useful financial statements for management's review of operations. Owners and creditors, especially long-term creditors, find that the income statement yields significant information for determining investment value and creditworthiness. However, when analyzing the operating results of any entity, an income statement should be considered in conjunction with other financial statements as well as with the footnotes to those financial statements.

In this chapter, we will address the major elements of the income statement and consider its relationship with the balance sheet. We will also note the differences between income statements prepared for internal users and those for external users. The primary focus will be on the income statement prepared for internal users (managers) for a single property. The uniform system of accounts and the general approach to income statements in the hospitality industry will also be discussed. We will provide an in-depth discussion of the contents of the income statement, consider the uses of departmental statements and industry operating statistics, and discuss guidelines and techniques for analyzing income statements.

Finally, a brief overview of the income statements based on the *Uniform System of Accounts for Restaurants (USAR)* and the *Uniform System of Financial Reporting for Clubs (USFRC)* will be presented.

3.1 MAJOR ELEMENTS OF THE INCOME STATEMENT

The income statement for a single property reflects the revenues, expenses, gains, and losses for a period of time. **Revenue** represents the inflow of assets, reduction of liabilities, or a combination of both resulting from the sale of goods or services. For a hospitality operation, revenues generally include food sales, beverage sales, room sales, interest and dividends from investments, and rents received from lessees of retail space.

Expenses are defined as the outflow of assets, increase in liabilities, or a combination of both in the production and rendering of goods and services. Expenses of a hospitality operation generally include cost of goods sold (e.g., food and beverages), labor, energy, water, and waste, advertising, depreciation, and property taxes, to list a few.

Gains are defined as increases in assets, reductions in liabilities, or a combination of both resulting from a hospitality operation's incidental transactions and from all other transactions and events affecting the operation during the period, except those that count as revenues or investments by owners. For example, there may be a gain on the sale of equipment. Equipment is used by the business to provide goods and services and, when sold, only the excess proceeds over its net book value (purchase price less accumulated depreciation) are recognized as gain.

Finally, **losses** are defined as decreases in assets, increases in liabilities, or a combination of both resulting from a hospitality operation's incidental transactions and from other transactions and events affecting the operation during a period, except those that count as expenses or distributions to owners. In the equipment example above, if the proceeds were less than the net book value, a loss would occur and would be recorded as "loss on sale of equipment." Another example would be a loss from an act of nature, such as a tornado or hurricane. The loss reported is the reduction of assets less insurance proceeds received.

In the income statement for hospitality operations, revenues are reported separately from gains, and expenses are distinguished from losses. These distinctions are important in determining management's success in operating the hospitality property. Management is held accountable primarily for operations (revenues and expenses) and only secondarily (if at all) for gains and losses. Generally, gains and losses are shown near the bottom of the income statement before income taxes.

The income statements of large, multiunit hospitality businesses may also be affected by items such as discontinued operations, extraordinary gains and losses, and changes in accounting principles. Discontinued operations refers to operations of a segment of business that has been disposed of or, though still operating, will be disposed of in the future based on a formal plan of disposal. Extraordinary gains and losses are classified as extraordinary by their unusual nature and infrequency of occurrence. An extraordinary item is unusual in nature when the underlying event is highly abnormal and is clearly unrelated to the ordinary and typical activities of the hospitality company. The infrequency of occurrence of an extraordinary item is determined by judging that the underlying event would not reasonably be expected to recur in the foreseeable future. For example, a flood loss for a hotel near the Mississippi River may not be unusual, while casualty loss from a flood to a hotel located several miles from any river may meet the definition of extraordinary. The cumulative effect of a change in one method of accounting to another (such as from a straight-line method of depreciation to an accelerated method of depreciation) must be reported. Generally accepted accounting principles require that these additional items be reported on income statements as follows:

Income from continuing operations before taxes	$ XXX
Income tax expense	(XX)
Income from continuing operations	XXX
Discontinued operations (net of tax)	XX
Extraordinary gains and losses (net of tax)	XX
Cumulative effect of change in accounting principle (net of tax)	XX
Net income	$ XXX

Since 1997, the Financial Accounting Standards Board has required businesses to report comprehensive income in addition to net income.[1] This requirement relates primarily to the corporate level of large lodging firms. Comprehensive income includes net income plus other comprehensive income, as follows:

Net income		$ XXX
Other comprehensive income (net of tax):		
Foreign currency translation adjustments	$ XX	
Unrealized gains in securities	XX	
Pension liability adjustments	XX	
Other comprehensive income		XX
Comprehensive income		$ XXX

3.2 RELATIONSHIP WITH THE BALANCE SHEET

The income statement covers a period of time, while the balance sheet is prepared as of the last day of the accounting period. Thus, the income statement reflects operations of the hospitality property for the period between balance sheet dates. The result of operations—net income or loss for the period—is added to the proper equity account and shown on the balance sheet at the end of the accounting period.

3.3 INCOME STATEMENTS FOR INTERNAL AND EXTERNAL USERS

Hospitality properties prepare income statements for both internal users (managers) and external users (creditors, owners, etc.). These statements differ substantially. The income statements provided to external users are relatively brief, providing only summary detail about the results of operations. Income statements for external users are often called **summary income statements**, even though the word "summary" does not usually appear on the form. Exhibit 3.1 is the income statement presentation of Hyatt Hotels Corporation and its subsidiaries from a recent annual report. Hyatt's consolidated statement of income shows the following items:

- Revenues
- Costs and expenses
- Operating income
- Equity earnings
- Interest expense
- Gain (loss) on asset dispositions and impairment
- Asset impairments
- Net income
- Earnings per share

HYATT HOTELS CORPORATION AND SUBSIDIARIES
CONSOLIDATED STATEMENTS OF INCOME (LOSS)
For the Years Ended December 31, 2020, December 31, 2019, and December 31, 2018
(in millions of dollars, except per share amounts)

	2020	2019	2018
REVENUES:			
Owned and leased hotels	$ 513	$ 1,848	$ 1,918
Management, franchise, and other fees	239	608	552
Contra revenue	(30)	(22)	(20)
Net management, franchise, and other fees	209	586	532
Other revenues	58	125	48
Revenues for the reimbursement of costs incurred on behalf of managed and franchised properties	1,286	2,461	1,956
Total revenues	2,066	5,020	4,454
DIRECT AND SELLING, GENERAL, AND ADMINISTRATIVE EXPENSES:			
Owned and leased hotels	627	1,424	1,446
Depreciation and amortization	310	329	327
Other direct costs	65	133	48
Selling, general, and administrative	321	417	320
Costs incurred on behalf of managed and franchised properties	1,375	2,520	1,981
Direct and selling, general, and administrative expenses	2,698	4,823	4,122
Net gains (losses) and interest income from marketable securities held to fund rabbi trusts	60	62	(11)
Equity earnings (losses) from unconsolidated hospitality ventures	(70)	(10)	8
Interest expense	(128)	(75)	(76)
Gains (losses) on sales of real estate and other	(36)	723	772
Asset impairments	(62)	(18)	(25)
Other income (loss), net	(92)	127	(49)
INCOME (LOSS) BEFORE INCOME TAXES	(960)	1,006	951
BENEFIT (PROVISION) FOR INCOME TAXES	257	(240)	(182)
NET INCOME (LOSS)	(703)	766	769
NET INCOME (LOSS) AND ACCRETION ATTRIBUTABLE TO NONCONTROLLING INTERESTS	—	—	—
NET INCOME (LOSS) ATTRIBUTABLE TO HYATT HOTELS CORPORATION	$ (703)	$ 766	$ 769
EARNINGS (LOSSES) PER SHARE—Basic			
Net income (loss)	$ (6.93)	$ 7.33	$ 6.79
Net income (loss) attributable to Hyatt Hotels Corporation	$ (6.93)	$ 7.33	$ 6.79
EARNINGS (LOSSES) PER SHARE—Diluted			
Net income (loss)	$ (6.93)	$ 7.21	$ 6.68
Net income (loss) attributable to Hyatt Hotels Corporation	$ (6.93)	$ 7.21	$ 6.68
Net income (loss)	$ (703)	$ 766	$ 769
Other comprehensive income (loss), net of taxes:			
Foreign currency translation adjustments, net of tax (benefit) expense of $2, $—, and $(1) for the years ended December 31, 2020, December 31, 2019, and December 31, 2018, respectively	38	8	52
Unrecognized pension (cost) benefit, net of tax (benefit) expense of $—, $(1), and $1 for the years ended December 31, 2020, December 31, 2019, and December 31, 2018, respectively	2	(4)	2
Unrealized gains on available-for-sale debt securities, net of tax expense of $— for the years ended December 31, 2020, December 31, 2019, and December 31, 2018.	—	1	—
Unrealized losses on derivative activity, net of tax benefit of $(8), $(5), and $— for the years ended December 31, 2020, December 31, 2019, and December 31, 2018, respectively	(23)	(14)	(1)
Other comprehensive income (loss)	17	(9)	53
COMPREHENSIVE INCOME (LOSS)	(686)	757	822
COMPREHENSIVE INCOME (LOSS) AND ACCRETION ATTRIBUTABLE TO NONCONTROLLING INTERESTS	—	—	—
COMPREHENSIVE INCOME (LOSS) ATTRIBUTABLE TO HYATT HOTELS CORPORATION	$ (686)	$ 757	$ 822

Source: United States Securities and Exchange Commission. (2021). *Form 10-K.* Retrieved from https://www.sec.gov/Archives/edgar/data/1468174/000146817421000011/h-20201231.htm

We have already stated that notes, which generally appear after the financial statements in the financial report, are critical to interpreting the numbers reported on the income statement.

Although the amount of operating information shown in the income statement and accompanying footnotes may be adequate for external users to evaluate the hospitality property's operations, management requires considerably more information. Management also needs this information more frequently than outsiders. In general, the more frequent the need to make decisions, the more frequent the need for financial information. Management's information needs are met, in part, by detailed monthly income statements that reflect budget numbers and report performance for the most recent period, the same period a year ago, and year-to-date numbers for both the current and past year.

If any difference between the year-to-date numbers and the originally budgeted numbers is expected, the income statements of many firms in the hospitality industry also show the latest forecast of results (reforecasting). Management is then able to compare actual results against the most recent forecasts.

Management's need for financial information on a monthly basis may be met, to a large degree, by using an income statement and accompanying departmental statements that are contained in the various uniform systems of accounts. In addition to the monthly income statement, a more frequent major report prepared for management is the **daily report of operations**.

Ultimately, however, hospitality managers require even more information than is provided by daily reports and monthly statements. Exhibit 3.2 lists various management reports and the frequency, content, comparisons, intended readers, and purpose of each report. Even this list does not include all reports required by the various levels of management in a hospitality operation. For example, two major financial statements, the balance sheet and the statement of cash flows, are absent from the list.

3.4 UNIFORM SYSTEMS OF ACCOUNTS

Uniform systems of accounts are standardized accounting systems prepared by various segments of the hospitality industry.[2] A uniform system of accounts provides a turnkey system for new entrants into the hospitality industry by offering detailed information about accounts, classifications, formats, and the different kinds, contents, and uses of financial statements and reports. For example, the *Uniform System of Accounts for the Lodging Industry (USALI)*, 11th Revised Edition contains not only the basic financial statements, but also more than 20 supplementary departmental operating statements, appendices covering financial ratios and operating metrics, and a revenue and expense guide.

A uniform system of accounts also allows for a more reasonable comparison of the operational results of similar hospitality properties. When various establishments follow a uniform system of accounts, the differences in accounting among these hospitality properties are minimized, thus ensuring comparability.

A uniform system of accounts is a time-tested system. The *Uniform System of Accounts for Hotels (USAH)* was first produced in 1925–26 by a designated group of accountants for the Hotel Association of New York City. Since then, the *USAH* has been revised many times by committees, beginning with New York City accountants and, later, by accountants from across the United States. In 1961, to meet the needs of its members, the American Hotel & Lodging Association appointed the National Association of Accountants to develop the *Uniform System of Accounts and Expense Dictionary for Small Hotels, Motels, and Motor Hotels (USASH)*, which also was revised a number of times. Then, in 1996, the Hotel Association of New York City and the American Hotel & Lodging Association combined their efforts to produce a single, updated, and authoritative uniform

Exhibit 3.2 **Management Reports**

Report	Frequency	Content	Comparisons	Who Gets It	Purpose
Daily Reports of Operations	Daily, on a cumulative basis for the month, the year to date.	Occupancy, average rate, revenue by outlet, and pertinent statistics.	To operating plan for current period and to prior year results.	Top management and supervisors responsible for day to day operation.	Basis for evaluating the current health of the enterprise.
Weekly Forecasts	Weekly.	Volume in covers, occupancy.	Previous periods.	Top management and supervisory personnel.	Staffing and scheduling; promotion.
Summary Report— Flash	Monthly at end of month (prior to monthly financial statement).	Known elements of revenue and direct costs; estimated departmental indirect costs.	To operating plan; to prior year results.	Top management and supervisory personnel responsible for function reported.	Provides immediate information on financial results for rooms, food and beverages, and other.
Cash Flow Analysis	Monthly (and on a revolving 12-month basis).	Receipts and disbursements by time periods.	With cash flow plan for month and for year to date.	Top management.	Predicts availability of cash for operating needs. Provides information on interim financing requirements.
Labor Productivity Analysis	Daily, weekly, monthly.	Dollar cost; manpower hours expended; hours as related to sales and services (covers, rooms occupied, etc.).	To committed hours in the operating plan (standards for amount of work to prior year statistics).	Top management and supervisory personnel.	Labor cost control through informed staffing and scheduling. Helps refine forecasting.
Departmental Analysis	Monthly (early in following month).	Details on main categories of income; same on expense.	To operating plan (month and year to date) and to prior year.	Top management and supervisors by function (e.g., rooms, each food and beverage outlet, laundry, telephone, other profit centers).	Knowing where business stands, and immediate corrective actions.
Room Rate Analysis	Daily, monthly, year to date.	Actual rates compared to rack rates by rate category or type of room.	To operating plan and to prior year results.	Top management and supervisors of sales and front office operations.	If goal is not being achieved, analysis of strengths and weaknesses is prompted.
Return on Investment	Actual computation, at least twice a year. Computation based on forecast, immediately prior to plan for year ahead.	Earnings as a percentage rate of return on average investment or equity committed.	To plan for operation and to prior periods.	Top management.	If goal is not being achieved, prompt assessment of strengths and weaknesses.
Long-Range Planning	Annually.	5-year projections of revenue and expenses. Operating plan expressed in financial terms.	Prior years.	Top management.	Involves staff in success or failure of enterprise. Injects more realism into plans for property and service modifications.
Exception Reporting	Concurrent with monthly reports and financial statements.	Summary listing of line item variances from predetermined norm.	With operating budgets.	Top management and supervisors responsible for function reported.	Immediate focusing on problem before more detailed statement analysis can be made.
Guest History Analysis	At least semi-annually; quarterly or monthly is recommended.	Historical records of corporate business, travel agencies, group bookings.	With previous reports.	Top management and sales.	Gives direction to marketing efforts.
Future Bookings Report	Monthly.	Analysis of reservations and bookings.	With several prior years.	Top management, sales and marketing, department management.	Provides information on changing guest profile. Exposes strong and weak points of facility. Guides (1) sales planning and (2) expansion plans.

system of accounts—the *Uniform System of Accounts for the Lodging Industry (USALI)*. The current 11th Revised Edition of the USALI was released in 2014.

This uniform system of accounts can be adapted for use by large and small hospitality operations. The *USALI* contains many more accounts and classifications than will generally be used by a single hotel or motel. Therefore, each facility simply selects the schedules and accounts that are required for its use and ignores the others.

The *USALI* is designed to be used at the property level rather than the corporate level of a hotel. The format of the income statement is based on **responsibility accounting**. That is, the presentation is organized to focus attention on departmental results such as the rooms and food and beverage departments. The income statements prepared at the corporate level, where more than one lodging property is owned by the lodging corporation, would probably be considerably different and would include sale of properties, corporate overhead expenses, and so on, not necessarily shown on an individual lodging property's income statement. Our discussion of income statements for management will focus primarily on the *USALI*, although, as stated earlier, income statements for the *USAR* and the *USFRC* will also be presented near the end of this chapter.

3.5 APPROACH TO HOSPITALITY INDUSTRY INCOME STATEMENTS

In many industries, the basic income statement format consists of the following:

	Revenues
Less:	Cost of goods sold
Equals:	Gross profit
Less:	Overhead expenses
Less:	Financing costs and income taxes
Equals:	Net income

For wholesale and retail firms, the cost of goods sold is the cost of goods purchased for resale, while for manufacturers, it is a combination of labor, raw materials, and overhead expenses incurred in the manufacturing process. The expenses subtracted from gross profit to equal net income consist of all other expenses, such as administration and selling expenses, depreciation, and income taxes.

By contrast, the income statement format in the *USALI* approach consists of the following:

	Revenues
Less:	Direct operating expenses
Equals:	Departmental operating income
Less:	Overhead expenses
Less:	Financing costs and income taxes
Equals:	Net income

Direct operating expenses include not only the cost of goods sold, but also the direct labor expense and other direct expenses. Direct labor expense is the expense of personnel working in the profit centers, such as the rooms department and the food department. Other direct expenses include supplies used by these revenue-producing departments. Therefore, everything else being the same, gross profit would exceed departmental operating income, since direct operating expenses include direct labor and other direct expenses in addition to cost of goods sold.

The income statements, including the supplementary schedules, based on the *USALI* provide separate line reporting by profit center; that is, sales and direct expenses are shown separately for the rooms department, the food and beverage department, and so forth. In addition, the overhead expenses are divided among undistributed operating expenses, management fees, nonoperating expenses, interest, depreciation, and amortization. The undistributed operating expenses are further detailed on the income statement by major service centers such as sales and marketing and property operation and maintenance. The detail provided by both profit centers and service centers reflects reporting by areas of responsibility and is commonly referred to as responsibility accounting.

Thus, the *USALI* income statement and the supplementary schedules are useful to managers in the hospitality industry because they are designed to provide the information necessary to evaluate the performance of managers of the lodging facility by area of responsibility.

3.6 SUMMARY OPERATING STATEMENT

The 11th Revised Edition of the *USALI* contains two summary operating statements. The first one, as shown in Exhibit 3.3, is for management companies (operators). The top part of the statement includes some key performance indicators, such as rooms available, rooms sold, occupancy percentage, average daily rate (ADR), rooms revenue per available room (RevPAR), and total revenue per available room (Total RevPAR). The detailed calculations of some of these metrics will be discussed in Chapter 5. This statement requires the combining of the food and beverage departments and the combining of all other operated departments that are shown on this statement as other operated departments.

The undistributed operating expenses section contains lines for administrative and general; information and telecommunication systems; sales and marketing; property operation and maintenance; and energy, water, and waste.

Total department profit less total undistributed expenses equals gross operating profit (GOP); GOP less management fees equals income before nonoperating income and expenses. Subtracting the nonoperating income and expenses then results in earnings before interest, taxes, depreciation, and amortization (EBITDA). Income taxes are then subtracted to yield net income. Finally, the amount transferred to the replacement reserve is subtracted to provide EBITDA less replacement reserve.

The statement for operators is a summary *operating* statement rather than a summary income statement because it does not include several elements (depreciation, amortization, interest expense, and income tax expense) needed to calculate net income. The *USALI* has a second version of this statement designed for owners that includes all of these missing elements and concludes with net income. While the *USALI* calls this a summary operating statement for owners, it is in effect a summary income statement. Many users may prefer the greater detail of the statement for owners.

3.7 CONTENTS OF THE INCOME STATEMENT

While the *USALI*'s summary operating statement for owners is essentially one way to organize a summary income statement, this text will use an alternate statement format that allows for additional detail, which is useful for teaching purposes (see Exhibit 3.4). (Appendix B presents the *USALI*'s versions of the various departmental statements used to support the income statement; these statements are discussed in the next section.)

The first section of Exhibit 3.4, operated departments, reports net revenue by department for every major revenue-producing department. Net revenue is the result of subtracting allowances from related revenues. Allowances (shown on the departmental statements) include adjustments for service problems. That is, when the hotel reduces the price of a guestroom because the guest encountered some problem with the room, the reduction is treated as an allowance. (Allowances do not include posting errors. For example, if a hotel charges

---

Exhibit 3.3   Summary Operating Statement (for Operators) per *USALI*

Summary Operating Statement [For Operators]

	PERIOD OF					
	CURRENT PERIOD			YEAR-TO-DATE		
	ACTUAL	FORECAST/ BUDGET	PRIOR YEAR	ACTUAL	FORECAST/ BUDGET	PRIOR YEAR
ROOMS AVAILABLE:						
ROOMS SOLD:						
OCCUPANCY:						
ADR:						
ROOMS REVPAR:						
TOTAL REVPAR:						

	PERIOD OF											
	CURRENT PERIOD						YEAR-TO-DATE					
	ACTUAL		FORECAST/ BUDGET		PRIOR YEAR		ACTUAL		FORECAST/ BUDGET		PRIOR YEAR	
	$	%[1]	$	%[1]	$	%[1]	$	%[1]	$	%[1]	$	%[1]
OPERATING REVENUE												
Rooms												
Food and Beverage												
Other Operated Departments												
Miscellaneous Income												
TOTAL OPERATING REVENUE												
DEPARTMENTAL EXPENSES												
Rooms												
Food and Beverage												
Other Operated Departments												
TOTAL DEPARTMENTAL EXPENSES												
TOTAL DEPARTMENTAL PROFIT												
UNDISTRIBUTED OPERATING EXPENSES												
Administrative and General												
Information and Telecommunications Systems												
Sales and Marketing												
Property Operation and Maintenance												
Utilities												
TOTAL UNDISTRIBUTED EXPENSES												
GROSS OPERATING PROFIT												
MANAGEMENT FEES												
INCOME BEFORE NON-OPERATING INCOME AND EXPENSES												
NON-OPERATING INCOME AND EXPENSES												
Income												
Rent												
Property and Other Taxes												
Insurance												
Other												
TOTAL NON-OPERATING INCOME AND EXPENSES												
EARNINGS BEFORE INTEREST, TAXES, DEPRECIATION, AND AMORTIZATION												
REPLACEMENT RESERVE												
EBITDA LESS REPLACEMENT RESERVE												

[1] All revenues and expenses should be shown as a percentage of total operating revenue, except departmental expenses, which should be shown as a percentage of their respective departmental revenue.

Source: *Uniform System of Accounts for the Lodging Industry,* 11th Rev. Ed. (Austin, TX: Hospitality Financial and Technology Professionals, 2018).

guests $100 for their rooms when it should have charged a group rate of $80, the subsequent $20 correction of this posting error is treated as a direct reduction of revenue rather than as an allowance.) Income earned from other activities, such as investments, is shown as miscellaneous income. If these amounts are significant, they should be reported separately. See the Miscellaneous Income Schedule in Appendix B for more examples.

For each department generating revenues, three major categories of direct expenses are reported: cost of sales, labor costs and related expenses, and other expenses. Cost of sales is normally determined as follows:

	Beginning inventory
Plus:	Inventory purchases
Equals:	Goods available for sale
Less:	Ending inventory
Equals:	Cost of goods consumed
Less:	Goods used internally
Equals:	Cost of goods sold

Beginning inventory is the value of the inventory at the start of the accounting period. Inventory purchases include the purchase cost of goods for sale plus the related shipping cost. An important, but relatively small, category of direct expense is "goods used internally." For example, food may be provided free of charge to employees (employee meals), to entertainers (entertainers—complimentary food), to guests for promotional purposes (promotion—food), or to other departments. In each case, the cost of food transferred must be charged to the proper account of the benefiting department and subtracted in the calculation of cost of food sold. For example, cost of employee meals for

Exhibit 3.4	**Summary Income Statement**					
		Net Revenue	Cost of Sales	Labor Costs and Related Expenses	Other Expenses	Profit (Loss)
Operated Departments		$	$	$	$	$
Rooms						
Food and Beverage						
Golf Course and Pro Shop						
Health Club/Spa						
Parking						
Other Operated Departments						
Miscellaneous Income						
Total Operated Departments						
Undistributed Operating Expenses						
Administrative and General						
Information and Telecommunications Systems						
Sales and Marketing						
Property Operation and Maintenance						
Utilities						
Total Undistributed Expenses						
Totals						
Gross Operating Profit						
Management Fees						

(Continued)

	Net Revenue	Cost of Sales	Labor Costs and Related Expenses	Other Expenses	Profit (Loss)
Income before Nonoperating Income and Expenses					
Income					
Rent					
Property and Other Taxes					
Insurance					
Other					
Total Nonoperating Income and Expenses					———
Earnings before Interest, Taxes, Depreciation, and Amortization (EBITDA)					
Interest					
Depreciation					
Amortization					
Total Interest, Depreciation, and Amortization					——— ———
Income before Income Taxes					
Income Taxes					
Net Income					$ _____

the rooms department is subtracted to determine cost of food sold. The cost of employee meals for rooms department employees is shown as an expense in the rooms department.

The second major direct expense category of operated departments is "labor costs and related expenses." This category includes the salaries and wages of employees working in the designated operated departments (for example, servers in the food department). Salaries, wages, and related expenses of departments not generating revenues but providing service, such as marketing, are recorded by service departments. The category of "related expenses" includes all payroll taxes and benefits relating to employees of each operated department. For example, in the rooms department, the front office manager's salary and related payroll taxes and benefits would be included in the "labor costs and related expenses" of the rooms department.

The final major expense category for the operated departments is "other expenses." This category includes only other direct expenses. For example, the 30 major other expense categories for the rooms department (per the *USALI*) include, but are not limited to, cleaning supplies, commissions, complimentary services and gifts, contract services, guest relocation, guest transportation, laundry and dry cleaning, linen, operating supplies, reservations, training, and uniform costs. Expenses such as marketing, administration, and general transportation are recorded as expenses of service departments. They benefit the rooms department and other profit centers, but only on an indirect basis.

Net revenue less the sum of cost of sales, labor costs and related expenses, and other expenses results in departmental profit or loss. The departmental profit or loss is shown on the income statement for each operated department.

The second major section of the income statement is undistributed operating expenses. This section includes five general categories: administrative and general expenses, information and telecommunications systems, sales and marketing, property operation and maintenance, and utilities. These expense categories are related to the various service departments. In the income statement, two of the expense elements—labor costs and related expenses, and other expenses—are shown for each category.

The administrative and general expense category includes service departments such as the general manager's office and the accounting office. In addition to salaries, wages, and related expenses of service department personnel covered by administrative and general, other expenses include, but are not limited to, credit card commissions, professional fees, and provision for doubtful accounts. The administrative and general statement in Appendix B at the end of this book represents the categories for such expenses.

The information and telecommunications systems category in a service center has been created to consolidate all system-related technology expenses. Sales and marketing expenses include costs relating to personnel working in the areas of sales and marketing. The sales and marketing schedule in Appendix B presents the line items for this schedule. Franchise fees are also included in this schedule for lodging operations that are franchised.

The fourth major category of undistributed operating expenses is property operation and maintenance. Included in property operation and maintenance are labor costs and related expenses of the property operation and maintenance personnel and the various supplies used to maintain the buildings, grounds, furniture, fixtures, and equipment.

The final category of undistributed operating expenses is utilities. The recommended schedule includes separate listings of the various utilities, such as electricity, gas, oil, steam, sewer, and water.

Subtracting the total undistributed operating expenses from the total operated departments profit results in gross operating profit (GOP).

Operating management is considered fully responsible for all revenues and expenses reported to this point on the income statement, as they generally have the authority to exercise their judgment to affect all these items. However, the management fees and the income and expenses that follow in the rest of the income statement are the responsibility primarily of the hospitality property's board of directors or owners. The items listed (primarily expenses) on this part of the statement generally relate directly to decisions the board or owner makes, rather than to management decisions.

Management fees are the cost of using an independent management company to operate the hotel or motel. Management fees often consist of a basic fee calculated as a percentage of sales and an incentive fee calculated as a percentage of GOP.

The next section is called nonoperating income and expenses. The income listed here relates to decisions by the owners of the hotel, not management. Rental income from billboards on a hotel or antennas on the hotel are examples. Also included as income is the rental space in the hotel for retail purposes.

Similarly, the expenses listed in this section are considered to be outside the direct control of management. Many of these expenses are referred to as **capacity costs,** as they relate to the physical plant or the capacity to provide goods and services to guests. Capacity costs include rent, property taxes, insurance, and depreciation and amortization. (Depreciation and amortization are not shown until the next section.) Rent includes the cost of renting real estate and other major items that, if they had been purchased, would have been recorded as fixed assets. Rental of miscellaneous equipment for specific functions such as banquets is to be shown as a direct expense of the food and beverage department.

Property taxes include real estate taxes, personal property taxes, and other taxes (but not income and payroll taxes) that cannot be charged to guests. Insurance expense is the cost of insuring the facilities, including contents, for damage caused by fire or other catastrophes, and the cost of liability insurance.

Other expenses include gain/loss on sale of fixed assets and owner expenses. A gain or loss on sale of property results from a difference between the proceeds from the sale and the carrying value (net book value) of the fixed asset. For example, suppose that a 15-unit motel that cost $600,000 and was depreciated by $450,000 was sold for $200,000. The gain in this case is determined as follows:

$$\text{Net Book Value} = \text{Cost} - \text{Accumulated Depreciation}$$
$$= \$600,000 - \$450,000$$
$$= \underline{\underline{\$150,000}}$$
$$\text{Gain} = \text{Proceeds} - \text{Net Book Value}$$
$$= \$200,000 - \$150,000$$
$$= \underline{\underline{\$50,000}}$$

On the income statement, gains are added while losses are subtracted.

The total of nonoperating income and expenses is subtracted from the income before nonoperating income and expenses to equal EBITDA (earnings before interest, taxes, depreciation, and amortization). Interest, depreciation, and amortization are then subtracted from EBITDA, resulting in income before taxes. Interest expense is the cost of borrowing money and is based on the amounts borrowed, the interest rate, and the length of time for which the funds are borrowed.

Depreciation of fixed assets and amortization of other assets are also shown on the summary income statement following EBITDA. The depreciation methods and useful lives of fixed assets are normally disclosed in footnotes.

Finally, income taxes are subtracted from income before income taxes to determine net income.

3.8 DEPARTMENTAL STATEMENTS

Departmental statements, supplementary to the income statement and referred to as **schedules,** provide management with detailed information by operated departments and service centers. Each of these schedules is included in Appendix B at the end of this book.

Exhibit 3.5 illustrates an abbreviated operated department schedule using the rooms department of the Vacation Inn. The operated department schedule reflects both revenues and direct expenses.

The expenses are subdivided on the rooms department schedule between "labor costs and related expenses" and "other expenses." Under labor costs and related expenses, salaries, wages, and bonuses and payroll-related expenses are shown. Employee benefits may include the cost of health insurance paid by the lodging operation and similar benefits.

Other expenses include direct expenses of the rooms department. According to the USALI, over 30 expense categories are shown under other expenses of the rooms department. All other rooms department expenses should be classified in these categories if the USALI is to be followed. When a classification is not used, it should not be shown on the rooms department schedule. Exhibit 3.5 does not include a few categories shown on the USALI model statement. For example, guest transportation is not included in this schedule.

Totals from the rooms department schedule and other operated department schedules are reflected on the income statement. In the rooms department illustration in Exhibit 3.5, the following totals are carried from the department schedule to the property's summary income statement:

■ Net Revenue	$ 1,041,200
■ Labor Costs and Related Expenses	$ 185,334
■ Other Expenses	$ 79,080
■ Departmental Profit	$ 776,786

Exhibit 3.5   Rooms Department Schedule

Vacation Inn	Schedule 1
Rooms	
For the year ended Dec. 31, 20X1	
Revenue	
Transient Rooms Revenue	$ 543,900
Group Rooms Revenue	450,000
Contract Rooms Revenue	48,000
Other Rooms Revenue	2,000
Allowances	(2,700)
Total Rooms Revenue	1,041,200
Expenses	
Labor Costs and Related Expenses	
Salaries and Wages	159,304
Payroll Taxes	10,420
Employee Benefits	15,610
Total Labor Costs and Related Expenses	185,334
Other Expenses	
Cleaning Supplies	3,200
Commissions	5,124
Contract Services	3,100
Guest Supplies	5,126
Guest Transportation	4,900
Laundry and Dry Cleaning	12,706
Linen	9,494
Miscellaneous	3,000
Operating Supplies	12,742
Reservations	9,288
Training	4,315
Travel—Meals and Entertainment	4,685
Uniforms	1,400
Total Other Expenses	79,080
Total Expenses	264,414
Departmental Profit	$ 776,786

Note: This is an abbreviated schedule.

Exhibit 3.6 is the Vacation Inn's summary income statement. The above figures from the rooms department schedule are reflected in the top row of figures on the income statement.

In contrast to the profit center schedules prepared by the revenue-producing operated departments of a hospitality operation, a service center schedule reports only expenses by area of responsibility. Although these activity areas do not generate revenues, they do provide service to the operated departments and, in some cases, to other service centers. Exhibit 3.7 illustrates a service center departmental schedule by using the property operation and maintenance schedule of the Vacation Inn. The three numbers that are carried over to the Vacation Inn's income statement (Exhibit 3.6) for this department are total labor costs and related expenses of $31,652, other expenses of $49,312, and total expenses of $80,964. Notice that the total expenses of service departments are shown on the income statement under the Profit (Loss) column.

| Exhibit 3.6 | Summary Income Statement–Vacation Inn |

Vacation Inn
Summary Income Statement
For the year ended Dec. 31, 20X1

	Schedule	Net Revenue	Cost of Sales	Labor Costs and Related Expenses	Other Expenses	Profit (Loss)
Operated Departments						
Rooms	1	$ 1,041,200	$ -0-	$ 185,334	$ 79,080	$ 776,786
Food and Beverage	2	653,193	254,953	232,849	73,329	92,062
Miscellaneous Income	3	25,000	-0-	-0-	-0-	25,000
Total Operated Departments		1,719,393	254,953	418,183	152,409	893,848
Undistributed Operating Expenses						
Administrative and General	4			74,200	48,000	122,200
Information and Telecommunications Systems	5			30,044	20,209	50,253
Sales and Marketing	6			33,231	33,585	66,816
Property Operation and Maintenance	7			31,652	49,312	80,964
Utilities	8			-0-	68,752	68,752
Total Undistributed Operating Expenses				169,127	219,858	388,985
Gross Operating Profit		$ 1,719,393	$ 254,953	$ 587,310	$ 372,267	504,863
Rent, Property Taxes, and Insurance	9					200,861
EBITDA						304,002
Interest Expense	10					52,148
Depreciation and Amortization	11					115,860
Income before Income Taxes						135,994
Income Tax	12					48,707
Net Income						$ 87,287

3.9 LODGING INDUSTRY OPERATING STATISTICS

A sale of $x by any operated department increases total revenues by that amount, but the increase in the total operated department *income* from additional sales of $x depends on the operated department making the sale. The different effects on the bottom line are caused by the direct expenses of the department generating the sale.

The difference between an operated department's revenues and its direct expenses is referred to as departmental income. The operated department contributing most to the lodging property's ability to pay overhead costs and generate profit is the one that has the greatest departmental income.

CBRE Hotels Research, an international firm providing specialized services to establishments in the hospitality industry, recently released figures showing that the average hotel reports rooms departmental income of 74.1 percent of total room

Exhibit 3.7	**Property Operation and Maintenance Schedule**	

Vacation Inn	Schedule 7
Property Operation and Maintenance	
For the year ended Dec. 31, 20X1	

Labor Costs and Related Expenses	
Salaries and Wages	$ 27,790
Payroll Taxes	1,642
Employee Benefits	2,220
Total Labor Costs and Related Expenses	31,652
Other Expenses	
Building	8,900
Electrical and Mechanical Equipment	8,761
Engineering Supplies	1,981
Furniture and Equipment	14,322
Grounds Maintenance and Landscaping	6,241
Operating Supplies	2,651
Painting and Wallcovering	2,499
Swimming Pool	2,624
Uniforms Costs	652
Waste Removal	681
Total Other Expenses	49,312
Total Expenses	$ 80,964

Note: This is an abbreviated schedule. A full schedule per the *USALI* is shown in Appendix B.

revenues, while the food and beverage departmental income is only 30.1 percent of total food and beverage revenues.[3] Therefore, all things being the same, a manager would rather have an additional sale of $x made in the rooms department than in any other operated department, because the contribution toward overhead costs and profit would be greater than from any other operated department. That is, based on CBRE's figures, a sale of $100 in the rooms department would result in a departmental income of $74.10. A similar sale in the food and beverage department would result in a departmental income of only $30.10.

Exhibit 3.8 provides statistics revealing the percentage distribution of revenues and expenses for the average hotel/motel. These statistics support the preceding discussion of the greater desirability of rooms sales compared with sales in any other department. However, do not consider these averages to be the norm. They are only averages and are based on lodging establishments that CBRE selected on a judgmental, not random, basis. The operated departments of a particular hotel will most likely produce different percentages. However, of more than 1,000 hotels and motels in the CBRE study, significant numbers noted in Exhibit 3.8 for 2019 include the following:

- Rooms revenues approximate 69.9 percent of total revenues.

- Food and beverage revenues approximate 23.4 percent of total revenues.

- Total operated department income approximates 63.3 percent of total revenues.

- Undistributed operating expenses approximate 25.5 percent of total revenues.

- Gross operating profit approximates 37.7 percent.

Exhibit 3.8 | Comparative Results of Operations

	2019 Percent of Revenue	2018 Percent of Revenue
Revenues		
Rooms	69.9%	70.2%
Food and Beverage	23.4%	23.5%
Other Operated Departments	4.7%	4.5%
Miscellaneous Income	1.9%	1.8%
Total Operating Revenue	100%	100%
Departmental Expenses*		
Rooms	25.9%	25.7%
Food and Beverage	69.9%	69.2%
Other Operated Departments	48.1%	49.8%
Total Departmental Revenue	36.7%	36.5%
Total Departmental Profit	**63.3%**	**63.5%**
Undistributed Operating Expenses		
Administrative and General	7.9%	7.7%
Information and Telecommunications Systems	1.4%	1.5%
Sales and Marketing	9.0%	8.8%
Property Operation and Maintenance	4.2%	4.1%
Utilities	3.0%	3.0%
Total Undistributed Expenses	25.5%	25.1%
Gross Operating Profit	**37.7%**	**38.4%**
Management Fees	**3.6%**	**3.6%**
Income before Nonoperating Income and Expenses	**34.2%**	**34.7%**
Nonoperating Income and Expenses		
Income	--	--
Rent	2.3%	2.3%
Property and Other Taxes	3.6%	3.5%
Insurance	0.9%	0.8%
Other	1.2%	1.1%
Total Nonoperating Income and Expenses	7.9%	7.8%
EBITDA (Earnings before Interest, Taxes, Depreciation, and Amortization)	**26.2%**	**26.9%**
Percent of Occupancy		75.1%
Average Daily Rate		$ 178.36
RevPAR		$ 139.99
Average Size (Rooms)		206

Source: *Trends in the Hotel Industry - US Edition* 2020 (Atlanta: CBRE Hotels Research), p. 61.
*Expressed as a percent of departmental revenue.

Finally, industry averages vary widely by type of lodging establishment. Exhibit 3.9 is a comparison of statistics covering full-service, limited-service, resort, suite, and convention hotels. Again, the reader is cautioned that the percentages shown are not norms or standards, but statistics based on a judgmental sample.

Hospitality industry statistics for the various segments of the industry are published annually by the National Restaurant Association, CBRE, and PBMares and are listed in Exhibit 3.10. These publications are generally available upon request to hospitality industry executives.

Exhibit 3.9   Sales and Expenses as a Percentage of Revenues - 2019

Summary Operating Statement

	Full-Service Hotels	Limited-Service Hotels	Suite Hotels with Food & Beverage	Suite Hotels without Food & Beverage	Convention Hotels	Resort Hotels
Revenues						
Rooms	72.3%	96.7%	78.9%	96.3%	59.6%	52.0%
Food and Beverage	22.7%	-	16.4%	-	34.5%	33.7%
Other Operated Departments	3.2%	2.1%	3.2%	2.8%	4.4%	10.8%
Miscellaneous Income	1.7%	1.2%	1.5%	1.0%	1.5%	3.5%
Total Operating Revenue	100%	100%	100%	100%	100%	100%
Departmental Expenses*						
Rooms	25.7%	27.4%	25.4%	24.0%	28.1%	25.0%
Food and Beverage	73.7%	-	63.8%	-	65.5%	68.0%
Other Operated Departments	44.5%	53.5%	47.8%	44.2%	34.3%	56.1%
Total Departmental Revenue	36.8%	27.6%	32.0%	24.3%	40.9%	42.0%
Total Departmental Profit	**63.2%**	**72.4%**	**68.0%**	**75.7%**	**59.1%**	**58.0%**
Undistributed Operating Expenses						
Administrative and General	8.5%	8.6%	7.6%	8.4%	7.2%	6.7%
Information and Telecommunications Systems	1.5%	1.3%	1.1%	1.2%	1.6%	1.4%
Sales and Marketing	9.6%	12.5%	12.5%	10.5%	7.3%	6.7%
Property Operation and Maintenance	4.2%	4.7%	4.2%	4.5%	4.0%	4.2%
Utilities	2.9%	3.7%	3.5%	3.6%	2.6%	2.8%
Total Undistributed Expenses	26.6%	30.8%	28.9%	28.2%	22.8%	21.8%
Gross Operating Profit	**36.6%**	**41.6%**	**39.2%**	**47.4%**	**36.4%**	**36.3%**
Management Fees	**3.4%**	**3.5%**	**3.1%**	**3.9%**	**4.0%**	**3.5%**
Income before Nonoperating Income and Expenses	**33.2%**	**38.1%**	**36.1%**	**43.6%**	**32.3%**	**32.8%**
Nonoperating Income and Expenses						
Income	0.1%	0.1%	0.1%	-	-	-
Rent	2.1%	5.8%	3.2%	6.2%	1.0%	1.3%
Property and Other Taxes	4.1%	4.0%	3.1%	4.0%	3.5%	2.3%
Insurance	0.8%	1.1%	0.7%	0.9%	0.7%	1.1%
Other	1.2%	0.1%	0.5%	0.7%	0.9%	1.8%
Total Nonoperating Income and Expenses	8.1%	10.9%	7.3%	11.8%	6.1%	6.6%
EBITDA (Earnings before Interest, Taxes, Depreciation, and Amortization)	**25.0%**	**27.1%**	**28.7%**	**31.8%**	**26.2%**	**26.2%**

Source: *Trends in the Hotel Industry - US Edition 2020* (Atlanta: CBRE Hotels Research), pp. 67, 78, 89, 100, 111, 122.
*Expressed as a percent of departmental revenue.

Exhibit 3.10   Major Hospitality Statistical Publications

Publication	Industry	
	Segment	Firm
Hotel Horizons	Lodging	CBRE
Trends in the Hotel Industry—US	Lodging	CBRE
Trends in the Hotel Spa Industry	Lodging/Spa	CBRE
Trends in the Canadian Hotel Industry	Lodging	CBRE
Caribbean Trends in the Hotel Industry	Lodging	CBRE
Clubs in Town and Country	Clubs	PBMares
Restaurant Operations Report	Restaurant	NRA

3.10 ANALYSIS OF INCOME STATEMENTS

The analysis of income statements enhances the user's knowledge of the hospitality property's operations. This can be accomplished by horizontal analysis, vertical analysis, base-year comparisons, and ratio analysis.

Since much less financial information is available to owners (stockholders and partners who are not active in the operation) and creditors than is available to management, their analytical approaches will generally differ.

Horizontal analysis compares income statements for two accounting periods in terms of both absolute and relative variances for each line item in a way similar to the analysis of comparative balance sheets. The user should investigate any significant differences. Another common comparative analysis approach is to compare the most recent period's operating results with the budget by determining absolute and relative variances.

Exhibit 3.11 illustrates the horizontal analysis of operating results of the Vacation Inn for years 20X1 and 20X2. In this comparative analysis, 20X1 is considered the base. Because the revenues for 20X2 exceed revenues for 20X1, the dollar difference is shown as positive. If 20X2 revenues had been less than 20X1 revenues, the difference would have been shown as negative. Actual 20X2 expenses increased compared with 20X1, resulting in a positive difference. This should be expected, since as revenues increase, expenses should also increase. If actual 20X2 expenses had decreased compared with 20X1, the differences would have been shown as negative. The percentage differences in this statement are determined by dividing the dollar difference by the base (that is, the 20X1 numbers).

Another approach in analyzing income statements is vertical analysis. The product of this analysis is also referred to as **common-size income statements** (vertical analysis). These statements result from reducing all amounts to percentages using total sales as a common denominator. Exhibit 3.12 illustrates two common-size income statements for the Vacation Inn.

Exhibit 3.11 Comparative Income Statements

Vacation Inn
Comparative Income Statements

	20X1	20X2	Difference $	Difference %
Total Revenue	$ 1,719,393	$ 1,883,482	$ 164,089	9.54%
Rooms—Revenue	1,041,200	1,124,300	83,100	7.98%
Labor Costs & Related Expenses	185,334	192,428	7,094	3.83%
Other Expenses	79,080	84,624	5,544	7.01%
Departmental Profit	776,786	847,248	70,462	9.07%
Food & Beverage—Revenue	653,193	733,182	79,989	12.25%
Cost of Sales	254,953	285,752	30,799	12.08%
Labor Costs & Related Expenses	232,849	265,909	33,060	14.20%
Other Expenses	73,329	84,236	10,907	14.87%
Departmental Profit	92,062	97,285	5,223	5.67%
Miscellaneous Income	25,000	26,000	1,000	4.00%
Total Operated Departments	893,848	970,533	76,685	8.58%
Undistributed Operating Expenses				
Administrative and General	122,200	135,131	12,931	10.58%
Info. and Telecom. Systems	50,253	60,571	10,318	20.53%
Sales and Marketing	66,816	69,760	2,944	4.41%
Property Operation and Maintenance	80,964	84,465	3,501	4.32%
Utilities	68,752	76,000	7,248	10.54%
Total Undistributed Operating Expenses	388,985	426,267	37,282	9.58%
Gross Operating Profit	504,863	544,266	39,403	7.80%
Rent, Property Taxes, and Insurance	200,861	210,932	10,071	5.01%
EBITDA	304,002	333,334	29,332	9.65%
Interest Expense	52,148	61,841	9,693	18.59%
Depreciation and Amortization	115,860	118,942	3,082	2.66%
Income before Income Taxes	135,994	152,551	16,557	12.17%
Income Taxes	48,707	57,969	9,262	19.02%
Net Income	$ 87,287	$ 94,582	$ 7,295	8.36%

Vertical analysis allows for more reasonable comparisons of two or more periods when the activity for the two periods was at different levels. For example, assume the following:

	20X1	20X2
Food sales	$500,000	$750,000
Cost of food sales	150,000	225,000

A $75,000 increase in cost of sales may at first appear to be excessive. However, vertical analysis reveals the following:

	20X1	20X2
Food sales	100%	100%
Cost of food sales	30%	30%

In this example, vertical analysis suggests that despite the absolute increase in cost of sales from 20X1 to 20X2, the cost of food sales has remained constant

Exhibit 3.12 Common-Size Income Statements

Vacation Inn
Common-Size Income Statements

	20X1	20X2	Percentages 20X1	Percentages 20X2
Total Revenue	$ 1,719,393	$ 1,883,482	100.0%	100.0%
Rooms—Revenue	1,041,200	1,124,300	60.6%	59.7%
Labor Costs & Related Expenses	185,334	192,428	10.8%	10.2%
Other Expenses	79,080	84,624	4.6%	4.5%
Departmental Profit	776,786	847,248	45.2%	45.0%
Food & Beverage—Revenue	653,193	733,182	38.0%	38.9%
Cost of Sales	254,953	285,752	14.8%	15.2%
Labor Costs & Related Expenses	232,849	265,909	13.5%	14.1%
Other Expenses	73,329	84,236	4.3%	4.5%
Departmental Profit	92,062	97,285	5.4%	5.2%
Miscellaneous Income	25,000	26,000	1.5%	1.4%
Total Operated Departments	893,848	970,533	52.0%	51.5%
Undistributed Operating Expenses				
Administrative and General	122,200	135,131	7.1%	7.2%
Info. and Telecom. Systems	50,253	60,571	2.9%	3.2%
Sales and Marketing	66,816	69,760	3.9%	3.7%
Property Operation and Maintenance	80,964	84,465	4.7%	4.5%
Utilities	68,752	76,000	4.0%	4.0%
Total Undistributed Operating Expenses	388,985	426,267	22.6%	22.6%
Gross Operating Profit	504,863	544,266	29.4%	28.9%
Rent, Property Taxes, and Insurance	200,861	210,932	11.7%	11.2%
EBITDA	304,002	333,334	17.7%	17.7%
Interest Expense	52,148	61,841	3.0%	3.3%
Depreciation and Amortization	115,860	118,942	6.7%	6.3%
Income before Income Taxes	135,994	152,551	7.9%	8.1%
Income Taxes	48,707	57,969	2.8%	3.1%
Net Income	$ 87,287	$ 94,582	5.1%	5.0%

at 30 percent of sales for both years. The relatively large dollar increase from 20X1 to 20X2 can be attributed to the higher level of activity during the 20X2 period rather than to unreasonable increases in the cost of sales.

Vertical analysis allows more meaningful comparisons among hospitality operations in the same industry segment but differing substantially in size. This common-size analysis also allows comparisons to industry standards, as discussed previously. However, a note of caution is offered at this point. Industry averages are simply that—averages. They include firms of all sizes from vastly different locations operating in entirely different markets. The industry averages reflect neither any particular operation nor an average operation, and they certainly do not depict an ideal operation.

A third approach to analyzing income statements is base-year comparisons. This approach allows a meaningful comparison of income statements for several periods. A base period is selected as a starting point and its figures are assigned a value of 100 percent. All subsequent periods are compared with the base on a percentage basis. Exhibit 3.13 is a **comparative income statement** (also known as horizontal analysis) that illustrates the base-year comparison of the Vacation

Exhibit 3.13 Base-Year Comparison Income Statements

Vacation Inn
Base-Year Comparison Income Statements

	20X0	20X1	20X2
Total Revenue	100.0%	107.5%	117.7%
Rooms—Revenue	100.0%	104.1%	112.4%
Labor Costs & Related Expenses	100.0%	104.7%	108.7%
Other Expenses	100.0%	105.4%	112.8%
Departmental Profit	100.0%	103.8%	113.3%
Food & Beverage—Revenue	100.0%	108.9%	122.2%
Cost of Sales	100.0%	110.8%	124.2%
Labor Costs & Related Expenses	100.0%	110.9%	126.6%
Other Expenses	100.0%	104.8%	120.3%
Departmental Profit	100.0%	102.3%	108.1%
Miscellaneous Income	100.0%	104.2%	108.3%
Total Operated Departments	100.0%	103.7%	112.6%
Undistributed Operating Expenses			
Administrative and General	100.0%	101.8%	112.6%
Info. and Telecom. Systems	100.0%	102.6%	123.6%
Sales and Marketing	100.0%	106.1%	110.7%
Property Operation and Maintenance	100.0%	108.0%	112.6%
Utilities	100.0%	114.6%	126.7%
Total Undistributed Operating Expenses	100.0%	106.0%	116.1%
Gross Operating Profit	100.0%	102.0%	110.0%
Rent, Property Taxes, and Insurance	100.0%	101.4%	106.5%
EBITDA	100.0%	102.4%	112.2%
Interest Expense	100.0%	100.3%	118.9%
Depreciation and Amortization	100.0%	102.5%	105.3%
Income before Income Taxes	100.0%	103.0%	115.6%
Income Taxes	100.0%	101.5%	120.8%
Net Income	100.0%	103.9%	112.6%

Inn for 20X0–20X2 (with 20X0 as the base). Note that some percentages increase quite dramatically.

A fourth approach to analyzing income statements is **ratio analysis**. Ratio analysis gives mathematical expression to a relationship between two figures and is computed by dividing one figure by the other figure. Financial ratios are compared with standards in order to evaluate the financial condition of a hospitality operation. Since vertical analysis is a subset of ratio analysis, there is considerable overlap between these two approaches.

3.11 *USAR* AND *USFRC*

Operations of a commercial foodservice outlet or a club differ from operations of a lodging business and, therefore, the financial information as presented in financial statements also differs. The income statement recommended for commercial foodservice operations is prescribed in the *Uniform System of Accounts for Restaurants (USAR)*, published by the National Restaurant Association. Exhibit 3.14 is the summary statement of income for the hypothetical Steak-Plus Restaurant.

Exhibit 3.14 *USAR* Summary Statement of Income

Steak-Plus Restaurant
Statement of Income
For the year ended Dec. 31, 20X1

	Amounts	Percentage*
Sales:		
Food	$ 800,000	78.0
Beverage	200,000	19.5
Merchandise & Other	25,000	2.5
Total Sales	1,025,000	100.0
Cost of Sales:		
Food	240,000	30.0
Beverage	60,000	30.0
Merchandise & Other	10,000	40.0
Total Cost of Sales	310,000	30.2
Labor:		
Management	100,000	9.8
Staff	160,000	15.6
Employee Benefits	60,000	5.9
Total Labor	320,000	31.2
Prime Cost	630,000	61.5
Other Controllable Expenses:		
Direct Operating Expenses	60,000	5.9
Music & Entertainment	3,000	0.3
Marketing	30,000	2.9
Utilities	40,000	3.9
General & Administrative Expenses	50,000	4.9
Repairs & Maintenance	18,000	1.8
Total Other Controllable Expenses	201,000	19.6
Controllable Income	185,000	18.1
Noncontrollable Expenses:		
Occupancy Costs	80,000	7.8
Equipment Leases	6,000	0.6
Depreciation & Amortization	20,000	2.0
Total Noncontrollable Expenses	106,000	10.3
Restaurant Operating Income	79,000	7.7
Corporate Overhead	3,000	0.3
Interest Expense	2,000	0.2
Other (Income)/Expense	(2,000)	(0.2)
Income before Income Taxes	$ 76,000	7.4

Format based on *Uniform System of Accounts for Restaurants,* 8th Edition (Washington, DC: National Restaurant Association, 2012), p. 3.
*All percentages are calculated as a percentage of total sales except cost of sales for food, beverage, and merchandise & other, which are based on their respective sales.

Exhibit 3.15 Country Club Statement of Activities

**COUNTRY CLUB
STATEMENT OF ACTIVITIES
(In Departmental Form)**
(Internal)

	Schedule	Period Ended
MEMBERSHIP REVENUE		
Membership dues	$	$
Initiation fees (see discussion section 1)		
Unused food and other minimums		
Total membership revenue		
COST OF SPORTS ACTIVITIES		
Golf operations income (loss)	E	
Less golf course maintenance	G	
Golf shop	F	
Net golf profit (expense)		
Racquet sports	H	
Racquet shop	I	
Fitness/spa	K	
Aquatic sports	J	
Other sports activities		
Net cost of sports activities		
Membership revenue available for clubhouse operations and fixed charges		
CLUBHOUSE OPERATING INCOME (LOSS)		
Food	A	
Beverage	B	
Social events	C	
Overnight rooms	D	
Locker rooms	L	
Special-purpose funds	N	
Marina	M	
Other operating departments	P	
Rentals and other revenue	Q	
Total clubhouse operating income (loss)		
UNDISTRIBUTED OPERATING EXPENSES		
Administrative and general	R	
Clubhouse	S	
Information technology	O	
Marketing and membership	T	
Facility maintenance	U	
Energy costs	U	
Total operating expenses		
Clubhouse operations and undistributed operating expenses		
INCOME BEFORE FIXED CHARGES		
FIXED CHARGES		
Rent	X	
Property taxes and other municipal charges		
Insurance		
Interest		
Depreciation and amortization		
Total fixed charges		

(Continued)

```
┌─────────────────────────────────────────────────────────────────────┐
│                          COUNTRY CLUB                                 │
│                    STATEMENT OF ACTIVITIES                            │
│                       (In Departmental Form)                          │
│                            (Internal)                                 │
│ INCOME (LOSS) BEFORE MEMBERSHIP AND OTHER ACTIVITIES                   │
│ MEMBERSHIP AND OTHER ACTIVITIES                                       │
│       Initiation fees                                                 │
│       Membership certificates issued                                  │
│       Membership certificates redeemed                                │
│       Nonoperating expenses                                           │
│       Capital assessments                                             │
│       Investment income, net of applicable taxes      _____    _____│
│       Other                                                           │
│ INCREASE (DECREASE) IN UNRESTRICTED NET                               │
│    ASSETS (MEMBERS' EQUITY)                                           │
│ UNRESTRICTED NET ASSETS, BEGINNING OF PERIOD          _____    _____│
│ UNRESTRICTED NET ASSETS, END OF PERIOD          $     _____  $ _____│
│                                                       ══════    ══════│
└─────────────────────────────────────────────────────────────────────┘
```

Source: *Uniform System of Financial Reporting for Clubs*, 7th Ed. (Washington, DC: Club Managers Association of America, 2012).

Most private clubs are organized as not-for-profit organizations. Their major focus is providing services to club members. A significant part of all clubs' revenue derives from membership dues and initiation fees. The bottom line of a club's statement of activities is increase (decrease) in unrestricted net assets. The statement of activities for club operations is prescribed by the *Uniform System of Financial Reporting for Clubs (USFRC)*, created by the Club Managers Association of America. As with *USALI* and *USAR*, this statement of activities has several supporting schedules. The *USFRC* includes separate forms for country and city clubs. Exhibit 3.15 shows the form for country clubs.

The benefits of the *USAR* and the *USFRC* are similar to those of the *USALI*. That is, both the *USAR* and the *USFRC*:

■ Provide for uniform classification and presentation of operating results.

■ Allow for easier comparisons with foodservice industry statistics *(USAR)* and club industry statistics *(USFRC)*.

■ Provide turnkey accounting systems.

■ Are time-tested systems prepared by some of the foodservice and club industries' best accounting minds.

The basic similarities and differences between the *USALI*'s, *USAR*'s, and *USFRC*'s income statement formats are as follows:

	USALI	USAR	USFRC
Sales segmented	Yes	Yes	Yes
Cost of sales segmented	Yes	Yes	No
Payroll and related costs segmented	Yes	No	No
Other direct costs segmented	Yes	No	No
Controllable expenses separated from fixed charges	Yes	Yes	Yes
Fixed charges segmented	Yes	Yes	Yes

The income statement, complete with all departmental statements, is generally considered the most useful financial statement for management. It highlights the important financial aspects of the property's operations over a period of time.

The income statement shows four major elements: revenues, expenses, gains, and losses. Revenues (increases in assets or decreases in liability accounts) and expenses (decreases in assets or increases in liability accounts) are directly related to operations, while gains and losses result from transactions incidental to the property's major operations.

In order to standardize income statements within the hospitality industry, the original *Uniform System of Accounts for Hotels* was written in 1925–26. Since then, there have been changes and revisions, the most recent being the 11th Revised Edition, the *Uniform System of Accounts for the Lodging Industry*, published in 2014. By using an accounting system based on a uniform system of accounts, the management of a new hotel has a turnkey accounting system for a complete and systematic accounting for the hotel's operations. The various uniform systems also facilitate comparison among operations of varying sizes in the hospitality industry.

In order to enhance the usefulness of the income statement, the format includes statements of departmental income showing the revenues produced by each profit center (operated department) and subtracting from each the corresponding direct operating expenses. Included in the direct operating expenses are not only the cost of goods sold, but also the direct labor costs and other direct expenses. Next, undistributed operating expenses, which consist of five major service center categories—administrative and general; information and telecommunications systems; sales and marketing; property operation and maintenance; and energy, water, and waste—must be subtracted to determine gross operating profit. This is followed by management fees and nonoperating income and expenses, which include rent, property taxes, fire insurance, and other nonoperating income and expenses. This category of expenses is subtracted from GOP to determine EBITDA. Interest expense, depreciation, and amortization are subtracted to yield income before income taxes. Finally, income taxes are subtracted to determine net income.

As a supplement to the income statement, several departmental income statements should be presented. These offer management additional insight into the operation of each department. The number of schedules necessary depends on the complexity of the lodging facility; the more cost and profit centers operated, the more supplemental statements should be presented. These departmental statements can be very useful for management. First, they can be used to compare the hotel's operations with industry averages, prior performance, and most important, budgeted standards or goals. Also, the relative profitability of various departments can be compared.

There are four major methods management can use to analyze the income statement. The first method is horizontal analysis, which considers both the relative and absolute changes in the income statement between two periods and/or between the budgeted and actual figures. Any major variances exceeding levels predefined by management can be further investigated to determine their causes. The next type of analysis is the vertical analysis, which reduces all items to a percentage of sales. These percentages, often referred to as common-size statements, can then be used to compare the results of the property's operations with either those of other lodging facilities or with industry standards. Again, any significant differences should be studied. The third method is base-year comparisons, in which two or more years are compared on a percentage basis with a base year set at 100 percent. The final method, ratio analysis, gives mathematical expression to a relationship between two figures and is computed by dividing one figure by the other figure. Financial ratios are compared with standards in order to evaluate the financial condition of a hospitality operation.

capacity costs—Fixed charges relating to the physical plant or the capacity to provide goods and services to guests.

common-size income statements—Income statements used in vertical analysis whose information has been reduced to percentages to facilitate comparisons.

comparative income statement—Horizontal analysis of income statements for two accounting periods in terms of both absolute and relative variances for each line item.

daily report of operations—A frequent major report prepared for management.

departmental statements—Supplements to the income statement that provide management with detailed financial information for each operating department and service center; also referred to as schedules.

expenses—Costs incurred in providing the goods and services offered.

gains—An increase in assets, a reduction in liabilities, or a combination of both resulting from incidental transactions and from all other transactions and events affecting the operation during the period, except those that count as revenues or investments by owners.

income statements—A report on the profitability of operations, including revenues earned and expenses incurred in generating the revenues for the period of time covered by the statement.

losses—A decrease in assets, an increase in liabilities, or a combination of both resulting from incidental transactions and from other transactions and events affecting the operation during a period, except those that count as expenses or distributions to owners.

ratio analysis—Ratio analysis gives mathematical expression to a relationship between two figures and is computed by dividing one figure by the other figure. Financial ratios are compared with standards in order to evaluate the financial condition of a hospitality operation.

responsibility accounting—The organization of accounting information (as on an income statement) that focuses attention on departmental results, such as the rooms and food departments.

revenue—The amount charged to customers in exchange for goods and services.

schedules—See "departmental statements."

summary income statements—Income statements intended for external users that lack the detail of supporting schedules.

uniform systems of accounts—Standardized accounting systems prepared by various segments of the hospitality industry offering detailed information about accounts; classifications; formats; the different kinds, contents, and uses of financial statements and reports; and other useful information.

1. What are the major differences between the balance sheet and the income statement?

2. Why are creditors interested in the income statement?

3. What are the major differences between a revenue and a gain?

4. What are three examples of direct operating expenses for the rooms department?

5. What is the difference between the income statement used in many non-hospitality industries and one prepared by a lodging facility?

6. How is the cost of food sold determined?

7. What are the advantages of the uniform systems of accounts?

8. What detailed expenses are included in the property operation, maintenance, and energy costs of the income statement?

9. Why are supplemental statements valuable to management?

10. What are the different techniques of income statement analysis?

11. How is the statement of income per the *USAR* similar to and different from the *USALI*'s income statement?

Problem 1

Barcelona Café sold two pieces of equipment during 20X2. Relevant information is as follows:

1. Sale of range
    Selling price = $600
    Original cost = $6,500
    Accumulated depreciation = $6,300

2. Sale of van
    Selling price = $4,500
    Original cost = $40,000
    Accumulated depreciation = $35,000

Required:

Determine the gain or loss on the sale of each piece of equipment.

Problem 2

The Avalon Café sold three pieces of equipment during 20X1, as follows:

1. A range costing $8,000 and depreciated down to $1,000 was sold for a "gain" of $500. How much cash was received?

2. A delivery van that originally cost $60,000 was depreciated using the straight-line method over a three-year life. Assume a salvage value of $3,000. At the end of exactly two years of use, the van was sold for $15,000. What was the gain or loss on the sale?

3. A computer that originally cost $4,000 was sold for $500 after the Avalon Café used it for a single year. It was being depreciated using the double declining balance method. Assume its estimated life when purchased was four years. What was the gain or loss on the sale?

Problem 3

The Tong Lee Inn had total revenues of $1 million for the month of June. Assume that the Tong Lee Inn's percentages for June were the same as the comparative results of operations information shown in Exhibit 3.8 for 2019.

Required:

Determine the amount of each of the following for June:

1. Rooms revenue

2. Total rooms expenses

3. Utilities

4. Administrative and general expenses

5. Food and beverage departmental income

6. Total food and beverage expenses

Problem 4

Joseph Lo, the owner of the JoLo Diner, has requested your assistance in determining some monthly expenses. He provides you with the following information:

	Food	Beverages
Beginning inventory, 1/1	$ 7,500	$ 2,750
Ending inventory, 1/31	$ 12,000	$ 3,500
Purchases	$ 43,250	$ 17,800
Employee meals	$ 600	—
Food transfers to beverage department	$ 250	—

Required:

Determine the following:

1. Cost of food used
2. Cost of food sold
3. Cost of beverages sold

Problem 5

As the controller for Vienna, a hotel with a large restaurant operation, you are responsible for monitoring costs. You have collected the following information concerning the food inventory and need to calculate the cost of food sold for the month of December.

Inventory, Dec. 1, 20X1	$25,869
Inventory, Dec. 31, 20X1	23,581
Purchases	79,540
Employee Meals:	
A. General manager	95
B. Food department	1,119
Transfers from the bar to kitchen	58
Promotional meals	326

Required:

1. Calculate the cost of food sold for December 20X1.
2. To which departments would each expense be charged?

Expense	Department
1. Cost of food sold	_____
2. Employee meals—general manager	_____
3. Employee meals—food department	_____
4. Promotional meals	_____

Problem 6

Several accounts from the Henderson Inn's general ledger that pertain to the rooms department are listed below. The accounts are in random order as follows:

Sales—transient—regular	$ 120,000
Salaries	15,000
Commissions	800
Uniforms	500
Linen expense	1,000
Sales—transient—groups	75,000
Wages	35,000
Payroll taxes	6,000
Operating supplies	2,500
Contract services	1,800
Laundry and dry cleaning	5,000
Fringe benefits	6,000
Other revenues	2,000
Allowances—rooms	800
Miscellaneous expenses	1,800

Required:

Prepare a rooms department schedule following the *USALI*. Use only classifications as shown on the prescribed schedule. Use Exhibit 3.5 as a guide.

Problem 7

The St. Bart's rooms department has revenue and expense accounts as follows:

Revenue:	
Transient—regular	$ 550,000
Transient—group	375,000
Other	50,000
Expenses:	
Allowances	$ 2,000
Salaries (management)	80,000
Wages (nonmanagement)	125,000
Payroll taxes	24,000
Workers' compensation	10,000
Health insurance	18,000
Commissions	2,000
Contract services	3,000
Laundry	5,500
Dry cleaning	2,000
Linen	7,500
Guest supplies	3,750
Cleaning supplies	1,950
Office supplies	1,350

Reservations	15,200
Printing and stationery	3,500
Training videos	550
Uniforms	1,870
Miscellaneous	670

Required:

Prepare the rooms department schedule for St. Bart in accordance with the USALI. Note: The rooms department has more individual accounts than should be shown on this schedule. Use Exhibit 3.5 as a guide.

Problem 8

Andrew Bromley is an excellent food manager, but needs your assistance in preparing the food department schedule for 20X8 according to the USALI.

Revenue information:	
Venue food revenue	$ 850,000
Service charges	45,000
Meeting room rentals	12,000
Allowances	2,000
Expense information:	
Food purchases	$ 300,000
Transfers from beverage department	500
Cost of employee meals	10,000
Complimentary food—marketing	1,000
Transfers to beverage department	300
Salaries (management)	70,000
Wages (nonmanagement)	200,000
FICA expense	20,000
SUTA expense	3,000
FUTA expense	1,000
Health insurance	25,000
Other employee benefits	10,000
Utensils	1,200
Uniform costs	5,400
Laundry	8,000
Operating supplies	20,500
Training	2,000
Uniform laundry	3,500
Contract services	25,000
China	6,500
Glassware	3,600
Licenses	1,500
Linen	5,400
Miscellaneous	3,200

In addition, the beginning food inventory totaled $15,000, while the ending food inventory totaled $18,000.

Required:

Prepare the food department schedule in accordance with the USALI.

Problem 9

The Warwick Motel's income statement for 20X6 is provided below:

Warwick Motel
Income Statement
For the year ended Dec. 31, 20X6

	Net Revenue	Cost of Sales	Labor Costs & Related Expenses	Other Expenses	Income (Loss)
Operated Departments					
Rooms	$ 380,000	$ —	$ 92,000	$ 30,000	$ 258,000
Food	180,000	54,000	69,000	20,000	37,000
Miscellaneous Income	1,000	—	—	—	1,000
Total Operated Departments	561,000	54,000	161,000	50,000	296,000
Undistributed Operating Expenses:					
Administrative and General			43,250	10,000	53,250
Info. & Telecom. Systems			20,000	10,000	30,000
Marketing				10,000	10,000
Prop. Op. Maint.				20,000	20,000
Utilities				27,000	27,000
Total Undist. Op. Exp.			63,250	77,000	140,250
Gross Operating Profit	$ 561,000	$ 54,000	$ 224,250	$ 127,000	155,750
Rent, Property Taxes, and Insurance					17,000
EBITDA					138,750
Interest Expense					21,000
Depreciation					30,000
Income before Income Taxes					87,750
Income Tax					35,100
Net Income					$ 52,650

Required:

Answer the following questions:

1. What is the total gross profit for 20X6?

2. What are the total overhead costs for 20X6?

3. What is the average tax rate for 20X6?

4. What is the amount of income the general manager is most likely responsible for during 20X6?

5. What is the labor cost percentage for 20X6?

6. What is the food cost percentage for 20X6?

Problem 10

The MacKenzie Inn (MKI) has two major operated departments: rooms and food. The following information is supplied to you as of December 31, 20X6:

Account	Account Balance
Rooms department—salaries and wages	$ 200,000
Food department—salaries and wages	180,000
Supplies and other—food department	40,000
Supplies and other—rooms department	100,000
Rooms sales	1,200,000
Interest income	?
Cost of food sold	?
Food sales	600,000
Miscellaneous income	50,000
Food purchases	360,000

Other information is as follows:

1. Two years ago, the MKI invested $200,000 in state of Colorado bonds. Interest is paid on the bonds at an annual rate of 9 percent.

2. The beginning and ending inventories of food were $8,000 and $9,000, respectively. Food consumed by the food and rooms department employees during the year (free of charge) totaled $2,000 and $1,000, respectively.

3. Fringe benefits and payroll taxes for all employees, *including* free food, are 20 percent of gross salaries and wages.

Required:

Prepare the top portion—that is, the operated departments section—of the income statement for the MKI. Follow the summary income statement shown in Exhibit 3.4.

Problem 11

The Meijer Motel has two major operated departments: rooms and food. The following information is supplied to you as of December 31, 20X6.

Account	Account Balance
Insurance (fire)	$ 5,000
Rooms department—salaries and wages	80,000
Food department—salaries and wages	60,000
Supplies—food department	20,000

Account	Account Balance
Room sales	380,000
Interest income	?
Interest expense	20,000
Cost of food sold	?
Food sales	175,000
A&G–salaries	60,000
Advertising	10,000
Maintenance—contract	30,000
Depreciation	20,000
Heat	15,000
Information and telecom. systems—contract	30,000
Power and lights	12,000
Franchise fee	20,000
Supplies and other—rooms department	30,000
Property taxes	12,000
A&G–other expense	10,000
Room allowances	5,000

1. Benefits and payroll taxes for all employees are 20 percent of gross salaries and wages.

2. The Meijer Motel pays an average of 20 percent of its pretax income to the various government units in the form of income taxes.

3. The management fee to be paid to the management company is 2 percent of net room revenue and 10 percent of GOP.

4. The food purchases totaled $50,000 during 20X6. Food inventory was $20,000 and $18,000 at the beginning and end of the year, respectively. The cost of employee meals totaled $3,000 for the year.

5. $100,000 was invested in a two-year certificate of deposit on October 1, 20X5. The annual rate of interest is 5 percent.

Required:

Prepare a summary income statement for the Meijer Motel for 20X6 in accordance with Exhibit 3.4 in this chapter.

Problem 12

The Salazar Sunset Inn (SSI) has three major operated departments: rooms, food, and beverages. The following information is supplied to you as of December 31, 20X6:

Account	Account Balance
Insurance (fire)	$ 20,000
Rooms department—salaries and wages	150,000
Food department—salaries and wages	160,000
Beverage department—salaries and wages	40,000
Management fees	50,000

Account	Account Balance
Supplies—food department	40,000
Cost of food sold	180,000
Cost of beverages sold	60,000
Room sales	1,000,000
Dividend income	15,000
Interest expense	85,000
Food sales	540,000
Beverage sales	200,000
A&G—wages	80,000
Supplies—beverage department	15,000
Advertising	30,000
Maintenance—contract	40,000
Information and telecom. systems—contract	20,000
Depreciation	50,000
Heat	40,000
Franchise fees	25,000
Power and lights	30,000
Amortization of initial franchise fee	5,000
Supplies and other—rooms department	80,000
Property taxes	50,000
A&G—other expense	40,000
Room—allowances	2,000

Required:

Prepare a summary income statement (see Exhibit 3.4). The SSI chooses to show food and beverage as two separate departments. Assume an average tax rate of 25 percent.

Problem 13

The general ledger of Sakura, a 100-seat restaurant, as of December 31, 20X3, includes revenue and expense accounts as follows:

Salaries	$ 175,000
Wages	280,000
Payroll taxes	32,000
Fringe benefits (excludes employee meals)	55,000
Employee meals	7,000
Food sales	1,200,000
Beverage sales	900,000
Food purchases	575,000
Beverage purchases	230,000
Direct operating expenses	100,000
Music	20,000
Marketing	30,000
Heat, light, and power	45,000

Rent	160,000
Interest expense	20,000
Depreciation	30,000
Repairs	38,000
Administrative and general	95,000

Other information:

Income tax rate—30 percent on pretax income

Inventories	1/1/X3	12/31/X3
Food	$30,000	$32,000
Beverage	15,000	17,000

Required:

Prepare Sakura's statement of income for 20X3 in accordance with the *USAR*. See Exhibit 3.14 for a guide.

Problem 14

The JW Motel (JWM) has two operated departments: rooms and food. The following information is supplied to you as of December 31, 20X2:

Account	Account Balance
Rooms department—salaries and wages	$ 350,000
Food department—salaries and wages	200,000
Management fees	?
Supplies and other—food department	40,000
Food purchases	220,000
Room sales	1,400,000
Interest expense	?
Cost of food sold	?
Food sales	500,000
A&G—salaries	100,000
Franchise fees	60,000
Maintenance—contract	60,000
Depreciation	80,000
Heat, light, and power	50,000
Water	20,000
Food—allowances	3,000
Information and telecom. systems—contract	20,000
Marketing expenses—advertising	30,000
Insurance (fire)	50,000
Supplies and other—room department	50,000
Property taxes	50,000
A&G—other expenses	40,000

Other information is as follows:

1. The JWM borrowed $1 million from the Red Cedar Bank on April 1, 20X2. The annual interest rate is 10 percent.

2. The beginning and ending inventories of food were $5,000 and $7,000, respectively. Food consumed by the food and A&G department employees during the year (free of charge) totaled $2,000 and $1,000, respectively.

3. Fringe benefits and payroll taxes for all employees, *including* free food, are 30 percent of gross salaries and wages.

4. The JWM pays an average of 25 percent of its pretax income to various government units in the form of income taxes.

5. The management fee to be paid to the management company is 2 percent of total net revenue and 5 percent of total income after undistributed operating expenses.

6. An investment in Marriott stock that cost $10,000 is sold for $15,000.

7. A van that cost $25,000 was sold for $2,000. Its net book value at the time of the sale was $5,000.

8. A one-year certificate of deposit was purchased at the Spartan National Bank; $100,000 was invested on September 1, 20X2. The annual interest rate is 6 percent.

Required:

Prepare an income statement for 20X2 for the JWM based on the format of Exhibit 3.4.

Problem 15

The Milford Motel (MM) has two major operated departments: rooms and food. The following information is supplied to you as of December 31, 20X7:

Account	Account Balance
Insurance (fire)	$ 20,000
Rooms department—salaries and wages	300,000
Food department—salaries and wages	200,000
Management fees	?
Supplies and other—food department	40,000
Food purchases	200,000
Room sales	1,210,000
Interest expense	?
Cost of food sold	?
Food sales	450,000
A&G—salaries and wages	120,000
Franchise fees	20,000
Maintenance—contract	40,000
Information and telecom. systems—contract	30,000
Depreciation	80,000
Heat, light, and power	50,000
Water	20,000

Account	Account Balance
Rooms—allowances	10,000
Marketing expenses—advertising	50,000
Rent expenses	10,000
Supplies and other—room department	50,000
Property taxes	40,000
A&G—other expenses	60,000

Other information is as follows:

1. The MM borrowed $1 million from the Red Cedar Bank on July 1, 20X7. The annual interest rate is 12 percent.

2. The beginning and ending inventories of food were $7,000 and $5,000, respectively. Food consumed by the food and rooms department employees during the year (free of charge) totaled $1,000 and $3,000, respectively.

3. Fringe benefits and payroll taxes for all employees, excluding free food, are 30 percent of gross salaries and wages.

4. The MM pays an average of 30 percent of its pretax income to various government units in the form of income taxes.

5. The management fee to be paid to the management company is 2 percent of net room sales and 10 percent of total GOP.

6. An investment in JMB stock that cost $10,000 was sold for $8,000.

7. A computer that cost $15,000 was sold for $2,000. Its accumulated depreciation at the time of sale was $12,000.

Required:

Prepare an income statement for 20X7 for the MM based on the format of Exhibit 3.4.

Problem 16

Tanner Tidbits' August and September 20X1 condensed income statements are as follows:

	August	September
Food sales	$ 180,000	$ 182,000
Cost of food sales	63,000	65,000
Labor	65,500	68,800
Laundry	9,000	4,200
China, glass, silver	3,000	1,100
Other	19,000	25,500
Total expenses	159,500	164,600
Net income	$ 20,500	$ 17,400
Customers were served as follows:		
Food	14,000	15,000

Required:

1. Convert the two income statements to common-size income statements.

2. Based on the information provided (including customer information), comment regarding the operating performance of Tanner Tidbits for the two months.

Problem 17

Jonathan Mulhurn, the founder of J's Place, wants to analyze the year's operations for 20X2 by comparing them with the 20X1 results. To aid him, prepare a comparative income statement using the 20X1 and 20X2 information available.

J's Place
Income Statement
For the years ending Dec. 31, 20X1 and 20X2

	20X1	20X2
Revenues		
Rooms	$ 988,000	$ 1,041,000
Food	614,000	636,000
Gift Shop	45,000	52,000
Total	1,647,000	1,729,000
Direct Expenses		
Rooms	250,000	283,000
Food	476,000	502,100
Gift Shop	65,000	68,000
Total Operated Department Income	856,000	875,900
Undistributed Operating Expenses		
Administrative and General	163,000	175,000
Information and Telecommunications Systems	30,000	62,000
Marketing	65,000	67,500
Property Operation and Maintenance	69,000	68,000
Utility Costs	101,000	102,000
Gross Operating Profit	428,000	401,400
Rent, Property Taxes, and Insurance	200,000	200,000
EBITDA	228,000	201,400
Interest	55,000	52,000
Depreciation and Amortization	116,000	116,000
Income before Income Taxes	57,000	33,400
Income Taxes	17,100	10,500
Net Income	$ 39,900	$ 22,900

Required:

Prepare the comparative income statement for J's Place. Note: Rearrange the income statement to conform to the format in Exhibit 3.11.

Problem 18

The Black Beach Motel (BBM) has three operated departments—rooms, food, and gift shop. The following information is supplied to you as of December 31, 20X1.

Account	Account Balance
Insurance (fire)	$ 20,000
Rooms department—salaries and wages	100,000
Food department—salaries and wages	80,000
Gift shop—salaries and wages	5,000
Supplies—food department	30,000
Food purchases	80,000
Room sales	600,000
Interest income	?
Interest expense	50,000
Cost of food sold	?
Food sales	300,000
A&G—wages	40,000
Advertising	8,000
Maintenance—contract	25,000
Information and telecommunications systems—contract	15,000
Depreciation	60,000
Heat	15,000
Power and lights	12,000
Supplies and other—rooms department	40,000
Property taxes	12,000
A&G—other expenses	20,000
Gift shop sales	16,000
Gift shop—cost of sales	10,000
Gift shop—other expenses	3,000
Management fee	?
Marketing—wages	20,000
Rent	5,000

Other information:

1. The BBM invested $100,000 on April 1, 20X1, in a certificate of deposit earning an annual rate of 8 percent.

2. The beginning and ending inventories of food were $4,000 and $6,000 respectively. Food consumed by the department employees during the year (free of charge) was as follows:

Rooms	$ 600
Food	1,000
A&G	300

3. Benefits and payroll taxes for all employees, excluding free food, are 25 percent of gross salaries and wages.

4. The BBM pays an average of 30 percent of its pretax income to the various government units in the form of income taxes.

5. The management fee to be paid to the management company is 5 percent of total sales and 8 percent of total income before management fees and fixed charges.

Required:

Prepare a summary income statement for 20X1 for the Black Beach Motel based on the format of Exhibit 3.4.

Problem 19

Aiden's Lodge has two major operated departments: rooms and food. The following information is supplied to you as of December 31, 20X2:

Account	Account Balance
Insurance (fire)	$?
Rooms department—salaries and wages	90,000
Food department—salaries and wages	60,000
Supplies and other—food department	20,000
Food purchases	65,000
Room sales	550,000
Interest income	?
Cost of food sold	?
Food sales	250,000
A&G—salaries	60,000
Advertising	12,000
Maintenance—contract	25,000
Information and telecommunications systems	15,000
Depreciation	40,000
Electricity	15,000
Heating oil	12,000
Amortization of intangible asset	5,000
Supplies and other—rooms department	30,000
Property taxes	15,000
A&G—other expense	15,000
Franchise fees	?
Rooms—allowances	1,000

Other information is as follows:

1. Aiden's Lodge invested $30,000 on July 1, 20X2, in Daytona Aircraft Bonds. The funds were invested at an annual interest rate of 12 percent.

2. The beginning and ending inventories of food were $5,000 and $4,000, respectively. Food consumed by the food and rooms department employees during the year (free of charge) totaled $500 and $300, respectively.

3. Fringe benefits and payroll taxes for all employees, inclusive of employee meals, are 20 percent of gross salaries and wages.

4. Aiden's Lodge pays an average of 30 percent of its pretax income to the various government units in the form of income taxes.

5. The management fee to be paid to the management company is 2 percent of net room sales and 6 percent of total income before management fees and fixed charges.

6. Fire insurance protection was secured on June 1, 20X1, for a two-year period of coverage from July 1, 20X1, through June 30, 20X3. The two-year premium was $36,000.

7. Franchise fees (a marketing expense) are paid to World Lodge Corporation at a rate of 3 percent of net room sales and 2 percent of net food sales.

Required:

Prepare an income statement for 20X2 for Aiden's Lodge based on the format of Exhibit 3.4.

Problem 20

The Tuscany's partially completed condensed comparative income statements are as follows:

	20X1	20X2	Difference $	%
Total Revenues	$ 1,000,000	$ 1,200,000		
Rooms—Revenues	600,000			25.0
Labor Costs & Related Expenses		120,000	10,000	
Other Expense	60,000			10.0
Department Income				
Food—Revenues	400,000		40,000	
Cost of Sales		130,000	15,000	
Labor Costs & Related Expenses	75,000			10.0
Other Expense			3,500	10.0
Department Income				
Gift Shop—Revenues	50,000	55,000		
Cost of Sales	40,000			12.0
Labor Costs & Related Expenses			2,000	14.0
Other Expense		6,000	1,000	
Department Income				
Total Operated Department Income				
Undistributed Operating Expenses:				
Administrative & General	100,000			11.0
Information & Telecommunications Systems	25,000	28,000	3,000	12.0
Sales & Marketing		75,000	5,000	
Property Maintenance	45,000		10,000	
Utilities				30.0
Total Undistributed Operating Expenses	250,000		32,000	
Management Fees		40,000	3,000	
Income before Nonoperating Expenses				
Rent, Property Taxes, & Insurance	100,000			6.0

	20X1	20X2	Difference $	Difference %
EBITDA	208,714	312,914	———	———
Interest		60,000	20,000	———
Depreciation	———	———	5,000	20.0
Income before Income Taxes	———	———		
Income Taxes			6,000	10.0
Net Income				

Required:

Complete the above comparative income statements.

Problem 21

Listed below is financial information for the Harby Hotel for the year ended December 31, 20X2:

Account	Account Balance
Commissions—Rooms Department	$ 23,500
Marketing Expense	111,800
Ending Food Inventory	53,000
Depreciation and Amortization Expense	91,000
Net Room Revenue	1,560,000
Cost of Sales—Gift Shop	41,974
Rent Expense	148,200
Rooms Reservation Expense	13,500
Fire Insurance Expense	10,400
Income Taxes—40% pretax rate	?
Employee Benefits—Rooms Department	51,000
Food Revenues	858,000
Proceeds from Sale of Equipment*	10,000
Contract Cleaning—Rooms Department	5,800
Administrative and General Expenses (total)	270,400
Property Taxes	70,200
Food Purchases	328,400
Payroll—Gift Shop	25,600
Linen Expense—Rooms Department	8,600
Other Expense—Gift Shop	9,360
Beginning Food Inventory	38,900
Revenues—Gift Shop	119,600
Miscellaneous Income	62,400
Information and Telecommunications Systems	55,120
Salaries and Wages—Rooms Department	209,000
Interest Expense	98,800
Free Food—Employees**	12,300

Account	Account Balance
Laundry and Dry Cleaning—Rooms Department	24,800
Other Expenses—Food Department	93,600
Other Expenses—Rooms Department	130,000
Property Operation and Maintenance (total)	118,440
Payroll—Food Department	93,600
Utilities (total)	159,500

* Equipment sold cost $15,000 and had been depreciated by $8,000.
** This has already been recorded as an expense in the appropriate departments, except in the determination of the cost of food sold.

Required:

1. Determine the cost of food sold.

2. Prepare a summary income statement following the format of Exhibit 3.4.

Problem 22

The Kaminski Motel (KM) has two major operated departments: rooms and food. The following information is supplied to you as of December 31, 20X2:

Account	Accounts Balance
Insurance (fire)	$?
Rooms Department—Salaries and Wages	90,000
Food Department—Salaries and Wages	60,000
Supplies and Other—Food Department	20,000
Food Purchases	65,000
Room Sales	550,000
Interest Income	?
Cost of Food Sold	?
Food Sales	250,000
Administrative and General—Salaries	60,000
Advertising	12,000
Maintenance—Contract	40,000
Depreciation	40,000
Electricity	15,000
Interest Expense	30,000
Information and Telecommunications Systems	12,000
Amortization of Intangible Assets	5,000
Supplies and Other—Rooms Department	30,000
Property Taxes	15,000
Administrative and General—Other Expenses	15,000
Franchise Fees	?
Room—Allowances	1,000

Other information is as follows:

1. The KM invested $30,000 on July 1, 20X2, in Daytona Aircraft Bonds. The funds were invested at an annual interest rate of 12 percent.

2. The beginning and ending inventories of food were $5,000 and $4,000, respectively. Food consumed by the food and rooms department employees during the year (free of charge) totaled $500 and $300, respectively.

3. Fringe benefits and payroll taxes for all employees, inclusive of employee meals, are 20 percent of gross salaries and wages.

4. The KM pays an average of 30 percent of its pretax income to the various government units in the form of income taxes.

5. The management fee to be paid to the management company is 2 percent of net rooms sales and 6 percent of GOP.

6. Fire insurance protection was secured on June 1, 20X1, for a two-year period of coverage from July 1, 20X1, through June 30, 20X3. The two-year premium was $36,000.

7. Franchise fees (a marketing expense) is paid to Best Eastern Corporation at a rate of 3 percent of net rooms sales and 2 percent of net food sales.

Required:

Prepare the modified income statement for 20X2. Use Exhibit 3.4 as a guide. Round to the nearest $1.

Problem 23

Westlake, a 100-seat fusion restaurant, has the following accounts in its general ledger as of December 31, 20X5:

Salaries	$ 250,000
Wages	325,000
Payroll taxes	45,000
Fringe benefits (excludes employee meals)	75,000
Employee meals	8,500
Food sales	1,600,000
Beverage sales	650,000
Food purchases	670,000
Beverage purchases	330,000
Direct operating expenses	90,000
Music	20,000
Marketing	15,000
Heat, light, and power	40,500
Rent	144,000
Interest expense	22,120
Depreciation	35,000
Repairs	30,000
Administrative and general	92,000

In addition, the beginning and ending balances of the two inventory accounts of food and beverage of Westlake are listed below.

Income tax rate—30 percent on pretax income.

Inventories	1/1/X5	12/31/X5
Food	$25,000	$23,500
Beverage	11,600	13,580

Required:

Prepare a statement of income for Westlake for 20X5 in accordance with the *USAR*. See Exhibit 3.14 for a guide. Please note that the income tax rate for Westlake is 30 percent on its pretax income.

Problem 24

The January and February 20X6 condensed income statement of Candy, Crepes & Coffee, as well as the customer counts, are as follows:

	January	February
Food Sales	$ 120,000	$ 145,000
Cost of Food Sales	35,640	41,560
Labor	30,250	31,580
Operating Supplies	5,600	5,800
China, Glass, Silver	1,200	1,250
Rent	5,000	5,000
Other	12,550	13,250
Total Expenses	90,240	98,440
Net Income	$ 29,760	$ 46,560
Customer Count	14,120	15,250

Required:

1. Convert the two income statements to common-size income statements.

2. Based on the information provided (including customer information), comment regarding the operating performance of Candy, Crepes & Coffee for the two months.

Problem 25

Dale Janik, founder of DJ by the Bay, wants to analyze the year's operations for 20X8 by comparing them with the 20X7 results. To aid him, prepare a comparative income statement using the 20X7 and 20X8 information available.

DJ by the Bay
Comparative Income Statements
For the Years Ended Dec. 31, 20X7 and 20X8

	20X7	20X8
Rooms		
Revenue	$ 1,156,478	$ 1,251,477
Expenses	298,400	305,411
Department Income	858,078	946,066
Food		
Revenue	725,840	727,890
Expenses	498,710	500,100
Department Income	227,130	227,790
Gift Shop		
Revenue	40,050	50,120
Expenses	58,200	55,110
Department Income	–18,150	–4,990
Total Operated Department Income	1,067,058	1,168,866
Undistributed Operating Expenses		
Administrative and General	210,560	211,540
Information and Telecom. Systems	32,000	35,000
Sales and Marketing	75,000	76,500
Property Operations and Maintenance	71,000	70,500
Utilities	121,500	122,400
Total Undistributed Operating Expenses	510,060	515,940
Income before Nonoperating Expenses	556,998	652,926
Rent	250,000	250,000
EBITDA	306,998	402,926
Depreciation and Amortization	135,000	142,000
Interest Expense	25,000	27,000
Income before Income Taxes	146,998	233,926
Income Taxes	44,099	70,178
Net Income	$ 102,899	$ 163,748

Prepare the comparative income statement for DJ by the Bay.

4

THE STATEMENT OF CASH FLOWS

Chapter 4 Outline

Competencies

1. Explain the purposes of the statement of cash flows and how the statement is used by hospitality managers. (pp. 142–144)

2. Identify cash flows as reported on the statement of cash flows in terms of operating activities, investing activities, and financing activities. (pp. 144–146)

3. Explain the direct and indirect methods of converting net income to net cash flow from operations. (pp. 146–148)

4. Describe the four-step approach to preparing the statement of cash flows. (pp. 148–163)

5. Identify issues involved in the analysis of statements of cash flows. (p. 164)

accrual basis

cash equivalents

cash inflows

cash outflows

direct method

indirect method

statement of cash flows (SCF)

KEY TERMS

Traditionally, the principal financial statements used by hospitality operations have been the income statement and the balance sheet. The balance sheet shows the financial position of the business at the end of the accounting period. The income statement reflects the results of operations for the accounting period. Although these statements provide extensive financial information, they do not provide answers to certain questions, such as the following:

1. How much cash was provided by operations?
2. What amount of property and equipment was purchased during the year?
3. How much long-term debt was borrowed during the year?
4. What amount of funds was raised through the sale of capital stock?
5. What amount of dividends was paid during the year?
6. How much was invested in long-term investments during the year?

The statement of cash flows (SCF) is designed to answer these questions and many more. The Financial Accounting Standards Board (FASB), which is the current accounting rule-making body, has mandated that the SCF be included with the other financial statements issued to external users only since 1988. It replaced a poorly understood financial statement, and hospitality managers welcomed the change.

Our discussion of this addition to the collection of major financial statements will address the definition of cash, the relationship of the SCF to other financial statements, the purposes and uses of the SCF, a classification of cash flows, alternative formats that may be used for the SCF, a four-step approach for preparing the SCF, and a comprehensive illustration of the preparation of the statement.

4.1 THE PURPOSE OF THE STATEMENT OF CASH FLOWS

The **statement of cash flows (SCF)** shows the effects on cash of a business's operating, investing, and financing activities for the accounting period. It explains the change in cash for the accounting period; that is, if cash increases by $5,000 from January 1, 20X1 (the beginning of the accounting period) to December 31, 20X1 (the end of the accounting period), the SCF will reflect the increase in the sum of cash from the firm's various activities.

For purposes of this statement, cash is defined to include both cash and cash equivalents. **Cash equivalents** are short-term, highly liquid investments, such as U.S. Treasury bills and money market accounts. Firms use cash equivalents for investing funds temporarily not needed for operating purposes. Generally, these short-term investments are made for 90 days or less. Since cash and cash equivalents are considered to be the same, transfers between cash and cash equivalents are not considered to be cash receipts or cash disbursements for SCF purposes.

The major purpose of the SCF is to provide relevant information regarding the cash receipts and disbursements of a hospitality business to help users (investors, creditors, managers, and others) to:

1. Assess the organization's ability to generate positive future net cash flows. Although users of financial statements are less interested in the past than in the future, many users, especially external users, must rely on historical financial information to assess an operation's future abilities. Thus, the investor interested in future cash dividends will review the SCF to determine past sources and uses of cash to evaluate the firm's ability to pay future dividends.

2. Assess the firm's ability to meet its obligations. Users of financial statements want to determine the firm's ability to pay its bills as they come due. If a firm has little likelihood of being able to pay its bills, then suppliers will most likely not be interested in selling the firm their goods and services.

3. Assess the difference between the enterprise's net income and cash receipts and disbursements. The SCF allows a user to quickly determine the major net sources of cash and how much relates to the enterprise's operations. Investors, creditors, and other users generally prefer enterprises that are able to generate cash from operations (i.e., from their primary purpose for being in business), as opposed to those generating cash solely from financing and investing activities (i.e., activities that are incidental to the primary purpose).

4. Assess the effect of both cash and noncash investing and financing during the accounting period. Investing activities relate to the acquisition and disposition of noncurrent assets, such as property and equipment. Financing activities relate to the borrowing and payment of long-term debt and sale and purchase of capital stock. Noncash activities (i.e., transactions involving no cash) include such transactions as the acquisition of a hotel in exchange for stock or long-term debt.

The three major user groups of the SCF are management (internal) and investors and creditors (external). Management may use the SCF to (1) assess the firm's liquidity, (2) assess its financial flexibility, (3) determine its dividend policy, and (4) plan investing and financing needs. Investors and creditors will most likely use the SCF to assess the firm's (1) ability to pay its bills as they come due, (2) ability to pay dividends, and (3) need for additional financing, including borrowing debt and selling capital stock.

The SCF in Relation to Other Financial Statements

The relationship of the SCF to other financial statements is shown in Exhibit 4.1. The statement of retained earnings, mentioned in Exhibit 4.1, reflects results of operations and dividends declared, and reconciles the retained earnings accounts of two successive balance sheets. Net income from the income statement is transferred to the retained earnings account when the temporary accounts (revenues and expenses) are closed at the end of the accounting period. In addition, net income is shown on the SCF when the SCF is prepared using the indirect approach (which is discussed later in this chapter). Finally, the SCF indirectly reconciles all accounts other than cash on the balance sheet by showing the sources and uses of cash.

Exhibit 4.1 Relationship of SCF to Other Financial Statements

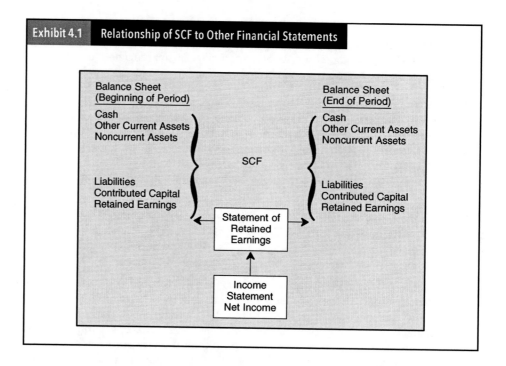

4.2 CLASSIFICATION OF CASH FLOWS

The SCF classifies **cash inflows** (cash received by a hospitality organization during an accounting period) and **cash outflows** (cash disbursed received by a hospitality organization during an accounting period) as operating, investing, and financing activities. Both cash inflows and outflows are included within each category. Exhibit 4.2 presents classifications of cash flows under the various activities, which are further described as follows:

- **Operating Activities:** This category includes cash transactions related to revenues and expenses. Revenues (cash inflows) include sales of food, beverages, and other goods and services to lodging guests, as well as interest and dividend income. Expenses (cash outflows) are for operational cash expenditures, including payments for salaries, wages, taxes, supplies, and so forth. Interest expense is also included as an operations cash outflow.

- **Investing Activities:** These activities relate primarily to cash flows from the acquisition and disposal of all noncurrent assets, especially property, equipment, and investments. Also included are cash flows from the purchase and disposal of marketable securities (short-term investments).

- **Financing Activities:** These activities relate to cash flows from the issuance and retirement of debt and the issuance and repurchase of capital stock. Cash inflows include cash received from issues of stock and both short-term and long-term borrowing. Cash outflows include repayments of loans (although the interest expense portion of the debt payment is an operating activity) and payments to owners for both dividends and any repurchase of stocks. Payments of accounts payable, taxes payable, and the various accrued expenses, such as wages payable, are not payments of loans under financing activities, but they are classified as cash outflows under operating activities.

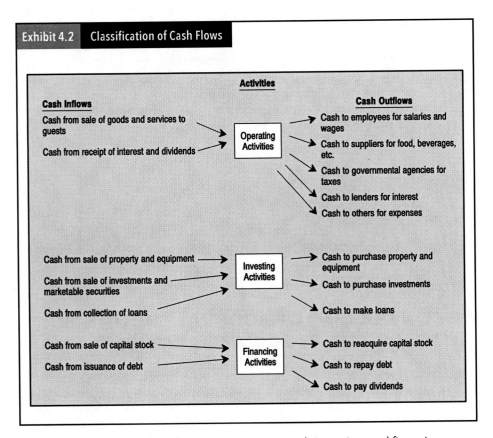

Exhibit 4.2   Classification of Cash Flows

Activities

Cash Inflows

Cash from sale of goods and services to guests

Cash from receipt of interest and dividends

→ Operating Activities →

Cash Outflows

Cash to employees for salaries and wages

Cash to suppliers for food, beverages, etc.

Cash to governmental agencies for taxes

Cash to lenders for interest

Cash to others for expenses

Cash from sale of property and equipment

Cash from sale of investments and marketable securities

Cash from collection of loans

→ Investing Activities →

Cash to purchase property and equipment

Cash to purchase investments

Cash to make loans

Cash from sale of capital stock

Cash from issuance of debt

→ Financing Activities →

Cash to reacquire capital stock

Cash to repay debt

Cash to pay dividends

Finally, hospitality enterprises engage in noncash investing and financing activities, such as the exchange of capital stock for a hotel building. Since this represents only an exchange, no cash transaction has occurred. Therefore, these noncash activities are not shown on the SCF. However, since a major purpose of the SCF is to include financing and investing activities, and since these activities will affect future cash flows, they must be disclosed on a separate schedule to the SCF. Thus, the user of financial information is provided with a complete presentation of investing and financing activities. Exhibit 4.3 is an example of a supplementary schedule of noncash investing and financing activities of the Gateway Inn.

The basic format of the SCF is shown in Exhibit 4.4. Generally, cash flows from operating activities are shown first. The indirect or direct approaches (to be discussed later) may be used to show cash flows from operating activities. Cash flows from investing and financing activities follow. Individual cash outflows and inflows are shown in each section. For example, long-term debt may increase by $100,000 due to the payment of $50,000 and subsequent borrowing of $150,000. Each cash flow should be shown rather than netting the two flows. Finally, as stated above, a supplementary schedule of noncash investing and financing activities to the SCF must be included.

Exhibit 4.3   Schedule of Noncash Investing and Financing Activities–Gateway Inn

Common stock exchanged for long-term debt	$100,000
Capital lease obligations incurred for use of equipment	50,000
Total	$150,000

Exhibit 4.4 Basic Format of the SCF

Cash Flows from Operating Activities (direct or indirect approaches may be used)	$XX
Cash Flows from Investing Activities (list cash inflows and outflows)	XX
Cash Flows from Financing Activities (list cash inflows and outflows)	XX
Net Increase (Decrease) in Cash	XX
Cash at the beginning of the period	XX
Cash at the end of the period	$XX
Schedule of Noncash Investing and Financing Transactions List individual transactions	$XX

4.3 CONVERSION OF ACCRUAL INCOME TO NET CASH FLOWS FROM OPERATIONS

A major purpose of the SCF is to show net cash flows from operations. The income statement is prepared on an **accrual basis**; that is, revenues are recorded when earned, not when cash is received from guests, and expenses are recorded when incurred, not necessarily when cash is disbursed. Consequently, there may be little correlation between net income and cash flow. Consider the hypothetical Wales Inn, which had $2 million in sales for 20X1. Its accounts receivable (AR) from guests totaled $100,000 at the beginning of the year and $110,000 at the end of the year. The cash received from sales during 20X1 is determined as follows:

$$\text{Cash receipts from sales} = \text{Sales} - \text{Increase in AR}$$
$$\textit{or} + \text{Decrease in AR}$$
$$= \$2,000,000 - \$10,000$$
$$= \underline{\$1,990,000}$$

Thus, even though the Wales Inn had sales of $2 million as reported on its income statement, it would show cash receipts from sales on its SCF as $1,990,000 following the direct method, discussed next.

Direct and Indirect Methods

There are two methods for converting net income to net cash flow from operations—the direct and the indirect methods. The **direct method** shows cash receipts from sales and cash disbursements for expenses. This method requires that each item on the income statement be converted from an accrual basis to a cash basis, as were the sales of the Wales Inn, above. Another example of this conversion process for the Wales Inn is payroll expense. Assume that the Wales Inn reported $700,000 as payroll expense for 20X1, and its balance sheet's accrued payroll account at the beginning of the year showed $15,000 and at the end of the year showed $20,000. Its cash disbursement for payroll for 20X1 is determined as follows:

$$\text{Cash disbursement for payroll expense} = \frac{\text{Payroll expense} - \text{Increase in Accrued payroll}}{\text{or} + \text{Decrease in accrued payroll}}$$

$$= \$700,000 - \$5,000$$

$$= \underline{\$695,000}$$

So, even though payroll expense for the year totaled $700,000 as shown on the income statement, only $695,000 was disbursed during the year.

Some expenses shown on the income statement do not involve any direct cash disbursement and are simply ignored when using the direct method. For example, depreciation expense is only an adjustment to help match expenses to revenues. Depreciation does not entail any cash, so it is ignored when using the direct method. The same approach is taken for amortization expense and gains and losses on the sale of property and equipment. The basic formats of cash flows from the operating activities section of the SCF for both the direct and indirect methods are shown in Exhibit 4.5.

The FASB prefers the direct approach. However, most hospitality businesses use the indirect method because the information needed to prepare it is more

---

Exhibit 4.5   Basic Formats of the Net Cash Flow from Operating Activities Sections

Operating Activities

Direct Method

Cash Flows from Operating Activities:		
Cash receipts from sales		$ XXX
Interest and dividends received		XXX
Total		XXX
Cash Disbursements for:		
Payroll	$ XXX	
Purchases of inventory	XXX	
Other expenses	XXX	
Interest expense	XXX	
Income taxes	XXX	XXX
Net Cash Flows from Operating Activities		$ XXX

Indirect Method

Cash Flows from Operating Activities:		
Net Income		$ XXX
Adjustments to reconcile net income to net cash flows from operating activities:		
Depreciation expense	$ XXX	
Gain on sale of property	(XXX)	
Loss on sale of investments	XXX	
Increase in accounts receivable	(XXX)	
Decrease in inventories	XXX	
.		
.		
.		
Increase in accrued payroll	XXX	XXX
Net Cash Flows from Operating Activities		$ XXX

readily available than that needed for using the direct method. For that reason, the major focus in this chapter will be the indirect method.

The **indirect method** for determining net cash flows from operations starts with net income. Net income is then adjusted for noncash items included on the income statement. The most common noncash expense deducted to determine net income is depreciation. Therefore, since depreciation is subtracted to compute net income on the income statement, it is added back to net income to compute net cash flows from operating activities. Other items on the income statement that must be added or subtracted include amortization expense and gains and losses on the sale of noncurrent assets and marketable securities (a current asset also known as short-term investments).

To illustrate the addback of a loss on the sale of investments, assume that the Wales Inn sold a parcel of undeveloped land (an investment) in 20X1 for $200,000 that originally cost $250,000. The journal entry to record the sale was as follows:

Cash	200,000	
Loss on sale of investments	50,000	
Investment in land		250,000

The $200,000 of cash inflow will be shown as an investing activity on the SCF; however, the loss on sale of investments of $50,000 was included on the income statement in determining net income. Since it was subtracted in determining the Wales Inn's net income and it did not use cash, it must be added back to net income to determine the net cash flows from operating activities for the SCF.

In addition, in order to determine the net cash flows from operating activities using the indirect method, the Wales Inn's net income must be adjusted for sales that were recorded but which guests did not pay for during 20X1. This adjustment is accomplished by subtracting the increase in accounts receivable of $10,000 from net income on the SCF (as discussed previously). There are several similar adjustments that must be made using the indirect method. These will be discussed in detail and illustrated in the next section of this chapter.

Regardless of the method used, the result will show the same amount of net cash provided by operating activities. The FASB requires that firms using the indirect method report the amount of interest expense and taxes paid in separate disclosures.

4.4 PREPARING THE SCF

The principal sources of information needed for preparing the SCF are the income statement, the statement of retained earnings, and two successive balance sheets from the beginning and end of the accounting period. In addition, details of transactions affecting any change in noncurrent balance sheet accounts must be reviewed. For example, if a comparison of two successive balance sheets shows the building account has increased by $5 million, the account must be analyzed to determine the reason(s) for the changes. Simply reflecting the net change of $5 million on the SCF is generally not acceptable.

A four-step approach for preparing the SCF is as follows:

1. Determine the net cash flows from operating activities.

2. Determine the net cash flows from investing activities.

3. Determine the net cash flows from financing activities.

4. Present the cash flows by activity on the SCF.

Exhibits 4.6 and 4.7 contain balance sheets and a condensed income statement and statement of retained earnings for the Simple Hotel. These will be used to illustrate this four-step approach. (A more comprehensive illustration will be shown later in the chapter.) The preparation of the SCF is illustrated using the indirect method for showing net cash flows from operating activities.

Step 1: Net Cash Flows from Operating Activities

To determine the net cash flow from operating activities using the indirect method, we focus first on the income statement by starting with net income of $500,000. Next, we need to adjust net income for items on the income statement that did not provide or use cash. In particular, depreciation expense and the gain on the sale of the investment are considered. Since depreciation was subtracted on the income statement to determine net income, it must be added to net income on the SCF to determine net cash flow from operating activities. Since the gain on the sale of investments is not a cash flow (the proceeds from the

Exhibit 4.6	Balance Sheets for the Simple Hotel

Simple Hotel
Balance Sheets
December 31, 20X1 and 20X2

Assets		20X1	20X2
Current Assets:			
Cash		$ 5,000	$ 10,000
Accounts Receivable		30,000	26,000
Inventory		10,000	12,000
	Total	45,000	48,000
Investments		50,000	300,000
Property and Equipment:			
Land		200,000	200,000
Building		10,000,000	10,000,000
Equipment		1,000,000	1,100,000
Less: Accum. Depreciation		(5,000,000)	(5,500,000)
	Total	6,200,000	5,800,000
Total Assets		$ 6,295,000	$ 6,148,000
Liabilities and Owners' Equity			
Current Liabilities:			
Accounts Payable		$ 6,000	$ 6,500
Accrued Payroll		4,000	4,500
Income Taxes Payable		7,000	6,000
Dividends Payable		10,000	15,000
	Total	27,000	32,000
Long-Term Debt		4,500,000	3,750,000
Owners' Equity:			
Capital Stock		1,000,000	1,250,000
Retained Earnings		768,000	1,116,000
	Total	1,768,000	2,366,000
Total Liabilities and Owners' Equity		$ 6,295,000	$ 6,148,000

Simple Hotel
Condensed Income Statement and Statement of Retained Earnings
For the Year Ended December 31, 20X2

Sales	$7,000,000
Cost of Goods Sold	1,000,000
Payroll Expenses	2,450,000
Other Expenses	2,400,000
Depreciation Expense	500,000
Income Taxes	250,000
Gain on the Sale of Investments	100,000
Net Income	500,000
Retained Earnings—12/31/X1	768,000
Dividends Declared	152,000
Retained Earnings—12/31/X2	$1,116,000

Other Information:

1. No property and equipment were disposed of during 20X2.

2. Investment and equipment purchases during 20X2 were made with cash. No funds were borrowed.

3. Investments costing $50,000 were sold for $150,000, resulting in a $100,000 gain on the sale of investments during 20X2.

4. Long-term debt of $250,000 was converted to capital stock in a noncash transaction during 20X2. No other capital stock was issued, and there were no repurchases of capital stock.

5. Interest expense paid during the year totaled $400,000.

sale of investments of $150,000 are an investing activity on the SCF and will be discussed later), the gain of $100,000 must be subtracted from net income on the SCF. Thus, the net cash flows from operating activities are determined at this point as follows:

Net Cash Flows from Operating Activities:		
Net income		$ 500,000
Adjustments to Reconcile Net Income to		
Net Cash Flows from Operating Activities:		
Depreciation expense	$ 500,000	
Gain on sale of investments	(100,000)	400,000
Partial net cash flows from operating activities		$ 900,000

The second type of adjustment includes changes in current accounts from the balance sheet. The cash account is not considered, since we are essentially looking at all other balance sheet accounts to determine what caused the change in cash for purposes of the SCF. In addition, the current liability account dividends payable is not considered in determining cash flows from operating activities, as dividends payable relate to financing activities and will be considered later. The change in the remaining five current accounts is fully considered as follows:

| | Balances—Dec. 31 | | Change in |
Account	20X1	20X2	Account Balance
Current Assets:			
Accounts Receivable	$ 30,000	$26,000	$ 4,000 (dec.)
Inventory	10,000	12,000	2,000 (inc.)
Current Liabilities:			
Accounts Payable	6,000	6,500	500 (inc.)
Accrued Payroll	4,000	4,500	500 (inc.)
Income Taxes Payable	7,000	6,000	1,000 (dec.)

A brief explanation follows for each of the above current accounts, including how the change affects net cash flow from operating activities.

Accounts receivable relate directly to sales, which were $7 million for the Simple Hotel for 20X2. Sales on account result in cash inflows when the hotel guests pay their bills. However, under accrual accounting, the sale is recorded when services are provided. Most of the sales during 20X2 resulted in cash as the guests paid their accounts, but at year-end, the accounts receivable account balance was $26,000. Analysis of the account will reveal how much cash resulted from sales as follows:

Accounts Receivable			
12/31/20X1 Balance	$ 30,000	Cash received	$ 7,004,000
Sales to hotel guests	7,000,000		
12/31/20X2 Balance	$ 26,000		

Alternatively, the cash receipts from hotel guests could be determined as follows:

Cash receipts from hotel guests = AR beginning balance

+ Sales − AR ending balance

= $30,000 + $7,000,000 − $26,000

= $7,004,000

In preparing the SCF, we need to show a decrease in accounts receivable of $4,000, which is added to net income as an increase in cash to determine net cash flows from operating activities.

The change in the balances of the inventory account is an increase of $2,000. Inventory relates to the purchases and cost of goods sold (food and beverages) accounts. Remember, cost of goods sold is the cost of food and beverage inventory sold, not the cash disbursed for purchases. Therefore, we need to determine the purchases for the year as follows:

	Ending inventory	$ 12,000
+	Cost of goods sold	1,000,000
	Goods available for sale	1,012,000
−	Beginning inventory	10,000
	Purchases	$1,002,000

The $2,000 increase in inventory causes the accrual-basis cost of goods sold to be $2,000 less than purchases. By assuming that purchases is the cash amount paid for purchases, we must show a decrease in cash flows from operating activities of $2,000. However, not all purchases were made with cash. The $500 increase in accounts payable represents the difference between purchases on account and cash paid to suppliers during 20X2. An increase in accounts payable means the amount of cash paid was less than the amount of purchases. Thus, the $500 increase in accounts payable must be added back to the accrual-basis net income to determine net cash flows from operating activities. An analysis of the accounts payable account shows this as follows:

Accounts Payable

		1/1/20X2 Balance	$ 6,000
Payments to suppliers	$1,001,500	Purchases	1,002,000
		12/31/20X2 Balance	$ 6,500

The increase in the accrued payroll account of $500 represents the difference between the accrual-basis payroll costs of $2,450,000 and the cash payments to personnel of $2,449,500. This determination is apparent in the analysis of the accrued payroll account as follows:

Accrued Payroll

		12/31/20X1 Balance	$ 4,000
Payments for payroll	$ $2,449,500	Payroll expense	2,450,000
		12/31/20X2 Balance	$ 4,500

Since the payroll payments were $500 less than the payroll expense, the $500 increase in accrued payroll is added back to the accrual-basis net income to determine net cash flows from operations.

Finally, the decrease of $1,000 in income taxes payable represents the difference between the accrual-basis income taxes of $250,000, shown on the condensed income statement of the Simple Hotel, and the $251,000 paid, as determined by the analysis of the income taxes payable account as follows:

Income Taxes Payable

		12/31/20X1 Balance	$ 7,000
Income taxes paid	$ 251,000	Income tax expense	250,000
		12/31/20X2 Balance	$ 6,000

In reality, the $7,000 of income taxes due at the beginning of 20X1 were paid along with $244,000 of income taxes for 20X2. The remaining $6,000 of taxes for 20X2 will be paid in early 20X3. However, since income taxes paid during 20X2 exceed income tax expenses for 20X2 by $1,000, the $1,000 must be subtracted from the accrual-basis net income to determine the net cash flows from operations.

In addition to differences from year-to-year in the payment of income taxes, a hospitality enterprise may have deferred income taxes over several years. The details of the account for deferred income taxes are beyond the scope of this chapter.

The Simple Hotel's SCF's net cash flows from operating activities based on the above would reflect the following:

Net Cash Flows from Operating Activities:

Net income	$ 500,000
Adjustments to Reconcile Net	
Income to Net Cash Flows from Operating Activities:	
Depreciation expense	$ 500,000
Gain on sale of investments	(100,000)

Decrease in accounts receivable	4,000	
Increase in inventory	(2,000)	
Increase in accounts payable	500	
Increase in accrued payroll	500	
Decrease in income taxes payable	(1,000)	402,000
Net Cash Flows from Operating Activities		$902,000

In general, the rules for accounting for changes in current accounts in determining net cash flows provided by operating activities are as follows:

- A decrease in a current asset is added to net income.

- An increase in a current asset is deducted from net income.

- A decrease in a current liability is deducted from net income.

- An increase in a current liability is added to net income.

Step 2: Net Cash Flows from Investing Activities

Step 2 of the four-step approach to preparing an SCF focuses on investing activities. In general, attention must be directed to noncurrent assets of the Simple Hotel.

The investment account increased by $250,000. Further analysis of this account is as follows:

Investments			
12/31/20X1 Balance	$ 50,000	Sale of investments	$ 50,000
Purchase of investments	300,000		
12/31/20X2 Balance	$ 300,000		

The analysis reveals both a sale of $50,000 of investments and a purchase of investments of $300,000. Thus, cash of $300,000 was used to purchase investments, which is a use of cash in the investing activities section of the SCF. However, further analysis of the sale of investments shows the journal entry to record this transaction as follows:

Cash	150,000	
Investments		50,000
Gains on sale of investments		100,000

The entry clearly shows a cash inflow of $150,000. Thus, this source of cash should be shown as an investing activity. Notice that the cost of investments sold ($50,000) and the gain on the sale of investments ($100,000) has no impact on net cash flow from investing activities.

There were no changes in the land and building accounts, as no purchases or sales were made during 20X2. Therefore, cash was not affected.

We will look next at the equipment account. According to note #1 under other information, no equipment was disposed of during 20X2. Thus, the $100,000 difference must be due to purchases of equipment. The $100,000 of equipment is shown as a use of cash in determining net cash flows from investing activities.

The Simple Hotel's final noncurrent account is accumulated depreciation, which increased by $500,000, the exact amount of depreciation expense for the year. Because depreciation does not affect cash, under the indirect method the $500,000 is added back to the accrual-basis net income as discussed under Step 1.

The change in no way affects investing activities of the Simple Hotel.

Now that the noncurrent asset accounts of the Simple Hotel have been analyzed, the investing activities section of the SCF would reflect the following:

Net Cash Flows from Investing Activities:	
Proceeds from sale of investments	$ 150,000
Purchase of investments	(300,000)
Purchase of equipment	(100,000)
Net cash flows from investing activities:	$(250,000)

Step 3: Net Cash Flows from Financing Activities

To determine the net cash flows from financing activities, we must turn our attention to the noncurrent liabilities and owners' equity accounts. First, the change in the long-term debt account is a decrease of $750,000. The analysis of the long-term debt is as follows:

Long-Term Debt (LTD)

		12/31/20X1 Balance	$4,500,000
Conversion to Common Stock	$250,000		
Payment of LTD	500,000		
		12/31/20X2 Balance	$3,750,000

The above analysis is based on notes #2 and #4 under other information. Note #4 reveals that $250,000 of LTD was converted to capital stock. This is a noncash transaction and will be shown only in a supplementary schedule to the SCF. Note #2 indicates no funds were borrowed; therefore, the remaining $500,000 reduction in LTD had to be due to payment of LTD. The $500,000 payment is a cash outflow from financing activities.

The next account to be analyzed is capital stock. The increase for 20X2 is $250,000, which is due to the exchange of capital stock for LTD, as discussed above. According to note #4 under other information, there were no other capital stock transactions. Since this change in capital stock did not involve cash, it is not shown on the SCF. However, since it is a financing activity, it is shown on a supplementary schedule as mentioned above.

The final account to be analyzed is retained earnings. The statement of retained earnings at the bottom of the income statement reflects the detailed changes in this account as follows:

Retained Earnings

		12/31/20X1 Balance	$ 768,000
		Net income	500,000
Dividends declared	$152,000		
		12/31/20X2 Balance	$1,116,000

The net income has already been accounted for in the SCF as an operating activity. The declaration of $152,000 of dividends is not a cash activity by itself. For the SCF, the focus is on dividend payments, not dividend declaration. When dividends are declared, they are recorded as a reduction in retained earnings and as an increase in dividends payable, a current liability account. Therefore, to determine the amount of dividends paid during 20X2, we analyze the dividends payable account as follows:

Dividends Payable

		12/31/20X1 Balance	$ 10,000
		Dividends declared	152,000
Dividends paid	$147,000		
		12/31/20X2 Balance	$ 15,000

Effectively, the $5,000 increase in the dividends payable account results in dividends declared during 20X2 exceeding dividends paid by $5,000. The $147,000 of dividends paid is shown in the SCF as a financing activity.

Another way to view dividends paid is that the $10,000 beginning balance of dividends payable was paid during 20X2 since it is a current liability. Further, that of the $152,000 of dividends declared in 20X2, $137,000 was paid, that is, all of the dividends declared except for the ending balance of $15,000. Thus, $10,000 from the beginning balance of $137,000 of dividends declared in 20X2 were paid in 20X2, totaling $147,000.

The Simple Hotel's SCF financing activity section would show the following:

Net Cash Flows from Financing Activities:	
Payment of long-term debt	$(500,000)
Payment of cash dividends	(147,000)
Net cash flows from financing activities	$(647,000)

Step 4: Presenting Cash Flows by Activity

We now are ready to prepare the SCF based on the analysis in Steps 1–3. The SCF for the Simple Hotel is shown in Exhibit 4.8. The three activities show cash flows as follows:

Operating activities provided cash	$ 902,000
Investing activities used cash	(250,000)
Financing activities used cash	(647,000)
Total	$ 5,000

The result is a bottom line of $5,000 cash inflow. The Simple Hotel's operating activities provided large enough cash inflows to cover the outflows for investing and financing.

In the preparation of the SCF, the net increase in cash of the Simple Hotel per the SCF is added to the Simple Hotel's cash at the beginning of 20X2 to equal the cash at the end of 20X2. The $5,000 net increase in cash per the SCF equals the $5,000 increase in cash per the Simple Hotel's successive balance sheets (Exhibit 4.6). This does not *prove* that the SCF is prepared correctly; however, if the $5,000 increase per the SCF had *not* been equal to the change per the successive balance sheets, we would know that we had improperly prepared the SCF. We would then need to locate our mistake and make the correction. Thus, this is at least a partial check on the SCF's accuracy.

Further, notice the supplementary schedule to the SCF, which shows the noncash exchange of capital stock of $250,000 for long-term debt and the supplementary disclosure of the amounts of interest and income taxes paid during 20X2.

Exhibit 4.8   SCF for the Simple Hotel

Simple Hotel
Statement of Cash Flows
For the Year Ended December 31, 20X2

Net Cash Flow From Operating Activities:

Net income		$ 500,000
Adjustments to reconcile net income to		
net cash flows from operating activities:		
Depreciation	$ 500,000	
Gain on sale of investments	(100,000)	
Decrease in accounts receivable	4,000	
Increase in inventory	(2,000)	
Increase in accounts payable	500	
Increase in accrued payroll	500	
Decrease in income taxes payable	(1,000)	402,000
Net cash flow from operating activities		902,000
Net Cash Flow From Investing Activities:		
Sale of investments	$ 150,000	
Purchase of investments	(300,000)	
Purchase of equipment	(100,000)	
Net cash flow from investing activities		(250,000)
Net Cash Flow From Financing Activities:		
Payment of long-term debt	$ (500,000)	
Dividends paid	(147,000)	
Net cash flow from financing activities		(647,000)
Net Increase in Cash During 20X2		5,000
Cash at the beginning of 20X2		5,000
Cash at the end of 20X2		$ 10,000

Supplementary Schedule of Noncash Financing and Investing Activities

Exchange of capital stock for long-term debt	$ 250,000

Supplementary Disclosure of Cash Flow Information:

Cash paid during the year for:	
Interest	$ 400,000
Income Taxes	$ 251,000

4.5 A COMPREHENSIVE ILLUSTRATION

To provide a comprehensive illustration of the preparation of an SCF with accompanying explanations, the Evangel Inn's financial statements, as shown in Exhibits 4.9 and 4.10, will be used. The Evangel Inn's SCF for 20X7 is shown in Exhibit 4.11.

Exhibit 4.9   Evangel Inn Balance Sheets

Evangel Inn
Balance Sheets
December 31, 20X6 and 20X7

Assets	20X6	20X7
Current Assets:		
Cash	$ 20,000	$ 60,000
Marketable Securities	20,000	25,000
Accounts Receivable	90,000	115,000
Inventory	15,000	20,000
Prepaid Expenses	15,000	5,000
Total Current Assets	160,000	225,000
Investments	150,000	450,000
Property and Equipment:		
Land	450,000	450,000
Buildings	2,000,000	2,000,000
Equipment	500,000	610,000
Less: Accum. Depr.	(1,000,000)	(1,300,000)
Net Property and Equipment	1,950,000	1,760,000
Other Assets—Franchise Fees	100,000	90,000
Total Assets	$2,360,000	$2,525,000
Liabilities and Owners' Equity		
Current Liabilities:		
Accounts Payable	$ 25,000	$ 35,000
Current Maturities of Long-Term Debt	50,000	50,000
Wages Payable	15,000	15,000
Dividends Payable	20,000	15,000
Total Current Liabilities	110,000	115,000
Long-Term Debt	1,000,000	1,050,000
Owners' Equity:		
Common Stock	1,160,000	1,285,000
Retained Earnings	100,000	225,000
Less: Treasury Stock	(10,000)	(150,000)
Total Owners' Equity	1,250,000	1,360,000
Total Liabilities and Owners' Equity	$2,360,000	$2,525,000

The net cash flows provided by operating activities for the Evangel Inn for 20X7 are $700,000. The explanation and/or source is as follows:

Item	Explanation and/or Source
1. Net income $330,000	From 20X7 income statement.
2. Depreciation expense $340,000	Depreciation is a noncash flow shown on the income statement. It must be added back to net income, as it was subtracted from revenues to determine net income. To confirm this amount, the accumulated depreciation account is analyzed as follows:

Accumulated Depreciation

	12/31/20X6 Balance	$1,000,000
Accumulated depreciation written off with sale of equipment $40,000		
	12/31/20X7 Balance	$1,300,000

3. Amortization expense $10,000	The amortization expense relates to write-off of franchise fees recorded originally as another asset. Like depreciation, it is a noncash expense subtracted to determine net income; therefore, it must be added back to net income to determine net cash flows provided by operating activities.
4. Gain on sale of equipment $20,000	The sale of equipment resulted in a gain of $20,000, as shown on the income statement. The $80,000 received per note #1 is shown as an investing activity. The gain shown on the income statement is not a cash figure, so the $20,000 must be subtracted from net income in the SCF.
5. Loss on sale of investments $50,000	The loss on the sale of investments is shown as an investing activity. The loss shown is not a cash figure, so the $50,000 must be added to net income in the SCF.
6. Changes in current assets and liabilities: Increase in accounts receivable $25,000; increase in inventory $5,000; decrease in prepaid expenses $10,000; increase in accounts payable $10,000.	The changes in the current accounts are added or subtracted from net income as follows: 1) *increases* in current assets and decreases in current liabilities are *subtracted*; 2) *decreases* in current assets and *increases* in current liabilities are *added*. The marketable securities current asset account, current maturities of long-term debt, and dividends payable are considered in preparing the investing and financing activity sections of the SCF, as these accounts do not relate to operating activities.

Exhibit 4.10 Evangel Inn Income Statement

Evangel Inn
Condensed Income Statement
For the Year Ended 20X7

Revenues:	
Sales	$2,700,000
Interest Income	80,000
Total Revenues	2,780,000
Expenses:	
Salaries and Wages	750,000
Depreciation	340,000
Amortization (franchise fees)	10,000
Interest Expense	100,000
Other Expenses	1,140,000
Income Before Gain and Losses and Income Taxes	440,000
Gain on Sale of Equipment	20,000
Loss on Sale of Investments	(50,000)
Income Taxes	80,000
Net Income	$ 330,000

Other Information:

1. Equipment costing $100,000 was sold for $80,000 during 20X7.

2. Investments costing $100,000 were sold during 20X7 for a loss of $50,000.

3. Dividends of $205,000 were declared during 20X7.

4. Treasury stock of $140,000 was purchased during 20X7.

5. Long-term debt of $100,000 was converted to common stock during 20X7.

6. Common stock of $35,000 was sold during 20X7.

7. Long-term debt of $200,000 was borrowed during 20X7.

8. Marketable securities of $5,000 were purchased during 20X7.

Exhibit 4.11 Evangel Inn SCF

Evangel Inn
Statement of Cash Flows
For the Year of 20X7

Cash Flow Provided by Operating Activities:		
Net Income		$ 330,000
Adjustments to Reconcile Net Income to		
Net Cash Flows Provided by Operating		
Activities:		
Depreciation expense	$ 340,000	
Amortization expense	10,000	
Gain on sale of equipment	(20,000)	
Loss on sale of investments	50,000	
Increase in accounts receivable	(25,000)	
Increase in inventory	(5,000)	
Decrease in prepaid expenses	10,000	
Increase in accounts payable	10,000	370,000
Net Cash Flows from Operating Activities		700,000
Cash Flow Provided by Investing Activities:		
Proceeds from sale of equipment	$ 80,000	
Proceeds from sale of investment	50,000	
Purchase of marketable securities	(5,000)	
Purchase of equipment	(210,000)	
Purchase of investments	(400,000)	
Net Cash Flows from Investing Activities		(485,000)
Cash Flow Provided by Financing Activities:		
Payment of long-term debt	$ (50,000)	
Borrowing—long-term debt	200,000	
Purchase of treasury stock	(140,000)	
Proceeds from sale of common stock	25,000	
Payment of dividends	(210,000)	
Net Cash Flows from Financing Activities		(175,000)
Increase in Cash		40,000
Cash at the beginning of 20X7		20,000
Cash at the end of 20X7		$ 60,000

**Supplementary Schedule of Noncash Investing
and Financing Activities**

Exchange of Common Stock for Long-Term Debt		$ 100,000

Supplementary Disclosure of Cash Flow Information:

Cash paid during the year for:	
Interest	$ 100,000
Income Taxes	$ 80,000

The investing activities section of the SCF relates to investment and property and equipment for the Evangel Inn. The activity to be shown in the SCF relates to investment and equipment transactions as follows:

Item	Discussion
1. Proceeds from sale of equipment	According to note #1, equipment was sold for $80,000.
2. Purchase of equipment	The equipment account, as shown on the successive balance sheets for 20X6 and 20X7, shows a $110,000 increase in 20X7. However, since equipment costing $100,000 was sold during 20X7, then $210,000 was purchased in 20X7. Analysis of the equipment account below supports this conclusion.

Equipment

Balance 12/31/20X6	$ 500,000	Cost of equipment sold	$100,000
Purchases during 20X7	210,000		
Balance 12/31/20X7	$610,000		

3. Proceeds from sale of investments $50,000	According to note #2, $100,000 of investments were sold at a loss of $50,000. Therefore, the proceeds are determined by subtracting the loss from the cost as follows:

Cost of investments sold	$100,000
Loss on sale of investments	(50,000)
Proceeds from sale	$ 50,000

4. Purchase of investments $400,000	Investments, according to the 20X6 and 20X7 balance sheets, increased by $300,000; however, during 20X7, $100,000 of investments were sold. Thus, purchases were $400,000, based on the analysis of the investment account as follows:

Investments

Balance 12/31/20X6	$150,000	Sale of investments	$100,000
Purchase of investments	400,000		
Balance 12/31/20X7	$450,000		

5. Purchase of marketable securities	According to note #8, marketable securities of $5,000 were purchased in 20X7.

The financing activities of the Evangel Inn during 20X7 resulted in a net cash outflow of $175,000, as well as the noncash exchange of $100,000 of Evangel's common stock for long-term debt as shown on the Supplementary Schedule of Noncash Investing and Financing Activities at the bottom of Exhibit 4.11. The individual sources and uses of cash flows in the financing activities section of the Evangel Inn's SCF are explained as follows:

Item	Discussion
1. Payment of long-term debt $50,000	The payment of debt is determined by analyzing both the LTD and current maturities of LTD accounts as follows:

Current Maturities of LTD

		12/31/20X6 Balance	$ 50,000
Payment of LTD	$50,000	Reclassification of LTD	50,000
		12/31/20X7 Balance	$ 50,000

Long-Term Debt

		12/31/20X6 Balance	$1,000,000
Reclassification of LTD	$ 50,000		
Converted to common stock	100,000	Borrowing during 20X7	200,000
		12/31/20X7 Balance	$1,050,000

The current maturities of LTD account showed $50,000 payable on Dec. 31, 20X6. By definition, current liabilities must be paid within one year; therefore, we can safely assume that the $50,000 balance at Dec. 31, 20X6, was paid in 20X7. The balance at the end of 20X7 is a $50,000 reclassification of LTD that occurred during 20X7. In other words, the $50,000 of LTD due in 20X8 is shown as current maturities of LTD on Dec. 31, 20X7.

Item	Discussion
2. Borrowed long-term debt $200,000	Note #7 reports $200,000 was borrowed during 20X7. The analysis of the long-term debt above confirms the $200,000 of new debt.
3. Purchase of treasury stock $140,000	The analysis of the treasury stock account confirms the purchase, according to note #4, of $140,000 as follows:

Treasury Stock

	12/31/20X6 Balance	$ 10,000
	Purchase	140,000
	12/31/20X7 Balance	$150,000

Item	Discussion
4. Proceeds from sale of common stock $25,000	Note #6 reveals $25,000 of common stock was sold during 20X7. This is confirmed by analyzing the common stock account as follows:

Common Stock

12/31/20X6 Balance	$1,160,000
Issued to retire LTD	100,000
Issued for cash	25,000
12/31/20X7 Balance	$1,285,000

The $100,000 of common stock issued for debt is a noncash transaction and is reported on the Schedule of Noncash Investing and Financing Activities shown at the bottom of Exhibit 4.11.

Item	Discussion
5. Payment of dividends $210,000	During 20X7, $205,000 of dividends were declared; however, for the SCF purposes, the $210,000 amount paid must be determined and shown. Analysis of the dividends payable account reveals that $210,000 was paid as follows:

Dividends Payable

	12/31/20X6 Balance	$20,000
	Dividends declared	205,000
Dividends paid $210,000		
	12/31/20X7 Balance	$15,000

In essence, the dividends declared in 20X6 and payable at the end of 20X6 of $20,000 were paid in 20X7. In addition, $190,000 of the $205,000 of dividends declared in 20X7 were paid in 20X7, leaving $15,000 dividends to be paid in 20X8 and shown as a current liability on Evangel Inn's balance sheet at the end of 20X7.

Thus, the net total of cash flows for operating, investing, and financing activities for the Evangel Inn for 20X7 is $40,000, which equals the increase in cash of $40,000 as reflected on the Evangel Inn's 20X6 and 20X7 balance sheets.

Interpreting the Results

The Evangel Inn's SCF lends insight to the user as follows:

- While net income increased by $330,000, cash flows from operations increased by $700,000. The major difference as shown on the SCF is depreciation expense of $340,000.

- Cash flows from operations were sufficient to allow the Evangel Inn to (1) use $485,000 in net investing activities, (2) use $175,000 in net financing activities, and (3) provide an increase in cash of $40,000 during 20X7.

- In addition, noncash activities occurred in the noncash exchange of $100,000 of common stock for $100,000 of long-term debt.

4.6 ANALYSIS OF STATEMENTS OF CASH FLOWS

Unlike the balance sheet and income statement, the SCF is generally not analyzed by itself. Rather, figures from the SCF are compared with specific balance sheet and income statement numbers. For example, the operating cash flow to total liabilities ratio is determined by dividing operating cash flows from the SCF by average total liabilities from the balance sheet.

A few reasons appear to exist for the comparative lack of analysis of the SCF. First, management tends to focus on operations (which are reflected on the income statement) and on resources used in operations (which are shown on the balance sheet). Though cash is critical to business, corporate officials often handle the cash activities. Second, the FASB has required that this statement be issued only since 1987. As we continue to issue this statement, more analysis will no doubt be conducted on the cash flow numbers.

Though a common-size SCF could possibly be prepared, it may be useless. What figure would be the base figure of 100 percent? Net sales and total assets from the income statement and balance sheet, respectively, serve that purpose. However, since the SCF is divided into three distinct, independent sections, no similar base figure appears reasonable. A comparative SCF could also be prepared. However, the results reflecting details of some sections would be relatively useless. For example, how would the change in accounts receivable be shown? Assume that in 20X1 accounts receivable increased by $10,000 and that during 20X2 accounts receivable decreased by $15,000. On the SCF, the increase is shown as a negative figure, while the decrease is shown as a positive figure. The change over the two periods is $25,000, yet the change in the accounts receivable balance over the two periods is a decrease of $5,000.

Useful analysis over time on a comparative basis would examine the changes in the net cash flows from each activity. An example is as follows:

	20X1	20X2	Difference $	Difference %
Net cash flows from:				
Operations	$ 300,000	$ 350,000	$ 50,000	16.67%
Investing	(400,000)	(300,000)	100,000	25.00%
Financing	150,000	100,000	(50,000)	33.33%
Change in cash	$ 50,000	$ 150,000	$100,000	200.00%

This analysis clearly reflects the changes in cash from the major activities. The user does not get lost in meaningless detail.

The SCF is an FASB–mandated financial statement that must be issued with other financial statements released to external users. It reflects the inflow and outflow of cash for a period of time.

The SCF must show operating, investing, and financing activities. Operating activities reflect cash flows as they relate to revenues and expenses. Investing activities relate to changes in marketable securities and noncurrent asset accounts. Commonly included in these activities are the purchase and sale of property and equipment. Financing activities relate to changes in dividends payable, current maturities of long-term debt, long-term debt, and equity accounts. The sale of common stock and payment of long-term debt are two examples of financing activities. The net sum of the three activities shown on the SCF must equal the change in the cash amount shown on the two successive balance sheets.

There are two basic approaches to preparing the SCF—the direct and indirect methods. The difference between the two approaches is reflected only in the operating activities section of the SCF. The indirect approach starts with net income and includes various adjustments made to determine net income which did not affect cash. Other adjustments for the indirect approach are the changes in current accounts related to operations. The direct approach shows the direct sources of cash, such as cash receipts from sales, and direct uses of cash, such as disbursements for payroll. Most hospitality firms use the indirect approach because it is easier to prepare.

accrual basis—System of reporting revenues and expenses in the period in which they are considered to have been earned or incurred, regardless of the actual time of collection or payment.

cash equivalents—Short-term, highly liquid investments, such as U.S. Treasury bills and money market accounts.

cash inflows—Cash received by a hospitality organization during an accounting period.

cash outflows—Cash disbursed by a hospitality organization during an accounting period.

direct method—One of two methods for converting net income to net cash flow from operations. This method shows cash receipts from sales and cash disbursements for expenses and requires that each item on the income statement be converted from an accrual basis to a cash basis.

indirect method—One of two methods for converting net income to net cash flow from operations. This method starts with net income and then adjusts for noncash items included on the income statement.

statement of cash flows (SCF)—Explains the change in cash for the accounting period by showing the effects on cash of a business's operating, investing, and financing activities for the accounting period.

1. What is the major purpose of the SCF?

2. How do different users of the SCF use this statement?

3. What are the three major classifications of cash flows in the SCF?

4. What are the two alternative approaches to preparing the SCF?

5. How do the two methods of preparing the SCF differ?

6. What supplementary information must be provided when the indirect approach is used in preparing the SCF?

7. How are changes in the various current balance sheet accounts shown on an SCF prepared using the indirect approach?

8. Where is the $10,000 loss on the sale of an investment shown on the SCF prepared using the indirect approach?

9. How does the sum of the cash flows from the three major classifications on the SCF relate to the change in balance sheet accounts from two successive balance sheets?

10. How is the exchange of common stock for long-term debt shown on the SCF?

Problem 1

The MSU Corporation has engaged in several transactions, listed below:

1. Sold food and beverages for cash
2. Sold food and beverages on credit
3. Exchanged its common stock for long-term bonds
4. Sold common stock
5. Issued a stock dividend
6. Paid salaries and wages owed to employees
7. Sold investments for a gain
8. Paid a cash dividend
9. Purchased a 60-day treasury bill
10. Sold land at a loss
11. Obtained a long-term mortgage
12. Received dividends from an investment
13. Paid for food and beverage supplies
14. Paid long-term debt
15. Purchased equipment

Required:

Identify each transaction as (1) an operating activity, (2) an investing activity, (3) a financing activity, (4) a noncash transaction, or (5) none of the above.

Problem 2

The Shaw Restaurant's balance sheets for 20X4 and 20X5 reveal the following amounts for its current accounts:

	20X4	20X5
Current Assets:		
Cash	$ 540	$ 750
Accounts Receivable	14,000	14,642
Food Inventory	6,211	6,001
Prepaid Insurance	3,422	4,158
Total	$24,173	$25,551
Current Liabilities:		
Accounts Payable	$ 4,158	$ 5,674
Accrued Expenses	2,414	2,176
Advanced Deposits	1,600	1,951
Total	$ 8,172	$ 9,801

Assume Shaw Restaurant's depreciation expense and net income for 20X4 and 20X5 were $5,200 and $31,452, respectively.

Required:

Prepare the cash from operating activities section of the SCF.

Problem 3

Unclassified Balance Sheets
Bread & Butter Café
Dec. 31, 20X1 and 20X2

	20X1	20X2
Cash	$ 15,000	$ 30,000
Marketable Securities	24,000	30,000
Accounts Receivable	25,000	26,000
Inventory	22,000	18,000
Prepaid Expenses	8,000	25,000
Equipment	420,000	555,000
Accumulated Depreciation	(180,000)	(200,000)
Total Assets	$ 334,000	$ 484,000
Current Liabilities:		
Accounts Payable	$ 16,000	$12,000
Accrued Expenses	10,000	16,000
Dividends Payable	23,000	25,000
Mortgage Payable (current)	20,000	26,000
Mortgage Payable (long-term)	150,000	195,000
Common Stock	120,000	140,000
Treasury Stock	(20,000)	(30,000)
Retained Earnings	15,000	100,000
Total Liabilities and Owners' Equity	$ 334,000	$ 484,000

Other information:

1. Assume the net income for 20X2 was $70,000.

2. Assume marketable securities costing $5,000 were sold for $8,000 during 20X2.

3. Assume equipment costing $30,000, with a net book value of $10,000, was sold at a loss of $5,000 during 20X2.

Required:

Prepare the cash flow from investing activities section of the SCF for 20X2.

Problem 4

The Washington Inn has incurred various activities, described in each situation below:

1. During 20X2, the Washington Inn's total payroll expense was $725,000. The payroll payable account at the beginning and end of 20X2 equaled $6,000 and $8,000, respectively. What were the total cash disbursements for payroll during 20X2?

2. The insurance expense for 20X2 was $12,000. Prepaid insurance was $3,000 at the beginning of 20X2 and $4,000 at the end of 20X2. The prepaid insurance account is debited when insurance premiums are paid and insurance expense is recorded as time passes. What was the amount of total insurance premiums paid during 20X2?

3. The utility expense was $35,000 during 20X2. The accrued utility expense was $4,000 and $5,000 at the beginning and end of the year, respectively. What was the total amount paid to the utility company during 20X2?

4. During 20X2, all equipment purchased was obtained by using excess cash of the Washington Inn. The equipment account had a beginning balance of $200,000 and an ending balance of $250,000. During 20X2, equipment that cost $20,000 was sold for $5,000. A loss of $2,000 was recorded on this sale. How much was expended during the year for equipment?

5. The balance of marketable securities was $20,000 and $25,000 at the beginning and end of 20X2, respectively. Marketable securities were sold during 20X2 for $8,000 and a gain on the sale of $3,000 was recorded. How much was expended during 20X2 for marketable securities?

Problem 5

The Eppley Hotel has incurred various activities, as described in each situation below:

1. During 20X3, the Eppley Hotel had cash sales of $900,000 and sales on account of $3.24 million. During the same year, accounts receivable—hotel guests increased by $10,000. Determine the cash received from hotel guests during 20X3.

2. During 20X3, the Eppley Hotel's board of directors declared cash dividends of $140,000. The dividends payable account was $5,000 at the beginning of the year and $15,000 at the end of the year. Determine the dividends paid by the Eppley Hotel during 20X3.

3. During 20X3, the Eppley Hotel had cost of food used of $500,000. During the year, food inventory increased by $7,000 and the related suppliers payable accounts decreased by $6,000. Determine the cash payments for food purchases during 20X3.

4. During the year, the Eppley Hotel's long-term debt of $2 million on January 1, 20X3, increased by $500,000 to $2.5 million on December 31, 20X3. Also during 20X3, $240,000 of long-term debt was converted to common stock, and $30,000 of long-term debt was reclassified as current debt. Determine the amount of cash that was borrowed and recorded as long-term debt during 20X3.

5. The Eppley Hotel's income tax expense for 20X3 was $35,000. Its income taxes payable account on the balance sheet was $4,000 at the beginning of the year and $5,000 at the end of the year. Determine the amount of income taxes paid during 20X3.

Problem 6

Hotel 222's current account balances at the beginning and end of the year were as follows:

Current Assets:	Beg.	End	Current Liabilities:	Beg.	End
Cash	$ 12,000	$ 15,000	Accounts payable	$42,000	$ 60,000
Accounts receivable	100,000	85,000	Wages payable	20,500	12,000
Food inventory	18,000	25,000	Interest payable	9,000	6,500
Prepaid expenses	5,000	11,000	Taxes payable	5,400	500
Total	$135,000	$136,000	Total	$76,900	$ 79,000

In addition, the hotel had total revenue of $3.75 million and expenses of $2,900,400, which include depreciation of $75,200 during the year.

Required:

Construct the cash from operating activities section of the SCF.

Problem 7

Frederick Bayard, owner of Bayshore Inn, is confused regarding the calculation of cash flows for the SCF and has requested your assistance. He provides you information and his requests as follows:

	March 31	
	20X3	20X4
1. Selected current asset accounts:		
Accounts receivable	$ 100,000	$ 132,000
Food inventory	45,000	38,000

What is the impact on cash flow of the change in each account and where would each be shown on the SCF?

	March 31	
2. Mortgage accounts:		
Mortgage payable (current)	$ 30,000	$ –0–
Mortgage payable (long-term)	800,000	1,000,000

How much cash was borrowed and how much was paid to retire debt during 20X4? Where will these amounts be shown on the SCF?

	March 31	
3. Selected current liability accounts:		
Accounts payable	$ 45,000	$ 50,000
Wages payable	20,000	18,000

What is the impact of the change of each account on cash flow and where will each be shown on the SCF?

	March 31	
4. Dividends and retained earnings:		
Retained earnings	$ 450,000	$630,000
Dividends payable	60,000	40,000

Assume net income for the year was $200,000 and that only net income and dividends declared affect retained earnings.

What amount of dividends were paid during 20X4 and where will the amount be shown on the SCF?

	March 31	
	20X3	20X4
5. Equipment:		
Equipment	$690,000	$750,000

During 20X4, only a van was sold, for $7,000. The van originally cost $25,000 and was depreciated by $22,000 when sold.

What was the gain on the sale of the van and where is it shown on the SCF? Where are the proceeds from the sale shown on the SCF? What was the amount of equipment purchased during 20X4 and where will it be shown on the SCF?

Problem 8

Farm Fresh Produce is undertaking a major expansion that has been financed with new equity and debt issues. During the past year, the corporation borrowed $10 million for a term of 15 years. It is only required to pay interest expense for the next two years on this loan. FLFC sold 100,000 shares of $1 par value stock at $85 per share.

Farm Fresh Produce paid off old debt with a $950,000 payment, which included interest expense for the year of $50,000. Finally, the corporation paid dividends of $1 on all its outstanding 2.5 million shares of common stock in December.

Required:

Prepare the corporation's cash from financing section of the SCF.

Problem 9

In 20X6, Hotel Calais earned net income of $408,000. Included on its income statement for 20X6 was depreciation expense of $120,000. Its current asset and liability accounts at the beginning and end of 20X6 had balances as follows:

	March 31	
	20X5	20X6
Cash	$ 35,000	$ 45,000
Accounts receivable	122,000	137,000
Food inventory	38,000	48,000
Prepaid insurance	3,000	8,000
Accounts payable	55,000	70,000
Accrued payroll	15,000	18,000
Taxes payable	12,000	14,000
Dividends payable	30,000	45,000
Current maturities of LTD	50,000	60,000

In addition, sales of equipment and investments during 20X6 were as follows:

1. A range costing $10,000 with a $1,000 net book value (NBV) at the time of sale was sold for $2,500.

2. Investments costing $60,000 were sold for $70,000.

3. A van with an NBV of $5,000 was sold for $4,000.

Required:

Prepare the cash flows from the operating activities section of the SCF.

Problem 10

You have been hired by D. Smith, a successful entrepreneur, to prepare a statement of cash flows for his two-year-old hotel, the Illini Inn. The following are copies of the condensed balance sheets and the income statement of the Illini Inn.

Illini Inn
Condensed Balance Sheets
Dec. 31, 20X1 and 20X2

	20X1	20X2
Cash	$ 30,000	$ 40,000
Accounts Receivable	190,000	225,000
Inventory	30,000	35,000
Property and Equipment (net)	1,400,000	1,500,000
Other Assets	200,000	100,000
Total Assets	$1,850,000	$1,900,000
Accounts Payable	$ 140,000	$ 185,000
Wages Payable	10,000	15,000
Current Maturities of LTD	50,000	50,000
Long-Term Debt	1,000,000	950,000
Total Liabilities	1,200,000	1,200,000
Owners' Equity	650,000	700,000
Total Liabilities and Owners' Equity	$1,850,000	$1,900,000

Illini Inn
Condensed Income Statement
For the year ended Dec. 31, 20X2

Sales	$1,600,000
Cost of Goods Sold	200,000
Contribution Margin	1,400,000
Undistributed Operating Expenses	950,000
Gross Operating Profit	450,000
Depreciation Expense	200,000
Amortization Expense	100,000
Income before Tax	150,000
Income Tax	50,000
Net Income	$ 100,000

Additional information:

1. Equipment was purchased for $300,000.

2. Dividends of $50,000 were declared and paid during 20X2.

3. Long-term debt of $50,000 was reclassified as current at the end of 20X2.

Required:

Prepare the SCF, with supplementary disclosures, for the Illini Inn using the indirect method.

Problem 11

The operations of the Molehill, a small lodging operation, are becoming more complex. Susan Strat, the owner, has asked for your help in preparing her statement of cash flows. She is able to present you with condensed balance sheets and some additional information.

The Molehill
Condensed Balance Sheets
Dec. 31, 20X1 and 20X2

	20X1	20X2
Cash	$ 10,000	$ $ 8,000
Accounts Receivable	26,500	22,500
Investments	10,000	20,000
Equipment	200,000	320,000
Accumulated Depreciation	(20,000)	(59,000)
Total Assets	$ 226,500	$ 311,500
Current Liabilities:		
Accounts Payable	$ 18,000	$ 21,000
Mortgage Payable (current)	5,000	22,000
Dividends Payable	5,000	8,000
Noncurrent Liabilities:		
Mortgage Payable	75,000	110,000
Common Stock	50,000	70,000
Retained Earnings	73,500	80,500
Total Liabilities and Owner's Equity	$ 226,500	$ 311,500

Additional information:

1. Equipment costing $20,000 and fully depreciated (to $0) was sold for $5,000.

2. Long-term investments costing $10,000 were sold for $12,000.

3. Common stock was sold and long-term debt was borrowed during 20X2. There were no noncash financing or investing activities during 20X2.

4. Income before gain on the sale of equipment for 20X2 totaled $15,000. The firm's average tax rate is 15 percent.

5. Assume all current liabilities are paid on a timely basis.

6. Assume all long-term debt is reclassified as a current liability on December 31 of the year prior to its payment.

7. Assume the change in retained earnings is due only to dividends declared and net income from operations. Dividends declared during 20X2 totaled $10,000.

Required:

Prepare the SCF using the indirect method.

Problem 12

The operations of The Freida, a small lodging operation, are becoming more complex. Ms. Martin, the owner, has asked for your help in preparing her statement of cash flows. She is able to present you with condensed balance sheets and some additional information.

The Freida
Condensed Balance Sheets
Dec. 31, 20X1 and 20X2

	20X1	20X2
Cash	$ 10,000	$ 6,000
Accounts Receivable	26,500	25,500
Investments	10,000	5,000
Equipment	200,000	325,000
Accumulated Depreciation	(20,000)	(40,000)
Total Assets	$226,500	$321,500
Current Liabilities:		
Accounts Payable	$ 18,000	$ 21,000
Mortgage Payable (current)	5,000	5,000
Dividends Payable	5,000	5,000
Noncurrent Liabilities:		
Mortgage Payable (long-term)	75,000	70,000
Notes Payable	–0–	40,000
Common Stock	50,000	100,000
Retained Earnings	73,500	80,500
Total Liabilities and Owner's Equity	$226,500	$321,500

Additional information:

1. Equipment costing $20,000, depreciated to one-half its cost, was sold for $8,000.

2. Common stock, purchased as a long-term investment for $5,000, was sold for $8,000.

3. Dividends declared during 20X2 totaled $7,000.

4. Equipment costing $145,000 was purchased during 20X2.

5. Depreciation expense for 20X2 totaled $30,000.

6. Long-term debt of $5,000 was reclassified as current at the end of 20X2.

7. Common stock of $50,000 was sold and long-term debt of $40,000 (note payable) was borrowed during 20X2.

8. The Freida generated net income of $14,000 during 20X2.

Required:

Prepare the SCF as requested by Ms. Martin using the indirect method.

Problem 13

The condensed balance sheets of the Spartan Inn are as follows:

Spartan Inn
Condensed Balance Sheets
Dec. 31, 20X1 and 20X2

Assets	20X1	20X2
Current Assets:		
Cash	$ 30,000	$ 40,000
Marketable Securities	50,000	50,000
Accounts Receivable	100,000	95,000
Inventory	20,000	25,000
Total Current Assets	200,000	210,000
Investments	100,000	60,000
Property and Equipment:		
Land	500,000	500,000
Building	5,000,000	6,000,000
Equipment	1,000,000	1,100,000
Accumulated Depreciation	(1,600,000)	(2,000,000)
Net Property and Equipment	4,900,000	5,600,000
Total Assets	$ 5,200,000	$ 5,870,000
Liabilities and Owners' Equity		
Current Liabilities:		
Accounts Payable	$ 60,000	$ 70,000
Dividends Payable	30,000	50,000
Current Portion of LTD	100,000	130,000
Total	190,000	250,000
Long-Term Debt	4,000,000	4,370,000
Capital Stock	700,000	700,000
Retained Earnings	310,000	550,000
Total Liabilities and Owners' Equity	$ 5,200,000	$ 5,870,000

Spartan Inn
Condensed Income Statement
For the year ended Dec. 31, 20X2

Sales	$6,000,000
Cost of Sales	1,000,000
Gross Profit	5,000,000
Depreciation	400,000
Other Expenses (except depreciation)	4,500,000
Net Operating Income	100,000
Gain on Sales of Investments	300,000
Income Taxes	110,000
Net Income	$ 290,000

Additional information:

1. Dividends declared during 20X2 totaled $50,000.

2. No investments were purchased during 20X2.

3. The current portion of long-term debt at the end of 20X2 was reclassified from noncurrent during 20X2.

4. No equipment or buildings were sold during 20X2.

5. Long-term debt was borrowed to partially finance the building purchase.

Required:

Prepare the Spartan Inn's SCF for 20X2 using the indirect method.

Problem 14

Use the information in Problem 13 for the Spartan Inn. Additional information is as follows:

    Total labor expense for 20X2 was $2 million.

    Interest expense for 20X2 was $450,000.

Required:

Prepare the Spartan Inn's SCF for 20X2 using the direct method.

Problem 15

Biola Chemistry is the owner of the BC Café, whose summary financial statements are shown below.

Balance Sheets

	Dec. 31	
	20X5	20X6
Assets:		
Cash	$ 15,000	$ 2,000
Inventory	6,000	15,000
Land	50,000	50,000
Building	300,000	300,000
Equipment	50,000	110,000
Accumulated depreciation	(50,000)	(80,000)
Total Assets	$ 371,000	$ 397,000
Liabilities and Owner's Equity:		
Accounts payable	$ 10,000	$ 8,000
Notes payable—long term	200,000	220,000
Common stock	100,000	100,000
Retained earnings	61,000	69,000
Total Liabilities and Owner's Equity	$ 371,000	$ 397,000

Income Statement and Retained Earnings

	20X6
Sales	$ 1,000,000
Cost of food sold	350,000
Payroll costs	400,000
Depreciation expense	30,000
Other expenses	160,000
Net income	60,000
Retained earnings—Jan. 1, 20X6	61,000
Less: Dividends declared	(52,000)
Retained earnings—Dec. 31, 20X6	$ 69,000

Other information:

1. No equipment was sold during 20X6.

2. No long-term debt was paid off during 20X6.

Required:

Explain to Biola how her company had net income of $60,000 for 20X6 but cash dropped by $13,000 during 20X6.

Problem 16

The operations of the Fishtail, a small foodservice operation, are becoming more complex. Treva Trout, the owner, has asked for your help in understanding the condensed balance sheets and additional information provided.

The Fishtail
Condensed Balance Sheets
Dec. 31, 20X1 and 20X2

	20X1	20X2
Cash	$ 10,000	$ 12,000
Accounts Receivable	15,000	18,500
Prepaid Expenses	21,500	20,000
Equipment	200,000	325,000
Accumulated Depreciation	(20,000)	(64,000)
Total Assets	$226,500	$311,500
Current Liabilities:		
Accounts Payable	18,000	21,000
Mortgage Payable (current)	5,000	15,000
Dividends Payable	5,000	18,000
Noncurrent Liabilities:		
Mortgage Payable	95,000	110,000
Common Stock	90,000	100,000
Treasury Stock	(40,000)	(30,000)
Retained Earnings	53,500	77,500
Total Liabilities and Owner's Equity	$226,500	$311,500

Additional information:

1. A range costing $8,000 with a net book value of $3,000 was sold for $4,000.

2. Dividends paid during 20X2 totaled $20,000.

3. There were no noncash transactions during 20X2.

4. Retained earnings is only affected by the results of operations (net income) and dividends declared.

Required:

1. What amount of dividends was declared in 20X2?

2. What was the net income for 20X2?

3. What was the depreciation expense for 20X2?

4. What were the equipment purchases for 20X2?

5. What was the amount of funds borrowed during 20X2?

Problem 17

The operations of the Great Rae Café, a small foodservice operation, are becoming more complex. Natalie Rae, the owner, has asked for your help in understanding the condensed balance sheets and the additional information provided.

The Great Rae Café
Condensed Balance Sheets
Dec. 31, 20X1 and 20X2

	20X1	20X2
Cash	$ 15,000	$ 12,000
Accounts Receivable	15,000	14,000
Inventory	25,000	20,000
Investments (noncurrent)	110,000	105,000
Equipment	240,000	320,000
Accumulated Depreciation	(20,000)	(50,000)
Total Assets	$385,000	$ 421,000
Current Liabilities:		
Accounts Payable	$ 18,000	$ 10,000
Note Payable	10,000	10,000
Dividends Payable	5,000	10,000
Noncurrent Liabilities:		
Note Payable	152,000	171,000
Common Stock	200,000	200,000
Treasury Stock	(40,000)	(50,000)
Retained Earnings	40,000	70,000
Total Liabilities and Owner's Equity	$385,000	$ 421,000

Additional information:

1. Investments costing $10,000 were sold for $5,000.

2. Dividends paid during 20X2 totaled $30,000.

3. The café's van, which cost $20,000, was sold for $5,000. Its net book value on the date of sale was $3,000.

4. Marketable securities purchased during 20X2 for $5,000 were sold for a gain of $2,000 during 20X2.

5. Assume that the retained earnings account is affected only by dividends declared and the result of operations (net income).

6. Assume current liabilities are paid on a timely basis.

7. Assume the current amount of notes payable was reclassified from the noncurrent notes payable.

Required:

1. What amount of dividends was declared during 20X2?

2. What amount of the note payable was paid during 20X2?

3. What impact did the change in inventory during 20X2 have on cash?

4. What impact did the change in accounts payable during 20X2 have on cash?

5. What was the net income for 20X2?

6. What amount of investments was purchased during 20X2?

7. What was the depreciation expense for 20X2?

8. What was the amount of working capital at the beginning of 20X2?

9. What amount of cash was received on the sale of marketable securities during the year?

10. What amount of treasury stock was sold during 20X2?

Problem 18

The operations of the Bloated Goat Café, a small foodservice operation, are becoming more complex. Sharon Nanny, the owner, has asked for your help in understanding the condensed balance sheets and the additional information provided.

The Bloated Goat Café
Condensed Balance Sheets
Dec. 31, 20X1 and 20X2

	20X1	20X2
Cash	$ 15,000	$ 12,000
Accounts Receivable	15,000	14,000
Inventory	25,000	20,000
Investments (noncurrent)	10,000	5,000
Equipment	240,000	320,000
Accumulated Depreciation	(20,000)	(50,000)
Total Assets	$ 285,000	$321,000

The Bloated Goat Café
Condensed Balance Sheets
Dec. 31, 20X1 and 20X2

Current Liabilities:		
Accounts Payable	$ 18,000	$ 10,000
Note Payable (current)	10,000	10,000
Dividends Payable	5,000	10,000
Noncurrent Liabilities:		
Note Payable	152,000	171,000
Common Stock	100,000	100,000
Treasury Stock	(40,000)	(50,000)
Retained Earnings	40,000	70,000
Total Liabilities and Owner's Equity	$ 285,000	$321,000

Additional information:

1. Investments costing $10,000 were sold for $15,000.

2. Dividends paid during 20X2 totaled $10,000.

3. The cafe's van, which cost $20,000, was sold for $5,000. Its net book value on the date of sale was $3,000.

4. Assume that the retained earnings account is affected only by dividends declared and the results of operations (net income).

5. Assume current liabilities are paid on a timely basis.

Required:

1. What amount of dividends was declared during 20X2?

2. What amount of the note payable was paid during 20X2?

3. What impact did the change in inventory during 20X2 have on cash?

4. What impact did the change in accounts payable during 20X2 have on cash?

5. What were the results of operations for 20X2?

6. What amount of investments was purchased during 20X2?

7. What was the depreciation expense for 20X2?

Problem 19

Jayoung Sohn has provided you with the December 31, 20X3, balance sheet and the month of December 20X3 statement of cash flows as follows:

Balance Sheet
Dec. 31, 20X3

Assets:	
Cash	$ 10,000
Inventory	20,000
Equipment	300,000
Accumulated depreciation	(50,000)
Total Assets	$ 280,000

Balance Sheet
Dec. 31, 20X3

Liabilities and Owner's Equity:

Accounts payable	$ 15,000
Long-term debt	200,000
J. Sohn, capital	65,000
Total Liabilities and Owner's Equity	$ 280,000

Statement of Cash Flows
For the Month of December 20X3

Cash flow from operations:	
Net income	$ 10,000
Adjustments:	
Depreciation expense	10,000
Increase in inventory	(5,000)
Decrease in accounts payable	(5,000)
Cash flow from operations	$10,000
Cash flow from investing activities:	
Purchase of equipment	(10,000)
Sale of equipment	5,000
Cash flow and investing activities	(5,000)
Cash flow from financing activities:	
Borrowed long-term debt	8,000
Owner's withdrawal	(5,000)
Cash flow provided by financing activities	3,000
Increase in cash	8,000
Cash on Nov. 30, 20X3	2,000
Cash on Dec. 31, 20X3	$ 10,000

Other information:

Equipment costing $15,000 with accumulated depreciation of $10,000 was sold for $5,000.

Required:

Jayoung misplaced the balance sheet for Nov. 30, 20X3. You are to prepare it based on the above financial statements and other information.

Problem 20

The Hawkeye Hotel's balance sheet for December 31, 20X5, is provided below.

Hawkeye Hotel
Balance Sheet
Dec. 31, 20X5

Current Assets		
Cash	$	12,540
Marketable Securities		100,000
Accounts Receivable		73,811
Food Inventory		10,833
Prepaid Insurance		4,318
Total Current Assets		201,502
Property and Equipment, at Cost		
Land		262,000
Building		1,572,805
Equipment		213,843
		2,048,648
Less Accumulated Depreciation		303,227
		1,745,421
Total Assets		$ 1,946,923
Current Liabilities		
Notes Payable	$	–0–
Mortgage Payable—Current		50,000
Accounts Payable		18,776
Accrued Wages		6,843
Total Current Liabilities		75,619
Long-Term Liabilities		
Mortgage Payable		950,695
Owners' Equity		
Common Stock, No Par, Authorized 100,000		
Shares, Issued 75,000 Shares		750,000
Retained Earnings		170,609
Total Liabilities and Owners' Equity		$ 1,946,923

The Hawkeye Hotel's general ledger as of December 31, 20X6, contained the following accounts:

	DR	CR
Cash	$ 19,278	
Accounts receivable	75,000	
Allowance for doubtful accounts		$ 1,211
Food inventory	11,936	
Prepaid insurance	4,667	
Land	262,000	
Building	1,927,817	
Equipment	241,470	

	DR	CR
Accumulated depreciation		411,137
Accounts payable		6,821
Accrued wages		7,953
Notes payable		25,000
Mortgage payable (current)		50,000
Mortgage payable (long-term)		1,105,399
Common stock		750,000
Retained earnings		107,109
Room revenues		1,349,866
Food revenues		753,722
Gift shop revenues		73,936
Other sales		1,006
Interest income		785
Room expenses:		
Labor	450,000	
Other	115,037	
Food expenses:		
Cost of sales	225,000	
Labor	220,000	
Other	139,161	
Gift shop expenses:		
Cost of sales	52,470	
Labor	22,000	
Other	2,000	
Administrative and general:		
Labor	150,677	
Other	100,000	
Marketing expense	45,000	
Property operation and maintenance:		
Labor	42,000	
Other	10,000	
Information and telecommunications systems:		
Labor	30,000	
Other	10,000	
Utilities	57,478	
Property taxes	80,000	
Fire insurance expense	31,462	
Interest expense	161,087	
Depreciation expense	110,225	
Gain on sale of equipment		3,000
Income taxes	51,180	
Total	$ 4,646,945	$ 4,646,945

Additional information:

1. Equipment costing $6,750 with accumulated depreciation of $2,315 was sold for $7,435.

2. The mortgage payable—current balance of $50,000 at the end of 20X6—was reclassified from noncurrent liabilities during 20X6.

3. An addition to the building during 20X6 cost $355,012.

4. Equipment purchases during 20X6 totaled $34,377.

5. Dividends paid during 20X6 totaled $63,500.

Required:

1. Prepare a comparative balance sheet for the Hawkeye Hotel.

2. Prepare the Hawkeye Hotel's income statement for 20X6 in accordance with the USALI.

3. Prepare the SCF for the Hawkeye Hotel for 20X6 using the indirect approach.

Problem 21

The Hemisphere Hotel has engaged in several activities (generally transactions), listed as follows:

1. Room sales totaled $20,500 for the day.

2. Repurchased its own capital stock for possible reissue in the future.

3. Invested in a Treasury bond.

4. Exchanged its own capital stock for a 100-room hotel building.

5. Sold common stock.

6. Purchased food and beverages on account.

7. The board declared a 2-for-1 stock split.

8. Paid income taxes of $25,000.

9. Sold long-term investments at a loss of $15,000.

10. The board declared a cash dividend of $1 per common share payable 30 days in the future.

11. Paid interest expense as part of a $150,000 mortgage payment.

12. Received $500 from interest from a certificate of deposit from a local bank.

13. Purchased new light fixtures for one of the restaurants for $140,000 cash.

14. Paid for guest supplies costing $5,000.

15. Paid salaries totaling $20,000 for the month.

Required:

Identify each activity as (1) an operating activity, (2) an investing activity, (3) a financing activity, (4) a noncash activity, or (5) none of the above.

Problem 22

The operations of Lakeside Lodge, a small lodging operation, are becoming more complex. Mimi Wong, the owner, has asked for your help in preparing her statement of cash flows. She is able to present you with condensed balance sheets and some additional information.

Lakeside Lodge
Condensed Balance Sheets
Dec. 31, 20X1 and 20X2

	20X1	20X2
Cash	$ 10,000	$ 6,000
Accounts Receivable	46,500	45,500
Investments	20,000	25,000
Building	2,000,000	2,000,000
Equipment	200,000	325,000
Accumulated Depreciation	(200,000)	(250,000)
Total Assets	$2,086,500	$2,151,000
Current Liabilities:		
Accounts Payable	$ 18,000	$ 21,000
Mortgage Payable (current)	55,000	55,000
Dividends Payable	25,000	25,000
Noncurrent Liabilities:		
Mortgage Payable (long-term)	1,575,000	1,520,000
Note Payable	-0-	40,000
Common Stock	200,000	300,000
Retained Earnings	213,500	190,500
Total Liabilities and Owner's Equity	$2,086,500	$2,151,500

Additional information:

1. Equipment costing $25,000, depreciated to one-half its cost, was sold for $8,000.

2. Common stock, purchased as a long-term investment for $5,000, was sold for $8,000.

3. Dividends declared during 20X2 totaled $50,000.

4. Equipment costing $150,000 was purchased during 20X2.

5. Depreciation expense for 20X2 totaled 35,000.

6. Long-term debt of $55,000 was reclassified as current at the end of 20X2.

7. Common stock of $100,000 was sold during 20X2.

8. The North Shore Motel generated net income of $37,000 during 20X2.

Required:

Prepare the cash from financing activities section of the SCF.

Problem 23

The Willow Corporation has engaged in several transactions, listed as follows:

1. Sold food for cash

2. Purchased stocks in another hotel corporation as an investment

3. Exchanged its common stock for long-term bonds

4. Sold common stock

5. Issued a stock dividend

6. Paid salaries to managers

7. Sold investments at a loss

8. Paid a cash dividend

9. Purchased a 90-day treasury bill

10. Sold equipment for a gain

11. Paid interest

12. Received interest from an investment

13. Paid office supplies

14. Paid mortgage

15. Purchased a truck for delivery equipment

Required:

Identify each transaction as (1) an operating activity, (2) an investing activity, (3) a financing activity, (4) a noncash activity, or (5) none of the above.

Problem 24

The balance sheets for Blue Mountain Grille for the years ending December 31, 20X1 and 20X2, are listed below. In addition, selected key accounts from its income statement for the year ending December 31, 20X2, are also included.

Blue Mountain Grille
Balance Sheets
Year Ending Dec. 31, 20X1 and 20X2

Assets	20X2	20X1
Current assets		
Cash	$ 580,230	$ 288,140
Accounts receivable	375,000	485,000
Inventories	200,000	180,000
Prepaid expenses	35,000	40,000
Total Current Assets	$ 1,190,230	$ 993,140
Property, plant, and equipment		
Land	$300,000	$400,000
Building	860,000	700,000
Equipment	430,000	450,360
	1,590,000	1,550,360

Blue Mountain Grille
Balance Sheets
Year Ending Dec. 31, 20X1 and 20X2

Less: Accumulated depreciation	(300,000)	(270,000)
Total property, plant, and equipment	1,290,000	1,280,360
Total Assets	$2,480,230	$2,273,500

Liabilities

Current liabilities

Accounts payable	$ 142,000	$ 200,000
Interest payable	2,000	4,500
Total current liabilities	$ 144,000	$ 204,500

Long-term liabilities

Long-term note payable	76,000	150,000
Total Liabilities	$ 220,000	$ 354,500

Stockholders' Equity

Common stock ($1 par)	$ 700,230	$ 700,000
Paid-in capital in excess of par	800,000	501,000
Retained earnings	760,000	718,000
Total Stockholders' Equity	$ 2,260,230	$ 1,919,000
Total Liabilities and Equity	$ 2,480,230	$ 2,273,500

The income statement for the year ending December 31, 20X2, included the following selected key amounts:

Net income	$ 250,000
Sales	2,400,000
Cost of food sold	1,200,000
Salaries and wages expense	400,000
Advertising expense	150,000
Depreciation expense	35,000
Income tax expense	20,000
Utilities expense	12,000
Interest expense	7,800
Loss on sale of land	22,450

Required:

Prepare the cash from operating activities section of the SCF.

Problem 25

Albright Hotel Company is expanding its portfolio and has always used a balanced approach by using debt and equity prudently. In the last year, Albright took out a $20 million loan for a term of 10 years and has negotiated to pay interest for the first three years. It then used the funds to purchase a select service hotel. In addition, Albright also sold 100,000 shares of $1 par value stock at $110 per share. Albright made an $800,000 payment on some old debt, plus interest expense on that debt at $50,000. At the end of the year, Albright also declared dividends of $1 per share on all its outstanding common stocks of 3 million shares.

Required:

Prepare the corporation's cash from financing section of the SCF.

5

RATIO ANALYSIS

Chapter 5 Outline

Competencies

1. Identify standards against which the results of ratio analysis may be compared. (pp. 193–194)

2. Explain the function and purposes of ratio analysis. (pp. 194–196)

3. Identify common classes of ratios and describe the general purpose of each. (p. 196)

4. Calculate common liquidity ratios and describe how creditors, owners, and managers view them. (pp. 196–205)

5. Calculate common solvency ratios and describe how creditors, owners, and managers view them. (pp. 205–210)

6. Calculate common activity ratios and describe how creditors, owners, and managers view them. (pp. 210–217)

7. Calculate common profitability ratios and describe how creditors, owners, and managers view them. (pp. 217–225)

8. Calculate common operating ratios and explain how managers use them to evaluate operational results. (pp. 225–235)

9. Summarize the limitations of ratio analysis and describe the usefulness of financial ratios. (pp. 235–237)

accounts receivable turnover

acid-test ratio

activity ratios

asset turnover

average collection period

average daily rate (ADR)

average occupancy per room

average room rate

beverage cost percentage

complimentary occupancy

current ratio

debt-equity ratio

debt service coverage ratio

double occupancy

earnings per share (EPS)

EBITDA

EBITDA margin ratio

EBITDA per available room

financial leverage

fixed charge coverage ratio

flex ratio

flow through ratio

food cost percentage

gross operating profit per available room (GOPAR or GOPPAR)

gross operating profit margin ratio

gross return on assets (GROA)

inventory turnover

labor cost percentage

liquidity ratios

long-term debt to total capitalization ratio

multiple occupancy

number of times interest earned ratio

operating cash flows to current liabilities ratio

operating cash flows to total liabilities ratio

operating efficiency ratio (gross operating profit margin ratio)

operating ratios

paid occupancy

price/earnings (PE) ratio

profit margin

profitability ratios

property and equipment turnover

ratio analysis

residual income

return on assets (ROA)

return on common stockholders' equity

return on owners' equity (ROE)

RevPAR

seat turnover

solvency ratio

solvency ratios

TRevPAC

TRevPAR

working capital turnover ratio

Financial statements issued by hospitality establishments contain a lot of financial information. A thorough analysis of this information requires more than simply reading the reported facts. Users of financial statements need to be able to interpret the reported facts to discover aspects of the hospitality property's financial situation that could otherwise go unnoticed. This is accomplished through **ratio analysis**, which is the comparison of related facts and figures, most of which appear on the financial statements. A ratio gives mathematical expression to a relationship between two figures and is computed by dividing one figure by the other figure. By bringing the two figures into relation with each other, ratios generate new information. In this way, ratio analysis goes beyond the figures reported in a financial statement and makes them more meaningful, more informative, and more useful. In particular, ratio analysis generates indicators for evaluating different aspects of a financial situation.

Ratio analysis can provide users of financial statements with answers to questions such as the following:

1. Is there sufficient cash to meet the establishment's obligations for a given time period?

2. Are the profits of the hospitality operation reasonable?

3. Is the level of debt acceptable in comparison with the stockholders' investment?

4. Is the inventory usage adequate?

5. How do the operation's earnings compare with the market price of the hospitality property's stock?

6. Are accounts receivable reasonable in light of credit sales?

7. Is the hospitality establishment able to service its debt?

In this chapter, we will first explain the different kinds of standards against which ratios are compared in order to evaluate the financial condition of a hospitality operation. We will also discuss the variety of functions or purposes that ratio analysis serves in interpreting financial statements and the ways in which different ratios are expressed in order to make sense of the information they provide. The remainder of the chapter is devoted mostly to a detailed discussion of the ratios most commonly used in the hospitality industry.

5.1 RATIO STANDARDS

Ratio analysis is used to evaluate the favorableness or unfavorableness of various financial conditions. However, the computed ratios alone do not say anything about what is good or bad, acceptable or unacceptable, reasonable or unreasonable. By themselves, ratios are neutral and simply express numerical relationships between related figures. In order to be useful as indicators or measurements of the success or well-being of a hospitality operation, the computed ratios must be compared against some standard. Only then will the ratios become meaningful and provide users of financial statements with a basis for evaluating the financial conditions.

There are basically three different standards that are used to evaluate the ratios computed for a given operation for a given period: ratios from a past period, industry averages, and budgeted ratios. Many ratios can be compared with corresponding ratios calculated for the prior period in order to discover any significant changes. For example, paid occupancy percentage (discussed later in this chapter) for the current year may be compared with paid occupancy percentage of the prior year in order to determine whether the lodging operation is succeeding in selling more of its available rooms this year than it had previously. This comparison may be useful in evaluating the effectiveness of the property's current marketing plans. Industry averages provide another useful standard against which to compare ratios. After calculating the return on investment (discussed later in this chapter) for a given property, investors may want to compare this with the average return for similar properties in their particular industry segment. This may give investors an indication of the ability of the property's management to use resources effectively to generate profits for the owners in comparison with other operations in the industry. In addition, managers may want to compare the paid occupancy percentage or food cost percentage for their own operation with industry averages in order to evaluate their abilities to compete with other operations in their industry segment. Published sources of average industry ratios are readily available.

While ratios can be compared against results of a prior period and against industry averages, ratios are best compared against planned ratio goals. For example, in order to more effectively control the cost of labor, management may project a goal for the current year's labor cost percentage (also discussed in this chapter) that is slightly lower than the previous year's levels. The expectation of a lower labor cost percentage may reflect management's efforts to improve scheduling procedures and other factors related to the cost of labor. By comparing the actual labor cost percentage with the planned goal, management is able to assess the success of its efforts to control labor cost.

Different evaluations may result from comparing ratios against these different standards. For example, a food cost of 33 percent for the current period may compare favorably with the prior year's ratio of 34 percent and with an industry average of 36 percent, but may be judged unfavorably when compared with the operation's planned goal of 32 percent. Therefore, care must be taken when evaluating the results of operations using ratio analysis. It is necessary to keep in mind not only which standards are being used to evaluate the ratios, but the purposes of the ratio analysis as well.

5.2 PURPOSES OF RATIO ANALYSIS

Managers, creditors, and investors often have different purposes in using ratio analysis to evaluate the information reported in financial statements.

Ratios help managers monitor the operating performances of their operations and evaluate their success in meeting a variety of goals. By tracking a limited number of ratios, hospitality managers are able to maintain a fairly accurate perception of the effectiveness and efficiency of their operations. In a foodservice operation, most managers compute food cost percentage and labor cost percentage in order to monitor the two largest expenses of their operations. In lodging operations, occupancy percentage is one of the key ratios that managers use on a daily basis. Management often uses ratios to express operational goals. For example, management may establish ratio goals as follows:

■ Maintain a 1.25-to-1 current ratio.

■ Do not exceed a debt-equity ratio of 1 to 1.

■ Maintain return on owners' equity of 15 percent.

■ Maintain property and equipment turnover of 1.2 times.

These ratios, and many more, will be fully explained later in this chapter. The point here is to notice that ratios are particularly useful to managers as indicators of how well goals are being achieved. When actual results fall short of goals, ratios help indicate where a problem may be. In the food cost percentage example presented earlier, in which an actual ratio of 33 percent compared unfavorably against the planned 32 percent, additional research is required to determine the cause(s) of the 1 percent variation. This 1 percent difference may be due to cost differences, sales mix differences, or a combination of the two. Only additional analysis will determine the actual cause(s). Ratio analysis can contribute significant information to such an investigation.

Creditors use ratio analysis to evaluate the solvency of hospitality operations and to assess the riskiness of future loans. For example, the relationship of current assets to current liabilities, referred to as the current ratio, may indicate an establishment's ability to pay its upcoming bills. In addition, creditors sometimes use ratios to express requirements for hospitality operations as part of the conditions set forth for certain financial arrangements. For example, as a condition of a loan, a creditor may require an operation to maintain a current ratio of 2 to 1.

Investors and potential investors use ratios to evaluate the performance of a hospitality operation. For example, the dividend payout ratio (dividends paid divided by earnings) indicates the percentage of earnings paid out by the hospitality establishment. Potential investors primarily interested in stock growth may shy away from investing in properties that pay out large dividends.

Ratios are used to communicate financial performance. Different ratios communicate different results. Individually, ratios reveal only part of the overall financial condition of an operation. Collectively, however, ratios are able to communicate a great deal of information that may not be immediately apparent from simply reading the figures reported in financial statements.

Finally, rather than evaluating a ratio for a single period, consider the same ratio over a period of time. Consider a monthly food cost percentage of 31 percent, 31.3 percent, 31.7 percent, 32 percent, and 32.2 percent over five months. From a cost perspective, the trend of this ratio should cause management to pause and consider what might be causing this change.

5.3 WHAT RATIOS EXPRESS

In order to understand the information communicated by the different kinds of ratios used in ratio analysis, it is necessary to understand the various ways in which ratios express financial information. Different ratios are read in different ways. For example, many ratios are expressed as *percentages*. An illustration is the food cost percentage, which expresses the cost of food sold in terms of a percentage of total food sales. If total food sales for a given year are $430,000, while the cost of food sold is $135,000, then the result of dividing the cost of food sold by the total food sales is 0.314. Because the food cost percentage is a ratio expressed as a percentage, this figure is multiplied by 100 to yield a 31.4 percent food cost. Another example is paid occupancy percentage, resulting from rooms sold divided by rooms available for sale. If a lodging property has 100 rooms available for sale and sells only 50 of them, then 50 divided by 100 yields 0.5, which is then multiplied by 100 to be expressed as a percentage (50 percent).

Some other ratios are expressed on a *per unit basis*. For example, the average breakfast check is a ratio expressed as a certain sum per breakfast served. It is calculated by dividing the total breakfast sales by the number of guests served during the breakfast period. Thus, on a given day, if 100 guests were served breakfast and the total revenue during the breakfast period amounted to $490, then the average breakfast check would be $4.90 per meal ($490 ÷ 100).

The proper way to express still other ratios is as a *turnover* of so many times. Seat turnover is one such ratio, determined by dividing the number of guests served during a given period by the number of restaurant seats. If the restaurant in the previous example had a seating capacity of 40, then seat turnover for the breakfast period in which it served 100 guests would be 2.5 (100 ÷ 40). This means that, during that breakfast period, the restaurant used its entire seating capacity 2.5 times.

Finally, some ratios are expressed as a *coverage* of so many times. The denominator of such a ratio is always set at 1. The current ratio, determined by dividing current assets by current liabilities, is one of the ratios expressed as a coverage of so many times. For example, if a hospitality operation reported current assets of $120,000 and current liabilities of $100,000 for a given period, then the operation's current ratio at the balance sheet date would be 1.2 to 1 (120,000 ÷ 100,000). This means that the hospitality operation possessed sufficient current assets to cover its current liabilities 1.2 times. Put another way, for every $1 of current liabilities, the operation had $1.20 of current assets.

The proper way to express the various ratios used in ratio analysis depends entirely on the particular ratio and the nature of the significant relationship it expresses between the two facts it relates. The ways in which different ratios are expressed are a function of how we use the information that they provide. As we discuss the ratios commonly used in the hospitality industry, pay attention to how each is expressed.

5.4 CLASSES OF RATIOS

Ratios are generally classified by the type of information that they provide. Five common ratio groupings are as follows:

1. Liquidity

2. Solvency

3. Activity

4. Profitability

5. Operating

Liquidity ratios reveal the ability of a hospitality establishment to meet its short-term obligations. **Solvency ratios**, on the other hand, measure the extent to which the enterprise has been financed by debt and is able to meet its long-term obligations. **Activity ratios** reflect management's ability to use the property's assets, while several **profitability ratios** show management's overall effectiveness as measured by returns on sales and investments. Finally, **operating ratios** assist in the analysis of hospitality establishment operations.

The classification of certain ratios may vary. For example, some texts classify the inventory turnover ratio as a liquidity ratio, but this text and some others consider it to be an activity ratio. Also, profit margin could be classified as an operating ratio, but it is generally included with the profitability ratios.

Knowing the meaning of a ratio and how it is used is always more important than knowing its classification. We will now turn to an in-depth discussion of individual ratios. For each ratio discussed, we will consider its purpose, the formula by which it is calculated, the sources of data needed for the ratio's calculation, and the interpretation of ratio results from the varying viewpoints of owners, creditors, and management.

Exhibits 5.1 through 5.4, financial statements of the hypothetical Grand Hotel, will be used throughout our discussion of individual ratios.

5.5 LIQUIDITY RATIOS

The ability of a hospitality establishment to meet its current obligations is important in evaluating its financial position. For example, can the Grand Hotel meet its current debt of $214,000 as it becomes due? Several ratios can be computed that suggest answers to this question.

Current Ratio

The commonest liquidity ratio is the **current ratio**, which is the ratio of total current assets to total current liabilities and is expressed as a coverage of so many times. Using figures from Exhibit 5.1, the 20X2 current ratio for the Grand Hotel can be calculated as follows:

$$\text{Current Ratio} = \frac{\text{Current Assets}}{\text{Current Liabilities}}$$

$$= \frac{\$338,000}{\$214,000}$$

$$= \underline{1.58} \text{ times or 1.58 to 1}$$

Exhibit 5.1   Balance Sheets

Balance Sheets
Grand Hotel
Dec. 31, 20X0, 20X1, 20X2

ASSETS	20X0	20X1	20X2
Current Assets:			
Cash	$ 20,000	$ 21,000	$ 24,000
Short-Term Investments	60,000	81,000	145,000
Accounts Receivable (net)	100,000	90,000	140,000
Inventories	14,000	17,000	15,000
Prepaid Expenses	13,000	12,000	14,000
Total Current Assets	207,000	221,000	338,000
Investments	43,000	35,000	40,000
Property and Equipment:			
Land	68,500	68,500	68,500
Buildings	810,000	850,000	880,000
Furniture and Equipment	170,000	190,000	208,000
	1,048,500	1,108,500	1,156,600
Less: Accumulated Depreciation	260,000	320,000	381,000
Total Net Property and Equipment	788,500	788,500	775,500
Other Assets—Operating Equipment	11,500	20,500	22,800
Total Assets	$ 1,050,000	$ 1,065,000	$ 1,176,300
LIABILITIES AND OWNERS' EQUITY			
Current Liabilities:			
Accounts Payable	$ 60,000	$ 53,500	$ 71,000
Accrued Income Taxes	30,000	32,000	34,000
Accrued Expenses	70,000	85,200	85,000
Current Portion of Long-Term Debt	25,000	21,500	24,000
Total Current Liabilities	185,000	192,200	214,000
Long-Term Debt:			
Mortgage Payable	425,000	410,000	400,000
Deferred Income Taxes	40,000	42,800	45,000
Total Long-Term Debt	465,000	452,800	445,000
Total Liabilities	650,000	645,000	659,000
Owners' Equity:			
Common Stock	55,000	55,000	55,000
Paid-in Capital in Excess of Par	110,000	110,000	110,000
Retained Earnings	235,000	255,000	352,300
Total Owners' Equity	400,000	420,000	517,300
Total Liabilities and Owners' Equity	$ 1,050,000	$ 1,065,000	$ 1,176,300

This result shows that for every $1 of current liabilities, the Grand Hotel has $1.58 of current assets. Thus, there is a cushion of $0.58 for every dollar of current debt. A considerable shrinkage of inventory and receivables could occur before the Grand Hotel would be unable to pay its current obligations. By comparison, the 20X1 current ratio for the Grand Hotel was 1.15. An increase in the current ratio from 1.15 to 1.58 within one year is considerable and would no doubt please creditors. However, would a current ratio of 1.58 please all interested parties?

Exhibit 5.2 Income Statements

Income Statements
Grand Hotel
For the years ended Dec. 31, 20X1 and 20X2

	20X1	20X2
Total Revenue	$ 1,300,000	$ 1,352,000
Rooms:		
Revenue	$ 780,000	$ 810,000
Labor Costs and Related Expenses	135,000	145,000
Other Direct Expenses	62,500	60,000
Departmental Income	582,500	605,000
Food and Beverages:		
Revenue	430,000	445,000
Cost of Sales	142,000	148,000
Labor Costs and Related Expenses	175,000	180,000
Other Direct Expenses	43,400	45,000
Departmental Income	69,600	72,000
Gift Shop:		
Revenue	40,000	42,000
Cost of Sales	30,000	31,000
Labor Costs and Related Expenses	10,000	10,500
Other Direct Expenses	5,000	4,500
Departmental Income	(5,000)	(4,000)
Miscellaneous Income	50,000	55,000
Total Operated Departments Income	697,100	728,000
Undistributed Operating Expenses:		
Administrative and General	75,000	76,500
Information and Telecommunications Systems	30,000	32,000
Sales and Marketing	51,500	55,000
Property Operation and Maintenance	62,250	67,500
Utilities	80,250	81,500
Total Undistributed Operating Expenses	302,000	312,500
Gross Operating Profit	395,100	415,500
Nonoperating Expenses:		
Rent	20,000	20,000
Property Taxes	20,000	24,000
Insurance	5,500	6,000
Total Nonoperating Expenses	45,000	50,000
EBITDA	349,600	365,500
Depreciation	60,000	61,000
Interest Expense	54,000	60,000
Income before Income Tax	235,600	244,500
Income Taxes	94,300	97,800
Net Income	$ 141,300	$ 146,700

Exhibit 5.3   Statement of Cash Flows

Statement of Cash Flows
Grand Hotel
For the years ended December 31, 20X1 and 20X2

	20X1	20X2
Cash Flows from Operating Activities	$ 141,300	$ 146,700
Net Income		
Adjustments to reconcile net income to net		
cash provided by operations:		
Depreciation expense	60,000	61,000
Inc./Dec. in accounts receivable (net)	10,000	(50,000)
Inc./Dec. in inventories	(3,000)	2,000
Inc./Dec. in prepaid expenses	1,000	(2,000)
Inc./Dec. in accounts payable	(6,500)	17,500
Increase in income taxes	2,000	2,000
Inc./Dec. in accrued expenses	15,200	(200)
Inc./Dec. in deferred taxes	2,800	2,200
Net cash from operating activities	222,800	179,200
Cash Flows from Investing Activities:		
Purchase of short-term investments	(21,000)	(64,000)
Sale of investments	8,000	–0–
Purchase of buildings	(40,000)	(30,000)
Purchase of furniture and equipment	(20,000)	(18,000)
Purchase of operating equipment	(9,000)	(2,300)
Purchase of investments	–0–	(5,000)
Net cash from investing activities	(82,000)	(119,300)
Cash Flows from Financing Activities:		
Payment of dividends	(121,300)	(49,400)
Payment of long-term debt	(25,000)	(21,500)
Borrowed long-term debt	6,500	14,000
Net cash from financing activities	(139,800)	(56,900)
Net Increase in Cash	$ 1,000	$ 3,000

Additional information

Investments of $8,000 were sold at cost in 20X1.

Owners/stockholders normally prefer a low current ratio to a high one, because stockholders view investments in most current assets as less productive than investments in noncurrent assets. Since stockholders are primarily concerned with profits, they prefer a relatively low current ratio.

Creditors normally prefer a relatively high current ratio, as this provides assurance that they will receive timely payments. A subset of creditors, lenders of funds, believe adequate liquidity is so important that they often incorporate a minimum working capital requirement or a minimum current ratio in loan agreements. Violation of this loan provision could result in the lender demanding full payment of the loan.

Management is caught in the middle, trying to satisfy both owners and lenders while, at the same time, maintaining adequate working capital and sufficient liquidity to ensure the smooth operation of the hospitality establishment. Management is able to take action affecting the current ratio. In the case of the Grand Hotel, a current ratio of 2 could be achieved by selling

Grand Hotel Statement of Retained Earnings and Other Information Dec. 31, 20X1 and 20X2

	20X1	20X2
Retained earnings—beginning of the year	$ 235,000	$ 255,000
Net income	141,300	146,700
Dividends declared	(121,300)	(49,400)
Retained earnings—end of the year	$ 255,000	$ 352,300

Other Information

	20X1	20X2
Rooms Sold	20,500	21,000
Paid Guests	23,500	24,000
Rooms Occupied by Two or More People	2,400	2,500
Complimentary Rooms	150*	160*
Shares of Common Stock Outstanding	55,000	55,000
Food Customers	55,500	56,000
Food Sales	$ 280,000	$ 300,000
Beverage Sales	$ 150,000	$ 145,000

*Assume one guest per complimentary room

$90,000 worth of short-term investments on the last day of 20X2 and paying current creditors.[1] Other possible actions to increase a current ratio include:

- Obtaining long-term loans
- Obtaining new owners' equity contributions
- Converting noncurrent assets to cash
- Deferring declaring dividends and leaving the cash in the business

An extremely high current ratio may mean that accounts receivable is too high because of liberal credit policies and/or slow collections, or it may indicate that inventory is excessive. Since ratios are indicators, management must follow through by analyzing possible contributing factors.

Acid-Test Ratio

A more stringent test of liquidity is the **acid-test ratio**. The acid-test ratio measures liquidity by considering only "quick assets"—cash and near-cash assets. Excluded from current assets are inventories and prepaid expenses in determining the total quick assets. In many industries, inventories are significant and their conversion to cash may take several months. The extremes appear evident in the hospitality industry. In some hospitality operations, especially quick-service restaurants, food inventory may be entirely replenished twice a week. On the other hand, the stock of certain alcoholic beverages at some foodservice operations may be replaced only once in three months.

The difference between the current ratio and the acid-test ratio is for the most part a function of the amount of inventory relative to current assets. In some operations, the difference between the current ratio and the acid-test ratio will be minor, while in others, it will be significant. Using relevant figures from Exhibit 5.1, the 20X2 acid-test ratio for the Grand Hotel is computed as follows:

$$\text{Acid-Test Ratio} = \frac{\text{Cash, Short-Term Investments, Notes Receivable, and Accounts Receivable}}{\text{Current Liabilities}}$$

$$= \frac{\$309,000}{\$214,000}$$

$$= \underline{\underline{1.44}}$$

The 20X2 acid-test ratio reveals quick assets of $1.44 for every $1 of current liabilities. This is an increase of 0.44 times over the 20X1 acid-test ratio. Although the acid-test ratio was 1.0 for 20X1, the Grand Hotel was not in difficult financial straits. Many hospitality establishments are able to operate efficiently and effectively with an acid-test ratio of 1 or less, for they have minimal amounts of both inventory and accounts receivable.

The viewpoints of owners, creditors, and managers toward the acid-test ratio parallel those held toward the current ratio. That is, owners of hospitality operations prefer a low ratio (generally less than 1), creditors prefer a high ratio, and management is again caught in the middle.

Operating Cash Flows to Current Liabilities Ratio

A fairly new ratio made possible by the statement of cash flows is **operating cash flows to current liabilities**. The operating cash flows are taken from the statement of cash flows, while current liabilities come from the balance sheet. This measure of liquidity compares the cash flow from the firm's operating activities to its obligations at the balance sheet date that must be paid within 12 months. Using the relevant figures from Exhibits 5.1 and 5.3, the 20X2 operating cash flows to current liabilities ratio is computed as follows:

$$\text{Operating Cash Flows to Current Liabilities Ratio} = \frac{\text{Operating Cash Flows}}{\text{Average Current Liabilities}}$$

$$= \frac{\$179,200}{0.5(\$192,200 + \$214,000)}$$

$$= 0.882 \text{ or } \underline{88.2\%}$$

The 20X2 ratio of 88.2 percent shows that only $.882 of cash flow from operations was provided by the Grand Hotel during 20X2 for each $1.00 of current debt at the end of 20X2. The prior year's ratio was 118 percent. This dramatic change should cause management to consider reasons for the change and be prepared to take appropriate action.

All users of ratios would prefer to see a high operating cash flow to current liabilities, as this suggests operations are providing sufficient cash to pay the firm's current liabilities.

Accounts Receivable Turnover

In hospitality operations that extend credit to guests, accounts receivable is generally the largest current asset. Therefore, in an examination of a property's liquidity, the "quality" of its accounts receivable must be considered.

In the normal operating cycle, accounts receivable is converted to cash. The **accounts receivable turnover** measures the speed of the conversion. The faster the accounts receivable is turned over, the more credibility the current and acid-test ratios have in financial analysis.

This ratio is determined by dividing revenue by average accounts receivable. A refinement of this ratio uses only charge sales in the numerator; however, quite often charge sales figures are unavailable to outsiders (stockholders, potential stockholders, and creditors). Regardless of whether revenues or charge sales are used as the numerator, the calculation should be consistent from period to period. Average accounts receivable is the result of dividing the sum of the beginning-of-the-period and end-of-the-period accounts receivable by two. When a hospitality operation has seasonal sales fluctuations, a preferred approach (when computing the *annual* accounts receivable turnover) is to sum the accounts receivable at the end of each month and divide by 12 to determine the average accounts receivable. Exhibit 5.5 uses relevant figures from Exhibits 5.1 and 5.2 to calculate the 20X2 accounts receivable turnover for the Grand Hotel. The accounts receivable turnover of 11.76 indicates that the total revenue for 20X2 is 11.76 times the average receivables. This is lower than the Grand Hotel's 20X1 accounts

Exhibit 5.5   Accounts Receivable Turnover

$$\text{Accounts Receivable Turnover} = \frac{\text{Total Revenue}}{\text{Average Accounts Receivable*}}$$

$$= \frac{\$1,352,000}{\$115,000}$$

$$= 11.76 \text{ times}$$

$$\text{*Average Accounts Receivable} = \frac{\text{Accounts Receivable at Beginning and End of Year}}{2}$$

$$= \frac{\$90,000 + \$140,000}{2}$$

$$= \$115,000$$

Exhibit 5.6   Aging of Accounts Receivable Schedule

Aging of Accounts Receivable Schedule
Grand Hotel
December 31, 20X2

Firm Name	Total	Days Outstanding				
		0–30	31–60	61–90	91–120	Over 120 days
Ace Co.	$600	$400	$200	$–0–	$–0–	$–0–
Acem Corp.	400	100	–0–	300	–0–	–0–
Ahern, Jim	100	100	–0–	–0–	–0–	–0–
America, Inc.	1,000	950	–0–	–0–	–0–	50
Armadillo Co.	50	–0–	–0–	–0–	50	–0–
.						
.						
.						
Zebra Zoo Equip.	80	80	–0–	–0–	–0–	–0–
Total	$145,000	$115,000	$18,000	$7,000	$4,000	$1,000

receivable turnover of 13.68. Management would generally investigate this difference. The investigation may reveal problems, or that changes in the credit policy and/or collection procedures significantly contributed to the difference.

Although the accounts receivable turnover measures the overall rapidity of collections, it fails to address individual accounts. This matter is resolved by preparing an aging of accounts receivable schedule that reflects the status of each account. In an aging schedule, each account is broken down to the period when the charges originated. Like credit sales, this information is generally available only to management. Exhibit 5.6 illustrates an aging of accounts receivable schedule. Since few hospitality establishments charge interest on their accounts receivable, the opportunity cost of credit sales is the investment dollars that could be generated by investing cash. However, credit terms are extended with the purpose of increasing sales. Therefore, theoretically, credit should be extended to the point where the bad debt and additional collection costs of extending credit to one more guest equal the additional profit earned by extending credit to one more guest.

Owners prefer a high accounts receivable turnover, as this reflects a lower investment in nonproductive accounts receivable. However, they understand how a tight credit policy and an overly aggressive collections effort may result in lower sales. Nonetheless, everything else being the same, a high accounts receivable turnover indicates that accounts receivable is being managed well. Suppliers, like owners, prefer a high accounts receivable turnover, because this means that hospitality establishments will have more cash readily available to pay them. Long-term creditors also see a high accounts receivable turnover as a positive reflection of management.

Management desires to maximize the sales of the hospitality operation. Offering credit helps maximize sales. However, management also realizes that offering credit to maximize sales may result in more accounts receivable and in selling to some less creditworthy customers. One result of management's decision to offer credit is a lower accounts receivable turnover. On the other hand, while management may see a lower accounts receivable turnover as a consequence of higher sales, it should not lose sight of the fact that it also must maintain the operation's cash flow—that is, it must effectively collect on the credit sales.

Average Collection Period

A variation of the accounts receivable turnover is the **average collection period**, which is calculated by dividing the accounts receivable turnover into 365 (the number of days in a year). This conversion simply translates the turnover into a more understandable result. For the Grand Hotel, the average collection period for 20X2 is as follows:

$$\text{Average Collection Period} = \frac{365}{\text{Accounts Receivable Turnover}}$$
$$= \frac{365}{11.76}$$
$$= \underline{31} \text{ days}$$

The average collection period of 31 days means that on an average of every 31 days throughout 20X2, the Grand Hotel was collecting all its accounts receivable. The 31 days is a four-day increase over the 20X1 average collection period of 27 days.

What should be the average collection period? Generally, the time allowed for average payments should not exceed the terms of sale by more than 7 to 10 days.

Therefore, if the terms of sale are *n*/30 (entire amount is due in 30 days), the maximum allowable average collection period is 37 to 40 days.

The above discussion assumes that all sales are credit sales. However, many hospitality operations have both cash and credit sales. Therefore, the mix of cash and credit sales must be considered when the accounts receivable turnover ratio uses revenue, rather than credit sales, in the numerator. This is accomplished by allowing for cash sales. For example, if sales are 50 percent cash and 50 percent credit, then the maximum allowable average collection period should be adjusted. An adjusted maximum allowable average collection period is calculated by multiplying the maximum allowable average collection period by credit sales as a percentage of total sales.

In the previous example of a maximum allowable collection period of 37 to 40 days and 50 percent credit sales, the adjusted maximum allowable average collection period for the Grand Hotel in 20X2 was 18.5 to 20 days (37 to 40 days × 0.5). Generally, only management can make this adjustment, because the mix of sales is unknown by other interested parties.

The average collection period preferred by owners, creditors, and management is similar to their preferences for the accounts receivable turnover, because the average collection period is only a variation of the accounts receivable turnover. Therefore, owners and creditors prefer a lower number of days, while management prefers a higher number of days (as long as cash flow is sufficient).

Working Capital Turnover Ratio

The final liquidity ratio presented here is the **working capital turnover ratio**, which compares working capital (current assets less current liabilities) to revenue. For most businesses, the higher the revenue, the greater the amount of working capital required. Thus, as the revenue rises, working capital is expected to rise also. Exhibit 5.7 uses relevant figures from Exhibits 5.1 and 5.2 to calculate the working capital turnover ratio in 20X2 for the Grand Hotel.

For the Grand Hotel, a working capital turnover of 17.70 means that working capital of $76,400 was "used" 17.70 times during the year. Everything else being the same, the lower the current ratio, the greater the working capital turnover ratio. Therefore, those establishments in segments of the hospitality industry with virtually no credit sales and a low level of inventory will generally have an extremely high working capital ratio.

Owners prefer this ratio to be high, as they prefer a low current ratio, thus low working capital. Creditors prefer a lower working capital turnover ratio than owners because they prefer a relatively high current ratio. Management's

Exhibit 5.7	Working Capital Turnover

$$\text{Working Capital Turnover} = \frac{\text{Revenue}}{\text{Average Working Capital}}$$

$$= \frac{\$1,352,000}{\$76,400^*}$$

$$= \underline{17.70} \text{ times}$$

	Working Capital(WC)	=	Current Assets − Current Liabilities
WC (20X2)	$124,000	=	$338,000 − $214,000
WC (20X1)	28,800	=	221,000 − 192,200

*Average Working Capital = ($124,000 + $28,800) ÷ 2 = $76,400

preferences fall between owners and creditors. Management desires to maintain an adequate amount of working capital to cover unexpected problems, yet management also desires to maximize profits by using available funds to make long-term investments.

5.6 SOLVENCY RATIOS

Solvency ratios measure the degree of debt financing by a hospitality enterprise and are partial indicators of the establishment's ability to meet its long-term debt obligations. These ratios reveal the equity cushion that is available to absorb any operating losses. Primary users of these ratios are outsiders, especially lenders, who generally prefer less risk rather than more risk. High solvency ratios generally suggest that an operation has the ability to weather financial storms.

Owners like to use debt instead of additional equity to increase their return on equity already invested. This process is commonly referred to as **financial leverage**. Financial leverage is used when the return on the investment exceeds the cost of the debt used to finance an investment. When using debt to increase their leverage, owners are, in essence, transferring part of their risk to creditors.

As a further explanation of the concept of leverage, let us consider the following example. Assume that total assets of a lodging facility are $100, earnings before interest and taxes (EBIT) are $50, and interest is 15 percent of debt. Further assume that two possible combinations of debt and equity are $80 of debt and $20 of equity, and the reverse ($80 of equity and $20 of debt). Further assume a tax rate of 40 percent. The return on equity for each of the two combinations is calculated in Exhibit 5.8.

The calculations in Exhibit 5.8 reveal that each $1 invested by stockholders in the high debt/low equity combination earns $1.14, while every $1 invested by stockholders in the low debt/high equity combination earns only $0.35.

This class of ratios includes three groups—those based on balance sheet information, those based on income statement information, and those based primarily on statement of cash flow information. The first three ratios to be examined (the solvency ratio, the debt-equity ratio, and long-term debt to total

| Exhibit 5.8 | Return on Equity |

	High Debt / Low Equity	High Equity / Low Debt
Debt	$ 80.00	$ 20.00
Equity	$ 20.00	$ 80.00
EBIT	$ 50.00	$ 50.00
Interest (15%)	12.00*	3.00**
Income before taxes	38.00	47.00
Income taxes	− 15.20	− 18.80
Net income	$ 22.80	$ 28.20

Return per $1 of equity:

$$\frac{\text{Net income}}{\text{equity}} = \frac{\$22.80}{\$20} = \$1.14 \qquad \frac{\$28.20}{\$80} = \$0.35$$

*Debt times interest rate = interest expense
$80 × .15 = $12

**$20 × .15 = $3

capitalization ratio) are based on balance sheet information. The following two ratios, the number of times interest earned ratio and the fixed charge coverage ratio, are based on information from the income statement. The final two ratios are the debt service coverage and operating cash flows to total liabilities ratios.

Solvency Ratio

A hospitality enterprise is solvent when its assets exceed its liabilities. Therefore, the **solvency ratio** is simply total assets divided by total liabilities. The solvency ratio in 20X2 for the Grand Hotel is determined as follows:

$$\text{Solvency Ratio} = \frac{\text{Total Assets}}{\text{Total Liabilities}}$$

$$= \frac{\$1,176,300}{\$659,000}$$

$$= \underline{1.78} \text{ times}$$

Thus, at the end of 20X2, the Grand Hotel has $1.78 of assets for each $1 of liabilities or a cushion of $0.78. The Grand Hotel's assets could be discounted substantially ($0.78 ÷ $1.78 = 43.8%) and creditors could still be fully paid. The Grand Hotel's solvency ratio at the end of 20X1 was 1.65 times. The 20X2 ratio would be considered more favorable from the perspective of creditors.

The greater the leverage (use of debt to finance the assets) used by the hospitality establishment, the lower its solvency ratio. Owners prefer to use leverage in order to maximize their return on their investments. This occurs as long as the earnings from the creditor-financed investment exceed the cost of the establishment's borrowing. Creditors, on the other hand, prefer a high solvency ratio, as it provides a greater cushion should the establishment experience losses in operations. Managers must satisfy both owners and creditors. Thus, they desire to finance assets so as to maximize the return on owners' investments, while not unduly jeopardizing the establishment's ability to pay creditors.

Debt-Equity Ratio

The **debt-equity ratio**, one of the commonest solvency ratios, compares the hospitality establishment's debt to its net worth (owners' equity). This ratio indicates the establishment's ability to withstand adversity and meet its long-term debt obligations. Figures from Exhibit 5.1 can be used to calculate the Grand Hotel's debt-equity ratio for 20X2:

$$\text{Debt-Equity Ratio} = \frac{\text{Total Liabilities}}{\text{Total Owners' Equity}}$$

$$= \frac{\$659,000}{\$517,300}$$

$$= \underline{1.27} \text{ to } 1$$

The Grand Hotel's debt-equity ratio of 1.27 to 1 at the end of 20X2 indicates for each $1 of owners' net worth, the Grand Hotel owed creditors $1.27. The debt-equity ratio for 20X1 for the Grand Hotel was 1.54 to 1. Thus, relative to its net worth, the Grand Hotel reduced its 20X1 debt.

Owners view this ratio similarly to the way they view the solvency ratio. That is, they desire to maximize their return on investment by using leverage. The greater the leverage, the higher the debt-equity ratio. Creditors generally would favor a lower debt-equity ratio because their risk is reduced as net worth increases relative to debt. Management, as with the solvency ratio, prefers a middle position between creditors and owners.

Long-Term Debt to Total Capitalization Ratio

Still another solvency ratio is **long-term debt to total capitalization ratio**, the calculation of long-term debt as a percentage of the sum of long-term debt and owners' equity, commonly called total capitalization. This ratio is similar to the debt-equity ratio except that current liabilities are excluded in the numerator, and long-term debt is added to the denominator of the debt-equity ratio. Current liabilities are excluded because current assets are normally adequate to cover them; therefore, they are not a long-term concern. Figures from Exhibit 5.1 can be used to calculate the 20X2 long-term debt to total capitalization ratio for the Grand Hotel:

$$\text{Long-Term Debt to Total Capitalization Ratio} = \frac{\text{Long-Term Debt}}{\text{Long-Term Debt and Owners' Equity}} \times 100$$

$$= \frac{\$445,000}{\$962,300} \times 100$$

$$= \underline{\underline{46.24\%}}$$

Long-term debt of the Grand Hotel at the end of 20X2 is 46.24 percent of its total capitalization. This can be compared to 51.88 percent at the end of 20X1. Creditors would prefer the lower percentage because it would indicate a reduced risk on their part. Owners, on the other hand, would prefer the higher percentage because of their desire for high returns through the use of leverage.

Number of Times Interest Earned Ratio

The **number of times interest earned ratio** is based on financial figures from the income statement and expresses the number of times interest expense can be covered. The greater the number of times interest is earned, the greater the safety afforded the creditors. Since interest is subtracted to determine taxable income, income taxes are added to net income and interest expense (earnings before interest and taxes, abbreviated as EBIT) to form the numerator of the ratio, while interest expense is the denominator. Figures from Exhibit 5.2 can be used to calculate the 20X2 number of times interest earned ratio for the Grand Hotel:

$$\text{Number of Times Interest Earned Ratio} = \frac{\text{EBIT}}{\text{Interest Expense}}$$

$$= \frac{\$304,500}{\$60,000}$$

$$= \underline{\underline{5.08}} \text{ times}$$

The result of 5.08 times shows that the Grand Hotel could cover its interest expense by over five times. The number of times interest earned ratio in 20X1 for the Grand Hotel was 5.36 times. This two-year trend suggests a slightly riskier position from a creditor's viewpoint. However, in general, a number of times interest earned ratio of greater than 4 reflects a sufficient amount of earnings for a hospitality enterprise to cover the interest expense of its existing debt.

All parties (owners, creditors, and management) prefer a relatively high ratio. Owners are generally less concerned about this ratio than creditors, as long as interest obligations are paid on a timely basis and leverage is working to their advantage. Creditors, especially lenders, also prefer a relatively high ratio, because this indicates that the establishment is able to meet its interest payments. To the lender, the higher this ratio, the better. Management also prefers a high ratio. However, since an extremely high ratio suggests leverage is probably not being optimized for the owners, management may prefer a lower ratio than do lenders.

The number of times interest earned ratio fails to consider fixed obligations other than interest expense. Many hospitality firms have long-term leases that require periodic payments similar to interest. This limitation of the number of times interest earned ratio is overcome by the fixed charge coverage ratio.

Fixed Charge Coverage Ratio

The **fixed charge coverage ratio** is a variation of the number of times interest earned ratio that considers leases as well as interest expense. Hospitality establishments that have obtained the use of property and equipment through leases may find the fixed charge coverage ratio to be more useful than the number of times interest earned ratio. This ratio is calculated the same as the number of times interest earned ratio, except that lease expense (rent expense) is added to both the numerator and denominator of the equation.

Exhibit 5.9 uses figures from Exhibit 5.2 to calculate the 20X2 fixed charge coverage ratio for the Grand Hotel. The result indicates that earnings prior to lease expense, interest expense, and income taxes cover lease and interest expense 4.06 times. The Grand Hotel's fixed charge coverage ratio for 20X1 was 4.18 times. The change of 0.12 times reflects a minor decrease in the Grand Hotel's ability to cover its fixed costs of interest and lease expense. The viewpoints of owners, creditors, and management are similar to the views they hold regarding changes in the number of times interest earned ratio.

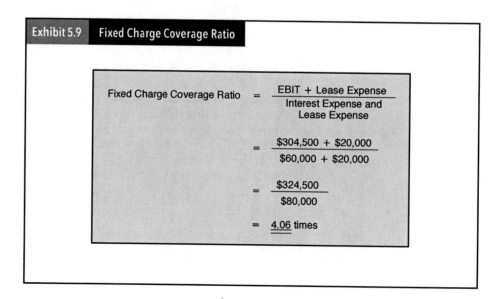

Exhibit 5.9   Fixed Charge Coverage Ratio

$$\text{Fixed Charge Coverage Ratio} = \frac{\text{EBIT} + \text{Lease Expense}}{\text{Interest Expense and Lease Expense}}$$

$$= \frac{\$304,500 + \$20,000}{\$60,000 + \$20,000}$$

$$= \frac{\$324,500}{\$80,000}$$

$$= \underline{4.06}\ \text{times}$$

Debt Service Coverage Ratio

The **debt service coverage ratio** measures the extent to which a property generates sufficient adjusted net operating income (net operating income less cash transfers to replacement reserves) to cover its debt obligations, including both interest and principal payments.

The ratio is calculated as follows:

$$\text{Debt Service Coverage Ratio} = \frac{\text{Net Operating Income} - \text{Cash Transfers to Replacement Reserves}}{\text{Debt Service Payment}}$$

Figures from Exhibits 5.2 and 5.3 are used to calculate the 20X2 debt service coverage ratio for the Grand Hotel in Exhibit 5.10. The result for 20X2 indicates that the debt payment could be made 3.74 times. This is a slight improvement over the debt service coverage ratio of 3.62 times for 20X1. All users of financial information prefer this ratio to be relatively high.

Operating Cash Flows to Total Liabilities Ratio

The final solvency ratio presented in this chapter, the **operating cash flows to total liabilities ratio**, uses figures from both the statement of cash flows and the balance sheet by comparing operating cash flows to average total liabilities. Both the debt-equity and long-term debt to total capitalization ratios are based on static numbers from the balance sheet. This ratio overcomes the deficiency of using debt at a point in time by considering cash flow for a period of time.

Figures from Exhibits 5.1 and 5.3 are used to calculate the 20X2 operating cash flows to total liabilities ratio for the Grand Hotel as follows:

$$\begin{aligned} \text{Operating Cash Flows to Total Liabilities Ratio} &= \frac{\text{Operating Cash Flows}}{\text{Average Total Liabilities}} \\ &= \frac{\$179,200}{0.5(\$645,000 + \$659,000)} \\ &= 0.275 \text{ or } \underline{27.5\%} \end{aligned}$$

Exhibit 5.10 Debt Service Coverage Ratio

$$\text{Debt Service Coverage Ratio} = \frac{\text{Net Operating Income Cash Transfers to Replacement Reserves}}{\text{Debt Service Payment}}$$

$$\text{Debt Service Coverage Ratio} = \frac{\$304,500^*}{\$81,500^{**}} = \underline{3.74} \text{ times}$$

*   Since the Grand Hotel is not managed by a management company, there is no required cash transfer to replacement reserves so only net operating income from Exhibit 2 is used.

** This includes both the interest expense of $60,000 (Exhibit 2) and the reduction in long-term debt of $21,500 (Exhibit 3).

The 20X1 operating cash flows to total liabilities ratio is 34.4 percent; thus, the Grand Hotel's ability to meet its long-term obligations with operating cash flows has deteriorated from 20X1 to 20X2.

All users of financial information prefer this ratio to be relatively high; that is, the cash flow from operations should be high relative to total liabilities, given that the amount of debt used is optimal.

5.7 ACTIVITY RATIOS

Activity ratios measure management's effectiveness in using its resources. Management is entrusted with inventory and fixed assets (and other resources) to generate earnings for owners while providing products and services to guests. Since the fixed assets of most lodging facilities constitute a large percentage of the operation's total assets, it is essential to use these resources effectively. Although inventory is generally not a significant portion of total assets, management must adequately control it in order to minimize the cost of sales.

Inventory Turnover

The **inventory turnover** shows how quickly the inventory is being used. All things being the same, generally, the quicker the inventory turnover the better because inventory can be expensive to maintain. Maintenance costs include storage space, freezers, insurance, personnel expense, recordkeeping, and, of course, the opportunity cost of the funds tied up in inventory. Inventories held by hospitality operations are highly susceptible to theft and must be carefully controlled.

Inventory turnovers should generally be calculated separately for food supplies and for beverages. Some foodservice operations will calculate several beverage turnovers based on the types of beverages available.

Exhibit 5.11 is a condensed food and beverage department statement of the Grand Hotel, with food and beverage operations for 20X2 shown separately. Figures from this statement will be used to illustrate the food and beverage turnover ratios.

Exhibit 5.12 shows the calculation of the 20X2 food inventory turnover for the Grand Hotel. The food inventory turned over 12.2 times during 20X2, or approximately once per month. The speed of food inventory turnover generally depends on the type of foodservice operation. A quick-service restaurant generally experiences a much faster food turnover than does a fine-dining establishment. In fact, a quick-service restaurant may have a food inventory turnover in excess of 200 times for a year. A norm used in the hotel industry for hotels that have several different types of restaurants and banquets calls for food inventory to turn over four times per month.

Although a high food inventory turnover is desired because it means that the foodservice establishment is able to operate with a relatively small investment in inventory, too high a turnover may indicate possible stockout problems. Failure to provide desired food items to guests may not only immediately result in disappointed guests but may also result in negative goodwill if this problem persists. Too low of an inventory turnover suggests that food is overstocked, and, in addition to the costs to maintain inventory previously mentioned, the cost of spoilage may become a problem.

Exhibit 5.13 uses figures from Exhibit 5.11 to calculate the 20X2 beverage turnover for the Grand Hotel. The beverage turnover of 4.67 means that the beverage inventory of $6,000 required restocking approximately every 78 days. This is calculated by dividing 365 days in the year by the beverage turnover

Exhibit 5.11 Condensed Food and Beverage Department Statement

Condensed Food and Beverage Department Statement
Grand Hotel
For the year 20X2

	Food	Beverage
Sales	$ 300,000	$ 145,000
Cost of sales:		
Beginning inventory	11,000	6,000
Purchases	120,000	28,000
Less: Ending inventory	9,000	6,000
Cost of goods used	122,000	28,000
Less: Employee meals	2,000	0
Cost of goods sold	120,000	28,000
Gross Profit	180,000	117,000
Expenses:		
Payroll and related expenses	135,000	45,000
Other expenses	30,000	15,000
Total expenses	165,000	60,000
Departmental income	$ 15,000	$ 57,000

Exhibit 5.12 Food Inventory Turnover

$$\text{Food Inventory Turnover} = \frac{\text{Cost of Food Used}}{\text{Average Food Inventory*}}$$

$$= \frac{\$122,000}{\$10,000}$$

$$= 12.2 \text{ times}$$

$$\text{*Average Food Inventory} = \frac{\text{Beginning and Ending Inventories}}{2}$$

$$= \frac{\$11,000 + \$9,000}{2}$$

$$= \$10,000$$

---

of 4.67. Not all beverage items are sold evenly; thus, some items would have to be restocked more frequently. A norm used in the hotel industry for hotels having several different types of lounges and banquets calls for beverage inventory to turn over 1.25 times per month or 15 times per year.

All parties (owners, creditors, and management) prefer high inventory turnovers to low ones, as long as stockouts are avoided. Ideally, as the last inventory item is sold, the shelves are being restocked.

Exhibit 5.13   Beverage Turnover

$$\text{Beverage Turnover} = \frac{\text{Cost of Beverages Used}}{\text{Average Beverage Inventory*}}$$

$$= \frac{\$28,000}{\$6,000}$$

$$= \underline{4.67} \text{ times}$$

$$\text{*Average Beverage Inventory} = \frac{\text{Beginning and Ending Inventories}}{2}$$

$$= \frac{\$6,000 + \$6,000}{2}$$

$$= \$6,000$$

Property and Equipment Turnover

The **property and equipment turnover** (sometimes called the fixed asset turnover) is determined by dividing average total property and equipment into total revenue for the period. A more precise measurement would be to use only revenues related to property and equipment usage in the numerator. However, revenue by source is not available to many financial analysts, so total revenue is generally used.

This ratio measures management's effectiveness in using property and equipment. A high turnover suggests the hospitality enterprise is using its property and equipment effectively to generate revenues, while a low turnover suggests the establishment is not making effective use of its property and equipment and should consider disposing of part of them.

A limitation of this ratio is that it places a premium on using older (depreciated) property and equipment, since their book value is low. Further, this ratio is affected by the depreciation method employed by the hospitality operation. For example, an operation using an accelerated method of depreciation will show a higher turnover than an operation using the straight-line depreciation method, all other factors being the same.

Exhibit 5.14 uses figures from Exhibits 5.1 and 5.2 to calculate the 20X2 property and equipment turnover ratio for the Grand Hotel. The turnover of 1.73 reveals that revenue was 1.73 times the average total property and equipment. For 20X1, the Grand Hotel's property and equipment turnover was 1.65 times. The change of 0.08 times, although fairly minor, is viewed as a positive trend.

All parties (owners, creditors, and management) prefer a high property and equipment turnover. Management, however, should resist retaining old and possibly inefficient property and equipment, even though they result in a high property and equipment turnover. The return on assets ratio (discussed under profitability ratios) is a partial check against this practice.

Exhibit 5.14   Property and Equipment Turnover

$$\text{Property and Equipment Turnover} = \frac{\text{Total Revenue}}{\text{Average Property and Equipment*}}$$

$$= \frac{\$1,352,000}{\$782,000}$$

$$= \underline{1.73} \text{ times}$$

$$\text{*Average Property and Equipment} = \frac{\text{Total Property and Equipment at Beginning and End of Year}}{2}$$

$$= \frac{\$788,500 + \$775,500}{2}$$

$$= \$782,000$$

Asset Turnover

Another ratio to measure the efficiency of management's use of assets is the **asset turnover**. It is calculated by dividing total revenue by average total assets. The two previous ratios presented, inventory turnover and property and equipment turnover, concern a large percentage of the total assets. The asset turnover examines the use of total assets in relation to total revenue. Limitations of the property and equipment ratio are also inherent in this ratio to the extent that property and equipment make up total assets. For most hospitality establishments, especially lodging businesses, property and equipment constitute the majority of the operation's total assets.

Exhibit 5.15 uses figures from Exhibits 5.1 and 5.2 to calculate the 20X2 asset turnover ratio for the Grand Hotel. The asset turnover of 1.21 indicates that each $1 of assets generated $1.21 of revenue in 20X2. The asset turnover ratio for 20X1 was 1.23. Thus, there was virtually no change for the two years.

As with the property and equipment turnover, all concerned parties (owners, creditors, and management) prefer this ratio to be high, because a high ratio means effective use of assets by management, subject to the limitations of using old (depreciated) assets as discussed previously.

Both the property and equipment turnover and the asset turnover ratios are relatively low for most hospitality segments, especially for hotels and motels. The relatively low ratios are due to the hospitality industry's high dependence on fixed assets and its inability to quickly increase output to meet maximum demand. It is common for many hotels and motels to turn away guests four nights per week due to excessive demand, and operate at an extremely low level of output (less than 50 percent) the three remaining nights.

Five additional measures of management's ability to efficiently use available assets are paid occupancy percentage, complimentary occupancy, average occupancy per room, multiple occupancy, and seat turnover. Although these ratios are not based on financial information, they are viewed as excellent measures of management's effectiveness in selling space, whether it be rooms in a lodging facility or seats in a foodservice establishment.

Paid Occupancy Percentage

Paid occupancy is a major indicator of management's success in selling its "product." It refers to the percentage of rooms sold in relation to rooms available

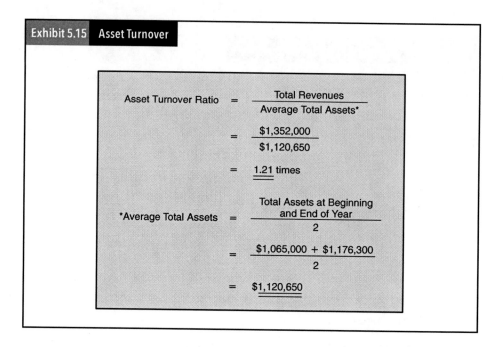

Exhibit 5.15 Asset Turnover

$$\text{Asset Turnover Ratio} = \frac{\text{Total Revenues}}{\text{Average Total Assets*}}$$

$$= \frac{\$1,352,000}{\$1,120,650}$$

$$= \underline{1.21 \text{ times}}$$

$$\text{*Average Total Assets} = \frac{\text{Total Assets at Beginning and End of Year}}{2}$$

$$= \frac{\$1,065,000 + \$1,176,300}{2}$$

$$= \underline{\$1,120,650}$$

for sale in hotels and motels. In foodservice operations, it is commonly referred to as seat turnover, and is calculated by dividing the number of people served by the number of seats available. Seat turnover is commonly calculated by meal period. In most foodservice facilities, different seat turnovers are experienced for different dining periods. The occupancy percentage for lodging facilities and the seat turnovers for foodservice facilities are key measures of facility utilization.

Using the "Other Information" listed in Exhibit 5.4, the annual paid occupancy of the Grand Hotel can be determined by dividing total paid rooms occupied by available rooms for sale. If the Grand Hotel had 80 rooms available for sale each day, its paid occupancy percentage for 20X2 is calculated as indicated in Exhibit 5.16.

Exhibit 5.16 Paid Occupancy Percentage

$$\text{Paid Occupancy} = \frac{\text{Paid Rooms Occupied}}{\text{Available Rooms*}}$$

$$= \frac{21,000}{29,200}$$

$$= \underline{71.92\%}$$

$$\text{*Available Rooms} = \text{Rooms Available per Day} \times 365 \text{ Days}$$

$$= 80 \times 365$$

$$= \underline{29,200}$$

The Grand Hotel's 20X2 annual paid occupancy percentage of 71.92 percent was an improvement over the 20X1 annual occupancy percentage of 70.21 percent, when 20,500 rooms were sold. This percentage does not mean that every day 70.21 percent of the available rooms were sold, but rather that on the average 70.21 percent were sold. For example, a hotel experiencing 100 percent paid occupancy Monday through Thursday and 33 percent paid occupancy Friday through Sunday would end up with a combined result of 71.29 percent.

There are many factors affecting paid occupancy rates in the lodging industry, such as location within an area, geographic location, seasonal factors (both weekly and yearly), rate structure, and type of lodging facility, to mention a few.

Among other uses, the paid occupancy percentage allows hotel operators to track their operating results by computing their hotel's market penetration. The calculation of market penetration also depends on something called market share. *Market share* refers to the number of rooms in a hotel calculated as a percentage of the total rooms in the hotel's market set—that is, the total number of rooms available within a hotel's market area. Assume the Brymon Lodge has 100 rooms and directly competes with four other lodging properties with a total of 900 rooms. Thus, the market set has 1,000 rooms and the market share for the Brymon Lodge would be 10 percent. If research shows that the market set has an aggregate occupancy of 65 percent, then, on a daily basis, an average of 650 rooms are sold by hotels in that market set. The market share on a daily basis for the Brymon Lodge would be 65 rooms per day.

Market penetration is the percentage of demand for rooms for a hotel within a particular market set. It is calculated by dividing the total rooms occupied in the hotel by that hotel's fair share of demand. For example, assume that for the month of June, the Brymon Lodge sold 1,860 rooms. The fair share for June for the Brymon Lodge is 1,950 rooms, determined by multiplying the 10 percent market share of 650 rooms by 30 days. The Brymon Lodge's June sales of 1,860 rooms are only 95.38 percent (1,860 rooms divided by 1,950 rooms) of its fair share of demand.

The result for the Brymon Lodge is likely unacceptable. Hotels strive to equal or exceed their competitors and achieve a market penetration of 100 percent or better. What could have gone wrong? There could be many factors, including:

- Location
- Wrong franchise
- Wrong data regarding the market set
- Lack of marketing effort
- Lack of sales effort
- Wrong amenity mix
- Reputation problems

Complimentary Occupancy

Complimentary occupancy, as stated in the *Uniform System of Accounts for the Lodging Industry*, is determined by dividing the number of complimentary rooms for a period by the number of rooms available. Using figures from the "Other Information" section of Exhibit 5.4, the 20X2 complimentary occupancy for the Grand Hotel is calculated as follows:

$$\text{Complimentary Occupancy} = \frac{\text{Complimentary Rooms}}{\text{Rooms Available}} \times 100$$

$$= \frac{160}{29,200} \times 100$$

$$= \underline{\underline{0.55\%}}$$

Average Occupancy per Room

Another ratio to measure management's ability to use the lodging facilities is the **average occupancy per room** ratio. This ratio is the result of dividing the number of guests by the number of rooms occupied. Generally, as the average occupancy per room increases, the room rate also increases.

Using figures from the "Other Information" section of Exhibit 5.4, the 20X2 average occupancy per room for the Grand Hotel can be calculated as follows:

$$\text{Average Occupancy per Room} = \frac{\text{Number of Guests}}{\text{Number of Rooms Occupied by Guests}}$$

$$= \frac{24,160}{21,160}$$

$$= \underline{\underline{1.14}} \text{ guests}$$

The Grand Hotel's 20X2 average occupancy per room was 1.14 guests. The 20X1 average occupancy per room was slightly higher at 1.15 guests.

The average occupancy per room is generally the highest for resort properties, where it can reach levels in excess of two guests per room and is lowest for transient lodging facilities.

Multiple Occupancy

Another ratio used to measure multiple occupancy of rooms is **multiple occupancy**, sometimes less accurately called **double occupancy**. This ratio is similar to the average occupancy per room. It is determined by dividing the number of rooms occupied by more than one guest by the number of rooms occupied by guests.

Using figures from the "Other Information" section of Exhibit 5.4, the multiple occupancy of the Grand Hotel for 20X2 can be calculated as follows:

$$\text{Multiple Occupancy} = \frac{\text{Rooms Occupied by Two or More People}}{\text{Rooms Occupied by Guests}} \times 100$$

$$= \frac{2,500}{21,160} \times 100$$

$$= \underline{\underline{11.81\%}}$$

The multiple occupancy for the Grand Hotel during 20X2 indicates 11.81 percent of the rooms sold were occupied by more than one guest. The 20X1 multiple occupancy for the Grand Hotel was 11.62 percent; therefore, a minor increase in multiple occupancy has occurred.

Owners, creditors, and management all prefer high occupancy ratios—paid occupancy percentage, average occupancy per room, and multiple occupancy.

The higher the occupancy ratios, the greater the use of the facilities. These ratios are considered to be prime indicators of a lodging facility's level of operations. Occupancy ratios are generally computed on a daily basis and are recorded on the daily report of operations.

Seat Turnover

A nonfinancial ratio used to measure the "occupancy" of a foodservice facility is **seat turnover**. The greater the seat turnover, the greater the use of the foodservice facility. This ratio is calculated by dividing the number of people served (sometimes called *covers*) by the number of seats in the foodservice facility. Assume the Grand Hotel has a single foodservice outlet with 100 seats. Assume further that the 56,000 customers (see Exhibit 5.4) in 20X2 were served in the 100-seat facility. The 20X2 seat turnover is calculated as follows:

$$\text{Food Service Seat Turnover} = \frac{\text{Customers Served in 20X2}}{\text{Number of Seats} \times \text{Number of Days Open}}$$

$$= \frac{56,000}{100 \times 365}$$

$$= \underline{\underline{1.53}} \text{ times}$$

The seat turnover of 1.53 means that each seat was "used" 1.53 times during the measured unit or period (in this case, per day). This compares favorably to the facility's seat turnover of 1.52 times for 20X1. Seat turnover would be computed for each meal period each day.

Of course, to compute and use the seat turnover ratio, foodservice operations must track the actual number of customers served. This can be more complex than it sounds, because it often is *not* simply a matter of counting every customer. Managers must define what the operation considers to be a customer. Must a customer purchase a full meal? Is someone who orders only a cup of coffee or only a dessert counted as a customer? The definition of a customer may even vary by meal period. The results of seat turnover calculations will depend on the definition chosen.

5.8 PROFITABILITY RATIOS

Profitability ratios reflect the results of all areas of management's responsibilities. All the information conveyed by liquidity, solvency, and activity ratios affect the profitability of the hospitality enterprise. The primary purpose of most hospitality operations is the generation of profit. Owners invest for the purpose of increasing their wealth through dividends and through increases in the price of capital stock. Both dividends and stock price are highly dependent on the profits generated by the operation. Creditors, especially lenders, provide resources for hospitality enterprises to use in the provision of services. Generally, future profits are required to repay these lenders. Managers are also extremely interested in profits because their performance is, to a large degree, measured by the operation's bottom line. Excellent services breed goodwill, repeat customers, and other benefits that ultimately increase the operation's profitability.

The profitability ratios we are about to consider measure management's overall effectiveness as shown by returns on sales (profit margin and operating efficiency ratio), returns on assets (return on assets and gross return on assets), return on owners' equity (return on owners' equity and return on common stockholders' equity), the relationship between net income and the market price of the hospitality establishment's stock (price earnings ratio), and the relationships between **EBITDA** (earnings before interest, taxes, depreciation, and amortization) and total operating revenues (EBITDA margin ratio) and available rooms.

Profit Margin

Hospitality enterprises are often evaluated in terms of their ability to generate profits on sales. **Profit margin**, a key ratio, is determined by dividing net income by total revenue. It is an overall measurement of management's ability to generate sales and control expenses, thus yielding the bottom line. In this ratio, net income is the income remaining after all expenses have been deducted, both those controllable by management and those directly related to decisions made by the board of directors.

Using figures from Exhibit 5.2, the 20X2 profit margin of the Grand Hotel can be determined as follows:

$$\text{Profit Margin} = \frac{\text{Net Income}}{\text{Total Revenue}} \times 100$$

$$= \frac{\$146,700}{\$1,352,000} \times 100$$

$$= \underline{\underline{10.85\%}}$$

The Grand Hotel's 20X2 profit margin of 10.85 percent has remained nearly constant from the 20X1 figure of 10.87 percent.

If the profit margin is lower than expected, then expenses and other areas should be reviewed. Poor pricing and low sales volume could be contributing to the low ratio. To identify the problem area, management should analyze both the overall profit margin and the operated departmental margins. If the operated departmental margins are satisfactory, the problem would appear to be with overhead expense.

Operating Efficiency Ratio

The **operating efficiency ratio** (also known as the **gross operating profit margin ratio**) is a better measure of management's performance than the profit margin. This ratio is the result of dividing gross operating profit by total revenue. Gross operating profit is the result of subtracting expenses generally controllable by management from revenues. Nonoperating expenses include management fees and fixed charges. These expenses are directly related to decisions made by the board of directors, not management. Fixed charges are expenses relating to the capacity of the hospitality firm, including rent, property taxes, insurance, and depreciation. Although these expenses are the result of board of directors' decisions and thus beyond the direct control of active management, management can and should review tax assessments and insurance policies and quotations, and make recommendations to the board of directors that can affect the facility's total profitability. In calculating the operating efficiency ratio, interest expense and income taxes are also excluded, since these are beyond the control of management. Using figures from Exhibit 5.2, the 20X2 operating efficiency ratio of the Grand Hotel can be calculated as follows:

$$\text{Operating Efficiency Ratio} = \frac{\text{Gross Operating Profit}}{\text{Total Revenue}} \times 100$$

$$= \frac{\$415,500}{\$1,352,000} \times 100$$

$$= \underline{30.73\%}$$

The operating efficiency ratio shows that nearly \$0.31 of each \$1 of revenue is available for fixed charges, interest expense, income taxes, and profits. The Grand Hotel's operating efficiency ratio was 30.39 percent for 20X1.

The next group of profitability ratios compares profits to either assets or owners' equity. The result in each case is a percentage and is commonly called a return.

Gross Operating Profit per Available Room

Gross operating profit per available room (GOPAR or GOPPAR) measures management's ability to produce profits by generating sales and controlling the operating expenses over which they have the most control. GOPAR is determined as follows:

$$\text{GOPAR} = \frac{\text{Gross Operating Profit}}{\text{Number of Available Rooms}}$$

This ratio may be useful in relating gross operating profits on a proportional basis across properties within a competitive set of comparable property groups. Because GOPAR is calculated before any deduction for management fees, this ratio can be used to compare comparable properties that are operated by a third-party management company with owner-operated properties.

Using figures from Exhibits 5.2 and 5.16, the Grand Hotel's 20X2 GOPAR is \$14.23 (\$415,500 ÷ 29,200). This compares favorably with its GOPAR for 20X1 of \$13.53.

EBITDA Margin Ratio

As discussed in the *USALI*, the **EBITDA margin ratio** measures management's overall ability to produce profits by generating revenue and controlling all operated department expenses, undistributed operating expenses, management fees, and nonoperating income and expenses. This ratio is calculated by dividing EBITDA by total revenue:

$$\text{EBITDA Margin Ratio} = \frac{\text{EBITDA}}{\text{Total Revenue}}$$

Using figures from Exhibit 5.2, the Grand Hotel's 20X2 EBITDA margin ratio is 27.03 percent (\$365,500 ÷ \$1,352,000). This is a slight increase over the 20X1 EBITDA margin ratio of 26.89 percent (\$349,600 ÷ \$1,300,000).

EBITDA per Available Room

EBITDA per available room is similar to the EBITDA margin ratio except that it measures the monetary amount of EBITDA in terms of the number of available rooms. As with the EBITDA margin ratio, it reveals management's ability to generate revenues and control expenses.

For the Grand Hotel, the EBITDA per available room was $12.52 for 20X2 ($365,500 ÷ 29,200) and $11.97 for 20X1 ($349,600 ÷ 29,200). This represents an increase of $0.55 from 20X1 to 20X2.

Return on Assets

The **return on assets (ROA)** ratio is a general indicator of the profitability of the hospitality enterprise's assets. Unlike profit margin, operating efficiency, gross operating profit, and EBITDA that draw only from income statement data, this ratio compares bottom-line profits to the total investment, that is, to the total assets. It is calculated by dividing net income by average total assets. This ratio, or a variation of it, is used by several large conglomerates to measure the performances of their subsidiary corporations operating in the hospitality industry.

Using figures from Exhibits 5.1 and 5.2, the Grand Hotel's 20X2 return on assets is calculated in Exhibit 5.17. The Grand Hotel's 20X2 ROA is 13.09 percent, which means there was 13.09 cents of profit for every dollar of average total assets. The 20X1 ROA was 13.36 percent. Therefore, there was a slight decline in ROA from 20X1 to 20X2.

A very low ROA may result from inadequate profits or excessive assets. A very high ROA may suggest that older assets require replacement in the near future or that additional assets need to be added to support growth in revenues. The determination of low and high is usually based on industry averages and the hospitality establishment's own ROA profile that is developed over time.

ROA may also be calculated by multiplying the profit margin ratio by the asset turnover ratio:

$$\text{Profit Margin} \times \text{Asset Turnover} = \text{ROA}$$

$$\frac{\text{Net Income}}{\text{Total Revenue}} \times \frac{\text{Total Revenue}}{\text{Average Total Assets}} = \frac{\text{Net Income}}{\text{Average Total Assets}}$$

Gross Return on Assets

Calculating the **gross return on assets (GROA)** is a variation of the ROA. This ratio measures the rate of return on assets regardless of financing methods. The

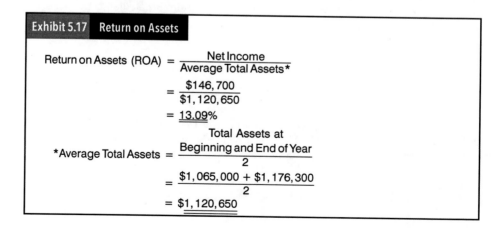

Exhibit 5.17   Return on Assets

$$\text{Return on Assets (ROA)} = \frac{\text{Net Income}}{\text{Average Total Assets*}}$$

$$= \frac{\$146,700}{\$1,120,650}$$

$$= \underline{13.09\%}$$

$$\text{*Average Total Assets} = \frac{\text{Total Assets at Beginning and End of Year}}{2}$$

$$= \frac{\$1,065,000 + \$1,176,300}{2}$$

$$= \underline{\$1,120,650}$$

calculation of ROA uses net income as its numerator and, therefore, includes the cost of debt financing of the assets. The computation of the GROA, on the other hand, ignores any debt financing by using income before interest and income taxes (EBIT)—also known as net operating income—as its numerator. Interest is excluded because it is a financing cost. Income taxes are not considered because interest expense is deductible in calculating the operation's tax liability.

Using figures from Exhibits 5.1 and 5.2, the Grand Hotel's GROA for 20X2 can be calculated as follows:

$$\text{Gross Return on Assets} = \frac{\text{EBIT [Net Operating Income]}}{\text{Average Total Assets}} \times 100$$

$$= \frac{\$304,500}{\$1,120,650} \times 100$$

$$= \underline{\underline{27.17\%}}$$

The Grand Hotel's GROA of 27.17 percent indicates a gross return of 27.17 cents for each dollar of average total assets for 20X2. This is a slight decline from 20X1, when GROA was 27.39 percent.

Return on Owners' Equity

A key profitability ratio is the **return on owners' equity (ROE)**. The ROE ratio compares the profits of the hospitality enterprise to the owners' investment. It is calculated by dividing net income by average owners' equity. Included in the denominator are all capital stock and retained earnings.

Exhibit 5.18 uses relevant figures from Exhibits 5.1 and 5.2 to calculate the 20X2 ROE for the Grand Hotel. In 20X2, for every one dollar of owners' equity, 31.30 cents was earned. The 20X1 ROE for the Grand Hotel was even higher, at 34.46 percent. To the owner, this ratio represents the end result of all management's efforts. The ROE reflects management's ability to produce for the owners.

An alternative calculation of ROE considers both ROA and average total assets to average owners' equity. For 20X2, the calculation for the Grand Hotel is as follows:

$$\text{ROE} = \text{ROA} \times \frac{\text{Average Total Assets}}{\text{Average Total Owners' Equity}}$$

$$= 13.09\% \times \frac{\$1,120,650}{\$468,650}$$

$$= \underline{\underline{31.30\%}}$$

Thus, the lower the owners' equity relative to total assets (i.e., the greater the financial leverage), the greater the ROE.

Return on Common Stockholders' Equity

A few hospitality enterprises have issued preferred stock in addition to common stock. When preferred stock has been issued, a variation of the ROE is the **return on common stockholders' equity**. It is necessary to compute this ratio only when more than one class of stock has been issued. Common stockholders are

Return on Owners' Equity

$$\text{Return on Owner's Equity (ROE)} = \frac{\text{Net Income}}{\text{Average Owner's Equity*}} \times 100$$

$$= \frac{\$146,700}{\$468,650} \times 100$$

$$= \underline{31.30\%}$$

$$\text{*Average Owners' Equity} = \frac{\text{Owners' Equity at Beginning and End of Year}}{2}$$

$$= \frac{\$420,000 + \$517,300}{2}$$

$$= \underline{\$468,650}$$

concerned with what is available to them—net income less preferred dividends paid to preferred stockholders. The ROE ratio is adjusted as follows:

$$\text{Return on Common Stockholders' Equity} = \frac{\text{Net Income} - \text{Preferred Dividends}}{\text{Average Common Stockholders' Equity}}$$

Since the Grand Hotel has not issued preferred stock, the calculation of this ratio is not further illustrated because it would be the same as the previously calculated ROE.

The return to common stockholders is enhanced with the issuance of preferred stock when the return on investment from the use of the preferred stockholders' funds exceeds the dividends paid to preferred stockholders. From a common stockholder's viewpoint, any time debt or preferred stock can be issued at a "cost" less than the return from investing these "outside funds," the return to common stockholders is increased.

Earnings per Share

A common profitability ratio shown on hospitality establishments' income statements issued to external users is **earnings per share (EPS)**. The EPS calculation is a function of the capital structure of the hospitality enterprise. If only common stock has been issued (i.e., there are no preferred stock or convertible debt or similar dilutive securities), then EPS is determined by dividing net income by the average common shares outstanding. When preferred stock has been issued, preferred dividends are subtracted from net income and the result is divided by the average number of common shares outstanding. If any dilutive securities have been issued, the EPS calculation is much more difficult and is beyond the scope of this chapter.[2]

Using figures from Exhibits 5.2 and 5.4, the 20X2 EPS for the Grand Hotel can be calculated as follows:

$$\text{Earnings per Share} = \frac{\text{Net Income}}{\text{Average Common Shares Outstanding}}$$

$$= \frac{\$146,700}{55,000}$$

$$= \underline{\$2.67} \text{ per share}$$

In 20X1, the Grand Hotel's EPS was $2.57. Thus, the Grand Hotel's EPS has increased by $0.10 from 20X1 to 20X2.

An increase in EPS must be viewed cautiously. The reduction of common stock outstanding by the issuing establishment's purchase of its own stock (treasury stock) will also result in an increased EPS, all other things being equal. Further, EPS is expected to increase as a hospitality enterprise reinvests earnings in its operations because a larger profit can then be generated without a corresponding increase in shares outstanding.

Price/Earnings Ratio

Financial analysts often use the **price/earnings (PE) ratio** in presenting investment possibilities in hospitality enterprises. The PE ratio is shown daily in the *Wall Street Journal* for many stocks listed on the New York Stock Exchange. It is computed by dividing the market price per share by the EPS.

Assume that the market price per share of the Grand Hotel is $25 at the end of 20X2. The PE ratio for the Grand Hotel at the end of 20X2 is calculated as follows:

$$
\text{Price/Earnings Ratio} = \frac{\text{Market Price per Share}}{\text{Earnings per Share}}
$$
$$
= \frac{\$25}{\$2.67}
$$
$$
= \underline{\underline{9.36}}
$$

The Grand Hotel's PE ratio of 9.36 indicates that if the 20X2 EPS is maintained, it would take 9.36 years for earnings to equal the market price per share at the end of 20X2.

The PE ratio for different hospitality enterprises may vary significantly. Factors affecting these differences include relative risk, stability of earnings, perceived earnings trend, and perceived growth potential of the stock.

Viewpoints Regarding Profitability Ratios

Owners, creditors, and management obviously prefer high profitability ratios. Owners prefer high profitability ratios because they indicate good returns from their investments. They are most concerned about ROE (return on common stockholders' equity if preferred stock has been issued) because ROE measures the precise return on their investments. Although other profitability measures are important to the owner, the ROE is the "bottom line." Other profitability ratios may be relatively low and the ROE may still be excellent. For example, the profit margin could be only 2 percent, but the ROE could be 20 percent, based on the following:

Sales	$ 100
Net Income	$ 2
Owners' Equity	$ 10
Profit Margin	2%
ROE	20%

If the profitability ratios are not as high as other available investments (with similar risks), stockholders may become dissatisfied and eventually move their funds to other investments. This move, if not checked, will result in lower stock prices, and may pose difficulties for the hospitality enterprise when it desires to raise funds externally.

Creditors also prefer high, stable, or even growing profitability ratios. Although they desire stockholders to receive an excellent return (as measured by ROE), they will look more to the ROA ratio because this ratio considers all assets, not simply claims to a portion of the assets as does ROE. A high and growing ROA represents financial safety and, further, indicates competent management. A high ROA also generally means high profits and cash flow, which suggests safety to the creditor and low risk to the lender.

Managers must keep both creditors and owners happy. Therefore, all profitability ratios are especially important to them. Everything else being the same, the higher the profitability ratios, the better. High ratios also indicate that management is performing effectively and efficiently.

Profitability Evaluation of Segments

In chain operations, hotel managers may be evaluated based on the ROA of their individual hotels. A hotel manager may hesitate to replace inefficient equipment with new, more efficient equipment because the replacement may lower income and ROA through an increased asset base and increased depreciation. Rather than using ROA to evaluate the performance of individual hotels, corporate headquarters should consider using **residual income** as an alternative measure. Simply stated, residual income is the excess of a hotel's net income over a minimum return set by the holding company. The minimum return is calculated as a percentage of the hotel's asset base. When residual income is the basis of hotel management performance evaluation, hotel managers are encouraged to maximize residual income rather than ROA.

To illustrate this concept, assume that A&B Corporation owns two hotels— Hotel A and Hotel B—and requires a 10 percent return on Hotel A's average total assets. Further assume that Hotel A has $5 million of average assets and generates net income of $600,000. The residual income of $100,000 is determined as follows:

Hotel A's net income	$ 600,000
Less: Minimum required return:	
$5,000,000 × 0.10	(500,000)
Residual Income	$ 100,000

Now let us assume for purposes of illustration that Hotel B is evaluated on its residual income base, while Hotel A is evaluated on an ROA of 10 percent. Further assume that each hotel is earning an ROA of 12 percent prior to proposed rooms expansions at the beginning of the year, costing $1 million each, which are expected to yield $110,000 at each property.

If Hotel A makes the $1 million investment and $110,000 of profits are earned (which is an 11 percent return), Hotel A's ROA will slip from 12 percent to 11.83 percent as shown in Exhibit 5.19. It appears that Hotel A's manager performance is lower. Therefore, since Hotel A's manager is evaluated based on ROA, he or she probably will reject the expansion opportunity, even though overall profits would be increased.

On the other hand, Hotel B's general manager, being evaluated on residual income, would welcome the expansion opportunity since the residual income for Hotel B increases by $10,000 as shown in Exhibit 5.19.

Exhibit 5.19   Investment Evaluations: ROA versus Residual Income

Hotel A	Current	Proposed	Total
Net Income	$600,000	$110,000	$710,000
Average Total Assets	$5,000,000	$1,000,000	$6,000,000
ROA	12%	11%	11.83%
Hotel B			
Average Total Assets	$4,000,000	$1,000,000	$ 5,000,000
Net income	$ 480,000	$ 110,000	$ 590,000
Minimum required return (0.10 × avg. total assets)	(400,000)	(100,000)	(500,000)
Residual income	$ 80,000	$ 10,000	$ 90,000

Although residual income appears to resolve the problem of evaluating managers using ROA, its major disadvantage is that it cannot be used to compare the performance of hospitality operations of different sizes.

5.9 OPERATING RATIOS

Operating ratios assist management in analyzing the operations of a hospitality establishment. Detailed information necessary for computing these ratios is normally not available to creditors or even owners not actively involved in management. These ratios reflect the actual mix of sales (revenues) and make possible comparisons to sales mix objectives. Further, operating ratios relate expenses to revenues and are useful for control purposes. For example, food cost percentage is calculated and compared to the budgeted food cost percentage to evaluate the overall control of food costs. Any significant deviation is investigated to determine the cause(s) for the variation between actual results and planned goals.

There are literally hundreds of operating ratios that could be calculated. Consider the following:

■ Departmental revenues as a percentage of total revenue (sales mix)

■ Expenses as a percentage of total revenue

■ Departmental expenses as a percentage of departmental revenues

■ Revenues per room occupied, meal sold, and so forth

■ Annual expenses per room, and so forth

Exhibit 5.20 suggests over 200 useful operating ratios.

Further, the *USALI* suggests many operating metrics covering 34 ratios. A limited number of operating ratios are covered later in this chapter. The reader desiring more detail should consult the *USALI*.

This section will consider only some of the most critical operating ratios, several relating to revenues and several relating to expenses. The revenue ratios include the mix of sales, average room rate, revenue per available room, revenue per available customer, and average foodservice check. The expense ratios include food cost percentage, beverage cost percentage, and labor cost percentage.

Mix of Sales

Hospitality establishments, like enterprises in other industries, attempt to generate sales as a means of producing profits. In the lodging segment of the hospitality industry, sales by the rooms department provide a greater contribution toward overhead costs and profits than the same amount of sales in other departments. In a foodservice operation, the sales mix of entrées yields

Exhibit 5.20 Selected Operating Ratios Useful in Analysis

CERTAIN OPERATING RATIOS USEFUL IN ANALYSIS	% of Total Revenues	% of Depart. Revenues	% of Depart. Total Cost	% Change from Prior Period	% Change from Budget	Per Available Room	Per Occupied Room	Per Available Seats	Per Cover/Guest	Per Square Foot	Per Full-time Equiv. Employee	% of Total Salaries & Wages	Per Unit Produced or Used
Total Revenues				•	•	•	•				•	•	
Rooms													
Revenue	•			•	•	•	•				•		
Salary, Wages & Burden		•	•	•	•	•	•						•
Other Expenses		•	•	•	•	•	•						
Departmental Profit		•		•	•	•	•						
Food													
Revenue	•			•	•	•	•	•	•	•	•		
Cost of Sales		•	•	•	•				•				
Salary, Wages & Burden		•	•	•	•			•	•				•
Other Expenses		•	•	•	•				•				
Departmental Profit		•		•	•			•	•	•	•		
Beverage													
Revenue	•			•	•	•	•	•	•	•	•		
Cost of Sales		•	•	•	•								
Salary, Wages & Burden		•	•	•	•			•					•
Other Expenses		•	•	•	•								
Departmental Profit		•		•	•			•		•	•		
Minor Departments													
Revenue	•			•	•								
Cost of Sales		•		•	•								
Salary, Wages & Burden		•		•	•								•
Other Expenses		•		•	•								
Departmental Profit		•		•	•								
Administrative & General													
Salary, Wages & Burden	•			•	•	•	•					•	
Other Expenses	•			•	•	•	•						
Departmental Total Cost	•			•	•	•	•						
Marketing													
Salary, Wages & Burden	•			•	•	•	•					•	
Other Expenses	•			•	•	•	•						
Departmental Total Cost	•			•	•	•	•						

(Continued)

(Continued)

CERTAIN OPERATING RATIOS USEFUL IN ANALYSIS

	% of Total Revenues	% of Depart. Revenues	% of Depart. Total Cost	% Change from Prior Period	% Change from Budget	Per Available Room	Per Occupied Room	Per Available Seats	Per Cover/Guest	Per Square Foot	Per Full-time Equiv. Employee	% of Total Salaries & Wages	Per Unit Produced or Used
Property Operation & Maintenance													
Salary, Wages & Burden	●			●	●	●	●					●	
Other Expenses	●			●	●	●	●						
Subtotal Maintenance	●			●	●	●	●						
Energy Cost	●			●	●	●	●						●
Departmental Total Cost	●			●	●	●	●						
House Laundry													
Salary, Wages & Burden	●			●	●	●	●					●	●
Other Expenses	●			●	●	●	●						●
Departmental Total Cost	●			●	●	●	●						●
Food & Beverage (or Outlets)													
Revenue	●	●		●	●	●	●						
Salary, Wages & Burden		●		●	●							●	
Other Expenses		●		●	●								
Departmental Total Cost		●		●	●								
Total Other Expenses	●			●	●	●	●						
Payroll Burden Items	●			●	●						●	●	
Total Salary & Wages	●			●	●	●	●				●		
Capital Expenses													
Property Taxes	●			●	●	●	●			●			●
Insurance	●			●	●	●	●						●
Rent/Lease	●			●	●	●	●						
Interest	●			●	●	●	●						●
Management Fee	●			●	●	●	●						
Debt Service	●			●	●	●	●						●
FF&E Reserve/Replacement	●			●	●	●	●						

Exhibit 5.21   Sales Mix

Departments	Sales	Percentage of Total
Rooms	$ 810,000	59.9%
Food	300,000	22.2
Beverage	145,000	10.7
Telecommunications	42,000	3.1
Rentals and Other Income	55,000	4.1
Total	$1,352,000	100.0%

a given contribution. The same sales total in a different sales mix will yield a different (possibly lower) contribution toward overhead and profits. Therefore, it is essential for management to obtain the desired sales mix. To determine the sales mix, departmental revenues are totaled and percentages of the total revenue are calculated for each operated department.

Using figures from Exhibits 5.2 and 5.4, Exhibit 5.21 shows the 20X2 sales mix for the Grand Hotel. The sales mix of a hospitality operation is best compared with the establishment's objectives, as revealed in its budget. A second standard of comparison is the previous period's results. A third involves a comparison with industry averages.

An evaluation of revenue by department is accomplished by determining each department's average sale. For the rooms department, the ratio is the average room rate. For the foodservice department, it is the average foodservice check.

Average Room Rate

A key rooms department ratio is the **average room rate**, often called the **average daily rate** or simply **ADR**. Most hotel and motel managers calculate the ADR even though rates within a property may vary significantly from single rooms to suites, from individual guests to groups and conventions, from weekdays to weekends, and from busy seasons to slack seasons.

Using figures from Exhibits 5.2 and 5.4, the 20X2 ADR for the Grand Hotel can be calculated as follows:

$$\text{ADR} = \frac{\text{Rooms Revenue}}{\text{Number of Rooms Sold}}$$

$$= \frac{\$810,000}{21,000}$$

$$= \underline{\$38.57}$$

The ADR for 20X2 is a $0.52 improvement over the 20X1 ADR of $38.05 ($780,000 ÷ 20,500 rooms sold). The best standard of comparison to use in evaluating an actual average room rate is the rate budgeted as the goal for the rooms department's operation during the period. This average rate should also be calculated individually for each market segment: business groups, tourists, airline crews, and other categories of guests served.

Revenue per Available Room

Traditionally, many hoteliers have placed heavy reliance on paid occupancy percentage as a quick indicator of activity and possibly performance. Others have looked at the ADR as an indication of the quality of an operation. However, paid occupancy percentage and average room rate by themselves are somewhat meaningless. A hotel may have a paid occupancy of 80 percent and an ADR of $40, while a close competitor has a paid occupancy of 70 percent and an ADR of $60. Which hotel is in the preferable condition?

The combination of paid occupancy percentage and ADR is called revenue per available room (**RevPAR**) and is calculated as follows:

$$\text{RevPAR} = \frac{\text{Rooms Revenue}}{\text{Available Rooms}}$$

or

$$\text{RevPAR} = \text{Paid Occupancy Percentage} \times \text{ADR}$$

Using the above example, the hotel with an 80 percent paid occupancy and the $40 ADR has a RevPAR of $32 ($40 × 80%), while its competitor has a RevPAR of $42 (70% × $60). Everything else being the same, one prefers the hotel with the higher RevPAR. In this example, the RevPAR leads us to choose the hotel with the higher ADR, but this will not always be the case. Suppose, for example, that the second hotel in the above example had a paid occupancy of 50 percent instead of 70 percent; its RevPAR would then be $30 ($60 × 50%) and the RevPAR ratio would then favor the hotel with the higher occupancy percentage.

Based on information in Exhibits 5.2, 5.4, and 5.16, the Grand Hotel's RevPAR for 20X2 is $27.74, while its RevPAR for 20X1 is $26.71. Thus, RevPAR increased by $1.03 in 20X2 over 20X1.

RevPAR is an improvement over simply looking at occupancy percentage or ADR separately. Many industry executives prefer this combined statistic.

Total Revenue per Available Room

Many hotels have other services and amenities offered to their guests besides the hotel room. These can include food and beverage, business services, spa and health clubs, parking, a golf course, or other operated departments. Therefore, besides a metric measuring rooms revenue, full-service hotels also calculate **total revenue per available room (TRevPAR)**, which measures the overall revenue an available hotel room earns. This ratio can assist hotels to gauge how their other departments, besides rooms, are contributing to the revenue of the entire property. For example, Hotels A and B have the same number of rooms and very similar other operated departments with the following revenue statistics:

	Hotel A	Hotel B
Number of rooms	300	300
Number of rooms sold	74,460	82,125
Occupancy percentage	68%	75%
Rooms sales	$ 12,285,900	$ 15,193,125
Revenue per available room (RevPAR)	$ 112.20	$ 138.75
Food and beverage revenue	$ 5,425,725	$ 2,052,030
Health club revenue	$ 893,520	$ 628,256
Parking revenue	$ 595,680	$ 903,375
Other operated departments revenue	$ 726,730	$ 396,664
Total revenue	$ 19,927,555	$ 19,173,450
Total revenue per available room (TRevPAR)	$ 182.00	$ 175.00

Hotel B enjoys a higher RevPAR at $138.75 than Hotel A's $112.20. In addition, Hotel B also has a higher occupancy, at 75 percent, compared to Hotel A's 68 percent. If the ADR is calculated, Hotel B also has a higher ADR, at $185, rather than Hotel A, at $165. Thus, in all three major key performance indicators, Hotel B is performing better than Hotel A. However, when the revenues of other departments are tallied, Hotel A has total revenue of $19.9 million, translating to a TRevPAR of $182, whereas Hotel B's total revenue is only $19.2 million, or a TRevPAR of $175. Thus, if compared at the total revenue level, Hotel A performed better. This is another reason why management and owners should look at various indicators when assessing the financial performance of their operations.

Total Revenue per Available Customer

Instead of focusing on revenue from room sales, **total revenue per available customer (TRevPAC)** measures the overall revenue received from the average hotel guest and is used for decision-making situations affecting operations. For example, assume that a lodging facility has sales proposals from two different groups for three-day stays as follows:

	Group A	Group B
Number of guests	50	50
Room sales	50	50
ADR	$ 90	$ 95
Daily food sales per guest	$ 30	–0–
Daily beverage sales per guest	$ 20	–0–

From an ADR perspective, the decision would be to accept Group B. From a daily TRevPAC perspective, clearly the decision would be to accept Group A because $140 of revenue would be received daily from each member of Group A, while only $95 of revenue would be received from each member of Group B.

For the Grand Hotel, the TRevPAC for 20X2 is determined as follows:

$$TRevPAC = \frac{Total\ Revenue\ from\ Hotel\ Guests}{Total\ Number\ of\ Guests}$$

$$= \frac{\$1,352,000}{24,000}$$

$$= \underline{\$56.33}$$

The TRevPAC of $56.33 assumes that all hotel revenue for the Grand Hotel during 20X2 was received from the 24,000 paid guests. This compares favorably with the TRevPAC for 20X1 of $55.32.

Average Foodservice Check

A key foodservice ratio is the average foodservice check. This ratio is determined by dividing total food revenue by the number of food customers during the period. Using figures from Exhibit 5.4, the average foodservice check for 20X2 for the Grand Hotel can be calculated as follows:

$$\frac{Average\ Foodservice}{Check} = \frac{Total\ Food\ Revenue}{Number\ of\ Food\ Customers}$$

$$= \frac{\$300,000}{56,000}$$

$$= \underline{\$5.36}$$

The $5.36 average foodservice check in 20X2 is a $0.31 increase over the Grand Hotel's average foodservice check of $5.05 for 20X1 ($280,000 ÷ 55,500 food customers). The average foodservice check is best compared with the budgeted amount for 20X2. An additional comparison relates this ratio to industry averages. Additional average checks should be calculated for beverages. Management should also calculate the average check by different dining areas and/or by various meal periods.

Food Cost Percentage

The **food cost percentage** is a key foodservice ratio that compares the cost of food sold to food sales. Most foodservice managers rely heavily on this ratio for determining whether food costs are reasonable.

Using figures from Exhibit 5.11, the 20X2 food cost percentage for the Grand Hotel is determined as follows:

$$\text{Food Cost Percentage} = \frac{\text{Cost of Food Sold}}{\text{Food Sales}} \times 100$$

$$= \frac{\$120,000}{\$300,000} \times 100$$

$$= \underline{\underline{40\%}}$$

The Grand Hotel's 20X2 food cost percentage of 40 indicates that of every $1 of food sales, $0.40 goes toward the cost of food sold. This is best compared with the budgeted percentage for the period. A significant difference in either direction should be investigated by management. Management should be just as concerned about a food cost percentage that is significantly lower than the budgeted goal as it is about a food cost percentage that exceeds budgeted standards. A lower food cost percentage may indicate that the quality of food served is lower than desired, or that smaller portions are being served than are specified by the standard recipes. A food cost percentage in excess of the objective may be due to poor portion control, excessive food costs, theft, waste, spoilage, and so on.

Beverage Cost Percentage

A key ratio for beverage operations is the **beverage cost percentage**. This ratio results from dividing the cost of beverages sold by beverage sales.

Using figures from Exhibit 5.11, the 20X2 beverage cost percentage for the Grand Hotel can be calculated as follows:

$$\text{Beverage Cost Percentage} = \frac{\text{Cost of Beverages Sold}}{\text{Beverage Sales}} \times 100$$

$$= \frac{\$28,000}{\$145,000} \times 100$$

$$= \underline{\underline{19.31\%}}$$

The 20X2 beverage cost percentage of 19.31 percent for the Grand Hotel means that for each $1 of beverage sales, $0.19 is spent on the cost of beverages served. As with the food cost percentage ratio, this ratio is best compared with the goal set for the period in question. Likewise, any significant variances must be investigated to determine the cause(s). Refinements of this ratio would be beverage cost percentage by type of beverage sold and by beverage outlet.

Labor Cost Percentage

The largest expense in hotels, motels, clubs, and many restaurants is labor. Labor expense includes salaries, wages, bonuses, payroll taxes, and fringe benefits. A general **labor cost percentage** is determined by dividing total labor costs by total revenue. This general labor cost percentage is simply a benchmark for making broad comparisons. For control purposes, labor costs must be analyzed on a departmental basis. The rooms department labor cost percentage is determined by dividing rooms department labor cost by room revenue. The food and beverage department labor cost percentage is determined by dividing food and beverage department labor cost by food and beverage revenue. Other operated department labor cost percentages are similarly determined.

Exhibit 5.22 uses figures from Exhibit 5.2 to calculate the 20X2 operated department labor cost percentages for the Grand Hotel. These show the food and beverage department with the highest labor cost percentage at 40.45 percent. In most lodging firms, this is the case. The standard of comparison for these ratios is the budgeted percentages. Since labor costs are generally the largest expense, they must be tightly controlled. Management must carefully investigate any significant differences between actual and budgeted labor cost percentages.

Ratios for other expenses are usually computed as a percentage of revenues. If the expenses are operated department expenses, then the ratio is computed with the operated department revenues in the denominator and the expense in the numerator. An overhead expense ratio will consist of the overhead expense divided by total revenue. For example, marketing expense percentage is determined by dividing the marketing expense by total revenue. Using figures for the Grand Hotel in 20X2 found in Exhibit 5.2, the marketing expense percentage is 4.07 percent (marketing expenses of $55,000 ÷ total revenue of $1,352,000).

Flow Through and Flex

As revenues in a hospitality business increase or decrease, the ability of ownership and management to keep as much of the revenue as profit is measured by the flow through and flex ratios, respectively. When a hotel brings in more revenue than budgeted, it is good news. All hotels would prefer making more revenue in the top line. However, a higher level of revenue does not guarantee a higher level of profit will "flow through" and be reflected in the GOP, EBITDA, or bottom line. Therefore, the **flow through ratio** is an important topic for management to understand.

For example, Hotel A and Hotel B are in a similar class, with a similar number of rooms, amenities, and services. Hotel A has prudent management with good scheduling plans, cross-trained employees, and prearranged additional on-call service staff who are also aware and trained with the service standards of Hotel A. With a sudden increase in rooms sold and thus an increase in rooms revenue, Hotel A is able to adjust its staffing level to meet the demand. Hotel B has good customer service ratings but does not have the bandwidth of employees. With a

Exhibit 5.22	Operated Department Labor Cost Percentages

Labor Cost Percentage	=	$\dfrac{\text{Labor Cost by Department}}{\text{Department Revenues}}$	X 100

Department	Total Labor Cost	÷	Total Revenue	=	Labor Cost Percentage
Rooms	$ 145,000		$ 810,000		17.90%
Food & Beverage	180,000		445,000		40.45%
Telecommunications	10,500		42,000		25.00%

sudden unexpected increase in demand, Hotel B has to work all its housekeeping staff overtime, incurring a much higher labor cost. In addition, the staff was so tired that their service level suffered. With a higher labor cost, the profit is not proportional to the revenue.

Flow through ratios can be calculated for the entire hotel, for each department (rooms flow or food and beverage flow), and at different profit measurement levels of the income statement, starting from the gross operating profit level, EBITDA, and net income. For example, the formula for a GOP flow through ratio is the difference between the actual GOP and budgeted GOP in the numerator divided into the difference between actual revenue and budgeted revenue in the denominator. Simply changing the GOP to EBITDA or net income will result in the other flow through ratios.

$$\text{Flow Through Ratio} = \frac{\text{Actual} - \text{Budgeted}}{\text{Actual Revenue} - \text{Budgeted Revenue}}$$

$$\text{GOP Flow Through Ratio} = \frac{\text{Actual GOP} - \text{Budgeted GOP}}{\text{Actual Revenue} - \text{Budgeted Revenue}}$$

Thus, effective management will yield positive flow through ratios, while ineffective management may bring in more revenues but at the end lose money for the owners, resulting in a negative flow through ratio. Consider the GOP and revenue data for Hotel Austin and Hotel Boston, below:

Hotel Austin	Actual	Budgeted	Variance
Revenue	$ 320,000	$ 280,000	$ 40,000
GOP	220,000	210,000	10,000

Using the flow through formula:

$$\text{GOP Flow Through Ratio} = \frac{\text{Actual GOP} - \text{Budgeted GOP}}{\text{Actual Revenue} - \text{Budgeted Revenue}}$$

$$= \$10,000 \div \$40,000$$

$$= +25\%$$

This means with a positive flow through percentage of 25 percent, for every dollar of additional revenue, Hotel Austin can flow 25 percent of that revenue to the GOP.

Hotel Boston	Actual	Budgeted	Variance
Revenue	$ 320,000	$ 280,000	$ 40,000
GOP	220,000	230,000	(10,000)

Using the flow through formula:

$$\text{GOP Flow Through Ratio} = \frac{\text{Actual GOP} - \text{Budgeted GOP}}{\text{Actual Revenue} - \text{Budgeted Revenue}}$$

$$= (\$10,000) \div \$40,000$$

$$= -25\%$$

In this case, with a negative percentage, this means even though Hotel Boston brought in $40,000 more in revenue, it was spending more on expenses. Its management is not able to retain any of the increased revenue and even lost another $10,000 in the GOP line.

Again, the flow through ratio measures when revenue increases relative to budget or the previous period, the percentage of incremental profit that "flows" to the gross operating profit or other profit lines from each additional dollar of top line revenue.

On the other hand, what happens when a hotel brings in less revenue than budgeted? In this case, a hotel will have to "flex" its revenues to absorb costs so that the profit levels can be maintained. In other words, when the revenue variance is negative, a hotel is in a flex situation, resulting in the calculation of the **flex ratio**.

Like flow through, flex ratios can also be calculated for the entire hotel or for each department, or at different profit measurement levels of the income statement. Since flexing is the opposite of flow through, the formula for a GOP flex ratio is "1 minus" the flow through ratio:

$$\text{Flex Ratio} = 1 - \left[\frac{\text{Actual} - \text{Budgeted}}{\text{Actual Revenue} - \text{Budgeted Revenue}} \right]$$

$$\text{GOP Flex Ratio} = 1 - \left[\frac{\text{Actual GOP} - \text{Budgeted GOP}}{\text{Actual Revenue} - \text{Budgeted Revenue}} \right]$$

Similarly, changing the GOP to EBITDA or net income will result in the other flex ratios. Consider the GOP and revenue data for Hotel Charlotte and Hotel Denver, below. Both hotels experienced a flex situation, as their actual revenue is less than budgeted:

Hotel Charlotte	Actual	Budgeted	Variance
Revenue	$280,000	$320,000	($40,000)
GOP	215,000	210,000	5,000

For Hotel Charlotte, using the flex formula:

$$\text{GOP Flex Ratio} = 1 - \left[\frac{\text{Actual GOP} - \text{Budgeted GOP}}{\text{Actual Revenue} - \text{Budgeted Revenue}} \right]$$

$$= 1 - [\$5,000 \div (\$40,000)]$$

$$= 1 - [(12.5\%)]$$

$$= +112.5\%$$

A flex ratio that is over 100 percent means Hotel Charlotte is able to flex its resources, and not only not to lose money from having less revenue, but manages to even earn more in its GOP!

Hotel Denver	Actual	Budgeted	Variance
Revenue	$ 280,000	$ 320,000	$ (40,000)
GOP	180,000	230,000	(50,000)

For, Hotel Denver, using the flex formula:

$$\text{GOP Flex Ratio} = 1 - \left[\frac{\text{Actual GOP} - \text{Budgeted GOP}}{\text{Actual Revenue} - \text{Budgeted Revenue}} \right]$$

$$= 1 - [(\$50,000) \div (\$40,000)]$$

$$= 1 - [125\%]$$

$$= -25\%$$

In this case, with a negative percentage, this means Hotel Denver not only lost revenue but was not able to flex its resources, and ended with a loss of 25 percent over its revenue loss in its GOP. Again, flex ratios measure when revenue decreases relative to budget or the previous period – the percentage of profit that is "flexed" or saved as revenue drops.

Besides comparing actual and budgeted figures, flow through and flex ratios can also be calculated between actual current and previous periods or years, and also budgeted numbers of current and previous periods or years. The use of these ratios can assist management to spot inefficiencies and take actions to enhance the profit of the hotel.

5.10 LIMITATIONS OF RATIO ANALYSIS

Ratios are extremely useful to owners, creditors, and management in evaluating the financial condition and operations of hospitality establishments. However, ratios are only indicators. Ratios do not resolve problems or even reveal exactly what the problem is. At best, when they vary significantly from past periods, budgeted standards, or industry averages, ratios only indicate that there *may be* a problem. Much more investigation and analysis are required.

Ratios are meaningful when they result from comparing two *related* numbers. Food cost percentage is meaningful because of the direct relationship between food costs and food sales. A goodwill to cash ratio may be somewhat meaningless due to the lack of any direct relationship between goodwill and cash.

Ratios are most useful when compared with a standard. A food cost percentage of 32 percent is of little use until it is compared with a standard such as past performance, industry averages, or the budgeted percentages.

Ratios are often used to compare different hospitality establishments. However, many ratios, especially operating ratios, will not result in meaningful comparisons if the two firms are in completely different segments of the industry. For example, comparing ratios for a luxury hotel to ratios for a quick-service restaurant would serve no meaningful purpose.

In addition, if the accounting procedures used by two separate hospitality establishments differ in several areas, then a comparison of their ratios will likely show differences related to accounting procedures as well as to financial positions or operations.

No single ratio tells the entire story. Several ratios are often useful in understanding the financial picture of a hospitality business. Generally, the same ratios should be viewed over a series of time periods.

The analyst also must be aware of events that do not directly affect the financial statements. For example, unrecorded contracts, lawsuits, lines of credit, and hotel group reservations will affect a company's financial condition, often with no immediate direct impact on the financial statements. The analyst must carefully weigh these matters and their potential impact on the firm's financial statements. Finally, financial ratios are generally computed from figures in the financial statements. These figures are based on historical costs. Over time, the effects of inflation render these figures less useful. For example, an ADR of $55 in 20X9 for a given lodging property is not necessarily a better performance than $40 in 20X1; if the inflation rate was greater than 37.5 percent for the 20X1–X9 time period, $55 in 20X9 is worth less than $40 in 20X1. Ratios that are most affected by inflation include those that contain property, equipment, or owners' equity in either the numerator or denominator. In addition, depreciation, since it relates to the historical cost of property and equipment, is often "understated," so income figures involving depreciation expense are often "overstated."

Accountants have used some fairly sophisticated techniques, such as restating the financial statements in constant dollars of equal purchasing power, to overcome this limitation in ratio analysis. However, as desirable as this correction is, it is often not used because of the major effort and time required to use it. An alternative approach is to apply an inflation correction factor to ratios that are affected by inflation. For example, using the above ADR example, assume that inflation for the 20X1–X9 period was 50 percent. The comparison of ADRs for 20X1 and 20X9 would be as follows:

20X1 (historical)	$ 40
20X1 (adjusted)	$ 60*
20X9	$ 55
*$40 × 150% = $60	

Thus, it is clear that the 20X1 ADR is preferred to the 20X9 ADR when inflation is considered.

Even though these limitations are present, a careful use of ratios that acknowledges their shortcomings will result in an enhanced understanding of the financial position and operations of hospitality establishments.

5.11 USEFULNESS OF FINANCIAL RATIOS

Research has been conducted to determine the usefulness of ratios to various users.[3] The following results are based on surveys of hotel general managers (GMs) and financial controllers who were requested to rate individually the usefulness of 45 different ratios to potential users of these ratios. Specifically, they were asked to rate the usefulness of each of these ratios to GMs, corporate executives, owners, and bankers on a scale of most important to least important. The results were then compiled by class of ratios and by users and are summarized as follows:[4]

	Users			
Class of Ratios	GMs	Corporate Executives	Owners	Bankers
Operating	1 (1)	2 (2)	3 (5)	4 (4)
Solvency	4 (5)	3 (3)	1 (2)	1 (1)
Activity	1 (2)	2 (5)	3 (4)	4 (5)
Profitability	4 (3)	2 (1)	1 (1)	3 (2)
Liquidity	3 (4)	1 (4)	2 (3)	4 (3)

The interpretation of the above table is as follows:

■ The parenthetic numbers show the relative ranking of usefulness of the classes of ratios to each user group. For example, GMs considered operating ratios most useful (1), followed by activity ratios (2), and so forth.

■ The nonparenthetic numbers reveal the relative usefulness of a class of ratios across the various user groups. For example, the survey results suggest operating ratios are considered most useful by GMs, followed by corporate executives, then owners and bankers.

■ Owners and bankers are tied in their rating of solvency ratios.

In addition, the survey of GMs revealed that across all user groups the 10 most useful ratios were:

1. Profit margin
2. Occupancy percentage—month-to-date
3. Cost of labor percentage
4. Daily occupancy percentage
5. ADR
6. Total revenue percentage change from budget
7. Cost of food sold percentage
8. Cost of beverage sold percentage
9. Room sales to total sales
10. Operating efficiency ratio

Ratio analysis permits investors, creditors, and operators to receive more valuable information from the financial statements than they could receive from reviewing the absolute numbers reported in the documents. Vital relationships can be monitored to determine solvency and risk, performance in comparison with other periods, and dividend payout ratios. A combination of ratios can be used to efficiently and effectively communicate more information than that provided by the statements from which they are calculated.

There are five major classifications of ratios: liquidity, solvency, activity, profitability, and operating. Although there is some overlap among these categories, each has a special area of concern. Exhibit 5.23 lists the ratios presented in this chapter and the formulas by which they are calculated. It is important to be familiar with the types of ratios in each category, to know what each ratio measures, and to be aware of the targets or standards against which they are compared.

For example, a number of liquidity ratios focus on the hospitality establishment's ability to cover its short-term debts. However, each person examining the establishment's financial position will have a desired performance in mind. Creditors desire high liquidity ratios, which indicate that loans will probably be repaid. Investors, on the other hand, like lower liquidity ratios since current assets are not as profitable as long-term assets. Management reacts to these pressures by trying to please both groups.

The five ratio classifications vary in importance among the three major users of ratios. Creditors focus on solvency, profitability, and liquidity; investors and owners consider these ratios, but highlight the profitability ratios. Management uses all types of ratios, but is especially concerned with operating and activity ratios because they can be used in evaluating the results of operations.

It is important to realize that a percentage by itself is not meaningful. It is only useful when it is compared with a standard: an industry average, a ratio from a past period, or a budgeted ratio. It is the comparison against budget ratios that is the most useful for management. Any significant difference should be analyzed to determine its probable cause(s). Once management has fully investigated areas of concern revealed by the ratios, then corrective action can be taken to rectify any problems.

	Ratio	Formula
1.	Current ratio	Current assets/current liabilities
2.	Acid-test ratio	Cash, marketable securities, notes, and accounts receivable/current liabilities
3.	Operating cash flows to current liabilities ratio	Operating cash flows/average current liabilities
4.	Accounts receivable turnover	Revenue/average accounts receivable
5.	Average collection period	365/accounts receivable turnover
6.	Working capital turnover	Revenue/average working capital
7.	Solvency ratio	Total assets/total liabilities
8.	Debt-equity ratio	Total liabilities/total owners' equity
9.	Long-term debt to total capitalization ratio	Long-term debt/long-term debt and owners' equity
10.	Number of times interest earned ratio	EBIT/interest expense
11.	Fixed charge coverage ratio	EBIT + lease expense/interest expense and lease expense
12.	Debt service coverage ratio	Net operating income − cash transfers for replacement reserves/debt service payment
13.	Operating cash flows to total liabilities ratio	Operating cash flows/average total liabilities
14.	Inventory turnover:	
	Food inventory turnover	Cost of food used/average food inventory
	Beverage turnover	Cost of beverages used/average beverage inventory
15.	Property and equipment turnover	Total revenue/average property and equipment
16.	Asset turnover	Total revenues/average total assets
17.	Paid occupancy percentage	Paid rooms occupied/rooms available
18.	Complimentary occupancy	Complimentary rooms/rooms available
19.	Average occupancy per room	Number of room guests/number of rooms occupied
20.	Multiple occupancy percentage	Rooms occupied by two or more people/rooms occupied by guests

Exhibit 5.23   List of Ratios

Ratio		Formula
21.	Seat turnover	Customers/number of seats
22.	Profit margin	Net income/total revenue
23.	Operating efficiency ratio (gross operating profit margin ratio)	Gross operating profit/total revenue
24.	Gross operating profit per available room	Gross operating profit/available rooms
25.	EBITDA margin ratio	EBITDA/total operated department revenues
26.	EBITDA per available room	EBITDA/available rooms
27.	Return on assets	Net income/average total assets
28.	Gross return on assets	EBIT/average total assets
29.	Return on owners' equity	Net income/average owners' equity
30.	Return on common stockholders' equity	Net income − preferred dividend/average common stockholders' equity
31.	Earnings per share	Net income/average common shares outstanding
32.	Price/earnings ratio	Market price per share/earnings per share
33.	Mix of sales	Departmental revenues are totaled; percentages of total revenue are calculated for each
34.	ADR	Rooms revenue/number of rooms sold
35.	RevPAR	Paid occupancy percentage × ADR
36.	TRevPAR	Total revenue from hotel guests/number of available rooms
37.	TRevPAC	Total revenue from hotel guests/number of hotel guests
38.	Average foodservice check	Total food revenue/number of food customers
39.	Food cost percentage	Cost of food sold/food sales
40.	Beverage cost percentage	Cost of beverages sold/beverage sales
41.	Labor cost percentage	Labor cost by department/department revenues
42.	GOP flow through	(Actual GOP − budgeted GOP)/(Actual revenue − budgeted revenue)
43.	GOP flex	1 − [(Actual GOP − budgeted GOP)/ (Actual revenue − budgeted revenue)]

accounts receivable turnover—A measure of the rapidity of conversion of accounts receivable into cash; calculated by dividing revenue by average accounts receivable.

acid-test ratio—Ratio of total cash and near-cash current assets to total current liabilities.

activity ratios—A group of ratios that reflect management's ability to use the property's assets and resources.

asset turnover—An activity ratio that measures the efficiency of management's use of assets. Total revenues divided by average total assets.

average collection period—The average number of days it takes a hospitality operation to collect all its accounts receivable; calculated by dividing the accounts receivable turnover into 365 (the number of days in a year).

average daily rate (ADR)—A key rooms department operating ratio. Rooms revenue divided by number of rooms sold. Also called average room rate.

average occupancy per room—An activity ratio measuring management's ability to use the lodging facilities. The number of guests divided by the number of rooms sold.

average room rate—See average daily rate.

beverage cost percentage—A ratio comparing the cost of beverages sold to beverage sales; calculated by dividing the cost of beverages sold by beverage sales.

complimentary occupancy—The number of complimentary rooms for a period divided by the number of rooms available.

current ratio—Ratio of total current assets to total current liabilities expressed as a coverage of so many times; calculated by dividing current assets by current liabilities.

debt-equity ratio—Compares the debt of a hospitality operation to its net worth (owners' equity) and indicates the operation's ability to withstand adversity and meet its long-term obligations; calculated by dividing total liabilities by total owners' equity.

debt service coverage ratio—Measures the extent to which a property generates sufficient adjusted net operating income to cover its debt obligations; calculated by dividing net operating income less cash transfers to replacement reserves by the debt service payment.

double occupancy—The number of rooms occupied by more than one guest divided by the number of rooms occupied by guests. More accurately called multiple occupancy.

earnings per share (EPS)—A ratio providing a general indicator of the profitability of an operation by comparing net income to the average common shares outstanding. If preferred stock has been issued for the operation, then preferred dividends are subtracted from net income before calculating EPS.

EBITDA—A company's earnings before interest, taxes, depreciation, and amortization.

EBITDA margin ratio—A ratio calculated by dividing EBITDA by total revenue.

EBITDA per available room—A ratio calculated by dividing EBITDA by the number of rooms available in the hotel.

financial leverage—The use of debt in place of equity dollars to finance operations and increase the return on the equity dollars already invested.

fixed charge coverage ratio—A variation of the number of times interest earned ratio that considers leases as well as interest expense. Lease expenses and earnings before interest and income taxes divided by interest expense and lease expense.

flex ratio—Measures when revenue decreases relative to budget or the previous period, the percentage of profit that is "flexed" or saved as revenue drops.

flow through ratio—Measures when revenue increases relative to budget or the previous period, the percentage of incremental profit that "flows" to the gross operating profit or other profit lines from each additional dollar of top line revenue.

food cost percentage—A ratio comparing the cost of food sold to food sales; calculated by dividing the cost of food sold by total food sales.

gross operating profit per available room (GOPAR or GOPPAR)—A ratio that expresses gross operating profit on a per-room basis. Gross operating profit divided by available rooms.

gross operating profit margin ratio—See operating efficiency ratio.

gross return on assets (GROA)—Measures the rate of return on assets regardless of financing methods. Earnings before interest and income taxes divided by average total assets.

inventory turnover—A ratio showing how quickly a hospitality operation's inventory is moving from storage to productive use; calculated by dividing the cost of food or beverages used by the average food or beverages inventory.

labor cost percentage—A ratio comparing the labor expense for each department by the total revenue generated by the department; total labor cost by department divided by department revenues.

liquidity ratios—A group of ratios that reveal the ability of an establishment to meet its short-term obligations.

long-term debt to total capitalization ratio—A solvency ratio showing long-term debt as a percentage of the sum of long-term debt and owners' equity. Long-term debt divided by long-term debt and owners' equity.

multiple occupancy—The number of rooms occupied by more than one guest divided by the number of rooms occupied by guests. Sometimes called double occupancy.

number of times interest earned ratio—A solvency ratio expressing the number of times interest expense can be covered. Earnings before interest and taxes divided by interest expense.

operating cash flows to current liabilities ratio—A liquidity ratio that compares the cash flow from the firm's operating activities to its obligations at the balance sheet date that must be paid within 12 months. Operating cash flows divided by average current liabilities.

operating cash flows to total liabilities ratio—A solvency ratio that uses figures from both the statement of cash flows and the balance sheet. Operating cash flows divided by average total liabilities.

operating efficiency ratio (gross operating profit margin ratio)—A measure of management's ability to generate sales and control expenses; calculated by dividing gross operating profit by total revenue. Also called gross operating profit margin ratio.

operating ratios—A group of ratios that assist in the analysis of hospitality establishment operations.

paid occupancy—A measure of management's ability to efficiently use available assets. The number of rooms sold divided by the number of rooms available for sale.

price/earnings (PE) ratio—A profitability ratio used by financial analysts when presenting investment possibilities. The market price per share divided by the earnings per share.

profit margin—An overall measure of management's ability to generate sales and control expenses; calculated by dividing net income by total revenue.

profitability ratios—A group of ratios which reflect the results of all areas of management's responsibilities.

property and equipment turnover—A ratio measuring management's effectiveness in using property and equipment to generate revenue; calculated by dividing average total property and equipment into total revenue generated for the period. Sometimes called fixed asset turnover.

ratio analysis—The comparison of related facts and figures.

residual income—The excess of a hotel's net income over an established minimum return.

return on assets (ROA)—A ratio providing a general indicator of the profitability of a hospitality operation by comparing net income to total investment; calculated by dividing net income by average total assets.

return on common stockholders' equity—A variation of return on owners' equity that is used when preferred stock has been issued. Net income less preferred dividends paid to preferred stockholders divided by average common stockholders' equity.

return on owners' equity (ROE)—A ratio providing a general indicator of the profitability of an operation by comparing net income to the owners' investment; calculated by dividing net income by average owners' equity.

RevPAR—Revenue per available room. A combination of paid occupancy percentage and average daily rate. Room revenues divided by available revenues or, alternatively, paid occupancy percentage times average daily rate.

seat turnover—An activity ratio measuring the rate at which people are served. The number of people served divided by the number of seats available.

solvency ratio—A measure of the extent to which an operation is financed by debt and is able to meet its long-term obligations; calculated by dividing total assets by total liabilities.

solvency ratios—A group of ratios that measure the extent to which the enterprise has been financed by debt and is able to meet its long-term obligations.

TRevPAC—Total revenue per available customer; calculated by dividing the total revenue from hotel guests by the total number of guests.

TRevPAR—Total revenue per available room; calculated by dividing the total revenue from hotel guests by the total number of rooms available.

working capital turnover ratio—A liquidity ratio that compares working capital (current assets less current liabilities) to revenue.

1. How does ratio analysis benefit creditors?

2. If you are investing in a hotel, which ratios would be most useful? Why?

3. What are the limitations of ratio analysis?

4. How do the three user groups of ratio analysis react to the solvency ratios?

5. What is leverage, and why may owners want to increase it?

6. What do activity ratios highlight?

7. How is the profit margin calculated? How is it used?

8. Which standard is the most effective for comparison with ratios?

9. What does the ratio expression "turnover" mean?

10. Of what value is the food sales/total sales ratio to the manager of a hotel? To a creditor?

Problem 1

Indicate the effects of the transactions listed below on each of the following: total current assets, working capital (CA − CL), and current ratio. Indicate increase with "+," indicate decrease with "−," and indicate no effect or effect cannot be determined with "0." Assume an initial current ratio of greater than 1.0.

	Total Current Assets	Working Capital	Current Ratio
1. Room is sold for cash.			
2. Equipment is sold at more than its net book value for a gain.			
3. Food is sold on account.			
4. A cash dividend is declared.			
5. Accrued utility is paid.			
6. Treasury stock is purchased.			
7. A fully depreciated fixed asset is retired.			
8. Equipment is purchased with long-term notes.			
9. Utility expenses are paid (they were not previously accrued).			
10. A cash dividend is paid.			

Problem 2

McDaniel's Place has selected financial ratios for 20X1–X3 as follows:

	20X1	20X2	20X3
Current ratio	1.1	1.15	1.2
Accounts receivable turnover	13	12	11
Inventory turnover	24	23	22
Asset turnover	1.3	1.4	1.5
Debt-equity ratio	1.5	1.4	1.3
Times interest earned	3.8	3.9	4.0

Sales for the three years were $1 million, $1.4 million, and $1.6 million, respectively.

Required:

1. Assume total assets did not change during 20X3. Determine the total debt at the end of 20X3.

2. If cost of sales were 20 percent of total sales, what was the average inventory for 20X3?

3. Comment on the changing liquidity of McDaniel's Place over the three-year period.

4. Comment on the changing solvency of this business over the three-year period.

◦ Problem 3

The Anchor Resort is managed by Inns, Inc. The management contract requires 5 percent of total revenue to be transferred to the replacement reserves to cover future renovations and equipment replacements. Anchor's debt service payment is $10,000 per month. The lodging property has 250 guestrooms, an ADR of $100, and a paid occupancy of 70 percent. Its room revenue is 75 percent of its total revenue and its net operating income is 15 percent of its total revenue.

Required:

1. Determine the Anchor's annual total revenue. $\cancel{K} 8 3 2, 8 66, 667$

2. Determine the Anchor's annual net operating income.

3. Determine the Anchor's debt service coverage ratio for the year.

Problem 4

The Lansing Club has annual revenues of $10 million and all sales are on account. Good credit and collection performance in the club industry result in a 35-day accounts receivable collection period (ACP). Assume a year has 365 days.

Required:

1. Determine the maximum receivables balance the club can tolerate and still receive a good rating for credit and collections.

2. If the Lansing Club is currently collecting receivables in 40 days, by how much must the receivable balance be reduced to achieve an ACP of 35 days?

Problem 5

The Madrid Hotel has the following ratios:

Return on equity:	12 percent
Total asset turnover:	1.5 times
Return on sales:	5 percent

The total assets of the Madrid Hotel equal $6 million. Assume the balance sheet numbers at the beginning and end of the year are the same.

Required:

1. Determine the firm's total annual sales.

2. Determine the firm's net income.

3. Determine the amount of the firm's total debt.

Problem 6

Part A:

The Ambassy Hotel, a 100-room limited-service operation, has provided you with the following data for the months of May and June:

	May	June
Single rooms sold	900	1,050
Double rooms sold	1,700	1,510
Room revenue	$ 221,000	$ 202,720
Number of paid guests	4,620	4,453

Required:

1. Compute the paid occupancy for May.

2. What was the monthly ADR for June?

3. What was the monthly RevPAR for May?

4. What was the average number of guests per double room during June? (Assume only one guest stayed in each single room.)

Part B:

The Bogdin Café's beginning and ending food inventory for 20X4 total $10,000 and $14,000, respectively. Activity during 20X4 was as follows:

(1) Food purchases	$ 160,000
(2) Employee meals	$ 3,000
(3) Promotional meals	$ 2,000
(4) Food sales	$ 500,000

Required:

1. Compute the food cost percentage.

2. Compute the food inventory turnover for 20X4.

Part C:

Selected financial ratios for the Cambridge's Club for 20X3–X5 are as follows:

	20X3	20X4	20X5
Current ratio	1.1	1.3	1.4
Accounts receivable turnover	24	22	20
Profit margin	5%	6%	7%
Inventory turnover	15	16	17

Required:

Comment on the changing liquidity of the Dodger's Club from 20X3 to 20X5. Be specific using the relevant ratios above.

Problem 7

Selected financial ratios for the Kensington Lodge for 20X5–X7 are as follows:

	20X5	20X6	20X7
Debt equity	1.2	1.4	1.6
Times interest earned	4.0	3.8	3.6
Return on assets	7%	8%	9%
Fixed charge coverage	3.0	3.1	3.2
Operating efficiency ratio	20%	24%	28%

Required:

1. Which ratios are not solvency ratios?

2. From the balance sheet perspective, how is the solvency of the Kensington Lodge changing from 20X5–X7?

3. From the income statement perspective, how is the solvency of this operation changing from 20X5–X7?

4. From a financing perspective, using loans and/or operating leases, what appears to be changing over this three-year period?

Problem 8

The Campanella Club (CC) has food sales of $4.5 million and a food cost of 40 percent. The CC's current ratio is 1.8, its food inventory turnover ratio is 16, and its average collection period is 45 days. Assume a year has 360 days.

Required:

Complete the current section of the CC's balance sheet.

Cash	$ 150,000
Accounts Receivable	$ _____
Food Inventory	$ _____
Total Current Assets	$ _____
Accounts Payable	$ _____
Accrued Expenses	$ 100,000
Total Current Liabilities	$ _____

▾ Problem 9

Hotel 1776 has provided the following selected financial information:

Balance Sheet	
Cash	$ 100,000
Property and equipment	$ 2,000,000
Income Statement	
Room sales	$ 2,000,000
Food sales	700,000

Cost of food sold	250,000
Net income	300,000
Ratios	
Current ratio	1.4
Food inventory turnover	12 times
Average collection period	20 days
Solvency ratio	2.5

Assumptions:

1. The balance sheet amounts are the same at the beginning and end of the year.

2. All sales are credit sales.

3. A year has 365 days.

4. Current assets consist of cash, food inventory, and accounts receivable.

5. Cash equals $100,000.

6. Total assets consist of current assets and property and equipment.

Required:

1. Calculate the amount of accounts receivable.

2. Calculate the amount of food inventory.

3. Calculate the amount of current liabilities.

4. Calculate the total amount of debt.

5. Calculate the total amount of owners' equity.

Problem 10

The following information applies to the Wills Wayside Inn, which is a 200-room lodging facility:

Current ratio	1 to 1
Acid-test ratio	0.8 to 1
Accounts receivable	$60,000
Operating efficiency ratio	30 percent
Total current liabilities	$100,000
Accounts receivable turnover	10 times
Labor costs	$400,000

Assume the following:

1. The accounts receivable turnover is based on *charge* sales *only*, which represents 50 percent of total sales.

2. The balances of all balance sheet accounts did *not* change from the beginning to the end of the year.

Required:

Determine each of the following:

1. Quick assets.

2. Total sales.

3. Total income after undistributed operating expenses.

4. Labor cost percentage.

5. During June, 4,500 rooms are sold. Assume two rooms are not available each day for legitimate business purposes; that is, they are not available for sale. What is the paid occupancy percentage?

6. If total assets equal $1 million at the end of the year, what is the total assets turnover?

Problem 11

The Hershiser Hotel is considering expansion. The proposed expansion is estimated to cost $20 million. Financing options are (1) all equity, (2) all debt, and (3) one-half debt and one-half equity. The expected annual income from the expansion before any interest and income taxes is $2 million. Assume an annual interest rate of 8 percent and a marginal tax rate of 30 percent. Further assume that 500,000 shares of common stock are outstanding, that additional shares can be sold for $100 per share with any equity financing, and that forecasted net income for the year related to current operations (before any expansion) is $2 per share based on the 500,000 shares outstanding.

Required:

Determine the expected annual increase in earnings per share for the Hershiser Hotel for each of the financing options.

Problem 12

Select ratios for the Erskine Hotel for the past three years are as follows:

	20X1	20X2	20X3
EPS	$ 2.40	$ 2.50	$ 2.60
PE ratio (last day of the year)	11	12	13
Profit margin	7%	6%	5%
Return on assets	12%	12.5%	13%
Debt-equity ratio	1 to 1	1.2 to 1	1.4 to 1

Further, assume (1) that the total assets have not changed over the three-year time period, and (2) that the average shares of capital stock outstanding for each year of the three-year period equals 1 million shares.

Required:

1. Determine the change in market price of the capital stock from the end of 20X1 to the end of 20X3.

2. What are the total assets at the end of each year?

3. What is the return on owners' equity for 20X3? (Hint: A = L + E.) For this question, assume that the total owners' equity did not change during the year.

Problem 13

The LaSorda Inn's condensed income statement for 20X3 and 20X4 is as follows:

	20X3	20X4
Rooms revenue	$ 3,450,000	$ 3,675,000
Rooms department expenses	1,450,000	1,500,000
Undistributed operating expenses	800,000	875,000
Gross operating profit	1,200,000	1,300,000
Insurance, property taxes, and depreciation	400,000	450,000
Interest expense	100,000	90,000
Income before income taxes	700,000	760,000
Income taxes	210,000	228,000
Net income	$ 490,000	$ 532,000

The LaSorda Inn has 100 guest rooms, and its paid occupancy percentage was 78 percent and 80 percent for 20X3 and 20X4, respectively. Assume all rooms in the hotel were available for sale.

Required:

1. Calculate the following for 20X3 and 20X4.
   a. Profit margin
   b. RevPAR
   c. ADR
   d. GOPAR
   e. Operating efficiency ratio
   f. Times interest earned ratio

2. Briefly comment on the changes in each ratio from 20X3 to 20X4.

Problem 14

You are the new manager of the Duke Snider Motel. In order to better understand the motel's financial situation, you decide to examine the financial statements for the year just ended (20X4). The motel's balance sheet and condensed income statement are as follows:

Duke Snider Motel
Balance Sheet
Dec. 31, 20X4

Assets
Current Assets:
Cash	$ 95,000
Accounts Receivable	100,000
Inventories	5,000
Total Current Assets	200,000

Property and Equipment:
Land	60,000
Building (net)	300,000

Duke Snider Motel
Balance Sheet
Dec. 31, 20X4

Furniture and Equipment (net)	80,000
Total Property and Equipment	440,000
Total Assets	$ 640,000
Liabilities and Owners' Equity	
Current Liabilities	$ 210,000
Long-Term Liabilities:	
Note from Owner	40,000
Mortgage Payable	80,000
Total Liabilities	330,000
Owners' Equity	
Common Stock	100,000
Retained Earnings	210,000
Total Owners' Equity	310,000
Total Liabilities and Owners' Equity	$ 640,000

Duke Snider Motel
Condensed Income Statement
For the year ended Dec. 31, 20X4

Sales	$ 1,500,000
Cost of Goods Sold	200,000
Operating Expenses	800,000
Contribution Margin	500,000
Undistributed Operating Expenses	125,000
Gross Operating Profit	375,000
Interest	120,000
Other Nonoperating Expenses	162,000
Income before Taxes	93,000
Income Tax	27,900
Net Income	$ 65,100

Required:

Calculate the following ratios:

1. Current ratio

2. Acid-test ratio

3. Debt-equity ratio

4. Number of times interest earned ratio

5. Operating efficiency ratio

6. Profit margin

7. Return on owners' equity (assume that the only change in owners' equity during 20X4 is the net income of $65,100)

8. Return on total assets (assume that total assets were $640,000 on January 1, 20X4)

Problem 15

The Henri, a 350-room hotel, has provided you with the following data for the months of April and May:

	April	May
Single rooms sold	2,600	2,418
Double rooms sold	4,200	4,478
Room revenue	$ 496,000	$ 439,000
Number of paid guests	9,900	9,910

Required:

1. Compute the following for June and July:
   a. Paid occupancy percentage
   b. Multiple occupancy percentage
   c. Average number of guests per double room sold (assume that only one guest stayed in each single room sold)
   d. Monthly ADR
   e. Monthly RevPAR

2. Was the financial performance of Henri better in April or May? (Assume that fixed costs were constant and that the variable costs per room sold remained constant. Support your answer with detailed discussion.)

Problem 16

The Gibson Hotel is a 300-room facility with several profit centers. The hotel is open throughout the year, and generally about 2 percent of the rooms are being repaired or renovated at all times; therefore, assume that they are unavailable for sale. During 20X1, the hotel sold 87,800 rooms and experienced an average occupancy per room of 1.32 people. The accounting department has supplied you with the following information concerning the food department:

Ending inventory	$ 35,000
Consumption by employees (free of charge)	5,000
Cost of sales	312,000
Food cost percentage	35 percent
Food inventory turnover	10 times

Required:

Determine the following:

1. Occupancy rate for 20X1

2. Number of paid guests for 20X1

3. Beginning inventory of food

4. Food sales

5. Multiple occupancy percentage (assume that no more than two persons occupied a double room)

Problem 17

Donna Drysdale, co-owner of Drysdale Pizza, provides you with the following information for 20X3 and 20X4:

	20X3	20X4
Food sales	$ 800,000	$850,000
Other sales	50,000	60,000
Total sales	850,000	910,000
Cost of food sold	160,000	170,000
Cost of other sales	20,000	24,000
Total cost of sales	180,000	194,000
Gross profit	670,000	716,000
Controllable expenses:		
Salaries and wages	160,000	170,000
Employee benefits	50,000	55,000
Other expenses	150,000	170,000
Income before occupation costs, interest, and depreciation	310,000	321,000
Depreciation expense	80,000	80,000
Interest expense	80,000	75,000
Occupation costs	40,000	45,000
Income before income taxes	110,000	121,000
Income taxes	30,000	35,000
Net income	$ 80,000	$ 86,000

Other Data	20X2	20X3	20X4
Rent expense	–	$10,000	$11,000
Food customers served	–	66,667	65,385
Food inventory at year-end	$4,800	$ 5,000	$ 5,300
Employee meals*	–	$ 1,500	$ 1,550

*Included as part of employee benefits.

Required:

1. Determine the following for 20X3 and 20X4:
   a. Average foodservice check
   b. Food cost percentage
   c. Labor cost percentage
   d. Labor cost per customer served
   e. Number of times interest earned
   f. Operating efficiency ratio
   g. Fixed charge coverage ratio
   h. Profit margin

2. Was Drysdale Pizza more efficient in 20X3 or 20X4? Support your answer with figures and discussion.

Problem 18

Some of the Evangel Inn's financial statements from 20X6 and 20X7 are as follows:

Evangel Inn
Balance Sheets
Dec. 31, 20X6 and 20X7

Assets	20X6	20X7
Current Assets:		
Cash	$ 20,000	$ 60,000
Marketable Securities	20,000	25,000
Accounts Receivable	90,000	115,000
Inventory	15,000	20,000
Prepaid Expenses	15,000	5,000
Total Current Assets	160,000	225,000
Investments	150,000	450,000
Property and Equipment:		
Land	450,000	450,000
Buildings	2,000,000	2,000,000
Equipment	500,000	610,000
Less: Accumulated Depreciation	(1,000,000)	(1,300,000)
Net Property and Equipment	1,950,000	1,760,000
Other Assets—Franchise Fees	100,000	90,000
Total Assets	$ 2,360,000	$ 2,525,000
Liabilities and Owners' Equity		
Current Liabilities:		
Accounts Payable	$ 25,000	$ 35,000
Current Maturities of Long-Term Debt	50,000	50,000
Wages Payable	15,000	15,000
Dividends Payable	20,000	15,000
Total Current Liabilities	110,000	115,000
Long-Term Debt	1,000,000	1,050,000
Owner's Equity:		
Common Stock	1,160,000	1,285,000
Retained Earnings	100,000	225,000
Less: Treasury Stock	(10,000)	(150,000)
Total Owners' Equity	1,250,000	1,360,000
Total Liabilities and Owners' Equity	$ 2,360,000	$ 2,525,000

Evangel Inn
Condensed Income Statement
For the year ended 20X7

Revenues	
Sales	$ 2,700,000
Interest Income	80,000
Total Revenues	2,780,000

Evangel Inn
Condensed Income Statement
For the year ended 20X7

Expenses:

Salaries and Wages		750,000
Depreciation		340,000
Amortization (franchise fees)		10,000
Interest Expense		100,000
Other Expenses		1,140,000
Income before Gains and Losses and Income Taxes		440,000
Gain on Sale of Equipment		20,000
Loss on Sale of Investments		(50,000)
Income Taxes		80,000
Net Income	$	330,000

Additional information:

1. Equipment costing $100,000 was sold for $80,000 during 20X7.

2. Investments costing $100,000 were sold during 20X7, for a loss of $50,000.

3. Dividends of $205,000 were declared during 20X7.

4. Treasury stock of $140,000 was purchased during 20X7.

5. Long-term debt of $100,000 was converted to common stock during 20X7.

6. Common stock of $35,000 was sold during 20X7.

7. Long-term debt of $200,000 was borrowed during 20X7.

8. Marketable securities of $5,000 were purchased during 20X7.

Evangel Inn
Statement of Cash Flows
For the year 20X7

Cash Flow Provided by Operating Activities:		
Net Income		$ 330,000
Adjustments to Reconcile Net Income to Net Cash Flows Provided by Operating Activities:		
Depreciation expense	$ 340,000	
Amortization expense	10,000	
Gain on sale of equipment	(20,000)	
Loss on sale of investments	50,000	
Increase in accounts receivable	(25,000)	
Increase in inventory	(5,000)	
Decrease in prepaid expenses	10,000	
Increase in accounts payable	10,000	370,000
Net Cash Flows from Operating Activities:		700,000

Evangel Inn
Statement of Cash Flows
For the year 20X7

Cash Flow Provided by Investing Activities:

Proceeds from sale of equipment	$ 80,000	
Proceeds from sale of investments	50,000	
Purchase of marketable securities	(5,000)	
Purchase of equipment	(210,000)	
Purchase of investments	(400,000	
Net Cash Flows from Investing Activities:		(485,000)

Cash Flow Provided by Financing Activities:

Payment of long-term debt	(50,000)	
Borrowing—long-term debt	200,000	
Purchase of treasury stock	(140,000)	
Proceeds from sale of common stock	25,000	
Payment of dividends	(210,000)	
Net Cash Flows from Financing Activities:		(175,000)
Increase in Cash		40,000
Cash at the beginning of 20X7		20,000
Cash at the end of 20X7		$ 60,000

Supplementary Schedule of Noncash Investing and Financing
Activities Exchange of Common Stock for Long-Term Debt
Supplementary Disclosure of Cash Flow Information

Cash paid during the year for:

Interest	100,000
Income Taxes	80,000

Required:

Compute the following ratios for the Evangel Inn:

1. Current ratio for 20X6 and 20X7

2. Acid-test ratio for 20X6 and 20X7

3. Accounts receivable turnover for 20X7

4. Return on assets for 20X7

5. Return on owners' equity for 20X7

6. Labor cost percentage for 20X7

7. Average tax rate for 20X7

8. Solvency ratio for 20X6 and 20X7

9. Operating cash flows to total liabilities ratio for 20X7

10. Operating cash flows to current liabilities for 20X7

11. Profit margin for 20X7

Problem 19

The Mantle Inn commenced operations on January 1, 20X1, and has been operating for two years. Assume that you are the new assistant manager and desire to gain some insight into the inn's financial condition. Balance sheets and condensed income statements for the first two years are as follows:

Balance Sheets
Mantle Inn
Dec. 31, 20X1 and 20X2

Assets	20X1	20X2
Current Assets:		
Cash	$ 10,000	$ 15,000
Marketable Securities	–0–	50,000
Accounts Receivable	55,000	60,000
Inventories	10,000	12,000
Total Current Assets	75,000	137,000
Property and Equipment:		
Land	100,000	100,000
Building (net)	1,950,000	1,900,000
Furniture and Equipment (net)	240,000	200,000
Total Property and Equipment	2,290,000	2,200,000
Total Assets	$ 2,365,000	$ 2,337,000
Liabilities and Owners' Equity		
Current Liabilities	$ 55,000	$ 60,000
Long-Term Debt	1,300,000	1,250,000
Total Liabilities	1,355,000	1,310,000
Owners' Equity		
Common Stock	1,000,000	1,000,000
Retained Earnings	10,000	27,000
Total Owners' Equity	1,010,000	1,027,000
Total Liabilities and Owners' Equity	$ 2,365,000	$ 2,337,000

Condensed Income Statements
Mantle Inn
For the years ended Dec. 31, 20X1 and 20X2

	20X1	20X2
Sales	$ 1,200,000	$ 1,400,000
Operated Department Expense	620,000	700,000
Operated Department Income	580,000	700,000
Undistributed Operating Expenses	380,000	400,000
Gross Operating Profit	200,000	300,000
Nonoperating Expenses	185,000	200,000
Income Taxes	5,000	45,000
Net Income	$ 10,000	$ 55,000

Required:

1. Calculate the following ratios for both years:
   a. Current ratio
   b. Solvency ratio
   c. Profit margin
   d. Operating efficiency

2. Calculate for 20X2 the following ratios:
   a. Property and equipment turnover ratio
   b. Total assets turnover ratio
   c. Accounts receivable turnover ratio
   d. Number of days accounts receivable outstanding
   e. Return on total assets
   f. Return on owners' equity

Problem 20

Musial Enterprises consists of four hotels. The corporation's required annual return for each hotel is 12 percent of each hotel's average total assets. The net income and average total assets for each hotel are as follows:

	Gibson Hotel	Brock Hotel	Smith Hotel	Carey Hotel
Net income	$ 2,700,000	$ 4,500,000	$ 3,000,000	$ 3,000,000
Average total assets	$ 20,000,000	$ 15,000,000	$ 25,000,000	$ 18,000,000

Each hotel has the opportunity to expand. The cost of expansion per hotel is $5 million, and the expected annual after-tax profit per hotel is $650,000.

Required:

1. Determine the ROA for each hotel before the expansion consideration.

2. If the expansion is based on maintaining or improving a hotel's ROA, which hotels would be expanded? Why?

3. Calculate the residual income for each hotel before and after the proposed expansion.

Problem 21

The owner of the Martin Motel and Restaurant has asked you to prepare an income statement and balance sheet based on the following:

1. Accounts receivable = $10,000

2. Accounts payable = $15,000

3. Current assets consist of cash, accounts receivable, and inventory

4. Current liabilities consist of only accounts payable

5. Current ratio = 1.2 to 1

6. Acid-test ratio = 0.8 to 1

7. Accounts receivable turnover = 30 times (all sales are credit sales)

8. Food inventory turnover = 9.625 times

9. Beverage inventory turnover = 6.3525 times

10. Property and equipment turnover = 13/47 times

11. Depreciation expense = 10 percent of book value at year-end

12. Long-term debt = 9 times accounts payable

13. Interest rate = 10 percent

14. Tax rate = 20 percent

15. Average room rate = $20

16. Average food and beverage check = $5

17. Size of motel = 25 rooms

18. Occupancy percentage = 80 percent

19. Number of food and beverage checks = 30,800

20. Undistributed operating expenses = 33⅓ percent of total revenue

21. Food cost percentage = 40 percent

22. Beverage cost percentage = 22 percent

23. Food and beverage labor and other cost percentage = 30 percent

24. Rooms labor and other cost percentage = 40 percent

25. Food sales = 62½ percent of total food and beverage sales

26. Debt-equity ratio = 1 to 1

27. Return on owners' equity = 1.330667 percent

Assume that the balance sheet at the beginning of the year is the same as at the end of the year.

Note: For this problem, food and beverage is a single combined department.

Problem 22

Part A:

The Hudson Hotel, a 100-room limited-service operation, has provided you with the following data for the months of September and October:

	September	October
Single rooms sold	1,000	950
Double rooms sold	1,600	1,610
Room revenue	$ 221,000	$ 222,720
Number of paid guests	4,520	4,653

Required:

1. Compute the paid occupancy for September.

2. What was the monthly ADR for October?

3. What was the monthly RevPAR for September?

4. What were the average number of guests per double room during October? (Assume that only one guest stayed in each single room.)

Part B:

The Ausmus Café's beginning and ending food inventory for 20X4 total $12,000 and $14,000, respectively. Activity during 20X4 was as follows:

(1) Food purchases	$ 160,000
(2) Employee meals	$ 3,000
(3) Promotional meals	$ 2,000
(4) Food sales	$ 480,000
(5) Transfers to the beverage department	$ 100

Required:

1. Compute the food cost percentage.

2. Compute the food inventory turnover for 20X4.

Part C:

Selected financial ratios for the Tiger's Club for 20X3–X5 are as follows:

	20X3	20X4	20X5
Current ratio	1.1	1.2	1.3
Accounts receivable turnover	24	22	20
Profit margin	5%	6%	7%
Inventory turnover	15	16	17

Required:

Comment on the changing liquidity of the Tiger's Club from 20X3 to 20X5. Be specific, using the relevant ratios above.

Problem 23

Surfside Lodge has just hired Joseph Lee as the new director of finance to start the new year. Joseph asked the owner about the flow through and flex ratios from last year, 20X8, to the year that just ended, 20X9. The owner has never calculated such ratios. Joseph looked at the statements and prepared the following for the owner.

	20X9	20X8
Operating Revenue		
Rooms	$ 645,921	$ 589,600
Food and Beverage	300,611	256,500
Total Operating Revenue	946,532	846,100
Departmental Expenses		
Rooms	195,877	135,608
Food and Beverage	275,936	192,375
Total Department Expenses	471,813	327,983
Undistributed Operating Expenses		
Administrative and General	121,255	101,532

	20X9	20X8
Information and Telecommunications Systems	50,147	10,153
Sales and Marketing	82,114	67,688
Property Operation and Maintenance	38,671	32,152
Energy, Water, and Waste	39,812	24,537
Total Undistributed Expenses	331,999	236,062
Gross Operating Profit	$ 139,814	$ 91,921

Required:

1. Would Joseph be preparing the GOP flow through or flex ratios or both? Why?

2. Calculate the proper GOP flow through or GOP flex ratio.

3. How is Surfside Lodge's performance in this most recent year, 20X9?

Problem 24

Hotel Lansing has the following summary operating statement, with accounts from all operating revenues to the gross operating profit. The current period of 20XX, the budgeted amounts, and the variance are included.

	20XX	Budget	Variance
Operating Revenue:			
Rooms	$ 201,533	$ 189,000	$ 12,533
Food and Beverage	56,884	57,000	(116)
Other Operated Departments	15,681	12,500	3,181
Miscellaneous Income	1,103	1,250	(147)
Total Operating Revenue	275,201	259,750	15,451
Departmental Expenses:			
Rooms	50,383	45,500	4,883
Food and Beverage	44,370	41,232	3,138
Other Operated Departments	15,932	12,400	3,532
Total Department Expenses	110,685	99,132	11,553
Undistributed Operating Expenses:			
Administrative and General	24,840	23,000	1,840
Information and Telecommunications Systems	2,674	2,800	(126)
Sales and Marketing	26,685	30,000	(3,315)
Property Operation and Maintenance	11,705	12,000	(295)
Energy, Water, and Waste	6,381	7,000	(619)
Total Undistributed Expenses	72,285	74,800	(2,515)
Gross Operating Profit	$ 38,400	$ 24,332	$ 14,068

Required:

1. Is this a flow through or flex situation?

2. Calculate either the GOP flow through or GOP flex ratio.

3. What does this ratio say about the financial performance of Hotel Lansing?

Problem 25

The management company of Oaks Resort shares the budgeted and actual 20X9 figures with its owners. The year 20X9 was particularly challenging, and neither revenue nor GOP made the budgeted level. In addition, Oaks had to replace some air conditioning units. While it was a planned replacement project, one unit simply failed and thus a new unit had to be replaced rather than being maintained.

	20X9	Budget
Operating Revenue:		
Rooms	$ 633,250	$ 775,420
Food and Beverage	297,412	275,500
Total Operating Revenue	930,662	1,050,920
Departmental Expenses:		
Rooms	211,541	217,118
Food and Beverage	269,855	206,625
Total Department Expenses	481,396	423,743
Undistributed Operating Expenses:		
Administrative and General	125,326	126,110
Information and Telecommunications Systems	48,522	12,611
Sales and Marketing	80,124	84,074
Property Operation and Maintenance	70,521	39,935
Energy, Water, and Waste	30,021	30,477
Total Undistributed Expenses	354,514	293,207
Gross Operating Profit	$ 126,882	$ 130,536

Required:

1. Did the Oaks Resort experience a flow through or flex situation in 20X9?

2. Calculate either the GOP flow through or GOP flex ratio.

3. What does the result indicate?

6

BASIC COST CONCEPTS

Chapter 6 Outline

Competencies

1. Define various types of costs and explain how they change in response to changes in sales volume. (pp. 266–272)

2. Use various methods to estimate the fixed and variable elements of a mixed cost. (pp. 272–277)

3. Explain how fixed and variable cost factors influence purchasing decisions. (pp. 277–279)

4. Distinguish direct costs from indirect costs. (p. 279)

5. Identify overhead costs and explain how they may be allocated to profit centers. (pp. 279–283)

6. Describe controllable, differential, relevant, sunk, opportunity, average, incremental, standard, and out-of-pocket costs. (pp. 283–291)

7. Describe activity-based costing and decision-making situations using cost concepts. (pp. 288–291)

KEY TERMS

activity-based costing (ABC)

average cost

avoidable costs

capacity fixed costs

controllable costs

cost allocation

differential costs

discretionary fixed costs

fixed costs

high/low two-point method

incremental cost

indifference point

mixed costs

multiple allocation base approach (MABA)

opportunity cost

out-of-pocket costs

overhead costs

regression analysis

relevant costs

scatter diagram

single allocation base approach (SABA)

standard costs

step costs

sunk cost

variable costs

The word *cost* is used in many different contexts and may convey very different meanings. For example, each of the following expressions uses the term to refer to something different: the cost of a dishwasher was $5,000; the labor cost for the period was $10,000; the cost of damages to the hotel from the hurricane approximated $10,000. In the first expression, cost refers to the purchase price of an asset; one asset (cash) was given in exchange for another asset (the dishwasher). The second expression uses cost to refer to an expense for the period; cash (an asset) was paid to employees for services they provided. In this case, assets were not directly exchanged; rather, cash was paid for labor services rendered by employees to generate revenues and accounts receivable. The accounts receivable, when collected, result in cash. In the third expression, the cost due to the hurricane refers to a loss—a dissipation of assets without the receipt of other assets either directly or indirectly. Obviously, the term cost may have a variety of meanings. In this chapter, we will generally use cost to mean expenses.

Managers must understand many cost concepts, including those in the following questions:

1. What are the hotel's fixed costs?

2. Which costs are relevant to purchasing a new computer?

3. What are the variable costs of serving a steak dinner?

4. What is the opportunity cost of adding 25 rooms to the motel?

5. What is the standard cost of catering a banquet for 500 people?

6. What are the hotel's controllable costs?

7. How are fixed cost portions of mixed costs determined?

8. How are costs allocated to operated departments?

9. Which costs are sunk costs in considering a future purchase?

10. Which costs are relevant to pricing a lobster dinner?

In this chapter, we will discuss a variety of cost concepts. We will consider costs in relation to sales volume and operated departments. We will also discuss the separation of mixed costs into fixed and variable elements, provide a simplified approach to the problem of cost allocation, and consider the concept of relevant costs in decision-making. Appendix C at the end of the book contains a detailed discussion of more advanced approaches to cost allocation, including illustrations of the direct and step methods of cost allocation.

6.1 GENERAL NATURE OF COST

Cost, considered as an expense, is the reduction of an asset, generally for the ultimate purpose of increasing revenues. Costs include cost of food sold, labor expense, supplies expense, utilities expense, marketing expense, rent expense, depreciation expense, insurance expense, and many others. Because the profit margin for most hospitality operations is less than 10 percent, more than 90 percent of their revenues (ultimately cash) is used to pay these expenses or costs. From management's viewpoint, there are several different types of costs. It is essential that managers understand both the types of costs and their applications.

6.2 COSTS IN RELATION TO SALES VOLUME

One way of viewing costs is to understand how they change with changes in the activity (sales) of the hospitality operation. In this context, costs can be seen as fixed, variable, step, or mixed (partly fixed and partly variable).

Fixed Costs

Fixed costs are those that remain constant in the short run, even when sales volume varies. For example, room sales may increase by 5 percent or food sales may decline by 10 percent while, in both cases, the fixed costs remain constant. The graph in Exhibit 6.1 plots costs along the vertical axis and sales volume along the horizontal axis. The graph shows that total fixed costs remain constant even when sales volume increases.

Common examples of fixed costs include salaries, rent expense, insurance expense, property taxes, depreciation expense, and interest expense. Certain fixed costs may be reduced if a lodging facility closes for part of the year. For example, insurance and labor expenses may be avoided during the shutdown. Fixed costs that may be avoided when a company shuts down are called **avoidable costs**.

Fixed costs are often classified as either capacity or discretionary costs. **Capacity fixed costs** relate to the ability to provide goods and services. For a hotel, the capacity fixed costs relate to the ability to provide a number of rooms for sale. The fixed costs include, but are not limited to, depreciation, property taxes, and certain salaries. There is a quality dimension related to capacity fixed costs. For example, if the hotel were to eliminate its swimming pool or air-conditioning system, it could still provide the same number of rooms, but at a lower level of service.

Discretionary fixed costs do not affect a lodging establishment's current capacity. They are costs that managers may choose to avoid during the short run, often to meet a budget. However, continued avoidance will generally cause problems for the hospitality operation. Discretionary fixed costs include educational seminars for executives, charitable contributions, employee training programs, and advertising. Generally, reducing such costs has no immediate effect on operations. However, if these programs continue to be curtailed, sales and various expenses may be seriously affected. During a financial crisis, discretionary fixed costs are likelier to be cut than capacity fixed costs because they are easier to restore and have less immediate impact.

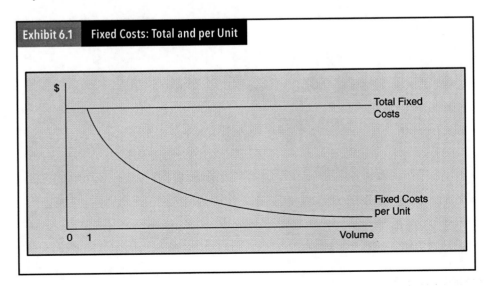

Exhibit 6.1 Fixed Costs: Total and per Unit

Fixed costs can also be related to sales volume by determining the average fixed cost per unit sold. For example, if fixed costs total $10,000 for a period in which 2,000 rooms are sold, the average fixed cost per room sold is $5 ($10,000 ÷ 2,000 rooms). However, if 3,000 rooms are sold during the period, then the average fixed cost per room sold is $3.33 ($10,000 ÷ 3,000 rooms). As the sales volume increases, the fixed cost per unit decreases. The graph in Exhibit 6.1 also illustrates this relationship.

Although they are constant in the short run, all fixed costs change over longer periods. For example, the monthly lease payment on a machine may increase about once per year. Therefore, from a long-term perspective, all fixed costs may be viewed as variable costs.

Variable Costs

Variable costs change proportionally with the volume of business. For example, if food sales increase by 10 percent, the cost of food sold may also be expected to increase by 10 percent. Exhibit 6.2 depicts total variable costs and variable costs per unit as each relates to sales volume. Total variable costs (TVC) are determined by multiplying the variable cost per unit by the number of unit sales. For example, the TVC for a foodservice operation with a variable cost per meal of $3 and 1,000 projected meal sales would be $3,000.

Theoretically, total variable costs vary with total sales, whereas unit variable costs remain constant. For example, if the cost of food sold is 35 percent, then the unit cost per $1 of sales is $0.35, regardless of sales volume. The graph in Exhibit 6.2 shows that unit variable costs are really fixed—that is, the cost per sales dollar remains constant. In actuality, of course, a business should be able to take advantage of volume discounts as its sales increase beyond some level. When this occurs, the cost of sales should increase at a slower rate than sales.

In truth, few costs, if any, vary in *exact* proportion to total sales. However, several costs come close to meeting this criterion and may be considered variable costs. Examples include the cost of food sold, cost of beverages sold, some labor costs, and supplies used in production and service operations. Management fees and franchise fees can also be considered as variable costs.

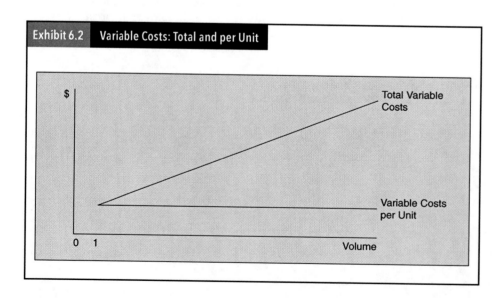

Exhibit 6.2   Variable Costs: Total and per Unit

Step Costs

Step costs are constant within a range of activity but different among ranges of activity. Exhibit 6.3 illustrates this relationship. Supervisor salaries are typical step costs. For example, if a housekeeping supervisor is able to oversee no more than 15 room attendants, then the operation must add another supervisor upon adding the sixteenth room attendant. This new supervisor would be able to supervise an additional 14 room attendants.

Step costs resemble fixed costs when one step includes the operation's probable range of activity. In Exhibit 6.3, for example, Range 2 might be a hotel's expected range of activity. In such cases, step costs are considered fixed costs for analytical purposes. When there are many steps and the cost differences between steps are small, then step costs, for analytical purposes, are considered mixed costs (to be discussed next).

Mixed Costs

Many costs are partly fixed and partly variable—that is, they are a mix of both fixed and variable cost elements. These costs are sometimes referred to as semi-variable or semi-fixed. In this chapter, we will refer to costs that are partly fixed and partly variable as **mixed costs**.

The mixed cost's fixed element is determined independently of sales activity, while the variable element is assumed to vary proportionally with sales volume. As with variable costs, the variable element of mixed costs may not vary in exact proportion to sales activity. However, the assumption of a linear relationship between variable cost elements and sales volume is generally accepted because any difference is usually considered insignificant. However, this assumption is reasonable only across a relevant range of activity. For example, the relevant range for a hotel *may* be paid occupancy levels between 40 percent and 95 percent. Outside of this range, the variable cost-sales relationship *may* be different.

The graph in Exhibit 6.4 depicts the two elements (fixed and variable) of mixed costs. The portion of the vertical axis below point A represents fixed costs, while the difference between the slopes of the total mixed costs and fixed cost lines reflects the variable element of total mixed costs. The graph in Exhibit 6.5 shows a decrease in unit mixed costs as sales volume increases. This decrease is not as dramatic as the decrease in fixed costs per sales unit (Exhibit 6.1) because the variable element in mixed costs increases with each unit sold, therefore increasing total mixed costs.

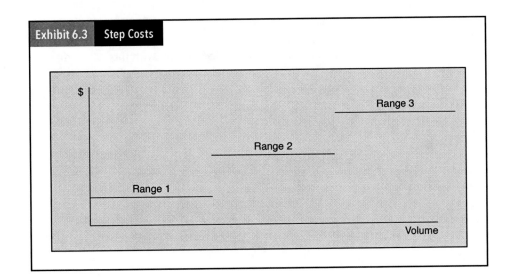

Exhibit 6.3 Step Costs

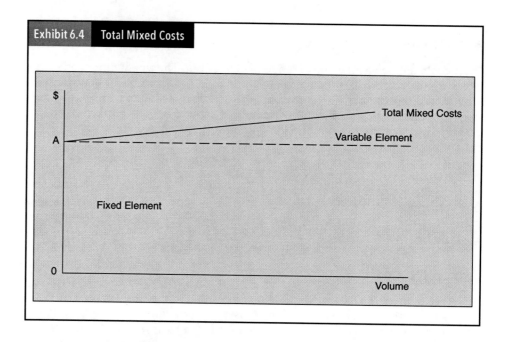

Exhibit 6.4 **Total Mixed Costs**

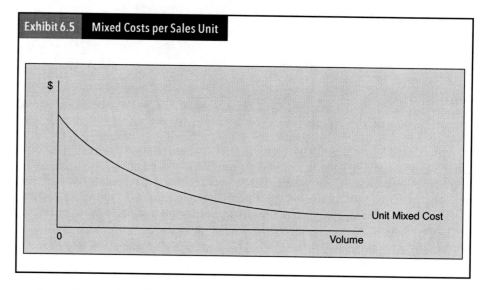

Exhibit 6.5 **Mixed Costs per Sales Unit**

Several examples of mixed costs, including a brief discussion of their fixed and variable elements, are listed in Exhibit 6.6.

Total mixed costs (TMC) for any cost can be estimated with the following equation:

$$TMC = \text{Fixed costs} + (\text{Variable cost per unit} \times \text{Unit sales})$$

Thus, a hotel with a franchise fee of $1,000 per month and $3 per room sold would estimate its franchise fees (a mixed cost) for a month with 3,500 projected room sales as follows:

$$\text{Franchise fees} = \$1,000 + (3,500 \times \$3)$$
$$= \underline{\underline{\$11,500}}$$

Exhibit 6.6	Fixed and Variable Elements of Mixed Costs	
	Elements	
Mixed Cost	**Fixed**	**Variable**
1. Telephone expense	Cost of system/rental of system	Cost of calls
2. Building lease	Fixed cost per square foot of space rented	Percentage of revenue in addition to fixed amount
3. Automobile lease	Fixed cost/day	Additional charge per mile automobile is driven
4. Executive remuneration	Base pay	Bonuses based on sales
5. Repair and maintenance	Minimum amount required to maintain lodging firm at low occupancy	Additional maintenance required with higher occupancy levels

Total Costs

Total costs (TC) for a hospitality establishment consist of the sum of its fixed, variable, step, and mixed costs. If step costs are included in either fixed or mixed costs, the TC may be determined by the following equation:

$$TC = \text{Fixed costs} + (\text{Variable cost per unit} \times \text{Unit sales})$$

An estimation of TC for a rooms-only lodging operation that sells 1,000 rooms and has total fixed costs of $20,000 and variable costs per unit of $20 is $40,000.

$$TC = \$20,000 + (1,000 \times \$20)$$
$$= \underline{\underline{\$40,000}}$$

Total costs are depicted graphically in Exhibit 6.7.

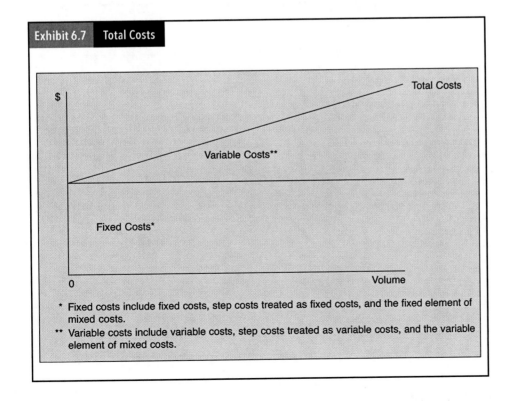

Exhibit 6.7	Total Costs

* Fixed costs include fixed costs, step costs treated as fixed costs, and the fixed element of mixed costs.

** Variable costs include variable costs, step costs treated as variable costs, and the variable element of mixed costs.

The equation for TC corresponds to the general equation for a straight line, which is as follows:[1]

$$y = a + bx$$

where
y = value of the dependent variable (total costs)
a = the constant term (total fixed costs)
b = slope of the line (variable cost per unit)
x = the value of the independent variable (units sold)

6.3 DETERMINATION OF MIXED COST ELEMENTS

When making pricing, marketing, and expansion decisions, management needs to estimate the fixed and variable elements of each mixed cost. We will consider three methods of estimating mixed cost elements: the high/low two-point method, the scatter diagram, and regression analysis. The maintenance and repair expense of the hypothetical Mayflower Hotel for 20X1 will be used to illustrate all three methods. Exhibit 6.8 presents the monthly repair and maintenance expense together with rooms sold by month for the Mayflower Hotel.

High/Low Two-Point Method

The simplest approach to estimating the fixed and variable elements of a mixed cost is the **high/low two-point method**. This approach is simple because it bases the estimation on data from only two periods in the entire time span of an establishment's operations. The method consists of the following eight steps:

Exhibit 6.8	Monthly Repair and Maintenance Expense

20X1 Monthly Repair and Maintenance Expense
Mayflower Hotel

Month	Repair and Maintenance Expense	Rooms Sold
January	$ 6,200	1,860
February	6,100	1,820
March	7,000	2,170
April	7,500	2,250
May	8,000	2,480
June	8,500	2,700
July	7,900	2,790
August	8,600	2,800
September	7,000	2,100
October	6,000	1,900
November	6,500	1,800
December	5,900	1,330
Total	$85,200	26,000

1. Select the two extreme periods (such as months) of sales activity (e.g., rooms sold) in the time span under consideration (such as 1 year). If an extreme value is due to an event beyond management's control and does not represent normal operations, consider the next value. For example, if a country club is closed for the month of January, the value for the next lowest month should be used. Extreme values may only be apparent when charted on a scatter diagram, which we will discuss shortly.

2. Calculate the differences in total mixed cost and activity for the two periods.

3. Divide the mixed cost difference by the activity difference to determine the variable cost per activity unit (e.g., each room sold).

4. Multiply the variable cost per activity unit by the total activity for the period of lowest (or highest) sales to arrive at the total variable cost for the period of lowest (or highest) activity.

5. Subtract the result in Step 4 from the total mixed cost for the period of lowest activity to determine the fixed cost for that period.

6. Check the answer in Step 5 by repeating Steps 4 and 5 for the period with the greatest activity.

7. Multiply the fixed cost per period by the number of periods in the time span to calculate the fixed costs for the entire time period.

8. Subtract the total fixed costs from the total mixed costs to determine the total variable costs.

The high/low two-point method is illustrated below using data from Exhibit 6.8:

1. High month—August
   Low month—December

2.

	Repair and Maintenance Expense	Rooms Sold
August	$8,600	2,800
December	5,900	1,330
Difference	$2,700	1,470

3. Variable Cost per Room Sold $= \dfrac{\text{Mixed Cost Difference}}{\text{Rooms Sold Difference}}$

   $= \dfrac{\$2,700}{1,470}$

   $= \$1.8367$

This result means that for every additional room sold, the hotel will incur repair and maintenance variable costs of $1.8367.

4. Total Variable Cost of Repair and Maintenance Expense for December $=$ December Rooms Sold $\times$ Variable Cost

   $= 1,330 \times 1.8367$

   $= \$2,442.81$

5. Total Fixed Cost of Repair and Maintenance Expense for December = Total Repair and Maintenance Cost for December–Variable Repair and Maintenance Cost for December

$$= \$5,900 - \$2,442.81$$

$$= \underline{\$3,457.19}$$

6. Check results by using the high month, August.

Variable Cost $= 2,800 \times 1.8367$

$$= \underline{\$5,142.76}$$

Fixed Cost $= \$8,600.00 - \$5,142.76$

$$= \underline{\$3,457.24}$$

Compare the result in Step 5 with Step 6 as follows:

Fixed Costs—Step 6 $3,457.24

Fixed Costs—Step 5 $-3,457.19$

             $\underline{0.05}$ (minor difference due to rounding)

7. Calculate total fixed costs for the year.

Total Fixed Costs = Fixed Costs per Month $\times$ 12 Months

$$= \$3,457.19 \times 12$$

$$= \underline{\$41,486.28}$$

8. Determine total variable costs of repair and maintenance expense for the year.

Total Variable Costs = Total Mixed Costs – Total Fixed Costs

$$= \$85,200 - \$41,486.28$$

$$= \underline{\$43,713.72}$$

The high/low two-point method considers only two extreme periods and is a fairly simple way of estimating the variable and fixed elements of mixed costs. This approach assumes that the extreme periods are a fair reflection of the high and low points for the entire year; therefore, the results will be inaccurate to the degree that the two periods fail to represent fairly the high and low points of activity. The scatter diagram, though tedious, is a more accurate approach.

Scatter Diagram

The **scatter diagram** is a detailed approach to determining the fixed and variable elements of a mixed cost. The steps involved in this method are as follows:

1. Prepare a graph with the independent variable (sales volume) on the horizontal axis and the dependent variable (cost) on the vertical axis.

2. Plot data on the graph by periods.

3. Draw a straight line through the points, keeping an equal number of points above and below the line.

4. Extend the line to the vertical axis. The intersection indicates the fixed costs for the period.

5. Multiply the fixed costs for the period by the number of periods to determine the fixed costs for the time span.

6. Determine total variable costs by subtracting total fixed costs (Step 5) from total mixed costs.

7. Determine variable costs per sales unit by dividing total variable costs by total units sold.

Exhibit 6.9 is a scatter diagram of the maintenance and repair expense of the Mayflower Hotel. The scatter diagram was graphed with rooms sold as the independent variable (horizontal axis) and repair and maintenance expense as the dependent variable (vertical axis). Each monthly repair and maintenance expense was plotted and a straight line was drawn through the points. The line might vary depending on who draws it; however, it should approximate a "best fit." In this case, there are five points above the line, five points below the line, and two points on the line. The line intersects the vertical axis at $3,300. This is the fixed cost approximation per month. The estimated annual fixed costs are $39,600 ($3,300 × 12 months). Therefore, total variable repair and maintenance costs are $45,600, determined by subtracting total fixed costs of $39,600 from total costs of $85,200. Variable repair and maintenance costs per room sold is $1.75, determined by dividing the total variable costs of $45,600 by the number of rooms sold for the year (26,000).

The scatter diagram is an improvement over the high/low two-point approach because it includes data from all periods in the time span under consideration. In our example, the calculations use data from 12 months of a year. However, these calculations are time consuming, and the placement of the straight line between the data points is an approximation rather than a precise measurement. Regression analysis (discussed next) is a still more accurate approach. However, since an assumption when using regression analysis is a linear relationship between the two variables, a scatter diagram is still useful for determining linearity.

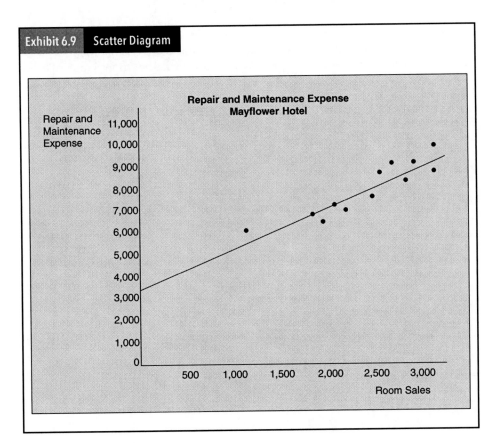

Exhibit 6.9   Scatter Diagram

Regression Analysis

Regression analysis is a mathematical approach to fitting a straight line to data points perfectly—that is, the difference in the distances of the data points from the line is minimized. The formulas used in regression analysis allow us to make the calculations without plotting points or drawing lines.

As stated earlier, the formula for a straight line is $y = a + bx$. In our Mayflower Hotel example, y stands for repair and maintenance expense, x stands for rooms sold, a stands for the fixed cost element, and b stands for the variable cost per room sold. Therefore, the total repair and maintenance expense (y) for any period is the fixed cost element (a) plus the variable cost per room sold (b) multiplied by the number of rooms sold (x).

Once we know the monthly fixed cost element of the repair and maintenance expense, we multiply that figure by 12 months to calculate the annual total fixed cost element. The formula for determining the monthly fixed cost element is as follows:

$$\text{Fixed Costs} = \frac{(\sum y)(\sum x^2) - (\sum x)(\sum xy)}{n(\sum x^2) - (\sum x)^2}$$

The formula is explained as follows:

$\sum$ is the Greek letter sigma, which is read, and means, "the sum of." So, $\sum x$ and $\sum y$ mean the sum of all x values and the sum of all y values, respectively. $\sum xy$ means the sum of all x and y values that are multiplied together.

y stands for the dependent variable.

x stands for the independent variable.

n stands for the number of periods in the time span.

Exhibit 6.10 presents the calculated values for the Mayflower Hotel. Putting these values into the formula reveals that the monthly fixed cost element of repair and maintenance expense is $2,719.57.[2] Fixed cost per month multiplied by 12 equals the total fixed element of repair and maintenance expense for 20X1 ($32,634.84).

The total variable costs are determined by subtracting total fixed costs from total costs. Using the total cost figure for the Mayflower Hotel's repair and maintenance expense found in Exhibit 6.8, we can calculate the total variable cost element as follows:

Repair and Maintenance Expense	$85,200.00
Total Fixed Cost Element	−32,634.84
Total Variable Cost Element	$52,565.16

The variable cost per room sold is determined by solving for the value of b using the formula for a straight line:

$$y = a + bx$$
$$85,200 = 32,634.84 + b(26,000)$$
$$b = \$2.02 \text{ per room sold}$$

These computations, performed manually, are too complex for practical application. Many computers and hand-held financial calculators have programs available to perform these calculations. The user simply enters the appropriate data. However, because this is so easy, there is a tendency for the user to feed raw data into the calculator or computer and accept the output as truth.

Exhibit 6.10 Calculating Values for Fixed Cost Elements

Determination and Calculation of Values for Repair and Maintenance Fixed Cost Elements
Mayflower Hotel

Month	(x) Rooms Sold	(y) Repair and Maintenance Expense	x^2	xy
January	1,860	$ 6,200	3,459,600	11,532,000
February	1,820	6,100	3,312,400	11,102,000
March	2,170	7,000	4,708,900	15,190,000
April	2,250	7,500	5,062,500	16,875,000
May	2,480	8,000	6,150,400	19,840,000
June	2,700	8,500	7,290,000	22,950,000
July	2,790	7,900	7,784,100	22,041,000
August	2,800	8,600	7,840,000	24,080,000
September	2,100	7,000	4,410,000	14,700,000
October	1,900	6,000	3,610,000	11,400,000
November	1,800	6,500	3,240,000	11,700,000
December	1,330	5,900	1,768,900	7,847,000
Totals	$\Sigma x = 26,000$	$\Sigma y = \$85,200$	$\Sigma x^2 = 58,636,800$	$\Sigma xy = 189,257,000$

The cliché "garbage in, garbage out" applies here. The user should select variables that have a logical relationship. For example, repair and maintenance expense and number of meals served may not be a meaningful relationship. If more guests dine in a hotel's restaurant, repair and maintenance expense in foodservice operations will increase, but dining in the restaurant does not affect repair and maintenance in other departments. Rooms sold, or even number of hotel guests, relates more logically to repair and maintenance expense.

As with the high/low two-point method, values representing abnormal operating conditions should not be included in regression analysis.

Evaluation of the Results

The three methods demonstrated to estimate the fixed and variable elements of the Mayflower Hotel's repair and maintenance expense produced the following results:

	Fixed	Variable	Total
High/low two-point method	$41,486.28	$43,713.72	$85,200
Scatter diagram	39,600.00	45,600.00	85,200
Regression analysis	32,634.84	52,565.16	85,200

The difference between the fixed cost amounts determined by the simplest (the high/low two-point method) and the most complex (regression analysis) methods is $8,851.44. This difference is more than 25 percent of the figure reached by regression analysis. Regression analysis is the most precise method and easily performed with a financial calculator or a computer. However, the major determination of which method to use is based on cost-benefit considerations.

6.4 FIXED VERSUS VARIABLE COSTS

Many goods and services may be purchased on either a fixed or variable cost arrangement. For example, a lease may be either fixed (offered at a fixed price) or variable (offered at a certain percentage of revenues). Management's decision to select a fixed or variable cost arrangement is based on the cost-benefit considerations involved. Under a truly fixed arrangement, the cost remains the same regardless of activity and, therefore, management is able to lock in a maximum amount. Under a variable arrangement, the amount paid depends on the level of activity. The level of activity at which the period cost is the same under either arrangement is called the **indifference point**. Some may also call this the natural breakpoint. An example follows to illustrate this concept.

Assume that a foodservice operation has the option of signing either an annual fixed lease of $48,000 or a variable lease set at 5 percent of revenue. The indifference point is determined as follows:

$$\text{Variable Cost Percentage} \times \text{Revenue} = \text{Fixed Lease Cost}$$
$$0.05 \, (\text{Revenue}) = 48,000$$
$$\text{Revenue} = \frac{48,000}{0.05}$$
$$\text{Revenue} = \underline{\underline{\$960,000}}$$

When annual revenue is $960,000, the lease expense will be $48,000, regardless of whether the lease arrangement is fixed or variable. Therefore, if annual revenue is expected to exceed $960,000, then management should select a fixed lease in order to minimize its lease expense. On the other hand, if annual revenue is expected to be less than $960,000, a variable lease will minimize lease

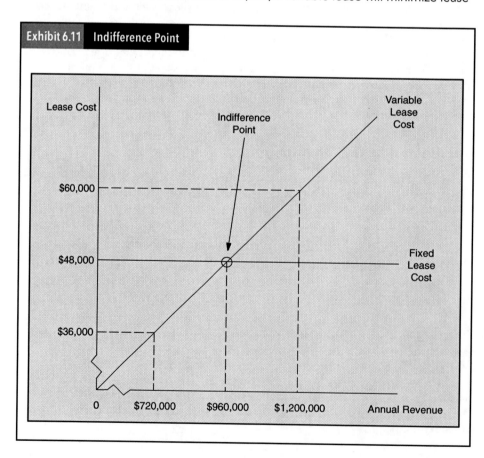

Exhibit 6.11   Indifference Point

expense. Exhibit 6.11 is the graphic depiction of this situation. A review of Exhibit 6.11 suggests the following:

1. Using a variable lease results in an excess lease expense at any revenue point to the *right* of the indifference point. For example, using the previous illustration, if revenue is $1.2 million, the lease expense from a variable lease is $60,000, or $12,000 more than for a fixed lease of $48,000 annually.

2. Using a fixed lease results in an excess lease expense at any revenue point to the *left* of the indifference point. For example, using the previous illustration, if revenue is $720,000, the lease expense is still $48,000, or $12,000 more than for a variable lease.

6.5 DIRECT AND INDIRECT COSTS

When we talk about expenses, certain expenses are called direct while other expenses are implied to be indirect. Direct and indirect expenses are discussed as they pertain to the operated departments (profit centers) within a lodging establishment. In other words, the "objects" of direct/indirect expenses are considered to be the operated departments that generate income and incur expenses, such as the rooms department and the food department. For example, direct costs of the rooms department may include payroll and related expenses, commissions, contract cleaning, guest transportation, laundry and dry cleaning, linen, operating supplies, reservations, uniforms, and other expenses as well. In this context, undistributed operating expenses, management fees, nonoperating expenses such as property taxes and depreciation, and income taxes may be considered indirect (overhead) expenses.

However, depending on the object of the incurred expenses, many costs may be both direct and indirect. In general, a direct cost is one readily identified with an object, whereas an indirect cost is not readily identified with an object. Therefore, whether a cost is direct or indirect depends on the context of the discussion and, in particular, on whether the object incurring the cost can be identified in the discussion's context. For instance, when speaking of the service center formed by the general manager's department, the general manager's salary can be ascribed as a direct cost of the service center and can be classified as a subset of administrative and general expense. However, in the context of discussing all operated departments (profit centers) and other service centers (e.g., the marketing department), the general manager's salary would be ascribed as an indirect cost of these other departments because the object of this cost in those departments cannot be directly identified.

This distinction is important because department heads are responsible for the direct costs of their departments since they exercise control over them; however, they normally are not responsible for indirect costs.

6.6 OVERHEAD COSTS

Overhead costs include all costs other than the direct costs incurred by profit centers. Thus, overhead costs are indirect costs when the cost objectives are the profit centers. Overhead costs include the undistributed operating expenses (administrative and general, information and telecommunications systems, sales and marketing, property operation and maintenance, and utility costs), management fees, and nonoperating expenses (insurance, rent, depreciation, property taxes, etc.). In the broadest sense, financing costs such as interest expenses and income taxes can also be considered overhead costs, though technically they do not relate directly or indirectly to production.

Generally, overhead costs are not distributed to profit centers. This is because these expenses are regarded as indirect costs, not readily ascribed to objects in the operated departments. However, management and the board of directors of a hospitality establishment may want to distribute overhead costs among the profit centers. This process is commonly called **cost allocation**.

Allocation of Overhead Costs

Appendix C at the end of the book discusses and illustrates advanced cost allocation approaches. For our purposes here, however, we will consider a simplified approach that allocates overhead costs using a single allocation base (such as square footage). This method is referred to as the **single allocation base approach (SABA)**. We will illustrate this approach with the hypothetical Walters Motor Inn, whose unallocated income statement for a typical month is shown in Exhibit 6.12.

As the exhibit shows, the monthly net income for the entire operation is $4,500. The rooms and food and beverage departments have generated departmental incomes of $40,000 and $8,500, respectively. The only overhead cost that will not be allocated among departments is income tax. All other costs will be allocated based on square footage. The square footage of the rooms department is 40,000, while the food and beverage department occupies 15,000 square feet. Therefore, 72.73 percent of the overhead costs will be allocated

---

Exhibit 6.12 Sample Unallocated Income Statement

Unallocated Income Statement
Walters Motor Inn

	Rooms	Food & Beverage	Total
Revenue	$ 60,000	$ 40,000	$ 100,000
Cost of Sales	0	16,000	16,000
Payroll & Related Expenses	14,000	11,000	25,000
Other Direct Expenses	6,000	4,500	10,500
Total Expenses	20,000	31,500	51,500
Departmental Income	$ 40,000	$ 8,500	48,500
Undistributed Operating Expenses:			
Administrative & General			12,000
Sales & Marketing			3,000
Property Operation and Maintenance			2,000
Utility Costs			4,000
Gross Operating Profit			27,500
Insurance			3,000
Depreciation			18,000
Total Insurance and Depreciation			21,000
Income before Income Taxes			6,500
Income Taxes			2,000
Net Income			$ 4,500

---

to the rooms department and 27.27 percent will be allocated to the food and beverage department.

Exhibit 6.13 illustrates this allocation. Exhibit 6.14 shows the allocated income statement of the Walters Motor Inn. The rooms department's bottom line after cost allocation is $9,453, while the food and beverage department's bottom line is $(2,953).

If an allocation base other than square footage had been used, there would have been different cost allocation amounts and, therefore, different departmental income reported after allocation. For example, the Walters Motor Inn employs 14 people in the rooms department and 20 people in the food and beverage department. If the SABA had used the number of employees in each department as the allocation base, the rooms department would absorb 41.18 percent of the overhead costs, while the food and beverage department would absorb 58.82 percent. The Walters Motor Inn allocated income statement, in very abbreviated form, would now appear as follows:

	Rooms	Food & Beverage	Total
Departmental Income	$ 40,000	$ 8,500	$ 48,500
Overhead Costs Allocated	17,296	24,704	42,000
Post Allocation Departmental Income	$ 22,704	$ (16,204)	$ 6,500

The above figures show that a different allocation base results in different allocated amounts and, therefore, in different departmental incomes following allocation. Ideally, costs should be allocated based on their actual usage by the profit centers and the nature of the expense involved. For example, if the hotel is leased on a square footage basis, then square footage is a suitable allocation base for the hotel's rent expense. On the other hand, since the general manager's supervisory role is often their primary role in managing the hotel, the general manager's salary may be allocated based on the number of employees supervised or even payroll expense by department.

Exhibit 6.13 Overhead Costs

Overhead Costs
Walters Motor Inn

Overhead Cost Area[2]	Overhead Cost	Percentage		Amount[1]	
		Rooms	Food & Bev.	Rooms	Food & Bev.
A & G	$ 12,000	72.73%	27.27%	$ 8,728	$ 3,272
Sales & Marketing	3,000	72.73	27.27	2,182	818
POM	2,000	72.73	27.27	1,455	545
Utility Costs	4,000	72.73	27.27	2,909	1,091
Insurance	3,000	72.73	27.27	2,182	818
Depreciation	18,000	72.73	27.27	13,091	4,909
Total	$42,000			$30,547	$11,453

[1]All amounts are rounded to the nearest $1.
[2]A & G = administrative & general; POM = property operation and maintenance.

Exhibit 6.14 Sample Allocated Income Statement

Allocated Income Statement
Walters Motor Inn

	Rooms	Food & Beverage	Total
Revenue	$60,000	$40,000	$100,000
Cost of Sales	0	16,000	16,000
Payroll & Related Expenses	14,000	11,000	25,000
Other Direct Expenses	6,000	4,500	10,500
Total Expenses	20,000	31,500	51,500
Departmental Income	40,000	8,500	48,500
Allocated Overhead Costs:			
Administrative & General	8,728	3,272	12,000
Sales & Marketing	2,182	818	3,000
Property Operation & Maintenance	1,455	545	2,000
Utility Costs	2,909	1,091	4,000
Insurance	2,182	818	3,000
Depreciation	13,091	4,909	18,000
Total	30,547	11,453	42,000
Income before Income Taxes	$ 9,453	$(2,953)	6,500
Income Taxes			2,000
Net Income			$ 4,500

Using different allocation bases to allocate different overhead costs among departments is referred to as the **multiple allocation base approach (MABA).** MABA is generally preferable to SABA because MABA allocates overhead costs on the basis of an observed relationship between the cost and the profit center. Appendix C at the end of the book contains a discussion of two multiple allocation base approaches.

After Cost Allocation

As Exhibit 6.14 shows, the food and beverage department of the Walters Motor Inn shows a $2,953 loss after cost allocation. Assuming the cost allocation was reasonable, what should be done, if anything? Management should consider at least four factors when deciding what to do about an underperforming department:

1. The underperforming department's income

2. The extent to which the overhead costs allocated to the underperforming department are fixed

3. The extent to which the presence and performance of the department affects other profit centers

4. Operating alternatives for the underperforming department

In our example, management of the Walters Motor Inn might propose closing the food and beverage department; however, this would result in the loss of the department's income of $8,500. Furthermore, assuming that the allocated overhead costs would be incurred anyway, the $11,453 allocated to the food and beverage department would be reallocated to the rooms department. (To the extent that some of these costs could be avoided, closing down a "losing" department would be favorable to the overall profit picture. However, other factors must be considered.) The Walters Motor Inn would thus incur a $2,000 pretax loss by closing the food and beverage department, determined as follows:

Income before income taxes (per Exhibit 6.14)	$ 6,500
Loss of food and beverage department income	(8,500)
Net result	$ (2,000)

Management must also consider the food and beverage department's impact on other profit centers. For example, if the food and beverage department is closed, sales in the rooms department, and thus rooms income, might decrease. The final consideration is how the food and beverage operation is being managed. Perhaps a new menu, renovations, or other changes might correct the department's performance problems.

6.7 CONTROLLABLE COSTS

Managers should generally hold their subordinates responsible only for those costs they can control; to do otherwise may be counterproductive. Controlling costs means using judgment and authority to regulate costs—that is, keeping costs within certain limits rather than eliminating them. **Controllable costs** are costs over which a person is able to exert an influence. For example, the food department manager may be able to influence food usage, personnel preparing and serving food, and supplies used in food production and service. Therefore, cost of food sold, payroll expense, and food and service supplies expense are controllable costs for the food department manager. On the other hand, the food department manager generally has no control over rent paid for the space the restaurant occupies. However, the board of directors may be able to control the rent expense; therefore, from the board's perspective, rent is a controllable expense.

Several costs cannot be easily influenced or changed in the short run; these costs are often considered noncontrollable. However, such costs can be regulated over the long run and from this perspective can be viewed as controllable. In general, all costs are controllable given sufficient time and input from a high enough level of management.

The income statement is organized on a responsibility accounting basis. The direct expenses of each profit center are those costs that the respective department heads control. For example, the food and beverage department manager has authority over (and can therefore control) cost of sales, payroll and related expenses, and other direct expenses of the food and beverage department. Exhibit 6.15 is a table listing several costs as they relate to the general manager's ability to control them.

The general manager and department managers should be held accountable for costs they control. First, the controllable fixed costs incurred should be compared to the amounts budgeted for the period. Second, the controllable variable costs should be compared to the product of the variable unit costs times the unit sales. For example, assume that a food and beverage department's costs are budgeted at $2,000 of fixed costs per month and $3 per meal served. Further assume that 3,000 meals were served during the month and that the actual costs incurred were $2,200 for fixed costs and $9,300 for variable costs. A quick review reflects the following:

	Budget	Actual	Difference
Fixed costs	$ 2,000	$ 2,200	$200
Variable costs	9,000	9,300	300
	$11,000	$11,500	$500

The manager's performance reflects actual costs of $500 in excess of the budget. (In practice, costs and expenses are shown by account, rather than being categorized simply as fixed and variable.)

6.8 DIFFERENTIAL COSTS

In a decision-making situation, costs that differ between two alternatives are called **differential costs**. By focusing on differential costs, decision-makers can narrow the set of cost considerations to those that make a difference between two alternatives.

For example, suppose management is considering the installation of a front office computer to replace two obsolete posting machines. In this situation, differential costs include the purchase price of the computer and any other costs associated with the new computer that differ from the costs involved in using the existing posting machines. Such costs might include labor, utilities, supplies, and insurance. Costs that remain the same with or without the new computer are nondifferential and need not be considered in the decision-making process.

6.9 RELEVANT COSTS

Relevant costs are those that must be considered in a decision-making situation. In order for a cost to be relevant, it must be differential, future, and quantifiable. The differential criterion demands that the cost between two or more alternatives be different, as just explained in Section 6.8. The future characteristic demands that the cost must not have already occurred, but must be incurred only after the decision is made. Finally, relevant costs must be quantifiable. An unquantifiable preference for Machine A over Machine B is not a cost consideration in the decision-making process. The following example illustrates the concept of relevant costs.

Happy Harry, owner of Harry's Place, has been approached by a salesperson selling ranges. The salesperson wants to sell Happy Harry a new range and provides the following information:

Cost of new range	=	$5,000
Estimated useful life of new range	=	6 years
Annual operating costs:		
Electricity	=	$800
Repairs	=	$200
Labor	=	$25,000
Estimated salvage value after 6 years	=	$500

Happy Harry believes his present range, with a major repair job, should last for six more years. In order to make a rational and informed decision, Happy Harry compiles the following data on his present range:

Original cost	=	$2,000
Estimated cost of required major repair	=	$1,200
Estimated salvage value now	=	$300
Estimated salvage value after 6 years	=	$100
Annual operating costs:		
Electricity	=	$700
Repairs	=	$500
Labor	=	$25,000

The relevant costs are listed in Exhibit 6.16. All of these costs are relevant because they are differential, future, and quantifiable. The original cost of the present range is irrelevant because it is not a future cost (but rather a *sunk cost*, discussed next), and the cost of labor is irrelevant because it is not differential. (The process of selecting an alternative is discussed later in this chapter.)

Exhibit 6.16	Relevant Costs–Happy Harry's

	Alternatives	
Cost	Buy New	Keep Old
Cost of new range	$5,000	–
Electricity (annually)	800	$ 700
Repairs (annually)	200	500
Salvage value of present range now	300	–
Salvage value of range (end of sixth year)	500	100
Major repair job	–	1,200

6.10 SUNK COSTS

A **sunk cost** is a past cost relating to a past decision. A sunk cost may be differential yet irrelevant because it is not future. In the case of Happy Harry's decision, the original cost of the old range, $2,000, is a sunk cost.

In many decision-making situations, management will review financial records to determine the net book value (cost less accumulated depreciation) of a fixed asset that is to be replaced. This suggests that many managers consider the net book value of a fixed asset (rather than its original cost) the sunk cost. However, in this chapter, we will consider *both* the original cost and the net book value sunk costs. The relevant cost in replacing a fixed asset is the asset's current value. The current $300 value of Happy Harry's old range and its projected value of $100 at the end of six years are both relevant costs since they are differential, future, and quantifiable.

6.11 OPPORTUNITY COSTS

The cost of the best foregone opportunity in a decision-making situation is the **opportunity cost**. Opportunity costs are among the relevant cost considerations in decision-making situations. If the decision-making process is rational, then the opportunity cost is less than the value associated with the outcome of the decision. For example, let's assume that $100,000 may be invested in one of three ways:

Investment	Annual Return
XYZ Corporation Bonds	10%
ABC Company Preferred Stock	12%
Uninsured Time Certificate of Deposit	9%

Assume that all three alternatives involve the same amount of risk—that is, the degree of certainty of receiving the specified return is the same for all three investment choices. Further assume that the ability of each investment to be converted into cash is the same for all three alternatives. Everything else being the same, the rational choice is to invest in ABC Company Preferred Stock. The best foregone opportunity is the investment in XYZ Corporation Bonds. Therefore, the opportunity costs associated with making the rational choice amount to $20,000 over 2 years ($100,000 × 10% × 2). The choice is a rational one because the return on the alternative selected ($24,000 from ABC stock) exceeds the opportunity costs of $20,000. The potential return of 9 percent on the Uninsured Time Certificate of Deposit is not an opportunity cost because it is not the best foregone opportunity. However, it is a relevant cost because it is future, differential, and quantifiable.

6.12 AVERAGE AND INCREMENTAL COSTS

The **average cost** to provide products and services is determined by dividing the total production and service costs by the quantity of production. For example, a foodservice operation may be able to produce the average meal served at breakfast for $3. The production costs include fixed, variable, and mixed costs. The calculation is as follows:

Cost of food (variable)	$ 200
Cost of labor (mixed)	200
Cost of supplies (variable)	10
Utilities (mixed)	10
Depreciation (fixed)	10
Other (mixed)	20
Total	$ 450
Number of meals produced	150

Average cost = $450 ÷ 150 = $3.00

The cost to produce and serve the next breakfast (number 151) is called the **incremental cost**. Incremental costs include the variable costs of food and supplies, as well as the variable portion of the mixed costs. Without providing detail, we will use $2 as the incremental cost. Thus, in this case, the incremental cost per meal is less than the average cost. In some cases, fixed costs or at least the fixed element of a mixed cost would have to be included in the incremental cost calculation. For example, if we wanted to know the cost of producing and serving 150 additional meals, we would include the cost of additional supervision and so on.

A common difference encountered between average and incremental costs concerns income taxes. To illustrate the difference, consider a simplified graduated tax rate as follows:

Taxable Income	Tax Rate
$20,000 and under	15%
Greater than $20,000	25%

The incremental taxes and average taxes paid on each dollar of taxable income up to $20,000 is $0.15. Taxes on income in excess of $20,000 will be $0.25 for each dollar of taxable income. Thus, the incremental tax on the 25,000th dollar is $0.25, while the average tax on $25,000 is 17 percent, calculated as follows:

Taxes on the first $20,000:	$20,000 × 0.15 =	$3,000
Taxes on the next $5,000:	$ 5,000 × 0.25 =	$1,250
Total taxes		$4,250

Average tax = $4,250 ÷ $25,000 = 0.17

6.13 STANDARD COSTS

Standard costs are a forecast of what actual costs should be under projected conditions. These standards may serve as comparisons for control purposes and as evaluations of productivity. Generally, standard costs are established on a unit basis. For example, standard recipe costs consider the planned cost of a food serving such as a dinner or an à la carte item. Assume that the standard recipe cost for a dinner is $4.50. If 100 dinners are served, then the budgeted cost is $450. An actual food cost of $475 reveals a $25 variance. If the variance is significant, it is investigated to determine the probable cause(s) and appropriate corrective action.

6.14 OUT-OF-POCKET COSTS

Most often when one refers to **out-of-pocket costs** or expenses, one is referring to cash payments that employees incurred on behalf of the business they work for as work-related expenses. Such expenses will be reimbursed by the company later. Examples of out-of-pocket costs can include parking fees, gasoline, tolls, or a business lunch with a client.

However, in managerial accounting, out-of-pocket costs are expenses that can either be incurred or avoided, which are to be decided by management, and will require a future outlay of cash. These costs are most relevant in the managerial decision-making process, as management has to decide whether there are enough cash reserves to fund an out-of-pocket expense in the future. The most common example is a management decision about purchasing new equipment. Therefore, the *USALI* advocates a replacement reserve account for management to plan for future out-of-pocket expenses. If these expenses are not planned properly, the cash balance of a hotel may be depleted by such out-of-pocket expenses and may even force hotels into bankruptcy by overstretching the hotel's cash resources. It is also important to note that not all equipment or assets purchases are out-of-pocket expenses, as in certain cases, hotels may trade like assets as a like-kind exchange with another company, where no cash is involved.

6.15 ACTIVITY-BASED COSTING

As seen in Chapter 3, a hotel has many undistributed expenses, from administrative and general to marketing and sales, just to name a few. These expenses are not distributed because the existing methods are either too costly or time consuming, or because the bases are never equitable in the eyes of all departments or parties involved. **Activity-based costing (ABC)** is a method to allocate indirect or overhead costs to related products and services based on the premise that products and services have relationships with costs and the undistributed activities. The ABC method has been around for more than 60 years and is used widely in manufacturing.[3] It is therefore reasonable to believe that ABC would be applicable to the hospitality industry, as businesses with undistributed expenses of over 15 percent of total costs would be prime candidates for ABC adoption.[4]

Attempts have been made to adopt ABC in the hospitality industry. The process of applying it starts with the principle that guests consume "activities" in hotels, restaurants, clubs, and other hospitality operations and that such activities consume resources. To be more concrete, let us look at a restaurant as an example.[5] To begin the ABC process, the restaurant first needs to:

1. Identify all that the activities need to create the product – the food that is sold. Of course, this depends on how extensive the menu is; every product will need to be analyzed fully, be it a breakfast, lunch, or dinner item. The activities can include but are not limited to setting specifications of products needed; receiving, storing, cooking, and preparing the food; serving, table setup, side work, and cleaning; and greeting customers: seating them, taking the order, general guest service, and cashing out the guests.

2. Identify all activity centers. In a restaurant, it may be front of the house and back of the house.

3. Classify activities into the activity centers and group them; these will become each menu item's bill of activity.

4. Collect all overhead cost information and assign it into homogeneous cost pools, such as labor cost pool (all labor and benefits related expenses), direct operating expense cost pool (uniforms, supplies, laundry, etc.), or facility-sustaining cost pool (repair and maintenance, utility, marketing, depreciation, insurance, accounting, etc.).

5. Assign cost pools to the activity centers to calculate the respective cost pool rate by dividing the total overhead costs in each cost pool by the total cost drivers. In this example, as the facility-sustaining cost pool cannot be related directly to a menu item, the cost pool rate is not calculated.

6. Calculate second-stage cost drivers by dividing total costs of each activity center into activity cost driver pool. The ABC method defines activities into four levels of second-stage cost drivers: unit-based, batch-based, product-related, and facility-sustaining. So, at each level, the two activity centers of front and back of the house will appear, with their respective activities.

7. Multiply the cost driver rate by the number of cost drivers to determine the final cost, and this will be the bill of activity for each menu item.

While ABC is embraced in manufacturing and has been studied and applied in hospitality, it has not been extensively utilized. This is mostly due to the herculean effort needed to implement and maintain the entire ABC system: The interviews, surveys, and observation of the staff to determine the time allocations for multiple activities are time consuming, and the need for constant updates of the data and system can be cost prohibitive. For example, productivity of employees fluctuates a lot more than a robot on a production line. Hospitality operations are more complex that one can imagine. Thus, in the last decade, there have been attempts to modify ABC to time-driven ABC (TDABC), where time is used as the primary cost driver. As our industry is always trying to find new ways to monitor costs and be more efficient, we shall see whether TDABC will be more accepted than its predecessor in the years to come.

6.16 DECISION-MAKING SITUATIONS

Many situations call on management to make decisions using the cost concepts presented in this chapter. Several of these decision-making situations are listed as follows:

1. Which piece of equipment should be purchased?

2. What prices should be set for the hospitality operation's goods and services?

3. Can the hospitality operation ever afford to sell goods and services below cost?

4. During what time periods of a day should the hospitality establishment remain open?

5. When should a seasonal resort close?

6. Which business segment of the hospitality operation should receive the largest amount of funds?

7. Where should the hospitality enterprise expand?

In attempting to answer these and other cost-related questions, remember that there is no definitive method of evaluating costs. However, when applied

Exhibit 6.17   Illustration of Relevant Costs in Management Decisions

	Desktop Computers	
	#1	#2
Costs—Hardware	$1,850	$2,750
Annual operating costs:		
Electricity	100	100
Supplies	200	200
Maintenance contract	200	100
Repairs (not covered by maintenance contract)	50	50
Software	2,000	1,800

correctly, the cost concepts presented in this chapter are useful in clarifying and helping to resolve these problems.

Illustration of Relevant Costs in Management Decisions

The selection process used to purchase a desktop computer will illustrate the application of relevant costs to a decision-making situation. Suppose a hotel wants to purchase a new desktop computer to be used by the controller for planning purposes. Even though the controller should become more productive by using the computer, their salary will not change because of the purchase. The costs associated with the purchase of either computer #1 or computer #2 are listed in Exhibit 6.17. Other information to consider includes the following:

1. Each computer is expected to have a useful life of 5 years, after which it would be considered worthless.

2. The different timing of costs that may be associated with each computer is ignored in this example, as well as any income tax implications.

3. The controller likes the appearance of computer #2 better; however, they are unable to place any value on this preference.

4. The value to the hotel of the controller's increased productivity is the same regardless of which desktop computer is purchased.

Exhibit 6.18   Cost Analysis Solution

Cost Analysis		
	Desktop Computers	
Relevant Cost	#1	#2
Hardware	$1,850	$2,750
Operating costs—maintenance contract for 5 years		
$200 × 5	1,000	–
$100 × 5	–	500
Software	2,000	1,800
Total cost	$4,850	$5,050

The irrelevant costs are the nondifferential ones, which include electricity, supplies, and repairs. All other costs listed for the two computers are relevant because they are future, differential, and quantifiable. The controller's preference for desktop computer #2 is not directly considered since it has not been quantified. The value of the controller's increased productivity has not been quantified since it is nondifferential between the two computers. In either case, the value to the hotel of this increase in productivity is expected to far exceed the cost of the computer.

Exhibit 6.18 presents a cost analysis useful in deciding which computer to purchase. Based on the lower cost, desktop computer #1 would be selected. If the $200 difference between desktop computers #1 and #2 were considered immaterial, then desktop computer #2 most likely would be purchased due to the controller's unquantified preference for it.

This chapter highlighted the variety of definitions the term *cost* can have in the accounting world. In general, a cost as an expense is the reduction of an asset incurred with the intention of increasing revenues. Such costs include labor costs, cost of food sold, depreciation, and others.

There are many specific types of costs. A fixed cost is one that remains constant over a relevant range of operations for the short term. A variable cost is one that changes directly with the level of activity. Depreciation is usually considered a fixed expense, while cost of food sold is assumed to be variable. Many costs are mixed, a combination of fixed and variable elements. For example, telephone expense can be divided into a fixed portion (the cost of the system) and a variable portion (the cost of making calls). Step costs are constant within a range of activity but vary among ranges of activity.

Three methods of determining the fixed and variable elements of mixed costs were presented in this chapter. The simplest is the high/low two-point method, which examines the cost differences between the periods of lowest and highest activity. A scatter diagram can be used to visualize the relationship between all periods' activities and costs. Regression analysis, the most sophisticated method addressed, uses equations to determine the appropriate fixed–variable relationship. Several types of costs are important in decision-making situations. Differential costs are useful when comparing two or more options; they are the costs that differ among the options. Relevant costs must be differential costs. In addition, relevant costs must be quantifiable and incurred in the future. Sunk costs are not considered in decision-making situations because they were incurred in the past. Other costs include controllable costs. Controllable costs are costs that can be regulated. All costs before management fees and fixed charges are generally considered under the general manager's control.

Understanding the relationships among the different types of costs can be very beneficial to a hospitality manager. Different purchase or lease options can be more easily analyzed, operations can be monitored against standards, and costs can be broken into their fixed and variable portions in order to forecast future expenses.

activity based costing (ABC)—A method to allocate indirect or overhead costs to related products and services based on the premise that products and services have relationships with costs and the undistributed activities.

average cost—Total production and service costs divided by the quantity of production.

avoidable costs—Costs that are not incurred when a hospitality operation shuts down (for example, when a resort hotel closes for part of the year).

capacity fixed costs—Fixed charges relating to the physical plant or the capacity to provide goods and services to guests.

controllable costs—Costs over which a manager is able to exercise judgment and hence should be able to keep within predefined boundaries or limits.

cost allocation—The process of distributing expenses among various departments.

differential costs—Costs that differ between two alternatives.

discretionary fixed costs—Costs that managers may in the short run choose to avoid. These costs do not affect an establishment's capacity.

fixed costs—Costs that remain constant in the short run even though sales volume varies; examples include salaries, rent expense, and insurance expense.

high/low two-point method—The simplest approach to estimating the fixed and variable elements of a mixed cost. It bases the estimation on data from two extreme periods.

incremental cost—The cost to produce one more unit; includes the variable costs and the variable portion of the mixed costs.

indifference point—The level of activity at which the cost is the same under either a fixed or a variable cost arrangement.

mixed costs—Costs that are a mixture of both fixed and variable costs.

multiple allocation base approach (MABA)—The use of different allocation bases to allocate different overhead costs among departments.

opportunity cost—Cost of foregoing the best alternative opportunity in a decision-making situation involving several alternatives.

out-of-pocket costs—Cash payments that employees incurred on behalf of a business as work-related expenses and for which they will be reimbursed by the company later.

overhead costs—All expenses other than the direct costs of profit centers; examples include undistributed operating expenses, management fees, fixed charges, and income taxes.

regression analysis—A mathematical approach to fitting a straight line to data points such that the differences in the distances of the data points from the line are minimized; used in forecasting when a dependent variable (e.g., restaurant covers) to be forecasted is thought to be causally related to one or more independent variables (e.g., rooms sold).

relevant costs—Costs that must be considered in a decision-making situation; must be differential, future, and quantifiable.

scatter diagram—A graphic approach to determining the fixed and variable elements of a mixed cost.

single allocation base approach (SABA)—The allocation of overhead costs among departments using a single allocation base (such as departmental square footage).

standard costs—Forecasts of what actual costs should be under projected conditions; a standard of comparison for control purposes or for evaluations of productivity.

step costs—Costs that are constant within a range of activity, but different among ranges of activity.

sunk cost—Past costs relating to a past decision; for example, the net book value of a fixed asset.

variable costs—Costs that change proportionately with sales volume.

1. What are some of the different meanings of *cost*?

2. What is the difference between overhead costs and indirect costs?

3. What is an opportunity cost?

4. Which technique is the most accurate method of determining the fixed and variable elements of a mixed cost? Why?

5. What are the two definitions of sunk costs?

6. Which hotel costs are fixed in the short run? In the long run?

7. Why would you consider allocating costs to the profit centers?

8. How are relevant costs defined? What is an irrelevant cost? Give an example.

9. Why are differential costs considered in a decision-making situation?

10. What is the difference between average costs and incremental costs?

Problem 1

Beth O'Brien has $160,000 of taxable income. The tax table is as follows:

Taxable Income	Tax Rate
< $20,000	10%
$20,000–$50,000	20%
> $50,000	30%

Required:

1. What is her total tax liability? $41,000.00
2. What is her average tax rate? 23.62%

Problem 2

Paragon Hospitality invested in a 20-acre plot of land for future development 10 years ago. It purchased this land for $200,000 and it could be sold today for $1 million. Paragon Hospitality's average and incremental tax rates are 22 percent and 30 percent, respectively. Paragon Hospitality is considering building a new lodging facility on this land.

Required:

What is the opportunity cost of this investment?

Problem 3

Kate Wilkinson, who owns the Sugar Sweet Café, is negotiating with the lessor regarding the lease of the building for the next five years. The lessor has proposed the following lease payment alternatives:

1. Monthly fixed lease payment of $2,400
2. Monthly fixed lease payment of $1,000 plus 2.5 percent of net sales
3. Monthly variable lease payment of 6.5 percent of net sales

Required:

1. What is the indifference point among the three proposals?
2. If expected average annual net sales are $350,000, which lease payment alternative should be recommended to Kate Wilkinson?
3. If expected average annual net sales are $500,000, which lease payment alternative should be recommended to Kate Wilkinson?

Problem 4

The following monthly income statement has been prepared by Dwayne Kris, CPA, for Troy Caballo, the owner of the Caballo Inn. As Mr. Caballo's private consultant, you are asked to explain several cost relationships.

Caballo Inn
Income Statement
For the month ended Jan. 31, 20X1

	Net Revenues	Cost of Sales	Payroll and Related Expense	Other Expenses	Income (Loss)
Rooms	$105,430	$ –0–	$ 20,000	$ 1,450	$ 83,980
Food	52,400	18,864	15,000	1,000	17,536
Beverage	26,720	6,680	10,000	12,400	(2,360)
Other	4,000	–0–	–0–	–0–	4,000
	$188,550	$ 25,544	$ 45,000	$ 14,850	103,156

Undistributed Operating Expenses:	
Administrative and General	20,890
Sales and Marketing	3,400
Property Operation and Maintenance	5,080
Utility Costs	15,400
Gross Operating Profit	58,386

Nonoperating Expenses:	
Rent	5,400
Property Taxes	1,220
Insurance	2,000
EBITDA	49,766
Depreciation	5,500
Interest Expense	3,330
Income before Income Taxes	40,936
Income Taxes	15,136
Net Income	$ 25,800

Required:

1. What are the direct expenses of the rooms department?

2. What is the total of the overhead expenses for the period?

3. Which costs are controllable by the general manager or people under their supervision?

4. Which costs are considered fixed?

5. What is the relationship of the cost of sales to sales?

Problem 5

Sherrie Calab, the manager of the Hotel 88, desires to know the breakdown of the electric costs between variable and fixed categories. She provides you with the following information:

Month	Electric Expenses	Occupancy Percentage
January	$ 6,600	62%
April	6,600	68%
August	8,200	78%
December	5,500	50%

Required:

Use the high/low two-point method for the following:

1. Determine the variable costs per 1 percent of occupancy.

2. Estimate the fixed costs per month.

3. What is the estimated total electric expense at 62 percent occupancy? Why does this differ from the $6,200 shown above for January?

Problem 6

Tiffany Lee, owner of Tiff's Place, wants to analyze labor costs in her restaurant operations and has asked you for assistance. The operating statistics for the previous year are as follows:

	Number of Customers	Labor Costs
January	4,000	$ 15,500
February	2,300	10,450
March	3,700	18,500
April	4,450	19,000
May	4,400	19,000
June	4,800	20,250
July	5,000	21,575
August	3,900	17,050
September	3,800	17,000
October	3,100	15,500
November	2,900	15,250
December	3,000	16,650

Required:

1. Using the high/low two-point method, determine the variable labor cost per customer.

2. What is the monthly fixed labor cost at Tiff's Place?

3. What is your estimate of total labor costs if 3,900 customers are served during the month? (Base this on your analysis in parts 1 and 2 above.)

Problem 7

Doug Litwiller is interested in renting space from D&T Associates for a foodservice business. D&T Associates has provided three alternatives, as follows:

1. $2,000 fixed rent per month

2. $1,000 fixed rent per month plus 2 percent of sales

3. $1,500 fixed rent per month plus 4 percent of monthly sales in excess of $37,500

Required:

1. Determine the indifference point.

2. Graph the three alternatives using Exhibit 6.11 as a guide.

3. If the average monthly sales are forecast to be $80,000, what will the total lease cost be under each alternative and which do you recommend?

Problem 8

The Lanai Motel's costs at two different sales levels are as follows:

	Monthly Room Sales	
	2,000	3,000
Payroll:		
Salaries	$15,000	$15,000
Wages	40,000	60,000
Employee benefits	9,200	10,700
Supplies	2,000	3,000
Utilities	8,000	8,000
Other operating costs	4,000	5,000
Building rent	9,000	9,000
Interest expense	2,500	2,500
Insurance	3,650	3,650

Required:

1. Identify each cost as fixed, variable, or mixed.

2. What are the total estimated monthly fixed costs?

3. What are the total estimated variable costs per room sold?

4. Develop a single equation to estimate total costs at various levels of activity.

5. Project the total costs if 3,500 rooms are sold.

Problem 9

Xavier Garcia is requesting your assistance in determining a cost equation for forecasting his expenses for his Maple Leaf Restaurant. He provides costs at two extremes, as follows:

	Monthly Covers	
	4,000	8,000
Cost of food sold	$12,000	$24,000
Salaries	12,000	12,000
Wages	10,000	20,000
Employee benefits	6,000	8,000
Supplies	3,000	6,000
Utilities	2,000	3,000
Rent	2,000	4,000
Other operating costs	4,000	5,000
Insurance	2,500	2,500
Depreciation	1,800	1,800
Property taxes	2,250	2,250

Required:

1. Identify each cost as fixed, variable, or mixed.

2. What are the estimated monthly fixed costs (including the fixed portion of mixed costs)?

3. What are the estimated variable costs per cover sold?

4. Develop a single equation to estimate costs at various levels of activity.

5. Project the total costs if 5,200 covers are sold, using the equation from part 4.

Problem 10

The Food Artist Restaurant currently has a variable lease that is 8 percent of its total revenue. An alternative approach is $160,000 per year. Assume its average and marginal tax rates are 35 percent and 40 percent, respectively.

Required:

1. Determine its indifference point.

2. If its annual sales are expected to be $3.8 million, which type of lease do you recommend? Provide figures to support your recommendation.

3. Assume the Food Artist Restaurant's indifference point is $1.5 million. What is the net of tax cost of making an error in signing a variable lease when its annual sales are $1.7 million?

Problem 11

The Pie Pizza House has provided you with the following information on its costs at various levels of monthly sales.

Monthly sales in units	3,000	6,000	9,000
Cost of food sold	$ 4,500	$ 9,000	$ 13,500
Payroll costs	3,500	5,000	6,500
Supplies	600	1,200	1,800
Utilities	360	420	480
Other operating costs	1,500	3,000	4,500
Building rent	1,500	1,500	1,500
Depreciation	300	300	300
Total	$12,260	$ 20,420	$ 28,580

Required:

1. Identify each cost as variable, fixed, or mixed.

2. Develop an equation to estimate total costs at various levels of activity.

3. Project total costs with monthly sales of 8,000.

Problem 12

Dylan's Place needs a new paper copier. Dylan Owen, the owner, has two alternatives:

	Buy	Lease
Cost of equipment	$ 20,000	–
Semi-annual equipment rental	–	$ 4,000
Salvage value in three years	2,000	–
Annual costs:		
Labor	35,000	35,000
Supplies	4,000	4,000
Utilities	2,000	2,000
Interest expense	1,000	–
Repairs	1,500	–

Additional information:

Assume that the paper copier has a three-year life.

Required:

1. Which costs are irrelevant?

2. Prepare a three-year cost schedule for each alternative and include only relevant costs. (Ignore income taxes and the time value of money.)

3. Which alternative do you recommend?

Problem 13

Tauras Inn needs new laundry equipment. Paul Torres, the owner, is faced with the following two alternatives:

	Buy	Lease
Cost of equipment	$ 22,000	–
Semi-annual equipment rental	–	$ 3,000
Salvage value in five years	1,000	–
Annual costs:		
Labor	18,000	18,000
Supplies	1,900	1,900
Utilities	3,500	3,500
Interest expense	1,500	–
Repairs	200	–

Additional information:

Assume that the laundry equipment has a five-year life.

Required:

1. Which costs are irrelevant?

2. Prepare a five-year cost schedule for each alternative. (Ignore income taxes and the time value of money.)

3. Which alternative do you recommend?

Problem 14

The unallocated income statement of Harper Inn is shown below:

Unallocated Income Statement
Harper Inn
For the month of January 20X4

	Rooms	Food	Total
Revenue	$ 70,000	$ 30,000	$100,000
Cost of Sales	-0-	12,000	12,000
Labor Costs and Related Expenses	16,000	10,000	26,000
Other Direct Expenses	6,000	4,000	10,000
Total Expenses	22,000	26,000	48,000
Departmental Income	$ 48,000	$ 4,000	$ 52,000

Undistributed Operating Expenses:	
Administrative and General	8,000
Sales and Marketing	4,000
Property Operation and Maintenance	2,000
Utility Costs	2,000
Gross Operating Profit	36,000

Unallocated Income Statement
Harper Inn
For the month of January 20X4

Nonoperating Expenses:	
Rent	6,000
Insurance	3,000
Property taxes	2,000
EBITDA	25,000
Depreciation	10,000
Income before Income Taxes	15,000
Income Taxes	6,000
Net Income	$ 9,000

Assume the square footage of the rooms department totals 50,000, while the square footage of the food department totals 10,000.

Required:

1. Using square footage and the SABA, prepare a fully allocated income statement.

2. What do the results from part 1 suggest?

Problem 15

Consider the following monthly income statement for the Double K Hotel:

Double K Hotel
Income Statement

	Rooms	Food	Gift Shop	Total
Revenue	$500,000	$500,000	$2,000	$1,002,000
Cost of Sales	–0–	180,000	1,000	181,000
Labor Costs and Related Expenses	120,000	130,000	400	250,400
Other Direct Expenses	40,000	45,000	100	85,100
Departmental Income	$340,000	$145,000	$ 500	$ 485,500

Undistributed Expenses:	Payroll & Related	Other	Total
Administrative and General	$60,000	$ 30,000	$ 90,000
Sales and Marketing	45,000	25,000	70,000
Property Operation and Maintenance and Utility Costs	30,000	40,000	70,000
Insurance	–	10,000	10,000
Depreciation	–	80,000	80,000
Total Undistributed Expenses			320,000
Income before Income Taxes			165,000
Income Taxes			50,000
Net Income			$115,500

Indirect expenses will be allocated based on the number of employees, who are distributed as follows:

Department	Number of Employees
Rooms	55
Food	70
Gift Shop	½
Administrative and General	20
Marketing	15
Property Operation and Maintenance and Utility Costs	10

Required:

Prepare a fully allocated income statement using the single allocation basis approach to cost allocation.

Problem 16

The owner of the Double K Hotel in Problem 15 would like to develop a fully allocated income statement using the step method. (The unallocated income statement is presented in Problem 15.) Indirect expenses will be allocated on the following bases:

Indirect Expense	Basis
Insurance	Book value of fixed assets
Depreciation	Square footage
Property Operation and Maintenance and Utility Costs	Square footage
Marketing	Ratio of sales
Administrative and General	Number of employees

Additional information:

Department	Book Value of Fixed Assets	Square Footage	Number of Employees
Rooms	$ 8,000,000	120,000	55
Food	3,000,000	20,000	70
Gift Shop	20,000	500	½
Administrative and General	400,000	6,000	20
Sales and Marketing	200,000	4,000	15
Property Operation and Maintenance and Utility Costs	1,500,000	10,000	10

Service department expenses should be allocated in the following order:

1. Administrative and General

2. Property Operation and Maintenance and Utility Costs

3. Sales and Marketing

Required:

Prepare a fully allocated income statement for the Double K Hotel using the step method. Note: Appendix C at the end of the book discusses and illustrates the step method.

Problem 17

Upset Ulysses is at it once again after he received the fully allocated monthly income statement for his lodging operation, USG Inn. He does a little research and asks for your advice. He sees three alternatives for the lounge operations, as follows:

1. Continue the lounge operations as is.

2. Close the lounge and expand the restaurant.

3. Lease the lounge space to Lounge Lease Inc. (LLI), which would run the lounge operation.

The following table summarizes USG Inn's monthly fully allocated income statement:

	Rooms	Food	Lounge	Total
Sales	$300,000	$100,000	$100,000	$500,000
Expenses	100,000	50,000	80,000	230,000
Department profit	200,000	50,000	20,000	270,000
Allocated overhead	100,000	40,000	30,000	170,000
Pretax income	$100,000	$ 10,000	$ (10,000)	100,000
Income taxes				25,000
Net income				$ 75,000

Additional information:

1. Closing the lounge would reduce overhead costs by $10,000 per month. Leasing the lounge to LLI would reduce the overhead costs by $5,000 per month.

2. The lounge space can be leased to LLI for 6 percent of sales. Ulysses believes this firm will be able to generate $1 million of annual sales.

3. If the lounge is closed, room sales are expected to decrease by 3 percent; however, restaurant profits are expected to increase by 10 percent. Assume that department expenses of rooms, food, and lounge are all variable except for $50,000 of the rooms department expenses, which are fixed.

4. Assume the cost to convert the lounge space to restaurant space (alternative #2 above) is $48,000 and the equipment will have a four-year life.

5. Assume the lounge space equipment if sold will provide an annual cash flow of $6,000 per year.

Required:

1. Prepare a comparative analysis using only relevant numbers to determine which alternative is preferred. Show all of your work.

2. Specify which alternative is preferred and explain why.

Problem 18

Sara Rose, owner of Rose Inn, is confused by the fully allocated financial statements that suggest the Rose Inn's lounge is losing money. As she sees it, there are three alternatives:

1. Continue the lounge operation as is.

2. Close the lounge and convert the space to a small meeting room.

3. Lease the space to Bevco.

The following table summarizes the Rose Inn's fully allocated monthly income statements:

	Rooms	Food	Lounge	Total
Departmental profit	$150,000	$ 30,000	$ 10,000	$190,000
Allocated overhead	100,000	25,000	15,000	140,000
Pretax income	$ 50,000	$ 5,000	$ (5,000)	50,000
Income taxes				20,000
Net income				$ 30,000

Additional information:

1. Closing the lounge would reduce overhead costs by $7,000. Leasing the lounge to Bevco would reduce overhead costs by $2,000.

2. The space can be leased to Bevco for 5 percent of sales. Bevco is a reputable operator, and Sara Rose believes that it will operate the lounge as effectively as Rose Inn has done in the past. Annual forecasted lounge sales are expected to be $150,000.

3. If the lounge is closed, room profits are expected to decrease by 2 percent, while food department profits are expected to increase by 20 percent.

4. The cost to convert the lounge for alternative use is assumed to be equal to the market value of the lounge equipment.

5. The lounge space, if used for small meetings, is expected to yield pretax profits of $3,000.

Required:

Based on the above information, recommend the best alternative to Sara Rose. Support your solution with numbers.

Problem 19

Peter John Star, owner of The Big Star Hotel, is confused by the fully allocated financial statements that suggest The Big Star Hotel's lounge is losing money. As he sees it, there are three alternatives:

1. Continue the lounge operation as is.

2. Close the lounge and expand the restaurant.

3. Lease the space to Philip Inc., a management company.

The following table summarizes the Big Star Hotel's fully allocated monthly income statements.

	Rooms	Restaurant	Lounge	Total
Revenues	$250,000	$100,000	$40,000	$390,000
Departmental expenses*	100,000	70,000	20,000	190,000
Departmental profit	150,000	30,000	20,000	200,000
Allocated overhead	100,000	25,000	30,000	155,000
Pretax income	$ 50,000	$ 5,000	($ 10,000)	45,000
Income taxes				20,000
Net income				$ 25,000

*All departmental expenses are assumed to be variable.

Additional information:

1. Closing the lounge would reduce monthly overhead costs by $10,000. Leasing the lounge to Philip Inc. would reduce monthly overhead costs by $5,000.

2. The space can be leased to Philip Inc. for 10 percent of sales. Philip Inc. is a reputable operator, and Peter John believes that it will operate the lounge as effectively as The Big Star Hotel has done in the past. Annual forecasted lounge sales are expected to be $550,000.

3. If the lounge is closed, room profits are expected to decrease by 2 percent, while food department sales are expected to increase by 20 percent.

4. The cost to convert the lounge for alternative use is expected to be $60,000. Assume that the life of the equipment is 5 years and that it will have no salvage value.

5. If the lounge is closed, the unneeded equipment can be sold on a contract over 5 years and $500 will be received each month.

Required:

Based on the above, advise Peter John Star. Use relevant numbers to support your recommendation.

Problem 20

Tammy's Motor Inn has been open for 5 months, and Tammy Weaver, the general manager, is conducting some cost analyses. She has not yet determined the amount of fixed and variable expenses the inn is incurring. The following is a summary of room sales and expenses incurred each month.

	Number of Rooms	Costs
June	3,488	$122,319
July	3,842	128,940
August	3,584	124,320
September	3,333	119,431
October	3,261	117,642

1. Using regression analysis, determine the fixed cost per month for Tammy's Motor Inn.

2. What is the variable cost per room?

3. If Tammy's Motor Inn expects to sell 3,666 rooms in January of the next year, what are the fixed costs, total variable costs, and total expenses?

Problem 21

Julie Schmidt has requested your help in determining a cost equation for forecasting expenses for her Midstate Inn. She provides cost at two extremes, as follows:

	Monthly Occupancies	
	50%	80%
Salaries	$100,000	$100,000
Wages	150,000	240,000
Benefits	60,000	80,000
Supplies	10,000	16,000
Utilities	7,000	8,000
Marketing	8,000	12,800
Depreciation	5,000	5,000
Property taxes	2,000	2,000
Other expenses	15,000	17,000

Required:

1. Identify each cost as fixed, variable, or mixed.

2. What are the total estimated fixed costs (including the fixed portion of mixed costs)?

3. What are the estimated variable costs per 1 percent occupancy?

4. Develop a single equation to estimate costs at various occupancy percentages.

Problem 22

Matthew College needs a new dishwashing machine. The college could substantially overhaul its existing dishwasher as well. The existing dishwasher originally cost $25,000. Details for the alternatives are as follows:

	Keep	Replace
Cost of new dishwasher	–	$30,000
Salvage value of existing dishwasher:		
Today	$ 2,000	–
In five years	4,000	–
Major one-time overhaul costs	10,000	–

	Keep	Replace
Salvage value of new dishwasher		10,000
Annual costs:		
Labor	30,000	30,000
Utilities	2,000	1,000
Repairs	1,000	300

Additional information:

Assume that both options would have a five-year life.

Required:

1. Which costs are sunk?

2. Which costs are irrelevant?

3. Prepare a schedule of relevant costs for each alternative. (Ignore income taxes and the time value of money.)

4. Which alternative do you recommend?

Problem 23

Susanne Benes is having some difficulties in determining an equation to estimate costs at her restaurant, SuzyB. She has some cost figures to share that are from her best and worst months in terms of number of guests served:

	Monthly Covers	
	3,000 guests served	6,000 guests served
Cost of food sold	$ 15,000	$ 30,000
Salaries	12,000	12,000
Wages	8,250	16,500
Employee benefits	7,500	10,650
Rent	4,000	4,000
Utilities	2,500	4,000
Other operating expense	5,000	7,250
Depreciation	1,500	1,500
Insurance	1,800	1,800
Property taxes	2,000	2,000

Required:

1. Identify each cost as fixed, variable, or mixed.

2. What are the estimated monthly fixed costs (including the fixed portion of mixed costs)?

3. What are the estimated variable costs per guests served?

4. Develop a single equation to estimate costs at various levels of guests served.

5. Project the total costs if 5,500 guests are served using the equation from part 4.

Problem 24

Spartan Country Club is looking at a new point of sale system for its food venues. The board receives many quotes and has narrowed them down to the final two, where one is to purchase the POS and the other is to lease the system. If purchased, this system will have a five-year useful life. The various costs for both options are listed below:

	Buy	Lease
Cost of equipment	$ 32,000	
Annual rental fee		$ 8,000
Salvage value in 5 years	2,000	
Other annual costs:		
Wages	30,000	30,000
Supplies	8,950	8,950
Utilities	3,100	3,100
Repairs and maintenance	500	

Required:

1. Which costs are relevant?

2. Prepare a five-year cost schedule for each alternative and include only relevant costs. (Ignore income tax and the time value of money.)

3. Which alternative is best for Spartan Country Club?

Problem 25

A few months ago, the DeLoziers bought The Mountain Lodge, a nice, select service hotel, at a perfect location right outside a state park. Phil, the owner and also general manager, is trying to understand the cost structure of his property. He would like to determine the amount of fixed and variable costs of the lodge, with the information below regarding the number of rooms sold and also the expenses for each month.

	Number of Rooms Sold	Costs
July	2,666	119,970
August	2,759	140,875
September	2,340	110,988
October	2,232	109,878
November	2,102	106,222
December	2,588	117,231

Required:

1. Using regression analysis, determine the fixed cost per month for The Mountain Lodge.

2. What is the variable cost per room?

3. If Phil expects to sell 2,635 rooms in March of next year, what will be the total fixed costs, total variable costs, and total expenses?

7

COST-VOLUME-PROFIT ANALYSIS

Chapter 7 Outline

Competencies

1. Define cost-volume-profit analysis and identify its major assumptions and limitations. (pp. 314–317)

2. Use CVP equations in both single- and multiple-product environments to determine the revenue required to reach specified profit levels as well as the following variables: units sold, fixed costs, selling price, and variable cost per unit. (pp. 317–333)

3. Explain what operating leverage is and how it affects a hospitality operation's profits and exposure to risk. (pp. 333–334)

4. Explain the concept of investment driven breakeven and calculate the investment breakeven point. (pp. 334–336)

KEY TERMS

breakeven analysis

breakeven point

contribution margin (CM)

contribution margin ratio (CMR)

cost-volume-profit (CVP) analysis

investment driven breakeven analysis

margin of safety

operating leverage

profit-volume graph

sensitivity analysis

weighted average contribution margin ratio (CMR_w)

Cost-volume-profit analysis is a set of analytical tools used to determine the revenues required at any desired profit level. Many businesspeople refer to cost-volume-profit (CVP) analysis as a **breakeven analysis**. However, the breakeven point of a firm is only one point among an infinite number of possible points that can be determined. When properly used, CVP analysis provides useful information about the structure of operations and answers many types of questions such as the following:

1. What is the breakeven point?

2. What is the profit at any given occupancy percentage above the breakeven point?

3. How will a $50,000 increase in property taxes next year affect the sales breakeven point?

4. How much must room sales increase next year to cover the increase in property taxes and/or other expenses and still achieve the desired profit?

5. How many rooms must be sold to achieve a $100,000 profit?

6. What is the effect on profit if prices, variable costs, or fixed costs increase?

This chapter begins with a definition of CVP analysis, followed by a clarification of both the assumptions of the CVP model and the limitations of CVP as an analytical tool. Next, we will describe the relationships depicted in the CVP model, namely the relationships among revenues, variable costs, fixed costs, and levels of activity. We will then illustrate CVP analysis by discussing both the simple situation of a single product offering and the more complex multiple product situation. We will also discuss the effects of income taxes within the CVP model and modify the basic model to more adequately reflect cash flow considerations. Finally, we will consider the topic of the relative mix of fixed and variable costs through a discussion of operating leverage.

7.1 CVP ANALYSIS DEFINED

Cost-volume-profit (CVP) analysis (or breakeven analysis) is a management tool that expresses the relationships among various costs, sales volume, and profits in either graphic or equation form. The graphs or equations assist management in making decisions. CVP is applicable to all businesses. Even for concepts such as ghost kitchen and virtual restaurants, where the fixed costs are much less than traditional restaurants, a different cost structure does not negate the need of a solid breakeven analysis. A simple example may be used to illustrate this process.

Assume that the manager of the Red Cedar Inn, a 10-room motel, would like to know what price must be charged in order to make a profit of $4,000 in a 30-day period. The available information is as follows:

■ Variable costs per room sold equal $20.

■ If the average price is between $70 and $80, 250 rooms can be sold.

■ Fixed costs for a 30-day period are $10,000.

Given these three pieces of information, using CVP analysis the manager is able to calculate that the selling price must average $76 in order to attain the goal of a $4,000 profit in a 30-day period. This selling price is determined on the basis of the CVP model by working through the calculations of the following formula:

$$\text{Selling Price} = \frac{\text{Variable Costs}}{\text{per Room}} + \frac{\text{Desired Profit} + \text{Fixed Costs}}{\text{Number of Rooms to be Sold}}$$

$$= \$20 + \frac{\$4,000 + \$10,000}{250}$$

$$= \underline{\$76}$$

Since the selling price of $76 suggested by the CVP analysis is within the range of $70 to $80 required to sell the specified number of rooms, the manager will be able to reach the desired goal of a $4,000 profit in 30 days by establishing the price at $76. The Red Cedar Inn's summarized operations budget for the 30-day period is as follows:

Room sales (250 × $76)		$19,000
Variable costs (250 × $20)	$ 5,000	
Fixed costs	10,000	15,000
Profit		$ 4,000

CVP Assumptions, Limitations, and Relationships

CVP analysis, like all mathematical models, is based on several assumptions. When these assumptions do not hold in the actual situations to which the model is applied, then the results of CVP analysis will be suspect. The commonest assumptions are as follows:

1. Fixed costs remain fixed during the period being considered. Over time, fixed costs do change. However, it is reasonable to assume that fixed costs remain constant over a short time span, such as one year.

2. Variable costs fluctuate in a linear fashion with revenues during the period under consideration. That is, if revenues increase x percent, variable costs also increase x percent.

3. Revenues are directly proportional to volume—that is, they are linear. As unit sales increase by x percent, revenues increase by x percent. This relationship is shown in Exhibit 7.1.

4. Mixed costs can be properly divided into their fixed and variable elements. All costs can be assigned to individual operated departments. This assumption limits the ability of CVP analysis to consider joint costs. These are costs that simultaneously benefit two or more operated departments. Joint costs, or a portion thereof, are not eliminated by discontinuing the offering of services such as food, beverage, telephone, and so forth. Therefore, for the purposes of CVP analysis, joint costs cannot be assigned to individual operated departments. Because of the existence of joint costs, the **breakeven point**, the level of sales volume at which total revenues equal total costs, cannot be determined by operated department. However, it can still be determined for the entire operation.

5. The CVP model considers only quantitative factors. Qualitative factors, such as employee morale, guest goodwill, and so forth, are not considered. Thus, management must carefully consider these qualitative factors before making any final decisions.

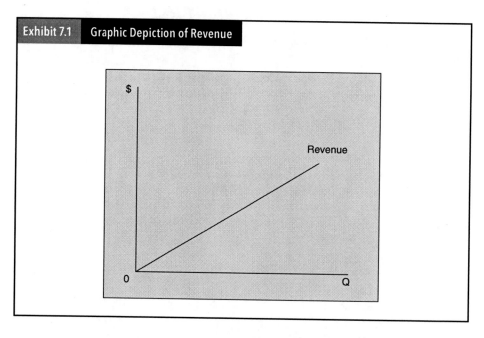

Exhibit 7.1   Graphic Depiction of Revenue

The cost-volume-profit relationships depicted in CVP equations and graphs consist of fixed costs, variable costs, and revenues. The relationships of fixed costs, variable costs, and revenues to volume and profits are graphically illustrated by Exhibit 7.2. The CVP graph shows dollars on the vertical axis and volume (rooms sales) on the horizontal axis. The fixed cost line is parallel to the horizontal axis from Point A. Thus, the amount of the fixed costs theoretically would equal the loss the hospitality operation would suffer if no sales took place. The variable cost line is the broken straight line from Point 0. This suggests that there are no variable costs when there are no sales, and the straight line suggests that variable costs change proportionately with sales. The sum of variable costs and fixed costs equals total costs. The total cost line is drawn from Point A parallel to the variable cost line. This suggests that total costs increase only as variable costs increase, and that variable costs increase only from increased sales.

The revenue line commences at Point 0 and reflects a linear relationship between revenue and units sold. Point B is the intersection of the total cost line and the revenue line. At Point B, revenues equal total costs; this is the breakeven point represented graphically. The vertical distance between the revenue line and the total cost line to the right of Point B represents profit, while the vertical distance between these two lines to the left of Point B represents operating loss.

In this way, the CVP model shows the relationship of profit to sales volume and relates both to costs. As the volume of sales increases and reaches the point where the amount of revenues generated by those sales equals the total costs of generating them, then the hospitality operation arrives at its breakeven point. As the volume of sales increases past the breakeven point, the amount of revenues generated by those sales increases at a faster rate than the costs associated with those sales. Thus, the growing difference between revenues and cost measures the increase of profit in relation to sales volume.

It is important to stress again that the CVP model of the relations of costs, sales volume, and profit is based entirely on its assumptions about the relationship of costs and revenues to sales volume. Although both costs and revenues are assumed to increase in direct linear proportion to the increase of sales volume, revenues must increase at a faster rate than costs if the business is to succeed; in other words, revenues must exceed variable costs. When this is true, both revenues and costs increase in proportion to sales, but they do so at different rates. It is because of this difference in growth rates of revenues and

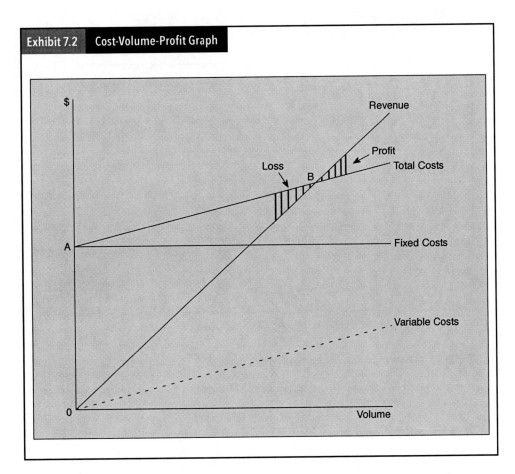

Exhibit 7.2   Cost-Volume-Profit Graph

costs in relation to sales that the total revenue and total cost lines are bound to intersect and reach a balance (breakeven point) as sales increase.

7.2 CVP EQUATION—SINGLE PRODUCT

The CVP graph, although appealing in its simplicity, is not sufficiently precise, and it is often time-consuming to manually construct a graph for each question to be solved using CVP analysis. However, computers can produce these graphs quickly and easily. As an alternative, CVP analysis uses a series of equations that express the mathematical relationships depicted in the graphic model.

A CVP equation expresses the cost-volume-profit relationships and is illustrated in Exhibit 7.3. At the breakeven point, net income is zero and the equation is simply shown as follows:

$$0 = SX - VX - F$$

The equation may be rearranged to solve for any one of the four variables, as follows:

		Equation	Determines
X	$=$	$\dfrac{F}{S-V}$	Units sold at breakeven
F	$=$	$SX - VX$	Fixed costs at breakeven
S	$=$	$\dfrac{F}{X} + V$	Selling price at breakeven
V	$=$	$S - \dfrac{F}{X}$	Variable cost per unit price at breakeven

A CVP analysis equation expresses the cost-volume-profit relationships as follows:

$$I_n = SX - VX - F$$

where:

I_n	=	Net income
S	=	Selling price
X	=	Units sold
V	=	Variable cost per unit
F	=	Total fixed cost

therefore:

SX	=	Total revenue
VX	=	Total variable costs

This CVP equation assumes the sale of a single product, such as rooms or meals. Most hospitality firms sell a vast array of goods and services. However, before turning to this more complex situation, let's look at an illustration of this simple CVP analysis equation through the following example.

CVP Illustration—Single Product

The Michael Motel, a 30-room budget motel, has the following cost and price structure:

- Annual fixed costs equal $187,500.

- Average selling price per room is $40.

- Variable cost per room sold equals $15.

What is the number of room sales required for the Michael Motel to break even?

$$X = \frac{F}{S-V} \qquad \text{(equation for units sold at breakeven)}$$

$$= \frac{\$187,500}{\$40 - \$15}$$

$$= \underline{\underline{7,500}} \text{ rooms}$$

Exhibit 7.4 depicts the breakeven point of the Michael Motel at 7,500 rooms. The total revenue at the breakeven point is shown as $300,000 (the result of multiplying the selling price per room by the number of rooms sold).

What is the occupancy percentage at breakeven for the Michael Motel?

$$\text{Occupancy Percentage} = \frac{\text{Rooms Sold}}{\text{Rooms Available}}$$

$$= \frac{7,500}{365 \times 30}$$

$$= \underline{\underline{68.49\%}}$$

If the proprietor desires the Michael Motel to earn profits of $50,000 for the year, how many rooms must be sold? This can be determined by modifying the equation for units sold at breakeven.

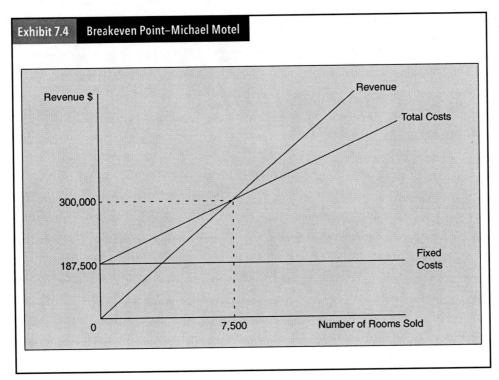

Exhibit 7.4   Breakeven Point–Michael Motel

$$X = \frac{F + I_n}{S - V} \qquad \text{(equation for units sold at \$50,000 profit level)}$$

$$= \frac{\$187,500 + \$50,000}{\$40 - \$15}$$

$$= \underline{9,500} \text{ rooms}$$

Therefore, for $50,000 to be earned in a year, the Michael Motel must sell 2,000 rooms beyond its breakeven point. The profit earned on these additional sales is the result of the selling price less variable cost per room multiplied by the excess rooms ($40 − $15 = $25; $25 × 2,000 = $50,000).

The difference between selling price and variable cost per unit is often called **contribution margin (CM)**. In this example, the CM is $25—for each room sold, $25 is available to cover fixed costs and then contribute toward profits once the fixed costs have been covered. Beyond the breakeven point, 2,000 additional rooms sales result in a $50,000 profit (rooms sales beyond breakeven × CM = profit).

Exhibit 7.5 is a graphic depiction of the $50,000 of net income. When total revenue is $380,000 (9,500 × $40), expenses equal $330,000 (calculated by multiplying $15 by 9,500 and then adding $187,500), resulting in a $50,000 net income. The distance between the total revenue line and the total cost line at the 9,500 rooms point represents the net income of $50,000.

Likewise, if rooms sales are less than the 7,500 breakeven point, $25 (CM) is lost per room not sold. For example, we can calculate the loss for the year if the Michael Motel sells only 6,500 rooms. Based on the above information, the answer should be $25,000 (CM × rooms less than breakeven). Using the general formula, the proof is as follows:

$$I_n = SX - VX - F \text{ (general formula)}$$

$$= \$40(6,500) - \$15(6,500) - \$187,500$$

$$= \underline{-\$25,000}$$

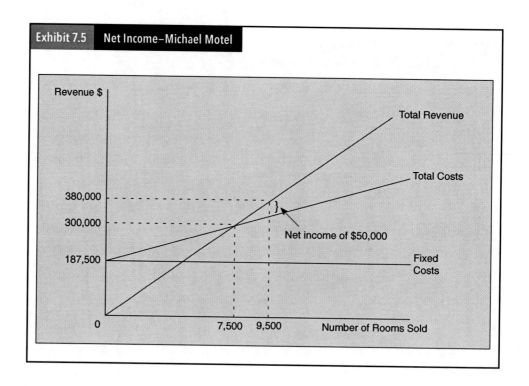

Thus, a loss of $25,000 would be incurred when rooms sales are only 6,500 for the year.

Margin of Safety

The **margin of safety** is the excess of budgeted or actual sales over sales at breakeven. For the Michael Motel above, the level of sales when net income of $50,000 is earned is $380,000. Since the breakeven sales were $300,000, the margin of safety for the Michael Motel when $50,000 of profit is generated is $80,000 and 2,000 rooms, as follows:

	Breakeven	Profit of $50,000	Margin of Safety
Sales—$	$300,000	$380,000	$80,000
Sales—Rooms	7,500	9,500	2,000

Sensitivity Analysis

Sensitivity analysis is the study of the sensitivity of the CVP model's dependent variables (such as room sales) to changes in one or more of the model's independent variables (such as variable costs and selling prices). The CVP model shows how the dependent variable will respond to a proposed change.

Again, we will use the Michael Motel to illustrate this concept. Assume that the Michael Motel's fixed costs increase by $25,000. How many more rooms must be sold in order to earn $50,000 of net income? (Assume that selling price and variable costs percentage remain constant.)

$$\text{Increased Rooms Sales} = \frac{\text{Increase in Fixed Costs}}{\text{Contribution Margin}}$$

$$= \frac{\$25{,}000}{\$25}$$

$$= \underline{\underline{1{,}000}}$$

Thus, a $25,000 increase in fixed costs (the independent variable) will require an increase in room sales of 1,000 units (the dependent variable) to cover the increased fixed costs and still make $50,000 in profits.

The proof is as follows:

Increased sales			
	1,000 rooms × $40	=	$40,000
Increased variable costs			
	1,000 rooms × $15	=	15,000
Increased fixed costs		=	25,000
Bottom line impact		=	$ –0–

7.3 CVP EQUATION—MULTIPLE PRODUCTS

Many hospitality operations, especially hotels, sell more than just a single product. In order to determine the operation's breakeven point (or any profit level) using CVP analysis, a different CVP equation is required. This equation is illustrated in Exhibit 7.6.

The **contribution margin ratio (CMR)** results from dividing CM by the selling price. (Remember that CM is determined by subtracting the variable cost per unit from the selling price.) Using the Michael Motel illustration, CMR is determined as follows:

$$\text{CMR} = \frac{\text{CM}}{\text{S}}$$

$$= \frac{\$40 - \$15}{\$40}$$

$$= \underline{0.625}$$

The CMR means that for every $1 of sales for the Michael Motel, 62.5 percent or $0.625 is contributed toward fixed costs and/or profits. However, recall that in a multiple product situation, more than just rooms are being sold. Therefore, the CMR must be a **weighted average contribution margin ratio (CMR$_w$)**. That is, an average CMR for all operated departments must be weighted to reflect the relative contribution of each department to the establishment's ability to pay fixed costs and generate profits.

Exhibit 7.6   Cost-Volume-Profit Analysis Equation–Multiple Products

$$R = \frac{F + I_n}{CMR_w}$$

where F   =   Total fixed costs
      I_n =   Net income
       R   =   Revenue at desired profit level
   CMR_w =   Weighted average contribution margin ratio

Exhibit 7.7   Weighted Average Contribution Margin Ratio

$$CMR_w = \frac{R_1}{TR} \times \frac{(R_1 - TV_1)}{R_1} + \frac{R_2}{TR} \times \frac{(R_2 - TV_2)}{R_2} + \frac{R_3}{TR} \times \frac{(R_3 - TV_3)}{R_3} +$$

$$\cdots + \frac{R_n}{TR} \times \frac{(R_n - TV_n)}{R_n}$$

where R_1 = Revenue for operated department 1
R_2 = Revenue for operated department 2
R_3 = Revenue for operated department 3
R_n = Revenue for operated department n
TR = Total revenue
TV_1 = Total variable cost for operated department 1
TV_2 = Total variable cost for operated department 2
TV_3 = Total variable cost for operated department 3
TV_n = Total variable cost for operated department n

Exhibit 7.8   Partial Income Statement–Michael Motel

Operated Department	Revenue		Variable Costs		Contribution Margin
Rooms	$300,000	(R_1)	$112,500	(TV_1)	$187,500
Coffee Shop	100,000	(R_2)	87,500	(TV_2)	12,500
	$400,000	(TR)	$200,000	(TV)	$200,000

The weighted average CMR can be determined from more than one formula. In the more complex formula, a CMR is determined for each operated department and the weighted average of the various CMRs is determined as illustrated in Exhibit 7.7. To illustrate this calculation of CMR_w, assume that the Michael Motel adds a coffee shop. Exhibit 7.8 shows a partial income statement for the Michael Motel after the first year the coffee shop has been in operation. Using the equation in Exhibit 7.7, the CMR_w of 0.5 for the Michael Motel is determined as follows:

$$CMR_w = \frac{R_1}{TR} \times \frac{R_1 - TV_1}{R_1} + \frac{R_2}{TR} \times \frac{R_2 - TV_2}{R_2}$$

$$= \frac{\$300,000}{\$400,000} \times \frac{(\$300,000 - \$112,500)}{\$300,000} + \frac{\$100,000}{\$400,000} \times \frac{(\$100,000 - \$87,500)}{\$100,000}$$

$$= 0.75(0.625) + 0.25(0.125)$$

$$= \underline{\underline{0.5}}$$

Alternatively, the CMR_w can sometimes be determined using a simpler formula, using total revenues and total variable costs, as follows:

$$C_w = \frac{TR - TV}{TR}$$

$$= \frac{\$400,000 - \$200,000}{\$400,000}$$

$$= \underline{\underline{0.5}}$$

The simpler formula is easier to use when you know the breakdown of fixed and variable costs for the entire property. However, when calculating the effects of various changes within departments (e.g., the sales mix), the formula in Exhibit 7.7 allows you to substitute figures more easily.

To further illustrate the use of the CMR_w formula, assume that forecasted activity at the Michael Motel shows the variable cost percentage of the rooms department dropping to 30 percent. Since the CMR equals one minus the variable cost percentage, the new rooms department CMR would be 0.7. Assuming the same sales mix (75 percent rooms, 25 percent coffee shop), the formula can be used to revise the CMR_w as follows:

$$\text{Revised } CMR_w = 0.75\,(0.7) + 0.25(0.125)$$

$$= \underline{0.55625}$$

CVP Illustration—Multiple Products

The following series of questions and answers uses the Michael Motel to illustrate how the CVP calculations are used to analyze profit levels, sales mix, and breakeven points in the more complex, and also more typical, situations where hospitality operations sell multiple goods and services. Consider the following information for the Michael Motel:

- Annual fixed costs are $300,000.

- Sales mix is 75 percent rooms, 25 percent coffee shop.

- The Rooms Department CMR is 0.6 and the Coffee Shop CMR is 0.2.
  What is revenue when the Michael Motel breaks even?

$$R = \frac{F}{CMR_w} \quad \text{(equation for revenue at the breakeven point)}$$

$$= \frac{\$300,00}{0.5}$$

$$= \underline{\$600,000}$$

Therefore, the Michael Motel's breakeven point is reached when revenue is $600,000. Since, in this application of CVP analysis, multiple products are being sold, the breakeven point is expressed in dollars, not units sold, which is used when analyzing single product/service operations.

What is the Michael Motel's total revenue when a profit of $50,000 is earned?

$$R = \frac{F + I_n}{CMR_w}$$

$$= \frac{\$300,00 + \$50,000}{0.5}$$

$$= \underline{\$700,000}$$

In order for the Michael Motel to earn $50,000, its revenue must increase by $100,000 beyond its breakeven sales of $600,000. Alternatively, the additional revenues beyond breakeven could have been determined as follows:

$$\text{Revenue Beyond Breakeven} = \frac{I_n}{CMR_w}$$

$$= \frac{\$50,000}{0.5}$$

$$= \underline{\$100,000}$$

Failure to reach breakeven sales will result in a loss of $0.50 for every $1 of sales that falls short of breakeven. For the Michael Motel, total sales of $580,000 will result in a $10,000 loss determined as follows:

$$I_n = R(CMR_w) - F$$
$$= \$58,000 \ (0.5) - \$300,000$$
$$= -\$10,000$$

Additional Questions and Solutions

Question: If net income is to be $75,000, how much must *rooms* revenue be, given a ratio of 75 percent of rooms revenue to total revenue?

$$R = \frac{F + I_n}{CMR_w}$$
$$= \frac{\$300,000 + \$75,000}{0.5}$$
$$= \$750,000$$
$$\text{Rooms Revenue} = 0.75R$$
$$= 0.75(\$750,000)$$
$$= \$562,500$$

In this situation, rooms revenue must be $562,500. A total revenue of $750,000 is required to yield a net income of $75,000, and 75 percent of this total revenue represents the contribution of the rooms department.

Question: If room prices increase by 20 percent and the related variable costs and the number of rooms sold remain constant, what is the revised breakeven point?

In this situation, we can expect that the price change will affect the rooms department's relative contribution to the operation's ability to meet fixed costs or profit goals. Therefore, the CMR_w must first be recalculated. This is accomplished by recalculating the CMR for the rooms department and then determining the revised CMR_w. The 20 percent room price increase not only increases the CMR for the rooms department, but it also changes the sales mix for the Michael Motel.

$$\text{Revised CMR for Rooms} = \frac{\$300,000(1.20) - \$120,000}{\$300,000(1.20)}$$
$$= \frac{\$360,000 - \$120,000}{\$360,000}$$
$$= \text{⅔ or } 0.6667$$
$$CMR_w = \frac{\$360,000}{\$460,000} \ (0.6667) + \frac{\$100,000}{\$460,000} \ (0.2)$$
$$= 0.5653$$
$$\text{Revenue} = \frac{F}{CMR_w}$$
$$= \frac{\$300,000}{0.5653}$$
$$= \$530,691.67$$

Thus, the effect on breakeven of a 20 percent rooms price increase is to reduce the amount of revenue needed to break even from $600,000 to $530,961.67.

Question: If the sales mix changes to 60 percent rooms and 40 percent food from the prior mix of 75 percent rooms and 25 percent food, what happens to the breakeven point?

Again, the CMR_w must first be revised. The revised CMR_w is divided into total fixed costs to yield the new breakeven point.

$$\text{Revised } CMR_w = 0.6(0.6) + 0.4(0.2)$$

$$= \underline{0.44}$$

$$\text{Revenue} = \frac{F}{CMR_w}$$

$$= \frac{\$300,000}{0.44}$$

$$= \underline{\$681,818.18}$$

Thus, the changes in sales mix result in a reduction in the weighted average CMR from 0.50 to 0.44. This reduction, in turn, results in an increase of $81,818.18 in the amount of revenue needed for the operation to break even.

Question: If fixed costs increase by $40,000 and all other factors remain constant, what is the revised breakeven point? (Assume a CMR_w of 0.5.)

In this situation, F is simply increased from $300,000 to $340,000. The new total for fixed costs is then divided by the CMR_w of 0.5 in order to calculate the new breakeven point.

$$\text{Revenue} = \frac{\$340,000}{0.5}$$

$$= \underline{\$680,000}$$

The breakeven point when revenues equal $680,000 could have been determined by dividing the increased fixed costs of $40,000 by 0.5 (the CMR_w) and adding the result ($80,000) to the original breakeven revenue of $600,000.

Question: If fixed costs increase by $40,000, variable costs decrease by five percentage points, and all other factors remain constant, what is the revised breakeven point?

If variable costs decrease by five percentage points, then CMR_w increases by the same five percentage points. Thus, the revised CMR_w is 0.55.

$$\text{Revised } CMR_w = \text{Prior } CMR_w + \text{Variable Cost Decrease}$$

$$= 0.5 + 0.05$$

$$= \underline{0.55}$$

$$\text{Revenue} = \frac{\$340,000}{0.55}$$

$$= \underline{\$618,181.82}$$

7.4 INCOME TAXES AND CVP ANALYSIS

Up to this point, the CVP model has treated all costs as either fixed or variable in relation to revenues. However, income taxes vary, not with revenues, but with pre-tax income. Rather than simply treating income tax as a variable expense (which it is not), management can adjust the CVP equations to reflect this relationship between income taxes and pretax income. The CVP equations reflect this refinement by substituting I_b, the notation for pretax income, in place of I_n. When I_n and the tax rate (t) are known, I_b can be determined with the following formula:

$$I_b = \frac{I_n}{1 - t}$$

For example, assume that the Michael Motel desires to earn $50,000 of net income ($I_n$) and its tax rate is 20 percent. Pretax income (I_b) is determined as follows:

$$I_b = \frac{\$50,000}{1 - 0.2}$$

$$= \$62,500^*$$

*Proof:

Pretax income	$62,500
Taxes (20%)	−12,500
Net Income	$50,000

The CVP equation is now altered for income taxes as follows:

$$R = \frac{I_b + F}{CMR_w}$$

This revised CVP analysis equation can be illustrated using the Michael Motel. Assume the following situation:

- Desired net income equals $60,000.
- Annual fixed costs equal $300,000.
- Tax rate equals 20 percent.
- CMR_w equals 0.5.

From this information, we can calculate the pretax income as follows:

$$I_b = \frac{\$60,000}{1 - 0.2}$$

$$= \$75,000$$

Once we calculate the pretax income as $75,000, we can then use the revised CVP equation to arrive at the breakeven point:

$$R = \frac{I_b + F}{CMR_w}$$

$$= \frac{\$75,000 + \$300,000}{0.5}$$

$$= \$750,000^*$$

*Proof:

Revenue	$ 750,000
Variable costs (50%)	−375,000
Fixed costs	−300,000
Pretax income	75,000
Income taxes	− 15,000
Net income	$ 60,000

When an enterprise breaks even, its net income and pretax income both equal zero. Therefore, the breakeven point for a given operation is the same regardless of the tax rate. This same CVP calculation can also be applied to and computed at a departmental or other level in a hotel.

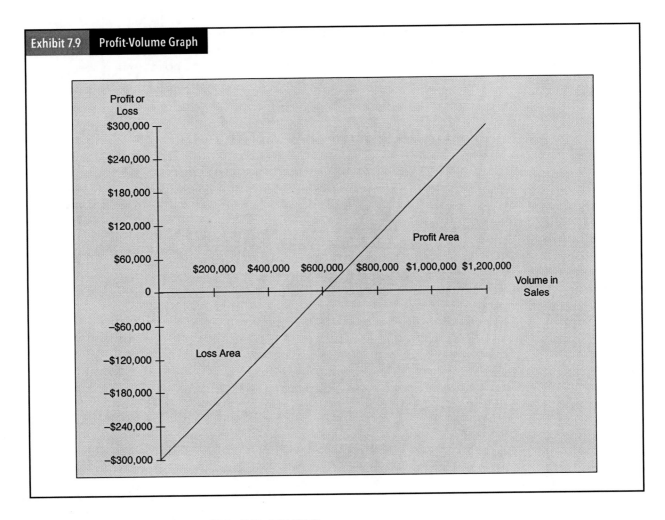

| Exhibit 7.9 | Profit-Volume Graph |

7.5 PROFIT-VOLUME GRAPHS

In CVP graphs such as Exhibit 7.2, profits and losses are represented by the vertical difference between the total revenue and total cost lines at any point. When management desires to focus on the impact on profits of changes in sales volume, a **profit-volume graph** is often used, because it more clearly depicts the relationship between volume and profits. In this graph, revenues and costs are not shown.

Exhibit 7.9 is the profit-volume graph (for the Michael Motel), which is used to illustrate the CVP analysis when a firm has multiple products. The breakeven point is reached when sales equal $600,000, as calculated earlier. If sales are $0, then losses are $300,000, which is the total amount of fixed costs. Likewise, if $300,000 of profit is to be earned, then total sales would have to be $1.2 million. Although the graph shows this result, one must question if this point is outside the Michael Motel's possible range of activity. If rooms revenue is 75 percent and the selling price per room is $40, then 22,500 rooms would have to be sold, determined as follows:

$$\text{Required Rooms Sales in Units} = \frac{\text{Rooms Revenue}}{\text{Room Selling Price}}$$

$$= \frac{0.75(\$1,200,000)}{\$40}$$

$$= \underline{22,500}$$

However, we established earlier in this chapter that the Michael Motel is a 30-room property. The total rooms it could sell in a year is 10,950; thus, 22,500 is beyond its reach. It would have to expand its size or increase its prices to achieve sales of $1.2 million and net income of $300,000. The point to remember is do not blindly use these analytical tools.

7.6 CASH FLOW CVP ANALYSIS

In addition to applying CVP analysis to evaluate profit levels, sales mixes, and pretax incomes, managers and owners are also interested in evaluating various levels of cash flow. They are interested in knowing the amount of revenues required to produce a sufficient flow of cash to reach such benchmarks as the breakeven point and other cash flow levels. The CVP analysis equations previously demonstrated may be modified to provide answers to these questions. The cash flow CVP equation is illustrated in Exhibit 7.10.

The application of CVP analysis to problems involving cash flow can be illustrated using the Michael Motel in light of the following information:

- Fixed costs equal $300,000.

- Tax rate equals 20 percent.

- CMR_w equals 0.5.

- Desired positive cash flow (after taxes) is $30,000.

- Noncash expenses equal $10,000. (This is depreciation expense for the period.)

- Nonexpense cash disbursements equal $20,000. (This could be debt reduction payments for the period.)

In this situation, we can calculate the total revenue required to yield the desired positive cash flow (CF_d) of $30,000. But first, we need to calculate the desired cash flow before taxes:

Exhibit 7.10	Cash Flow Cost-Volume-Profit Analysis Equation

$$R = \frac{CF_b + F - NCE + NECD}{CMR_w}$$

where CF_b = Desired cash flow before taxes.

  F = Fixed costs (including depreciation).

  NCE = Noncash expenses—expenses that do not entail cash payments, such as depreciation and amortization.

  NECD = Nonexpense cash disbursements—cash payments that do not relate directly to expenses. Nonexpense cash disbursements are for loan payments excluding interest expense, payments for fixed assets, etc. Payment for accounts payable, payroll payable, etc., are considered to relate "directly" to expense; thus, they would not be included in this figure.

$$CF_b = \frac{CF_d + NECD - NCE}{1 - t} - NECD + NCE$$

$$= \frac{\$30,000 + \$20,000 - \$10,000}{1 - 0.2} - \$20,000 + \$10,000$$

$$= \underline{\underline{\$40,000}}$$

We can now calculate the total revenue required to yield the desired cash flow before taxes by using the following formula:

$$R = \frac{CF_b + F - NCE + NECD}{CMR_w}$$

$$= \frac{\$40,000 + \$300,000 - \$10,000 + \$20,000}{0.5}$$

$$= \underline{\underline{\$700,000}}$$

Therefore, the Michael Motel must have total revenues of $700,000 in order to generate sufficient cash internally to make its payments and to attain the desired positive cash flow level. The proof of our calculations appears in Exhibit 7.11.

Alternatively, the total revenue at which the Michael Motel has breakeven cash flow (i.e., CF_d equals 0) can be determined. First, we need to calculate the desired cash flow before taxes, as follows:

$$CF_b = \frac{CF_d + NECD - NCE}{1 - t} - NECD + NCE$$

$$= \frac{0 + \$20,000 - \$10,000}{1 - 0.2} - \$20,000 + \$10,000$$

$$= \underline{\underline{\$2,500}}$$

Now we calculate total revenue required to yield a breakeven cash flow, as follows:

$$R = \frac{CF_b + F - NCE + NECD}{CMR_w}$$

$$= \frac{\$2,500 + \$300,000 - \$10,000 + \$20,000}{0.5}$$

$$= \underline{\underline{\$625,000}}$$

Therefore, the Michael Motel requires revenue of $625,000 to yield sufficient cash so that it does not have to borrow working capital funds. The revenue required for a breakeven cash flow of $625,000 is $25,000 greater than the breakeven revenue of $600,000 as computed previously. This difference is due to the excess of the required pretax cash flow and NECD over NCE, determined as follows:

$$\text{Difference in Revenue} = \frac{CF_b + NECD - NCE}{CMR_w}$$

$$= \frac{\$2,500 + \$20,000 - \$10,000}{0.5}$$

$$= \underline{\underline{\$25,000}}$$

7.7 COMPREHENSIVE PROBLEM

The Smith Hotel will be used to more fully illustrate CVP analysis. Exhibit 7.12 contains the income statement for the Smith Hotel for the year ended December 31, 20X1.

Exhibit 7.11   Cash Flow–Michael Motel

Cash receipts (revenue)	$700,000
Cash disbursements:	
Variable costs	350,000
Fixed costs	290,000*
Nonexpenses (reduction in debt)	20,000
Income taxes	10,000**
Positive cash flow	$ 30,000

* Total fixed costs less depreciation equals fixed costs cash disbursements
($300,000 − $10,000 = $290,000).

** Income Taxes = (Revenue − Variable Costs − Fixed Costs) (Tax Rate)
Income Taxes = ($700,000 − $350,000 − $300,000) (0.2)
Income Taxes = $50,000 (0.2)
Income Taxes = $10,000

Exhibit 7.12   Income Statement–Smith Hotel

Summary Income Statement
Smith Hotel
For the year ended December 31, 20X1

	Revenue	Cost of Sales	Payroll and Related Expenses	Other Expenses	Income (Loss)
Operating Departments:					
Rooms	$4,000,000	$ 0	$ 500,000	$ 300,000	$3,200,000
Food	1,200,000	350,000	550,000	150,000	150,000
Beverage	600,000	150,000	150,000	50,000	250,000
Telephone	200,000	160,000	30,000	10,000	0
Total	$6,000,000	$ 660,000	1,230,000	510,000	3,600,000
Undistributed Operating Expenses:					
Administrative and General			200,000	40,000	600,000
Sales and Marketing			100,000	300,000	400,000
Property Operation and Maintenance			100,000	100,000	200,000
Utility Costs			0	400,000	400,000
Gross Operating Profit	$6,000,000	$ 660,000	$ 1,630,000	$ 1,710,000	2,000,000
Rent, Property Taxes, and Insurance					200,000
EBITDA					1,800,000
Depreciation					500,000
Interest Expense					1,000,000
Income before Income Taxes					300,000
Income Taxes					60,000
Net Income					$ 240,000

For CVP analysis, expenses need to be identified as either variable or fixed.
For illustration purposes, the direct expenses of the operated departments
for the Smith Hotel are assumed to be variable, while overhead costs—the
undistributed operating expenses, fixed charges (rent, property taxes, insurance,

Exhibit 7.13 Relationship of Revenues, Variable Costs, and Contribution Margin – Smith Hotel

Relationship of Revenues, Variable Costs, and Contribution Margin
Smith Hotel
For the year ended December 31, 20X1

	Revenue	Variable Costs	Contribution Margin
Rooms	$4,000,000	$ 800,000	$3,200,000
Food	1,200,000	1,050,000	150,000
Beverage	600,000	350,000	250,000
Telephone	200,000	200,000	0
Total	$6,000,000	$2,400,000	3,600,000
Fixed Costs			3,330,000
Income Before Income Taxes			300,000
Income Taxes			60,000
Net Income			$ 240,000

and depreciation), and interest expense—are assumed to be fixed costs. Income tax is a function of income before income taxes. These assumptions are shown in Exhibit 7.13.

Given this information, we will now use CVP analysis to calculate each of the following situations for the Smith Hotel:

1. Weighted average contribution margin ratio

2. Breakeven point

3. Total revenue to yield a net income of $500,000

4. Rooms revenues when profit equals $500,000

5. Breakeven point if fixed costs increase by $300,000

6. Breakeven point if fixed costs increase by $300,000 and revenues increase 10 percent for each department through price increases

Situation #1: Determine the CMR_w.

From Exhibit 7.13, the CMR_w may be determined as follows:

$$CMR_w = \frac{\text{Contribution Margin*}}{\text{Total Revenue}}$$

$$= \frac{\$3,600,000}{\$6,000,000}$$

$$= \underline{0.6}$$

*Total operated departments income

Situation #2: Determine the breakeven point.

$$R = \frac{F}{CMR_w}$$

$$= \frac{\$3,300,000}{0.6}$$

$$= \underline{\$5,500.000}$$

Situation #3: Determine the total revenue required to yield $500,000 of net income. (Assume that the sales mix remains constant.)

First, the effect of income taxes on net income must be accounted for, assuming the Smith Hotel's income tax rate of 20 percent. The amount of income before income taxes that the hotel must generate in order to achieve the desired net income of $500,000 can be determined as follows:

$$I_b = \frac{I_n}{1-t}$$

$$= \frac{\$500,000}{1-0.2}$$

$$= \$625,000$$

Second, the total revenue needed to yield this amount of income before income taxes is calculated as follows:

$$R = \frac{I_b + F}{CMR_w}$$

$$= \frac{\$625,000 + \$3,300,000}{0.6}$$

$$= \$6,541,666.67$$

Situation #4: Determine the amount of room revenue when the Smith Hotel makes $500,000 of net income.

First, from the information provided on the Smith Hotel's summary income statement (Exhibit 7.12), we can determine the relative contribution of rooms revenue to total revenue.

$$\frac{Rooms\ Revenue}{Total\ Revenue} = \frac{\$4,000,000}{\$6,000,000}$$

$$= 0.6667$$

Second, we can then multiply 0.6667 by the total revenue and arrive at the required rooms revenue as part of the total revenue for the Smith Hotel to achieve $500,000 of net income.

$$Rooms\ Revenue = \$6,541,666.67 \times 0.6667$$

$$= \$4,361,329.17$$

Situation #5: Determine the breakeven point for the Smith Hotel if fixed costs increase by $300,000 and all other things remain constant.

The breakeven point is determined as follows:

$$R = \frac{F}{CMR_w}$$

$$= \frac{\$3,600,000}{0.6}$$

$$= \$6,000.000$$

Note that the Smith Hotel's breakeven point increases from $5.5 million to $6 million when its fixed costs increase by $300,000. Alternatively, the new breakeven point could have been determined by dividing the increased fixed costs ($300,000) by the CMR_w and adding the result to the previously calculated breakeven point of $5.5 million as follows:

$$R = \$5,500,000 + \frac{\$300,000}{0.6}$$

$$= \$6,000,000$$

Situation #6: Determine the breakeven point for the Smith Hotel if fixed costs increase by $300,000 and revenues increase 10 percent for each department through price increases. Assume that all factors remain constant.

First, a revised CMR_w must be determined as follows:

	Total Revenue	Total Contribution Margin
Prior	$ 6,000,000	$ 3,600,000
Increase	600,000	600,000
Revised	$ 6,600,000	$ 4,200,000

$$\text{Revised } CMR_w = \frac{\text{Revised Total Contribution Margin}}{\text{Revised Total Revenue}}$$

$$= \frac{\$4,200,00}{\$6,600,000}$$

$$= \underline{0.6364}$$

Then the total fixed costs are increased by $300,000 to $3.6 million, and the breakeven point is determined as follows:

$$R = \frac{F}{CMR_w}$$

$$= \frac{\$3,600,000}{0.6364}$$

$$= \$5,656,819.61$$

7.8 OPERATING LEVERAGE

Operating leverage is the extent to which an operation's expenses are fixed rather than variable. If an operation has a high level of fixed costs relative to variable costs, it is said to be highly levered. Being highly levered means a relatively small increase in sales beyond the breakeven point results in a relatively large increase in net income. However, failure to reach the breakeven point results in a relatively large net loss.

If an operation has a high level of variable costs relative to fixed costs, it is said to have low operating leverage. A relatively small increase in sales beyond the breakeven point results in a small increase in net income. On the other hand, failure to reach the breakeven point results in a relatively small net loss.

For example, consider the cost structures of two hospitality operations illustrated in Exhibit 7.14. Note that both properties will break even when their revenues equal $500,000. However, Property A has a CMR of 0.4, while Property B has a CMR of 0.6. This reveals that, for each revenue dollar over the shared breakeven point, Property A will earn only $0.40 while Property B will earn $0.60. On the other hand, for each revenue dollar under the breakeven point, Property A loses only $0.40 while Property B loses $0.60. Both properties identify the same breakeven point as the difference between revenues and expenses, and, for both properties, the costs of failure equal the rewards of success. They both risk as much as they gain, but for Property B, the stakes are higher. Property B is more highly levered than Property A.

Exhibit 7.15 is a graphical representation of the cost structures of Properties A and B and reflects their identical breakeven points. However, it is the vertical

Exhibit 7.14   Cost Structures of Properties A and B

	Property A		Property B	
	$	%	$	%
Revenues	$500,000	100%	$500,000	100%
Variable costs	300,000	60	200,000	40
Fixed costs	200,000	40	300,000	60
Net income	$ 0	0%	$ 0	0%

distance between the total revenue and total cost lines that measures the degree of profitability for each property. Since Property B is more highly levered, the distance between the total cost and total revenue lines is greater at all operating levels compared to Property A, except at the breakeven point.

The degree of operating leverage desired by a hospitality property reflects the degree of risk that the operation desires to take. All other things being the same, the more highly levered the operation, the greater the risk. However, the greater the risk, the greater the expected returns, as reflected in Exhibit 7.15. For example, if sales are $300,000 below the breakeven point, Property A loses only $120,000 ($300,000 × 0.4), while the more highly levered Property B loses $180,000 ($300,000 × 0.6). However, if sales are $300,000 over the breakeven point for both operations, Property A earns only $120,000 of profit, while Property B generates $180,000 of profit.

Exhibit 7.16 contains the profit-volume graph for Properties A and B. Notice that both properties break even when sales equal $500,000. When sales of $1 million are generated, Property B earns $300,000, while Property A earns only $200,000; however, when sales are zero, Property B loses $300,000, while Property A loses only $200,000.

HotStats estimates the breakeven occupancy for all U.S. properties at 37.3 percent, ranging from 39.4 percent for select-service properties to 34.4 percent for luxury properties. As breakeven is a function of costs and room rates and they both are very different in various parts of the world, these breakeven occupancy percentages are lower in other regions, with Europe at 34.5 percent, Asia Pacific region at 33.2 percent, and Middle East, the lowest, at 22.4 percent.[1]

7.9 INVESTMENT DRIVEN BREAKEVEN

In addition to the traditional operating and interest payment breakeven analysis, HVS is also advocating the use of **investment driven breakeven analysis**.[2] In this case, besides the normal fixed, variable, and mixed costs, the investment driven analysis considers the cost of debt of a hotel property and calculates the sales level at which a hotel is unlikely to default on its interest payment, or where EBITDA equals the interest payment of the subject hotel. If the loan the hotel obtains requires a repayment of both the principal and interest, then EBITDA will be set to equal to the debt service and not just the interest payment of a hotel property.

Exhibit 7.15   Operating Leverages of Properties A and B

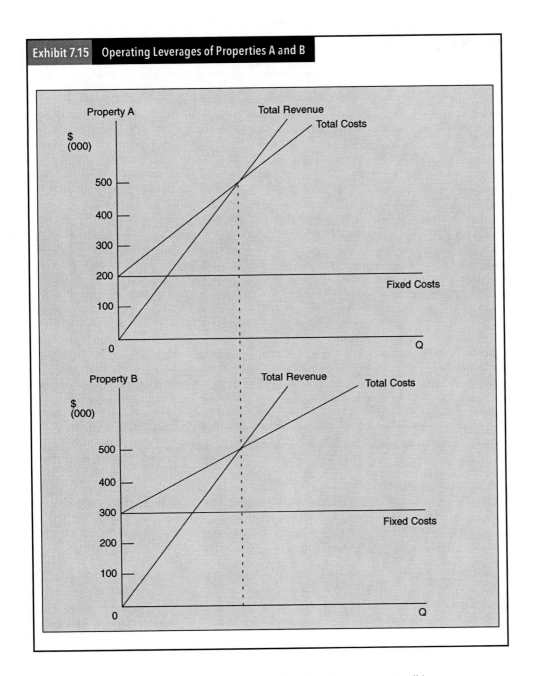

Using the CVP formula, the investment drive breakeven point will be calculated as follows:

Investment Breakeven Point = [Fixed Operating Expenses
+ Annual Interest Payments
+ (Equity Investment × Equity Yield)]
÷ (1 − Variable Costs, or Gross Margin)

Thus, the usefulness of the CVP formula can be extended to assist managers, owners, and operators to make operating, investing, and financing decisions.

Exhibit 7.16 Profit-Volume Graph for Properties A and B

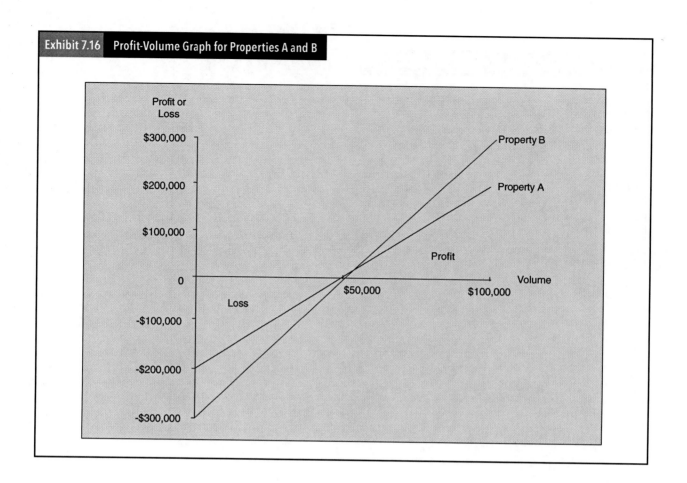

Managers use CVP analysis as an analytical tool to examine the relationships among costs, revenues, and sales volume. By expressing these relationships in graphic form or by using mathematical equations, management can determine an operation's breakeven point, sales requirements for a specified net income level, and/or the mix of sales within the operation.

In order to use CVP analysis to determine the breakeven point, various relationships must be assumed. First, fixed costs are constant; they will not fluctuate within the range of operating activity being studied. Also, both variable costs and revenues fluctuate linearly with sales volume; that is, a percentage increase in sales volume (e.g., rooms sold) will result in the same percentage increase in revenues and variable expenses. In a "shutdown" situation (when sales are zero), there are no variable costs or revenues, but the fixed costs will be at their constant level; therefore, the theoretical bottom line for such a shut-down period will be a net loss equal to the fixed costs of the period.

The breakeven point is defined as the level of sales that generates revenues equal to total (fixed and variable) costs. CVP analysis allows management selling a single product/service (e.g., only rooms) to arrive at this breakeven level of revenues with the aid of the equation:

$$X = \frac{F}{S - V}$$

The $S - V$ element of the equation is the contribution margin, which is the amount of money generated by the sale that may be applied to cover fixed costs, or, beyond the breakeven point, to contribute to profit. Therefore, the equation reflects the fixed cost divided by the dollars provided to cover fixed costs per sales unit.

In the more complex situation where more than one good or service is sold, the CVP formula is as follows:

$$R = \frac{F + I_n}{CMR_w}$$

The CMR_w element of the equation reflects the weighted average of the CMRs for the profit centers. The CVP formulas for the multiple products operation may be used to determine breakeven points by substituting 0 for I_n. This formula may further be modified by substituting I_b for I_n to consider the effect of income taxes.

Once the CVP relationship is understood, it can become a vital tool offering aid in a number of situations. It can provide management with benchmark sales levels (such as the breakeven level, the amount needed to provide a specific net income, or the required level to provide for cash needs), prices, or sales mix. It can be used to examine the differences between levels of sales or costs. It can also be used to examine different cost structures, as the effect of differences in the CMR can be seen over different sales levels.

breakeven analysis—See cost-volume-profit analysis.

breakeven point—The level of sales volume at which total revenues equal total costs.

contribution margin (CM)—Sales less cost of sales for either an entire operating department or for a given product; represents the amount of sales revenue that is contributed toward fixed costs and/or profits.

contribution margin ratio (CMR)—The contribution margin divided by the selling price. Represents the percentage of sales revenue that is contributed toward fixed costs and/or profits.

cost-volume-profit (CVP) analysis—A set of analytical tools used by managers to examine the relationships among various costs, revenues, and sales volume in either graphic or equation form, allowing one to determine the revenue required at any desired profit level. Also called breakeven analysis.

investment driven breakeven analysis—An analysis that considers fixed, variable, and mixed costs and the cost of debt of a hotel property and calculates the sales level at which a hotel is unlikely to default on its interest payment, or where EBITDA equals the interest payment of the subject hotel.

margin of safety—The excess of budgeted or actual sales over sales at breakeven.

operating leverage—The extent to which an operation's expenses are fixed rather than variable; an operation that substitutes fixed costs for variable costs is said to be highly levered.

profit-volume graph—A graph that focuses on the impact on profits of changes in sales volume; revenues and costs are not shown.

sensitivity analysis—The study of the sensitivity of the CVP model's dependent variables (such as room sales) to changes in one or more of the model's independent variables (such as variable costs and selling prices).

weighted average contribution margin ratio (CMR_w)—In a multiple product situation, an average contribution margin for all operated departments that is weighted to reflect the relative contribution of each department to the establishment's ability to pay fixed costs and generate profits.

1. What are the assumptions underlying CVP analysis?

2. What does the term $S - V$ represent in the CVP equation? How does its use differ from that of the CMR?

3. Draw a CVP graph of the following operation: $F = \$10$; $S = \$1$; $V = \$0.50$. What is the meaning of the regions (between the total revenue and total cost lines) to the left and right of 20 units sold?

4. What is income before taxes for a hospitality operation that generates no sales during a period?

5. What is the advantage of using CVP equations instead of CVP graphs to express relationships?

6. How does CMR for a single department, or for an enterprise selling only one product/service, differ from a weighted average CMR (CMR_w)? How is CMR_w determined?

7. What part of the CVP equation used to determine the breakeven point must be changed in order to produce the answer in terms of sales dollars versus sales units? Why is this so?

8. What is the sales mix? How does it affect CMR_w?

9. Why should noncash expenses be subtracted in the CVP formula used to determine the revenue level at the cash flow breakeven point?

10. If, by changing an operation's sales mix, the CMR_w decreases, how is the breakeven level of sales affected?

Problem 1

The Michigan Café's average lunch sells for $15, while its variable costs per lunch average $9. It plans to advertise a Monday lunch special for $11. The special would cost Eastpointe $7.75 per meal (variable costs). An ad in the local paper to promote the special would cost Michigan $300.

Required:

1. What are the café's contribution margin (CM) and contribution margin ratio (CMR) to begin with? 40%

2. What are the CM and CMR based strictly on the lunch special-related price and cost? $3.25 and 21.53%

3. How many lunch covers must be sold to cover the promotion of the luncheon special? 93 lunch covers

Problem 2

The 150-room limited-service Vineyard Inn has an ADR of $85 and variable costs per room sold of $20. Assume there is no other sales activity. Its monthly fixed costs total $150,000.

Required:

1. How many rooms must be sold to break even? 2,307.69

2. What day of the month does it break even if it averages a paid occupancy percentage of 60 percent? Assume all 150 rooms are available for sale each day.

3. If variable costs are reduced by $3 and fixed costs increase by $72,000 annually, what are the monthly breakeven revenues? $2294.12

Problem 3

Bobby Randall has spent $550 for a tent, table, and chairs for his lemonade stand. He figures he can sell a glass of lemonade in the park to Little League players for an even $1. His cost per drink is estimated to be $0.30. He also has to cover napkins, cups, and other variable costs estimated to be $0.10 per glass of lemonade sold.

He will open his business on June 1 (a Monday) and be open five days each week for the summer months of June–August. He will pay his parents $2 each day to transport him and his materials to and from the park.

Bobby projects daily sales of 100 glasses of lemonade.

Required:

1. What is his contribution margin?

$\frac{2}{100} = 0.06$ $.30 + .10 + .02 .56B$

$1 - .42 = 0.58$

2. What is his breakeven point (in units), given that he wants to cover all of his costs? $X = \frac{F}{S-V}$ $= \frac{500}{1-0.42} = 649$

3. What day of the summer will he break even?

Problem 4

Evan Lee has acquired the Centennial, a 100-room, limited-service lodging property. Its costs are as follows:

Variable costs per room sold: $20

Monthly fixed costs: $120,000

Mixed costs:

	Low Month	High Month
	60% Occupancy	80% Occupancy
Repairs	$3,000	$3,500
Utilities	$4,000	$5,000

(Note: The mixed costs are not part of the variable and fixed costs above.)

Required:

1. Determine the variable cost per room, considering the mixed costs.

2. Determine the monthly fixed costs, considering the mixed costs.

3. What must the ADR be if the Centennial breaks even at the end of the twentieth day of each month? Assume an average paid occupancy of 75 percent.

Problem 5

The Crystal Hotel has room and food operations. The rooms operation provides 70 percent of the total revenue and has variable costs of 25 percent. The food operation provides 30 percent of the total revenue and has variable costs of 60 percent. The total annual fixed costs are $275,000.

Required:

1. What is the CMR for the rooms operation? 64.24%

2. What is the CMR for the food operation? -100%

3. What is the weighted average CMR for the Lucas Inn? 22.30%

4. What is the breakeven point? $1,833,333.33

5. If the average tax rate is 25 percent, what is the annual revenue required to achieve annual net income of $125,000? $3,555,555.56

Problem 6

The Mountain Lodge (a rooms-only property) cost its owners $4 million, of which they borrowed $1.5 million. The general manager estimates the following costs:

Variable costs per room sold:	20 percent of ADR
Annual fixed costs:	
Salaries	$ 250,000
Insurance	20,000
Depreciation	100,000
Interest	150,000
Other	75,000

In addition, the lodge's pretax income will be taxed at an average rate of 25 percent.

1. What is the monthly breakeven level of sales at the Mountain Lodge?

2. What amount of annual sales are required if the owners are to earn 20 percent of their investment in this property?

Problem 7

The ALAN, owned by Alex and Andy Cornwall, includes a 40-room lodging operation and coffee shop. The average annual revenue and variable expense figures for the past two years have been as follows:

	Rooms	Coffee Shop
Revenue	$ 700,000	$ 300,000
Variable expenses	120,000	200,000
The fixed costs are as follows:		
Rooms department	$ 55,000	
Coffee shop	65,000	
Overhead	300,000	

Required:

1. Assuming the sales mix remains constant, calculate the following:
   a. The annual revenue at the breakeven point.
   b. Total net income when total revenue equals $1.2 million. (Assume an income tax of 20 percent.)
   c. The required level of annual revenue when net income is $200,000. (Assume there are no income taxes.)

2. Answer the same questions as Part 1, but assume the sales mix has changed to 75 percent/25 percent for rooms/coffee shop.

Problem 8

Jack Benoit, owner of Benoit Inn, has requested your assistance in analyzing his 50-room rooms-only property. He provides you information as follows:

1. The average rooms sales price is $80.

2. Monthly fixed costs equal $30,000.

3. His variable costs per room sold equal $20.

Required:

1. Determine the Benoit Inn's breakeven point in revenue.

2. If revenues equal $650,000, what is the Benoit Inn's margin of safety in revenues and rooms sold?

3. If John desires his property to generate a pretax profit of $100,000, how many rooms must be sold?

4. What is the occupancy percentage for the Benoit Inn when pretax profit earned is $100,000?

Problem 9

George Patel, the owner/operator of the Riverside, is interested in determining the level of sales necessary to realize a net income of $550,000 next year. He has compiled records on each department's sales and costs and assumes that the sales mix will be the same next year. The major department, the rooms department, had sales of $2.5 million, and its contribution margin was $1.75 million. The coffee shop had sales of $750,000 and variable costs of $350,000. The restaurant had sales of $1.2 million and variable costs of $750,000. Mr. Patel assumes that the fixed costs will be $1.2 million.

Required:

1. What is the CMR_w?

2. What is the required level of total sales to generate $500,000 net income? (Assume that there are no income taxes.)

3. What is the required level of total sales to generate $500,000 net income if the income tax rate is 30 percent?

Problem 10

Justin Ainsley is considering expanding his company's operations into the hospitality industry. His company's goals include diversification, but also require an 18 percent return on investment after taxes. Mr. Ainsley has studied a hotel property that yields the following results:

1. The rooms department generates 80 percent of the sales and operates with a CMR of 0.74.

2. The food and beverage department generates the other 20 percent of sales and has a CMR of 0.45.

3. Fixed costs per year are estimated to be $340,000.

4. In order to purchase the hotel, Mr. Ainsley would have to invest $1.5 million.

5. Mr. Ainsley's tax rate is 30 percent.

Required:

What level of sales is required before Mr. Ainsley would recommend investing in the hotel to the company's board of directors?

Problem 11

The M & L Inn's summary income statement is as follows:

	Rooms	Food	Total
Revenues	$ 1,500,000	$ 500,000	$ 2,000,000
Variable Costs	300,000	400,000	700,000
Contribution Margin	$ 1,200,000	$ 100,000	1,300,000
Fixed Costs*			1,100,000
Pretax Income			200,000
Income Taxes			50,000
Net Income			$ 150,000

*Includes lease expense of $480,000

Required:

1. What is the breakeven point for the M & L Inn?

2. If the fixed cost lease is traded for a variable lease of 20 percent of total sales, what is the revised breakeven point for the M & L Inn?

Problem 12

The Myer Motel (MM), a rooms-only, 50-room lodging operation, has a cost structure as follows:

Monthly fixed costs = $20,000
Variable costs/room sold = $20
ADR = $60
Average tax rate = 20 percent

Required:

1. What is MM's CMR?

2. What is MM's breakeven point (in rooms sold)?

3. If MM is to make $10,000 of monthly after-tax profit, what must its total revenue be?

4. If the MM makes $10,000 of monthly profit during June, what day of the month does it break even? (Assume the number of rooms sold are the same each day.)

5. If MM's variable costs increased by 50 percent, how much must its ADR increase, all other things being the same?

Problem 13

The Mackinaw and Minier Hotels' summarized operating results are as follows:

	Mackinaw Hotel	Minier Hotel
1. CMR_w	60 percent	50 percent
2. Annual fixed costs	$1.2 million	$1 million
3. Tax rate	20 percent	20 percent

Required:

1. Compute each hotel's breakeven point.

2. Draw a profit-volume chart, including a profit-volume line, for each hotel for sales volumes ranging from $0 to $3 million.

3. Which hotel is riskier? Why?

Problem 14

Bob and Susan Menzel are planning to open a foodservice operation and have heard about operating leverage. They are forecasting annual sales and expenses as follows:

Annual sales	$ 500,000
Food costs—variable	30 percent
Wages	20 percent
Other	10 percent
Fixed costs	$ 100,000

They have the opportunity to sign a variable, mixed, or fixed lease for the space and equipment. The lease expense is in addition to the above listed expenses. The options are as follows:

Variable:	6 percent of sales
Mixed:	2 percent of sales plus $1,500 per month
Fixed:	$2,500 per month

Required:

1. Determine the level of sales required to break even for each lease option.

2. If the foodservice operation has annual sales of $700,000, what is the net income given each lease option?

3. If annual sales are only $400,000, which lease option do you recommend? Explain using numbers.

Problem 15

The Hazen's summary income statement is as follows:

	Rooms	Food	Total
Revenues	$ 1,500,000	$ 500,000	$ 2,000,000
Variable Costs	200,000	300,000	500,000
Fixed Costs	200,000	100,000	300,000
Contribution Margin	$ 1,100,000	$ 100,000	1,200,000
Variable Costs*			150,000
Fixed Costs**			800,000
Pretax Income			250,000
Income Taxes			100,000
Net Income			$ 150,000

* Management contract based on rooms revenue
** Includes depreciation expense of $500,000

Required:

1. What is the breakeven point for The Hazen?

2. If the sales mix changes to 60 percent room sales and 40 percent food sales, while total revenue remains $2 million, what is the breakeven point?

3. What is the level of total revenue at which The Hazen's cash flow is $0? Assume it plans to sell capital stock for $100,000 of cash and to pay dividends of $50,000.

4. The food department manager has proposed running a display ad costing $300 in the *State News* to get more Sunday brunch business. How many additional meals must be sold to make a $200 after-tax profit on this proposal? Assume an average price per meal of $12.

Problem 16

The KDJ Inn's summary income statement is as follows:

	Rooms	Food	Total
Revenues	$ 1,500,000	$ 500,000	$ 2,000,000
Variable Costs	300,000	400,000	700,000
Contribution Margin	$ 1,200,000	$ 100,000	1,300,000
Fixed Costs			1,000,000*
Pretax Income			300,000
Income Taxes			75,000
Net Income			$ 225,000

*Includes lease expense of $480,000

Required:

1. What is the breakeven point for the KDJ Inn?

2. If the fixed cost lease is traded for a variable lease of 20 percent of total sales, what is the revised breakeven point for the KDJ Inn?

3. If (independent of #2) the variable costs increase by 10 percent, by what percentage must sales increase in order for the KDJ Inn to earn its net income of $225,000?

4. If (independent of #2 and #3) the KDJ Inn is to earn net income of $300,000, what must its room sales equal? (Assume that the sales mix remains constant.)

Problem 17

Stephanie Miller, an experienced businessperson and consultant, realizes the importance of cash flow. Therefore, whenever she is requested to provide a client with a breakeven level of sales, she also provides a cash flow breakeven analysis. The client has provided Ms. Miller with the following information for BMS Inc.

BMS Inc.
Monthly Condensed Income Statement

Rooms Revenues		$ 100,000
Food Revenue		40,000
Total Revenue		140,000
Departmental Expenses		
Rooms	$ 20,000	
Food	20,000	
Total Departmental Expenses		40,000
Contribution Margin		100,000
Fixed Costs		
Interest Expense	10,000	
Depreciation	20,000	
Other Fixed Costs	50,000	
Total Fixed Costs		80,000
Income before Tax		20,000
Tax		5,000
Net Income		$ 15,000

Other information:

1. Assume the tax rate to be constant over any level of pretax income.

2. The monthly mortgage payment is $15,000, of which $10,000 is interest expense.

3. All inventories are purchased on a cash basis and are expensed when purchased since they are insignificant.

4. There is no major change in current assets, other than cash, or current liabilities from month to month.

Required:

You are to assist Ms. Miller in:

1. Determining the level of sales required to provide BMS with $40,000 net income

2. Determining the level of sales required to provide BMS with $20,000 positive cash flow for a month

Problem 18

The condensed income statement of the Allen Hotel (AH) is as follows:

	Revenue	Variable Costs	Fixed Costs	Dept. Income
Rooms	$ 5,000,000	$ 1,000,000	$ 500,000	$ 3,500,000
Food	2,000,000	800,000	500,000	700,000
Gift shop	400,000	150,000	100,000	150,000
Other	200,000	200,000	100,000	(100,000)
Total department income				4,250,000
Other variable expenses				950,000*
Other fixed costs				2,800,000**
Pretax income				500,000
Income taxes				100,000
Net income				$ 400,000

* Management fees and rent expense vary with rooms revenue
** Includes depreciation of $800,000

Required:

1. Compute the AH's weighted average CMR. Consider all variable costs.

2. Compute the AH's breakeven point.

3. If the AH desires to earn (net income) $500,000, what must its total food sales equal? Assume the sales mix is constant.

4. If the AH desires to generate pretax cash flow of $800,000, what must its total revenue equal? Assume its debt reduction payment is $300,000 for the year and it plans to purchase equipment for $100,000 using cash.

5. If the sales mix charges to rooms = 60 percent, food = 30 percent, gift shop = 5 percent, and other = 5 percent, what is the revised CMR_w?

Problem 19

The condensed income statement of the Colton Inn (CI) is as follows:

	Revenue	Variable Costs	Fixed Costs	Department Income
Room	$ 5,000,000	$ 1,000,000	$ 500,000	$ 3,500,000
Food	3,000,000	1,000,000	1,000,000	1,000,000
Other	500,000	200,000	100,000	200,000
Total department income				4,700,000
Other variable expenses*				500,000
Other fixed costs**				2,000,000
Pretax income				2,200,000
Income taxes				600,000
Net income				$ 1,600,000

* Rent (10 percent of room sales)
** Includes depreciation and amortization of $500,000

Required:

1. Compute the contribution margin ratio for the rooms department.

2. Compute the CI's weighted average CMR.

3. Compute the CI's breakeven point.

4. If the CI wants to make $1.5 million of net income, what must its rooms sales equal?

Problem 20

Keith and Sue's Dude Ranch (KSDR) is a 40-room hotel near Denver with a thirty-seat restaurant and stables (a profit center). Keith and Sue Cass, the owners, are interested in having you use CVP analysis to aid them in determining various sales levels for their resort. The following is a summary of the most recent annual income statement.

Keith and Sue's Dude Ranch
Condensed Income Statement for the year ended Dec. 31, 20X5

	Rooms	Food	Stables	Total
Revenues	$ 500,000	$ 200,000	$ 5,000	$ 705,000
Variable Expenses	150,000	150,000	4,000	304,000
Contribution Margin	$ 350,000	$ 50,000	$ 1,000	401,000
Fixed Costs				151,000
Income Tax				125,000
Net Income				$ 125,000

Required:

1. What is the food department's CMR?

2. What is the weighted average CMR for KSDR?

3. What is the breakeven point?

4. The Casses wish to increase net income by $30,000 and feel this can be done by increasing room sales *only*. Determine the necessary increase in room sales to meet this requirement.

5. Assume (independent of #4) that revenue from the stables can be increased, but only with a $500 increase in advertising (a fixed cost) for brochures to go in each room. What level of sales from the stables must be generated to cover this cost?

6. Assume that the brochures mentioned in #5 are used as a direct mailing. The cost would now be $1,500 to cover printing and mailing, but sales for each department would increase. Assuming that room sales, food sales, and stable revenue remain at a ratio of 5 to 2 to 0.05, how much must revenues increase for net income to remain constant?

Problem 21

The condensed income statement of the Sweetwater Hotel (SH) is as follows:

	Revenue	Variable Costs	Fixed Costs	Department Income
Rooms	$ 4,000,000	$ 800,000	$ 200,000	$ 3,000,000
Food	2,400,000	1,000,000	400,000	1,000,000
Gift Shop	300,000	150,000	100,000	50,000
Other	300,000	200,000	100,000	–0–
Total Department Income				4,050,000
Other Variable Expenses*				700,000
Other Fixed Costs**				2,800,000
Pretax Income				550,000
Income Taxes				200,000
Net Income				$ 350,000

 * Management Fees (10 percent of total sales)
** Includes depreciation of $1 million

Required:

1. Compute the SH's weighted average contribution margin ratio (CMR_w). Consider *all* variable costs.

2. Compute the SH's breakeven point.

3. Compute the total sales required to yield a *pretax* cash flow of $2 million. Assume a single payment during the accounting period to *reduce* the mortgage was for $200,000. Also assume other nonexpense cash disbursements of $100,000.

4. The gift shop manager has proposed the development of a promotional piece to boost gift shop sales. The brochure would be mailed to area residents. The development cost is $4,000, and the expected mailing cost is $0.50 per person. The mailing is expected to go to 10,000 people. If $2,000 of profit (net of tax and management fees) is to be realized on this project solely from increased gift shop sales, what is the required increase in gift shop sales?

5. Independent of #4, assume a sales mix as follows:

Rooms	50%
Food	35%
Other	5%
Gift Shop	10%
Total	100%

Assume the management fee remains at 10 percent of total revenue. What is the revised weighted average CMR?

Problem 22

The K&K Motel has 100 rooms and a swimming pool. Other activities, such as vending machine sales and telephone sales, are operated on a breakeven basis and may be ignored.

The cost structure of the K&K differs slightly by month based on season. The variable costs per occupied room are estimated as follows:

Housekeeping	$4.00
Operating supplies	2.00
Repair and maintenance	1.00
Utilities (summer)	0.50
Utilities (winter)	2.00
Pool/maintenance (summer)	0.50
Laundry	1.00

Fixed costs per month are estimated as follows:

Housekeeping—supervision	$ 2,000
Front office	3,000
Administration	6,000
Depreciation	5,000
Pool costs (summer)	2,000
Utilities	1,000
Insurance and other	2,500

Assume the average income tax rate is 30 percent of pretax income. The average daily rate of the K&K is estimated to be $35.

Required:

1. Compute the net income expected during June (a summer month) if 80 percent occupancy is achieved.

2. Compute the breakeven point in rooms sold during June. If 80 percent occupancy is achieved each night, on what day does the K&K break even?

3. Compute the net income expected during November (a winter month) if 70 percent occupancy is achieved.

4. Compute the breakeven point in rooms sold during November. If 70 percent occupancy is achieved each night, on what day does the K&K break even?

Problem 23

Susan and Thomas Taylor bought a small, select service property in a college town. While the hotel does not have a large number of rooms, it does have a sizable banquet area. And with Thomas's culinary background, they believe this is their perfect investment. They would like to determine the level of sales needed to net an income of $400,000 next year. From the records of the previous owner, they estimate the rooms department to generate $2 million, with a contribution margin of $1.5 million. The marketplace, which is a small coffee shop that also sell pastries and sundry items, to have sales of $850,000 and variable costs of $375,000. For the banquet space, they expect sales to reach $2.1 million and variable costs of $1.35 million. The total fixed costs are approximated at $1.1 million.

Required:

1. What is the CMR_w?

2. What is the required level of total sales to generate $400,000 net income? (Assume that there are no income taxes.)

3. What is the required level of total sales to generate $400,000 net income if an income tax rate of 34 percent is expected?

Problem 24

The Mark, a seaside resort, has the following income statement. The owner, Mark Valentini, would like your help on conducting a breakeven analysis. All departmental expenses are assumed to be variable costs.

Revenues	
Rooms	$ 3,000,000
Food and Beverage	4,230,500
Other	72,800
Total Revenues	7,303,300
Departmental Expense	
Rooms	770,100
Food and Beverage	3,228,717
Other	50,981
Total Departmental Expenses	4,049,798
Total Departmental Profit	3,253,502
Fixed Cost*	1,400,000
Income before Tax	1,853,502
Income Tax	593,120
Net Income	$ 1,260,382

*Includes rent expense of $600,000

Required:

1. What is the breakeven point for The Mark?

2. If the fixed rent is renegotiated for a variable lease of 10 percent of total revenues, what is the revised breakeven point for The Mark?

3. In addition to the new lease in #2, The Mark also needs to net an income of $800,000 for its investors. What must the hotel generate in room sales? (Assume that the sales mix remains constant.)

Problem 25

Lizzy Delo is about to open The Delo B&B, a small, fifty-room mountain resort with a restaurant. She has completed a breakeven analysis, but she has also heard about the cash flow breakeven analysis and is not sure how to complete one. Knowing you are a hospitality major and are learning managerial accounting, she is asking for your help. She has a monthly condensed income statement and also some additional information for you:

The Delo B&B

Revenues		
Rooms Revenue	$ 150,000	
Food Revenue	50,000	
Total Revenue		$ 200,000
Departmental Expenses		
Rooms Expense	25,000	
Food Expense	30,000	
Total Departmental Expenses		55,000
Total Departmental Profit		145,000
Fixed Costs		
Interest Expense	10,000	
Depreciation Expense	12,000	
Other Fixed Expenses	60,000	
Total Fixed Costs		82,000
Income before Tax		63,000
Tax		25200
Net Income		$ 37,800

1. Assume the tax rate to be constant over any level of pretax income.

2. The monthly mortgage payment is $12,000, of which $10,000 is interest expense.

3. As owner of a new business, she has to pay for all her inventory purchases on a cash basis and they are expensed when purchased.

4. On a monthly basis, there should be no major change in current assets, other than cash, or current liabilities.

5. Assume all operating department expenses are variable.

<u>Required:</u>

1. Determine the level of sales required to provide Lizzy and the hotel with $25,000 net income.

2. Determine the level of sales required to provide The Delo B&B with $30,000 positive cash flow for a month.

8

COST APPROACHES
TO PRICING

Competencies

1. Explain how the concept of price elasticity of demand applies to hospitality operations. (pp. 359–361)

2. Describe informal approaches to pricing and identify factors that modify cost approaches to pricing. (pp. 361–362)

3. Apply ingredient and prime ingredient markup approaches to pricing food and beverage items. (pp. 362–364)

4. Apply the $1 per $1,000 approach and the Hubbart Formula to pricing rooms. (pp. 364–368)

5. Describe the reasons for and process of discounting room rates, and define and apply revenue management. (pp. 368–374)

6. Use a bottom-up approach to pricing meals. (pp. 374–376)

7. Demonstrate how changes in sales mix affect gross profit. (pp. 376–378)

8. Explain the menu engineering approach to pricing food and beverage items. (pp. 379–384)

9. Identify the advantages and disadvantages of integrated pricing by hospitality operations. (p. 384)

KEY TERMS

elastic demand

Hubbart Formula

inelastic demand

ingredient markup

integrated pricing

markup

menu engineering

$1 per $1,000 approach

price elasticity of demand

prime ingredient markup

revenue management

unit elastic

Pricing is one of the most difficult decisions hospitality managers make. If prices are set too high, lower demand may result in reduced sales. When prices are set too low, demand may be high, but lowered sales revenue is likely to result in costs not being covered. Either way, the hospitality operation's profitability may be placed in jeopardy. How can a hospitality manager ensure that prices are neither too high nor too low?

Establishing prices that result in maximized revenues is extremely difficult. Some managers would suggest that the process of setting effective prices involves a bit of luck. Yet, while there may be no completely scientific method guaranteed to determine the best prices to maximize profits, good managers will seek to establish a rational basis for their pricing decisions. General approaches to the pricing problem provide ways of using relevant information and the manager's knowledge of the relationships among sales, costs, and profits to establish a reasonable basis for effective pricing.

Our discussion of cost approaches to pricing in this chapter will answer many of the important questions that come to mind regarding the pricing process, such as the following:

1. Which costs are relevant in the pricing decision?
2. What is the common weakness of informal pricing methods?
3. What are the common cost methods of pricing rooms?
4. What are common methods of pricing food and beverages?
5. How may popularity and profitability be considered in setting food prices?
6. Will departmental revenue maximization result in revenue maximization for the hospitality firm?
7. What is price elasticity of demand?
8. What is integrated pricing?

We will begin this chapter with a discussion of the importance of pricing and the need for profits by both profit-oriented and nonprofit-oriented operations. Next, we will explain and illustrate the concept of the price elasticity of demand. We will then consider a variety of approaches to pricing both rooms and meals, discuss the effect of sales mix on profits, and address the topic of integrated pricing.

8.1 THE IMPORTANCE OF PRICING

A major determinant of a hospitality establishment's profitability is its prices. Whether prices are set too low or too high, the result is the same—a failure to maximize profits. When prices are below what the market is willing to pay, the establishment will realize less revenues than it could generate through its operations. Alternatively, prices set too high will reduce sales and thereby fail to achieve the operation's potential for profit. Management's goal is to set prices that result in profit maximization.

Another factor to consider when setting prices is the "positioning" of the establishment's offerings within the marketplace. Prices set too low may tend to degrade the perceived quality of products, whereas inflated prices may tend to reduce the perceived value of products from the guest's perspective.

Profits should not result simply because revenues happen by chance or luck to exceed expenses. Profits should occur because revenues generated have been carefully calculated to exceed expenses incurred. The emphasis should not be defensive; that is, on keeping costs down to make a profit. Aggressive management should set out to generate sufficient revenues to cover costs. Cost containment is a respectable secondary objective *after* marketing efforts are undertaken to achieve a reasonably high level of sales.

In this chapter, prices will be approached from a cost perspective. However, this is not meant to suggest that noncost factors, such as market demand and competition, are irrelevant. In most situations, they are critical to the pricing decision.

For-profit operations desire to make profits for such reasons as expanding operations, providing owners with a return on capital invested, and increasing the share prices of stock. Many nonprofit operations must also make a profit (often called "revenues in excess of expenses" or, more formally, "increase in net assets") for expanding operations, replacing property and equipment, and upgrading services. Since both types of operations need to generate profits, their approaches to pricing will not necessarily be different. The differences generally relate to costs and type of demand. For example, some nonprofit foodservice operations, including some in the institutional setting, do not have to cover many capital costs such as interest expenses, property taxes, or depreciation. Further, the demand for the products and/or services may be different. The demand for foodservice in a hospital is quite different from the demand for foodservice in most hotels or restaurants. Many nonprofit operations have less direct competition, so they may have greater leeway in pricing their products and/or services.

The emphasis in this chapter will be on commercial (for-profit) operations. However, since we will be discussing cost-oriented approaches to pricing, our discussion will apply to nonprofit operations as well.

8.2 PRICE ELASTICITY OF DEMAND

The concept of the **price elasticity of demand** provides a means for measuring how sensitive demand is to changes in price. In general, as the selling price of a product or service decreases, everything else being the same, more will be sold. When the price of a product is increased, only rarely is more of the product sold, everything else being the same, and even then, there may be other factors that account for the increased demand.

The demand for a product or service may be characterized as **elastic** or **inelastic**. An elastic demand is where the percentage change in quantity demanded exceeds the percentage change in price. If the elasticity of demand exceeds 1, the demand is said to be elastic. That is, demand is sensitive to price changes. In other words, any additional revenues generated by the higher price are more than offset by the decrease in demand. When demand is elastic, a price increase will decrease total revenues. Up to a point, price decreases will increase total revenues. An inelastic demand is where the percentage change in price results in a smaller percentage change in quantity demanded. If elasticity of demand is less than one, demand is said to be inelastic. Every operation desires an inelastic demand for its products and/or services. When prices are increased, the percentage reduction in quantity demanded is less than the percentage of the price increase. Therefore, revenues will often—but not always—increase despite some decrease in the quantity demanded. If the elasticity of demand is exactly one, it is known as **unit elastic**. Any percentage change in price is accompanied by the same percentage change in quantity demanded.

Exhibit 8.1   Price Elasticity of Demand Formula

$$\text{Price Elasticity of Demand} = \dfrac{\dfrac{\Delta Q}{Q_o}}{\dfrac{\Delta P}{P_o}}$$

where:

ΔQ	=	Change in quantity demanded
Q_o	=	Base quantity demanded
ΔP	=	Change in price
P_o	=	Base price

Exhibit 8.1 illustrates the price elasticity of demand formula for mathematically determining whether the demand is elastic or inelastic. The base quantity demanded (Q_o) is the number of units sold during a given period before changing prices. The change in quantity demanded (ΔQ) is the change in the number of units sold during the period the prices were changed compared with the prior period. The base price (P_o) is the price of the product and/or service for the period prior to the price change. The change in price (ΔP) is the change in price from the base price. Strictly speaking, this equation will virtually always yield a negative number, since it is the result of dividing a negative change in quantity demanded by a positive price change or vice versa. (In other words, as price goes up, quantity demanded goes down and vice versa.) By convention, however, the negative sign is ignored.

Let's look at an example illustrating the calculation of price elasticity of demand. A budget motel sold 1,000 rooms during a recent thirty-day period at $60 per room. For the next thirty-day period, the price was increased to $66, and 950 rooms were sold. The demand for the budget motel over this time period is considered to be inelastic, since the calculated price elasticity of demand is less than one. The calculation of price elasticity of demand is as follows:

$$\text{Price Elasticity of Demand} = \frac{50}{1,000} \div \frac{6}{60}$$
$$= 0.05 \div 0.1$$
$$= \underline{\underline{0.5}}$$

In general, the demand for products and services in the lodging and the commercial foodservice segments of the hospitality industry is considered to be elastic. Generally, demand will be elastic where competition is high due to the presence of many operations and where the products and/or services offered are fairly standardized. On the other hand, where competition is low or nonexistent or where an operation has greatly differentiated its products and/or services, then demand may be inelastic. At the extreme, some resorts, clubs, high-check-average restaurants, and luxury hotels are known to have an inelastic demand for their products and services. Generally, quick-service restaurants and medium- and low-priced hotels/motels are considered to have elastic demand for their products and services. However, these are generalizations, and there are exceptions.

This analysis of demand/price relationships assumes that other things are the same. However, hospitality operations seldom increase prices without effectively advertising their products in an effort to counter potential decreased demand. Therefore, the concept of the price elasticity of demand tends to be more theoretical than practical in nature.

8.3 INFORMAL PRICING APPROACHES

There are several informal approaches to setting prices for selling food, beverages, and rooms. Since each of these approaches ignores the cost of providing the product, they are only briefly presented here as a point of departure for our discussion of more scientific approaches to setting prices.

Several managers price their products on the basis of what the competition charges. If the competition charges $80 for a room night, or an average of $20 for a dinner, then managers using competitive pricing set those prices as well. When the competition changes its prices, managers using this pricing approach follow suit. A variation of this approach is changing prices when the leading hospitality operation changes its prices.

Although these approaches may seem reasonable when there is much competition in a market, they ignore the many differences that exist among hospitality operations, such as location, product quality, atmosphere, customer goodwill, and so forth. In addition, they ignore the cost of producing the products and services sold. Hospitality operations must consider their own cost structures when making pricing decisions. A dominant operation with a low-cost structure may "cause" competitors to go bankrupt if those competitors ignore their own costs and price their products following the competitive approach.

Another informal pricing approach used by some managers is intuition. Intuitive pricing is based on what the manager feels the guest is willing to pay. Generally, managers using this approach rely on their experience regarding guests' reactions to prices. However, as with competitive pricing, intuition ignores costs and may result in a failure not only to generate a reasonable profit, but even to recover costs.

A third approach is psychological pricing. Here, prices are established on the basis of what the guest "expects" to pay. This approach may be used by relatively exclusive locations (such as luxury resorts) and by operators who think that their guests believe "the more paid, the better the product." Although psychological pricing does possess a certain merit, it fails to consider costs and, therefore, may not result in profit maximization.

Finally, the trial-and-error pricing approach first sets a product price, monitors guests' reactions, and then adjusts the price based on these reactions. This approach appears to consider fully the operation's guests. However, problems with this method include:

- Monitoring guests' reactions may take longer than the manager would like to allow.

- Frequent changes in prices based on guests' reactions may result in price confusion among guests.

- There are many outside, uncontrollable factors that affect guests' purchase decisions. An example illustrates this problem: A 10 percent price increase in rooms may appear to be too high if occupancy is down by more than 10 percent over the next 30 days. However, other factors that may be part of the consumer decision include competition, new lodging establishments, weather conditions (especially if the lodging facility is a resort), and so on.

- The trial-and-error approach fails to consider costs.

Although all of the informal price approaches have some merit, they are most useful only when coupled with the cost approaches we are now going to consider.

8.4 COST APPROACHES: FOUR MODIFYING FACTORS

Before looking at specific cost approaches to pricing, however, we need to set the stage. When pricing is based on a cost approach, four modifying factors to consider are historical prices, perceived price/value relationships, competition, and price rounding. These price modifiers relate to the pricing of nearly all products and services.

First, prices that have been charged in the past must be considered when pricing the hospitality operation's products. A dramatic change dictated by a cost approach may seem unrealistic to the consumer. For example, if a breakfast meal with a realistic price of $8.49 was mistakenly priced at $6.49 for five years, the foodservice operation may need to move slowly from $6.49 to $8.49 by implementing several price increases over a period of time.

Second, the guests must perceive that the product and/or service is reasonably priced in order to feel that they are getting a good value. Many guests today appear to be more value-conscious than ever. Most are willing to pay prices much higher than a few years ago, but they also demand value for the price paid. The perceived value of a meal includes not only the food and drink, but also the atmosphere, location, quality of service, and many other often intangible factors.

Third, the competition cannot be ignored. If an operation's product is viewed as substantially the same as a competitor's, then everything else being equal, the prices would have to be similar. For example, assume that an operation's price calculations for a gourmet burger may suggest a $6.50 selling price; however, if a strong nearby competitor is charging $4.50 for a very similar product, everything else being the same, then competition would appear to force a price reduction. However, remember that it is extremely difficult for *everything* else to be the same: The location is at least slightly different; one burger may be fresher, one may be grilled, and the other fried; and so on.

Finally, the price may be modified by price rounding. That is, the item's price will be rounded up to the nearest $0.25 or possibly up to $X.95.

8.5 MARKUP APPROACHES TO PRICING

A major method of pricing food and beverages is marking up the cost of the goods sold. The **markup** is designed to cover all nonproduct costs, such as labor, utilities, supplies, interest expense, taxes, and also to provide the desired profit.

Under the markup approaches to pricing are **ingredient markup** and **prime ingredient markup**. The ingredient markup approach considers all product costs. The prime ingredient markup considers only the cost of the major ingredient.

The four steps of the ingredient cost approach are as follows:

1. Determine the ingredient costs.

2. Determine the multiple to use in marking up the ingredient costs.

3. Multiply the ingredient costs by the multiple to get the desired price.

4. Determine whether the price seems reasonable based on the market.

The multiple determined in Step 2 is generally based on the desired product cost percentage. For example, if a product cost percentage of 40 percent is desired, the multiple would be 2.5, determined as follows:

$$\text{Multiple} = \frac{1}{\text{Desired Product Cost Percentage}}$$

$$= \frac{1}{0.4}$$

$$= \underline{\underline{2.5}}$$

The ingredient cost approach can be illustrated using the cost figures for a chicken dinner listed in Exhibit 8.2. Assuming a desired multiple of 4, the price of the chicken dinner is determined as follows:

How to Best Design Menus for the Web?

Foodservice is not just brick-and-mortar in today's world. If a customer physically walks into a restaurant and is being seated, chances are he or she will stay and place an order. Web-based dining is very different. With the increased use of online food delivery systems—where a potential customer can visit many websites first and finally decide on one; place an order via a smartphone, tablet, laptop, desktop, etc.; and either pick up the food or have it delivered—the importance of having a good web-based menu to "lock in" the customer with your website and not leave and shop at another is paramount.

Leib, Reynolds, Taylor, and Baker (2017) study the design of web-based menus, and share the following factors, in order of importance, that are crucial to web-menu design:

1. Trust: Clearly displaying the selling prices of menu items increases transparency and trust between the potential customer and the restaurant. In addition, simply presenting the dollar amount—such as "20" rather than "$20" or "twenty dollars"—results in higher check averages.

2. Familiarity and Recognizable Patterns: In terms of layouts, customers are more inclined to make a purchase when a web-based menu has recognizable patterns, such as grouping items into categories (appetizers, entrees, vegetables, starches, dessert), which makes navigating the site easier as well.

3. Brand Consistency: Among the three options of a) a traditionally strong brand consistency; b) a mix brand, where there are clear brand linkages and some new brand extensions; and c) a nouveau stance, where the menu is a complete departure from the brand image, customers prefer brand consistency when viewing a web-based menu.

4. "Psychological" Triggers: Since the customer cannot be physically present at the restaurant to see what the servers carry out to other patrons, images of food items and of the restaurant itself can give the customer a better idea of what they will be ordering and trigger a purchase decision. "A picture is worth a thousand words," still holds true.

5. Utility: Last, but not least, the ease of use is significant and essential. Simplicity is the key and providing menu links on the homepage or a subpage is a must.

Source: Thomas Leib, Dennis Reynolds, Jim Taylor, and William Baker, "Web-Based Menu Design: A Conjoint Value Analysis," *International Journal of Hospitality and Tourism Administration,* September 2017, pp. 1–13.

$$\text{Price} = \text{Ingredients Cost} \times \text{Multiple}$$

$$= \$2.13 \times 4$$

$$= \underline{\underline{\$8.52}}$$

If the result appears reasonable based on the market for chicken dinners, then the chicken dinner is sold for about $8.52. (In this instance, price rounding might set the price at $8.75 or $8.95.)

The prime ingredient approach differs only in that the cost of the prime ingredient is marked up rather than the total cost of all ingredients. In addition, the multiple used, all other things being equal, would be greater than the

Exhibit 8.2   Chicken Dinner Ingredients and Cost

Ingredient	Cost
Chicken—2 pieces	$ .89
Baked potato with sour cream	.29
Roll and butter	.11
Vegetable	.19
Salad with dressing	.50
Coffee—refills free	.15
Total cost	$2.13

multiple used when considering the total cost of all ingredients. The multiple used would generally be based on experience; that is, what multiple has provided adequate cost coverage and desired profit. Using the same chicken dinner example, the prime ingredient cost is chicken with a cost of $0.89. Using an arbitrary multiple of 9.5, the chicken dinner is priced at $8.46, calculated as follows:

$$\text{Price} = \text{Prime Ingredient Cost} \times \text{Multiple}$$
$$= \$0.89 \times 9.5$$
$$= \underline{\$8.46}$$

If the cost of chicken in the above example increases to $0.99 for the dinner portion, then the new price would be $9.41 ($0.99 × 9.5). The prime ingredient approach assumes that the costs of all other ingredients change in proportion to the prime ingredient; that is, when the prime ingredient's cost increases 10 percent, then other ingredient's costs have also increased 10 percent. When changes in the other ingredient's cost percentage differ from the prime ingredient's, then the product cost percentage will differ from the established goal.

8.6 PRICING ROOMS

Two well-known cost approaches to pricing rooms are the $1 per $1,000 approach and the Hubbart Formula approach.

$1 per $1,000 Approach

The **$1 per $1,000 approach** sets the price of a room at $1 for each $1,000 of project cost per room. This includes the hotel fully equipped. For example, assume that the average project cost of a hotel for each room was $120,000. Using the $1 per $1,000 approach results in a price of $120 per room. Doubles, suites, singles, and so on would be priced differently, but the average would be $120.

In emphasizing the project cost, this approach fails to consider the current value of facilities. A well-maintained hotel worth $100,000 per room today may have been constructed at $20,000 per room 40 years ago. The $1 per $1,000 approach would suggest a price of $20 per room; however, a much higher rate would appear to be appropriate. This approach also fails to consider all the services that guests pay for in a hotel complex, such as food, beverages, laundry, and so forth. If a hotel is able to earn a positive contribution from these services (and the successful ones do), then the need for higher prices for rooms is reduced. Although this method is based on cost, if the market value of the hotel is known, the same $1 to $1,000 of purchase price or market value is applicable.

Hubbart Formula

A more recently developed cost approach is the **Hubbart Formula**, which is a *bottom-up* approach to pricing rooms. In determining the average price per room, this approach considers costs, desired profits, and expected rooms sold. In other words, this approach starts with desired profit, adds income taxes, then adds interest expense, fixed charges, and management fees, followed by operating overhead expenses and direct operating expenses. It is called bottom-up because the first item, net income (profit), is at the bottom of the income statement. The second item, income taxes, is the next item from the bottom of the income statement, and so on. The approach involves the following eight steps:

1. Calculate the desired profit by multiplying the desired rate of return (ROI) by the owners' investment.

2. Calculate pretax profits by dividing desired profit (Step 1) by 1 minus tax rate.

3. Calculate interest expense, depreciation, amortization, nonoperating expenses, and management fees. This calculation includes estimating depreciation, interest expense, property taxes, insurance, amortization, rent, and management fees. If there is any nonoperating income, it should be subtracted at this point.

4. Calculate undistributed operating expenses. This calculation includes estimating administrative and general, information and telecommunications systems, sales and marketing, property operation and maintenance, and energy costs.

5. Estimate nonroom operated department income or losses; that is, food and beverage department income, gift shop department income or loss, and so forth.

6. Calculate the required rooms department income. The sum of pretax profits (Step 2), interest expense, depreciation, amortization, insurance, rent, property taxes, and management fees (Step 3), undistributed operating expenses (Step 4), and other operated department losses less other operated department income (Step 5) equals the required rooms department income.

7. Determine the rooms department revenue. The required rooms department income (Step 6) plus rooms department direct expenses of payroll and related expenses plus other direct expenses equals rooms department revenue.

8. Calculate the average room rate by dividing rooms department revenue (Step 7) by rooms expected to be sold.

Illustration of the Hubbart Formula

The Harkins Hotel, a 200-room hotel, is projected to cost $9.9 million inclusive of land, building, equipment, and furniture. An additional $100,000 is needed for working capital. The hotel is financed with a loan of $7.5 million at 12 percent annual interest, with the owners providing cash of $2.5 million. The owners desire a 15 percent annual return on their investment. A 75 percent occupancy is estimated; thus, 54,750 rooms will be sold during the year (200 × 0.75 × 365). The income tax rate is 40 percent. Additional expenses are estimated as follows:

Property taxes	$ 250,000
Insurance	50,000
Depreciation	300,000
Administrative and general	350,000
Information and telecommunications systems	100,000
Sales and marketing expense	200,000
Property operation and maintenance	340,000
Utility costs	250,000

The other operated departments' incomes are estimated as follows:

Food	$ 150,000
Beverage	60,000
Gift shop	20,000
Miscellaneous income	40,000

Rooms department direct expenses are $10 per room sold.

Exhibit 8.3 contains the calculations used in the Hubbart Formula and reveals an average room rate of $66.53.

The formula for calculating room rates for singles and doubles, where the doubles are sold at a difference of y from singles, is shown in Exhibit 8.4. For the Harkins Hotel, a double occupancy rate of 40 percent and a price difference of $10 would result in the calculation of single and double rates as follows:

$$\frac{\text{Doubles sold}}{\text{in one day}} = \text{Double occupancy rate} \times \text{Number of rooms} \times \text{Occupancy percentage}$$

$$= 0.4(200)(0.75)$$

$$= \underline{\underline{60}}$$

$$\frac{\text{Singles sold}}{\text{in one day}} = 150 - 60$$

$$= \underline{\underline{90}}$$

$$90x + 60(x + 10) = (\$66.53)(150)$$
$$90x + 60x + 600 = \$9,979.50$$
$$150x = \$9,379.50$$
$$x = \frac{\$9,379.50}{150}$$
$$x = \$62.53$$
$$\underline{\text{Single Rate}} = \$62.53$$
$$\underline{\text{Double Rate}} = \$62.53 + \$10.00$$
$$= \underline{\$72.53}$$

Exhibit 8.3 Calculation of Average Room Rate Using Hubbart Formula

Item	Calculation	Amount
Desired net income	Owners' Investment × ROI $2,500,000 × 0.15 = $375,000	$ 375,000
Pretax income	Pretax income $= \dfrac{\text{net income}}{1-t}$ Pretax income $= \dfrac{\$375,000}{1-0.4}$ Pretax income = $625,000	$ 625,000
Interest expense	Principal × int. rate × time = int. exp. $7,500,000 × 0.12 × 1 = $900,000	$ 900,000
Income before interest and taxes		1,525,000
Estimated depreciation, property taxes, and insurance		600,000
Income after undistributed operating expenses		2,125,000
Undistributed operating expense		1,240,000
Required operated departments income		3,365,000
Departmental results excluding rooms		
Less: Food income		150,000
Beverage income		60,000
Miscellaneous income		40,000
Gift shop department income		20,000
Rooms department income		3,095,000
Rooms department direct expense	54,750 × $10 = 547,500	547,500
Rooms revenue		3,642,500
	÷	54,750
Required average room rate		$ 66.53

Alternatively, the double rate could be set as a percentage of the single rate. When this is the case, the formula is slightly altered, as follows:

$$\binom{\text{Average}}{\text{rate}}\binom{\text{Rooms}}{\text{sold}} = \binom{\text{Doubles}}{\text{sold}}(x)\left(1 + \frac{\text{Percentage}}{\text{markup}}\right) + \binom{\text{Singles}}{\text{sold}}(x)$$

The percentage markup is simply the percentage difference of the double rate over the single rate. To illustrate this approach, we will again use the Harkins Hotel example. Assume a 40 percent double occupancy and a markup of 15 percent.

$$90x + 60(x)(1.15) = (\$66.53)(150)$$
$$90x + 69x = \$9,979.50$$
$$159x = \$9,979.50$$
$$x = \frac{\$9,979.50}{159}$$
$$x = \$62.76$$
$$\text{Single Rate} = \underline{\$62.76}$$
$$\text{Double Rate} = \$62.76(1.15)$$
$$= \underline{\$72.17}$$

The Hubbart Formula is most useful in setting target average prices as opposed to actual average prices. A lodging establishment does not generally earn profits in its first two or three years of operation. Thus, the average price determined using this formula is a target price at the point of profitability for the prospective property. As stated previously, even when this approach is used to set room prices, the four modifying factors must be considered. For example, assume that the average target price for a hotel is $75 when the average rate for competitive hotels is only $50. If the proposed hotel would be opening in two years, is the target price too high? By the end of the two years, the competitor's average price with annual 5 percent price increases would be $55.13 ($50.00 × 105% × 105%).

Since the proposed hotel would be new, a price premium could be expected; however, a difference of nearly $20, given a competitor's average price of just over $55, would appear to be too much. Therefore, a more reasonable price might be $65, which, after three years of successive price increases of 5 percent per year, would be increased to just over $75, as follows:

	Annual Increase at 5%	Selling Price
Initial room rate		$65.00
At the end of year X3	$3.25	$68.25
At the end of year X4	$3.41	$71.66
At the end of year X5	$3.58	$75.24

8.7 DISCOUNTING ROOM RATES

Discounting room rates is widely practiced in the lodging industry in the United States. The maximum rate a hotel would charge is known as the rack rate; however, due to seasonality and the inability to carry unsold rooms over to the next day, room rates are often discounted. The discounting may be very significant due to the minimal variable costs per room. A guestroom with a rack rate of $150 and variable costs of $20 results in a contribution toward fixed costs of $130. When the room rate is discounted to $100, a sizeable contribution toward fixed costs of $80 is still achieved. It certainly would appear that the hotel is better off selling the room for $100 than not at all. In addition, hotels often have a variety of additional goods and services to offer the guest once they have occupied the room. Many hotels have food, beverages, movies, and gift shop items for sale, which will generally be priced to make a profit.

At some hotels, there is no methodology for determining how discounts are offered, and it may appear to be at the whim of the hotel's reservations department or the front-office clerk when a potential guest shows up near the midnight hour. Rate cutting certainly can generate more rooms revenue, but it may not always translate into an increased net income for the lodging establishment. Several years ago, a 100-room mid-Michigan hotel generated significant room sales resulting in a 72 percent paid occupancy percentage but failed to generate a positive bottom line because its major room sales were to airline employees at deep discounts.

In order for a lodging operation to achieve the equivalent room revenue contribution margin (room revenue − marginal costs), an equivalent room occupancy (ERO) can be determined as follows:

$$\frac{\text{Equivalent Room}}{\text{Occupancy}} = \frac{\text{Current Occupancy}}{\text{Percentage}} \times \frac{\text{Rack Rate} - \text{Marginal Cost}}{\text{Rack Rate} \times (1 - \text{Discount Percentage}) - \text{Marginal Cost}}$$

$$\text{ERO} = \frac{\text{Current Occupancy}}{\text{Percentage}} \times \frac{\text{Current Contribution Margin}}{\text{Revised Contribution Margin}}$$

For example, consider Bruce & Lucy's, a 100-room inn, which has a rack rate for its rooms of $100 and a marginal cost of $20. The inn currently has a 60 percent paid occupancy percentage. The manager is considering discounting the rack rate by 20 percent. What new paid occupancy percentage must be achieved to yield the same amount of room contribution margin from room sales?

$$\text{ERO} = 0.60 \times \frac{100 - 20}{(100 \times 0.8) - 20}$$

$$\text{ERO} = 0.60 \times \frac{80}{60} = 80\%$$

Thus, in this case, a 20 percent room rate discount requires a 33⅓ percent increase in room occupancy to result in the same amount of room contribution margin. The proof is as follows:

	Rooms Sold	Price	Marginal Cost	Total Rooms Contribution Margin
Current situation	60	$ 100	$ 20	$4,800
Proposed situation	80	$ 80	$ 20	$4,800

A discount grid can assist management in evaluating room rate discounting strategies. For example, if a hotel's average room rate is $100 and its marginal costs per room equal $11, the grid in Exhibit 8.5 reflects the ERO to achieve an equivalent room revenue contribution margin given different room rate discount levels. The discount grid is prepared by first calculating the marginal cost of providing a guestroom and then using the ERO formula. Spreadsheet programs greatly simplify this process.

Exhibit 8.5　Sample Discount Grid

Rack Rate	$100.00
Marginal Cost	$11.00

Current Occupancy	Equivalent Occupancy Percent Required to Maintain Profitability if Rates Are Discounted by:						
	5%	10%	15%	20%	25%	30%	35%
100%	106.0%	112.7%	120.3%	129.0%	139.1%	150.8%	164.8%
95%	100.7%	107.0%	114.3%	122.5%	132.1%	143.3%	156.6%
90%	95.4%	101.4%	108.2%	116.1%	125.2%	135.8%	148.3%
85%	90.1%	95.8%	102.2%	109.6%	118.2%	128.2%	140.1%
80%	84.8%	90.1%	96.2%	103.2%	111.3%	120.7%	131.9%
75%	79.5%	84.5%	90.2%	96.7%	104.3%	113.1%	123.6%
70%	74.2%	78.9%	84.2%	90.3%	97.3%	105.6%	115.4%
65%	68.9%	73.2%	78.2%	83.8%	90.4%	98.1%	107.1%
60%	63.6%	67.6%	72.2%	77.4%	83.4%	90.5%	98.9%
55%	58.3%	62.0%	66.1%	70.9%	76.5%	83.0%	90.6%
50%	53.0%	56.3%	60.1%	64.5%	69.5%	75.4%	82.4%
45%	47.7%	50.7%	54.1%	58.0%	62.6%	67.9%	74.2%
40%	42.4%	45.1%	48.1%	51.6%	55.6%	60.3%	65.9%
35%	37.1%	39.4%	42.1%	45.1%	48.7%	52.8%	57.7%
30%	31.8%	33.8%	36.1%	38.7%	41.7%	45.3%	49.4%
25%	26.5%	28.2%	30.1%	32.2%	34.8%	37.7%	41.2%

Source: Michael L. Kasavana, *Managing Front Office Operations,* Tenth Edition (Lansing, MI: American Hotel & Lodging Educational Institute, 2017) p. 490.

8.8 REVENUE MANAGEMENT AND DYNAMIC PRICING

Revenue management can be broadly defined as the process of understanding, anticipating, and reacting to buying trends.[1] As this field has developed in the hotel industry, the original focus, which was solely on revenue, has shifted to include strong consideration of profit. Revenue management requires that the manager analyze the changing nature of the marketplace and the operation on a moment's notice. This is done by constantly reviewing the status of demand for the hotel and the available supply of rooms. There are several components that must be taken into consideration in this process in order to maximize both revenue and profit: the revenue channels supplying demand, the accurate forecasting of purchase patterns of the customers in those channels, and the types of customers or market segments available to generate demand. Pricing strategies are set based on *where* the customer buys (the revenue channel) and *who* the customer is (market segment). Some revenue channels cost more to operate. For example, the commission a hotel must pay a travel agent for a reservation is generally more than the cost of a reservation received on the hotel's website. Market segments comprise homogeneous groups of buyers whose purchase habits are indicated by their price sensitivity. Price sensitivity, or the elasticity of demand, helps to determine the price to be offered to each segment.

Recognizing that there are multiple revenue channels generating demand for a hotel's perishable product is critical to maximizing revenue as well as profit. Through "optimization," or determining the optimal mix of demand from these channels, a hotel can generate the highest probable revenue and profit.

Before it can do any of this, however, a hotel must determine the proper pricing for its product. In order to do this, consideration must be given to the dynamics of the distribution channels, purchase patterns, and market segments that make up the demand in a market. The market segment and revenue channel combination help the revenue manager set prices by creating reservation booking rules based on length of stay, number of days in advance the reservation is made prior to stay, and the market segment. A real-time demand forecast is an essential tool for pricing. By identifying the high and low demand periods for a hotel, it can be determined when prices can be increased and when they must be reduced. These periods may be seasonal time frames throughout the year, a weekly pattern that is evident from one day to the next, or simply demand variances between weekdays and weekend days.

Accurate demand forecasting allows a revenue manager to anticipate business and price the hotel appropriately before any bookings have been made. Understanding the normal demand patterns for a market helps predict future demand and establish pricing. Additional understanding of the type of customer generating demand is equally important. This is known as market segmentation. An example of some typical hotel market segments would be as follows: weekday corporate, corporate discount, weekend leisure, government, e-commerce, and group. Each of these segments can have unique demand patterns and price thresholds. By taking that into consideration along with the total demand expected for a particular time period, revenue managers can then determine the amount of their product they want to make available to any particular segment. Various statistics are used to forecast demand. Call volume, cancellations, no-show history, conversion percentage (the actual bookings divided by the number of inquiries), and booking pace (the speed and pattern at which the property is receiving reservations for a particular date) all assist the revenue manager in evaluating demand for the property.

Generally speaking, during a high-demand period, one would want to employ a sales strategy that restricts availability of discounted rates and limits business that is unlikely to produce high profits. Lower-demand periods allow the hotel to be more open to all business opportunities presented and willing to sell its inventory at a substantial discount.

Most of the time, however, demand is complex and a combination of many types of business are necessary to maximize revenue and profit.

Here is an example to demonstrate how a hotel might evaluate a business opportunity. A group would like to stay at a hotel. It is calling six months prior to its event and its needs are as follows:

- Fifty rooms for three nights
- Arrival on Sunday; departure on Wednesday
- Room rate of $100 per room per night
- One large meeting room for 50 people on Monday and Tuesday
- Light food and beverage needs for only morning and afternoon breaks
- $1,000-per-day budget for meeting space and food and beverage

The hotel has 200 rooms. Not including this group, it is forecasting to be at 50 percent occupancy on Sunday, with an average rate of $125; 90 percent occupancy on Monday, with an average rate of $130; and 95 percent occupancy on Tuesday, with an average rate of $127. The meeting room is available.

Based on that information, this group will definitely benefit the hotel on Sunday night. It appears, however, that it may not be as good of an opportunity when you consider the impact it will have on Monday and Tuesday.

The revenue from this opportunity is:

Room revenue:	150 room nights at $100 =	$ 15,000
Meeting room rental:		750
F&B revenue:		2,250
Total:		$ 18,000

The values for meeting room and food and beverage revenue must be estimated at this point based on the likely minimum per-person price possible for the morning and afternoon breaks. Assume this is $15 per person per day.

Because this group will cause the hotel to exceed its guestroom capacity on Monday and Tuesday, we must determine the revenue that this group will displace.

On Sunday there will be no displacement. However, on Monday the forecast indicates the hotel will have 180 occupied rooms, so 30 rooms will be displaced. On Tuesday the hotel will have 190 occupied rooms and the displacement will be 40 rooms.

30 rooms × $130 ADR	=	$3,900
40 rooms × $127 ADR	=	$5,080
Total revenue displaced	=	$8,980

By subtracting the displaced revenue from the anticipated room revenue that the group booking will generate, you can determine whether it is worth displacing the forecasted rooms. In this case, the total value of the group's room revenue is greater than the displaced revenue, so this would be a good opportunity to pursue from a guestroom standpoint.

We have not included the value of the meeting and F&B in the evaluation because the rooms revenue is positive. If it was not, however, the meeting and F&B revenue may be sufficient to make up for the deficiency in rooms revenue and still make taking the opportunity a good business decision.

Measuring Revenue Management Yield

Revenue management is about enhancing revenue. To measure revenue achievement, a yield statistic is calculated. The yield statistic is the ratio of actual room revenue to potential room revenue. There are several steps required to calculate the yield statistic:

1. Determine the potential average single rate.

2. Determine the potential average double rate.

3. Calculate the multiple paid-occupancy percentage.

4. Determine the rate spread.

5. Calculate the potential average rate.

6. Calculate the rate achievement factor.

7. Determine the yield statistic.

An illustration will demonstrate the process. Our hypothetical hotel is the Beck Inn. The Beck Inn has 150 hotel rooms, of which 75 have a single bed and 75 have two beds. The average daily rate is $90, and the inn is currently operating at an average paid occupancy of 60 percent. Management has set single and double rack rates for each room type as follows:

| | Prices | |
Room Type	Single	Double
One-bed room	$ 90	$ 110
Two-bed room	100	120

Thus, a one-bed room sold as a single has a targeted price of $90, but the same room sold as a double has a targeted price of $110.

The first calculation is the *potential average single rate*. It is computed by multiplying the number of rooms of each room type by its single rack rate and dividing the result by the 150 rooms of the Beck Inn, as follows:

Room Type	Number of Rooms	Single Rack Rate	Revenue @ 100% Paid Occupancy
One-bed	75	$ 90	$ 6,750
Two-bed	75	100	7,500
		Total	$14,250

$$\text{Potential average single rate} = \frac{\$14,250}{150}$$
$$= \$95$$

The *potential average double rate* is calculated in the same way, as follows:

Room Type	Number of Rooms	Double Rack Rate	Revenue @ 100% Paid Occupancy
One-bed	75	$ 110	$ 8,250
Two-bed	75	120	9,000
		Total	$17,250

$$\text{Potential average double rate} = \frac{\$17,250}{150}$$
$$= \$115$$

The next step is to determine the average proportion of rooms occupied by more than one person, which is called *multiple paid occupancy percentage*. This information indicates sales mix and helps in determining future demand. If 75 of the 150 rooms of the Beck Inn are normally occupied by more than one person, the multiple paid occupancy percentage is 50 percent.

The next step is to determine the *rate spread* between the various room types, which is simply the difference between the potential average single rate and the potential average double rate.

The rate spread for the Beck Inn is $115 – $95, or $20. The next step is to determine the *potential average rate*. This calculation is based on the potential average single rate, the multiple paid occupancy percent-age, and the rate spread. For the Beck Inn, the potential average rate is determined as follows:

$$\text{Potential average rate} = \left(\begin{array}{c} \text{Multiple paid} \\ \text{occupancy percentage} \end{array} \times \begin{array}{c} \text{Rate} \\ \text{spread} \end{array} \right) + \begin{array}{c} \text{Potential average} \\ \text{single rate} \end{array}$$

$$= (0.50 \times \$20) + \$95$$
$$= \underline{\$105}$$

Next, we must calculate the *rate achievement factor*. This factor expresses the difference between the property's actual average rate and its potential average rate. The rate achievement factor is calculated by dividing the actual average rate by the potential average rate. For the Beck Inn, the rate achievement factor is $90 ÷ $105, or 85.7 percent.

Now the yield statistic can be calculated. The yield statistic is determined by multiplying the paid occupancy percentage by the rate achievement factor. For the Beck Inn, the yield statistic is 60 percent × 0.857, or 51.42 percent. A yield statistic of 51.42 percent clearly shows that the Beck Inn is falling considerably short of its potential.

8.9 BOTTOM-UP APPROACH TO PRICING MEALS

A bottom-up approach similar to the Hubbart Formula may be used to determine the average meal price for restaurants. Seven steps for determining the average meal price are as follows:[2]

1. Determine desired net income by multiplying investment by desired return on owners' investment (ROI).

2. Determine pretax profit by dividing the desired net income by 1 minus the tax rate.

3. Determine interest expense.

4. Determine operating expenses.

5. Determine food revenue by first adding figures from Steps 2–4 and then dividing this sum by 1 minus the desired food cost percentage.

6. Determine meals to be served by multiplying days open by number of seats by seat turnover for the day.

7. Determine price of the average meal by dividing the total food revenue by the estimated number of meals to be served.

To illustrate the average restaurant meal price calculation, Morgans, a 100-seat restaurant, will be used. Information regarding Morgans is found in Exhibit 8.6. Given this information, Exhibit 8.7 shows that the average meal price for Morgans, inclusive of beverage sales, desserts, and so forth, is $18.22. In those calculations, total food revenue is determined by dividing total expenses and net income (prior to cost of food sold) by 1 minus the cost of food sold percentage. If management could turn the seats over faster, everything else being the same, then the average meal price required to provide the owners with the desired

Exhibit 8.6 **Essential Factors for Determining the Average Meal Price at Morgans**

Item	Amount	Other
Owner's investment	$200,000	Desired ROI = 12%
Funds borrowed	500,000	Interest Rate = 10%
Tax rate	–	30%
Operating expenses	600,000	Annual amount
Seat turnover	–	2 times per day
Days open (closed one day per week)	–	313 days
Desired food cost percentage	–	40%

Exhibit 8.7 **Calculation of Average Meal Price at Morgans**

Item	Calculation	Amount
Desired net income	$200,000 \times 0.12$	$ 24,000
Pretax profits	$\dfrac{24,000}{1-0.3} = \dfrac{24,000}{0.7}$	$ 34,286
Interest	$500,000 \times 0.10 \times 1$	50,000
Operating expenses		600,000
Total expenses and net income prior to cost of food sold		$ 684,286
Total food revenue	$\dfrac{684,286}{0.6}$	$1,140,477
Meals sold	$313 \times 100 \times 2$	62,600
Average meal price	$\$1,140,477 \div 62,600$	$ 18.22

12 percent return would be reduced. For example, if the seat turnover could be increased to three, then the average meal price is determined as follows:

$$\text{Average Meal Price} = \frac{\text{Food Revenue}}{\text{Meals Sold}}$$
$$= \frac{\$1,140,477}{93,900}$$
$$= \underline{\$12.15}$$

On the other hand, a less frequent turnover requires a higher average meal price, all other things being the same. For Morgans, a seat turnover of 1.5 requires an average meal price of $24.29.

The entire discussion of the bottom-up approach to pricing meals has centered on average meal prices. Few foodservice establishments price all meals at one price, or even all meals for a given meal period at one price. However, the average meal price per meal period can be determined as follows:

1. Calculate the revenue per meal period by multiplying the total food revenue by the estimated percentage of that total earned during that meal period.

2. Divide the revenue per meal period by the meals sold per meal period. (Meals sold per meal period is calculated by multiplying the days the foodservice business is open by the seat turnover by the number of seats.)

Exhibit 8.8	Sales Mix Alternatives and Number of Meals		

	Sales Mix Alternatives		
	#1	#2	#3
Chicken	500	300	200
Fish	200	300	300
Steak	300	400	500
Total	1,000	1,000	1,000

Once again, we will use Morgans to illustrate these calculations. Assume that management estimates the total food revenue to be divided between lunch and dinner revenue as 40 percent and 60 percent, respectively. Further assume that the luncheon seat turnover is 1.25 and the dinner seat turnover is 0.75. Using the total revenue for Morgans as calculated in Exhibit 8.8, the average meal prices by meal period are determined as follows:

Revenue per meal period :

Lunch 40% × \$1,140,477 = \$ 456,191

Dinner 60% × \$1,140,477 = 684,286

Total = \$1,140,477

Meals sold per meal period :

Lunch 313 × 100 × 1.25 = 39,125

Dinner 313 × 100 × 0.75 = 23,475

Average meal prices by meal period = $\dfrac{\text{Meal Period Revenue}}{\text{Meals Sold}}$

Lunch = $\dfrac{\$456,191}{39,125}$ = \$11.66

Dinner = $\dfrac{\$684,286}{23,425}$ = \$29.15

8.10 FOOD SALES MIX AND GROSS PROFIT

Traditionally, restaurateurs have placed heavy emphasis on food cost percentage. The multiple in the markup approach used to price meals for many restaurants has been set at 2.5 times, so that a 40 percent cost of food sold could be achieved. This emphasis resulted in many managers evaluating the profitability of their foodservice operations by reviewing the food cost percentage. However, the food cost percentage is not the best guide to evaluating food sales, as will be shown below.

Consider a restaurant that may sell one of three alternative sales mixes for the week as listed in Exhibit 8.8. Notice that in each sales mix the same number of meals is served. Exhibit 8.9 shows the total revenue, total cost of food sold, the gross profit, and food cost percentage for each alternative. The selling price and cost per meal remains constant for each menu item across the three alternative sales mixes.

Exhibit 8.10 compares the three alternatives. The sales mix with the lowest total food cost percentage is mix #1 at 39.56 percent, while mix #3 has the highest at 41.99 percent, or nearly 2.5 percent greater than mix #1. If the most desirable mix is based on food cost percentage, then mix #1 is selected. However, under

Exhibit 8.9 **Profitability of Three Sales Mix Alternatives**

	Selling Price	Cost Per Meal	Menu Item Food Cost Percentage	Meals Sold	Revenue	Total Cost of Food	Gross Profit
Alternative #1							
Chicken	$4.95	$1.65	33.33%	500	$2,475	$ 825	$1,650
Fish	6.95	2.75	39.57	200	1,390	550	840
Steak	9.95	4.45	44.72	300	2,085	1,335	1,650
Total				1,000	$6,850	$2,710	$4,140

$$\text{Food cost \%} = \frac{2,710}{6,850} = 39.56\%$$

	Selling Price	Cost Per Meal	Menu Item Food Cost Percentage	Meals Sold	Revenue	Total Cost of Food	Gross Profit
Alternative #2							
Chicken	$4.95	$1.65	33.33%	300	$1,485	$ 495	$ 990
Fish	6.95	2.75	39.57	300	2,085	825	1,260
Steak	9.95	4.45	44.72	400	3,980	1,780	2,200
Total				1,000	$7,550	$3,100	$4,450

$$\text{Food cost \%} = \frac{3,100}{7,550} = 41.06\%$$

	Selling Price	Cost Per Meal	Menu Item Food Cost Percentage	Meals Sold	Revenue	Total Cost of Food	Gross Profit
Alternative #3							
Chicken	$4.95	$1.65	33.33%	200	$ 990	$ 330	$ 660
Fish	6.95	2.75	39.57	300	2,085	825	1,260
Steak	9.95	4.45	44.72	500	4,975	2,225	2,750
Total				1,000	$8,050	$3,380	$4,670

$$\text{Food cost \%} = \frac{3,380}{8,050} = 41.99\%$$

Exhibit 8.10 **Comparison of Sales Mix Alternatives**

Sales Mix Alternative	Total Revenue	Total Cost of Food	Gross Profit	Food Cost %
1	$6,850	$2,710	$4,140	39.56%
2	7,550	3,100	4,450	41.06
3	8,050	3,380	4,670	41.99

mix #3, the gross profit is $4,670 compared to a low of $4,140 for mix #1. Gross profit generated by mix #3 is $530 more than the profit generated by mix #1. Therefore, all other things being the same, mix #3 is preferred, because a higher gross profit means a higher net income.

Exhibit 8.11 reveals the average gross profit for the three sales mix alternatives. The gross margin reflects the average gross profit per meal sold. The average gross margin under sales mix #3 ($4.67) is $0.53 and $0.22 higher than under mixes #1 and #2, respectively. Based on these results, fewer meals could be sold under mixes #2 and #3 than under mix #1, yet the gross profit under mix #1 still would be earned:

$$\frac{\text{Gross Profit of Mix \#1}}{\text{Gross Margin of Other Sales Mix Alternatives}}$$

Mix #2 to Mix #1

$$\frac{\$4,140}{\$4.45} = \underline{930.34}\ \text{meals}$$

Thus, under sales mix #2, 930.34 meals sold at an average gross margin of $4.45 yields $4,140 of gross profit, which is the same as that generated under mix #1 when 1,000 meals are sold.

Mix #3 to Mix #1

$$\frac{\$4,140}{\$4.67} = \underline{886.51}\ \text{meals}$$

Thus, under sales mix #3, 886.51 meals sold at an average gross margin of $4.67 yields $4,140, the same gross profit as that generated with mix #1 when 1,000 meals are sold.

These results are more clearly reflected in the graph found in Exhibit 8.12. The gross profit is related to meals sold in sales mixes #1 through #3. Gross profit increases progressively from sales mix #1 to sales mix #3. The same gross profit for sales mix #1 can be achieved by sales mixes #2 and #3 with fewer meals sold.

Exhibit 8.11	Average Gross Profit of Sales Mix Alternatives		
Sales Mix	**Gross Profit**	**Meals Sold**	**Gross Margin**
1	$4,140	1,000	$4.14
2	4,450	1,000	4.45
3	4,670	1,000	4.67

Exhibit 8.12 Gross Profit Graph of Three Sales Mix Alternatives

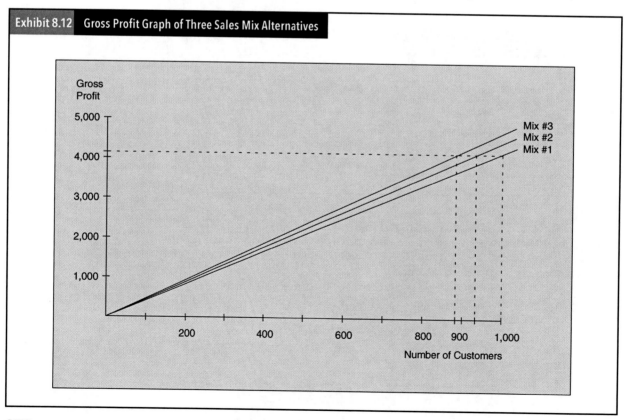

8.11 MENU ENGINEERING

One method of menu analysis and food pricing is called **menu engineering**.[3] This sophisticated and fairly complex approach considers both the profitability and popularity of competing menu items. The emphasis is on gross margin (called *contribution margin* by Kasavana and Smith). For all practical purposes, food cost percentages are ignored. The emphasis on gross margin rather than food cost percentage is based on the fact that managers bank dollars, not percentages.

Menu engineering requires the manager to know each menu item's food cost, selling price, and quantity sold over a specific period of time. The menu item's gross margin (selling price minus food cost) is characterized as either high or low in relation to the average gross margin for all competing menu items sold.

For example, if a menu item has a gross margin of $3 when the average gross margin for the menu is $3.50, then the menu item is classified as having a low gross margin. If the menu item has a gross margin of $4.50, then it is classified as high for profitability purposes.

Each menu item is further classified by popularity (high or low) based on the item's menu mix percentage; that is, the menu item count for each menu item as a percentage of the total menu items sold. Where *n* equals the number of competing menu items, the dividing point for determining high and low popularity is calculated as follows:

$$70\% \times \frac{1}{n}$$

Therefore, if there are 10 competing items on a menu, the dividing point is 7 percent, determined as follows:

$$70\% \times \frac{1}{10} = \underline{\underline{0.07}} \text{ or } \underline{\underline{7\%}}$$

Given a 10-item menu, any menu items with unit sales of less than 7 percent of the total items sold would be classified as having a low popularity, while any equal to or greater than 7 percent would be classified as having high popularity.

Using Menu Engineering: A 14-Step Approach*

1. First, the operator lists all menu entrées in column A. Only entrée items are listed. Do not list appetizers, desserts, or other side items. Do not list alcoholic beverage sales on this list. The ratio of food to beverage sales is a key to successful merchandising in most restaurants. The analysis of beverage sales, however, should be done separately. While we separate sales for the purposes of our menu analysis, the successful operator is always concerned with the guests' total expenditure.

2. The total number of items sold for each item is listed in column B, menu mix, and the total is recorded in column N.

3. Each item's menu mix percentage is determined by dividing the number sold in column B by the total in column N.

4. Each item's menu mix percentage is categorized as either high or low. Any item that is equal to or exceeds the percentage in column Q is classified as high. All others are classified as low. The MM percent category is recorded in column R.

5. Each item's standard food cost is listed in column D. An item's standard portion cost is composed of standard recipe costs, garnish cost, and supplemental food cost. Not all items, however, will have all three cost components.

6. Each item's published menu selling price is listed in column E.

7. The contribution margin for each item is listed in column F. Contribution margins are determined by subtracting the item's standard food cost (column D) from its selling price (column E).

8. In column G, the total menu food cost is determined by first multiplying each item's standard food cost (column D) by the number of items sold (column B). The sum of the amounts in column G is recorded in column I.

9. In column H, the total menu revenues are determined by multiplying the number of sales of each item (column B) by its selling price (column E). The sum of the amounts in column H is recorded in column J.

10. The total menu contribution margin is listed in column M. This is determined by first multiplying each item's contribution margin (column F) by the item's total number of items sold (column B). The contribution margin (by item) is recorded in column L. Then the sum of the item's contribution margins is recorded in column M.

11. The menu's average contribution margin is determined by dividing the total contribution margin (column M) by the total number of items sold (column N).

12. Each item's contribution margin is categorized as either high or low in column P, depending on whether or not the item's contribution margin exceeds the menu's average contribution margin.

13. All the data that has been gathered is used to classify each item into categories in column S. Each menu item is classified as either a Star, Plow Horse, Puzzle, or Dog. These classifications are standard marketing theory terms (see page 20).

14. In column T, the decisions made on each item are listed. Should the item be retained, repositioned, replaced, or repriced?

How to Use the Categories

Once you have grouped your menu into the four key categories, you are ready to make decisions. Each category must be analyzed and evaluated separately.

Stars. You must maintain rigid specifications for quality, quantity, and presentation of all Star items. Locate them in a highly visible position on the menu. Test them occasionally for price inelasticity. Are guests willing to pay more for these items, and still buy them in significant quantity? The Super Stars of your menu—highest-priced Stars—may be less price-sensitive than any other items on the menu. If so, these items may be able to carry a larger portion of any increase in cost of goods and labor.

Plow Horses. These items are often an important reason for a restaurant's popularity. Increase their prices carefully. If Plow Horses are highly price-sensitive, attempt to pass only the cost of goods increase on to the menu price. Or, consider placing the increase on to a Super Star item. Test for a negative effect on demand (elasticity). Make any price increase in stages (from $4.55 to $4.75, then to $4.95). Relocate nonsignature and low contribution margin Plow Horses to a lower profile position on the menu. Attempt to shift demand to more profitable items by merchandising and menu positioning. If the item is an image maker or signature item, hold its current price as long as possible in periods of high price sensitivity.

Determine the direct labor cost of each Plow Horse to establish its labor and skill intensiveness. If the item requires high skills or is labor-intensive, consider a price increase or substitution. Also, consider reducing the item's standard portion without making the difference noticeable. Merchandise the Plow Horse by packaging it with side items to increase its contribution margin. Another option is to use the item to create a "better value alternative." For example, prime rib can be sold by the inch, and steak can be sold by the ounce. This offers guests an opportunity to spend more and get more value.

Puzzles. Take them off the menu—particularly if a Puzzle is low in popularity, requires costly or additional inventory, has poor shelf life, requires skilled or labor-intensive preparation, and is of inconsistent quality. Another option is to reposition the Puzzle and feature it in a more popular location on the menu. You can try adding value to the item through Table d'Hôte packaging. Rename it. A Puzzle's popularity can be affected by what it is called, especially if the name can be made to sound familiar.

Another strategy is to decrease the Puzzle's price. The item may have a contribution margin that is too high and is facing price resistance. Care must be taken, however, not to lower the contribution margin to a point where the Puzzle draws menu share from a Star. Increase the item's price and test for inelasticity. A Puzzle that has relatively high popularity may be inelastic.

Or, limit the number of Puzzles you allow on your menu. Puzzles can create difficulties in quality consistency, slow production down, and cause inventory and cost problems. You must accurately evaluate the effect Puzzle items have on your image. Do they enhance your image?

Dogs. Eliminate all Dog items if possible. Foodservice operators are often intimidated by influential guests to carry a Dog on the menu. The way to solve this problem is to carry the item in inventory (assuming it has a shelf life) but not on the menu. The special guest is offered the opportunity to have the item made to order upon request. Charge extra for this service. Raise the Dog's price to Puzzle status. Some items in the Dog category may have market potential. These tend to be the more popular Dogs and may be converted to Puzzles.

Whenever possible, replace Dogs with more popular items. You may have too many items. It is not unusual to discover a number of highly unpopular menu items with little, if any, relation to other more popular and profitable items held in inventory. Do not be afraid to terminate Dogs, especially when demand is not satisfactory.

*The process described here differs slightly from the process used to complete the menu engineering worksheet in Exhibit 8.15. The differences are not significant.
Excerpted from an article by Donald Smith, Hospitality Publications, Okemos, Michigan.

The profitability and popularity classifications for each menu item result in four categories of menu items, as shown in Exhibit 8.13. In general, "Stars" should be retained, "Puzzles" repositioned, "Plow Horses" repriced, and "Dogs" removed from the menu. (For more discussion of management actions regarding the four classifications, see *Using Menu Engineering: A 14-Step Approach*.)

Exhibit 8.14 is a graphic illustration of menu engineering results containing menu items in the four classifications. Eight menu items, identified by letters corresponding to the following table, are shown on the graph.

Menu Item	Item Contribution Margin	Number Sold	Classification
A	$5.10	150	Star
B	$6.53	430	Star
C	$4.90	430	Plow Horse
D	$1.50	150	Plow Horse
E	$4.90	130	Dog
F	$1.50	90	Dog
G	$6.53	130	Puzzle
H	$5.10	90	Puzzle

In general, one prefers stars to dogs, puzzles, and plow horses. However, are stars *always* preferred to puzzles and plow horses? Specifically, is menu item A preferred to items C and G? Using the information for these menu items, we determine the following:

Exhibit 8.13 Profitability/Popularity Classification of Menu Items

Profitability	Popularity	Classification
High	High	Stars
High	Low	Puzzles
Low	High	Plow Horses
Low	Low	Dogs

Exhibit 8.14   Graph of Menu Engineering Results

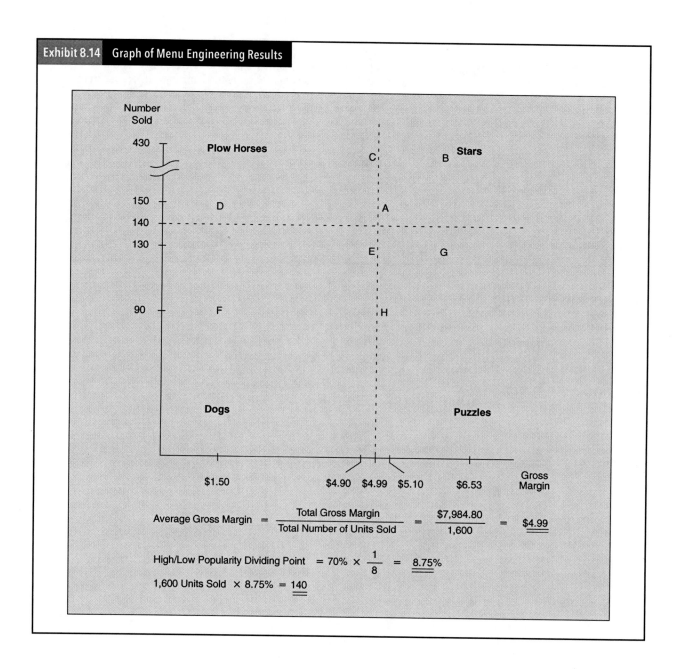

Menu Item	Classification	Item Contribution Margin	Number Sold	Total Item Contribution Margin
A	Star	$5.10	150	$ 765.00
C	Plow Horse	$4.90	430	$2,107.00
G	Puzzle	$6.53	130	$ 848.90

Menu items C and G provide $2,107 and $848.90 of contribution margin, respectively, compared to only $765 for item A. Thus, in this case, both items C and G (non-Star items) are preferred to the Star menu item A. Further, as can be seen in Exhibit 8.13, the Dog item E, with a total item contribution margin of $637, is nearly as profitable as the Star menu item A.

Exhibit 8.15 Menu Engineering Worksheet

Menu Engineering Worksheet

Restaurant: _____

Date: _____

Meal Period: _____

(A) Menu Item Name	(B) Number Sold (MM)	(C) Menu Mix %	(D) Item Food Cost	(E) Item Selling Price	(F) Item CM (E-D)	(G) Menu Costs (D*B)	(H) Menu Revenues (E*B)	(L) Menu CM (F*B)	(P) CM Category	(R) MM% Category	(S) Menu Item Classification	(T) Decision
Column Totals:	N					I	J	M				
						K = I/J		O = M/N		Q% = (100%/items)(70%)		

Additional Computations:

The key to this analysis is not simply to classify menu items but rather to consider total contribution margin. A menu may be analyzed using menu engineering and revised to eliminate all Dogs. However, if the total contribution margin is not increased, little, if anything, has been accomplished.

Exhibit 8.15 is a menu engineering worksheet useful for determining the classification of each menu item. Even when this form is used, however, a graph should be prepared for each menu analyzed to provide a better perspective of the relationships of menu items.

8.12 INTEGRATED PRICING

Many businesses in the hospitality industry, especially the lodging sector, have several revenue-producing departments. Allowing each profit center to price its products independently may fail to optimize the operation's profits. For example, suppose the swimming pool department manager decides to institute a direct charge to guests. This new pricing policy may maximize swimming pool revenues, but, at the same time, guests may choose to stay at other hotels where pool privileges are provided at no additional cost. Therefore, revenues would be lost from guests who selected competing hotels because of the new pool charge policy. Prices for all departments should be established such that they optimize the operation's net income. This will generally result in some profit centers *not* maximizing their revenues and thus their departmental incomes. This **integrated pricing** approach is essential and can only be accomplished by the general manager and profit center managers coordinating their pricing.

An optimal pricing structure can play a large role in the profitability of a hospitality operation. If rooms are underpriced, profits are lost. If meals are overpriced, demand may decrease, causing a decrease in profits. Management needs to be aware of these effects and set prices accordingly.

The relationship between the percentage change in price and the resulting percentage change in demand is called elasticity. In order to determine the price elasticity of demand for a product, the manager utilizes this formula:

$$\frac{\text{Change in Quantity Demanded}}{\text{Base Quantity}} \div \frac{\text{Change in Price}}{\text{Base Price}}$$

If the result (ignoring the negative sign) is greater than 1, the demand for the product is said to be elastic. In other words, a change in price results in a larger percentage change in the quantity demanded. Raising prices results in reduced revenues. Inelastic demand exists when the percentage change in price is greater than the percentage change in demand, and the formula results in an answer of less than 1. Every manager would prefer to have products with inelastic demand. When this is the case, raising prices results in increased revenues because the percentage decrease in demand is less than the percentage increase in prices.

There are a number of informal pricing methods. Some managers base prices on what the competition charges. Other managers assume that they intuitively know the price the public will accept. Still another method is psychological pricing, by which managers determine what they think customers expect to pay.

These methods, although frequently used, fail to examine costs. More technical methods, such as the markup and the bottom-up approaches, start with costs to determine prices that result in adequate net income.

The markup approach multiplies cost by a markup based on the desired product cost percentage. There are two variations of this approach. One sets a markup factor for the total cost of the meal. The other multiplies only the prime ingredient cost by a factor. The result of either of these approaches should be a price that will cover not only the food cost, but also the labor and other costs.

The Hubbart Formula is a method used to price rooms. It begins with the required return on the investment and adds to it the costs of operation, including taxes, management fees, depreciation, interest expense, property taxes, insurance, rent, undistributed operating expenses, and other departmental income.

Using this approach, departmental incomes (or losses) from other profit centers are added to (or subtracted from) the total indirect expenses of the hotel to determine the required rooms department income. The direct expenses of the rooms department plus the required rooms department income equal the required rooms department revenue. The average price per room is calculated by dividing the required rooms department revenue by the number of rooms expected to be sold during the period.

The cost approaches appear rigorous and objective; however, they generally are based on estimates. Further, when the proposed price is computed on the basis of one of the cost approaches presented, careful consideration must be given to prices being charged by the competition before the implementation of any price changes. Differences in price must be supported by a different offering, such as a better location, more amenities, and so on. Finally, in a multiproduct situation, such as a hotel, prices of the various products, food, beverages, and rooms, must be set on an integrated basis.

elastic demand—A situation in which the percentage change in quantity demanded exceeds the percentage change in price.

Hubbart Formula—A bottom-up approach to pricing rooms. In determining the average price per room, this approach considers costs, desired profits, and expected rooms sold.

inelastic demand—A situation in which a percentage change in price results in a smaller percentage change in quantity demanded.

ingredient markup—See "markup"; the ingredient markup approach considers all product costs.

integrated pricing—An approach to pricing in a hospitality operation having several revenue-producing departments that sets prices for goods and/or services in each profit center so as to optimize the entire operation's net income.

markup—An approach to pricing goods and services that determines retail prices by adding a certain percentage to the cost of goods sold. The markup is designed to cover all nonproduct costs (labor, utilities, supplies, interest expense, taxes, etc.) as well as desired profit. Ingredient markup is based on all ingredients. Prime ingredient markup bases the markup solely on the cost of the main ingredient.

menu engineering—A method of menu analysis and food pricing that considers both the profitability and popularity of competing menu items.

$1 per $1,000 approach—An approach to rooms pricing that sets the price of a room at $1 for each $1,000 of project cost per room.

price elasticity of demand—An expression of the relationship between a change in price and the resulting change in demand.

prime ingredient markup—See "markup"; the prime ingredient markup approach considers only the cost of the major ingredient.

revenue management—Selling rooms in a way that maximizes total revenues. Before selling a room in advance, the hotel considers the probability of being able to sell the room to other market segments that are willing to pay higher rates.

unit elastic—Elasticity of demand is exactly one (1). Any percentage change in price is accompanied by the same percentage change in quantity demanded.

1. What are four methods of informal pricing?

2. What disadvantages are inherent with informal pricing?

3. How is the cost markup factor often calculated?

4. What is the difference between the markup and the prime ingredient markup pricing methods?

5. What is price elasticity of demand?

6. What is the philosophy behind bottom-up pricing?

7. What does menu engineering consider in its review of menu items?

8. What is the relation between contribution margins and cost percentages?

9. How is the $1 per $1,000 approach used to price rooms?

10. Which pricing method is the most applicable for restaurants? Why?

Problem 1

Carroll Lewis, owner of the 100-seat CL's Café, provides you with cost and other information as follows:

Monthly fixed costs	=	$50,000
Variable cost percentage	=	50%
Owner's equity	=	$300,000
Desired ROI	=	20%
Average tax rate	=	30%

Required:

1. What are the monthly breakeven sales?

2. What are the monthly revenues when the desired profits are earned?

3. What is the average foodservice check if the seat turnover is an average of two per day for the 24 days it is open in February?

Problem 2

The Ramsey's, a lodging establishment, has 20 doubles and 10 single rooms. The average daily rate (ADR) is $60. Assume 24 rooms are sold each night.

Required:

Complete the following:

Room Rates for Doubles Compared with Singles		Assumed Sales Mix		ADR	
		Singles	Doubles	Singles	Doubles
1.	+$10	12	12		
2.	+$20	8	16		
3.	10% higher	10	14		
4.	30% higher	12	12		

Problem 3

The rack rate for the average room at the Felix and Brandon's Anniversary hotel is $120. The marginal cost per room is $15 and the paid occupancy percentage is 75 percent. Assume there are 100 guestrooms. Assume rooms are sold at the rack rate.

Required:

1. What is the daily room revenue?

2. What is the daily room contribution margin?

3. What is the equivalent room occupancy if the room rate is discounted 10 percent?

Problem 4

The owner/manager of the Motley has seen occupancy dip over the last six months to 55 percent and has requested your assistance with proposed room rate discounting. The marginal cost per room sold is $25 at the Motley and the average daily rate has been $95.

Required:

1. Determine the equivalent room occupancy (ERO) if the ADR is reduced by $10.

2. Determine the ERO if the ADR is reduced from $80 by 10 percent.

Problem 5

The owner of CDG desires to earn $15,000 of net income each month. Its monthly fixed costs equal $30,000 and its variable cost percentage is equal to 65 percent. It has 100 seats and is only open for lunch. Assume an average tax rate of 25 percent.

Required:

1. Calculate its average foodservice cover if the seat turnover is 30 times per month.

2. Calculate its average foodservice cover if the seat turnover is 45 times per month, desired profits are $25,000, and monthly fixed costs equal $45,000.

Problem 6

Nathan and Tucker are brothers and they have invested $600,000 in NT's Place. Their projected costs and activities are as follows:

Variable costs = 60%
Monthly fixed costs = $45,000
Monthly covers sold = 10,000
Average tax rate = 25%

Required:

1. What must the average foodservice check be to break even?

2. If a monthly profit of $5,000 is to be earned, what must the average foodservice check be?

Problem 7

Yoyo Redmond has just invested $200,000 of his own funds in a new family-style restaurant. He has borrowed $200,000 at 10 percent annual interest from his aunt, Ada. He desires a 20 percent return on his investment. The restaurant has 100 seats and is open 6 days per week (closed on Sundays). He believes he can achieve average seat turnovers as follows:

Breakfast = 1.5
Lunch = 1.6
Dinner = 1.1

His expected average tax rate is 15 percent. Assume the first day of the year is a Monday.

Cost estimates are as follows:

Annual Fixed Costs		Variable Costs	
Rent	$ 40,000	Food costs	35%
Insurance	8,000	Wage costs	20%
Depreciation	35,000	Supplies	9%
Salaries	180,000	Utilities	3%
Utilities	26,000	Other	5%
Other	30,000		

Required:

1. Determine the average check.

2. If the percentage sales by meal period are 20 percent, 30 percent, and 50 percent for breakfast, lunch, and dinner, respectively, what is the average check for each period?

Problem 8

A proposed economy hotel, Branson, is scheduled to open in two months. The owner, Luke Branson, seeks your advice on pricing. Although he knows he will have to modify your recommendations based on market prices, he desires a cost perspective. He gives you the following information:

Luke's investment	=	$2.5 million
Luke's desired ROI	=	20 percent
Luke's marginal tax rate	=	30 percent
Funds borrowed	=	$3.5 million
Interest rate	=	10 percent annual

Forecasted annual costs:

Depreciation, property taxes, and insurance	=	$500,000
Management fees	=	5 percent of room sales
Rooms department expenses	=	25 percent of room sales
Undistributed operating expenses	=	$300,000 + 5 percent of room sales

Assume:

- Nonroom profit centers generate $10,000 of annual department profit.

- Assume the Branson has 150 guestrooms, and it expects to have paid occupancy of 70 percent.

Required:

1. Determine the required ADR.

2. Assume the Branson has both single and double rooms. Further assume that 80 percent of rooms sold are doubles, and that doubles sell for $25 more than the price of a single. What is the average selling price of a double?

Problem 9

The Anthony, a family-style, 50-seat restaurant, revises its menu every six months. The revisions are based, in part, on the price elasticity of demand for its menu items. During the 30-day periods before and after the last menu revision, the selling prices and quantity sold of three items were as follows:

Item	Prior to Revision		After Revision	
	Price	Quantity	Price	Quantity
Super Burger	$ 7.95	450	$ 8.45	400
Golden Chicken	$ 8.45	800	$ 7.95	1,000
Ocean Delight	$ 9.45	600	$ 9.95	400

The above sales quantities have remained fairly constant each month since the last menu revision.

Required:

1. Compute the price elasticity of demand for each menu item.

2. Advise Kay Rae, the manager, of the implications of your results for each menu item.

Problem 10

The Brookeside Inn had an average dinner cover charge of $11.75 during the month of June, when 3,000 patrons were served. E.L. Brooke, the owner/ manager, increased the dinner menu prices by an average of $ 0.50 per item. During the first 30 days of July, the average cover charge was $12.25 for the 2,900 patrons who were served dinner.

Required:

1. Compute the price elasticity of demand.

2. How is demand characterized based on your calculations?

Problem 11

The 100-room O'Dea Hotel experienced a 65 percent paid occupancy and a rack rate of $130 for 20X5. The hotel has four market segments. The percentage of room nights and the percentage of rack rate for each segment are as follows:

	Percentage of Rooms Sold	Rack Rate Percentage
Business transient	40%	100%
Group	15	90
Tourist	35	85
Government	10	70

Required:

1. What is the average room rate per market segment?

2. What are the total sales for the year by market segment?

Problem 12

The proposed Harris Place (a 50-room, rooms-only lodging facility) is to be built in mid-Michigan. Jeremy Harris, the owner, is concerned about the average daily room rate (ADR), construction costs, borrowing costs, and their impact on profits. He provides you with the following information:

1. Proposed costs of the lodging facility:

Land	$ 400,000
Building	$ 2 million
Equipment	$ 1 million

2. Financing:

Equity (desired return on investment) (ROI = 15 percent)	$ 1 million
Debt (8 percent annual interest rate)	$ 2.4 million

3. The income tax rate is 40 percent.

4. Property taxes are $120,000 per year.

5. For fire insurance, the annual premium is $30,000.

6. Depreciation:
   Building: 40-year life, straight-line method, $0 salvage value
   Equipment: 10-year life, straight-line method, $0 salvage value

7. Undistributed operating expenses are $300,000 annually and 5 percent of total room revenue.

8. The management fee is 5 percent of rooms revenue.

9. The telephone department is expected to just break even.

10. Rooms department expenses equal $30,000 annually plus 15 percent of room sales.

11. Expected paid occupancy is 70 percent.

Required:

Determine the required ADR to achieve Jeremy Harris's goal of earning an ROI of 15 percent.

Problem 13

Josie's Place Inn, a proposed 30-room motel with a fully equipped restaurant, will cost $750,000 to construct. An estimated additional $50,000 will be invested in the business as working capital. Of the total $800,000 investment, $400,000 is to be secured from the Columbo Federal Bank at the rate of 10 percent interest. The projected occupancy rate is 80 percent for the year. The owners desire a 15 percent return on equity after the corporation pays income taxes of 25 percent. The estimated undistributable expenses, not including income taxes and interest expense, total $480,000. The estimated direct expenses of the rooms department are $7 for each room sold. Consider a year to have 365 days.

Required:

1. Determine the average price of a room using the Hubbart Formula, assuming the contribution from the restaurant department is $0.

2. If the double rooms are sold at a premium of $10 over singles, what is the price of singles and doubles? Assume a double occupancy rate of 40 percent.

3. If the restaurant generates a department profit of $20,000 per year, how much may average room rates be decreased and still meet the owners' financial goals?

Problem 14

The Cody Hotel, a proposed 100-room hotel with a fully equipped restaurant, will cost $10 million to construct. An estimated additional $200,000 will be invested in the business as working capital. Of the total $10.2 million investment, $8 million is to be secured from Detroit Federal Bank at an interest rate of 12 percent. The projected occupancy rate is 70 percent for the year. The owners desire a 15 percent return on equity after the corporation pays income taxes of 30 percent. The estimated undistributable expenses, not including income taxes and interest expense, total $1.2 million. The estimated direct expenses of the rooms department are 20 percent of room sales plus $100,000 for the year. Consider a year to have 365 days.

Required:

1. Determine the average price of a room using the Hubbart Formula, assuming the contribution from the restaurant department is $100,000.

2. If the double rooms are sold at a premium of 25 percent over singles, what is the price of singles and doubles? Assume a double occupancy rate of 80 percent.

3. If the restaurant incurs a department loss of $50,000 per year, how much should average room rates be increased (over #1) to still meet the owners' financial goals?

Problem 15

A proposed dinner-only restaurant, Snickers, is scheduled to open in two months. The owner, Betsy Lab, seeks your advice on pricing. Although she knows she will have to modify your recommendations based on market prices, she desires a cost perspective. She gives you the following information:

Betsy's investment	=	$500,000
Betsy's desired ROI	=	15 percent
Betsy's tax rate	=	35 percent
Funds borrowed	=	$500,000
Interest rate	=	10 percent annual
Forecasted annual costs:		
Occupation costs other than interest and depreciation	=	$100,000
Depreciation costs	=	$60,000
Controllable expenses	=	$750,000
Cost of food sales	=	35 percent of food sales

Snickers will have 150 seats and the average expected seat turnover per day is 1.0. The restaurant will be open 310 days per year.

Required:

1. Determine the average dinner check.

2. Assume nonfood business provides $20,000 of pretax profits each year. Determine the average dinner check.

Problem 16

Natalie's Café, a proposed 100-seat restaurant, is expected to have the following investment costs, annual sales, and expenses:

Natalie's investment	=	$300,000
Funds borrowed	=	$400,000
Average tax rate	=	25 percent
Nonoperating expenses (excluding interest)	=	$40,000
Depreciation	=	$60,000
Food costs	=	30 percent of food sales
Labor costs (variable)	=	15 percent of food costs
Labor costs (fixed)	=	$150,000
Other controllable costs	=	$100,000
ROI	=	15 percent
Interest rate	=	10 percent
Seat turnover	=	2 times per day
Days open	=	313

Required:

1. Determine the average price per meal.

2. Assume that the revenue is divided between lunch and dinner at 40 percent and 60 percent, respectively. Further, assume the lunch seat turnover averages 1.2 times per day, while dinner seat turnover averages 0.8 times per day. What are the average prices for lunch and dinner?

Problem 17

The Midday Cafe is located in the Midtown Mall, which is open from 10 a.m. to 5 p.m. each day. The cafe sells 10 different sandwiches as well as a variety of soft drinks. In a recent week, the following activity occurred:

Sandwich	Selling Price	Cost	Number Sold
Pork Barrel	$3.95	$1.30	50
Lamb Leg	3.75	1.00	40
Chicken Breast	3.95	1.40	150
Burger Delight	3.45	0.85	300
Super Burger	4.95	1.25	190
Roast Beef	4.95	1.50	250
Ocean Catch	4.45	1.20	200

Sandwich	Selling Price	Cost	Number Sold
Tuna Salad	3.50	0.60	175
Egg Salad	3.25	0.35	150
Cheese Mix	2.95	0.40	60

Required:

1. Determine the total sales revenue for sandwiches for the week.

2. Determine the total cost of sandwich sales for the week.

3. Determine the food cost percentage for the week.

4. Determine the average contribution margin for all sandwiches sold.

5. Using menu engineering, determine the classification of each sandwich.

Problem 18

The Lynn Inn, a 100-room lodging facility, is proposed for construction in the north-central part of the United States. The total cost of construction is $5 million. Another $200,000 is required for franchise costs and working capital purposes. Franchise costs of $100,000 are to be amortized over the first 5 years of operations. To simplify the problem, depreciation is calculated on a straight-line basis over 24 years (assume $200,000 of salvage value).

   The owners will borrow $3 million at an annual interest rate of 12 percent. The owners desire an 18 percent return on their equity investment. Other unallocable costs, except for management fees, total $1.5 million annually. Management fees are based on 3 percent of room sales.

   Assume that gift shop department and foodservice department profits total $0 and $300,000, respectively. Further assume that all room department costs are variable and total 25 percent of room revenues, and that the Lynn Inn can achieve a 70 percent occupancy rate for the first year. Finally, assume an average tax rate of 25 percent.

Required:

1. Determine the average room rate for the Lynn Inn.

2. Assume that gift shop department losses total $50,000. How much must the average room rate be modified to cover this loss?

3. Assume (independent of #2) that the Lynn Inn has singles, doubles, and suites. Further, the relationship between sales and prices are as follows:

	Price	Sales Mix
Singles	??	30%
Doubles	$10 premium over singles rate	50
Suites	125% of doubles rate	20
		100%

Determine the average room rate for suites and doubles.

Problem 19

Stan Rey, the manager of Masons, a casual dining facility, has just been exposed to the concept of analyzing a menu based on its gross profits rather than food cost percentage. The four major entrées at Masons and its selling prices (SP), food costs (FC), and contribution margins (CM) are as follows:

	SP	FC	CM
Chicken	$ 5.95	$1.78	$4.17
Fish	$ 6.95	$2.43	$4.52
Pork chops	$ 8.95	$3.58	$5.37
Steak	$11.95	$5.97	$5.98

Three alternative sales mixes are as follows:

	Sales Mixes		
	#1	#2	#3
Chicken	400	350	100
Fish	300	300	150
Pork chops	200	200	250
Steak	100	150	500
Total	1,000	1,000	1,000

Required:

1. Compute the total revenue, gross profit, and food cost percentage for each alternative.

2. How many meals would have to be sold for mixes #1 and #2 so that each would provide the gross profit earned with sales mix #3?

3. Which sales mix would you prefer? Why?

Problem 20

Barbara Rope, a wealthy investor, is considering investing $2 million in a 300-room hotel. Debt financing would total $8 million. She desires to know the average rate her hotel will have to charge, given the following alternatives:

	Alternatives				
	#1	#2	#3	#4	#5
Desired ROI	14 %	15 %	16 %	17 %	18 %
Interest rate	12 %	12 %	13 %	14 %	14 %
Tax rate	30 %	30 %	30 %	30 %	30 %
Estimated annual fixed charges (depreciation and nonoperating expenses)	$ 700,000	$ 700,000	$ 700,000	$ 700,000	$ 700,000

	Alternatives				
	#1	#2	#3	#4	#5
Management fees (% of room sales)	3 %	3 %	3 %	4 %	4 %
Undistributed operating expense	$3,000,000	$3,000,000	$3,500,000	$3,500,000	$3,500,000
Departmental profits:					
Food	$ 300,000	$ 300,000	$ 400,000	$ 450,000	$ 450,000
Other	$ 10,000	$ 10,000	$ 10,000	$ 10,000	$ 10,000
Variable costs per room sold	$ 15	$ 15	$ 20	$ 20	$ 20
Occupancy rate	65 %	70 %	65 %	75 %	80 %

Required:

Compute the average daily room rate for each alternative. To minimize the calculations, consider using a spreadsheet program.

Problem 21

Bobbie's Place has not changed its menu in three years. Recently, the owner, Bobbie Schmidt, read about menu engineering and desires your assistance in analyzing the dinner menu. The seven dinner entrées, their selling prices, costs, and the menu counts for a recent month are as follows:

	Selling Price	Food Cost	Number Sold
Sirloin steak	$ 9.95	$ 3.00	240
King crab	15.95	6.00	50
Lobster	18.45	8.00	60
Prime rib	14.50	4.25	300
Whitefish	8.75	2.50	80
New York strip	12.45	5.75	180
Chicken à la king	8.50	2.60	280

Required:

1. Complete a menu engineering worksheet using the format of Exhibit 8.15.

2. What recommendations would you offer the owner based on your analysis?

Problem 22

The K&S Restaurant desires to analyze its luncheon menu prior to making several changes. The manager, Louis Kass, has provided the following information:

	Selling Price	Food Cost	Number Sold
Hamburger Deluxe	$ 4.95	$ 1.50	180
Cheeseburger Deluxe	5.25	1.60	120
Turkey Sandwich	4.25	1.25	80
Ham and Cheese on Rye	6.25	1.70	220
Egg Salad Sandwich	3.95	1.10	50
Fishwich	4.50	1.30	80
Pizzaburger	3.00	0.85	100
Chicken Delight	6.25	2.10	140
Taco Salad	3.25	0.85	60
Chef Salad	3.95	1.25	100

Required:

1. Complete a menu engineering worksheet using the format of Exhibit 8.15. Alternatively, use a computerized menu engineering program.

2. Complete a second menu engineering worksheet after revising the menu as follows:
   A. Drop the poorest performing item (Dog) and allocate the units sold of this item to the Plow Horses on a *pro rata* basis.
   B. Lower the prices of Puzzle items by 5 percent and increase sales of each by 10 percent.
   C. Increase the prices of Plow Horses by 5 percent and decrease sales of each by 5 percent.
   D. Increase prices of each Star to either the next $X.45 or $X.95 and assume that the number sold of each remains constant.

3. Compare the results of menu engineering of #1 and #2 above with regard to the following:
   A. Number of items sold
   B. Total sales
   C. Average contribution margin
   D. Total contribution margin
   E. Number of Dogs and Stars after each analysis

Problem 23

Artisan, a fine-dining restaurant in the tourist section of the city, reviews and updates sections of its menu every few months to take advantage of the seasonal items and also offer its guests more choices. The decision for changes, besides product availability, is also based on what the guests are willing to pay: in other words, price elasticity of demand for the items. In addition, there is a trend in fine-dining restaurants to simply price their menu items rounded to the nearest dollar. The chef/owner of Artisan is well aware of her guests' preferences, and she always wants to assess the price elasticity of demand for the items. She shares the data with you on the appetizers, and the prices and the quantity ordered before and after 30 days of the menu price changes are indicated as follows:

	Item Prior to Revision		After Revision	
	Price	Quantity	Price	Quantity
Ahi Tuna and Shrimp Cocktail	$ 15.95	490	$ 19	450
Pan-Seared Pork Belly	$ 14.95	800	$ 17	600
Calamari Artisan	$ 13.95	600	$ 15	450
Texas Wedge Salad	$ 9.95	400	$ 11	300
French Onion Soup	$ 11.95	500	$ 13	475

Required:

1. Compute the price elasticity of demand for each menu item.

2. Advise the chef/owner of the implications of your results for each menu item.

Problem 24

The DeLoziers always wanted to build a small bed and breakfast on their property, which is tucked away in a nice, wooded area by a lake and yet is only a half-hour drive to the city. The proposed plan is a 20-room property with a restaurant for the convenience of the guests where breakfasts will be served. The construction cost is $1.8 million with an additional $50,000 as net working capital. Sixty percent of the total investment will be funded by a 6 percent loan, and the remainder will be from the savings of the couple. The estimated occupancy is 60 percent for the first year. The DeLoziers would like to see a 10 percent return on equity after tax and their tax rate is at 30 percent. With a 60 percent occupancy, the undistributed expenses, not including income taxes and interest expense, total $500,000. The estimated direct expense of the rooms department is $10 for each room sold. Consider a year to have 365 days.

Required:

Round all answers to the nearest whole number.

1. Determine the average price of a room using the Hubbart Formula, assuming there is no contribution from the restaurant department.

2. If the double rooms are sold at a premium of $20 over singles, what is the price of singles and doubles? Assume a double occupancy rate of 80 percent.

3. If the restaurant can generate a $40,000 profit per year, how much may average room rates be decreased and still meet the owners' financial goals?

Problem 25

Matt Kawasaki is contemplating buying this limited hotel at a beach resort. The 110-room property has a price tag of $15 million, but it has a strong occupancy of 85 percent as the weather is nice year-round. The purchase is going to be financed with an 8 percent loan for 75 percent of the project cost. Matt will use his own money for the other 25 percent, on which he would require a 15 percent after-tax return on investment at his personal tax rate of 30 percent. The estimated undistributed expense, not including income taxes and interest expense, is $1 million per year. In addition, the estimated direct expense of the rooms department is $15 for each room sold, $100,000 fixed for the year, but the hotel should also realize an annual miscellaneous income of $15,000.

Required:

Using the full calendar year of 365 days:

1. Determine the average price per room using the Hubbart Formula.

2. If double rooms are sold at a premium of 20 percent over singles, what are the prices of single and double rooms if the double occupancy is 80 percent?

9
FORECASTING METHODS

Chapter 9 Outline

Competencies

1. Describe the nature and limitations of forecasting and identify the kinds of patterns that emerge from the historical data of hospitality operations. (pp. 404–408)

2. Describe and apply various quantitative forecasting methods and explain how they differ from qualitative forecasting methods. (pp. 408–415)

3. Identify factors hospitality operations should consider when selecting a forecasting method. (pp. 415–417)

4. Describe the purpose of, and methods used to create, short-term forecasts in the lodging industry. (p. 417)

5. Describe forecasting in the club industry. (pp. 417–422)

KEY TERMS

capture ratios

causal forecasting approaches

coefficient of correlation

coefficient of determination

cyclical patterns

exponential smoothing

moving average

multiple regression analysis

naïve approach

qualitative forecasting methods

quantitative forecasting methods

seasonal pattern

smoothing constant

time series forecasting approaches

trend pattern

Every hospitality manager's job includes forecasting, which is the calculation and prediction of future events, such as sales for the following day, week, or month. Forecasting is necessary in order to plan the most effective and efficient ways to meet expected sales volume. For example, if the food and beverage manager of a hotel forecasts 500 dinner guests, then food, beverages, and other supplies must be obtained, and the appropriate personnel must be scheduled to prepare and serve the food and beverages to the guests. Generally, the accuracy of sales forecasts is a major determinant of the cost effectiveness of the hospitality operation. For example, if 400 meals are forecast and 500 guests show up, the food and beverage provisions and the number of employees scheduled to work may not be adequate. This may result in poor service and overtime wages. On the other hand, if 600 meals had been forecast, service would probably have been outstanding; however, due to possibly excessive labor costs, efficiency would have been reduced. The general topic of forecasting raises several questions, such as the following:

1. How important is forecasting?
2. Is forecasting limited to financial forecasts?
3. How is forecasting conducted by unit managers in the hospitality industry?
4. How does forecasting enable management to be successful?
5. What are the limitations to forecasting?
6. How does forecasting differ from planning?
7. What is the difference between seasonal and cyclical patterns?
8. How do quantitative and qualitative forecasting methods differ?
9. How is a moving average calculated?
10. When are causal forecasting approaches most useful in the hospitality industry?

This chapter begins by explaining the distinction between implicit and explicit forecasts. A general discussion of forecasting in the hospitality industry is followed by a discussion of the personnel who are responsible for preparing forecasts. Next, we turn to the nature of forecasting itself, focusing on the underlying patterns of data used in forecasts and providing an overview of various forecasting methods. The problem of selecting a forecasting method appropriate to individual hospitality operations is given special consideration. Finally, we will illustrate the chapter's discussion of forecasting by providing case studies of how forecasts are prepared by three different hospitality operations.

9.1 IMPLICIT VERSUS EXPLICIT FORECASTS

Some hospitality managers may insist that they do not believe in forecasting. However, their actions almost always prove otherwise. For example, when a manager decides to replace an inoperative piece of equipment, such as a range, they are implicitly forecasting that profits will be higher if a new range is purchased.

This intuitive approach to managing may be useful, since unforeseen events often occur and must be resolved quickly. However, managing in this fashion on a daily basis is less than optimal. It is generally more useful to forecast consciously. Implicit forecasts are unsystematic, imprecise, and difficult to evaluate rationally. Explicit forecasts are systematic, may be reasonably reliable and accurate, and are easier to evaluate rationally.

9.2 FORECASTING IN THE HOSPITALITY INDUSTRY

A major function of management is planning, and a subset of the planning function is forecasting. Forecasting is generally used to predict what will happen in a given set of circumstances. The forecast gives an idea of expected results if management makes no changes in the way things are done. In planning, forecasts are used to help make decisions about which circumstances will be most desirable for the hospitality operation. Thus, if a forecast shows rooms demand will decrease next month, management should prepare an action plan to prevent rooms sales from declining. After the action plan is completed, a new forecast must be made to reflect the expected impact of the action plan.

Planning, and thus forecasting, is pervasive in hospitality operations. In a hotel operation, rooms sales and food and beverage sales account for approximately 85 percent of the total sales activity of a hotel. Many operations, especially foodservice and lodging chains, forecast sales for several years in long-range operating budgets. At the other extreme, sales are forecast for months, days, parts of a day, and sometimes even on an hourly basis, since management must plan to service the forecasted sales.

Hospitality establishments also provide estimates of future activity in management reports to stockholders, which include both qualitative and quantitative forecasts. For example, Marriott International included the following in its 2020 annual report regarding the severe impact of the COVID-19 pandemic:

> As discussed in this Form 10-K, the COVID-19 pandemic is materially impacting our operations and financial results. COVID-19, and the volatile regional and global economic conditions stemming from it, and additional or unforeseen effects from the COVID-19 pandemic, could also give rise to or aggravate the other risk factors that we identify within Part I, Item 1A of this report, which in turn could materially adversely affect our business, liquidity, financial condition, and results of operations. Further, COVID-19 may also affect our operating and financial results in a manner that is not presently known to us or that we currently do not consider to present significant risks to our operations.[1]

9.3 PERSONNEL RESPONSIBLE FOR FORECASTING

Forecasting of sales and related expenses is the responsibility not only of the accounting department, but also of management personnel in other departments. For example, the year-ahead forecast should include input from (1) the sales director's forecast of group rooms business, (2) the front office manager's forecast of rooms occupancy from all other sources, (3) a joint forecast of rooms business by the sales director and front office manager, (4) the controller, and (5) the general manager and management team review.

Exhibit 9.1 reveals the results of research regarding the number of people involved in making short-term (three- to ten-day) forecasts. Across all properties surveyed, the range of the number of personnel involved in the three areas shown was one to six people. The larger the property, the greater the number of personnel involved with the forecast. For example, the megahotels (1,000 or more rooms) that responded use six people in their rooms forecast, while hotels with fewer than 150 rooms involve an average of two people.

Exhibit 9.1 | Personnel Involved in Making Short-Term Forecasts

	Rooms Forecast	Food & Beverage Forecast	Catering Forecast
Average number of personnel involved	3 people	3 people	2 people
Person responsible for final forecast	General manager (GM) and to a lesser extent the front office manager	Food and beverage director and to a lesser extent the GM	Director of catering and to a lesser extent the food and beverage director

9.4 THE NATURE OF FORECASTING

It is important to understand the nature and limitations of forecasting. First, forecasting deals with the future. A forecast made today is for activity during a future period, be it tonight's dinner sales or next year's rooms sales. The time period involved is significant. A forecast today for tomorrow's sales is generally much easier than an estimate today of next year's sales. The further removed the forecast period is from the date the forecast is made, the greater the difficulty in making the forecast and the greater the risk that the actual results will differ from the forecast. Second, forecasting involves uncertainty. If management were certain about what circumstances would exist during the forecasted period, the forecast preparation would be a trivial matter. Virtually all situations faced by managers involve uncertainty; therefore, judgments must be made and information gathered on which to base the forecast. For example, assume that rooms sales for a major hotel must be forecast for one year in advance. A manager (forecaster) may be uncertain about competition, guest demand, room rates, and so forth. Nevertheless, using the best information available and their best judgment, they forecast that x rooms at an average room rate of $\$y$ will be sold.

Third, forecasting generally relies on information contained in historical data. Historical activity (for example, past sales) may not be a strong indicator of future activity, but it is considered a reasonable starting point. When historical data appears to be irrelevant to the future time period, the forecasts should be modified appropriately. For example, a successful Summer Olympics might have a major impact on hotel occupancies for several months. However, in projecting future hotel occupancies after the end of the Summer Olympics, the recent historical information may well be much less relevant.

Fourth, by their nature, forecasts are generally less accurate than desired. However, rather than discarding forecasts due to their inaccuracy, management should consider using more sophisticated forecasting models when their cost is justified, updating forecasts as necessary, and/or planning more carefully on the basis of the forecasted projections.

Naïve forecasting models, such as using the most recent value plus x percent, may have been adequate in the past for small hospitality operations. However, more sophisticated models may be appropriate for larger properties. Forecasts should be revised as soon as there is a change in the circumstances on which the forecasts were based. For example, an enhanced food and beverage reputation due to favorable publicity may call for reforecasting next month's food and beverage sales.

Finally, management must plan to cover a deviation of an additional *x* percent from the forecasted levels. Experience may be the best indication of the required planning. For example, if actual sales historically have exceeded projected sales by 10 percent, management should order sufficient provisions and schedule labor to cover such a deviation for the projected activity.

9.5 UNDERLYING PATTERN OF THE DATA

Many forecasting methods assume that some pattern exists in past data that can be identified and used in making the forecast. The methods to be presented in this chapter make explicit assumptions about the type of underlying pattern. Thus, the forecaster must attempt to match the patterns with the most appropriate forecasting methods. Three types of patterns are trend, seasonal, and cyclical (discussed below and graphed for a hypothetical hotel in Exhibit 9.2).

The **trend pattern** is simply a projection of the long-run estimate of the activity being evaluated. The trend pattern of the data is often shown for several years. The trend of rooms sales in Exhibit 9.2 is an increasing one and could be determined by using methods presented later in this chapter.

A **seasonal pattern** exists when a series of data fluctuates over time according to some pattern. Business may vary regularly by season of the year, by month, by week, or even by the days of the week. Seasonal patterns exist in the hospitality industry primarily because of forces external to the industry. For example, many summer resort hotels experience high occupancy during

| Exhibit 9.2 | Underlying Patterns of Data for a Hypothetical Hotel |

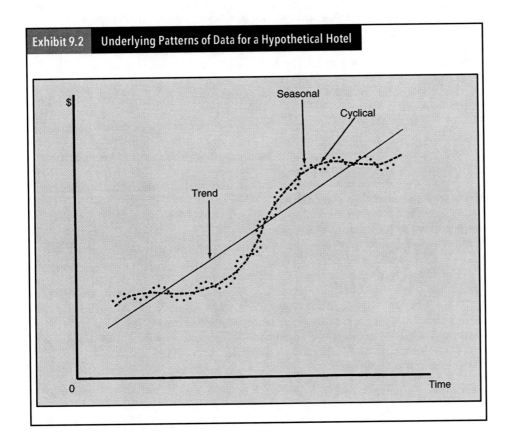

the summer months, but are closed during the off-season. The manager of a hospitality operation affected by seasonal business swings must fully appreciate this impact in order to manage efficiently.

The final underlying pattern of data is called cyclical. **Cyclical patterns** are movements about a trend line that generally occur over a period of more than one year. Exhibit 9.2 shows that the cyclical pattern is similar to a seasonal pattern except for the length of the pattern. The cyclical pattern is the most difficult to predict because, unlike a seasonal pattern, it does not necessarily repeat itself at constant intervals.

Finally, random variations are also present in all historical data. By definition, there is no pattern in random variations. They occur for reasons that the hospitality manager cannot anticipate regardless of the forecasting method. Therefore, the actual observed result is a combination of trend and randomness. As long as randomness exists, uncertainty will be present. However, when the forecaster is able to identify the exact pattern of the underlying data, the random deviations are minimized.

9.6 OVERVIEW OF FORECASTING METHODS

There are numerous ways to forecast, ranging from the simple, unsophisticated method of intuition to complex approaches such as econometric models, where sets of two or more multiple regression equations are used. Forecasting methods may be classified as shown in Exhibit 9.3.

The first breakdown is between informal and formal forecasting methods. Informal methods are based on intuition and lack systematic procedures transferable to other forecasters. Formal forecasting methods outline steps to be followed so they can be applied repeatedly. Formal forecasting methods are divided between **qualitative forecasting methods**, which emphasize human judgment, and **quantitative forecasting methods**, which rely on numbers and calculations such as causal and time series approaches to forecasting. The quantitative methods, which are the primary concern of this chapter, are further divided between causal and time series approaches.

The **time series approaches** always assume that a pattern recurs over time, which, when identified, may be used to forecast values for any subsequent time period. For example, if a seasonal pattern of December hotel occupancies of 30 percent below the monthly average has been identified, then the estimated hotel occupancy for December of the following year would most likely be 30 percent below the monthly average for that year.

Time series approaches assume that the underlying pattern can be identified solely on the basis of historical data from that series. They do not consider the potential effects of certain decisions, such as pricing and advertising, that the manager makes for the future periods. Time series approaches presented in this chapter include naïve methods and smoothing methods. The decomposition method is beyond the scope of this chapter.

The **causal approaches** assume that the value of a certain variable is a function of other variables. For example, the sale of food and beverages in a hotel is a function, among other things, of hotel occupancy. Thus, a food and beverage sales forecast is based in part on forecasted rooms sales. Causal methods include single and multiple linear regression, nonlinear regression, and econometric models. Only the single linear regression approach will be presented in this chapter.[2]

Exhibit 9.3	Forecasting Methods	

		Approaches	Brief Description
		Informal forecasting	Ad hoc, judgmental, or intuitive methods
Formal Forecasting	Quantitative Methods — Causal	**Regression Analysis**	Independent variables are related to the dependent variable using least squares: $y = A + Bx_1 + Cx_2$. Approaches include similar linear regression, multiple linear regression, and nonlinear regression.
		Econometrics	A system of interdependent regression equations describing one or more economic sectors.
	Quantitative Methods — Time Series	**Naïve**	Simple rules such as forecast equals last period's actual activity.
		Smoothing	Based on average past values of a time series (moving average) or weighting more recent past values of a time series (exponential smoothing).
		Decomposition	A time series that is broken down into trend, cyclical, seasonality, and randomness.
	Qualitative Methods	**Market Research**	Gathering information from potential customers regarding a "new" product or service.
		Juries of Executive Opinion	Top executives jointly prepare forecasts.
		Sales Force Estimates	A bottom-up approach to aggregating unit managers' forecasts.
		Delphi Method	A formal process conducted with a group of experts to achieve consensus on future events as they affect the company's markets.

Naïve Methods

The simplest time series approach to forecasting is the naïve approach, where the most recently observed value is used as a forecast and assumes there is no seasonality affecting sales. For example, a foodservice manager's sales projections of $50,000 for the current month may be based on the $50,000 in sales of the previous month. To take seasonality into account, a forecaster might use sales from the same month of the previous year as a base and either add or subtract a certain percentage.

For example, assume that a hotel's January 20X1 rooms sales totaled $150,000. The projection for January 20X2, using an anticipated 10 percent increase due to expected increased rooms sales and prices, would be $165,000, computed as follows:

$$\text{Base}(1 + 10\%) = \text{Forecast for January 20X2}$$
$$\$150,000(1.1) = \underline{\$165,000}$$

Although naïve methods are based on very simple rules, they may provide reasonably accurate forecasts, especially for estimates of up to one year. In some cases, more sophisticated methods do not sufficiently improve the accuracy of forecasts to justify their use—especially in light of their higher costs.

Moving Averages

In some cases, the major cause of variations among data used in making forecasts is randomness. Since managers do not make business decisions based on randomness that may never again happen, they attempt to remove the random effect by averaging or "smoothing" the data from specified time periods. One such approach to forecasting is the **moving average**, which is expressed mathematically as follows:

$$\text{Moving Average} = \frac{\text{Activity in Previous } n \text{ Periods}}{n}$$

where n is the number of periods in the moving average

This moving average method is illustrated using the contract foodservice operation at the Bank of Hospitality. Service Company, the contract feeding company, serves lunch five days per week at the Bank of Hospitality, and the manager needs to estimate sales for the thirteenth week. Exhibit 9.4 reveals weekly sales for weeks 1–12. Using a three-week moving average, the estimate for the number of meals to be served during the thirteenth week is 1,025, determined as follows:

$$\text{Three-Week Moving Average} = \frac{1,025 + 1,000 + 1,050}{3}$$

$$= \underline{1,025} \text{ meals}$$

Exhibit 9.4	Weekly Meals Served–Bank of Hospitality

Week	Actual Meals Served
1	1,000
2	900
3	950
4	1,050
5	1,025
6	1,000
7	975
8	1,000
9	950
10	1,025
11	1,000
12	1,050

As new weekly results become available, they are used in calculating the average by adding the most recent week and dropping the earliest week. In this way, the calculated average is a "moving" one because it is continually updated to include only the most recent observations for the specified number of time periods. For example, if 950 meals were served during week 13 at the Bank of Hospitality, then the forecast for week 14, using the three-week moving average, would be calculated as follows:

$$\text{Forecast for Week 14} = \frac{\text{Sum of Sales for Weeks 11–13}}{3}$$

$$= \frac{1{,}000 + 1{,}050 + 950}{3}$$

$$= \underline{\underline{1{,}000}} \text{ meals}$$

Alternatively, more weeks could be used to determine the weekly forecast. For example, a 12-week moving average to estimate meals to be sold during the thirteenth week results in a forecast of 994, determined as follows:

$$\text{Twelve-Week Moving Average} = \frac{\text{Actual Weekly Sales for Weeks 1–12}}{12}$$

$$= \frac{11{,}925}{12}$$

$$= 993.75, \text{rounded to } \underline{994}$$

It should be noted that the more periods averaged, the less effect the random variations will have on the forecast. This can be seen in the above illustration. The three-week moving average forecast for week 13 was 1,025 meals, compared to the 12-week moving average forecast of 994. In this case, since the actual sales during the thirteenth week turned out to be 950 meals, the 12-week moving average forecast of 994 was more accurate than the forecast based on only three weeks. The increased accuracy is due to minimizing the effect of random variations by using data covering a greater number of time periods.

Although the moving average approach to forecasting is often considered to be more accurate and reliable than the naïve methods, there are some disadvantages associated with this approach. One limitation is the need to store and continually update the historical data covering the most recent number of time periods used in calculating the moving average. This requirement would be quite costly for a large retail business, such as Walmart, which would have to keep track of sales data for a large number of different items. However, in the hospitality industry, the cost of storing and maintaining historical data for moving average forecasts is not unreasonable, since hotels and restaurants sell a comparatively small number of different items.

A more serious limitation is that the moving average method gives equal weight to each of the observations gathered over the specified number of time periods. Many managers would agree that the data from the most recent time periods contain more information about what will happen in the future and, therefore, should be given more weight than the older observations that are calculated into the moving average. The exponential smoothing approach to forecasting not only satisfies this concern by counting recent data more heavily than older data, but also eliminates the need for storing all of the historical data covering the specified time period.

Exponential Smoothing

A **smoothing constant** is a value used in the exponential smoothing forecasting method. It is determined by using forecasts from two consecutive previous periods and the actual demand from the earlier of these two periods. In other words, **exponential smoothing** is a forecasting method that uses this smoothing constant and recent actual and forecasted activity to estimate future activity.

This approach has widespread appeal among business forecasters. It essentially says, "If the forecast for a particular period was too high, reduce it for the next period; if it was too low, raise it." A major benefit of this approach is that data for only two prior periods need to be retained, as the calculation of the smoothing constant is based on these limited data.

When the exponential smoothing method is used, the hospitality manager requires only two types of readily available data:

1. The forecasts from the two previous periods

2. The actual activity during the earlier of the two previous periods

These data are used to determine the smoothing constant as follows:

$$\frac{\text{Smoothing}}{\text{Constant}} = \frac{\text{Period 2 Forecast} - \text{Period 1 Forecast}}{\text{Period 1 Actual Demand} - \text{Period 1 Forecast}}$$

For example, consider an elementary school foodservice that uses exponential smoothing. Its period 1 forecast and actual demand were 200 and 220, respectively. The period 2 forecast was 210. The smoothing constant is 0.5, determined as follows:

$$x = \frac{210 - 200}{220 - 200}$$
$$= \underline{0.5}$$

The smoothing constant requires the manager to identify what is a good response rate. The smoothing constant should be small if sales have been relatively stable in the past, and large if the product/service is experiencing rapid growth.

Once the smoothing constant has been determined, it can be inserted into the general formula for exponential smoothing, which is as follows:

$$\frac{\text{New}}{\text{Forecast}} = \frac{\text{Past}}{\text{Forecast}} + \frac{\text{Smoothing}}{\text{Constant}} \times \left(\frac{\text{Actual}}{\text{Demand}} - \frac{\text{Past}}{\text{Forecast}} \right)$$

Using the previous illustration with the Bank of Hospitality, the weekly sales will be projected for week 13 using the exponential smoothing method of forecasting. Assume that the forecasted sales for week 12 were 1,020 and that 0.1 is the smoothing constant. The forecasted sales for week 13 of 1,023 meals is determined as follows:

$$\frac{\text{Week 13}}{\text{Forecast}} = \frac{\text{Week 12}}{\text{Forecast}} + 0.1 \text{ (Week 12 Actual Sales} - \text{Week 12 Forecast)}$$
$$= 1,020 + 0.1 \text{ (1,050} - 1,020)$$
$$= \underline{1,023} \text{ meals}$$

The exponential smoothing method presented in this chapter is only one of several such approaches.[3] Exponential smoothing techniques are most useful when only short-term forecasts are required, and when reasonably accurate—rather than precise—forecasts are acceptable.

Causal Forecasting Approaches

Causal forecasting approaches include both single and multiple regression as well as econometric models. In this chapter, we will discuss only single regression analysis.

Regression analysis involves estimating an activity on the basis of other activities or factors that are assumed to be causes or highly reliable indicators of the activity. The activity to be forecasted (such as food sales) is the dependent, unknown variable, while the basis on which the forecast is made (such as room sales and/or advertising expenses) is the independent, known variable. Regression analysis is used to predict the dependent variable given the value of the independent variable.

The level of demand to be estimated is thought to depend on, or be closely related to, the independent variable. In order to forecast the operation's demand, the closeness of the variables needs to be determined. For example, how closely related are a lodging property's rooms sales to food sales in its restaurant operation? Two measures of closeness are the coefficient of correlation and the coefficient of determination. The **coefficient of correlation** is the measure of the relationship between the dependent and independent variables, such as food sales and rooms sales. The formula for determining the coefficient of correlation is as follows:

$$r = \frac{n\Sigma xy - \Sigma x \Sigma y}{\sqrt{[n\Sigma x^2 - (\Sigma x)^2][n\Sigma y^2 - (\Sigma y)^2]}}$$

where x is the independent variable
           y is the dependent variable
           n is the number of observations
           r is a positive relationship value[4] between 0 and 1

The closer the r value is to 1, the stronger the relationship between the dependent and independent variables being measured.

The square of the coefficient of correlation (r^2) is the **coefficient of determination**. This measure reflects the extent to which the change in the independent variable explains the change in the dependent variable.

Regression analysis is illustrated using data from the Forest Hotel. Exhibit 9.5 contains the number of room guests and meals served in the dining room for 20X1. Using this data, we can develop a regression equation that will allow us to forecast meals to be served based on our knowledge of the number of hotel guests. The regression formula is as follows:

$$y = a + bx$$

where y = Meals served
           a = Meals served to nonhotel registrants
           b = Average number of meals served to each hotel guest
           x = Number of hotel room guests

Given the data in Exhibit 9.5 and using formulas[5] and a computer spreadsheet program to determine a and b, the regression equation becomes:

$$y = 370 + 1.254(x)$$

This equation indicates that 370 people not registered as guests at the Forest Hotel dine there monthly and, further, that each registered room guest eats 1.254 meals at the hotel each day.

Assuming that the sales forecast for January 20X2, is 3,000 rooms at an average occupancy per room of 1.5 people, the projected meals to be sold is determined as follows:

Forecasted Meals Sold = 370 + 1.254(3,000)(1.5)

                        = 370 + 5,643

                        = 6,013

Exhibit 9.5   Room Guests and Meals Served

	x Room Guests	y Meals Served
January	4,060	5,200
February	4,100	5,360
March	4,200	5,720
April	4,250	5,430
May	4,200	5,680
June	4,150	5,520
July	4,300	5,800
August	4,350	5,910
September	4,400	6,020
October	4,200	5,840
November	4,080	5,510
December	3,600	5,020

The forecasted 6,013 meals to be sold during the first week of January 20X2, includes 370 meals for diners not registered as guests and 5,643 meals for hotel guests.

The coefficient of correlation (r) measures the relationship between hotel room guests and meals served. The r value for the above example is 0.8568, which suggests a strong relationship between the two variables. The coefficient of determination (r^2) for this example is 0.7341, which means that 73.41 percent of the change in meals served is explained by the change in hotel room guests.

Regression analysis forecasting used when two or more independent variables are related to the dependent variable is called **multiple regression analysis**. For example, the manager of the food and beverage department at a lodging operation may desire to forecast food sales on the basis of the number of room guests *and* advertising expenditures. Although multiple regression analysis is both interesting and challenging, it is beyond the scope of this chapter.[6]

The usefulness of these regression analysis techniques is a function of satisfactory dependent and independent variables. That is, the higher the correlation of the dependent and independent variables, the greater the probability regression analysis will yield meaningful forecasts.

Limitations of Quantitative Forecasting Methods

Although time series forecasting and causal forecasting can be quite useful, they have limitations. First, they are virtually useless when data is scarce, such as at the opening of a new hotel, restaurant, or club. In these instances, there is no sales history for the newly opened facility from which to collect the data needed to forecast demand. Second, they assume that historical trends will continue into the future and are unable to consider unforeseeable occurrences, such as wars or acts of terrorism, and their impact on lodging properties.

Qualitative Forecasting Techniques

When the limitations of quantitative approaches significantly affect a hospitality operation, qualitative forecasting methods are useful. These methods emphasize human judgment. Information is gathered in as logical, unbiased, and systematic a way as possible, and then judgment is brought to bear on the activity being forecasted. Qualitative forecasting methods include market research, jury of executive opinion, sales force estimates, and the Delphi method.

The market research method involves systematically gathering, recording, and analyzing data related to a hospitality operation's marketing of products and services. Large hotel chains generally conduct extensive market research before opening a new property to determine whether there is adequate demand. This market research provides data that can then be used in preparing formal sales forecasts.

The jury of executive opinion technique uses key financial, marketing, and operations executives to estimate sales for the forecast period. Generally, the person using this technique will provide the executives with expected economic conditions and changes in the establishment's services. The executives will then independently make their sales forecasts. The person using this technique will then reconcile differences among the executives' opinions.

The sales force estimates technique is similar to the jury of executive opinion in that opinions of corporate personnel are obtained. However, in this case, the input is from lower-echelon personnel who estimate their next year's sales. This approach is sometimes used by multiunit foodservice operations. Unit managers are polled, and their immediate superiors review and discuss these estimates with each unit manager. Then, the separate sales estimates are combined to create a sales forecast for the foodservice operation.

The Delphi method is used for making forecasts that are generally very futuristic in nature—for example, forecasting expected changes in international travel for the coming decade. This technique involves obtaining opinions from a group of experts to achieve consensus on future events that might affect an operation's markets. Rather than meeting together at one place, the group interacts anonymously. Questionnaires are often used. The responses are then analyzed and resubmitted to the experts for a second round of opinions. This process may continue for several rounds until the researcher is satisfied that consensus regarding the forecast has been achieved.

9.7 SELECTION OF A FORECASTING METHOD

The specific forecasting method that a hospitality operation adopts will depend on several factors. The two most important are the method's effectiveness in providing usable projections from available data and the cost of using the method. Different methods will be used for different purposes as suggested throughout this chapter. Small establishments lacking personnel with forecasting skills will probably adopt the less sophisticated, but still highly useful, naïve methods. On the other hand, large establishments may find the more sophisticated methods to be the most effective. Although these approaches may appear costlier, they may actually be less costly in the long run for large establishments.

In addition to the effectiveness and cost of different forecasting methods, other relevant factors include the following:

- Frequency with which forecasts will be updated
- Turnaround required for an updated forecast
- Size and complexity of the hospitality operation
- Forecasting skills of personnel involved in making forecasts
- Purposes for which the forecasts are made

9.8 SHORT-TERM FORECASTS IN THE LODGING INDUSTRY

Exhibit 9.6 is a survey summary of lodging industry short-term sales forecasting approaches by three profit centers: rooms, food (restaurants), and catering (banquets). Short-term forecasts in this research refer to forecasts covering from three to 10 days.

The major purpose of each short-term forecast is to allow for staffing and, in food and catering, for ordering the food supplies to service the dining guests. A distant last purpose is the motivation of personnel (i.e., using the short-term sales forecast as a target).

The methods used by the majority of respondents differ by profit center. Most hotels, especially those with reservation systems, forecast room sales using the rooms reservations at the time of the forecast plus an estimate for walk-ins. For example, a hotel may show 100 rooms reserved for the following Monday and add the average of walk-ins (say, 15) for the past four Mondays to equal a

Exhibit 9.6	Summary of Lodging Industry Short-Term Sales Forecasting Approaches by Three Profit Centers		
	Rooms	Food	Catering
Major purposes of forecast:	Staffing (98%) Motivating personnel (25%)	Staffing (100%) Order food (72%) Motivating personnel (19%)	Staffing (82%) Order food (72%) Motivating personnel (16%)
Methodology:	Room reservations plus estimated walk-ins (93%)	Prior period sales adjusted based on intuition (46%)	Booked catered events plus estimate of additional sales (90%)
	Prior period sales adjusted based on intuition (7%)	Meal reservations and estimate for walk-ins (28%) Capture ratios related to the rooms forecast (26%)	Prior period sales adjusted based on intuition (10%)
Expression of short-term forecast:	Daily number of rooms sold (80%)	Total covers (79%)	Total sales dollars (70%)
	Daily sales dollars (55%)	Total sales dollars (61%)	Total covers (67%)
	Daily number of rooms by type (35%)	Food covers by meal period (60%)	Sales dollars by catered event (47%)
	Daily sales dollars by type of room (20%)	Sales dollars by meal period (44%)	Covers by catered event (47%)

rooms sales forecast of 115 rooms. In this example, the short-term forecast is a combination of known sales plus a four-week moving average for the walk-ins.

A second approach is adjusting the prior period's sales based on intuitive expectations for the forecast period. Only seven percent of the lodging establishments reported using this approach, and the majority of these users (60 percent) were establishments with fewer than 150 rooms.

The most common approach used to forecast short-term food sales by hoteliers (46 percent) is using the prior period's sales figure and adjusting it for expected differences for the forecast period. For example, if 100 customers were served at the prior Monday evening dinner, the hotel's forecast for the coming Monday evening would be 100 plus or minus an adjustment for expected differences. These differences could be based on house guests, local events, weather forecasts, and other similar activities.

Twenty-eight percent of the hotels rely in part on meal reservations and estimated walk-ins, while 26 percent use **capture ratios**—that is, ratios based on hotel guests or some variation of hotel guests. For example, a hotel might estimate its dinner customers to be 40 plus one-quarter of the estimated house guests for the night. If the estimated house guests total 200, then the dinner customers forecasted equal 90, determined as follows:

$$\text{Forecasted dinner customers} = a + bx$$

where a = estimated customers for walk-ins (non-hotel guests)

b = percentage of hotel guests expected to eat dinner

x = hotel guest count for evening

$$\text{Forecasted dinner customers} = 40 + 0.25(200)$$
$$= \underline{\underline{90}}$$

The sales forecasting methods reported for catered events include two alternatives:

■ Ninety percent use the booked catered events plus an estimate for additional sales not booked when the forecast is made.

■ Ten percent use prior period catered sales adjusted for expected differences.

As Exhibit 9.6 shows, the short-term sales forecast is expressed in a variety of ways. For rooms, the most common way is rooms sold (80 percent); for food sales, the most common is total customers (79 percent); and for catering sales, the most common is the total forecasted catering sales dollars (70 percent), followed closely by total customers (67 percent). Many hotels express the sales forecasts in more than one way.

Most hoteliers compare their actual results to their short-term sales forecasts in order to determine their forecasting accuracy, so that in the future they can refine their forecasting method and allow for forecasting error in staffing and ordering supplies.

Exhibit 9.7 contains a summary of the accuracy of the short-term sales forecasts for rooms, food, beverage, and catering activities. The rooms and catering sales forecasting appear to be the most accurate, as 40 percent and 42 percent respectively are accurate to within plus or minus two percent or less, compared with 27 percent for restaurant food forecasts and 24 percent for beverage sales forecasts. At the other extreme, only seven percent of the hotels report their actual rooms sold differs by greater than five percent from their sales forecast, compared with 37 percent, 28 percent, and 40 percent for restaurant food, catering, and beverage forecasts, respectively. These results, especially in the restaurant food and beverage areas, clearly suggest that there is room for improvement.

Exhibit 9.7 | Accuracy of Short-Term Sales Forecasts

Degree of Accuracy of Short-Term Sales Forecast:*

	Rooms	Restaurant Food	Beverage	Catering
No difference	2%	1%	0%	5%
± 1.0% or less	20	12	8	15
± 1.1% –2%	18	14	16	22
± 2.1% –3%	17	18	18	13
± 3.1% –5%	36	18	18	17
± >5%	7	37	40	28
Total	100%	100%	100%	100%

*Based on the percentage difference between the short-term sales forecast and the actual sales.

9.9 FORECASTING METHODS IN THE CLUB INDUSTRY

Club executives were surveyed regarding the approaches they use to forecast the various major sales of their clubs (in particular, dining room, banquets, beverages, golf course, and tennis). Seven forecasting techniques were provided to potential respondents, as shown in Exhibit 9.8. The techniques listed in Exhibit 9.8 are abbreviated in the matrix shown in Exhibit 9.9.

Across all sales areas, "last year's actual revenues adjusted subjectively" is the most commonly used technique. Approximately 40 percent of clubs use this technique for the various sales areas. Just over 46 percent of the clubs use it to forecast tennis revenues, while 37 percent use it to forecast banquet food sales. The second most common choice for forecasting banquet food revenues is advanced bookings. Last year's actuals were used by nearly one of every four clubs for forecasting tennis revenues and by nearly one of every five clubs for forecasting golf revenues. Other techniques for other sales areas were used by less than 15 percent of the respondents.

The next two most common approaches across all sales areas clearly appear to be the prior year's budgeted dollar amounts multiplied by 1 plus x percent and the average of several past years' revenues multiplied by 1 plus x percent.

A review of techniques by size of club did not reveal any differences in forecasting techniques used. Each club differs, yet some common subjective adjustments most likely provide better forecasts than others. Though some techniques may appear to be more sophisticated than others, the best technique is the one that provides a forecast that is closest to the results that subsequently occur.

9.10 FORECASTING CASES

To illustrate forecasting in hospitality industry firms, three companies from different segments have contributed overviews of one facet of forecasting at their companies. The first case illustration from Oberoi Holdings, a Wendy's franchisee, serves as an example of an entrepreneurial enterprise and focuses on labor forecasting, from using a simple spreadsheet to two third-party back-office

Exhibit 9.8 **Seven Forecasting Techniques**

Technique	Example
1. Prior year's budgeted dollar amounts multiplied by 1 + x percent	Green fees for March 20X1 were budgeted at $10,000. The budget for green fees for March 20X2 is set at a 10 percent increase. The budgeted amount is $11,000 ($10,000 + 0.10 x $10,000 = $11,000).
2. Number of members by expected spending per member	A club's 1,000 members spent an average of $25.00 each for lunches during January 20X1. The expected spending by members in January of 20X2, on average, is $27.50 and membership has stabilized at 1,000. Therefore, luncheon sales for January 20X2 is budgeted to be $27,500 (1,000 x $27.50 = $27,500).
3. Expected units to be sold multiplied by expected selling price	A club budgets its dinner sales based on the forecasted number of customers and expected average dinner prices. The number of customers and the average dinner price during January 20X1 were 3,000 and $15.00, respectively. The forecast for January 20X2 is $49,600, based on 3,100 forecasted customers and an average expected selling price of $16.00.
4. Change in advance bookings from prior year	A club's advance banquet bookings in November 20X0 for January 20X1 totaled 20 events at an average of $5,000 per event, The club's advance bookings in November 20X1 for January 20X2 (when the 20X2 budget is being prepared) total 25 events; the average expected sales per booking is $5,500. Therefore, the banquet food sales are forecasted to be $137,500 (25 x $5,500 = $137,500).
5. Last year's actual revenues	A club's green fees for May 20X1 were $15,000. The same figure is used as the forecast for May 20X2, since green fees have not changed and the membership is stable at 400 golf members.
6. Last year's actual revenues are adjusted subjectively	A club's 20X1 tennis revenues were $5,000 during May. The forecast for May 20X2 is $6,000, based on the tennis pro's subjective consideration of expected participation, weather conditions, and anticipated changes in tennis fees.
7. Average of several past year's revenues multiplied by 1 + x percent	A club's beverage sales for the past three Aprils—20X1, 20X2, and 20X3—have been $16,000, $13,000, and $16,000, respectively. The average is $15,000. The manager forecasts the beverage sales to be $16,500 for April 20X4 based on the three-month average, plus a 10 percent increase ($15,000 + $15,000 × 0.1 = $16,500).

Exhibit 9.9   Forecasting Techniques Matrix

Forecasting Technique	Sales Areas (%)				
	Dining Room	Banquet	Beverage	Golf Course	Tennis
(1) Prior budget × (1 + x percent)	3.8%	9.3%	12.4%	4.5%	13.9%
(2) Number of members × expected spending per member	11.0	3.1	6.7	7.2	6.2
(3) Units × selling price	6.4	3.1	6.7	3.6	3.1
(4) Advanced bookings	0.9	29.9	3.8	2.4	1.5
(5) Last year's actuals	7.3	6.2	10.5	18.1	24.6
(6) Last year's actuals, adjusted subjectively	45.0	37.0	43.7	42.1	46.1
(7) Average of past years × (1 + x percent)	13.8	9.3	13.3	12.1	4.6
(8) Other	1.8	2.1	2.9	0.0	0.0
TOTAL	100.0%	100.0%	100.0%	100.0%	100.0%
Number of respondents	109	97	105	83	65

solutions. The second case, from Aramark, provides an example on the business and industry segment of the hospitality industry, focuses on daily to monthly, and, finally, annual forecasting at the unit level. A brief description of the calculation of the sales dollars is included. Finally, the Hilton Worldwide Holding Inc.'s illustration focuses on the forecast for the annual budget. Several forms used in this process are shown. The three cases cover three segments of the hospitality industry and three time periods—weekly, monthly, and annual. They are just a sampling of budgeting practices in hospitality corporations.

Wendy's—Labor Forecasting: A Franchisee's Perspective

With more than 6,500 outlets worldwide, Wendy's owns a number of its restaurants, but the vast majority are franchised operations. Franchisees follow Wendy's guidelines and make appropriate decisions to manage and grow the business. Ricki Oberoi, president of Oberoi Holdings, opened his first Wendy's restaurant in 1996. In 2021, with 27 Wendy's operations spread over five districts that employ over 800 hourly employees and managers, labor forecasting is an important element of his business. It is through diligent forecasting, time management, reforecasting, and controls that Oberoi is able to achieve labor costs below 25 percent consistently and become a successful entrepreneur.

A franchisee is able to select their own third-party back-office solution to assist in labor forecasting. When Oberoi was operating his first Wendy's in 1996, he and his director of operations, Edith Hernandez, used a simple spreadsheet to forecast its labor needs by using historical sales figures and hours worked by management and hourly staff to come up with a labor guide for various sales levels. When daily sales are projected, the required labor hours will be filled in. To assess the results, the actual hours used would be entered at the end of the day to calculate any variances to aid future decisions. Exhibit 9.10 shows three tables. Table 1 has the names of the morning and afternoon/evening managers scheduled for each day, then, the crew hours, shift hours (hourly management), and salary hours are entered to derive the total hours. The net sales figures are then divided by the total hours worked to calculate a dollar cost average. With this information over a period of time, a labor guide is then established, in Table 2, with the projected

Exhibit 9.10   Wendy's Labor Forecasting

Table 1

Store #

Week Ending

Day	AM Manager	PM Manager	Crew Hours	Shift Hours	Salary Hours	Total	Net Sales	Dollar Cost Average
Monday								
Tuesday								
Wednesday								
Thursday								
Friday								
Saturday								
Sunday								

Table 2

Sales	Hours/day Average	$/Man Hour	Weekly Total
$ 18,000	85	$ 30	595
$ 20,000	92	$ 31	644
$ 22,000	94	$ 33	658
$ 24,000	100	$ 34	700
$ 25,000	105	$ 35	735
$ 26,000	105	$ 35	735
$ 27,000	105	$ 36	735
$ 28,000	108	$ 36	756
$ 30,000	108	$ 38	756
$ 32,000	115	$ 40	805
$ 34,000	115	$ 42	805
$ 36,000	115	$ 45	805
$ 40,000	120	$ 48	840

Table 3

Day	Projected Sales	Required Man Hour	Hour Used	Variance
Monday				
Tuesday				
Wednesday				
Thursday				
Friday				
Saturday				
Sunday				
TOTAL				

Courtesy of Oberoi Holdings

sales levels and the corresponding hours/day average, $/man hour, and weekly totals (hours/day average multiplied by $/man hour). This guide is then used to populate the weekly labor needs, in Table 3. When the projected sales are entered for each day, then the required man hours can be entered. At the end of the day, the actual hours used are also recorded to calculate a variance.

However, as the franchise grew from one restaurant to 27, and with technological advances in the past two decades, labor forecasting has become a science. Now, Oberoi and his management team use two third-party back-office solution systems to forecast and schedule his 800 plus employees. Both back-office solutions have the Wendy's labor guide built into their systems, and management is also allowed to adjust the results. First, a sales forecast is developed to help drive the daily food and labor needs to maximize profitability. Each week, prior to finalizing a schedule, management reviews and adjusts each day's forecast by considering events, holidays, and promotions. In addition, on a daily basis, management will consider the weather or sales trends over the past few days to amend any labor needs. And, where applicable, management is also encouraged to evaluate and tweak an evening's forecast prior to the afternoon re-prep to further fine-tune food and labor needs. Exhibit 9.11 is a daily schedule where employees' names and work time and total hours will be posted.

Exhibit 9.11 Wendy's Daily Schedule

Daily Summary: 4/19/22

Projected Sales	4480	Guide	109	Schedule Dollars	1157	
Net Hours	111	Variance	2	Schedule Percent	25.81%	

Daily Schedule 4/19/22

Employees	Time	Hours	5am	6am	7am	8am	9am	10am	11am	12pm	1pm	2pm	3pm	4pm	5pm	6pm	7pm	8om	9pm	10pm	11pm	12am
Manny	6am-4pm	10		■	■	■	■	■	■	■	■	■	■									
Susan	9am-5pm	8					■	■	■	■	■	■	■	■								
Tommy	11am-5pm	6							■	■	■	■	■	■								
Juana	5:30am - 2pm	8.5	■	■	■	■	■	■	■	■	■											
Alfred	4pm-12:30am	8.5												■	■	■	■	■	■	■	■	■
Marcella	6am-3pm	9		■	■	■	■	■	■	■	■	■										
Carlos	11am-4pm	5							■	■	■	■	■									
Matteo	11am-6pm	7							■	■	■	■	■	■	■							
Tasha	5:30am-3pm	9.5	■	■	■	■	■	■	■	■	■	■										
Mohammad	4pm-10pm	6												■	■	■	■	■	■			
Luke	6pm-12:30am	6.5														■	■	■	■	■	■	■
John	5pm-10pm	5													■	■	■	■	■			
Leonard	4pm-12:30am	8.5												■	■	■	■	■	■	■	■	■
Martha	4pm- 10pm	6												■	■	■	■	■	■			
George	5pm-12:30am	7.5													■	■	■	■	■	■	■	■

Daily Data 4/19/22

To further consider the proper labor needs of not just one restaurant, but that of a district, Exhibit 9.12 shows an example of a district labor analysis. The crew hours, hourly management, and salary management hours are totaled, which are then compared to the labor guide from Wendy's to determine the guide variance. The scheduled hours are also listed as a comparison. The "crew $" is then divided by the sales of the day to obtain the "crew %," and also divided by the crew hours to obtain the crew average. The same processes are carried out for hourly management and salary management. Then, all the dollar amounts of the three categories are totaled and divided by the sales of the day to derive the total labor percentage per store. The column totals are then also calculated to obtain the results for the district. As districts are from different locations, the wages from each district may differ. Therefore, an analysis of labor comparison across districts, especially if the districts are from different states, should be performed with considerations, and wages and labor law may differ. Finally, crew OT and hourly management OT are recorded, as overtime can be detrimental to the labor cost and thus the profit; and this is one of the main reasons why labor forecasting is important.

Aramark—Forecasting by Directors of Foodservice

Aramark is a leading competitor in the contract foodservice segment of the hospitality industry, with its core market in the United States, supplemented by an additional eighteen-country footprint, employing approximately 247,000 associates. Aramark provides foodservice to many segments of the hospitality industry, including school and colleges, hospitals, correctional institutions, sports and entertainment facilities, and business and industry locations.

Aramark's higher education unit provides foodservice to private and public higher education institutions and uses a 4-4-5 cycle of 13 weeks per quarter to forecast. A monthly forecast for each month of the fiscal year is prepared for each operating account by the director of foodservice (DFS), using a third-party

Exhibit 9.12 **Wendy's District Labor Analysis**

Store ID	Crew Hours	Hourly Mgmt Hours	Mgmt Hours	Total Hours	Labor Guide	Guide Variance	Scheduled Hours	Crew $	Crew %	Crew Average	Hourly Mgmt $	Hourly Mgmt %	Mgmt Average	Mgmt $	Mgmt %	Total Labor $	Total Labor %	Crew OT	Hourly Mgmt OT	Total OT Hours
1005																				
1010																				
1018																				
1027																				
DISTRICT "A" TOTAL																				

Courtesy of Oberoi Holdings

product that provides infrastructure and applications capabilities. Historical data form the basis of the forecast and is composed of:

- Sales (number of customers, participation rate and declining balances of meal plans, sales by meal period, menu offerings)
- Food cost
- Labor cost
- Direct expenses

The historical data for each of the above categories are then adjusted by the DFS of the unit for known changes that will affect the next fiscal year. Sales are adjusted for selling price increases and changes in customer count and participation, as well as menu programs that will increase average check size. Food cost is adjusted for anticipated cost increases, menu changes, and food cost ratios. Labor is adjusted by the change in hours needed for each fiscal period and changes in anticipated wages and tax rates. Prior to the completion of the process, the DFS reviews the forecast with regional management to obtain confirmation of the assumptions and financial data used to develop the forecast. A summary forecast and a detailed forecast are compared to the actual results generated each month, and if an account has variances to forecast, appropriate action is taken by the DFS to correct the variances. These could include menu adjustments, selected price changes, and staffing adjustments. Key performance indicators such as total sales, total product cost, total labor cost, total direct expense, profit, and profit margin are also reviewed.

Exhibits 9.13 and 9.14 show two examples of forecasting forms used in a higher education Aramark account. Although this account is part of Aramark's higher education portfolio, it is also a hotel on campus rather than a regular university dining facility that only uses meal cards. Therefore, it has two forecasting components: (1) retail, which is the forecast of the restaurant in the hotel, and (2) catering, which is the forecast of the banquet operation. For the restaurant, the service days are first entered into a module in this third-party platform, where they are then pulled into a second module (Exhibit 9.13) to fill in the service days per week. If meal plans are accepted in this restaurant, the sales and the meal card swipes would then be entered to compute for the average check and also the subtotal of retail sales for food.

In the second section, the guest count (transactions per day) will be entered to be multiplied by number of service days pulled from the service day module to obtain the retail transactions. A forecasted average check amount will be entered for the module to calculate the total retail sales. At such time, the DFS

Exhibit 9.13 Forecast for Retail Sales

Years	Scenario	Entity
FY22	Forecast	ABC University - Restaurant

Forecast

	Weeks Total	Sept Week 1	Sept Week 2	Sept Week 3	Sept Week 4	Sept Week Total	Oct Week 1	Oct Week 2	Oct Week 3	Oct Week 4	Oct Week Total	Nov Week 1	Nov Week 2	Nov Week 3	Nov Week 4	Nov Week 5	Nov Week Total
Service Days																	
RETAIL SALES - MEALS/CASH EQUIVALENCY:																	
Daily Retail Meal Swipes																	
Meal Swipes																	
Avg Check (Retail value)																	
Retail Sales - Food																	
RETAIL SALES - CASH/CREDIT/DB:																	
Transactions Per Day																	
Retail Transactions																	
Avg Check																	
Retail Sales - (Calc)																	
TOTAL RETAIL SALES:																	
Total Transactions																	
Retail Sales - Food Total (Calc)																	

Courtesy of ARAMARK

Exhibit 9.14 Forecast of Catering Sales

Years	Scenario	Entity
FY22	Forecast	ABC University - Banquets

Forecast

		Forecast FY22 Year Total	Sept	Oct	Nov	Dec	Jan	Feb	Mar	Apr	May	Jun	Jul	Aug
CATERING														
RETAIL SALES - CATERING FOOD AND BEVERAGE	Catering													
	Concessions													
	Camps													
	Conferences													
OTHER SALES														
Sales-Other	Other													
Retail Transactions														

Courtesy of ARAMARK

will use these historical data to make adjustments for holidays and events such as graduation, sports, special events at the university, and big conferences booked with the hotel that do not have food included in the contact. The DFS will also assess events booked by repeat clients and whether their spending pattern will stay the same, increase, or decrease.

For catering, or banquets, the DFS will also start with historical data and functions already booked; then again, the director will look for the spending patterns of repeat clients to forecast the amount they may spend in addition to the contract booking. Catering is mostly done weekly, then rolled up to a monthly figure and totaled to an annual amount. The DFS will then meet with the general manager of the hotel to discuss the feasibility of the figures. Should the hotel desire an increase in catering sales, the director of sales will be brought in to discuss the details and what the sales team needs to do to drive the revenue to meet budget. Exhibit 9.14 shows the monthly summary page for catering, and divides it further into catering, concessions, camps, conferences, and other sales where applicable.

When the entire forecast is complete, the DFS will submit the result to the corporate office, where the forecast may be revised. If so, such revision is normally done on a semester basis, as this is a higher education account. For example, the summer months will normally be slower than the fall and spring semesters, and the budget should reflect these peak times. If major events, weather, school closures, and other factors affect university operations, or new functions are booked, the forecast will be adjusted.

Forecasting at Hilton Worldwide

Hilton Worldwide is one of the world's largest lodging companies. With over 6,500 properties representing over 1 million rooms in 119 countries and territories, Hilton has some of the world's most well-known hotels, including The Waldorf Astoria New York, Hilton Hawaiian Village Beach Resort and Spa, and the Palmer House Hilton. Hilton has 18 brands, ranging from its midscale brand Tru to its luxury Conrad Hotels and Waldorf Astoria Hotels & Resorts.

The annual forecast at each property begins in mid-summer and is completed in September. Several steps are taken at the property level to arrive at the forecast, which is prepared in conjunction with Hilton's business plan for the year.

Exhibit 9.15 is a monthly forecast for a full-service Hilton property, which also compares that particular forecasted period to a prior period and to the budget. Statistics, including occupancy (percentage), average (room) rate, RevPAR, gross operating profit per available room (GOPAR), and total cost per occupied room (TCOP) are shown at the top of the exhibit. In addition, key metrics, such as food cost margin, beverage cost margin, food revenue, beverage revenue, undistributed payroll cost, total customers, and average checks, are included to provide owners and management with a dashboard of important indicators. The forecast starts with comparing the numbers for the current period (Fcst 11+1) to the prior period (Fcst 10+2) in the first two columns to derive the differences in numbers and percentages in the third column (Fcst vs. Fcst 10+2). Then, the budget is shown in the fourth column to calculate the difference between the forecast and budget (fifth column—Fcst vs. Bud Owner Version). Finally, when the actual figures materialize, they will replace the current forecasted numbers in the "Act. Working" column to then calculate the difference between the forecasted and actual numbers and percentages.

Exhibit 9.15   Forecasting at Hilton

	Act FY-2		Fcst FY-1		Fcst vs Fcst FY-2			Bud Owner Version		Fcst vs Bud Owner Version			Act Wrkng		Fcst vs Act Wrkng	
	FY-2	%Rev	FY-1	%Rev	B/(W) FY-1 vs FY-2	%B/(W)	%Rev	FY-1	%Rev	B/(W) FY-1 vs FY-1	%B/(W)	%Rev	FY-1 Wrkng	%Rev	B/(W) FY-1 vs FY-1	%B/(W)
% Occupancy	73.1%		69.7%		3.4 pts		4.9%	71.3%		1.7 pts	2.4%		73.1%		0.0 pts	0.0%
ADR	184.2		181.8		2.4	1.3%		183.8		0.4	0.2%		184.2		0.0	0.0%
RevPAR	134.6		126.7		8.0	6.3%		131.1		3.5	2.7%		134.6		0.0	0.0%
GOPAR	66.9		60.7		6.2	10.2%		60.1		6.7	11.2%		66.9		0.0	0.0%
Total CPOR	240.5		235.8		(4.7)	(2.0%)		239.4		(1.1)	(0.5%)		240.5		0.0	0.0%
Trans Revenue	1,005,027	31.6%	1,119,611	37.7%	(114,584)	(10.2%)	38.1%	1,161,864		(156,838)	(13.5%)	31.6%	1,005,027	31.6%	0	0.0%
Group Revenue	634,380	20.0%	406,708	13.7%	227,672	56.0%	14.0%	425,708	49.0%	208,672	49.0%	20.0%	634,380	20.0%	0	0.0%
Permanent	181,780	5.7%	177,636	6.0%	4,144	2.3%	5.8%	177,780	5.8%	4,000	2.2%	5.7%	181,780	5.7%	0	0.0%
Other Operating Revenue	28,406	0.9%	36,288	1.2%	(7,883)	(21.7%)	1.2%	36,288	1.2%	(7,882)	(21.7%)	0.9%	28,406	0.9%	0	0.0%
Total Rooms Revenue	1,849,592	58.2%	1,740,243	58.7%	109,349	6.3%	59.1%	1,801,640	59.1%	47,952	2.7%	58.2%	1,849,592	58.2%	0	0.0%
Outlet (Dept) Operating Revenue	315,644	9.9%	284,733	9.6%	30,912	10.9%	9.2%	279,609	9.2%	36,036	12.9%	9.9%	315,644	9.9%	0	0.0%
Catering Operating Revenue - Local	548,853	17.3%	516,317	17.4%	32,537	6.3%	15.3%	467,641	15.3%	81,212	17.4%	17.3%	548,853	17.3%	0	0.0%
Catering Operating Revenue - Group	415,148	13.1%	375,623	12.7%	39,525	10.5%	14.7%	448,948	14.7%	(33,800)	(7.5%)	13.1%	415,148	13.1%	0	0.0%
Catering Operating Revenue - No Product	0	0.0%	0	0.0%			0.0%	0	0.0%	0		0.0%	0	0.0%	0	0.0%
Total Catering Operating Revenue	964,001	30.3%	891,939	30.1%	72,062	8.1%	30.1%	916,589	30.1%	47,412	5.2%	30.3%	964,001	30.3%	0	0.0%
Total FB Operating Revenue	1,279,645	40.2%	1,176,672	39.7%	102,973	8.8%	39.2%	1,196,198	39.2%	83,447	7.0%	40.2%	1,279,645	40.2%	0	0.0%
Total Other Operating Revenue	29,198	0.9%	27,399	0.9%	1,799	6.6%	0.9%	28,277	0.9%	921	3.3%	0.9%	29,198	0.9%	0	0.0%
Miscellaneous Income (D11500) Operating Revenue	21,315	0.7%	21,671	0.7%	(357)	(1.6%)	0.7%	21,918	0.7%	(604)	(2.8%)	0.7%	21,315	0.7%	0	0.0%
Operating Revenue	3,179,749	100.0%	2,965,985	100.0%	213,765	7.2%	100.0%	3,048,033	100.0%	131,716	4.3%	100.0%	3,179,749	100.0%	0	0.0%
Total Rooms Payroll, Taxes & Benefits	389,940	21.1%	375,497	21.6%	(14,443)	(3.6%)	22.6%	406,347	22.6%	16,407	4.0%	21.1%	389,940	21.1%	0	0.0%
Total Rooms Commissions/Fees/HHonors	36,374	2.0%	40,402	2.3%	4,028	10.0%	2.1%	38,634	2.1%	2,260	5.8%	2.0%	36,374	2.0%	0	0.0%
Total Rooms OthOpExp excl Comms/Fees/HH	159,976	8.6%	134,897	7.8%	(25,079)	(18.6%)	7.7%	139,067	7.7%	(20,909)	(15.0%)	8.6%	159,976	8.6%	0	0.0%
Total Rooms Operating Profit	1,263,302	68.3%	1,189,447	68.3%	73,855	6.2%	67.6%	1,217,592	67.6%	45,710	3.8%	68.3%	1,263,302	68.3%	0	0.0%
Rooms Margin Change/Flow - through					0.0 pts	67.5%				0.7 pts	95.3%				0.0 pts	
Total FB Payroll, Taxes & Benefits	660,534	51.6%	620,477	52.7%	(40,057)	(6.5%)	53.6%	641,127	53.6%	(19,406)	(3.0%)	51.6%	660,534	51.6%	0	0.0%
Total FB Cost of Sales	161,794	12.6%	146,299	12.4%	(15,495)	(10.6%)	13.1%	157,107	13.1%	(4,687)	(3.0%)	12.6%	161,794	12.6%	0	0.0%
Total FB Other Operating Expense	42,405	3.3%	49,471	4.2%	7,066	14.3%	4.0%	48,202	4.0%	5,796	12.0%	3.3%	42,405	3.3%	0	0.0%
Total FB Operating Profit	414,912	32.4%	360,425	30.6%	54,487	15.1%	29.2%	349,761	29.2%	65,150	18.6%	32.4%	414,912	32.4%	0	0.0%
F&B Margin/flow - through					1.8 pts	52.9%				3.2 pts	78.1%				0.0 pts	
Total Oth Op Payroll Taxes & Benefits	2,610	0.1%	1,847	0.1%	(763)	(41.3%)	0.1%	1,855	0.1%	(755)	(40.7%)	0.1%	2,610	0.1%	0	0.0%
Total Oth Op Other Operating Expense	2,822	0.1%	3,555	0.1%	734	20.6%	0.1%	4,337	0.1%	1,515	34.9%	0.1%	2,822	0.1%	0	0.0%
Total Operating Other Profit	13,852	0.4%	11,427	0.4%	2,425	21.2%	0.4%	11,262	0.4%	2,590	23.0%	0.4%	13,852	0.4%	0	0.0%
Miscellaneous Income (D11500) Operating Profit	21,315	0.7%	21,671	0.7%	(357)	(1.6%)	0.7%	21,918	0.7%	(439)	(2.8%)	0.7%	21,315	0.7%	0	0.0%
Total Operating Department Profit	1,713,380	53.9%	1,582,970	53.4%	130,410	8.2%	52.5%	1,600,533	52.5%	112,846	7.1%	53.9%	1,713,380	53.9%	0	0.0%
Operating Margin Change/Flow - through					0.5 pts	61.0%				1.4 pts	85.7%				0.0 pts	
A&G (less CC, Prog Fees)	166,957	5.3%	170,015	5.7%	3,058	1.8%	5.2%	159,853	5.2%	(7,105)	(4.4%)	5.3%	166,957	5.3%	0	0.0%
CC Commissions	83,640	2.6%	72,969	2.5%	(10,671)	(14.6%)	2.5%	74,976	2.5%	(8,663)	(11.6%)	2.6%	83,640	2.6%	0	0.0%
GS&B	0	0.0%					0.0%		0.0%			0.0%		0.0%		
Administrative & General	250,597	7.9%	242,984	8.2%	(7,613)	(3.1%)	7.7%	234,829	7.7%	(15,768)	(6.7%)	7.9%	250,597	7.9%	0	0.0%
Information and Telecommunications	45,088	1.4%	44,998	1.5%	(90)	(0.2%)	1.6%	47,427	1.6%	2,339	4.9%	1.4%	45,088	1.4%	0	0.0%
S & M Less Fees/HHonors/EDGE/PPC	173,884	5.5%	153,041	5.2%	(20,844)	(13.6%)	5.5%	167,078	5.5%	(6,807)	(4.1%)	5.5%	173,884	5.5%	0	0.0%
Program Fees	59,002	1.9%	55,514	1.9%	(3,488)	(6.3%)	1.9%	57,472	1.9%	(1,530)	(2.7%)	1.9%	59,002	1.9%	0	0.0%
HHonors	50,664	1.6%	41,766	1.4%	(8,898)	(21.3%)	1.4%	43,343	1.4%	(7,321)	(16.9%)	1.6%	50,664	1.6%	0	0.0%
EDGE/PPC	4,137	0.1%	3,699	0.1%	(439)	(11.9%)	0.1%	3,699	0.1%	(439)	(11.9%)	0.1%	4,137	0.1%	0	0.0%
Total Sales and Marketing	287,688	9.0%	254,019	8.6%	(33,669)	(13.3%)	8.9%	271,591	8.9%	(16,096)	(5.9%)	9.0%	287,688	9.0%	0	0.0%
Property Operations and Maint	157,852	5.0%	147,057	5.0%	(10,795)	(7.3%)	5.2%	157,104	5.2%	(748)	(0.5%)	5.0%	157,852	5.0%	0	0.0%
Utilities	53,500	1.7%	60,571	2.0%	7,070	11.7%	2.1%	63,552	2.1%	10,052	15.8%	1.7%	53,500	1.7%	0	0.0%
Total Overhead Expenses	794,726	25.0%	749,628	25.3%	(45,097)	(6.0%)	25.4%	774,504	25.4%	(20,222)	(2.6%)	25.0%	794,726	25.0%	0	0.0%
Gross Operating Profit	918,654	28.9%	833,342	28.1%	85,313	10.2%	27.1%	826,030	27.1%	92,625	11.2%	28.9%	918,654	28.9%	0	0.0%
GOP Margin Change/Flow - through					0.8 pts	39.9%				1.8 pts	70.3%				0.0 pts	
Base Management Fees	95,392	3.0%	88,985	3.0%	(6,407)	(7.2%)	3.0%	91,447	3.0%	(3,946)	(4.3%)	3.0%	95,392	3.0%	0	0.0%
Incentive Management Fees	49,396	1.6%	44,661	1.5%	(4,734)	(10.6%)	1.4%	44,075	1.4%	(5,321)	(12.1%)	1.6%	49,396	1.6%	0	0.0%
Other Management and Franchise Fees	0	0.0%	0	0.0%			0.0%	0	0.0%	0	150.0%	0.0%	0	0.0%	0	0.0%
Management and Royalty Fees	144,788	4.6%	133,647	4.5%	(11,141)	(8.3%)	4.4%	135,522	4.4%	(9,266)	(6.8%)	4.6%	144,788	4.6%	0	0.0%
Income Before Non-Operating Income and Expenses	773,866	24.3%	699,695	23.6%	74,171	10.6%	22.7%	690,508	22.7%	83,358	12.1%	24.3%	773,866	24.3%	0	0.0%

Exhibit 9.15 Forecasting at Hilton (Continued)

November section spans the Bud Owner Version, Fcst vs. Bud Owner Version, Act Working, and Fcst vs. Act Working column groups.

	Fcst 11+1 FY19	% Rev	Fcst 10+2 FY19	% Rev	Fcst vs. Fcst 10+2 (FY19 vs. FY19) Loc B/(W)	% B/(W)	Bud Owner Version FY19	% Rev	Fcst vs. Bud Owner Version (FY19 vs. FY19) Loc B/(W)	% B/(W)	Act Working FY19	% Rev	Fcst vs. Act Working (FY19 vs. FY19) Loc B/(W)	% B/(W)
Rent Costs	2,800	0.1%	2,800	0.1%	0	0.0%		0.0%	(2,800)		2,800	0.1%	0	0.0%
Insurance Expense	10,636	0.3%	10,636	0.4%	0	0.0%	10,340	0.3%	(297)	(2.9%)	10,636	0.3%	0	0.0%
Other Costs (OthCosts)	8,142	0.3%	8,017	0.3%	(125)	(1.6%)	10,142	0.3%	1,999	19.7%	8,142	0.3%	0	0.0%
NonOperating Income	14	0.0%	197	0.0%	(183)	(93.1%)	197	0.0%	(183)	(93.1%)	14	0.0%	0	0.0%
NonOperating Expense	21,578	0.7%	21,453	0.7%	(125)	(0.6%)	20,481	0.7%	(1,097)	(5.4%)	21,578	0.7%	0	0.0%
Operational EBITDA	**752,302**	**23.7%**	**678,438**	**22.9%**	**73,863**	**10.9%**	**670,223**	**22.0%**	**82,078**	**12.2%**	**752,302**	**23.7%**	**0**	**0.0%**
EBITDA Margin Change/Flow - through					0.8 pts	34.6%			1.7 pts	62.3%			0.0 pts	
Adjusted EBITDA	**752,302**	**23.7%**	**678,438**	**22.9%**	**73,863**	**10.9%**	**670,223**	**22.0%**	**82,078**	**12.2%**	**752,302**	**23.7%**	**0**	**0.0%**
All Other EBITDA Expense	**752,302**	**23.7%**	**678,438**	**22.9%**	**73,863**	**10.9%**	**670,223**	**22.0%**	**82,078**	**12.2%**	**752,302**	**23.7%**	**0**	**0.0%**
Accounting EBITDA (Less Replacement Reserve)							522,511	17.1%	522,511	100.0%				
Depreciation and Amortization	0	0.0%	0	0.0%							0	0.0%		0.0%
Total Interest, Depr and Amort	**0**	**0.0%**	**0**	**0.0%**	**73,863**	**10.9%**	**147,712**	**4.8%**	**604,589**	**409.3%**	**752,302**	**23.7%**	**0**	**0.0%**
Inc Before Taxes	**752,302**	**23.7%**	**678,438**	**22.9%**	**73,863**	**10.9%**	**147,712**	**4.8%**	**604,589**	**409.3%**	**752,302**	**23.7%**	**0**	**0.0%**
Net Inc Before Disc Ops	**752,302**	**23.7%**	**678,438**	**22.9%**	**73,863**	**10.9%**	**147,712**	**4.8%**	**604,589**	**409.3%**	**752,302**	**23.7%**	**0**	**0.0%**
Capital Reserve Stat (924955)		0.0%		0.0%			121,929	4.0%	(121,929)	(100.0%)		0.0%		0.0%
Owner Net Income (Excl Capital Reserve)	**752,302**	**23.7%**	**678,438**	**22.9%**	**73,863**	**10.9%**	**25,783**	**0.8%**	**726,518**	**999.9%**	**752,302**	**23.7%**	**0**	**0.0%**
Key Metrics														
TGCC	129.73		161.21		(31.48)	(19.5%)	196.48		(66.74)	(34.0%)	129.73		0.00	
Food Cost Margin	16.3%		17.1%		0.8 pts	5.0%	17.8%		1.6 pts	8.8%	16.3%		0.0 pts	
Beverage Cost Margin	18.2%		15.3%		(3.0) pts	(19.5%)	15.8%		(2.4) pts	(15.2%)	18.2%		0.0 pts	
Total Food Revenue	736,757	23.2%	647,329	21.8%	89,428	13.8%	670,328	22.0%	66,429	9.9%	736,757	23.2%	0	0.0%
Total Beverage Revenue	213,276	6.7%	213,686	7.2%	(410)	(0.2%)	210,711	6.9%	2,565	1.2%	213,276	6.7%	0	0.0%
Total Undistributed Payroll Cost	329,612	10.4%	315,657	10.6%	13,955	4.4%	315,159	10.3%	14,453	4.6%	329,612	10.4%	0	0.0%
Undistributed (less CC, HH, Prog, GS&B, EDGE, PPC)	218,469	6.9%	201,713	6.8%	16,756	8.3%	223,799	7.3%	(5,331)	(2.4%)	218,469	6.9%	0	0.0%
Total Operating Depts Payroll and Benefits Cost	1,118,411	35.2%	1,060,902	35.8%	(57,508)	(5.4%)	1,118,512	36.7%	101	0.0%	1,118,411	35.2%	0	0.0%
Total Undistributed Payroll Cost	378,814	11.9%	373,969	12.6%	(4,845)	(1.3%)	371,215	12.2%	(7,599)	(2.0%)	378,814	11.9%	0	0.0%
Total Hotel Payroll and Benefits Cost	1,497,224	47.1%	1,434,871	48.4%	(62,354)	(4.3%)	1,489,727	48.9%	(7,496)	(0.5%)	1,497,224	47.1%	0	0.0%
Payroll & Benefits % of Total Hotel Revenue	47.1%		48.4%		1.3 pts	2.7%	48.9%		1.8 pts	3.7%	47.1%		0.0%	0.0%
Total Occupied Rooms	10,092		9,702		390	4.0%	9,932		160	1.6%	10,092		0	0.0%
Total Occupied Rooms Exc Comps	10,042		9,574		468	4.9%	9,803		239	2.4%	10,042		0	0.0%
Total Available Rooms (919270)	13,740		13,740		0	0.0%	13,740		0	0.0%	13,740		0	0.0%
Total Net Revenue per Occupied Room	315.08		305.73		9.35	3.1%	306.91		8.17	2.7%	315.08		0.00	0.0%
Total Net Revenue per Available Room	231.42		215.88		15.54	7.2%	221.85		9.57	4.3%	231.42		0.00	0.0%
Total Customers	21,080		20,556		524	2.5%	18,207		2,873	15.8%	21,080		0	0.0%
Average Checks	44		39		5	13.9%	45		(1)	(1.9%)	44		0	0.0%

Courtesy of Hilton

Forecasting is simply the process of estimating the levels of some future activity, such as sales. After an initial sales forecast has been made, the hospitality operation must plan to ensure the desired outcome is achieved.

Forecasts may be implicit or explicit. Implicit forecasts are implied by the expectations reflected by managers' actions when no explicit forecast has been made. In this chapter, we focused on explicit forecasts; that is, on deliberate attempts to estimate levels of future activities. Explicit forecasting techniques provide managers with rational foundations for planning.

Since forecasting deals with the future, it inevitably involves uncertainty. In addition, since forecasts are based on historical data, they are predicated on the risky assumption that the past will be indicative of the future.

Patterns in existing data include trend, seasonal, and cyclical. A trend is simply the long-run projection of an activity being evaluated. Seasonal patterns exist when a series of data fluctuates according to a seasonal pattern, such as seasons of the year. Cyclical patterns represent movements along a trend line.

Forecasting methods covered in this chapter included both quantitative and qualitative approaches, with the emphasis on the former. Quantitative methods discussed included naïve methods, moving averages, exponential smoothing, and single regression analysis. Limitations of quantitative methods, such as scarce data and the inability to consider unforeseeable occurrences, sometimes render quantitative methods less useful. When these limitations are significant, qualitative methods may be used. The qualitative methods covered briefly in this chapter included market research, jury of executive opinion, sales force estimates, and the Delphi method.

Finally, forecasting techniques used by unit-level management at three hospitality operations were presented. The three operations—Oberoi Holdings as a franchisee of Wendy's, Aramark, and Hilton Worldwide Holdings Inc.—were intentionally selected from three different segments of the hospitality industry to illustrate different applications of forecasting methods; they are not necessarily representative of their respective segments.

capture ratios—Ratios based on hotel guests or some variation of hotel guests. For example, a hotel may estimate its dinner covers to be 40 plus one-quarter of the estimated house guests for the night.

causal forecasting approaches—Forecasts made on the assumption that the future value of one variable is a function of other variables.

coefficient of correlation—A mathematical measure of the relation between the dependent variable and independent variables used in causal forecasting methods. May be any number between −1 and +1, inclusive.

coefficient of determination—A measure that reflects the extent to which the change in the independent variable explains the change in the dependent variable. The square of the coefficient of correlation; a number between 0 and +1.

cyclical pattern—A pattern of data (e.g., sales activity) that fluctuates around a trend line according to some regular time period.

exponential smoothing—A forecasting method that uses a smoothing constant (a number between 0 and 1), along with recent actual and forecasted data, to reflect the relative stability or growth of the activity being forecasted.

moving average—Averaging data from specified time periods in a continually updating manner such that as new results become available, they are used in the average by adding the most recent value and dropping the earliest value.

multiple regression analysis—Regression analysis forecasting used when two or more independent variables are related to the dependent variable.

naïve approach—The most recently observed value is used as a forecast and assumes that there is no seasonality affecting sales.

qualitative forecasting methods—Forecasting methods that emphasize human judgment.

quantitative forecasting methods—Forecasting methods that emphasize the use of numbers and calculation. Causal and time series approaches are some examples.

seasonal pattern—A pattern of data (e.g., sales activity) that shows regular fluctuations within a time period (daily, weekly, monthly, yearly).

smoothing constant—A value used in the exponential smoothing forecasting method. Determined using forecasts from two consecutive previous periods and the actual demand from the earlier of these two periods.

time series forecasting approaches—Forecasts made on the assumption that an underlying pattern is recurring over time.

trend pattern—A pattern of data (for example, sales activity) characterized by a general direction whose long-run estimate is projected into the future.

1. What is the difference between implicit and explicit forecasts?
2. How do forecasting and planning differ?
3. What are the purposes and limitations of forecasting?
4. How do cyclical and seasonal patterns of data differ?
5. What are the differences between quantitative and qualitative forecasting methods?
6. How do causal forecasting methods differ from time series methods?
7. How is a moving average calculated?
8. When are exponential smoothing techniques most useful?
9. How can regression analysis be used to forecast food revenues based on occupancy percentage?

Problem 1

The Sinclair Hotel uses the simplest time series approach for forecasting monthly revenues. The current year's revenues by department are multiplied by $1 + x$ percent to forecast the next year's revenues. The current year's department revenues for January and percentage increases for the coming year are provided below.

Required:

Calculate monthly forecasted revenues by department below:

Department	20X1 Revenues	Percentage Increase	20X2 Forecasted Revenues
Rooms	$195,000	6%	_____
Food	55,500	4%	_____
Health Club and Spa	32,000	2%	_____

Problem 2

The Alerion Elementary School forecasts its lunch meals using the exponential smoothing method, discussed in this chapter. The recent results and forecasts have been as follows:

	Forecast	Actual Demand
Day 1	500	515
Day 2	520	525

Required:

1. Determine the smoothing constant.
2. Provide the forecast of lunch meals for Day 3.

Problem 3

The Douglas Hotel consists of 100 guestrooms and a 50-seat coffee shop. The average room rate is as follows:

Single rooms	$ 80
Double rooms	120
King suites	140

The monthly paid occupancy for April is forecast at 70 percent. The single and double occupancies are forecast to be 40 percent and 50 percent, respectively. The remainder of the rooms sold will be king suites.

The coffee shop is open for three meals each day and the average seat turnover and average check by meal period is as follows:

	Average Check	Seat Turnover
Breakfast	$ 9.50	1.2
Lunch	15.50	1.8
Dinner	23.50	0.6

In addition, other revenues average five percent of total revenue.

Required:

1. Calculate the forecast room revenues for April.

2. Calculate the forecast food revenues for April.

3. Calculate the other revenue for April.

Problem 4

The 150-seat Blue Ridge Café forecasts sales based on seat turnover and average selling price by meal period. Beverage revenues are estimated to equal 15 percent of food sales. The relevant information for food sales is as follows:

	Seat Turnover		Average Selling Price	
Day of Week	Breakfast	Lunch	Breakfast	Lunch
Sunday	0.5	1.2	$8.95	$15.50
Monday	1.1	1.5	9.25	14.25
Tuesday	1.3	1.4	9.25	14.25
Wednesday	1.4	1.6	9.25	14.25
Thursday	1.3	1.7	9.25	14.25
Friday	1.2	1.8	9.25	14.25
Saturday	0.8	0.8	7.50	10.50

Required:

1. Forecast the food sales by meal period and day of the week.

2. Forecast beverage sales by meal period and day of the week.

3. Forecast the monthly sales for February. Assume February has 28 days.

Problem 5

The North Aurelius Elementary School's lunch customers are forecast based on a moving average. The number of customers served by day for the first five weeks of the year are as follows:

	1	2	3	4	5
Monday	421	430	429	425	440
Tuesday	398	410	396	415	412
Wednesday	410	420	415	428	410
Thursday	398	412	396	410	405
Friday	440	435	445	438	441

439.8

709.5

Required:

1. Forecast the number of meals for each day of Week 6 using the five-week moving average method.

2. Forecast the number of meals for each day of Week 6 using the three-week moving average method.

3. Comment on the difference in the results of parts 1 and 2.

Problem 6

Kerry Normandy is forecasting sales of her 100-room, limited-service Normandy Inn. She forecasts by market segment. The most recent year's (20X3) percentage of rooms sold and average daily room rate (ADR) by market segment were as follows:

Segment	Percentage of Rooms Sold	ADR
Business	45%	$125
Group	5%	85
Tourist	50%	110

On an average day, her inn experiences a 72 percent paid occupancy. With considerable advertising, she believes she can achieve a daily paid occupancy of 75 percent. Further, she believes she can increase the business segment up to 55 percent at the expense of the tourist segment, which pays a lower rate. In addition, she projects ADR increases of five percent.

Required:

Forecast the room revenue for January 20X4.

Problem 7

FreshServ operates the lunch program at Edison Elementary School. The weekly sales forecast necessary for ordering food provisions and scheduling labor is based on a three-week moving average; that is, Monday's forecast is based on the average sales of the prior three Mondays. The forecast is modified based on a number of factors, including weather. The weather modification is that sales are expected to increase moderately as the school year progresses into cooler weather and to decrease moderately with warmer weather in the spring. In addition, rainy days result in significant increases in sales.

The sales for Weeks 4 through 6 were as follows:

	Week 4	Week 5	Week 6
Monday	$450	$470	$485
Tuesday	420	445	460
Wednesday	440	438	440
Thursday	430	445	540
Friday	410	420	435

Required:

Using the above results, answer the following questions:

1. What type of weather trend do the above figures suggest? Why?
2. Which day did it appear to rain?

Problem 8

This problem is a continuation of Problem 7. Karin Smith, manager of FreshServ, desires assistance in preparing the sales forecast for Week 7. To prepare the weekly sales forecast, the days' sales of the prior three weeks are averaged and modified by $20 for expected weather changes. In addition, if a rainy day is expected, an additional $70 of sales is expected.

Required:

Prepare the weekly sales forecast by day for Week 7. Assume that the winter season is approaching; that is, it is expected that Week 7 will be cooler than Week 6. Further, use $440 for sales for Wednesday of Week 6 in place of actual sales of $540. Finally, assume that Monday of Week 7 is expected to be a rainy day.

Problem 9

James Fee, manager of the Spruce Resort, has requested your assistance in forecasting the lodging and foodservice operations sales for April. The resort has single and double guestrooms.

Information provided is as follows:

Number of guestrooms	=	100
Number of dining room seats	=	80%
Estimated paid occupancy percentage	=	80%
Double occupancy percentage	=	60%
Average daily rate	=	$130
Average double room rate	=	single room rate + $30
Average occupancy per room:		
Single rooms	=	1
Double rooms	=	2.2
Breakfast sales capture ratios:		
Single room occupants	=	40%
Double room occupants	=	80%
Lunch sales seat turnover	=	1.5 times
Dinner sales seat turnover	=	0.7 times

Average foodservice checks:

Breakfast	$ 10.95
Lunch	15.50
Dinner	22.95

434 Hospitality Industry Managerial Accounting

Required:

1. What is the average single room rate?

2. Forecast the room sales for April.

3. Forecast the foodservice sales for April for each meal period.

Problem 10

The University Club forecasts its monthly luncheon sales based on historical trends and planned promotion. The January luncheon activity for the past three years has been as follows:

	Club Membership	Frequency	Average Guests/ Member Visit	Average Price	Total Luncheon Revenue
20X1	1,000	1.5	0.5	$8.00	$18,000.00
20X2	1,100	1.6	0.6	8.80	24,780.80
20X3	1,200	1.7	0.7	9.68	33,570.24

Assume for 20X4, promotional efforts will *double* the annual change in frequency experienced in recent years and the change in average guests per member visit; that membership will stabilize at the 20X3 level; and that the average luncheon price will increase by the same percentage experienced in the recent past.

Required:

Determine the forecasted luncheon revenue for 20X4 for the College Club.

Problem 11

The Blue Water Café forecasts its beverage sales based on food sales. Its food sales are estimated based on the trend of both customer counts and average foodservice check.

The historical data for the Blue Water Café for June 20X1–X3 is as follows:

	Customer Count	Average Foodservice Check	Beverage Sales
20X1	3,000	$10.00	$ 7,500
20X2	3,200	11.00	8,800
20X3	3,400	12.10	10,285

Required:

Forecast the food and beverage sales for June 20X4 based on the above information.

Problem 12

The Post Oak Inn forecasts customer counts for its 120-seat restaurant based on historical seat turnover information. It weights the past two years of data by 60 percent and 40 percent for the most recent two years; the 60 percent is applied to the most recent year. Then, the determined average customer count is increased by five percent as an estimate for the month of the next year.

Daily Seat Turnover

	20X1	20X2
January	1.00	1.05
February	1.02	1.04
March	1.03	1.06

Required:

1. Estimate the average daily seat turnovers per month for January–March 20X3.
2. Estimate the customer counts for January–March 20X3.

Problem 13

B.T. Marvel, the owner/manager of the 100-room Finney Motel, forecasts room revenues based on the number of room sales and expected ADR. The monthly room sales (in units) for July–September 20X3 were as follows:

July	2,480
August	2,542
September	2,325

B.T. believes the room sales for each month will increase by two occupancy points. In addition, B.T. expects the ADR for July–September will be $75, $78, and $72, respectively.

Required:

1. Forecast the expected number of rooms to be sold for each month; that is, July–September 20X4.
2. Forecast the room revenue for each of the three months.

Problem 14

Nate Tree, manager of the 150-room Pine Inn, uses regression analysis for forecasting the inn's coffee shop breakfast sales. The daily equations (where y stands for forecasted meals and x the number of lodging guests) and the paid single and double occupancy percentages are as follows:

	Equation	Occupancy	Double Occupancy
Sunday	$y = 30 + 0.2x$	30%	60%
Monday–Thursday	$y = 40 + 0.8x$	80%	40%
Friday	$y = 30 + 0.6x$	40%	50%
Saturday	$y = 80 + 0.1x$	20%	60%

Assume an average of two guests stay in a double room and a single guest stays in a single room.

Required:

1. Calculate total expected breakfast covers for a week.

2. Calculate the expected breakfast sales for the month of June when the first day of June is a Sunday and the average foodservice check for the month is $7.95.

Problem 15

The Groesbeck Golf Club forecasts its beverage sales for golfers based on the forecasted rounds of golf. The rounds of golf are forecast based on the number of golf members and expected rounds of golf per member. The number of golf members and expected rounds of golf for April–August 20X4 are as follows:

	Expected Number of Golf Members	Forecasted Average Rounds of Golf/Member
April	400	5
May	405	8
June	410	10
July	415	9
August	420	8

The expected beverage sales per round of golf is forecasted to be $3.

Required:

Forecast the monthly beverage sales for each month.

Problem 16

Part I

The Westsider has asked for your assistance in forecasting its room sales and foodservice sales. To forecast room sales for the week of May 18–24 (Week 4), it considers its group reservations and uses a moving average of the nongroup hotel guestrooms sold for the prior three weeks. This moving average then is increased by two percent. Data for the past three weeks are as follows:

	Nongroup Hotel Guestrooms			Week 4		
	Week 1	Week 2	Week 3	Group Reservations	Nongroup Guests	Total
Sunday	150	160	164	215	_____	____
Monday	250	270	290	240	_____	____
Tuesday	245	275	305	250	_____	____
Wednesday	250	270	260	240	_____	____
Thursday	240	240	249	200	_____	____
Friday	120	110	130	50	_____	____
Saturday	80	90	100	60	_____	____

Required:

Complete the two right columns above. Round your forecast to the nearest whole number.

Part II

To forecast its foodservice breakfast sales, the Westsider uses the following formula:

$$y = a + bx_1 + cx_2$$

where x_1 = hotel guests

x_2 = hotel guests at the economy motel adjacent to the Westsider

a = nonhotel (Westsider and the economy motel) guests eating breakfast

b = percentage of hotel guests expected to eat breakfast

c = percentage of economy motel guests that are expected to eat at the Westsider

Additional information:

1. x_2 = 80
2. b = 0.8
3. c = 0.3
4. a = 20

Required:

Forecast breakfast sales for Monday.

Problem 17

The Harris Hotel forecasts its breakfast customers based on (1) its prior night room guests count, (2) an estimated number of diners from the local community, and (3) an estimated number of guests who are staying at a nearby limited-service hotel and will have breakfast at the Harris. The formula used is as follows:

$$X = 30 + 0.8(B) + 0.2(C)$$

where X = forecasted breakfast customers

B = number of prior night room guests at the Harris Hotel

C = number of prior night room guests at the nearby limited-service hotel

The estimated numbers of hotel guests are as follows:

	B	C
Sunday	200	100
Monday	300	140
Tuesday	310	120
Wednesday	320	130

	B	C
Thursday	310	140
Friday	140	80
Saturday	100	90

Required:

1. Forecast the number of breakfast covers for Monday through Saturday.

2. Comment on the relevance of a three-period moving average and of the causal approach used by the Harris Hotel.

Problem 18

The Evergreen Hotel, a 200-room lodging facility, uses regression analysis to forecast dining room meals. Larry Spruce, the manager, has indicated the regression equations used are as follows:

$$y = 50 + 0.42x \quad \text{(breakfast)}$$
$$y = 200 + 0.21x \quad \text{(lunch)}$$
$$y = 450 + 0.35x \quad \text{(dinner)}$$

where y equals forecasted meals

x equals the number of hotel guests

Further, the average check in the hotel's dining room is expected to be as follows:

Breakfast	$ 3.25
Lunch	$ 6.50
Dinner	$12.95

Required:

Forecast daily sales by meal period when the occupancy percentage is expected to be 85 percent (all rooms are available for sale) and the average occupancy per room is expected to be 1.58.

Problem 19

The Marcus Motel uses the moving average approach to forecast its rooms sales for each week and linear regression for forecasting its food sales. The moving average approach utilizes the most recent five weeks of actual data. An adjustment is made for extremes as follows: If during the five weeks the actual rooms sold for a week differed by more than 30 percent from the budgeted room sales for that week, the actual is considered to be an extreme. In such cases, the extreme is ignored and the budgeted number of rooms sold is used in its place.

The rooms sold for the five preceding weeks were as follows:

	Rooms Budgeted	Rooms Sold
May 24–31	660	460
June 1–7	710	700
June 8–14	720	710
June 15–21	710	930
June 22–28	715	710
June 29–July 5	?	?

The average occupancy per room sold is expected to be 1.8 for June 29–July 5. The regression equations used to forecast the number of meals to be sold are as follows:

$$\text{Breakfast customers} = 50 + 0.8(x)$$
$$\text{Lunch customers} = 150 + 0.2(x)$$
$$\text{Dinner customers} = 60 + 0.6(x)$$

where x equals number of motel room guests not committed to food functions for that day.

Room guests committed to food functions (other than the restaurant) for June 29 are as follows:

Breakfast	50
Lunch	100
Dinner	–0–

Required:

1. Calculate the expected number of rooms to be sold for the week of June 29–July 5.

2. Calculate the number of meals to be sold for breakfast, lunch, and dinner in the motel's restaurant for June 29. Assume 100 rooms are sold for June 29.

Problem 20

The Grand Hotel has 300 rooms and is expected to have a 90 percent occupancy for Monday through Thursday nights, June 16–19, and 50 percent occupancy the remaining nights of the week. The average occupancy per room of the Grand Hotel is 1.6 on weekends (Friday–Sunday) and 1.4 on weekdays. The expected luncheon average prices are $4.95 for weekdays and $5.95 for weekends. The regression equations to estimate luncheon covers are as follows:

Lunch customers for weekdays = $50 + 0.6(x_1) + 0.1(x_2)$. Lunch customers for weekend days = $150 + 0.4(x_1) + 0.2(x_2)$.

x_1 = number of lodging guests at the Grand Hotel

x_2 = number of lodging guests at the Fairview Inn, a rooms-only lodging property

The projected room sales and average occupancy for the Fairview Inn for June 15–21 are as follows:

		Room Sales	Average Occupancy/Room
June 15	Sunday	60	1.2
June 16	Monday	80	1.1
June 17	Tuesday	80	1.05
June 18	Wednesday	80	1.05
June 19	Thursday	80	1.1
June 20	Friday	40	1.6
June 21	Saturday	30	2.0

Required:

Forecast the Grand Hotel's luncheon sales in dollars and customers for each day for June 15–21.

Problem 21

The Merry Motel uses the moving average approach to forecast its rooms sales for each week and linear regression for forecasting its food sales. The moving average approach utilizes the most recent five weeks of actual data. An adjustment is made for holidays as follows:

- If the holiday occurred during the prior five weeks, the week containing the holiday is adjusted by multiplying it by 110 percent.

- If the holiday occurs during the forecast week, the forecasted estimate based on the moving average is reduced by 10 percent.

The rooms sold for the five preceding weeks were as follows:

	Rooms Budgeted	Rooms Sold	Holidays
May 24–31	660	640	Memorial Day (May 30)
June 1–7	710	700	—
June 8–14	720	710	—
June 15–21	710	720	—
June 22–28	715	710	—
June 29–July 5	?	?	July 4

The average occupancy per room sold is expected to be 1.6 for June 29–July 5.

The regression equations used to forecast the number of meals to be sold are as follows:

Breakfast covers	=	50 +	0.8(number of hotel room guests)
Lunch covers	=	150 +	0.2(number of hotel room guests)
Dinner covers	=	60 +	0.6(number of hotel room guests)

Required:

1. Calculate the expected number of rooms to be sold for the week of June 29–July 5.

2. Calculate the number of meals to be sold for breakfast, lunch, and dinner for the week of June 29–July 5.

Problem 22

The Sunset Inn's room guests and breakfast customers served in 20X1 were as follows:

	Room Guests	Breakfast Customers
January	1,010	1,200
February	960	1,010
March	1,100	1,260
April	1,050	1,230
May	1,210	1,350
June	1,190	1,280
July	1,150	1,320
August	1,200	1,340
September	1,180	1,260
October	1,120	1,250
November	1,010	1,160
December	910	1,005

Required:

1. Determine the coefficient of correlation for the Sunset Inn based on the above data.

2. Determine a regression equation for forecasting breakfast customers based on the number of room guests.

3. If 1,050 room guests are forecasted for January, how many breakfast customers are forecasted to be served?

Problem 23

The Red and White Dessert & Café is a small, 80-seat eatery that serves breakfast and lunch. Its seat turnover statistics for the last quarter of the past two years are listed below. Ben, the owner, wants to be totally prepared for this year's holiday season, and these three months are historically the busiest months for the café due to holiday shoppers.

Ben wants to give more weight to the most recent year (20X2) at 70 percent and the other 30 percent to 20X1. He would then want to increase the count by 10 percent to estimate for the three months in this current year coming up.

| | Breakfast Seat Turnover | | Lunch Seat Turnover | |
	20X1	20X2	20X1	20X2
October	1.1	1.1	1.2	1.4
November	1.3	1.4	1.5	1.6
December	1.5	1.5	1.7	1.8

Required:

1. Estimate the average daily seat turnovers per month for October–December 20X3.

2. Estimate the customer counts for October–December 20X3. Please round customer count to the nearest whole number.

Problem 24

The Seascape Hotel is a nice, upscale, 100-room boutique hotel by the beach. The hotel forecasts its daily room sales based on the moving average of the prior four weeks' daily occupied rooms. It also makes the following adjustments to allow for holidays and rainy days:

1. If a holiday occurred during the prior four-week period, the day containing the holiday is adjusted by multiplying it by 0.8, as holidays bring larger crowds to the beach.

2. If a rainy day occurred during the prior four-week period, the day containing the holiday is adjusted up by multiplying it by 1.2, as sunny days bring larger crowds to the beach.

3. In estimating daily rooms sales for August, the moving average is increased by five percent, as families normally want to have a last break before school starts in September.

Room sales for the prior four weeks were as follows:

	July 1–7	July 8–14	July 15–21	July 22–28	July 29–Aug 4
Sunday	95	90	70 (Rain)	80	
Monday	80	88	85	78	
Tuesday	70	70	88	79	
Wednesday	100 (Holiday)	60	70	70	
Thursday	90	85	80	75	
Friday	95	94	90	85	
Saturday	96	94	95	86	

Required:

Calculate the expected room sales for the week of July 29–August 4. Round your answer to the nearest whole room. Show all of your work.

Problem 25

One-Eleven, a limited-service hotel, has the data for its total operating revenue and utility expense as follows. It plans to use its total operating revenue to predict its utility cost for budgeting purposes.

	Total Operating Revenue ($)	Utility Cost ($)
January	71,327	2,114
February	69,535	2,085
March	86,581	2,768
April	79,865	2,580
May	78,501	2,491
June	88,439	2,839
July	90,754	2,987
August	92,409	2,811
September	88,011	2,708
October	89,564	2,501
November	79,617	2,357
December	78,098	2,490

Required:

1. Using Excel, determine the coefficient of correlation for One-Eleven based on the above data.

2. Using Excel, determine a regression equation for forecasting utility expense based on the estimated total operating revenue.

3. If $85,000 of total operating revenue is expected for January, what will be the estimated utility expense using the regression equation?

10

OPERATIONS BUDGETING

Chapter 10 Outline

Competencies

1. Describe the purposes of budgeting for operations and identify the roles and responsibilities of those involved in the budgeting process. (pp. 448–451)

2. Explain the process of preparing an operations budget. (pp. 451–462)

3. Describe the budgeting control process and explain how significant variances are determined. (pp. 462–468)

4. Use information from budget reports to calculate and analyze several kinds of variances related to revenue, cost, volume, and labor. (pp. 468–477)

5. Describe the proper management response to the results of variance analysis. (pp. 477–478)

6. Understand the importance of reforecasting and budgeting at multiunit hospitality enterprises and lodging properties, with industry examples. (pp. 478-481)

KEY TERMS

capital budget

cash budget

cost of goods sold variance

incremental budgeting

operations budget

revenue variances

significance criteria

strategic planning

variable labor variance

variance analysis

zero-base budgeting (ZBB)

Every rational manager plans for the future. Some plans are formal and others are informal. Budgets are formal plans expressed in dollars. Budgets provide answers to many questions, including the following:

1. What are the forecasted revenues for the month?

2. What is the budgeted labor for the year?

3. How many rooms are expected to be sold during any given month, and what is the expected average room rate?

4. What is the budgeted rooms department operating income for the month?

5. What is the estimated depreciation for the year?

6. How close were actual food and beverage revenues to the budgeted amounts for the month?

7. What is the projected net income for the year?

This chapter is divided into two major sections. The first section investigates reasons for budgeting, the process of preparing the operations budget, and the idea of budgeting horizons. The second section focuses on budgetary control and on how hospitality operations use budget reports in the budgetary control process. The Sands Motel, a hypothetical small lodging operation, is used to illustrate both budget preparation and control.

10.1 TYPES OF BUDGETS

Hospitality operations prepare several types of budgets. The **operations budget**, the topic of this chapter, is also referred to as the revenue and expense budget, because it includes management's plans for generating revenues and incurring expenses for a given period. The operations budget includes not only operated department budgets (budgets for rooms, food, beverage, and other profit centers), but also budgets for service centers such as sales and marketing, accounting, and human resources. In addition, the operations budget includes the planned expenses for depreciation, interest expense, and nonoperating expenses. Thus, the operations budget is a detailed operating plan by profit centers, cost centers within profit centers (such as the housekeeping department within the rooms department), and service centers.[1] It includes all revenues and all expenses that appear on the income statement and related subsidiary schedules. Annual operating budgets are normally subdivided into monthly periods. Certain information is reduced to a daily basis for management's use in controlling operations. The operations budget enables management to accomplish two of its major functions: planning and control.

Two other types of budgets are the **cash budget** and the **capital budget**. The cash budget is management's plan for cash receipts and disbursements. Capital budgeting pertains to planning for the acquisition of equipment, land, and buildings.

10.2 BUDGETING HORIZONS

The annual operations budget must be subdivided into monthly plans in order for management to use it effectively as an aid in monitoring operations. The monthly plans allow management to measure the operation's overall performance several times throughout the year. Certain elements of the monthly plan are then reduced to weekly and daily bases. For example, many lodging operations have daily revenue plans that differ by property, by day of the week, and by season. The daily revenue is compared to these daily revenue goals on the daily report of operations. Any significant differences (variances) require analysis, determination of causes, and, if necessary, corrective action. (Variance analysis will be discussed later in Section 10.9.) In addition, every month all revenue and expense amounts are compared to the budgeted amounts, and all significant variances are analyzed and explained. Alternatives to the monthly breakdown of annual budgets are using 13 four-week segments or the 4-4-5 quarterly plan. The 4-4-5 plan consists of two four-week plans followed by one five-week, equaling the 13 weeks in a quarter. Four of these quarterly plans serve as the annual operations budget.

Many hospitality organizations also prepare operations budgets on a long-range basis. A common long-range period is five years. A five-year plan consists of five annual plans. The annual plans for the second through fifth years are much less detailed than the current year's annual plan. When long-range budgets are used, the next year's budget serves as a starting point for preparing the operations budget. The long-range budget procedure is used to review and update the next four years and add the fifth year to the plan.

Long-range planning, also referred to as **strategic planning**, is recognized as essential to the controlled growth of major hospitality organizations. It not only considers revenues and expenses (as do annual operating plans), but also evaluates and selects from among major alternatives those that provide long-range direction to the hospitality operation. Major directional considerations may include the following:

- Evaluating whether a proposed acquisition will have a positive effect on existing operations or whether it will hinder or detract from existing operations

- Determining whether the hospitality operation should expand into foreign markets

- Determining whether a quick-service restaurant chain should add breakfast to its existing lunch and dinner offerings

- Considering whether a single-property operation should add rooms or possibly expand to include another property

Recent research reveals that about one-third of the private clubs in the United States prepare long-range operating budgets. The most common long-range plans cover four years in the future.

10.3 REASONS FOR BUDGETING

Many small organizations in the hospitality industry have not formalized their operations budgets. Often, the overall goals, sales objectives, expense projections, and the desired bottom line remain "in the head" of the owner/ manager. However, there are many reasons every hospitality operation should use formalized budgeting. Several of these are briefly described as follows:

1. Budgeting requires management to examine alternatives before selecting a particular course of action. For example, there are pricing alternatives for each product and/or service sold. Also, there are many different marketing decisions that must be made, such as where to advertise, how much to

advertise, how to promote, when to promote, and so on. There are also several approaches to staffing, each of which will affect the quality of service provided. In nearly every revenue and expense area, several courses of action are available to hospitality operations. Budgeting provides management with an effective means of evaluating these alternatives.

2. Budgeting provides a standard of comparison. At the end of the accounting period, management is able to compare actual operating results to a formal plan. Significant variances should be analyzed to suggest the probable cause(s) that require additional investigation and possibly corrective action. While the preparation of budgets is independent of budgetary control, it is inefficient not to use budgets for control purposes. The focus of the last part of this chapter is on the control process.

3. Budgeting enables management to look forward, especially when strategic planning is concerned. Too often, management is either solving current problems or reviewing the past. Budgeting requires management to anticipate the future. Future considerations may be both external and internal. External considerations include the economy, inflation, and major competition. Internal considerations are primarily the hospitality operation's reactions to external considerations. Hospitality operations should aggressively attempt to shape their environment rather than merely reacting to it.

4. When participative budgeting is practiced, the budget process involves all levels of management. This involvement motivates the lower-level managers because they have real input in the process rather than being forced to adhere to budget numbers that are imposed upon them. Too often, autocratic budgeting approaches result in "unsuccessful" managers who blame the budget preparers (higher-level managers) instead of accepting responsibility for poor operating results.

5. The budget process provides a channel of communication whereby the operation's objectives are communicated to the lowest managerial levels. In addition, lower-level managers are able to react to these objectives and suggest operational goals such as rooms sold, rooms revenues, rooms labor expense, and so on. When the budget is used as a standard of comparison, the operating results are also communicated to lower-level managers. This allows for feedback to these managers. Further, lower-level managers are required to explain significant variances—why they exist, what the causes are, and what action is to be taken.

6. Finally, to the degree that prices are a function of costs, the budget process (which provides estimates of future expenses) enables managers to set their prices in relation to their expenses. Price changes can be the result of planning, thereby allowing such changes to be properly implemented. Price changes made on the spur of the moment often result in unprofessional price execution, such as penciled changes on menus, poorly informed service staff who misquote prices, and other similar situations.

In a recent study on club segment of the hospitality industry, 96.6 percent of the respondents share that their clubs use the operations budget as a means to monitor performance. Moreover, over half (55.7 percent) of the clubs compared the budgeted numbers to the actual revenue and expenses to gauge their performance.[2]

10.4 PERSONNEL RESPONSIBLE FOR BUDGET PREPARATION

The complete budget process includes both budget preparation and budgetary control. The major purpose of budgeting is to allow management to accomplish three of its functions: planning, execution, and control.

In most hospitality organizations, the board of directors approves the operating budget, the preparation of which has been delegated to the chief executive officer (CEO). The CEO generally enlists the controller to coordinate the budget preparation process. However, budgeting is not a financial function where bookkeepers, accountants, and the controller have the sole responsibility. The controller facilitates the budget preparation process by initially providing information to operating managers. The major input for the budget should come from operated department (profit center) managers working with their lower-level managers and from service department managers.

The controller receives the department managers' operating plans and formulates them into a comprehensive operating budget. This is then reviewed by the CEO and a budget committee (if one exists). If the comprehensive operating budget is satisfactory in meeting financial goals, the CEO presents it to the board of directors. The controller or chief financial officer often accompanies the CEO to assist the CEO as needed. If the operating budget is not satisfactory, then the elements requiring change are returned to the appropriate department heads for review and change. This process may repeat several times until a satisfactory budget is prepared.

The final budget should ideally be the result of an overall team effort rather than a decree dictated by the CEO. This participative management approach should result in maximizing departmental managers' motivation.

10.5 THE BUDGET PREPARATION PROCESS

The major elements in the budget preparation process are as follows:

- Financial and other objectives
- Revenue forecasts
- Expense forecasts
- Net income forecasts

The operations budget process begins with the board of directors establishing financial and other objectives. A major financial objective set by many organizations, both hospitality and business firms in general, is long-term profit maximization. Long-term profit maximization may mean that the operation does not maximize its profits for the next year. For example, in the next year, profits could be increased by reducing public relations efforts and major maintenance projects; however, in the long run, cuts in these programs may disturb the financial well-being of the hospitality establishment. An alternative objective set by institutional foodservice operations (e.g., hospital foodservice) is cost containment. Since many of these operations generate limited foodservice revenues, cost containment is critical to enable these operators to break even.

Another objective may be to provide high-quality service, even if it means incurring higher labor costs than allowable to maximize profits. Other objectives set by hospitality organizations have been to be the top establishment in one segment of the hospitality industry, to be the fastest-growing establishment, and/ or to be recognized as the hospitality operation with the best reputation. Many more objectives could be listed. The critical point is that the board must establish major objectives. These are then communicated to the CEO and are the basis for formulating the operations budget.

When a management company operates a hotel for independent owners, the owners' expectations for both the long and short term must be fully considered. Generally, the owners reserve the right to approve the operating budget. Therefore, failure to consider their views will most likely result in their rejection of the plan, as well as damaged relationships and the need to redo the budget. Several of the major hotel chains, such as Hilton, Starwood, and Marriott, manage many more hotels than they own. Thus, their management teams at the managed properties must work closely with the owners of each hotel.

Forecasting Revenue

Forecasting revenue is the next step in preparing the operations budget. In order for profit center managers (e.g., rooms department managers) to be able to forecast revenue for their departments, they must be provided with information regarding the economic environment, marketing plans, capital budgeting, and detailed historical financial operating results of their departments.

Information regarding the economic environment includes such items as:

- Expected inflation for the next year.

- Ability of the operation to pass on cost increases to guests.

- Changes in competitive conditions—for example, the emergence of new competitors, the closing of former competitors, and so on.

- Expected levels of guest spending for products/services offered by the hospitality operation.

- Business travel trends.

- Tourist travel trends.

- For international operations, other factors, such as expected wage/price controls and the political environment, may need to be considered.

In order for this information to be useful, it must be expressed in usable numbers. For example, regarding inflation and the ability of the operation to increase its prices, the information received by department heads may be phrased as follows: Inflation is expected to be 4 percent for the next year and prices of all products and services may be increased by an average maximum of 5 percent, with a 2.5 percent increase effective January 1 and July 1.

Marketing plans include, but are not limited to, advertising and promotion plans. What advertising is planned for the upcoming year, and how does it compare with the past? What results are expected from the various advertising campaigns? What promotion will be used and when during the budget year? What results can be expected? Are reduced room prices and complimentary meals part of the weekend promotion? Answers to these questions and many others must be provided in order for managers to be able to prepare their budgets.

Capital budgeting information includes the time of the addition of property and equipment. For an existing property, the completion date of guestroom renovation must be projected in order to effectively estimate room sales. The renovation of a hotel's restaurant, the addition of rooms, and so forth are areas that must be covered before projecting sales and expenses for the upcoming year.

Historical financial information should be detailed by department. The breakdown should be on at least a monthly basis, and in some cases, on a daily basis. Quantities and prices should both be provided. That is, the number of each type of room sold and the average selling price by market segment—business, group, tourist, and contract—should be provided. Generally, financial information for at least the two prior years is provided. The controller should be prepared to provide additional prior information as requested.

Historical financial information often serves as the foundation on which managers build their revenue forecasts. This type of budgeting has been called **incremental budgeting**. For example, rooms revenue of a hotel for 20X1 through 20X4 is shown in Exhibit 10.1. From year 20X1 to 20X4, the amount of revenue increased 10 percent for each year. Therefore, if future conditions appear to be similar to what they were in prior years, the rooms revenue for 20X5 would be budgeted at $1,464,100, which is a 10 percent increase over 20X4.

An alternative approach to budgeting revenue based on increasing the current year's revenue by a percentage is to base the revenue projection on unit sales and prices. This approach considers the two variables of unit sales and prices separately. For example, an analysis of the past financial information in Exhibit 10.2 shows that occupancy percentage increased 2 percent from 20X1 to 20X2, 1 percent from 20X2 to 20X3, and 2 percent from 20X3 to 20X4. The average room rates have increased by $2, $3, and $4 over the past three years, respectively. Therefore, assuming the future prospects appear similar, the forecaster may use a 1 percent increase in occupancy percentage and a $5 increase in average room rate as the basis for forecasting 20X5 rooms revenue. The formula for forecasting rooms revenue is as follows:

$$\text{Rooms Available} \times \text{Occupancy Percentage} \times \text{Average Rate} = \text{Forecasted Rooms Revenue}$$

$$36,500 \times 0.76 \times \$114 = \$3,162,360$$

This simplistic approach to forecasting rooms revenue is meant only to illustrate the process. A more detailed (and proper) approach would include further considerations, such as different types of rooms available and their rates, different room rates charged to different guests (e.g., convention groups, business travelers, and tourists), different rates charged on weeknights versus weekends, and different rates charged based on seasonality (especially for hotels subject to seasonal changes). In addition, managers of other profit centers, such as food, beverage, and the gift shop, must forecast their revenue for the year.

Although sales forecasting is often used for short-term forecasts, many of its concepts are relevant to forecasting revenue for the annual budget. In addition to relying on historical information, many hotels, especially convention hotels that have major conventions booked a year or more in advance, are able to rely in part on room reservations in forecasting both room and food and beverage sales. Still, for activities not reserved so far in advance, forecasting must be done.

Exhibit 10.1 Rooms Revenue Increases

	Amount	Increase over Prior Year Amount	%
20X1	$1,000,000	—	—
20X2	1,100,000	100,000	10
20X3	1,210,000	110,000	10
20X4	1,331,000	121,000	10

Exhibit 10.2   Rooms Revenue 20X1–20X4

Year	Rooms Sold	Occ. %	Average Room Rate	Rooms Revenues
20X1	25,550	70	$100	$2,555,000
20X2	26,280	72	102	2,680,560
20X3	26,645	73	105	2,797,725
20X4	27,375	75	109	2,983,875

Estimating Expenses

The next step in the budget formulation process is estimating expenses. Since expenses are categorized both in relation to operated departments (direct/indirect) and how they react to changes in volume (fixed/variable), the forecasting of expenses is similar to the approach used in forecasting revenue. However, before department heads are able to estimate expenses, they must be provided with information regarding the following:

- Expected cost increases for supplies, food, beverages, and other expenses
- Labor cost increases, including the cost of benefits and payroll taxes

Department heads of profit centers estimate their variable expenses in relation to the projected revenues of their departments. For example, historically, the food department may have incurred food costs at 35 percent of food sales. For the next year, the food department manager decides to budget at 35 percent. Therefore, multiplying projected food sales by 35 percent results in the projected cost of food sales. Other variable expenses may be estimated similarly.

An alternate way to estimate expense is based on standard amounts. For example, a hotel may have a work standard that requires room attendants to clean two rooms per hour. Given this standard, if 800 rooms sales are budgeted during a month, 400 labor hours would be budgeted for room attendants' labor. If the average hourly wage is $12 per hour, $4,800 in wages is budgeted for room attendants for the period. Employee benefits related to room attendants are additional costs that also must be considered.

Another example is guestroom amenities. If the typical amenity package includes soap, mouthwash, shampoo, and so forth and costs $2 per room, then when 800 rooms sales are forecasted, the guest amenities budget would be $1,600.

Fixed expenses are projected on the basis of experience and expected changes. For example, assume that supervisors in the food department were paid salaries of $85,000 for the past year. Further assume that the new salary level of the supervisors is $90,000 plus another half-time equivalent to be added at a cost of $25,000 for the next year. Thus, the fixed cost of supervisor salaries for the next year is set at $115,000. Other fixed expenses are similarly projected.

The service center department heads also estimate expenses for their departments. The service departments in a hotel comprise the general expense categories of administrative and general, marketing, property operation and maintenance, utility costs, human resources, information and telecommunications systems, security, and transportation. Service center department heads will estimate their expenses based on experience and expected changes. Generally, the historical amounts are adjusted to reflect higher costs. For example, assume that the accounting department salaries of a hotel for 20X1 were $150,000.

Further assume that salary increases for 20X2 are limited to an average of 5 percent. Therefore, the 20X2 accounting department salaries budget is set at $157,500.

A different budgeting approach, **zero-base budgeting (ZBB)**, is applicable in budgeting for service departments. ZBB, unlike the incremental approach, requires all expenses to be justified. In other words, the assumption is that each department starts with zero dollars (zero base) and must justify all budgeted amounts. Let's look at an example that illustrates the differences between the incremental and ZBB approaches to budgeting.

Assume that the marketing department of a hotel had a total departmental budget of $500,000 in 20X1. In 20X2, cost increases are expected to average 5 percent, and new advertising in the monthly city magazine is expected to cost $500 per month. Under the incremental approach, the marketing budget would be set at $531,000, determined as follows:

$$\$500,000 + \$500(12) + \$500,000(0.5) = \$531,000$$

Under ZBB, the marketing department would have to justify every dollar budgeted. That is, documentation would be required showing that all budgeted amounts are cost-justified. This means all payroll costs, supplies, advertising, and so forth would have to be shown to yield greater benefits than their cost.

The ZBB approach to budgeting in hotels appears to be limited to the service departments. However, since the total cost of these departments is approximately 25 percent of the average hotel's total revenue, the total amount can be considerable.

More detailed discussion of ZBB is beyond the scope of this chapter.[3]

Projecting Fixed Charges and Interest Expense

The next step in the budget formulation process is projecting fixed charges. In the *USALI*, several of these expenses are referred to as nonoperating expenses. Fixed charges include depreciation, insurance expense, property taxes, rent expense, and similar expenses. In addition, interest expense, if any, must be forecasted. These expenses are fixed and are projected on the basis of experience and expected changes for the next year.

Exhibit 10.3 illustrates how the interest expense budget for 20X2 is determined by estimating interest expense based on current and projected borrowings. Based on calculations in Exhibit 10.3, the interest expense budgeted for 20X2 is $107,000.

Even though the above-mentioned expenses are considered to be fixed, management and/or the board may be able to affect the fixed amounts for the year. For example, property taxes are generally based on assessed valuation and a property tax rate. Generally, a reduction in the assessed valuation will result in

Exhibit 10.3	Interest Expense Budget for 20X2			
Debt	**Principal**	**Interest Rate**	**Time**	**Amount**
Mortgage payment	$500,000	8%	Year	$ 40,000
Loan from partner A	500,000	12	Year	60,000
Working capital loans	200,000	7	6 mo.	7,000
			Total	$ 107,000

a reduction in the hotel's property taxes. Thus, if the property is over-assessed, management should pursue a reduction that, if successful, will lower the property tax expense. Some hotels have been successful in obtaining reductions in their assessments, thus reducing this "fixed" expense for the year.

The final step of the budget formulation process is for the controller to formulate the entire budget based on submissions from operated departments and service departments. The forecasted net income is a result of this process. If this bottom line is acceptable to the board of directors and/or the owners, then the budget formulation is complete. If the bottom line is not acceptable, then department heads are required to rework their budgets to provide a budget acceptable to the board and/or owners. Many changes may be proposed in this "rework" process, such as price changes, marketing changes, and cost reductions, to mention just a few. Often, the board or owner will provide a targeted bottom-line number before the budget is prepared. More often than not, budgets must be reworked several times before an acceptable budget is produced.

Budget Formulation Illustrated

A very simplified lodging example will be used to illustrate the preparation of an operations budget. The Sands Motel is a 20-room, limited-service lodging facility that has two profit centers: the rooms department and the pantry department. The Sands Motel also has two service centers: administration and a combined maintenance and utility cost department.

The board of directors has established the major financial goal of generating a minimum net income of 15 percent of sales. The income statements for the past three years are presented in Exhibit 10.4. An analysis of this financial information

Exhibit 10.4	Income Statements–Sands Motel

Income Statements Sands Motel
For the years 20X1–20X3

	20X1	20X2	20X3
Revenue:			
Rooms	$146,438	$158,634	$171,654
Pantry	2,962	3,466	4,246
Total	149,400	162,100	175,900
Departmental Expenses:			
Rooms:			
Payroll	21,966	23,000	27,465
Laundry	1,464	1,600	1,735
Linen	2,929	3,150	4,324
Commissions	1,470	1,578	1,650
All Other Expenses	1,500	2,380	2,575
Total	29,329	31,708	37,749
Pantry	2,850	3,350	4,285
Total	32,179	35,058	42,034
Departmental Income:			
Rooms	117,109	126,926	133,905
Pantry	112	116	(39)
Total	117,221	127,042	133,866

(continued)

Income Statements Sands Motel For the years 20X1–20X3	20X1	20X2	20X3
Undistributed Operating Expenses:			
Administration	27,470	30,105	32,795
Maintenance and Utility Costs	16,952	19,292	21,775
Total	44,422	49,397	54,570
Gross Operating Profit	72,799	77,645	79,296
Depreciation	15,000	15,000	15,500
Property Taxes	5,000	5,500	6,000
Insurance	5,000	5,000	5,000
Interest Expense	15,000	16,000	15,000
Income before Income Taxes	32,799	36,145	37,796
Income Taxes	9,840	10,844	11,339
Net Income	$ 22,959	$ 25,301	$ 26,457

Exhibit 10.5   Analysis of Income Statements–Sands Motel

Analysis of Income Statements Sands Motel For the years of 20X1–20X3	20X1	20X2	20X3
Rooms Sold	4,964	5,036	5,124
Occ. %	68	69	70
Average Rate	$29.50	$31.50	$33.50
Rooms Revenue	$146,438	$158,634	$171,654
Pantry revenue as a % of room revenue	2%	2.2%	2.5%
Rooms expenses %			
Payroll	15%	14.5%	16%
Laundry	1	1	1
Linen	2	2	2.5
Commissions	1	1	1
All other expenses	1	1.5	1.5
Total	20%	20%	22%
Administration			
Payroll			
Fixed	$20,000	$22,000	$24,000
Variable	3%	3%	2.5%
Other	2%	2%	2.5%
Maintenance and Utility Costs			
Maintenance			
Fixed	$4,000	$4,500	$5,000
Variable	3%	3%	3%
Utility Costs			
Fixed	$1,000	$1,500	$2,000
Variable	5%	5.2%	5.4%

Fixed Charges

  Depreciation—based on cost of fixed assets, expected lives, and straight-line method of depreciation
  Property taxes—historically has increased by $500 for 20X1 through 20X3
  Insurance—a three-year policy for 20X1–20X3 was quoted at $5,000 per year
  Interest expense—based on amount borrowed and prevailing interest rates
  Income taxes—based on 30% of income before income taxes

	20X1	20X2	20X3
Profit margin %	15.36%	15.61%	15.04%

appears in Exhibit 10.5. Economic environment information relevant to the Sands Motel in 20X4 is summarized as follows:

- No new firms are expected to compete with the Sands Motel.

- Overall consumer demand for motel rooms is expected to remain relatively constant.

- Inflation is expected to be about 5 percent in the next year. The major findings and projections for 20X4 are as follows:

Item	Analytical Findings	Projection for 20X4
1. Rooms Revenue		
Paid Occupancy	There is no new competition for next year, and the Sands has increased its paid occupancy one percentage point each year for the last three years. Assume a 1% increase in 20X4.	71%
Average Room Rate	This has increased by $2 each year, and the Sands Motel has still increased its occupancy percentage. An additional $2 increase appears to be reasonable for 20X4. Note: The $2 increase is 6% of the $33.50 average price for 20X3 and exceeds the expected inflation of 5%.	$35.50
2. Pantry Revenue %	This has increased from 0.2 percent to 2.5 percent. A 0.2% increase appears reasonable for 20X4.	2.7%
3. Rooms Expenses Payroll	This has fluctuated significantly due to labor unrest. Major pay increases this past year appear to be satisfying the two room attendants and part-time front office personnel. Keep the payroll percentage for 20X4 at 20X3 levels.	16%
Laundry	This has remained constant at 1% of rooms revenue for three years.	1%
Linen	A 0.5% increase was experienced in 20X3 due to major purchases. The prior 2% appears adequate for 20X4.	2%
Commissions	The average for the past three years has been 1%. Continue to use 1% as an estimate for 20X4.	1%
All Other Expenses	These have stabilized for the past two years at 1.5%. This appears reasonable.	1.5%
4. Pantry Expense	This has nearly equaled pantry revenue each year. A breakeven situation is reasonable for 20X4.	100% of pantry revenue

Item	Analytical Findings	Projection for 20X4
5. Administration		
Payroll	The fixed portion has increased approximately $2,000 per year from 20X1–20X3. A $3,000 increase is scheduled for 20X4 to reward the general manager. Variable labor (as a percentage of total revenue) is expected to be 3% for 20X4.	$27,000 and 3%
Other	Although this increased to 2.5% in 20X3, it is expected to return to the previous level of 2% in 20X4.	2%
6. Maintenance and Utility Costs		
Maintenance	The fixed portion of part-time workers' pay has increased $500 each year over three years. An increase of $1,000 is scheduled for 20X4. Variable maintenance of 3% appears adequate for 20X4.	$6,000 and 3%
Utility Costs	The fixed portion has increased approximately $500 each year since 20X1. Therefore, the estimated fixed portion should be increased accordingly for 20X4. The variable portion has increased 0.2% from 20X1–20X3. Utility costs are expected to be moderate in 20X4 and 5.4% appears reasonable.	$2,500 and 5.4%
7. Fixed Charges		
Depreciation	The accountant's calculation of depreciation for 20X4 is $15,000 for existing fixed assets and an additional $700 for a new computer to be purchased in 20X4.	$15,700
Property Taxes	This assessed valuation is expected to increase by 10% for 20X4. The tax rate is not expected to change; therefore, increase property taxes for 20X4 to $6,600.	$6,600
Insurance	The current three-year insurance policy expires on December 31. The new three-year policy requires a $6,000 premium each year.	$6,000
Interest Expense	The flexible interest rate, currently at 15%, is expected to average 14.5% for 20X4. The average debt outstanding for 20X4 will be $90,000. $90,000 × 0.145 = $13,050.	$13,050
Income Taxes	Income taxes for 20X1–20X3 were 30% of the income before income taxes. Due to reduced rates, the tax rate for 20X4 will be 25%.	25% of pretax income

Exhibit 10.6 Sample Operations Budget Worksheet

Operations Budget (Worksheet)
Sands Motel
For the year 20X4

	Calculation	Amount
Revenue:		
Rooms	365 × 20 × 0.71 × $35.50	$183,996
Pantry	$183,996 × 0.027	4,968
Total		188,964
Departmental Expenses:		
Rooms		
Payroll	183,996 × 0.16	29,439
Laundry	183,996 × 0.01	1,840
Linen	183,996 × 0.02	3,680
Commissions	183,996 × 0.01	1,840
All Other Expenses	183,996 × 0.015	2,760
Total		39,559
Pantry	(same as pantry revenue)	4,968
Departmental income:		
Rooms		144,437
Pantry		-0-
Total		144,437
Undistributed Operating Expenses:		
Administration	$27,000 + 0.05 ($188,964)	36,448
Maintenance and Utility Costs	$8,500 + 0.084 ($188,964)	24,373
Total		60,821
Gross Operating Profit		83,616
Insurance		6,000
Property Taxes		6,600
Depreciation		15,700
Interest Expense		13,050
Income before Income Taxes		42,266
Income Taxes	$42,266 × 0.30	12,680
Net Income		$ 29,586

The operations budget for 20X4 is shown in Exhibit 10.6. The projected 20X4 net income for the Sands Motel of $29,586 is 15.6 percent of sales, which exceeds the minimum requirement of 15 percent.

Flexible Budgets

The budgets we have discussed so far have been fixed (sometimes called static) in that only one level of activity was planned. However, no matter how sophisticated the budget process, it is improbable that the level of activity budgeted will be realized exactly. Therefore, when a fixed budget is used, variances from several budget line items, specifically for revenues and variable expenses, can almost always be expected. An alternative approach is to budget for several different levels of activity. For example, a hotel may budget at three paid occupancy levels, such as 69 percent, 71 percent, and 73 percent, even

Exhibit 10.7   Flexible Operations Budget–Sands Motel

Flexible Operations Budget
Sands Motel
For the year of 20X4

| | Activity Levels—Occupancy % | | |
	69%	71%	73%
Revenue:			
Rooms	$178,813	$183,996	$189,179
Pantry	4,828	4,968	5,108
Total	183,641	188,964	194,287
Departmental Expenses:			
Rooms	28,445	39,559	40,673
Pantry	4,828	4,968	5,108
Total	43,273	44,527	45,781
Departmental Income:			
Rooms	140,368	144,437	148,506
Pantry	0	0	0
Total	140,368	144,437	148,506
Undistributed Operating Expenses:			
Administration	36,182	36,448	36,714
Maintenance and Utility Costs	23,926	24,373	24,820
Total	60,108	60,821	61,534
Gross Operating Profit:	80,260	83,616	86,972
Insurance	6,000	6,000	6,000
Property Taxes	6,600	6,600	6,600
Depreciation	15,700	15,700	15,700
Interest	13,050	13,050	13,050
Income before Income Taxes	38,910	42,266	45,622
Income Taxes	11,673	12,680	13,687
Net Income	$ 27,237	$ 29,586	$ 31,935

though it believes that the level of activity is likeliest to be at the 71 percent level. With flexible budgeting, revenues and variable expenses change with each level of activity, while fixed expenses remain constant.

Exhibit 10.7 contains three condensed operations budgets for the Sands Motel. The flexible budgeting reflects occupancy at 69 percent, 71 percent, and 73 percent. The static budget for the Sands Motel (Exhibit 10.6) was based on 71 percent occupancy. The kinds of observations that should be made in relation to flexible budgeting reflected in Exhibit 10.7 include the following:

■ Revenues increase/decrease with occupancy.

■ Departmental expenses increase/decrease with occupancy.

■ Undistributed operating expenses increase/decrease only slightly, since a major portion of these expenses is fixed.

■ Fixed expenses remain constant as expected.

■ Net income changes with activity, but not as much as revenue.

■ Net income as a percentage of total revenue for the three levels of activity is as follows:

At 69% occupancy: $\dfrac{\text{Net Income}}{\text{Total Revenue}}$ = $\dfrac{27,237}{183,641}$ = <u>14.8</u>%

At 71% occupancy: $\dfrac{\text{Net Income}}{\text{Total Revenue}}$ = $\dfrac{29,586}{188,964}$ = <u>15.7</u>%

At 73% occupancy: $\dfrac{\text{Net Income}}{\text{Total Revenue}}$ = $\dfrac{31,935}{194,287}$ = <u>16.4</u>%

Therefore, the minimum required profit margin percentage of 15 percent can only be realized at the budgeted occupancy levels of 71 percent and 73 percent. Since 69 percent yields less than the targeted 15 percent profit margin, management may be requested to review the budget at 69 percent in an attempt to achieve the desired net income.

The flexible budget is relatively easy to prepare using computers. The relationship between revenues and expenses is expressed in formulas, and the computer, with minor human assistance, is able to do the rest. The major benefit of the flexible budget is to provide management and owners with bottom-line results for alternative levels of activity. Many activity levels can be projected.

As a note of caution, however, forecasters should realize that different levels of activity will most likely affect prices and possibly related expenses. For example, a room rate of $35.50 was used across the three occupancy levels in the Sands Motel's flexible operations budget. However, in order to increase occupancy above 73 percent, an average price reduction may be necessary, and a still greater price reduction may be required beyond 80 percent or some other higher number.

Budgeting for a New Lodging Property

The preceding discussion covers budgeting for an existing lodging property. However, a hotel in its first year lacks a historical base. How can it prepare its budget? Certainly, one source for budgeting for a hotel's first year is the lodging feasibility study (LFS) that is generally prepared to secure the financing for the property. This study provides a summary of operations, including sales, direct expenses of the profit centers, and operating overhead expenses. However, forecasters should not rely totally on these numbers for two major reasons. First, the study is prepared to secure financing, and the figures are not detailed by month, type of market, and so forth. Second, the LFS is prepared before the construction of the hotel, which is probably two years before the opening of the hotel; thus, the figures are somewhat dated. Nonetheless, it is a set of figures with which to start. These numbers should be updated on the basis of current room rates, labor costs, and other expenses.[4]

If a new hotel is part of a chain, cost information of similar properties can be obtained. When used cautiously, this information will be reasonably useful.

Finally, few if any new hotels or restaurants make a bottom-line profit their first year. Unexpected expenses arise until the "bugs" are worked out and the market realizes the property exists. Therefore, the initial budget should allow for these higher-than-normal costs and possibly lower-than-desired revenues. A critical need is to have sufficient cash to carry the new property to the point of cash breakeven, which often is delayed until the second or third year of operation.

10.6 BUDGETARY CONTROL

In order for budgets to be used effectively for control purposes, budget reports must be prepared periodically (generally on a monthly basis) for each level of financial responsibility. In a hotel, this would normally require budget reports for profit, cost, and service centers.

Budget reports may take many forms. Exhibit 10.8 is a consolidated profit and loss statement of a full-service Marriott Hotel. It shows the overall figures for operations month by month. All the numbers on this statement are supported by detailed supplementary schedules (not included in this book). Marriott follows the format recommended in the *USALI*.

Exhibit 10.9 is a departmental budget report for the rooms department of a Marriott Hotel. It provides a further breakdown of the elements that make up revenues, wages, benefits, and other expenses. This report, which is available to corporate management, also goes to the next level of management below the general manager and directors of finance and accounting.

In order for the reports to be useful, they must be timely and relevant. Budget reports issued weeks after the end of the accounting period are too late to allow managers to investigate variances, determine causes, and take timely action. Relevant financial information includes only the revenues and expenses for which the individual department head is held responsible. For example, including allocated overhead expenses such as administrative and general salaries on a rooms department budget report is rather meaningless from a control viewpoint because the rooms department manager is unable to affect these costs. Further, they detract from the expenses that the rooms department manager can take action to control. Relevant reporting also requires sufficient detail to allow reasonable judgments regarding budget variances. Of course, information overload (which generally results in management's failure to act properly) should be avoided. There are five steps in the budgetary control process, and they are detailed in Sections 10.7 to 10.10:

1. Determination of variances

2. Determination of significant variances

3. Analysis of significant variances

4. Determination of problems

5. Action to correct problems

10.7 DETERMINATION OF VARIANCES

Variances are determined by using the budget report to compare actual results to the budget. The budget report should disclose both monthly variances and year-to-date variances. Variance analysis generally focuses on monthly variances because the year-to-date variances are essentially the sum of monthly variances.

Exhibit 10.10 is the January 20X4 summary budget report for the Sands Motel. This budget report contains only monthly financial information and not separate year-to-date numbers, as January is the first month of the fiscal year for the Sands Motel.

Variances shown on this report include both dollar variances and percentage variances. The dollar variances result from subtracting the actual results from the budget figures. For example, rooms revenue for the Sands Motel was $14,940, while the budgeted rooms revenue was $15,620, resulting in a difference of $680. The difference is set in parentheses to reflect an unfavorable variance. Dollar variances are considered either favorable or unfavorable based on situations presented in Exhibit 10.11.

Exhibit 10.8 Consolidated Profit and Loss Statement–Full Service Marriott Hotel

Marriott International, Inc.
Consolidated Profit and Loss Statement
Full Service Business Unit
20x2 Budget as of December 31, 20x1
In Operating Currency - (000's)

Spread View - Budget NY

	January	February	March	April	May	June	July	August	September	October	November	December	Total	% of Total
SALES														
ROOMS	1,369	1,366	1,768	1,459	1,554	1,422	1,418	1,216	1,425	1,858	1,173	826	16,876	51.4%
RESTAURANTS	90	83	109	90	91	95	109	92	75	104	79	70	1,087	3.3%
LOUNGES	241	248	301	283	337	348	379	316	303	375	238	213	3,590	10.9%
AUDIO VISUAL	57	57	57	61	57	47	36	36	48	69	56	46	627	1.9%
BANQUET	975	852	1,033	770	1,022	828	533	708	520	787	700	571	9,299	28.3%
TOT FOOD & BEV	1,362	1,241	1,500	1,210	1,508	1,318	1,057	1,152	947	1,335	1,073	900	14,603	44.5%
LEISURE/RECREATION	0	0	1	2	6	6	5	5	3	2	1	0	41	0.1%
SPA	19	21	24	26	32	32	32	26	29	30	19	25	315	1.0%
MISCELLANEOUS INCOME	64	62	73	71	70	70	81	76	69	78	63	70	846	2.6%
OTHER DEPTS.	12	11	15	12	13	13	14	13	13	15	11	9	151	0.5%
TOTAL SALES	2,827	2,722	3,382	2,780	3,184	2,861	2,617	2,497	2,485	3,317	2,341	1,830	32,832	100.0%
DEPARTMENT PROFIT														
ROOMS	1,024	1,067	1,391	1,142	1,223	1,089	1,055	888	1,065	1,486	891	596	12,918	76.5%
RESTAURANTS	62	51	70	51	52	57	66	54	41	62	40	33	642	59.1%
LOUNGES	107	115	148	145	177	184	206	160	147	189	106	85	1,770	49.3%
AUDIO VISUAL	57	57	57	61	57	47	36	36	48	69	56	46	627	100.0%
BANQUET	711	616	741	539	732	582	327	464	326	550	468	367	6,421	69.1%
KITCHEN (% FOOD SALES)	(380)	(341)	(402)	(340)	(402)	(387)	(348)	(364)	(312)	(369)	(335)	(255)	(4,235)	(47.6%)
TOT FOOD & BEV	557	498	615	456	617	482	287	349	250	501	330	278	5,226	35.9%
LEISURE/RECREATION	(12)	(10)	(21)	(20)	(19)	(24)	(77)	(24)	(17)	(20)	(18)	(13)	(214)	(516.6%)
SPA	1	4	4	6	9	8	6	5	6	7	1	4	60	19.0%
MISCELLANEOUS INCOME	64	62	73	71	70	70	81	76	69	78	63	70	846	100.0%
OTHER DEPTS.	12	11	15	12	13	13	14	13	13	15	11	9	151	100.0%
TOT DEPT PROFIT	1,646	1,633	2,077	1,667	1,913	1,635	1,425	1,307	1,385	2,066	1,285	944	15,996	57.1%
UNDISTRIBUTED OPERATING EXP														
ADMINISTRATIVE & GENERAL	176	157	191	169	181	185	172	152	163	186	156	145	2,037	6.2%
INFORMATION & TELECOM SYSTEMS	92	80	87	83	88	84	80	79	77	95	87	100	1,034	3.2%
PROPERTY OPERATION & MAINT.	42	42	48	47	49	52	56	53	44	47	40	41	561	1.7%
UTILITIES	96	86	96	89	92	97	92	89	95	90	108	113	1,143	3.5%
CNTR TRAIN & RELOC	10	10	10	10	10	10	10	10	10	10	10	10	118	0.4%
SALES & MARKETING	233	193	220	199	215	210	190	193	177	215	191	170	2,405	7.3%
TOTAL UNDISTRIBUTED OP EXP	649	568	652	597	636	638	599	576	566	645	592	578	7,297	22.2%
GROSS OPERATING PROFIT	997	1,065	1,424	1,070	1,278	1,000	825	731	819	1,422	693	366	11,699	35.6%
GOP MARGIN	35.3%	39.1%	42.1%	38.5%	40.1%	34.9%	31.5%	29.4%	32.9%	42.9%	29.6%	20.0%	35.6%	
BASE MGMT FEE	85	82	101	83	96	86	79	75	75	100	70	55	985	3.0%
INCENTIVE MGMT FEE	0	0	9	(6)	34	(37)	0	0	0	0	0	0	0	0.0%
TOTAL MANAGEMENT FEES	85	82	111	77	130	48	79	75	75	100	70	55	985	3.0%
INCOME BEFORE NON-OP INC/EXP	912	983	1,314	993	1,148	951	747	656	744	1,322	623	311	10,704	32.6%
Non-Op Inc/Exp Excl. Owner Exp	216	214	237	228	230	228	246	236	222	243	210	221	2,731	8.3%
EBITDA Excluding Owner Expenses	696	770	1,077	765	917	723	501	420	522	1,079	413	90	7,974	24.3%
Owner Expenses	80	0	0	0	0	0	0	0	0	0	0	0	80	0.2%
EBITDA	616	770	1,077	765	917	723	501	420	522	1,079	413	90	7,894	24.1%
REPLACEMENT RESERVE	57	54	68	56	64	57	52	50	50	66	47	37	657	2.0%
EBITDA Less REPLACEMENT RESV	560	715	1,009	709	854	666	449	371	473	1,013	366	53	7,237	22.0%
Net Due To/(From) Owner	560	715	1,009	709	854	666	449	371	473	1,013	366	53	7,237	22.0%
Retained Profit/(Loss)	0	0	0	0	0	0	0	0	0	0	0	0	0	0.0%
MARRIOTT PROFIT CONTRIB														
BMF INCOME	265	255	317	261	299	268	245	233	233	311	219	172	3,078	3.0%
IMF INCOME	0	0	29	(20)	108	(117)	0	0	0	0	0	0	0	0.0%
OTHER MI INC/ (EXP)	(34)	(34)	(34)	(34)	(34)	(34)	(34)	(34)	(34)	(34)	(34)	(34)	(412)	(0.4%)
TOTAL MI PROFIT CONTRIB	231	221	312	206	372	117	211	199	199	277	185	137	2,666	2.6%
KEY STATISTICS														
ROOMS SOLD	7,013	6,507	8,535	7,097	7,504	7,491	8,108	7,169	7,211	8,339	6,324	5,161	86,457	
TOTAL OCCUPANCY	70.7%	72.6%	86.0%	73.9%	75.6%	78.0%	81.7%	72.3%	75.1%	84.1%	65.9%	52.0%	74.0%	
AVERAGE RATE	195.25	213.07	207.20	205.64	207.11	189.76	174.90	169.64	197.56	222.80	185.54	160.14	195.19	
ROOM REVPAR	138.04	154.74	178.27	152.01	156.68	148.08	142.94	122.59	148.39	187.29	122.23	83.31	144.48	
TOTAL REVPAR	284.94	303.76	340.88	289.59	320.97	298.01	263.82	250.67	258.86	334.42	243.84	184.48	281.10	

Courtesy of Marriott International.

Exhibit 10.9 Departmental Budget Report – Rooms Department

Marriott International, Inc.
Departmental Profit and Loss Statement
Full Service Business Unit
20x2 Budget as of December 31, 20x1
In Operating Currency - (000's)

Spread View - Budget NY

	January	February	March	April	May	June	July	August	September	October	November	December	Total	%
TOTAL OCC ROOMS	8,768	8,270	11,663	10,894	10,179	9,837	11,669	9,685	8,073	9,448	8,033	5,743	112,263	73.2%
OCC PT	67.3%	70.3%	89.6%	86.5%	76.2%	78.1%	89.6%	74.4%	64.1%	72.6%	63.6%	44.1%	73.2%	
DEPARTMENT SALES	3,664,363	3,682,447	4,964,691	4,388,360	4,539,323	4,160,429	3,890,516	3,216,623	3,276,278	4,150,377	3,328,016	2,507,013	45,768,837	
DEPARTMENT VOLUME	31,059	29,100	43,918	42,291	42,756	39,841	45,102	34,092	30,466	36,795	32,517	24,130	432,068	
ROOM	4,135,546	4,451,067	6,188,382	5,610,107	5,311,898	4,969,753	4,922,196	4,015,204	4,136,053	5,033,287	3,896,234	2,350,889	55,020,616	
FEES	(111,568)	(94,357)	(120,538)	(106,986)	(108,386)	(108,087)	(103,666)	(87,006)	(85,296)	(102,359)	(87,903)	(73,921)	(1,190,063)	
TELEPHONE	40,293	38,007	53,601	50,067	46,779	45,209	53,627	44,508	43,422	43,422	36,916	26,393	515,924	
FOOD	2,559,586	2,388,494	3,169,432	2,616,742	2,903,725	2,581,206	2,262,278	1,753,566	1,928,278	2,649,984	2,336,119	2,028,577	29,177,989	
BEVERAGE	791,068	727,812	1,005,024	903,659	1,191,416	1,067,282	1,002,519	907,662	916,923	916,923	835,555	646,828	10,539,262	
OTHER	1,309,747	1,256,707	1,524,793	1,374,888	1,452,480	1,351,373	1,126,180	1,024,691	1,041,012	1,340,564	1,106,926	990,312	14,906,693	
TOTAL SALES	3,664,383	3,682,447	4,964,691	4,388,360	4,539,323	4,160,829	3,890,516	3,216,623	3,276,278	4,150,377	3,328,016	2,507,013	45,768,837	
FOOD	167,759	157,743	206,609	192,167	202,246	191,413	203,012	130,948	166,658	194,753	173,848	111,387	2,098,541	17.1%
BEVERAGE	50,124	45,838	64,315	59,212	76,468	68,722	66,675	61,681	48,975	59,507	40,959	38,194	680,671	15.4%
OTHER	10,894	10,685	14,023	12,259	12,259	14,540	13,657	16,229	14,940	15,993	16,183	9,590	160,062	2.6%
TOTAL COST OF SALES	228,777	214,266	284,947	262,448	290,974	274,675	283,344	208,858	230,573	270,252	230,990	159,171	2,939,274	6.4%
SALARIES & WAGES	467,201	469,789	614,729	595,442	603,693	581,838	682,764	568,253	511,978	563,237	488,029	458,890	6,605,844	14.4%
MGMT SALARIES	227,926	239,654	273,509	263,574	271,476	258,485	269,231	252,879	234,922	279,921	232,618	232,527	3,036,720	6.6%
OVERTIME PREMIUM	11,556	13,169	23,118	17,413	20,546	19,876	21,905	20,501	11,567	17,267	17,157	12,660	206,935	0.5%
SERVICE CHARGE DISTRIBUTION	132,778	124,523	157,617	130,377	147,967	129,512	105,258	84,483	101,035	139,465	118,974	112,735	1,484,724	3.2%
CONTRACT/BUYOUT LBR	0	0	0	0	0	0	0	0	0	0	0	0	0	0.0%
BONUSES	29,600	27,380	32,507	31,530	31,506	31,087	31,626	31,033	31,335	31,261	30,927	31,380	371,172	0.8%
OTHER WAGES	3,664	6,211	7,627	7,561	5,956	7,074	8,630	8,082	6,059	6,160	6,274	5,852	79,369	0.2%
TOTAL SALARIES & WAGES	872,724	880,726	1,109,107	1,045,917	1,081,146	1,027,872	1,119,814	965,231	896,896	1,037,311	893,979	854,243	11,784,784	25.7%
HOURS & HRS POR	37,681	37,508	47,521	46,154	47,220	45,654	52,508	43,569	39,695	44,241	37,863	35,212	514,827	4.59
SALES/HOUR	97.25	98.18	104.47	95.08	96.13	91.14	74.09	73.83	82.54	93.81	87.90	71.20	88.90	
AVERAGE RATE	12.40	12.52	12.84	12.90	12.78	12.74	13.00	13.04	12.90	12.73	12.89	13.03	12.83	
NUMBER OF MANAGERS	44	0	0	0	0	0	0	0	0	0	0	0	44	
PAID TIME OFF	105,193	38,095	55,617	45,114	78,209	15,366	75,112	42,411	72,247	44,082	71,020	73,018	715,684	1.6%
TAX EXPENSE	85,858	91,058	82,218	74,769	79,859	73,871	78,928	65,000	61,933	68,893	64,623	60,841	885,651	1.9%
MED/PROF SHR	111,607	109,721	117,075	113,776	118,606	115,539	117,926	116,203	115,988	117,293	116,662	117,597	1,398,195	3.0%
ASSOC RELATIONS	9,678	9,678	9,678	9,678	9,678	9,678	9,678	9,678	9,678	9,678	9,678	9,678	116,132	0.3%
ASSOC FOOD	16,979	15,199	18,560	15,412	16,237	19,364	17,920	21,290	19,338	21,727	22,262	15,527	219,814	0.5%
WC EPL PREMIUM	9,123	10,140	13,267	9,902	10,279	11,173	9,969	10,271	9,175	9,884	10,937	11,708	125,838	0.3%
WC EPL DEDUCTIBLE	4,459	4,537	4,682	4,776	5,392	5,745	5,919	5,745	4,979	4,716	4,550	4,518	60,018	0.1%
OTHER BENEFITS	6,089	(30,866)	(2,843)	2,838	623	2,067	4,035	7,364	742	8,103	(1,385)	3,095	(728)	(0.0%)
TOTAL EMP COST	348,986	247,572	298,153	276,265	318,682	252,803	317,486	277,962	294,279	284,386	298,047	295,983	3,510,604	7.7%
% TO TOT WAGES	40.0%	28.1%	26.9%	26.4%	29.5%	24.6%	28.4%	28.8%	32.8%	27.4%	33.3%	34.6%	29.8%	
GROSS PROF AFT WG	2,213,877	2,339,883	3,272,484	2,803,731	2,848,523	2,605,479	2,170,072	1,764,572	1,854,531	2,558,428	1,905,000	1,197,615	27,534,195	60.2%
TOTAL CONTROLLABLES	829,726	757,459	931,637	853,187	905,103	835,459	855,606	813,415	822,350	918,942	647,729	621,480	9,792,093	21.4%
CONTROLLABLES CPV	26.71	26.03	21.21	20.17	21.17	20.97	18.97	23.86	26.99	24.97	19.92	25.76	22.66	
DEPT PROFIT/(EXP)	1,384,151	1,582,424	2,340,847	1,950,543	1,943,420	1,770,020	1,314,466	951,157	1,032,181	1,639,486	1,257,271	576,135	17,742,102	38.8%
TOTAL INV FACTORS	1,287,851	1,485,580	2,071,388	1,764,543	1,753,983	1,621,100	1,270,296	960,755	1,041,548	1,534,246	1,206,756	514,555	16,532,602	36.1%
DEPT NET PROFIT/(EXP)	96,301	96,843	269,459	186,000	189,437	148,920	44,170	(28,598)	(9,388)	105,240	50,515	61,580	1,209,500	2.6%
DEPARTMENT CPV	3.10	3.33	6.14	4.40	4.43	3.74	0.98	(0.87)	(0.31)	2.86	1.55	2.55	2.80	
STATISTICS	12,552,540	11,770,867	14,638,914	13,968,552	17,258,876	17,943,938	11,908,662	18,085,959	15,669,537	15,486,384	12,749,840	7,850,755	169,910,844	

Courtesy of Marriott International.

Exhibit 10.10   Summary Budget Report–Sands Motel

Summary Budget Report Sands Motel
For January 20X4

	Budget	Actual	Variances $	%
Revenue:				
Rooms	$ 15,620	$ 14,940	$ (680)	(4.35)%
Pantry	429	414	(15)	(3.50)
Total	16,049	15,354	(695)	(4.33)
Departmental Expenses:				
Rooms				
Payroll	2,500	2,243	257	10.28
Laundry	156	150	6	3.85
Linen	313	300	13	4.15
Commissions	156	150	6	3.85
All other expenses	234	200	34	14.53
Total	3,359	3,043	316	9.41
Pantry	422	380	42	9.95
Total	3,781	3,423	358	9.47
Rooms	12,268	11,911	(357)	(2.91)
Pantry	0	20	20	NA
Total	12,268	11,931	(337)	(2.75)
Undistributed Operating Expenses:				
Administration	3,052	2,961	91	2.98
Maintenance and Utility Costs	2,169	2,220	(51)	(2.35)
Gross Operating Profit:	7,047	6,750	(297)	(4.21)
Insurance	500	500	-0-	-0-
Property Taxes	550	550	-0-	-0-
Depreciation	1,308	1,308	-0-	-0-
Interest Expense	1,087	1,087	-0-	-0-
Income before Income Taxes	3,602	3,305	(297)	(8.25)
Income Taxes	1,081	99	289	8.23
Net Income	$ 2,521	$ 2,313	$ (208)	(8.25)%

Exhibit 10.11   Evaluating Dollar Variance Situations

	Situation	Variance
Revenues	Actual exceeds budget	Favorable
	Budget exceeds actual	Unfavorable
Expenses	Budget exceeds actual	Favorable
	Actual exceeds budget	Unfavorable

Percentage variances are determined by dividing the dollar variance by the budgeted amount. For rooms revenue (Exhibit 10.10), the (4.35 percent) is the result of dividing $(680) by $15,620.

Variances should be determined for all line items on budget reports along with an indication of whether the variance is favorable or unfavorable.

The kind of variance can be indicated by marking it "+" for favorable and "–" for unfavorable, "F" for favorable and "U" for unfavorable, or placing parentheses around unfavorable variances and showing favorable variances without parentheses, as shown in Exhibit 10.10. Some enterprises simply asterisk unfavorable variances.

10.8 DETERMINATION OF SIGNIFICANT VARIANCES

Virtually all budgeted revenue and expense items on a budget report will differ from the actual amounts, with the possible exception of fixed expenses. This is only to be expected because no budgeting process, however sophisticated, is perfect. However, simply because a variance exists does not mean that management should analyze the variance and follow through with appropriate corrective actions. Only significant variances require this kind of management analysis and action.

Criteria used to determine which variances are significant are called **significance criteria**. They are generally expressed in terms of both dollar and percentage differences. Dollar and percentage differences should be used jointly due to the weakness of each when used separately. Dollar differences fail to recognize the magnitude of the base. For example, a large hotel may have a $1,000 difference in rooms revenue from the budgeted amount. Yet the $1,000 difference based on a budget of $1 million results in a percentage difference of only 0.1 percent. Most managers would agree this is insignificant. However, if the rooms revenue budget for the period was $10,000, a $1,000 difference would result in a percentage difference of 10 percent, which most managers would consider significant. This seems to suggest that variances should be considered significant based on the percentage difference. However, the percentage difference also fails at times. For example, assume that the budget for an expense is $10. A dollar difference of $2 results in a 20 percent percentage difference. The percentage difference appears significant, but generally, little (if any) managerial time should be spent analyzing and investigating a $2 difference.

Therefore, the dollar and percentage differences should be used jointly in determining which variances are significant. The size of the significance criteria will differ among hospitality properties in relation to the size of the operation and the controllability of certain revenue or expense items. In general, the larger the operation, the larger the dollar difference criteria. Also, the greater the control exercised over the item, the smaller the criteria.

For example, a large hospitality operation may set significance criteria as follows:

Revenue	$1,000 and 4 percent
Variable expense	$500 and 2 percent
Fixed expense	$50 and 1 percent

A smaller hospitality operation may set significance criteria as follows:

Revenue	$200 and 4 percent
Variable expense	$100 and 2 percent
Fixed expense	$50 and 1 percent

Notice that the change in criteria, based on size of operation, is generally the dollar difference. Both significance criteria decrease as the item becomes more controllable.

To illustrate the determination of significant variances, the significance criteria above for a small hospitality operation will be applied to the Sands Motel's January 20X4 budget report (see Exhibit 10.10). The following revenue and expense items have significant variances:

1. The unfavorable $680 difference between the budgeted rooms revenue and the actual rooms revenue exceeds the dollar difference criterion of $200, and the unfavorable 4.35 percent percentage difference exceeds the percentage difference criterion of 4 percent.

2. The favorable $257 difference between the budgeted rooms payroll expense and the actual rooms payroll expense exceeds the dollar difference criterion of $100, and the favorable 10.28 percent difference exceeds the percentage difference criterion of 2 percent.

3. Several rooms expense variances, such as laundry, linen, and commissions, exceed the percentage difference criterion, but do not exceed the dollar difference criterion, so they are not considered significant; therefore, they will not be subjected to variance analysis.

10.9 VARIANCE ANALYSIS

Variance analysis is the process of analyzing variances in order to give management more information about variances. With this additional information, management is better prepared to identify the causes of any variances.

We will look at variance analysis for three general areas—revenue, cost of goods sold, and variable labor. The basic models presented in these areas can be applied to other similar areas. For each area, formulas, a graph, and an example will be provided. In addition, the two significant variances of the Sands Motel, rooms revenue and rooms payroll expense, will be analyzed.

Revenue Variance Analysis

Revenue variances occur because of price and volume differences. Thus, the variances relating to revenue are called *price variance* (PV) and *volume variance* (VV). The formulas for these variances are as follows:

$$\frac{\text{Price}}{\text{Variance}} = \frac{\text{Budgeted}}{\text{Volume}} \times \left(\frac{\text{Actual}}{\text{Price}} - \frac{\text{Budgeted}}{\text{Price}} \right)$$

$$PV = BV(AP - BP)$$

$$\frac{\text{Volume}}{\text{Variance}} = \frac{\text{Budgeted}}{\text{Price}} \times \left(\frac{\text{Actual}}{\text{Volume}} - \frac{\text{Budgeted}}{\text{Volume}} \right)$$

$$VV = BP(AV - BV)$$

A minor variance due to the interrelationship of the price and volume variance is the *price-volume variance* (P-VV), calculated as follows:

$$\frac{\text{Price-Volume}}{\text{Variance}} = \left(\frac{\text{Actual}}{\text{Price}} - \frac{\text{Budgeted}}{\text{Price}} \right) \times \left(\frac{\text{Actual}}{\text{Volume}} - \frac{\text{Budgeted}}{\text{Volume}} \right)$$

$$P\text{-}VV = (AP - BP)(AV - BV)$$

Exhibit 10.12   Rooms Revenue: Budget and Actual–Sample Motel

	Room Nights	Average Price	Total
Budget	400	$ 100	$ 40,000
Actual	450	90	40,500
Difference	50	$ 10	$500 (F)

These formulas are illustrated by using the Sample Motel, whose budget and actual monthly results for rooms revenue appear in Exhibit 10.12.

The budget variance of $500 is favorable. Variance analysis will be conducted to determine the general cause(s) of this variance—that is, price, volume, or the interrelationship of the two. The price variance for the Sample Motel is determined as follows:

$$PV = BP(AP - BP)$$
$$= 400(\$90 - \$100)$$
$$= -\$4,000 \text{ (U)}$$

The price variance of $4,000 is unfavorable because the average price charged per room night of $90 was $10 less than the budgeted average price of $100.

The volume variance is computed as follows:

$$VV = BP(AV - BV)$$
$$= \$100(450 - 400)$$
$$= \$5,000 \text{ (F)}$$

The volume variance of $5,000 is favorable, because 50 more rooms per night were sold than planned.

The price-volume variance is determined as follows:

$$P\text{-}VV = (AP - BP)(AV - BV)$$
$$= (\$90 - \$100)(450 - 400)$$
$$= -\$500 \text{ (U)}$$

The price-volume variance is due to the interrelationship of the volume and price variances. Ten dollars per room less than budgeted multiplied by the 50 excess rooms results in an unfavorable $500 price-volume variance.

The sum of the three variances equals the budget variance of $500 for room revenue as follows:

VV	$ 5,000 (F)
PV	−4,000 (U)
P-VV	−500 (U)
Total	$ 500 (F)

The price-volume variance in the analysis of revenue variances will be unfavorable when the price and volume variances are different—that is, when one is favorable and the other is unfavorable. When the price and volume variances are the same—that is, either both are favorable, or both are unfavorable—then the price-volume variance will be favorable.

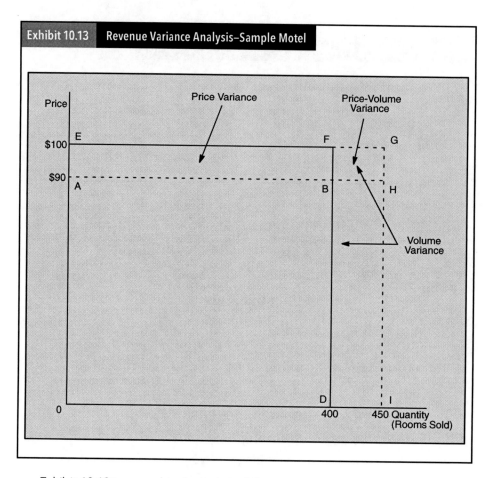

Exhibit 10.13 Revenue Variance Analysis–Sample Motel

Exhibit 10.13 is a graphic depiction of the revenue variance analysis for the Sample Motel. The rectangle 0EFD represents the budgeted amount. The rectangle 0AHI represents the actual amount of rooms revenue. The price variance is the rectangle AEFB. The volume variance is the rectangle DFGI. The price-volume variance is the rectangle BFGH.

Cost of Goods Sold Analysis

The **cost of goods sold variance** occurs because of differences due to cost and volume. That is, the amount paid for the goods sold (food and/or beverage) differs from the budget, and the total amount sold differs from the budgeted sales. The detailed variances related to the cost of goods are called the *cost variance* (CV), the *volume variance* (VV), and the *cost-volume variance* (C-VV). The formulas for these variances are as follows:

$$\text{Cost Varience} = \text{Budgeted Volume} \times \left(\text{Budgeted Cost} - \text{Actual Cost} \right)$$

$$\text{CV} = \text{BV(BC − AC)}$$

$$\text{Volume Variance} = \text{Budgeted Cost} \times \left(\text{Budgeted Volume} - \text{Actual Volume} \right)$$

$$\text{VV} = \text{BC(BV − AV)}$$

$$\text{Cost-Volume Variance} = \left(\text{Budgeted Cost} - \text{Actual Cost} \right) \times \left(\text{Budgeted Volume} - \text{Actual Volume} \right)$$

$$\text{C-VV} = \text{(BC − AC)(BV − AV)}$$

	Covers	Average Cost per Cover	Total Cost
Budget	3,000	$ 4.00	$12,000
Actual	3,200	4.10	13,120
Difference	200	$ 0.10	$ 1,120 (U)

Exhibit 10.14   Cost of Food Sold: Budget and Actual–Sample Restaurant

The cost-volume variance results from the interrelationship of the cost and volume variances.

The analysis of the cost of goods sold variance formulas is illustrated by using a foodservice example. The Sample Restaurant, open for dinner only, had cost of food sold results and budgeted amounts for January as shown in Exhibit 10.14. The budget variance of $1,120 is analyzed using variance analysis as follows:

The cost variance is determined as follows:

$$CV = BV(BC - AC)$$
$$= 3,000(\$4.00 - \$4.10)$$
$$= \$\underline{300} \ (U)$$

The cost variance of $300 is unfavorable because the cost per cover of 3,000 covers exceeded budget by $0.10.

The volume variance is determined as follows:

$$VV = BC(BV - AV)$$
$$= \$4(3,000 - \$3,200)$$
$$= -\$\underline{800} \ (U)$$

The volume variance of $800 is also unfavorable because excessive volume results in greater costs than budgeted. Remember that this is from an expense perspective. Excessive volume from a revenue perspective is favorable.

The cost-volume variance is determined as follows:

$$C\text{-}VV = (BC - AC)(BV - AV)$$
$$= (\$4.00 - \$4.10)(3,000 - 3,200)$$
$$= \$\underline{20} \ (U)$$

The cost-volume variance of $20 is also unfavorable, even though the mathematical sign of the result is positive. The cost-volume variance will be unfavorable when the other two variances (cost and volume) are the same—that is, when both are favorable or unfavorable. When the cost and volume variances differ—that is, when one is favorable and the other unfavorable—then the cost-volume variance will be favorable.

The sum of the three variances is $1,120:

Cost Variance	$ 300 (U)
Volume Variance	800 (U)
Cost-Volume Variance	20 (U)
Total	$1,120 (U)

This sum equals the $1,120 budget variance shown in Exhibit 10.14. These results show that of the total $1,120, only $300 was due to cost overruns. Further investigation should be undertaken to determine why there were excessive food costs of $300. The volume variance of $800 should be more than offset by the favorable volume variance for the Sample Restaurant food revenue. The cost-volume variance of $20 is due to the interrelationship of cost and volume. It is insignificant and requires no additional management attention.

Exhibit 10.15 is a graphic depiction of the cost of food sold variance analysis. The original budget of $12,000 for cost of food sold is represented by the rectangle 0ABC, while the actual food cost for the period is the rectangle 0DFH. Therefore, the difference between these two rectangles is the budget variance. The budget variance is divided among the three variances of cost, volume, and cost-volume. The cost variance is represented by the rectangle ADEB. The volume variance is represented by the rectangle BGHC. The cost-volume variance is represented by the rectangle BEFG.

Variable Labor Variance Analysis

Variable labor expense is labor expense that varies directly with activity. Variable labor increases as sales increase and decreases as sales decrease. In a lodging operation, the use of room attendants to clean rooms is a clear example of variable labor. Everything else being the same, the more rooms to be cleaned, the more room attendants' hours are necessary to clean the rooms; therefore, the greater the room attendants' wages. In a foodservice situation, servers' wages are generally treated as variable labor expense. Again, the greater the number of guests to be served food, the greater the number of servers; therefore, the

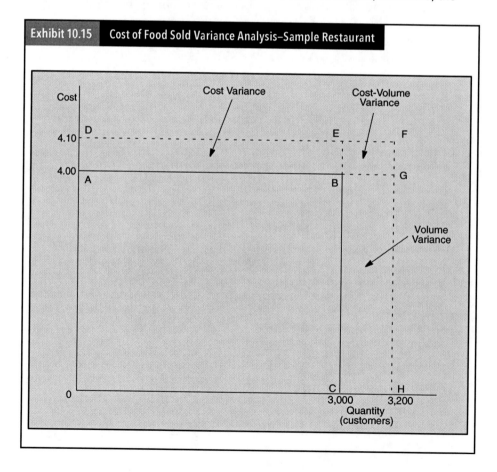

Exhibit 10.15   Cost of Food Sold Variance Analysis–Sample Restaurant

greater the server expense. The remainder of the discussion of labor in this section will pertain to variable labor, which we will simply call labor expense.

Labor expense variances result from three general causes—volume, rate, and efficiency. All budget variances for labor expense may be divided among these three areas. *Volume variances* (VV) result when there is a different volume of work than forecasted. *Rate variances* (RV) result when the average wage rate is different than planned. *Efficiency variances* (EV) result when the amount of work performed by the labor force on an hourly basis differs from the forecast. Of course, as with revenue variance analysis and with cost of goods sold variance analysis, there is a variance (called the *rate-time variance*) due to the interrelationship of the major elements of the labor budget variance. The formulas for these variances are:

$$VV = BR(BT - ATAO)$$
$$RV = BT(BR - AR)$$
$$EV = BR(ATAO - AT)$$
$$R\text{-}TV = (BT - AT)(BR - AR)$$

where the elements within these formulas are defined as follows:

- BR (Budgeted Rate)—the average wage rates budgeted per hour for labor services.

- BT (Budgeted Time)—hours required to perform work according to the budget. For example, if the work standard for serving meals is 15 customers per hour per server, then servers would require 40 hours (600 ÷ 15) to serve 600 meals.

- ATAO (Allowable Time for Actual Output)—hours allowable to perform work based on the actual output. This is determined in the same way as budgeted time, except that the work is actual versus budget. For example, if 660 meals were actually served, the allowable time given a work standard of 15 meals per hour would be 44 hours (660 ÷ 15).

- AR (Actual Rate)—the actual average wage rate paid per hour for labor services.

- AT (Actual Time)—the number of hours actually worked.

The calculation of these formulas is illustrated in Exhibit 10.16. The work standard for servers of the Sample Restaurant is serving 15 meals per hour. Therefore, on the average, a meal should be served every four minutes (60 ÷ 15).

Exhibit 10.16	Labor Expense: Budget and Actual–Sample Restaurant				
	Covers	Time/ Cover	Total Time	Hourly Wage	Total
Budget	3,000	4 min.	200 hrs.	$2.50	$500
Actual	3,200	5 min.	266 2/3 hrs.	2.40	640
Difference	200	1 min.	66 2/3 hrs.	0.10	$140 (U)

The volume variance is determined as follows:

$$VV = BR(BT - ATAO)$$
$$= \$2.50(200 - 213.33^*)$$
$$= -\$33.33 \text{ (U)}$$

*The ATAO of 213.33 is determined by dividing the work standard of 15 covers per hour into the 3,200 covers served.

The volume variance of $33.33 is unfavorable, because more covers were served than budgeted. Normally, the volume variance is beyond the control of the supervisor of personnel to which the labor expense pertains. Therefore, this should be isolated and generally not further pursued from an expense perspective. In addition, an unfavorable volume variance should be more than offset by the favorable volume variance for the related food sales.

The rate variance for the Sample Restaurant is determined as follows:

$$RV = BT(BR - AR)$$
$$= 200(\$2.50 - \$2.40)$$
$$= \$20 \text{ (F)}$$

The rate variance of $20 is favorable because the average pay rate per hour is $0.10 per hour less than the budgeted $2.50 per hour. The credit for this is normally given to the labor supervisor responsible for scheduling and managing labor.

The efficiency variance for the Sample Restaurant is determined as follows:

$$EV = BR(ATAO - AT)$$
$$= \$2.50(213.33 - 266.67)$$
$$= -\$133.35 \text{ (U)}$$

The efficiency variance of $133.35 is unfavorable, because an average of one minute was spent serving a meal than was originally planned. The supervisor must determine why this occurred. It could have been due to new employees who were inefficient because of work overload, or perhaps there were other factors. Once the specific causes are determined, the manager can take corrective action to ensure a future recurrence is avoided.

The rate-time variance is determined as follows:

$$R\text{-}TV = (BT - AT)(BR - AR)$$
$$= (200 - 266.67)(\$2.50 - \$2.40)$$
$$= -6.67 \text{ (F)}$$

The rate-time variance of $6.67 is favorable, even though the negative sign seems to indicate otherwise. This compound variance is favorable when the individual variances within it differ. In this case, the rate variance was favorable; however, the time variance was unfavorable.

The sum of the four variances equals the budget variance of $140 (U) as follows:

Volume Variance	$ 33.33 (U)
Rate Variance	20.00 (F)
Efficiency Variance	133.35 (U)
Rate-Time Variance	6.67 (F)
Total	$140.01 (U)

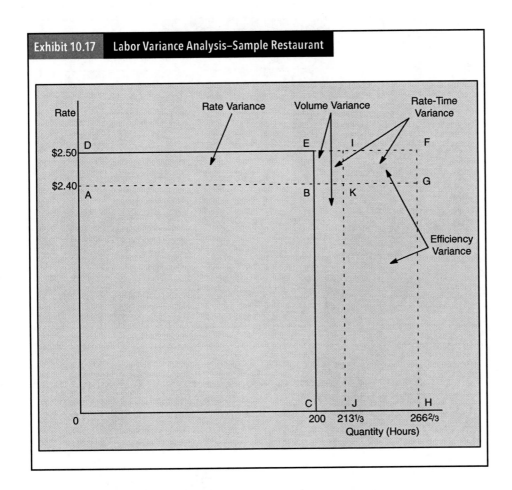

Exhibit 10.17 — Labor Variance Analysis–Sample Restaurant

The one-cent difference is due to rounding.

Exhibit 10.17 is a graphic depiction of the labor variance analysis of the Sample Restaurant. The budget for labor expense is represented by the rectangle 0DEC, while the actual labor expense is represented by the rectangle 0AGH. The rate variance is represented by the rectangle ADEB. The volume variance is represented by the rectangle CEIJ. The rectangle JIFH represents the efficiency variance. The rate-time variance is represented by the rectangle BEFG.

Variance Analysis of Sands Motel's Significant Variances

Exhibit 10.18 contains the analysis of the unfavorable rooms revenue variance of $680 identified earlier in the chapter for the Sands Motel. The breakdown is as follows:

Due to unfavorable volume differences	$887.50	(U)
Due to favorable price differences	220.00	(F)
Compound Variance	12.50	(U)
	$680.00	(U)

Management needs to investigate the causes of the failure to sell 25 additional rooms. This failure was partially offset by a favorable price variance.

Exhibit 10.18   Rooms Revenue Variance Analysis–Sands Motel

Analysis of Rooms Revenue Variance
Sands Motel
January 20X4

	Room Nights	Price	Total
Budget	440	$35.50	$15,620
Actual	415	36.00	14,940
Difference	25	$ 0.50	$ 680 (U)

Volume Variance
VV = BP (AV − BV)
VV = 35.50 (415 − 440)
VV = $887.50 (U)

Price Variance
PV = BV (AP − BP)
PV = 440 (36.00 − 35.50)
PV = $220 (F)

Price-Volume Variance
P-VV = (AV − BV)(AP − BP)
P-VV = (415 − 440) (36.00 − 35.50)
P-VV = $12.50 (U)

If the volume variance was due to controllable causes, such as price resistance or rooms being unavailable because they were out of order or simply not clean when potential guests desired them, then management action can be taken. If, on the other hand, the causes were beyond management's control, such as weather-related factors, then no specific management action appears to be required.

The other significant variance of the Sands Motel requiring analysis was rooms payroll, which was favorable during January 20X4, at $257. Assume that an analysis of rooms labor reveals the following:

	Budget	Actual	Difference
Room attendants	$ 737	$ 581	$156 (F)
Front office	1,763	1,662	101 (F)
	$ 2,500	$2,243	$257 (F)

Since the largest portion relates to room attendants' wages, only this portion is analyzed for illustrative purposes in Exhibit 10.19. The analysis of the $156 variance reveals favorable volume, rate, and efficiency variances.

When analyzing a variable labor variance, pay careful attention to each type of variance. Variable labor variance is a group of variances used to examine differences between budgeted and actual **variable labor expense**

Generally, a volume variance is beyond the scope of the labor supervisor's responsibility. For example, the $156 favorable room attendants' labor variance includes $41.88 of favorable volume variance. However, this results from fewer rooms being sold than budgeted—hardly a reason to praise the supervisor. Likewise, when more rooms are sold than budgeted, the room attendants' labor expense variance would contain an unfavorable volume variance. This portion of the total variance is not the fault of the supervisor and should be excluded when analyzing the budget variance.

Exhibit 10.19   Rooms Payroll Variance Analysis–Sands Motel

Analysis of Rooms Payroll Variance
Sands Motel
January 20X4

	Room Nights	Time/ Room	Total Time	Hourly Wages	Total
Budget	440	30 min.	220 hrs.	$3.35	$737
Actual	415	28 min.	193 2/3	3.00	581
Difference	25	2 min.	26 1/3 hrs.	$0.35	$156 (F)

Volume Variance
VV = BR (BT − ATAO)
VV = 3.35 (220 − 207.5)
VV = 3.35 (12.5)
VV = $41.88 (F)

Rate Variance
RV = BT (BR − AR)
RV = 220 (3.35 − 3.00)
RV = 220 (0.35)
RV = $77 (F)

Efficiency Variance
EV = BR (ATAO − AT)
EV = 3.35 (207.5 − 193.67)
EV = 3.35 (13.83)
EV = $46.33 (F)

Rate-Time Variance
R-TV = (BT − AT) (BR − AR)
R-TV = (220 − 193.67) (3.35 − 3.00)
R-TV = (26.33) (0.35)
R-TV = $9.22 (U)

Summation of Variances

Volume Variance	$41.88 (F)
Rate Variance	77.00 (F)
Efficiency Variance	46.33 (F)
Rate-Volume Variance	9.22 (U)
	155.99
Rounding Difference	0.01
Total	$156.00 (F)

10.10 DETERMINATION OF PROBLEMS AND MANAGEMENT ACTION

The next step in the budgetary control process is for management to investigate variance analysis results in an effort to determine the cause(s) of the variance. This is needed because the analysis of a revenue variance will reveal differences due to price and/or volume, but not *why* the price and/or volume variances exist. Similarly, the analysis of variable labor expense will reveal differences due to rate, efficiency, and volume but, again, not the exact cause(s) of the variances. Additional investigation by management is required.

For example, assume that the analysis of the room attendants' labor variance reveals that a significant portion of an unfavorable variance is due to rate. Management must investigate the rate variance to determine why the average rate paid was higher than budgeted. An unfavorable labor rate variance may be due to staffing problems, excessive overtime pay, or a combination of these two factors. It may have been due to the scheduling of more higher-paid room attendants than originally planned. There may be another reason. Each significant variance requires further management investigation to determine the cause(s).

The final step to complete the budgetary control process is taking action to correct a problem. For example, if a major cause of the rate variance for room attendants is that excessive overtime is paid, this may be controlled by requiring all overtime to be approved a specified number of hours in advance by the next highest management level.

10.11 REFORECASTING

Regardless of the extensive efforts and the sophisticated methods used in formulating operations budgets, most large hospitality properties reforecast their expected operations as they progress through the budget year. This reforecasting is necessary only when the actual results begin to vary significantly from the budget. Some organizations will start reforecasting at the beginning of the budget year and continue to reforecast every month for the entire year.

Reforecasting at Marriott International Inc.

For an example, we will look at how Marriott International Inc. reforecasts. At the property level, the director of finance and accounting is the main person in charge. Marriott's corporate office and the regional team provide each property with initial instructions and parameters in September to start the process. The director of finance and accounting will then work with department managers and the executive committee to set the budget. Once a draft budget is complete, the property will send the draft to the regional office team for approval. The regional team then works collaboratively with the property and makes necessary adjustments. The draft will then be sent to the corporate office team for the next level of approval. Once approved, which usually happens in October, based on each hotel's management agreement, many of the drafts will then be sent to the owners for final approval around November. There will be a period for the property to true up the numbers at year end, and thus the new budget is locked normally in mid-January of the following year.

As soon as the budget is locked in January, the revenue management team will start the reforecasting process for the rest of the year. The revenue management team uses a proprietary system known as One Yield to examine room pickup on a day-by-day basis, using an algorithm that includes data on market trends, citywide events, and historical bookings, to adjust the numbers. The reforecasting starts from readjusting rooms revenue and banquets revenue. These two figures will drive the rest of the revenues to be forecasted. The cost metrics will then be applied depending on the revenue levels. This reforecast is performed monthly where as soon as a month is completed, the remaining months of the year will be reforecast. The reforecast profit and loss statements and the departmental budgets are the same as seen in Exhibits 10.8 and 10.9 except that the month or months completed will now be populated by actual numbers and the upcoming months will be populated by reforecast numbers. The revenue management team then provides a 10-day forecast on a weekly basis for the hotel for operation, staffing, and other purposes, and the front office provides a four-day forecast daily for any further fine-tuning.

Exhibit 10.20 | Blank Operating Budget Template

Name of Hotel
Budgeted Monthly Operating Results
Date

Summary Operating Statement

	January Year	February Year	March Year	April Year	May Year	June Year	July Year	August Year	September Year	October Year	November Year	December Year	TOTAL
Statistical:													
Rooms Available:													
Rooms Sold:													
Occupancy:													
ADR:													
Rooms RevPAR:													
Operating Revenue													
Rooms													
Food and Beverage													
Minor Operated Department													
Miscellaneous Income													
Total Operating Revenue													
Departmental Expenses													
Rooms													
Food and Beverage													
Other Operated Departments													
Total Departmental Expenses													
Total Departmental Profit													
Undistributed Operating Expenses													
Administrative and General													
Information and Telecommunications Systems													
Sales and Marketing													
Property Operation and Maintenance													
Utilities													
Total Undistributed Expenses													
Gross Operating Profit													
Management Fees													
Income Before Non-Operating Income and Expenses													
Non-Operating Income and Expenses													
Income													
Rent													
Property and Other Taxes													
Insurance													
Other													
Total Non-Operating Income and Expenses													
Earnings Before Interest, Taxes, Depreciation, and Amortization													
Interest, Depreciation, and Amortization													
Debt Service													
Depreciation													
Amortization													
Total Interest, Depreciation, and Amortization													
Income Before Income Taxes													
Income Taxes													
Net Income													

10.12 BUDGETING AT MULTIUNIT HOSPITALITY ENTERPRISES

This chapter has been oriented toward operations budgeting at a single hotel property. However, both lodging and foodservice chains continue to increase their dominance in their respective hospitality segments. The chains in the foodservice industry account for more than 50 percent of foodservice sales, and in the lodging industry, giants such as Hilton, Marriott, and Hyatt experience billions in lodging sales annually.

Research on budgeting at multiunit foodservice and lodging chains has revealed the following significant results:[5]

1. A majority of companies develop their overall corporate budgets using the bottom-up approach. That is, managers develop individual budgets that are accumulated through successive company layers until an overall corporate budget is proposed. The most common reasons cited for using the bottom-up approach are (1) the need to increase the feeling of unit-level "ownership" in the budget, and (2) the ability of unit-level personnel to recognize specific problems affecting lower organizational levels.

2. A significant minority develop their budgets at the corporate level and then dictate the budgets to the lower levels in the corporate structure. The major reason cited for the top-down approach is that the sum of the individual restaurant budgets would not meet corporate expectations.

3. Several companies use a combination of the bottom-up and top-down approaches.

4. Whether the budgeting approach is bottom-up or top-down, most companies at the corporate level set financial goals before the budget process begins.

5. The major differences in budgeting by chains versus the single unit organization include:
   - Greater need for coordination
   - Greater volume of information to be processed
   - Use of more sophisticated and frequently computerized procedures; greater amount of time required
   - Unique procedures to allocate costs between organization levels
   - Greater extent of management attention to budget process

6. The percentage of lodging chains that reported allowable variance levels for selected costs is as follows:

	Percentage of Chains Reporting			
Allowable Variance	Food Costs	Beverage Costs	Labor Costs	Other Costs
< 1%	5%	5%	6%	6%
1–1.9%	26	28	23	6
2–2.9%	11	11	18	29
3–3.9%	5	6	12	18
4–4.9%	16	11	6	6
> 4.9%	5	6	6	6
No set amount	32	33	29	29
Total	100%	100%	100%	100%

For those lodging chains that set tolerance criteria for variable costs, 1–1.9 percent was most common for food costs, beverage costs, and labor costs, while 2–2.9 percent was most common for other costs. Foodservice chains generally have even lower tolerances than lodging chains.

10.13 BUDGETING AT LODGING PROPERTIES

The budgetary process at lodging corporations is built on strategic plans, short-term operating plans, and monthly budgets. Individual hotels participate by providing their numbers for the prospective year based on a review and evaluation of the competition and marketing plans. Generally, the numbers are developed at the hotel level and rolled up for the corporate operating budgets.

Exhibit 10.20 is a blank form for an operating budget template, while Exhibit 10.21 is a completed operating budget used by an independent management company, Inntegrated Hospitality Management Ltd., headquartered in Calgary, Alberta, Canada, for one of their clients. The format of the *Uniform System of Accounts for the Lodging Industry* (*USALI*) is followed closely. It is shown by month for the year on a single page, with the budgeted statistics of rooms available, rooms sold, occupancy percentage, ADR, and Rooms RevPAR on the top of the budget. These two exhibits are not meant to serve as models. Each lodging property will develop the format that best serves its budgeting purposes.

Exhibit 10.21	Annual Operating Budgeting by Month for a Small Boutique Hotel

Budgeted Monthly Operating Results
Year Ending December 31, 2019

Summary Operating Statement

	January 2019	February 2019	March 2019	April 2019	May 2019	June 2019	July 2019	August 2019	September 2019	October 2019	November 2019	December 2019	TOTAL
Statistical:													
Rooms Available:	1240	1160	1240	1200	1240	1200	1240	1240	1200	1240	1200	1240	14640
Rooms Sold:	700	665	673	630	796	861	1055	1060	1100	911	605	670	9726
Occupancy:	56.5%	57.3%	54.3%	52.5%	64.2%	71.8%	85.1%	85.5%	91.7%	73.5%	50.4%	54.0%	66.4%
ADR:	$ 203.36	$ 225.10	$ 233.30	$ 197.77	$ 242.70	$ 498.93	$ 462.77	$ 454.55	$ 394.20	$ 219.04	$ 191.06	$ 300.03	$ 320.40
Rooms RevPAR:	$ 114.80	$ 129.04	$ 126.62	$ 103.83	$ 155.80	$ 357.98	$ 393.72	$ 388.57	$ 361.35	$ 160.92	$ 96.32	$ 162.11	$ 212.86

	January 2019 $	February 2019 $	March 2019 $	April 2019 $	May 2019 $	June 2019 $	July 2019 $	August 2019 $	September 2019 $	October 2019 $	November 2019 $	December 2019 $	TOTAL $
Operating Revenue													
Rooms	142,353	149,691	157,014	124,595	193,193	429,582	488,218	481,824	433,623	199,545	115,590	201,019	3,116,247
Food and Beverage	71,970	68,371	70,161	64,773	81,840	89,490	108,469	108,983	113,095	93,663	63,170	70,161	1,004,145
Minor Operated Department	1,500	1,975	3,165	1,250	3,000	3,000	3,650	3,650	3,000	3,000	1,750	2,130	31,070
Miscellaneous Income	5,473	5,163	5,571	5,216	8,139	9,376	10,149	10,149	9,737	7,536	5,170	5,805	87,485
Total Operating Revenue	221,295	225,200	235,911	195,834	286,171	531,448	610,486	604,606	559,455	303,745	185,680	279,116	4,238,948
Departmental Expenses													
Rooms	55,162	58,005	60,343	48,281	74,862	166,463	189,184	186,707	168,029	77,324	44,791	77,895	1,207,546
Food and Beverage	61,174	58,115	59,637	55,057	69,564	76,067	92,198	92,635	96,131	79,614	53,694	59,637	853,523
Other Operated Departments	825	1,276	2,007	748	1,650	1,650	2,008	2,008	1,650	1,650	963	1,324	17,757
Total Departmental Expenses	117,161	117,397	122,487	104,085	146,076	244,179	283,390	281,350	265,810	158,588	99,448	138,856	2,078,826
Total Departmental Profit	104,135	107,803	113,425	91,749	140,095	287,269	327,096	323,256	293,645	145,157	86,232	140,260	2,160,122
Undistributed Operating Expenses													
Administrative and General	24,998	23,921	22,960	22,401	24,875	32,325	35,740	34,952	33,537	26,444	22,812	25,012	329,978
Information and Telecommunications Systems	6,381	5,406	5,432	9,319	10,059	10,386	10,591	6,569	6,400	5,581	5,787	5,586	87,497
Sales and Marketing	8,606	8,106	11,706	8,013	7,513	6,263	6,263	6,263	6,263	7,513	7,513	7,513	91,535
Property Operation and Maintenance	22,224	21,128	21,950	24,532	45,238	56,515	22,598	19,112	22,522	30,205	30,463	21,942	338,430
Utilities	16,148	10,770	15,583	7,538	10,363	6,450	6,050	4,150	9,683	13,920	14,453	16,680	131,785
Total Undistributed Expenses	78,356	69,332	77,631	71,802	98,047	111,939	81,243	71,046	78,405	83,663	81,028	76,733	979,225
Gross Operating Profit	25,778	38,471	35,794	19,947	42,048	175,329	245,853	252,210	215,241	61,494	5,204	63,527	1,180,897
Management Fees	6,639	6,756	7,072	5,875	8,585	15,943	18,315	18,138	16,784	9,112	5,570	8,373	127,168
Income Before Non-Operating Income and Expenses	19,139	31,715	28,717	14,072	33,463	159,386	227,538	234,072	198,457	52,382	(366)	55,153	1,053,729
Non-Operating Income and Expenses													
Income	0	0	0	0	0	0	0	0	0	0	0	0	0
Rent	6,700	6,700	6,700	6,700	6,700	6,700	6,700	6,700	6,700	6,700	6,700	6,700	80,400
Property and Other Taxes	4,125	4,125	4,125	4,125	4,125	4,125	4,125	4,125	4,125	4,125	4,125	4,125	49,500
Insurance	4,680	4,680	4,680	4,680	4,680	4,680	4,680	4,680	4,680	4,680	4,680	4,680	56,160
Other	0	0	0	0	0	0	0	0	0	116,000	0	0	116,000
Total Non-Operating Income and Expenses	15,505	15,505	15,505	15,505	15,505	15,505	15,505	15,505	15,505	131,505	15,505	15,505	302,060
Earnings Before Interest, Taxes, Depreciation, and Amortization	3,634	16,210	13,212	(1,433)	17,958	143,881	212,033	218,567	182,952	(79,123)	(15,871)	39,648	751,669
Interest, Depreciation, and Amortization													
Debt Service	20,000	20,000	20,000	20,000	20,000	20,000	20,000	20,000	20,000	20,000	20,000	20,000	240,000
Depreciation													
Amortization													
Total Interest, Depreciation, and Amortization	20,000	20,000	20,000	20,000	20,000	20,000	20,000	20,000	20,000	20,000	20,000	20,000	240,000
Income Before Income Taxes	(16,366)	(3,790)	(6,788)	(21,433)	(2,042)	123,881	192,033	198,567	162,952	(99,123)	(35,871)	19,648	511,669
Income Taxes	11,000	11,000	11,000	11,000	11,000	11,000	11,000	11,000	11,000	11,000	11,000	11,000	132,000
Net Income	(27,366)	(14,790)	(17,788)	(32,433)	(13,042)	112,881	181,033	187,567	151,952	(110,123)	(46,871)	8,648	379,669

Courtesy of Inntegrated Hospitality Management Ltd.

The budgetary process is valuable to the operation of a hospitality establishment. In order to formulate a budget, the establishment's goals must be stated, and each department must look ahead and estimate future performance. As the actual period progresses, management can compare operating results to the budget, and significant differences can be studied. This process forces management to set future goals and to strive to see that they become realized.

In order to formulate a budget, each department estimates its revenues and expenses. This is done by observing past trends and projecting them for another year. The manager must also take into account forces in the economy, new developments in the market, and other significant events that will affect the operation. These projections are then combined to form a budget for the next period's operations. At this point, the budgeted results are compared with the establishment's goals, and the budget is adjusted until these goals are met.

Once completed, the budget becomes a control tool. As the periods progress, management compares the budget with actual performance. The differences between each line item are calculated, and any significant differences are analyzed. Significance depends on both absolute dollar differences and percentage differences. The analysis includes dividing each line item into its components, including price and volume for revenues and rate, volume, and efficiency for labor. Management can then address any deficiencies and take corrective action to keep the operations heading toward the defined goals.

capital budget—Management's plan for the acquisition of equipment, land, and buildings.

cash budget—Management's plan for cash receipts and disbursements.

cost of goods sold variance—A group of variances used to examine differences between budgeted and actual amounts paid for goods sold and the total amount sold.

incremental budgeting—Forecasting budgets based on historical financial information.

operations budget—Management's detailed plans for generating revenue and incurring expenses for each department within the operation; also referred to as the revenue and expense budget.

revenue variances—A group of variances used to examine differences between budgeted and actual prices and volumes.

significance criteria—Criteria used to determine which variances are significant. Generally expressed in terms of both dollar and percentage differences.

strategic planning—Another name for long-range planning. It not only considers revenues and expenses but also evaluates and selects from among major alternative plans those that provide long-range direction to the hospitality operation.

variable labor variance—A group of variances used to examine differences between budgeted and actual variable labor expense.

variance analysis—Process of identifying and investigating causes of significant differences (variances) between budgeted plans and actual results.

zero-base budgeting (ZBB)—An approach to preparing budgets that requires the justification of all expenses; assumes that each department starts with zero dollars and must justify all budgeted amounts.

1. What are four future items that should be considered when formulating a budget?

2. How does a budget help an establishment to realize its operating goals?

3. How is the budget formulated?

4. Why should budgets be prepared at various levels of sales?

5. What constitutes a "significant" variance?

6. What do volume variances highlight for management?

7. Why is an increase in volume favorable in revenue analysis and unfavorable in cost analysis?

8. What does the formula $EV = BR(ATAO - AT)$ calculate?

9. What items should be considered when preparing the rooms revenue section of the budget?

10. What are three possible goals an establishment could set for its operations?

Problem 1

Adam Backett, manager of the Café 360, has asked for your assistance preparing the monthly budget for March 20X8. He provides you with the prior March actuals, as follows:

Sales	$150,000
Expenses:	
Labor (F)	17,000
Labor (V)	26,892
Cost of sales (V)	53,785
Supplies (V)	4,781
Energy (V)	3,914
Promotion (V)	1,942
Maintenance (F)	2,500
Maintenance (V)	1,793
Property taxes (F)	800
Depreciation (F)	1,000
Rent (F)	950
Insurance (F)	825
Subtotal	116,183
Net income	$ 33,817

Assume for 20X8 sales are expected to increase by 15 percent, fixed costs will increase by 5 percent, and variable costs will remain at the same percentage of sales as experienced in the prior March.

Required:

Prepare the budget for March 20X8.

Problem 2

Brandon McKay manages the MK Place, a 150-room limited-service hotel. He provides you with details for preparing the March 20X7 operating budget, as follows:

Expected paid occupancy percentage	=	80%
Double-room occupancy	=	80%
Single-room occupancy	=	20%
ADR	=	$110
Price of double rooms	=	$20 more than singles
Room revenue	=	95% of total revenue
Other revenue	=	5% of total revenue
Room expenses:		
Fixed	=	$6,000
Variable	=	$12 per room sold

Expected paid occupancy percentage	=	80%

Other expenses:

	Fixed	Variable (% of total revenue)
A&G	4,000	4%
Sales and marketing	1,000	5%
Property operation and maintenance	3,800	–
Energy costs	1,000	2.5%
Insurance	2,000	–
Property taxes	3,000	–
Depreciation	2,500	–
Interest	1,700	–

Income taxes = 25% of pretax income

Required:

Based on the above financial and operating information, prepare the operating budget for March 20X7.

Problem 3

The New Asian Diner, managed by Yani Chan, needs your assistance in preparing its 20X8 operating budget. Since the diner is a sole proprietorship, it will not pay income taxes. She provides you with the following information:

Food sales—estimated	$650,000
Other revenue	4% of total revenue

Expenses:	Fixed	Variable*
Labor	$90,000	10%
Cost of sales	–	33%
Supplies	–	3%
Energy	9,000	4%
Marketing	6,000	2%
Maintenance	4,000	3%
Property taxes	3,000	–
Depreciation	15,000	–
Property insurance	5,500	–
Rent	3,000	–

*as a percentage of food sales

Required:

Prepare the operating budget for 20X8.

Problem 4

The 100-room Delavan Inn's past three years of room sales for April are as follows:

Year	Rooms Sold	ADR	Room Revenues
20X1	$2,100	$45.00	$ 94,500
20X2	2,140	47.50	101,650
20X3	2,180	50.00	109,000

Required:

Analyze the past performance and project sales for April 20X4. Assume that the trends of rooms sold and ADR continue for April of 20X4.

Problem 5

JD's Eatery, a 50-seat restaurant, projects its seat turnover for June 20X2 as follows:

	Seat Turnovers		
Day of Week	Breakfast	Lunch	Dinner
Sunday	---------- Closed ----------		
Monday	1.4	1.5	0.8
Tuesday	1.2	1.3	0.6
Wednesday	1.4	1.4	0.6
Thursday	1.4	1.2	0.5
Friday	1.3	1.3	1.3
Saturday	1.5	1.8	1.5
Avg. Foodservice Check	$8.25	$12.85	$16.50

Required:

Determine the projected food sales by meal period for June 20X2. Assume that the first day of the month is a Sunday.

Problem 6

Horner's Corner projected 4,000 lunches to be sold for September at an average price of $5.50. The actual sales were 4,200 meals and food revenue of $24,990.

Required:

1. Determine the budget variance.

2. Determine the volume variance.

3. Determine the price variance.

Problem 7

The accountant at Pratt's Place analyzes only significant budget variances on a monthly basis. The criteria used to determine if the budget variances are significant are as follows:

Revenues	$5,000 and 4 percent
Fixed expenses	$100 only
Variable expenses	$500 and 2 percent

Selected revenues and expenses for October 20X2 are as follows:

	Budget	Actual	Dollar Variance	Percentage Variance	S/NS
Room sales	$200,000	$196,000	_____	_____	____
Food sales	50,000	56,000	_____	_____	____
Cost of food sold (V)	15,000	16,000	_____	_____	____
Labor (F)	10,000	9,700	_____	_____	____
Labor (V)	15,000	15,200	_____	_____	____
Supplies (V)	2,500	2,700	_____	_____	____
Franchise fees (V)	4,000	4,480	_____	_____	____
Depreciation (F)	6,000	6,000	_____	_____	____
Insurance (F)	2,000	2,050	_____	_____	____
Property taxes (F)	3,000	3,000	_____	_____	____

Required:

1. Complete the two variance columns above.

2. Identify each variance as either (S) significant or (NS) not significant.

Problem 8

Carlo Davidson is the rooms department manager of the Athletes Lodge. The wages budget for his department is divided between fixed and variable expenses. The work standard for room attendants is to clean two rooms per hour. The average wage rate per hour is $10. The variable wages budget for room attendants for June is $8,400 based on $10 per hour, 100 rooms, 30 days in the month, and 70 percent occupancy.

During June, room attendants worked 1,140 hours and the average hourly pay was $9.80. In addition, 2,300 rooms were cleaned.

Required:

1. Determine the budget variance for room attendant variable wage expense.

2. Is the budget variance determined in #1 above significant? Explain.

3. Rate Mr. Davidson's performance in managing the room attendants. Support your discussion with *specific numbers*.

Problem 9

Vanessa Trevino, the rooms department manager of Mont Blanc Hotel, is preparing a condensed 20X6 annual budget. She has the following information upon which to base her estimates:

- Estimated occupancy percentage: 75 percent
- Rooms: 100
- Average rate: $85
- Labor: Variable: $8/room
  Fixed: $100,000 (annual)
- Other operating expenses: $4.50/room

Required:

1. Prepare a condensed budget for the rooms department. (Assume that the hotel is open 365 days a year.)
2. The Mont Blanc's management requires that the department have a departmental profit of at least $1 million and 75 percent of revenue. Will Ms. Trevino's condensed budget projections be acceptable to the hotel's management?

Problem 10

The Clarkson, open 365 days a year, consists of a 100-room hotel with a 50-seat restaurant shop. Shirley Clarkson provides you with the following information:

1. Of the 100 rooms, 70 are doubles and 30 are singles.
2. The doubles are sold for $120 each and the singles are sold for $95 each.
3. Forecasted occupancy is 70 percent for doubles and 60 percent for singles.
4. The average occupancy per room is 1.6. (Only one person stays in a single, but two or more may stay in a double for $120 per night.)
5. Forty percent of those staying in the singles and 25 percent of those staying in the doubles eat breakfast in the restaurant. (There is no walk-in business for breakfast.) The average check is $8.80.
6. The lunch and dinner business have seat turnovers and average checks as follows:

	Lunch		Dinner	
	Turnover	Avg. Chk.	Turnover	Avg. Chk.
Mon.–Fri.	1.25	$11.00	1.0	$18.75
Saturday	0.5	$11.50	1.0	$22.50
Sunday	1.5	$12.00	0.5	$21.25

Required:

1. Forecast the amount of room sales for June 20X1.

2. Forecast the amount of breakfast sales for June 20X1. (Assume the first day of June is a Monday.)

3. Forecast the amount of lunch sales for June 20X1.

Problem 11

The Mason Inn Inc., a rooms-only property owned and managed by Donna Mason, had a profitable year in 20X7. Ms. Mason has requested your assistance preparing the 20X8 operating budget. Assume the lodging operation is open 365 days during 20X8. She provides you with the following information for 20X8:

	Number	Occupancy %	ADR
Room revenues:			
Single rooms	30	70%	$80
Double rooms	40	60	90
King rooms	30	80	100

Other revenue: 4 percent of total revenue
Room expenses:

	Fixed	Variable*
Labor	$100,000	15%
Supplies	–	$5 per room sold
Other room expenses	10,000	2%
* as a percentage of room sales		
Undistributed operating expenses:		
A&G	150,000	3%
Sales and marketing (except franchise fees)	30,000	6%
Franchise fees	–	6%
Maintenance	60,000	4%
Energy	30,000	4%
Fixed charges:		
Insurance	20,000	–
Property taxes	40,000	–
Depreciation	50,000	–

Interest expense:

The average amount of long-term debt for 20X8 is expected to be $1 million and the annual interest rate is 8 percent.

Income taxes:

The average tax rate is expected to be 20 percent.

Required:

Prepare the annual operating budget for 20X8.

Problem 12

Barbara Collins is the manager of Shives, a fine-dining restaurant, and is preparing next year's budget. She wants to examine three different levels of sales as follows: $700,000, $1 million, and $1.3 million. The following information upon which to make the calculations is provided:

- Food cost percentage: 45 percent
- Labor: Variable: 23 percent
  Fixed: $80,000
- Other operating expenses: 8 percent
- Fixed charges: $100,000
- Income taxes: 30 percent of pretax income

Required:

1. Prepare the condensed operating budget for Shives at the three levels of sales indicated above.

2. Comment briefly about the impact of different levels of sales on the restaurant's profits.

Problem 13

The Mica Motel (MM), open 365 days a year, consists of an 80-room motel with a 60-seat coffee shop. J.D. Mica provides you with the following information:

1. Of the 80 rooms, 60 are doubles and 20 are singles.

2. The doubles are sold for $22 each and the singles are sold for $18 each.

3. Forecasted occupancy is 84 percent for doubles and 78 percent for singles.

4. The average occupancy per room is 1.8. (Only one person stays in a single, but two or more may stay in a double for $22 per night.)

5. Forty percent of those staying in the singles and 20 percent of those staying in the doubles eat breakfast in the coffee shop. (There is no walk-in business for breakfast.) The average check is $2.80.

6. The lunch and dinner business have seat turnovers and average checks as follows:

	Lunch		Dinner	
	Turnover	Avg. Chk.	Turnover	Avg. Chk.
Mon.–Fri.	1.25	$4.20	1.0	$10.75
Saturday	0.5	4.50	1.0	12.50
Sunday	1.5	5.50	0.5	11.25

7. The first day of the year for which you are to prepare the budget is Monday.

8. The food cost percentage is estimated to be 35 percent.

9. The labor cost percentages are as follows:
    Rooms: 20 percent
    Food: 32 percent

10. Other direct expenses of the operated departments are as follows:
    Rooms: 10 percent
    Food: 12 percent

11. Undistributed operating expenses include:
    $100,000 of fixed expenses and the remainder is 10 percent of total revenue

12. Other fixed costs include the following:

Property taxes	$30,000
Depreciation	60,000
Interest	50,000

13. The MM's average income tax rate is 30 percent.

Required:

Prepare, in reasonable form, the operations budget for the year.

Problem 14

Herb Lang manages the local 150-seat restaurant. He requests your assistance with projecting sales for April 20X5. During April 20X4, average prices and seat turnovers were as follows:

	Seat Turnover		Average Meal Prices	
Day of Week	Lunch	Dinner	Lunch	Dinner
Sunday	1.0	0.5	$12.40	$15.00
Monday	2.2	1.0	10.95	14.20
Tuesday	2.1	1.1	10.80	14.30
Wednesday	2.0	1.2	10.70	14.40
Thursday	2.1	1.3	10.80	14.50
Friday	2.2	0.8	10.95	16.90
Saturday	0.5	0.4	9.50	15.20

Additional information is as follows:

1. Meal prices are expected to increase during 20X5 by 5 percent over 20X4 prices.

2. Additional promotion is expected to increase seat turnover by 0.1 each meal period each day. For example, the seat turnover on Sunday for the lunch period is expected to be 1.1 for 20X5.

3. Appetizers should constitute 4 percent of total sales.

4. Desserts should constitute 6 percent of total sales.

5. Beverages are part of each meal, and there is no separate charge.

Required:

1. Use a spreadsheet to show the expected sales for meals by day for each meal period. Assume the first day of April 20X4 is a Monday.

2. Determine the forecasted sales from appetizers and desserts for the month.

Problem 15

For the week of June 6, Melvin Mince, the manager of Melvin's Hotel in northwestern Illinois, budgeted 600 hours for room attendants to clean rooms. This budget was based on a work standard of cleaning one room every 36 minutes. The rooms attendants actually worked 660 hours cleaning 1,050 rooms. The budgeted wage rate for room attendants is $13.40 per hour. The wages paid to room attendants totaled $8,778.00.

Required:

1. What is the amount of the budget variance?

2. What is the amount of the volume variance?

3. What is the amount of the efficiency variance?

4. What is the amount of the rate variance?

Problem 16

Bill Smith is the dining room manager of the Cycle Club. The wages budget for his department is divided between fixed and variable expenses. The work standard for servers is to serve 10 meals per hour. The average wage rate per hour is $12. The variable wages budget for servers for the first week of February is $4,800, based on $12 per hour. Given the work standard, this is also based on serving 4,000 people. During the first week of February, the server wages totaled $5,200. During the first week of February, the average hourly pay was $11.50 per hour. In addition, 4,200 members were provided service by the servers.

Required:

1. Determine the budget variance for server variable wage expense.

2. Is the budget variance determined in #1 significant? Explain.

3. Rate Mr. Smith's performance in managing the servers. Support your discussion with specific numbers.

Problem 17

Part I

Holly's Hotel budgeted 800 room sales for the week ended March 10. The estimated average price per room was $88.50. The actual average price per room was 10 percent greater than anticipated, while room sales in units were 10 percent less than forecasted.

Required:

What is the budget variance for the week? Analyze the budget variance by calculating each revenue variance.

Part II

For the same week, Holly's Hotel's head housekeeper, based on the work standard, budgeted 400 hours for room attendants to clean the rooms sold. The actual hours worked totaled 380. The estimated average wage rate for the attendants is $14.00 per hour. The wages paid totaled $5,054.

Required:

1. Were the room attendants efficient?

2. How much was the rate variance?

3. Based on the above, how would you rate the head housekeeper, considering the dollars spent? Use figures to support your answer.

Problem 18

The Orleans Café appears to be having some difficulty controlling its food costs. The cafe's budgeted food cost percentage was 36 percent based on food sales of $120,000. However, the actual food sales were $136,000, and the actual food cost totaled $46,400. The proprietor, A.B. Schmidt, is concerned about the unfavorable food cost variance of $3,200. The number of covers budgeted and actually served totaled 15,000 and 16,000, respectively. The average foodservice check was budgeted for $8. The average foodservice check for the month was $8.50.

Required:

1. Analyze the food revenue variance of $10,000, showing the amounts that relate to volume and price.

2. Analyze the cost of food sold variance and determine the amounts relating to the cost variance, volume variance, and cost-volume variance.

Problem 19

R.K. Dwight is interested in long-term operations planning for the rooms department of her hotel, the Dwight Inn. The budget detail for 20X5 is as follows:

	Rooms	Occ. %	ADR	Total
Singles	50	60%	$55	$ 602,250
Doubles	100	75%	$65	1,779,375
Suites	50	80%	$70	1,022,000
			Total	$ 3,403,625

Payroll costs:
  Fixed labor costs (annual) $120,000
  Variable labor costs   12% of room sales
Other expenses: (as a percent of room sales)
  Commissions   2.0%
  Laundry   2.0%

Operating supplies	3.0%
Linen	0.5%
Uniforms	0.5%
All other	1.5%

Assume that the rooms department for years 20X6–20X9 is able to realize occupancy increases of 0.5 percentage points per year for each type of room sales (for example, singles would be 60.5 percent for 20X6), and that ADR increases of $2 per year can be realized for each type of room. Further assume that variable labor costs increase by 4 percent each year and fixed labor costs increase by 6 percent each year. Finally, assume that the other expense percentages are maintained over the five years of 20X5–20X9. Round all figures to the nearest dollar.

Required:

Prepare the five-year budget for the rooms department of the Dwight Inn.

Problem 20

Don Litwiller, general manager of the Mustang Ranch, is interested in flexible budgeting. The focus for 20X4 is to be limited to the rooms operations. He provides you with information as follows:

Number of guestrooms	150
ADR	$150
Payroll costs:	
Salaries	$20,000 per month
Wages (variable)	$15 per room sold
Payroll taxes	10 percent of salaries and wages
Fringe benefits	$2,000 per month, plus 3 percent of room sales
Other costs:	
Reservations	$3 per room sold
Commissions	3 percent of room revenue
Linen	2 percent of room revenue
Supplies	$5 per room sold
Other	$500 per month, plus 5 percent of room sales

Required:

Prepare flexible budgets for the rooms department for 20X4 based on 78 percent, 80 percent, and 82 percent paid occupancy levels.

Problem 21

The Hovious Inn is struggling to understand its unfavorable budget variance for cleaning rooms. The data are as follows:

	Rooms' Sales	Time to Clean a Room	Hourly Wage Rates	Total
Budget	1,000	30 minutes	$12.00	$6,000.00
Actual	1,100	28 minutes	$12.50	6,416.67

Required:

1. Determine the budget variance.

2. Determine the volume variance.

3. Determine the rate variance.

4. Determine the efficiency variance.

5. How would you rate the management of the room attendants?

Problem 22

John Miller, owner of the 150-seat Miller Café, requests your assistance in forecasting food revenues for January. The cafe is *not* open on holidays (January 1 and 15) and on Sundays. The first day of January is a Monday.

He provides you with the seat turnover by meal period and average foodservice price as follows:

	Breakfast	Lunch	Dinner
Monday	0.8	2.1	1.1
Tuesday	0.7	2.0	1.0
Wednesday	0.75	2.0	1.2
Thursday	0.8	2.1	1.1
Friday	0.8	1.9	1.0
Saturday	0.6	0.6	2.0
Average foodservice price	$9.50	$12.75	$18.25

Required:

1. Determine the forecasted breakfast revenues for January.

2. Determine the forecasted lunch revenues for January.

3. Determine the forecasted dinner revenues for January.

Problem 23

Gigi Cirino has been operating her namesake pizzeria, Gigi, for almost 10 years. The restaurant is a popular place. She started in a small unit with about 50 seats, and eventually expanded three years ago to a 120-seat restaurant after the next-door tenant moved out. She is now working on her operations budget for next year, 20X1, and has the following figures for her seat turnover by meal period on a daily basis; Tuesday seems to be the slowest day of the week, and dinner on Friday and Saturday are the busy times:

	Lunch	Dinner
Monday	1.10	0.95
Tuesday	0.50	0.75
Wednesday	0.90	0.80
Thursday	1.25	1.20
Friday	1.25	1.50
Saturday	1.75	1.75
Sunday	1.50	1.00

The average check for lunch last year was $20 and dinner was $32. Ms. Cirino is also expecting an increase of 5 percent in revenues for 20X1. As for the food cost, she has been running the place at 38 percent for a number of years. Last year, a consultant helped her control the cost down to 33 percent, and she believes she will be able to achieve 32 percent for 20X1. Ms. Cirino has always been good with her labor cost and she expects that to stay at 33 percent for 20X1, including the raise she wants to give to her shift supervisors. The other controllable expenses are expected to be at 15 percent of total sales, with a fixed cost of $175,000. Her average tax rate is at 28 percent, and 20X1 has 365 days, starting the new year on a Monday.

Required:

Prepare the operations budget for 20X1 for Gigi.

Problem 24

St. Aiden Hotel has the following information regarding its labor cost for the week ending February 16, 20X1:

It budgeted 900 hours for room attendants to clean 1,200 rooms. As the hotel's rooms are all suites, the budget was based on a work standard of cleaning one room every 45 minutes. The room attendants actually worked 910 hours, cleaning 1,250 rooms. The budgeted wage rate for room attendants is $10.50 and the actual wage paid per hour was $10.75.

Required:

1. What is the amount of the budget variance?

2. What is the amount of the volume variance?

3. What is the amount of the efficiency variance?

4. What is the amount of the rate variance?

5. What is the amount of the rate-time variance?

Problem 25

The Z opened two years ago and has been having a very difficult time meeting its labor budget. It has an unfavorable variance for the last eight months and the months previous to that were just meeting budget. The owner, Zachary Zane, is asking you to help him figure out what might be the issue. Given that a budget variance can be due to the volume of business, efficiency of the staff, the rate, and also rate-time, please assist Mr. Zane in the analysis of the data from the most recent month as shared below. The standard of cleaning a room is 30 minutes.

	Rooms Sold	Hours	Wage Rate
Budget	1,400	700	$11.00
Actual	1,500	740	12.50

Required:

1. Determine the budget variance.
2. Determine the volume variance.
3. Determine the efficiency variance.
4. Determine the rate variance.
5. Determine the rate-time variance.
6. How would you rate the management of the room attendants?

11

CASH MANAGEMENT

Chapter 11 Outline

Competencies

1. Explain what is meant by cash management and the cash conversion cycle, and calculate the effective interest rate. (pp. 502–504)

2. Distinguish between income and cash flows. (pp. 504–506)

3. Explain the function of and two approaches to cash budgeting. (pp. 507–516)

4. Explain how the following factors affect cash management: mobile payment, float, cash flow information, working capital, collection of accounts receivable, inventory control, current liabilities, trade credit, and cash discounts offered by suppliers. (pp. 517–522)

5. Identify critical elements in accounting for gift card sales. (pp. 522–525)

6. Describe issues involved in using various unsecured bank loans. (pp. 526–527)

7. Describe the importance of integrated cash management for multiunit operations. (pp. 527–528)

8. Describe an integrated cash management system. (p. 528)

KEY TERMS

adjusted net income approach

cash budgets

cash flows

cash management

cash receipts and disbursements approach

city ledger

collection float

effective cost

float

gift card breakage

imprest basis

income flows

integrated cash management system

lockbox system

net float

payment (or disbursement) float

trade credit

transaction motive

working capital

Cash management refers to the management of a hospitality operation's cash balances (currency and demand deposits), cash flow (cash receipts and disbursements), and short-term investments in securities. Cash management is critical to both large and small hospitality operations. Insufficient cash can quickly lead to bankruptcy. This chapter will address many questions regarding cash management, including the following:

1. What is the difference between income and cash flows?

2. What is contained in a cash budget?

3. How are cash receipts forecasted?

4. How do short-term and long-term cash budgeting approaches differ?

5. What are the relevant factors to consider when investing working capital funds?

6. What are compensating balances?

7. How does a lockbox system speed up cash flow?

8. Why is depreciation expense irrelevant in cash flow considerations?

9. Why are investors primarily interested in cash flow?

10. How are other (noncash) current assets related to cash flow?

Our discussion of cash management will identify the uses and importance of cash in a hospitality operation. We will consider the distinction between income and cash flows and explain what is meant by negative cash flow. We will discuss basic approaches to using cash budgets for planning purposes. We will also address the major areas of hospitality operations affecting the process of cash budgeting, such as management of working capital, including accounts receivable, inventory, current liabilities, gift card accounting, and unsecured bank loans. Finally, we will address the special aspects of integrated cash management for multiunit operations.

11.1 CASH AND ITS IMPORTANCE

As mentioned, **cash management** is the management of a hospitality operation's cash balances and cash flow, which includes both cash flowing in (cash receipts) and cash flowing out (cash disbursements) of the operations, and short-term investments in securities. In hospitality establishments, cash consists of petty cash funds, cash on hand for operational purposes, and cash in the bank. Cash on hand includes both house banks and undeposited cash receipts. Cash in the bank includes demand deposits. Some operations also consider time deposits and certificates of deposit as cash. In our discussion, all of these elements will be considered cash.

Petty cash funds are established for making minor cash purchases. These funds are normally maintained on an **imprest basis**—that is, they are replenished by the amount of disbursements since the previous replenishment.

House banks are maintained in order to facilitate cash transactions with guests. Each cash drawer should hold only as much as is needed to transact business. Added together, the house banks in a hotel may total several thousand dollars. Since house banks do not generate earnings, these cash balances should be minimized.

Ideally, the hospitality operation's cash balance in a demand deposit bank account should be zero. That is, daily deposits should equal disbursements from the account. However, cash received and cash disbursed are generally not uniform because the cash receipts for a day seldom equal the cash disbursements for the same day. Therefore, most operations maintain minimum balances in their checking accounts to cover checks drawn. The reason for keeping these cash balances is commonly referred to as a **transaction motive**.

The size of the checking account balance is also influenced by banks. Some banks demand that depositors maintain substantial amounts in their accounts to cover bank services and to serve as compensating balances for bank loans. For example, an operation receiving a loan for $100,000 may be required to maintain a 10 percent compensating balance. This means $10,000 must be maintained in the checking account. Since no interest is earned on the compensating balance, the **effective cost**, or true cost when all elements are considered, of the loan is higher than its stated interest rate. The effective cost is determined as follows:

$$\text{Effective Interest Rate} = \frac{\text{Annual Interest on Loan}}{\text{Loan} - \text{Compensating Balance Requirement}}$$

For example, assume that a hotel receives a one-year loan of $100,000 at 10 percent interest with a compensating balance requirement of $10,000. The effective interest rate is 11.1 percent, as illustrated below:

$$\text{Interest} = \text{Principal} \times \text{Rate} \times \text{Time}$$
$$= \$100,000 \times 10\% \times 1 \text{ year}$$
$$= \$10,000$$

$$\text{Effective Interest Rate} = \frac{\$10,000}{\$100,000 - \$10,000}$$
$$= 11.1\%$$

Aggressive financial managers attempt to keep cash balances as low as possible given in-house cash needs and banking requirements. The cost of maintaining excessive in-house cash or checking accounts is the opportunity cost. The opportunity cost equals the earnings available if the cash were invested. For example, if a hospitality operation has an average annual checking account balance of $40,000 when the bank requires only $25,000, the opportunity cost is the interest that could be earned on $15,000. At an interest rate of 6 percent, the opportunity cost is $900 annually ($15,000 × 0.06).

Investors also have a keen interest in an operation's cash position. Investors make money in two ways: they receive cash dividends and their wealth increases as the stock prices increase. However, corporations are able to pay cash dividends only as cash is available. Therefore, those investing in corporations for dividends will review financial statements, especially the statement of cash flows, to determine whether the operation has sufficient cash to pay dividends and whether it will be operated in a manner that will allow dividend payments in the future.

11.2 CASH CONVERSION CYCLE

A major objective of cash management is to operate a hospitality business with as little money "invested" in accounts receivables and inventories as possible. Cash is used to purchase inventory, say food, which is then sold. When the food is sold on account, essentially the investment moves from inventory to accounts receivable. Within a reasonable time, receivables are collected and the business once again has cash. This process is the cash conversion cycle. Generally, the shorter the process the better, as this minimizes the amount of cash required to operate the business. The cash conversion cycle is part of the larger operating cycle that starts with the purchase of inventory on account. The difference between the cash conversion cycle and the operating cycle is the payables

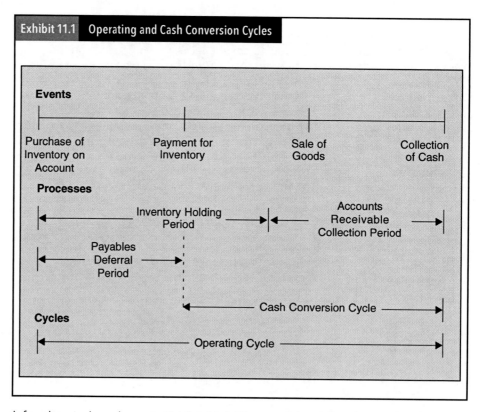

Exhibit 11.1   Operating and Cash Conversion Cycles

Events

Purchase of Inventory on Account — Payment for Inventory — Sale of Goods — Collection of Cash

Processes

Inventory Holding Period

Accounts Receivable Collection Period

Payables Deferral Period

Cycles

Cash Conversion Cycle

Operating Cycle

deferral period, as shown in Exhibit 11.1. The payables deferral period is the amount of time from the purchase of inventory on account until the business pays the supplier. The inventory holding period is the amount of time from when the inventory is purchased until it is sold, while the accounts receivable collection period (also called the receivables collection period) is the amount of time from the sale on account until the receivables are collected.

Just how are the lengths of a firm's operating and cash conversion cycles computed? Consider selected information for the Smoltz Foodservice Company, shown in Exhibit 11.2.

The operating cycle (OC) for the Smoltz Foodservice Company is the sum of the accounts receivable collection period (ARCP) and the inventory holding period (IHP), as follows:

$$OC = ARCP + IHP$$

$$= 29.2 \text{ days} + 30 \text{ days} = \underline{59.2} \text{ days}$$

The cash conversion cycle (CCC) for Smoltz is the OC less the payables deferral period:

$$CCC = 59.2 \text{ days} - 20 \text{ days} = \underline{39.2} \text{ days}$$

Thus, the Smoltz Foodservice Company has its cash invested for an average of 39.2 days at a time. Its financial executives should consider ways to reduce the CCC so that they can be more effective in managing cash.

11.3 DISTINCTION BETWEEN INCOME AND CASH FLOWS

Income flows result from operations generating revenues and incurring expenses. These flows are shown on the income statement and reflect the results of operations. **Cash flows** result from the receipt and disbursement of cash. It is

Exhibit 11.2   Select Operating Information for Smoltz Foodservice Co.

	December 31	
	20X1	20X2
Accounts receivable	$75,000	$85,000
Food inventory	28,000	32,000
Accounts payable	18,000	22,000
Food sales for 20X2	= 1,000,000	
Cost of food sold for 20X2	= 365,000	

$$\text{Payables deferral period} = \frac{\text{Average Accounts Payable}}{\text{Cost of Food Sold} \div 365}$$

$$\text{Payables deferral period} = \frac{(18,000 + 22,000) \div 2}{365,000 \div 365} = \frac{\$20,000}{\$1,000} = \underline{\underline{20}} \text{ days}$$

$$\text{Accounts collection period} = \frac{\text{Average Accounts Receivable}}{\text{Daily Sales}}$$

$$\text{Accounts collection period} = \frac{(75,000 + 85,000) \div 2}{1,000,000 \div 365} = \frac{\$80,000}{\$2,739.73} = \underline{\underline{29.2}} \text{ days}$$

$$\text{Inventory holding period} = \frac{\text{Average Food Inventory}}{\text{Cost of Food Sold} \div 365}$$

$$\text{Inventory holding period} = \frac{(28,000 + 32,000) \div 2}{365,000 \div 365} = \frac{\$30,000}{\$1,000} = \underline{\underline{30}} \text{ days}$$

possible for an operation to generate profits (income flow) yet have a negative cash flow (cash disbursements exceed cash receipts).

Exhibit 11.3 illustrates this situation. The statements are simplified for illustrative purposes. As the income statement shows, Rambles Restaurant generated net income flows of $15,000; however, cash disbursements exceeded cash receipts by $20,000. In this simplified illustration, the differences in income and cash flows are as follows:

Income Flows	Cash Flows
1. Depreciation $50,000.	1. Depreciation has no effect on cash flows.
2. Interest expense $25,000.	2. Interest expense is part of the mortgage payment of $50,000. The $25,000 difference between the mortgage payment and the interest expense is the principal reduction portion of the mortgage payment.

	Income Flows		Cash Flows

Income Flows

3. The purchase of equipment has no direct effect on income flows. The write-off (depreciation) will affect income flows over several years.

4. Dividends do not affect income flows.

Cash Flows

3. Payment of $50,000 for equipment purchase (purchased in the last month of the year).

4. Dividends paid of $10,000.

Therefore, the $110,000 *cash* outflows listed above (mortgage payment of $50,000, payment of $50,000 for equipment, and dividends of $10,000 paid) exceed the sum of the two *income* outflows (depreciation and interest expense) of $75,000. The difference of $35,000 ($110,000 − $75,000) is the same as the difference between the income flows (net income of $15,000) and cash flows (net cash outflow of $20,000). Note that all other cash flows and income flows are the same in this simplified example. In more complex situations, there are usually many additional differences between income and cash flows.

A hospitality operation may withstand negative cash flows for short periods of time if cash reserves are adequate to cover the deficits. However, over long periods, negative cash flows will most likely result in failure even if income flows are positive.

Most businesses, including hospitality establishments, have peaks and valleys in their operations. Generally, more cash is required during peak periods because cash is tied up in inventories and especially accounts receivable. Therefore, cash planning is important to ensure sufficient cash at all times. Cash planning is achieved by preparing cash budgets for several months in the future.

Exhibit 11.3 **Sample Condensed Income Statement and Cash Flow Statement–Rambles Restaurant**

Condensed Income Statement and Cash Flow Statement
Rambles Restaurant
For the year ended December 31, 20X3

Income Statement		Cash Flow Statement	
Sales	$ 600,000	Cash Receipts:	
Cost of Food Sold	200,000	Cash Sales	$ 300,000
Payroll Cost	200,000	Collection of Accounts	
Other Operating Expenses	100,000	Receivable	300,000
Depreciation	50,000	Total	600,000
Interest	25,000	Cash Disbursements:	
Income Taxes	10,000	Purchases of Food	200,000
Net Income	$ 15,000	Payment of Payroll	200,000
		Payment of Other Operating Costs	100,000
		Payment of Income Taxes	10,000
		Payment for Equipment	50,000
		Mortgage Payment	50,000
		Dividends Paid	10,000
		Total	620,000
		Excess Cash Disbursements	$ (20,000)

11.4 CASH BUDGETING

Cash budgets are prepared to reflect the estimated cash receipts and cash disbursements for the period. In certain situations, cash may be in short supply and a cash deficit may be projected. If the estimated cash receipts and beginning cash (estimated available cash) are not sufficient to cover projected cash disbursements, management must take action. Even if estimated available cash is greater than projected cash disbursements, the projected cash balance must be reviewed to determine if it is a sufficient buffer for any cash receipt shortfalls and/or unplanned cash disbursements. If the estimated cash balance is insufficient, the operation must plan to increase cash receipts, decrease cash disbursements, or do both. Management actions to cover temporary deficits may include obtaining short-term bank loans, obtaining loans from owners, deferring equipment purchases, and deferring dividend payments or a combination of such actions.

If the estimated cash balance at the end of the period appears excessive, then the excess cash should be temporarily invested. The six factors management should consider when investing excess cash are risk, return, liquidity, cost, size, and time:

- *Risk* refers to the probability of losing the investment. Management should generally take a minimum risk when investing, especially when investing short-run funds. For example, investments in government securities such as Treasury bills are considered risk-free.

- *Return* refers to the rate of return that can be received on the funds. Generally, the greater the risk and the longer the investment period, the greater the return.

- *Liquidity* refers to the ability to convert the investment to cash. When cash is invested temporarily, it should generally be invested in fairly liquid investments so it can be quickly liquidated as required.

- *Cost* refers to the brokerage cost of investing.

- *Size* refers to the amount of funds available for investing. In general, the more money available for investing, the higher the return.

- *Time* refers to the amount of time the excess funds are invested. Generally, the longer the investment time, the higher the return.

Because managers need to know in advance whether cash shortages or excesses are likely, they project cash flows when they prepare cash budgets. There are two basic approaches to cash budgeting: the cash receipts and disbursements approach and the adjusted net income approach. The method used depends primarily on the length of time for which the cash budget is prepared.

Cash Receipts and Disbursements Approach

The **cash receipts and disbursements approach** is useful when forecasting cash receipts for periods of up to six months. It shows the direct sources of cash receipts, such as cash sales, collection of accounts receivable, bank loans, sale of capital stock, and so forth. It also reveals the direct uses of cash, such as payment of food purchases, payroll, mortgage payments, and dividend payments. Because the cash receipts and disbursements method reflects the direct sources and uses of cash, it is easy to understand. However, it should generally not be used for periods exceeding six months. Projected figures beyond this point become

Exhibit 11.4   Cash Budget–Cash Receipts and Disbursements Approach

Cash Budget
Cash Receipts and Disbursements Approach
For the months of January–June 20X1

	January	February	March	April	May	June
Estimated Cash—						
Beginning	$	$	$	$	$	$
Estimated Cash Receipts:						
Cash Sales						
Collection of Accounts Receivable						
Proceeds from Bank Loans						
Proceeds from Sale of Fixed Assets						
Other						
Total						
Estimated Cash Available						
Estimated Cash Disbursements:						
Inventory						
Payroll						
Operating Expenses						
Taxes						
Insurance						
Mortgage Payments						
Dividends						
Other						
Total						
Estimated Cash Ending						
Minimum Cash Required						
Cash Excess or Shortage	$	$	$	$	$	$

increasingly unreliable, especially when actual operations differ significantly from the operations budget.

Exhibit 11.4 illustrates the basic format of a cash budget based on the cash receipts and disbursements approach. This format consists of two major sections: estimated cash receipts and estimated cash disbursements. Estimated cash receipts are added to the estimated beginning cash to project the estimated cash available for the period. Estimated cash disbursements are subtracted from estimated cash available to determine estimated ending cash. This figure is then compared to the minimum cash required to identify any shortage or excess. (The process of estimating cash receipts and cash disbursements will be presented later in this chapter.) The detail of the cash budget is a function of the desired information. For example, some users might desire the detail of payroll to be shown on the cash budget; thus, the breakdown could include salaries, wages, fringe benefits, and payroll taxes.

Adjusted Net Income Approach

The **adjusted net income approach** is generally preferable for budgeting cash for periods longer than six months. It also reflects the estimated cash balance for management's evaluation. In addition to its usefulness for longer periods of time, it emphasizes external, as opposed to internal, sources of funds. Exhibit 11.5 illustrates the format of a prepared cash budget using the adjusted net income approach.

The adjusted net income method is an indirect approach to cash budgeting because the sources and uses related to operations are indirect rather than direct; for example, neither direct sources from operations such as cash sales are shown, nor are direct uses for operations such as disbursements for payroll. This approach has two major sections: sources and uses. The sources section consists of internal and external sources. Internal sources are primarily cash from operations (chiefly reflected by net income plus income tax expense, depreciation, and other expenses that do not require cash). External sources

Exhibit 11.5	**Cash Budget–Adjusted Net Income Approach**

Cash Budget
Adjusted Net Income Approach
For the year ended December 31, 20X1

Cash—Beginning of Year $

Sources of Cash:
    Net Income $
    Add: Depreciation
           Amortization
           Other   _____

Other Sources:
    Proceeds from Bank Loans
    Sale of Fixed Assets
    Sale of Capital Stock
    Other   _____

        Total   _____

Uses of Cash:
    Increase in Accounts Receivable*
    Increase in Inventories*
    Decrease in Current Liabilities*
    Purchase of Fixed Assets
    Reduction in Long-Term Debt
    Other   _____

        Total   _____

Estimated Cash—End of Year   _____

Minimum Cash Requirement   _____

Cash Excess or Shortage $ _____

*Decreases in accounts receivable and inventories and increases in current liabilities would be sources of cash.

Note: When a hospitality firm *pays* an amount of income taxes that differs from what is shown on the income statement, the difference must be included on the cash budget. This may be easily accomplished by showing the amount of income tax expense in the sources section, similar to depreciation, and the amount of taxes paid in the uses section of the cash budget.

of funds include proceeds from bank loans and the sale of capital stock. The beginning cash and the sources of cash are totaled.

The uses of cash are subtracted from cash at the beginning of the year plus sources of cash to find the estimated cash at the end of year. This figure is compared with the minimum cash requirement to determine any excess or shortage.

The adjusted net income approach, much like the statement of cash flows prepared on an indirect basis, focuses directly on changes in accounts receivable, inventories, and current liabilities. This requires management to consider the amount of cash tied up in accounts receivable and inventory and cash provided by current liabilities. Therefore, this approach encourages closer management review of these working capital accounts.

From a practical viewpoint, both cash budgeting approaches are useful. The cash receipts and disbursements approach should be used for short-term budgets prepared on a monthly or weekly basis. The adjusted net income approach is useful for long-term budgets. Many hospitality establishments prepare cash budgets for long-range periods corresponding to each annual operations budget prepared for several years into the future.

Information for Cash Budgeting

The operations budget is the major source of information for preparing a cash budget. For example, estimated cash sales for a period are based on total sales for the period and the estimated percentage of the sales that is paid for with cash.

In addition to the operations budget, the following information is necessary to prepare a cash budget:

- Estimated percentages of cash and credit sales.

- Estimated collection experience for credit sales—that is, when the credit sales will be collected. For example, the collection experience may be 30 percent during the month of sale, 60 percent in the following month, and 10 percent in the second month after the sale.

- Estimated other cash receipts, including bank loans, sale of capital stock, and proceeds from sale of fixed assets and investments.

- Estimated payments for inventory items. For example, 10 percent of purchases may be paid during the month of purchase and 90 percent paid in the following month.

- Estimated payroll payments. A monthly payroll where all employees are paid on the last day of the month for that month means simply using the payroll expense estimates from the operations budget. Payroll distributed in any other way requires many more calculations.

- The payment schedules for other operating periods. Some operating expenses, such as utilities, are generally paid the month after they are expensed. Operating supplies are often paid for before the recognition of the expense when hospitality operations carry them as "supplies—inventory." Each type of expense must be reviewed to determine when the related cash expenditure is made.

- Expenses related to property and equipment (such as property taxes and insurance) which are often paid only once or twice per year. In these cases, the payment date, not the expense from the operations budget, should be considered.

- A schedule of debt payments (not part of the operations budget). This is required to determine total debt payments.

- Additional information including, but not necessarily limited to, forecasted dividend payments and forecasted property and equipment and investment purchases.

Illustration—Cash Receipts and Disbursements Approach

The Greenery, a 100-seat restaurant, will be used to illustrate the cash receipts and disbursements approach to cash budgeting. In this illustration, cash budgets will be prepared for the three-month period of April–June 20X1. Exhibit 11.6 contains The Greenery's operations budget for March–July 20X1.

At The Greenery, cash receipts and sales relationships are as follows:

1. Cash sales represent 50 percent of each month's sales. Therefore, the Greenery's estimated cash receipts from cash sales in April are $30,000 ($60,000 × 0.5).

2. Charge sales represent the remaining 50 percent. Twenty percent of the charge sales are collected in the month of sale, while the remaining 80 percent are collected in the following month. The Greenery's estimated cash receipts from April charge sales total $6,000 ($60,000 × 0.5 × 0.2). In addition, March charge sales collected in April yield $25,200 of cash receipts ($63,000 × 0.5 × 0.8).

3. The Greenery receives cash each month for the projected interest income as shown in Exhibit 11.6. Therefore, The Greenery's cash receipts from interest income total $2,000 for April.

The Greenery's cash disbursements and expenses have the following relationships:

1. Food purchases (cost of sales) are paid during the current month as follows:

    30 percent of cost of sales of previous month
    70 percent of cost of sales of current month

    The Greenery's cash disbursements for food during April total $20,300, as follows:

March cost of sales	×	0.3	= $21,000	× 0.3	= $ 6,300
April cost of sales	×	0.7	= $20,000	× 0.7	= $14,000
					$20,300

2. Salaries, wages, and benefits are paid in the month they are expensed. The April cash disbursements for salaries, wages, and benefits total $18,500.

3. With the exception of marketing, 50 percent of all remaining controllable expenses are paid in the month expensed. The other 50 percent are paid in the following month. The Greenery's April cash disbursements of $8,400 for these expenses are shown in Exhibit 11.7.

Exhibit 11.6 Operations Budget–The Greenery

Operations Budget
The Greenery
For the months of March–July, 20X1

	March	April	May	June	July
Sales	$63,000	$60,000	$65,000	$70,000	$75,000
Cost of Sales	21,000	20,000	21,700	23,400	25,000
Gross Profit	42,000	40,000	43,300	46,600	50,000
Interest Income	2,000	2,000	2,000	2,000	2,100
Total Income	44,000	42,000	45,300	48,600	52,100
Controllable Expenses:					
Salaries and Wages	17,000	16,000	18,000	19,000	20,000
Employee Benefits	3,000	2,500	3,000	3,000	3,500
Direct Operating Expenses	3,000	2,500	2,500	2,500	3,000
Marketing	4,000	4,200	4,000	4,500	5,000
Utility Costs	3,000	2,500	2,000	2,000	2,200
Administrative and General	2,000	1,800	1,700	1,800	2,000
Repairs and Maintenance	1,000	1,000	1,000	1,000	1,000
Income below Occupation					
Costs, Interest, and Depreciation	11,000	11,500	13,100	14,800	15,400
Occupation Costs	4,000	4,000	4,000	4,000	4,000
Interest	1,000	1,000	1,000	1,000	1,000
Depreciation	1,700	1,700	1,700	1,700	1,700
Income before Income Taxes	4,300	4,800	6,400	8,100	8,700
Income Taxes	1,400	1,600	2,100	2,700	2,900
Net Income	$ 2,900	$ 3,200	$ 4,300	$ 5,400	$ 5,800

Exhibit 11.7 Estimated Cash Disbursements–The Greenery

Estimated Cash Disbursements in April
for Various Controllable Expenses
The Greenery

	From March	For April	Total
Direct Operating Expenses	$1,500	$1,250	$2,750
Utility Costs	1,500	1,250	2,750
Administrative and General	1,000	900	1,900
Repairs and Maintenance	500	500	1,000
Total	$4,500	$3,900	$8,400

4. Marketing expense is paid for as follows: In January, $24,000 was paid to an advertising agency for $2,000 of advertising for each month of 20X1. The remaining marketing expense (per the operations budget) is paid for during the month it is expensed. Therefore, The Greenery has an actual cash disbursement in April of $2,200 ($4,200 – $2,000) for marketing expense.

5. Occupation costs of $4,000 per month are paid during the month incurred.

6. Interest expense of $1,000 for April is included in the mortgage payment of $2,000 per month.

7. Depreciation is a write-off of fixed assets and requires no cash flow.

8. Income taxes are paid quarterly. The tax expense for April–June is paid in June.

Other information includes the following:

1. Assume that cash at the beginning of April is $5,000.

2. Equipment costing $5,000 is scheduled for purchase in May and is to be paid for in June.

The Greenery's three-month cash budget for April–June 20X1 is shown in Exhibit 11.8. Exhibit 11.9 provides explanations for each cash budget line item.

The Greenery has a relatively healthy cash flow, as cash at the beginning of the quarter (April 1) of $5,000 is projected to increase to $18,070 by the end of the quarter (June 30). If the Greenery's management considers cash at the end of any month to be in excess of its cash needs, then it should invest the excess. Many hospitality operations establish a minimum cash balance requirement. Any cash over this amount is available to invest on a temporary basis (if needed for future operations) or paid to the owners. Ideally, the minimum cash balance could be $0 as long as daily cash inflow were equal to daily cash outflow. However, this ideal situation is seldom achieved, so a cushion is maintained.

Exhibit 11.8   Cash Budget–The Greenery

Cash Budget
The Greenery
For the months of April–June, 20X1

	April	May	June
Cash—Beginning of Month	$ 5,000	$ 12,800	$ 20,110
Estimated Cash Receipts:			
Cash Sales	30,000	32,500	35,000
Collection of Accounts Receivable	31,200	30,500	33,000
Interest Received	2,000	2,000	2,000
Total	63,200	65,000	70,000
Estimated Available Cash	68,200	77,800	90,110
Estimated Cash Disbursements:			
Food Purchases	20,300	21,190	22,890
Salaries, Wages, and Fringe Benefits	18,500	21,000	22,000
Direct Operating Expenses	2,750	2,500	2,500
Marketing	2,200	2,000	2,500
Utility Costs	2,750	2,250	2,000
Administrative and General	1,900	1,750	1,750
Repairs and Maintenance	1,000	1,000	1,000
Occupation Costs	4,000	4,000	4,000
Mortgage Payment	2,000	2,000	2,000
Income Taxes	0	0	6,400
Payment of Equipment Purchase	0	0	5,000
Total	55,400	57,690	72,040
Estimated Cash—End of Month	$ 12,800	$ 20,110	$ 18,070

Exhibit 11.9   Explanation of Cash Budget Line Items–The Greenery

Explanation of Cash Budget Line Items
The Greenery
April–June, 20X1

Monthly Budgets

Line Item	April	May	June
Cash—beginning of month (BOM)	*$5,000:* based on assumption provided	*$12,800:* cash-EOM, April 20X1	*$20,110:* cash-EOM, May 20X1
Cash sales	*$30,000:* April sales × .5 = 60,000 × .5 = $30,000	*$32,500:* May sales × .5 = 65,000 × .5 = $32,500	*$35,000:* June sales × .5 = 70,000 × .5 = $35,000
Collection of accounts receivable	*$31,200:* April sales × .5 × .2 = 60,000 × .5 × .2 = $6,000; March sales × .5 × .8 = 63,000 × .5 × .8 = $25,200	*$30,500:* May sales × .5 × .2 = 65,000 × .5 × .2 = $6,500; April sales × .5 × .8 = 60,000 × .5 × .8 = $24,000	*$33,000:* June sales × .5 × .2 = 70,000 × .5 × .2 = $7,000; May sales × .5 × .8 = 65,000 × .5 × .8 = $26,000
Interest received	*$2,000*	*$2,000*	*$2,000*
Estimated cash available	*$68,200:* cash-BOM + total estimated cash receipts = 5,000 + 63,200 = $68,200	*$77,800:* cash-BOM + total estimated cash receipts = 12,800 + 65,000 = $77,800	*$90,110:* cash-BOM + total estimated cash receipts = 20,110 + 70,000 = $90,110
Food purchases	*$20,300:* March exp. × .3 = 21,000 × .3 = $6,300; April exp. × .7 = 20,000 × .7 = $14,000	*$21,190:* April exp. × .3 = 20,000 × .3 = $6,000; May exp. × .7 = 21,700 × .7 = $15,190	*$22,890:* May exp. × .3 = 21,700 × .3 = $6,510; June exp. × .7 = 23,400 × .7 = $16,380
Salaries, wages, and fringe benefits	*$18,500:* 16,000 + 2,500 = $18,500	*$21,000:* 18,000 + 3,000 = $21,000	*$22,000:* 19,000 + 3,000 = $22,000
Direct operating expenses	*$2,750:* March exp. × .5 = 3,000 × .5 = $1,500; April exp. × .5 = 2,500 × .5 = $1,250	*$2,500:* April exp. × .5 = 2,500 × .5 = $1,250; May exp. × .5 = 2,500 × .5 = $1,250	*$2,500:* May exp. × .5 = 2,500 × .5 = $1,250; June exp. × .5 = 2,500 × .5 = $1,250
Marketing expenses	*$2,200:* April exp. − 2,000 = 4,200 − 2,000 = $2,200	*$2,000:* May exp. − 2,000 = 4,000 − 2,000 = $2,000	*$2,500:* June exp. − 2,000 = 4,500 − 2,000 = $2,500
Utility costs	*$2,750:* March exp. × .5 + April exp. × .5 = (3,000 × .5) + (2,500 × .5) = 1,500 + 1,250 = $2,750	*$2,250:* April exp. × .5 + May exp. × .5 = (2,500 × .5) + (2,000 × .5) = 1,250 + 1,000 = $2,250	*$2,000:* May exp. × .5 + June exp. × .5 = (2,000 × .5) + (2,000 × .5) = 1,000 + 1,000 = $2,000
Administrative and general	*$1,900:* March exp. × .5 + April exp. × .5 = (2,000 × .5) + (1,800 × .5) = 1,000 + 900 = $1,900	*$1,750:* April exp. × .5 + May exp. × .5 = (1,800 × .5) + (1,700 × .5) = 900 + 850 = $1,750	*$1,750:* May exp. × .5 + June exp. × .5 = (1,700 × .5) + (1,800 × .5) = 850 + 900 = $1,750
Repairs and maintenance	*$1,000:* March exp. × .5 + April exp. × .5 = (1,000 × .5) + (1,000 × .5) = 500 + 500 = $1,000	*$1,000:* April exp. × .5 + May exp. × .5 = (1,000 × .5) + (1,000 × .5) = 500 + 500 = $1,000	*$1,000:* May exp. × .5 + June exp. × .5 = (1,000 × .5) + (1,000 × .5) = 500 + 500 = $1,000
Occupation costs	*$4,000*	*$4,000*	*$4,000*
Mortgage payment	*$2,000*	*$2,000*	*$2,000*
Income taxes	$ 0	$ 0	*$6,400:* April-June exp. = 1,600 + 2,100 + 2,700 = $6,400
Purchase of equipment	$ 0	$ 0	*$5,000*
Estimated cash—EOM	*$12,800:* Est. available cash − est. cash disb. = 68,200 − 55,400 = $12,800	*$20,110:* Est. available cash − est. cash disb. = 77,800 − 57,690 = $20,110	*$18,070:* Est. available cash − est. cash disb. = 90,110 − 72,040 = $18,070

Exhibit 11.10   Projected Cash Available to Invest–The Greenery

Projected Cash Available to Invest
The Greenery
For the months of April–June, 20X1

	April	May	June
Cash—BOM	$ 5,000	$ 5,000	$ 5,000
Plus: Total Estimated Cash Receipts	63,200	65,000	70,000
Less: Total Estimated Disbursements	55,400	57,690	72,040
Preliminary Cash EOM	12,800	12,310	2,960
Less: Cash Cushion	5,000	5,000	5,000
Excess Cash for Investing	$ 7,800	$ 7,310	($2,040)*

*If the excess cash is invested in April and May, The Greenery should prepare to liquidate $2,040 of these investments to maintain the desired cash cushion of $5,000 at the end of June.

Assume that The Greenery maintains a cash cushion of $5,000 at the end of each month. Exhibit 11.10 presents the projected cash available to invest at the end of each month in the quarter. The Greenery is projected to have excess cash for investing of $7,800 and $7,310 in April and May, respectively. However, in June, temporary investments of $2,040 must be liquidated to provide the $5,000 minimum cash balance at the end of the month.

Illustration—Adjusted Net Income Approach

The adjusted net income approach can be used to prepare The Greenery's long-term cash budgets for 20X1–20X3. Exhibit 11.11 presents The Greenery's operations budgets for 20X1–20X3. Additional information required to prepare cash budgets using the adjusted net income approach is as follows:

1. Equipment acquisitions, which will be purchased with cash, are projected at $10,000 per year for 20X1–20X3.

2. Distributions to owners are projected at 50 percent of net income.

3. Mortgage payments are estimated to be $30,000 per year for 20X1–20X3, of which 50 percent is interest expense.

4. The annual change in various current assets and current liabilities is estimated as follows:

	20X1	20X2	20X3
Accounts receivable	+2,000	+3,000	+4,000
Inventory	+1,000	+1,500	+1,500
Current liabilities	+2,000	+3,000	+3,500

The Greenery's long-range cash budget for 20X1–20X3 is shown in Exhibit 11.12. Overall, the cash budget shows a substantial increase in cash—from $5,000 at the beginning of 20X1 to $87,150 at the end of 20X3. This fully considers the distribution of 50 percent of net income to owners, the cash purchase of $10,000 of equipment each year, and the reduction of long-term debt by $15,000 each year. The Greenery's management must consider the best uses of the excess funds reflected by the cash budget. The factors relevant to short-term investing are also appropriate in a long-term situation, although liquidity is less important.

Exhibit 11.11	Long-Range Operations Budget–The Greenery		
	20X1	20X2	20X3
Sales	$730,000	$850,000	$1,000,000
Cost of Sales	240,000	270,000	320,000
Gross Profit	490,000	580,000	680,000
Interest Income	25,000	30,000	35,000
Total Income	515,000	610,000	715,000
Controllable Expenses:			
Salaries and Wages	200,000	240,000	300,000
Employee Benefits	25,000	30,000	35,000
Direct Operating Expenses	28,000	30,000	32,000
Marketing	40,000	50,000	60,000
Utility Costs	30,000	35,000	40,000
Administrative and General	20,000	25,000	30,000
Repairs and Maintenance	12,000	14,000	16,000
Total	355,000	424,000	513,000
Income before Occupation Costs, Interest, and Depreciation	160,000	186,000	202,000
Occupation Costs	50,000	50,000	50,000
Interest	15,000	15,000	15,000
Depreciation	20,000	22,000	24,000
Income before Income Taxes	75,000	99,000	113,000
Income Taxes*	25,000	33,000	37,700
Net Income	$ 50,000	$ 66,000	$ 75,300

*The income tax paid each year is the same as the income tax expense in the long-range operations budget.

Exhibit 11.12	Long-Range Cash Budget–The Greenery		
	20X1	20X2	20X3
Cash—Beginning of Year	$ 5,000	$24,000	$ 52,500
Sources of Cash:			
Net Income	50,000	66,000	75,300
Add: Depreciation	20,000	22,000	24,000
Increase in Current Liabilities	2,000	3,000	3,500
Total	72,000	91,000	102,800
Uses of Cash:			
Increase in Accounts Receivable	2,000	3,000	4,000
Increase in Inventory	1,000	1,500	1,500
Distributions to Owners	25,000	33,000	37,650
Purchase of Fixed Assets	10,000	10,000	10,000
Reduction in Long-Term Debt	15,000	15,000	15,000
Total	53,000	62,500	68,150
Estimated Cash—End of Year	$24,000	$52,500	$ 87,150

11.5 MOBILE PAYMENT

Making payments for goods and services in cash is becoming less and less common. In 2020, mobile or digital payments represented about 45 percent of global e-commerce payment transactions, compared with the second-ranked option of credit cards, at 23 percent. The use of mobile payment is projected to exceed 50 percent by 2024.[1] Although most mobile payments in the hospitality industry are made in restaurants and coffee shops, hotels have also begun using this method of payment, with hotels in Las Vegas accepting mobile wallet payments for show tickets and hotel billing since 2017, utilizing Apple Pay, Android Pay, Google Wallet, and Samsung Pay.[2]

Mobile payment has a number of advantages for both the customers and the business. For customers, there is no need to carry checks or credit cards as everything is at the fingertips with a smartphone. The convenience, speed, efficiency are second to none. For merchants, upgrades to POS systems are necessary to accept such payment. The platforms a business selects—PayPal, Google Checkout, Payment, or even Alipay, for Chinese inbound tourists—are options that need to be considered.

Obviously, data security is a great concern; the Global Data Protection Regulation (GDPR) provides meaningful standards that merchants must follow. With 5G networking as the norm, mobile payment will only increase—enhancing the cash flow for many hospitality businesses.

11.6 FLOAT

The use of **float** is another element of cash management. Float is time between the subtraction or addition of cash to the company's books and the actual subtraction or addition to the company's bank account. For example, assume that The Greenery pays a supplier $1,000 on account. When the check is written, the cash is subtracted from the company's cash (general ledger) account. Assume that the check is mailed to the supplier, who receives it three days later. The supplier deposits the check the following day in its own bank, which is different from The Greenery's bank, and two days later the funds are deducted from The Greenery's bank account. The Greenery actually had use of the $1,000 for six days—from the day the check was written and deducted from the books until the day its bank paid the $1,000. This type of float is called **payment (or disbursement) float**. The Greenery benefits from this float, and any reasonable steps to increase payment float are to The Greenery's advantage.

On the other hand, when The Greenery deposits a guest's check into its bank account, it increases its cash account on the books but must wait to use the funds until its bank has received the funds from the guest's bank. This difference is called **collection float**. The difference between payment float and collection float is **net float**. Since management prefers a positive net float, it should take whatever legal actions it can (referred to as "playing the float") to increase payment float and decrease collection float.

11.7 CASH FLOW INFORMATION

A 2020 study revealed that 79.9 percent of lodging firms and over 80 percent of clubs found their cash budget moderately, very, or extremely useful. In addition, 38.5 percent of the hotels and 54.1 percent of clubs in this study prepared their cash budget on a monthly basis.[3]

Exhibit 11.13   Accounts Receivable and Payable Practices

Accounts Receivable Practices	Clubs (%)	Hotels (%)
Receive payments via credit cards	24.2	100.0[1]
Send invoices as soon as billing cycle closes	50.4[3]	98.6[2]
Send invoices via email	54.9[1]	98.6[2]
Send reminders after 30 days	30.8[6]	98.6[2]
Send second reminders after 60 days	28.6	98.6[2]
Suspend any further charges for delinquent accounts	NA	98.6[2]
Charge cancellation fees	NA	97.7
Send invoices via regular mail	44.0[4]	95.7
Hold monthly credit meetings to discuss 60-days-plus accounts	12.1	95.7
Require deposits	NA	95.3
Send second collection letters after 60 days	27.5	88.6
Receive payments via lock boxes	13.2	88.6
Send collection letters after 30 days	8.8	85.7
Post invoices on individual members' account online for immediate access by members	50.9[2]	NA
Suspend privileges after 90 days	40.7[5]	NA
Direct bill with members' credit card on file	14.3	NA
Suspend privileges after 60 days	13.2	NA

Accounts Payable Practices	Clubs (%)	Hotels (%)
Take 30-day terms, when possible, except for cash discount	35.2	97.1
Use technology to monitor cash level	20.9	95.7
Take all cash discounts offered by suppliers	53.8	95.7
Time all payments properly and delay paying bills until deadline	35.2	95.7
Less frequent payment of personnel (e.g., paying payroll every 2 weeks rather than every week)	6.6	80.0

Note: Superscripts indicate the top rankings among clubs and hotels, respectively.

Enhancing Cash Flows

Both lodging firms and clubs in this study were asked which accounts receivable and payable practices they use to enhance cash flows. Exhibit 11.13 lists such practices. The percentage of firms using each practice is shown.[4]

11.8 MANAGEMENT OF WORKING CAPITAL

The management of working capital is closely related to the management of cash. **Working capital** (current assets less current liabilities) is directly related to cash; Exhibit 11.14 depicts the effect of working capital on cash. These relationships assume that other activities (such as sales and expenses) remain constant. For example, if marketable securities decrease, cash increases, provided everything else remains the same. Therefore, it is imperative that hospitality managers understand the management of these elements of working capital.

Exhibit 11.14	The Effect of Working Capital on Cash

Increases in cash result as:

- marketable securities decrease
- accounts receivable decrease
- inventories decrease
- current liabilities increase

Decreases in cash result as:

- marketable securities increase
- accounts receivable increase
- inventories increase
- current liabilities decrease

11.9 ACCOUNTS RECEIVABLE

Accounts receivable arise from sales on account. Hospitality operations would prefer to transact only cash sales. However, in order to increase sales, credit is often extended to guests. Credit commences when the guest checks into a room without paying for the room. Credit continues until the guest pays the bill—at check-out or after leaving the hotel. Credit should be monitored while the guest stays at the hotel.[5]

Accounts receivable statements should be mailed on a regular basis, usually monthly. A series of collection letters should be used to speed collection of accounts receivable. Delinquent accounts should be turned over to collection agencies only after the hospitality operation has made all reasonable collection efforts. Collection agency fees may range from 30 percent to 50 percent of the delinquent amount.

A **lockbox system** speeds the flow of cash from accounts receivable to the bank. This system consists of a post office box from which bank personnel collect all incoming mail and deposit any checks directly in the property's bank account. This process may speed the cash flow from collection of accounts receivable by up to three days by decreasing collection float. In addition, it enhances control over mail cash receipts because company personnel do not have access to this cash. However, the bank does charge for this service, usually by the number of checks handled. If the operation receives many small payments, the cost of a lockbox system may exceed the benefits.

A formula for considering the costs and benefits of a lockbox system provides a breakeven amount. This is the amount of a receivables account which, when invested for the number of days cash flow is speeded up, yields income equal to the added variable cost of the lockbox system. The formula is as follows:

$$B = \frac{C}{I \times T}$$

where B = Breakeven Amount

C = Bank Charge per Item

I = Daily Interest Rate

T = Change in Time

An example may best illustrate this formula. Assume that a hotel needs to know the breakeven amount for a lockbox system. The bank charges $0.20 for each mail receipt processed, funds can be invested at 8 percent annually, and the lockbox system gets mail cash receipts to the bank two days faster. The breakeven amount per check is $456.25, determined as follows:

$$B = \frac{\$0.20}{\frac{0.08}{365} \times 2}$$

$$= \underline{\underline{\$456.25}}$$

That is, this hotel will benefit financially by using a lockbox system for processing mail receipts over $456.25. Therefore, this hotel should instruct its debtors with balances greater than $456.25 to mail their checks to its lockbox, while debtors owing less than $456.25 should send their payments to the hospitality operation for company personnel to process. This assumes that company personnel and related expenses are fixed and will not change by processing more or fewer mail cash receipts.

Accounts receivable, especially **city ledger** accounts, which are accounts that contain nonguest transactions, are monitored by the use of ratio analysis and the preparation of an aging schedule of accounts receivable. Three useful ratios are accounts receivable to sales, accounts receivable turnover, and number of days accounts receivable outstanding, which is a variation of the accounts receivable turnover. These ratios are useful in detecting changes in the overall accounts as they relate to sales.

An aging of accounts receivable is useful for monitoring delinquent accounts. Maximum efforts should be exerted to collect the oldest accounts. The aging schedule is also useful for estimating the uncollectible accounts at the end of the accounting period.

11.10 INVENTORY

Inventory is viewed by some as a necessary evil. Hospitality operations must maintain an inventory of food and beverages even though the cost of storing these items is relatively high. The benefit of having food and beverages for sale is obvious, however—they are generally sold at several times their cost.

The nonproduct costs of maintaining inventory need to be considered so that management will exercise tight control in this area. Several costs directly related to inventory include storage, insurance, and personnel. Inventory requires storage space, and many inventory items must be stored in temperature-controlled environments. Certain inventory items have a limited shelf life; thus, personnel need to monitor these items closely. Inventory must be counted periodically, which also requires personnel and therefore payroll dollars. Overall costs also increase when inventory items spoil and must be discarded. Insurance to cover inventory, although not expensive, is yet another cost. In addition to these costs, there is the opportunity cost of inventory. If funds were not tied up in inventory, they could be invested to provide a return to the hospitality operation. Therefore, management must closely monitor inventory to keep it at a minimum, while still having products available when customers wish to make purchases.

Assistance to foodservice operations in minimizing their inventories is available through computer programs that produce food purchase orders for required products. For example, when a 1,000-person banquet with ham as an entrée and various side dishes is entered into such a computer program, the program would produce an order for x pounds of ham and y cans of each side order. Since delivery is often available on short notice, these quantities can essentially be ordered on a "just-in-time" basis. The critical elements are forecasting meals to be served and using standard recipes.

Common means of monitoring inventory include the inventory ratios. The most commonly used ratio is inventory turnover, calculated by dividing cost of goods used by average inventory. This ratio should be computed not only for food but also for each category of beverages. The results are most meaningful when compared to the planned ratios and to ratios for past periods. These ratios can help management detect unfavorable trends. For example, food inventory turnovers of 2, 1.8, and 1.6 for three successive months suggest a major change in food inventory. Management should determine if the inventory is excessive and take the appropriate action to correct the situation.

11.11 CURRENT LIABILITIES

A large portion of current assets is financed by current liabilities in hospitality operations. The current ratio (computed by dividing current assets by current liabilities) of approximately 1 to 1 for hospitality operations, especially in the lodging sector, reflects this situation. **Trade credit** is free—that is, suppliers do not charge interest to hospitality operations for amounts owed in the normal course of business. Everything else being the same, the longer a property has to pay its bills, the greater its reliance on trade credit to finance its operations.

Current liabilities consist primarily of trade payables, taxes payable, accrued wages, and the current portion of long-term debt. The remainder of this section focuses on trade payables, as the other payables must generally be paid on stipulated dates.

Trade payables resulting from purchases on account generally require payment in 30 days. Sometimes, suppliers offer cash discounts to hospitality operations to encourage their customers to pay their accounts early. For example, a supplier may provide a 2 percent cash discount if the invoice is paid within 10 days of the invoice date. Thus, the terms of sale per the invoice are simply shown as 2/10, n/30. The n/30 means that if the discounted invoice is not paid within 10 days of the invoice date, then the entire amount (net) is due within 30 days of the invoice date. The effective interest rate of the cash discount is determined as follows:[6]

$$\text{Effective Interest Rate} = \frac{\text{Cash Discount}}{\text{Invoice Amount} - \text{Cash Discount}} \times \frac{\text{Days in Year}}{\text{Difference between End of Discount Period and Final Due Day}}$$

The following example illustrates the calculation of the effective interest rate. Assume that a hotel purchases a computer for $8,000 and is offered terms of 3/10, n/30. The effective interest rate of 56.45 percent is the result of:

$$\text{Effective Interest Rate} = \frac{\$240^*}{\$8,000 - \$240} \times \frac{365}{20}$$

$$= \underline{56.45\%}$$

$$^*\text{Cash Discount} = \$8,000 \times 0.03 = \$240$$

Thus, the hotel would be wise to pay the invoice within the cash discount period, even if it had to borrow funds to do so, as long as the annual interest rate on the loan were less than 56.45 percent.

Alternatively, assume that the terms of sale are 1/10, *n*/30 and that this hotel must pay interest at an annual rate of 20 percent.

$$\text{Effective Interest Rate} = \frac{\$80}{\$8,000 - \$80} \times \frac{365}{20}$$

$$= \underline{18.43\%}$$

If the hotel has the cash available and management considers 18.43 percent to be an attractive return on a short-term investment, the hotel should pay the invoice within the cash discount period. However, if the cash is not available, the hotel should not borrow to pay the invoice, since the effective interest rate of 18.43 percent is lower than the rate at which the hotel can borrow funds. In this situation, the hotel should not take the cash discount, but rather should pay the full $8,000 thirty days after the invoice date.

In general, management should pay bills only when they are due except when cash discounts are available for early payments and they result in lowering costs. The payment of invoices earlier than required results in a higher cost of doing business since the cash expended could have been invested. However, management must consider the intangible factor of supplier relations. Keeping on favorable terms with suppliers is especially advantageous when the hotel or restaurant occasionally needs special favors—such as receiving inventory two days sooner than normally available.

11.12 GIFT CARD ACCOUNTING

A major source of cash inflows for a hotel with a spa occur as a result of the sales of gift cards. Gift card sales occur throughout the year. However, substantial peaks occur during the winter holiday shopping season and before such holidays as Valentine's Day and Mother's Day.

Regulations regarding the sale and redemption of gift cards vary from state to state in the United States. At the writing of this text, according to the Consumers Union, roughly one half of the states' regulations do not allow expiration dates. Regulations regarding "use fees"—fees that decrease the face value amount of the card on a monthly or other stated time interval—also vary, with approximately 30 states not permitting any fees or limiting the fees to a small amount.

From a marketing perspective, gift cards offer a twofold opportunity: the person purchasing the card may or may not be a guest, and the person receiving the card is potentially a new guest. As a result, the capture of information from both the buyer and the recipient allows significant future marketing opportunities. Furthermore, many recipients of gift cards will purchase additional services or merchandise over and above the amount of the gift at the time of redemption.

From an accounting perspective, the sale of a gift card is not recorded as revenue, but rather as deferred revenue—gift cards, which is reflected as a liability on the balance sheet. In simple terms, the spa has done nothing yet to earn the money paid for the gift card; the sale cannot properly be recorded on the income statement as revenue until the spa earns it by providing the bearer with services or merchandise. Revenue is recorded at the time the gift card is redeemed. The following entry would record the cash sale of a gift card in the amount of $250:

Cash in Bank	250	
Deferred Revenue—Gift Cards		250

Various methods are used to record the sale of gift cards and certificates, including manual preparation of gift certificates by spa personnel, the use of an outside gift card processor, and the use of an in-house point-of-sale system. The sale of gift cards, the cash flow management issues involved, and the attendant accounting issues require adequate internal control and accurate recordkeeping, both for financial reporting and tax reporting purposes.

Ideally, a gift card sale should be created and recorded through the POS system and the gift card issued directly by the system. Contact information for both the buyer and the recipient should be obtained if possible. It is imperative that the date of sale, amount of the sale, and card control number be recorded in the Deferred Revenue—Gift Card database. It is also imperative that the database be capable of maintaining remaining/outstanding card balances, year of issue, amount used by card, small balance card amounts (i.e., $5 or less), and other pertinent information.

When the recipient uses the card to purchase services or products from the hotel spa, the revenue is earned. Assume that the recipient of the gift card sold for $250 used the card to pay for massage services of $100, a gratuity of $20, product sales of $75, and sales tax of $7.50. The entry to record the revenue is as follows:

Deferred Revenue—Gift Card	202.50	
Massage Revenue		100.00
Gratuity Payable		20.00
Revenue—Products		75.00
Sales Tax Payable		7.50

In this example, the card holder has a balance remaining of $47.50 that can be used at a later date. Never redeem a gift card balance for cash unless your state's regulations allow purchasers that option. Not only does giving cash back eliminate the opportunity to earn a profit on services and products provided, it creates an easy opportunity for fraud.

A material amount of gift card sales goes unused. A 2014 article in the *New York Post* reported that $44 billion of gift cards had been unredeemed since 2008.[7] Cards are not used for a variety of reasons. For example, the recipient may simply not be comfortable with visiting a spa; the card may be lost or forgotten; or the bearer may move away. Also, small balances are quite often forgotten or ignored and discarded. This unused gift card issue is referred to as **gift card breakage**. While some states have laws (escheat) governing unclaimed property that regulate gift card breakage, in most cases gift cards have no expiration dates and, while they remain unredeemed, represent an indefinite obligation of the hotel.

As time passes, the likelihood of gift card redemption decreases until, at some point, deferred revenue from gift card breakage should be realized and recorded by the spa. As the hotel measures historical patterns of redemption, each spa will be able to compute a gift card breakage estimate. It is recommended that at least four years of history be considered and that the gift card breakage remaining at the end of the fourth year be recorded as income to the spa.

Because of the nature of the redemption process, some portion of the gift card redemption takes place as a Current Deferred Revenue—Gift Card item and some other portion takes place as a Long-Term Deferred Revenue—Gift

Card. That is, a portion of the redemptions will occur in the next 12 months (current) and another portion will take place after the next 12 months (long-term). The historical pattern of redemption and breakage will allow the calculation of estimated current and long-term portions of the Deferred Revenue.

To understand the accounting and cash flow complexities of spa gift cards, let's assume the following multiple-year examples for the hypothetical Hotel Spa. To simplify the example a bit, we will recognize breakage revenue after three years instead of four.

- Gift card sales—20X7: $500,000
- Gift card sales—20X8: $600,000
- Gift card sales—20X9: $700,000
- Gift card redemptions in year of sale—Year 1:   40%
- Gift card redemptions subsequent year—Year 2:   30%
- Gift card redemptions—Year 3   10%
- Average gift card breakage (after Year 3)   20%

The table below demonstrates the determination and calculation of historical patterns and gift card breakage:

Description	20X9	20X8	20X7	Total
Deferred revenue from sales of gift cards	$ 700,000	$ 600,000	$ 500,000	$1,800,000
Gift card redemptions in 20X7			(200,000)	(200,000)
Gift card redemptions in 20X8		(240,000)	(150,000)	(390,000)
Gift card redemptions in 20X9	(280,000)	(180,000)	(50,000)	(510,000)
Deferred Revenue—Gift Cards: 12-31-X9	$ 420,000	$ 180,000	100,000	$ 700,000
Write-off of gift card breakage—20X7			100,000	100,000
Deferred Revenue—Gift Cards: 12-31-X9	$ 420,000	$ 180,000	$ –0–	$ 600,000

Deferred Revenue—Gift Cards for the three-year period in the above table—totals $1.8 million for the Hotel Spa. Hotel Spa's startup year was 20X7. Sales of gift cards for the year totaled $500,000. Redemptions of $200,000 (40 percent) left a balance at the end 20X7 in Deferred Revenue—Gift Cards of $300,000. From a cash-flow viewpoint, the Hotel Spa deposited into its bank account $300,000 in cash net of current year services rendered with an obligation to provide services at a later time. The deferred revenue for gift cards at the end of 20X8 is determined as follows:

20X7 Gift Card Sales	$ 500,000
20X8 Gift Card Sales	600,000
40% redemption of 20X7	(200,000)
30% redemption of 20X7 gift cards in 20X8	(150,000)
40% redemption of 20X8 gift cards in 20X8	(240,000)
Balance of Deferred Revenue—Gift Cards	$ 510,000

The same process is used to determine the total amount of deferred revenue—gift cards at the end of 20X9.

At the end of 20X9, Hotel Spa has $100,000 of the 20X7 gift card sales that are unredeemed and the redemption of the remaining cards is both unpredictable and unlikely. Although there is a chance that some holders of the remaining outstanding gift cards issued in 20X7 will appear at the hotel to redeem their cards, the vast majority will not. Therefore, in keeping with the three-year period of open redemption we established for this example, the $100,000 is concluded to be breakage, removed from Deferred Revenue—Gift Cards, and reported as income to the spa in 20X9. The entry to record the write-off of the 20X7 gift card breakage is as follows:

Deferred Revenue—Gift Cards	100,000	
Other Income		100,000

Historical patterns of redemption will allow the accounting for the current and long-term portions of deferred revenue—gift cards. See the table below:

Description	20X9	20X8	Total
Deferred Revenue—Gift Card balance 12/31/20X9	$420,000	$180,000	$ 600,000
20X8 cards to be redeemed in 20Y0 ($600,000 × 10%)		60,000	(60,000)
20X9 cards to be redeemed in 20Y0 ($700,000 × 30%)	210,000		(210,000)
Long-Term Portion—Deferred Revenue—Gift Cards	210,000	120,000	330,000
Current Portion—Deferred Revenue—Gift Cards	210,000	60,000	270,000

The Hotel Spa balance sheet for the year ended December 31, 20X9, will have a line item titled Current Portion Deferred Revenue—Gift Cards in the amount of $270,000 classified as a current liability. The lline item Long-Term Portion Deferred Revenue—Gift Cards in the amount of $330,000 will be classified as a long-term liability.

Based on the above, the Hotel Spa manager is able to draw the following conclusions regarding budgeting cash flow for 20Y0:

■ Revenue of $270,000 will be generated by the redemption of prior year gift cards.

■ Revenue from 20X9 gift card sales was $700,000 and the sales are trending up at $100,000. Therefore, $800,000 in gift card sales can be forecast for 20Y0.

■ The hotel will redeem $320,000 of the $800,000 gift card sales in 20Y0.

The condition of the economy can play a huge role in gift card cash flow planning. In times of recession, guests will slow down the purchase of gift cards, while the recipients of cards are more likely to use them to conserve their cash. As a result, the cushion or "gift card float" can disappear and cash flow can be squeezed severely. In periods of economic growth, the opposite is prone to occur. Sales of gift cards can result in large deferred revenue liabilities that can threaten the financial existence of a spa. A conservative risk management approach to limiting the risk involved is to maintain a "trust" bank account where cash or cash equivalents are held in the same amount as the balance in the Deferred Revenue—Gift Cards account. Balances in the trust account can be invested in order to generate income.

11.13 UNSECURED BANK LOANS

Bank loans are a major source of short-term financing for most hospitality firms. They come in a variety of forms and may be secured or unsecured.

A promissory note is the traditional bank lending arrangement. The borrower signs a note promising to repay the amount borrowed at a definite future date along with a specified amount of interest. The note also indicates the nature of supporting collateral, if any, and any other terms and conditions of the loan. When the agreement is signed, the bank generally credits the amount borrowed directly into the borrowing firm's checking account. The hospitality firm recognizes the cash and the liability, notes payable, on its books.

Interest is determined using the following formula:

$$\text{Interest} = \text{Principal} \times \text{Interest Rate} \times \text{Time}$$

where *principal* is the amount of the loan, *interest rate* is the annual interest rate, and *time* is the term of the loan stated as a portion of a year. For example, assume the Main Street Hotel borrows $100,000 for six months when the prime interest rate is 6 percent. Further assume the Main Street Hotel is charged interest at 2 percent over prime. The cost of this loan is $4,000, determined as follows:

$$\text{Interest Expense} = \$100,000 \times 0.08 \times 0.5$$

$$= \underline{\underline{\$4,000}}$$

A line of credit is a relatively informal, nonbinding agreement between the bank and the borrower that specifies the maximum amount that can be borrowed during a particular period, usually a year or less. For example, a hotel with a $50,000 line of credit could have up to five $10,000 promissory notes outstanding at any time during a year. However, because the agreement is nonbinding, the bank could reduce the line of credit at any time. For example, it could decide that the hotel's condition had deteriorated somewhat after $40,000 had been advanced, and refuse to loan the last $10,000. It could not, however, shorten the term of any note that had already been signed. An amount borrowed under a line of credit is said to take down the line by that amount. Interest is paid only on what is borrowed.

Credit lines are generally unsecured, meaning the loans are not backed by specific assets and the bank relies only on the general creditworthiness of the hotel for repayment. A revolving credit agreement is similar to a line of credit, except that the bank guarantees the availability of funds up to a maximum amount during the specified period. This is a binding line of credit. Like the line of credit, it is also generally unsecured.

The bank's commitment to advance funds up to a maximum amount carries a cost to the hospitality firm. The borrowing hotel is required to pay a commitment fee on the unborrowed balance of the agreement. Commitment fees are approximately 0.25 percent per year.

The interest rates on revolving credit agreements are generally variable. They're usually specified relative to the bank's prime rate. The interest rate on smaller firms' revolving debt is likely to be stated at prime plus 2 or 3 percent.

Consider an example. Assume the Wall Hotel has a $2 million revolving credit agreement with its bank at prime plus 2 percent based on a calendar year. Before April, it had borrowed $1 million that was outstanding for the entire month. On April 15, it borrowed another $500,000 (assume the funds were available on April 16). Prime is 7 percent and the bank's commitment fee is 0.25 percent annually. What bank charges will the Wall Hotel incur for the month of April?

The Wall Hotel payment will consist of the interest on money actually borrowed and the commitment fee for the unused balance of its revolving credit agreement. Its monthly interest rate is 0.75 percent, determined as follows:

$$(7\% + 2\%) \div 12 = \underline{0.75\%}$$

and the monthly commitment fee is

$$0.25\% \div 12 = \underline{0.0208\%}$$

In April, a loan of $1 million was outstanding for the entire month and an additional $500,000 was outstanding for 15 days. Hence, the interest charge is

$$(\$1,000,000 \times 0.0075) + \left(\$500,000 \times 0.0075 \times \frac{15}{30}\right) = \underline{\$9,375}$$

The unused balance of the revolving credit agreement was $500,000 for 15 days and $1 million for 15 days for an average of $750,000. The commitment fee is then:

$$\$750,000 \times 0.000208 = \$156$$

Thus, the total interest payment is $9,531.

In theory, a hospitality firm could maintain a balance of short-term debt all the time by borrowing on a new note to pay off each old one as it comes due. Doing that would make it possible to fund long-term projects with short-term money by refinancing the debt again and again throughout the life of the project. But this procedure can be rather risky for two reasons. First, if short-term interest rates increase, interest expense can increase quickly, putting a strain on the firm's profitability. Second, if refinancing funds become unavailable, a default on the short-term note is likely as the short-term note comes due. This kind of risk for a borrowing hospitality firm is also risky for the bank, because a defaulted hospitality firm is likely to mean a lending loss. Therefore, banks try to keep hospitality firms from falling into the trap of using short-term funds to support long-term projects.

The banks' approach is the *clean-up requirement*. They simply require that borrowers pay off all unsecured short-term debt periodically and remain out of debt for a specified period. Most clean-up requirements stipulate that hospitality firms be out of short-term debt for 30 to 45 days once a year.

11.14 INTEGRATED CASH MANAGEMENT FOR MULTIUNIT OPERATIONS

So far, our discussion of cash management could most easily be applied to a single-unit operation. However, for multiunit operations, an **integrated cash management system** should generally be installed.

An integrated cash management system consists of centralizing cash receipts and especially cash disbursements from the corporate office. Cash receipts, although initially received by the individual unit, are moved quickly to the corporate office. Cash disbursements, for the most part, are made from the corporate bank accounts. For example, payroll checks are prepared at the corporate office. Supplier invoices may also be paid from corporate accounts.

An integrated cash system's primary goal is to minimize the amount of cash the hospitality operation—both the corporate office and the individual facilities—holds. Cash balances at individual units may be reduced by having a centralized cash disbursement system. The checking accounts of individual units become, in essence, cash clearing accounts, maintained at balances just sufficient to facilitate required local disbursements. All excess cash is quickly transferred to the corporate accounts. More cash at the corporate level results in increased financial returns for two reasons. First, a large cash reserve increases the corporation's bargaining power with financial institutions. Second, the corporate office usually staffs more financial experts than individual operations can afford.

An integrated cash management system can pay real dividends. For example, assume that a chain's cash system is able to keep cash in its accounts (available for investment) for two days longer by increasing its net float. The interest earned for a chain with $1 billion of annual sales is $547,945, determined as follows:

$$\text{Interest} = \text{Principal} \times \text{Rate} \times \text{Time}$$
$$= \$100,000,000 \times 0.10 \times \frac{2}{365}$$
$$= \underline{\underline{\$547,945}}$$

An integrated cash management system results in better allocation of funds throughout the operation. When some properties need cash, they receive it from the corporate office rather than a local bank. Some experts suggest that an integrated cash system improves control over collection and disbursement procedures.[8] For example, individual properties may pay invoices before their due dates; however, a centralized system allows for proper monitoring of cash disbursements.

An integrated cash management system uses cash forecasting, including the preparation of cash budgets at both the unit and corporate levels. Both short- and long-term budgets should be prepared at both levels. The centralized system is designed to transfer as much cash as possible to corporate accounts. Some hospitality operations also have their own credit card systems, although most work directly with major credit card companies.

Cash is a very important asset for hospitality operations. Although it may not earn interest, cash is used to pay debts, make other disbursements, and facilitate guest transactions. Management must try to minimize the operation's cash holdings by investing them in revenue-producing assets while, at the same time, not jeopardizing its operations. This chapter highlighted a number of cash management tools, including cash budgets, the treatment of other current assets, and an integrated cash system.

Cash budgets are formulated to estimate the operation's future cash position. Two approaches, the cash receipts and disbursements approach and the adjusted net income approach, estimate the cash balance at the end of the period and give management the information necessary for planning.

The cash receipts and disbursements method is a direct approach that examines all cash inflows and outflows. Items found in this budget might include the amount of cash sales in the period, collection of accounts receivable, dividends and interest received, the operating expenses that were paid for during the period, and dividends paid. This type of budget is most useful for short-term periods because the estimates upon which it is based are less reliable the further the projections are made into the future.

The adjusted net income approach to cash budgeting is used for periods of over six months. The projected operations for each future year are adjusted to reflect cash flows. This approach also considers any expected changes in current accounts and any capital expenditures. Management should examine excess funds and determine the appropriate way to invest them.

Management must also monitor the activity in other current accounts in order to optimize the operation's liquidity position. Accounts receivable should be analyzed to ensure their timely collection. Inventory is expensive to store but is valuable to operations, so it should also be monitored. This is often done by analyzing the turnover ratio. Current liabilities should be studied with special consideration given to trade discounts. All of these procedures will aid management in cash control and overall operational efficiency.

An integrated cash system can minimize the total cash holdings of a multiunit corporation. This is accomplished by maintaining a central account to which almost all receipts are deposited and from which almost all disbursements are made. Even when hospitality operations have this central account, it is important for them to make budgets, both for the long- and short-term horizons, and constantly update them as information becomes available.

adjusted net income approach—One of two basic approaches to cash budgeting. It is generally preferable for budgeting cash for periods longer than six months.

cash budgets—Management's detailed plan for cash receipts and disbursements.

cash flows—A stream of receipts (inflows) and disbursements (outflows) resulting from operational activities or investments.

cash management—The management of a hospitality operation's cash balances (currency and demand deposits), cash flow (cash receipts and disbursements), and short-term investments in securities.

cash receipts and disbursements approach—One of two basic approaches to cash budgeting. It is useful when forecasting cash receipts for periods of up to six months. It shows the direct sources of cash receipts and the direct uses of cash.

city ledger—As opposed to the guest ledger, which contains all the accounts of the registered hotel guests, it contains all the accounts of nonguest transactions. It is also known as the house ledger.

collection float—The time between when a hospitality business deposits a guest's check (increasing its cash account on the books) and when the business can use the funds (i.e., when the bank receives the funds from the guest's bank).

effective cost—The true cost when all elements are considered.

float—The time between the subtraction or addition of cash to the company's books and the actual subtraction or addition to the company's bank account.

gift card breakage—The unused (unredeemed) portion of gift card sales.

imprest basis—Method of maintaining funds by replenishing the amount of disbursements since the previous replenishment.

income flows—Flow that results from operations generating revenues and incurring expenses. These flows are shown on the income statement and reflect the results of operations.

integrated cash management system—A cash management system for multiunit operations. It consists of centralizing cash receipts and especially cash disbursements from the corporate office.

lockbox system—A system used to speed the flow of cash from accounts receivable to the hospitality operation's bank accounts, consisting of a post office box from which bank personnel collect all incoming mail and deposit any checks directly in the operation's account with the bank.

net float—The difference between payment float and collection float.

payment (or disbursement) float—The time between when a hospitality business writes a check (decreasing its cash account on the books) and when the funds are actually deducted from the business's bank account. Also called disbursement float.

trade credit—Term for credit offered by suppliers who do not charge interest to hospitality operations for amounts owed in the normal course of business.

transaction motive—The rationale for maintaining adequate balances in checking accounts to meet checks drawn on those accounts.

working capital—Current assets minus current liabilities.

1. What is meant by an *imprest basis*?

2. How is cash used by hospitality operations?

3. What are three items that exemplify the differences between income and cash flows?

4. What are the two different types of cash budget formats? In what circumstances would you use each one?

5. What are five informational items needed to prepare a cash budget using the cash receipts and disbursements approach?

6. What should management consider when investing excess cash?

7. Why must you analyze other current asset accounts when using the adjusted net income approach to cash budgeting?

8. How soon should you turn delinquent accounts receivable over to a collection agency? Why?

9. What is the value of a lockbox system to a hospitality operation?

10. What is an integrated cash management system?

Problem 1

Angela Westmont is the owner/manager of the Canterra. Her accountant has suggested that all cash discounts should be taken. Assume the Canterra can borrow short-term funds at an annual interest rate of 8 percent.

Required:

1. Determine the effective rate of interest of the following terms of sale:
   a. 1/10, *n*/40
   b. 2/10, *n*/60
   c. 3/10, *n*/50

2. Do you agree with the accountant, given the above terms of sale and the borrowing interest rate for short-term loans as stated above?

Problem 2

Wilson Price, owner of the WP Hotel, is considering a lockbox system for some of his accounts receivable collections. He can program his computer to send statements with different return addresses depending on the amount of the balance. The bank charges $0.35 per item for lockbox service. Mr. Price can invest cash with the bank at an annual interest rate of 8 percent. He has estimated that using the lockbox would speed up collections by three days.

Required:

What is the breakeven amount—that is, the amount at which Mr. Price would be indifferent as to whether a customer sent the check directly to the motel or the post office lockbox?

Problem 3

The Charlotte Hotel has just signed a promissory note for $200,000 for six months. The annual interest rate is 10 percent. The compensating balance requirement is 15 percent. The loan amount plus interest must be paid in six months.

Required:

1. What will be the interest cost of this loan?

2. What will be the total loan payment at the end of the loan term?

3. Assuming the checking account balance would be zero without the loan, what is the effective interest rate of this note?

4. Assuming the Charlotte Hotel has a balance in its checking account of $8,000 throughout the loan period without the loan, what is the effective interest rate?

Problem 4

Patel Lodging Corporation (PLC) collects $21 million per year from major corporate clients. The average remittance check is $3,000. A lockbox system would shorten the float by two days but would cost $2,000 per year plus $0.20 per check. PLC's relevant interest rate is 7 percent.

Required:

Should PLC use this lockbox system? Use numbers to support your answer.

Problem 5

The River Rowing Club collects $8 million each year from its members. The average check written by these members is $800. The average float time is three days. The club's banker has proposed a lockbox arrangement that will reduce the float time to two days. The bank will charge a fixed fee of $3,000 per year plus $0.25 per check handled. The relevant interest rate to the club is 8 percent. Assume a 365-day year.

Required:

Should the River Rowing Club accept this lockbox proposal?

Problem 6

The Ralston Food Company (RFC) is interested in knowing the length of its operating cycle and cash conversion cycle. You are provided with the following information:

	December 31	
	20X4	20X5
Accounts receivable	$55,000	$65,000
Food inventory	25,000	40,000
Accounts payable	25,000	30,000

The food sales for 20X5 were $1.5 million and RFC's cost of food sold was 35 percent.

Required:

1. Determine RFC's operating cycle.

2. Determine RFC's cash conversion cycle.

Problem 7

Brady Inc. has a $20 million revolving credit agreement with its bank at an interest rate of prime plus 2 percent. The bank's commitment fee is 0.25 percent annually on the unused portion. The company's use of the credit agreement for the year just completed and the prime rates for each time period are as follows:

Quarter	Outstanding Balance	Prime Rate
First	$12 million	4.5%
Second	16 million	5%
Third	15 million	5.5%
Fourth	17 million	5%

Required:

Assume that the outstanding balance as reported exists for the entire quarter and that each quarter has 90 days in a 360-day year. Calculate the interest cost, including the commitment fee cost, of this revolving credit agreement.

Problem 8

The Grainger Lodge (GL) borrowed short-term funds of $180,000 from the Eastern Michigan Bank. The annual interest rate is 10 percent. The bank requires GL to have a compensating balance of $15,000 in its checking account.

Required:

1. Assuming GL historically has a zero cash bank balance, what is the effective interest rate of this loan?

2. Assume GL normally maintains $5,000 in its checking account, so only an additional $5,000 must be left in its checking account related to this loan. What is the effective interest rate?

Problem 9

May Cole is the manager of the Real Time Inn and has completed the operating budgets for the next three years, as shown below. She is now ready to prepare the cash budget.

	Operating Budgets 20X1–20X3		
	20X1	20X2	20X3
Sales	$1,000,000	$1,400,000	$1,800,000
Direct Expenses	450,000	650,000	750,000
Depreciation	100,000	100,000	100,000
Other Fixed Expenses	350,000	450,000	650,000
Income before Taxes	100,000	200,000	300,000
Income Tax	40,000	80,000	120,000
Net Income	$ 60,000	$ 120,000	$ 180,000

Additional information:

1. Dividends paid in a given year are estimated to be 50 percent of net income for that year but cash is not to be reduced to less than $150,000 at the end of any year.

2. The following is a summary of the only current accounts that are expected to change:

	20X1	20X2	20X3
Accounts Receivable	−10,000	+20,000	+20,000
Accounts Payable	+10,000	+15,000	+20,000

3. A major piece of equipment that costs $100,000 is scheduled for purchase during 20X3. May Cole would like to purchase the machine with cash and by borrowing long-term funds. The funding is to be 50/50.

4. The cash balance at the beginning of 20X1 is $20,000.

5. Assume that the income tax for each year is paid in the year it is shown as an expense.

Required:

Prepare cash budgets for 20X1–20X3 for the Real Time Inn using the adjusted net income approach.

Problem 10

The Murphy Motel's general manager, Bryan Murphy, has completed the operations budget for 20X6. He requests your assistance in developing equations for the cash budget. He provides sales information as follows:

January	$275,000	April	$312,000
February	$280,000	May	$308,000
March	$290,000	June	$315,000

The division of sales is as follows:

Cash sales	40%
Regular credit	60%

Regular credit accounts are collected as follows:

Month of sale	10%
Month after month of sale	60%
Second month after month of sale	20%
Third month after month of sale	9%
Bad debts	1%
Total	100%

Required:

Determine the amount of cash expected to be received during May 20X6. (Show all of your calculations.)

Problem 11

The Danforth Corporation had net income of $200,000 for 20X2. Its income statement reflected depreciation of $45,000 and amortization expense of $15,000. Accounts receivable decreased by $10,000 during 20X2, while accounts payable declined by $7,000. The mortgage payments for 20X2 totaled $85,000, of which $40,000 was interest expense. Dividends of $28,000 were paid during 20X2, while $35,000 of dividends were declared during 20X2.

Required:

Determine the net cash flow for 20X2. (Show all of your work.)

Problem 12

Use the following information to formulate a simplified cash budget for Heidi's Place:

	December	January	February	March
Sales	$ 40,000	$40,000	$ 50,000	$75,000
Inventory Purchases	15,000	17,000	18,000	30,000
Other Cash Expenses	15,000	15,000	22,000	37,000
Capital Purchases (with cash)	–0–	–0–	10,000	–0–

Sales:	Sixty percent of the sales are cash while the remaining 40 percent are credit sales. One-half of the credit sales are collected in the month of sale and one-half in the next month.
Inventory Purchases:	Eighty percent of the purchases are paid in the month of the purchase, while 20 percent are paid in the next month.
Other:	Assume that other cash expenses and capital purchases are paid for during the month indicated above (e.g., other cash expenses of $15,000 for December were paid in December).

Assume that the beginning cash balance of January 1 is $5,000.

Required:

Prepare a cash budget using the cash receipts and disbursements approach for the months of January through March.

Problem 13

Managers at the Topeka Corporation have just completed a long-range operations budget for 20X1–20X3. They are interested in their ability to buy fixed assets in 20X2 and 20X3 from cash generated by the business. They need tentative cash budgets for 20X1–20X3 to evaluate the situation. The following information is available:

Condensed Operations Budgets
Topeka Corporation
20X1–20X3

	20X1	20X2	20X3
Sales	$5,000,000	$6,000,000	$6,500,000
Operating expenses	4,000,000	5,000,000	6,000,000
Depreciation	500,000	500,000	500,000
Income before taxes	500,000	500,000	–0–
Income tax expense*	200,000	200,000	–0–
Net income	$ 300,000	$ 300,000	$ –0–

*The income tax expense is recorded on the books only. The amount paid each year is as follows:

	20X1	20X2	20X3
Income tax liability for each year	$150,000	$150,000	$ 50,000
Increase in accounts receivable	10,000	20,000	10,000
Increase in accounts payable	5,000	15,000	20,000
Increase in inventories	5,000	2,000	1,000
Expected distributions to partners (owners)	100,000	110,000	120,000

Required:

Prepare cash budgets for the Topeka Corporation for 20X1–20X3 using the adjusted net income approach.

Problem 14

The Mounds Motel's summarized three-year strategic operations budget is as follows:

	20X4	20X5	20X6
Sales	$ 1,500,000	$1,600,000	$ 1,700,000
Operating expenses	900,000	950,000	1,000,000
Depreciation	200,000	200,000	200,000
Other fixed charges	300,000	300,000	300,000
Income tax provision	20,000	40,000	80,000
Net income	80,000	110,000	120,000
The expected income tax payments each year are as follows:	$ –0–	$ 10,000	$ 30,000
Expected changes in current accounts:			
Accounts receivable	+30,000	+50,000	+80,000
Inventory	+5,000	+5,000	+5,000
Accounts payable	+5,000	+5,000	+5,000
Expected fixed asset acquisitions (with cash)	$ 200,000	$ 150,000	$ 200,000

The owners have invested $600,000 in the motel and would like a 10 percent return if possible. They would like 5 percent of projected sales for the following year in the motel operation for contingency. The cash balance at the beginning of 20X4 is $50,000. Projected sales for 20X7 are $1,800,000.

Required:

Prepare cash budgets for 20X4–20X6 and advise the owners.

Problem 15

Financial information for Strawberry's Place is as follows:
Cash at January 1, 20X1 is $10,000. The firm desires to maintain a minimum balance of $10,000 at the end of each month.
    Total monthly sales are as follows:

December	20X0	$120,000
January	20X1	150,000 (est.)
February	20X1	160,000 (est.)

    The sales are 40 percent cash and 60 percent credit card. Visa is the only acceptable credit card at Strawberry's, and assume the charges are converted to cash the day of the sale. The brokerage charge is 2 percent of the sale.
    Expected other income is $2,000 from interest to be received in February. In addition, in January, a range with a net book value of $300 is expected to be sold for cash, resulting in a $1,000 gain on the sale.

Food and beverages are paid for the month following the sale and average 40 percent and 25 percent, respectively. Food sales are four times beverage sales. Total sales consist of only food and beverage sales. Labor is paid for the last day of the month and averages 35 percent of sales.

Other expenses approximate $20,000 per month and are paid for in that month. In the month of January, $30,000 is expected to be expended on new equipment. Funding for this expenditure in part comes from a long-term loan of $15,000 from the Delaware Bank and Trust.

If the firm borrows working capital funds, it must do so on an incremental basis of $1,000.

Required:

Prepare the cash budgets for January and February 20X1.

Problem 16

The M&N Corporation, a consulting client of yours, has just completed its long-range operations budget for three years. The company has asked you to assess its ability to buy various pieces of equipment in 20X2 and 20X3. In order to respond, you need to prepare cash budgets for 20X1–20X3. Information provided to you is as follows:

	20X1	20X2	20X3
Sales	$5,000,000	$6,000,000	$6,500,000
Operating expense	4,000,000	5,000,000	6,000,000
Interest expense	100,000	90,000	80,000
Depreciation	400,000	410,000	420,000
Income before taxes	500,000	500,000	–0–
Income tax provision	200,000	200,000	–0–
Net income	$ 300,000	$ 300,000	$ –0–
Other information:			
Income tax payments	$ 150,000	$ 150,000	$ 50,000
Increase in accounts receivable	100,000	200,000	150,000
Increase in accounts payable	5,000	15,000	20,000
Reduction in LTD	100,000	110,000	120,000

Required:

Prepare a cash budget for 20X1–20X3. Assume cash on January 1, 20X1, equals $25,000.

Problem 17

The Redbird Restaurant's financial information for the months of July through September 20X2 is as follows:

	Budgeted sales
July	$60,000
August	70,000
September	65,000

In the past, cash and charge sales have been 40 percent and 60 percent, respectively, of total sales. Actual sales for May and June totaled $62,000 and $58,000, respectively. Collections on charge sales average 75 percent in the month following the sale and 25 percent in the second month after the sale. Food costs average 35 percent of total revenue. Thirty percent of food costs is paid in the month of sale, while the remaining 70 percent is paid in the following month. Payroll costs are paid at the end of each month and average 30 percent of total sales.

Other budgeted expenses are as follows:

	July	August	September
Interest—loans	$1,500	$1,495	$1,490
Depreciation	1,000	1,000	1,000
Property taxes	500	500	500
Insurance	400	400	400
Other expenses	2,000	2,000	2,000

The interest is part of Redbird's $2,000 monthly mortgage payment. Property tax payments of $3,000 are made in July and December. The annual insurance premium of $4,800 was paid in January. Other expenses are paid each month as the expense is incurred.

During August, a new cash register is to be purchased for $8,000. The old register will be sold at an expected loss of $500; its net book value at that time will be $1,000. If necessary, the Redbird Restaurant can borrow money from the Illinois State Bank on a six-month-note basis—that is, the note and interest would be paid in six months.

The cash balance on July 1, 20X2, is $5,000.

Required:

Prepare the Redbird Restaurant's cash budget for July through September 20X2 using the cash receipts and disbursements approach.

Problem 18

The financial information for the Soliz Café is as follows:

	Budgeted	
	Cash sales	Charge sales
August	$32,000	$16,000
September	26,500	13,000
October	28,000	13,000
November	28,000	12,000
December	30,000	15,000

Collection on charge sales averages 60 percent in the month following the sale, and the remaining 40 percent in the month following that. Purchases (cost of sales) average 35 percent of total revenue. Of that, 100 percent is paid in the month following purchase. Payroll is on a cash basis and is forecasted to be:

October	$15,000
November	15,500
December	16,000

Other budgeted expenses are as follows:

	October	November	December
Rent	$ 2,600	$2,600	$2,600
Insurance	200	200	200
Energy costs	400	500	600
Depreciation	900	900	900
Loan interest	400	400	400
Other expenses	1,200	1,000	1,400

The rent, energy costs, loan interest, and other expenses are paid in cash each month as the expense is occurred. The insurance expense, $2,400, is paid in November each year for the entire year.

The restaurant is making monthly payments of principal toward a bank loan. The amount is $1,000 per month. New equipment is to be purchased in November. The cash cost will be $6,600. At the same time, old equipment will be sold. The estimated gain on the sale is expected to be $800. The old equipment has a net book value of $1,200 and is to be sold for cash. In December, the restaurant owner plans to pay a Christmas bonus to his staff in the amount of $5,000.

Required:

Prepare the restaurant's cash budget for the months of October, November, and December. Assume the opening bank balance on October 1 is $3,000.

Problem 19

Claude Ziggy, owner of Ziggy's Diner, needs your assistance to prepare a cash budget for his restaurant. He estimates cash on July 1 will be $2,400. He wants to maintain a minimum of cash at the end of each month equal to one week's (seven days') disbursements for the next month, not including disbursements related to working capital loans. (Assume that disbursements are made evenly throughout a month.)

Total monthly sales are as follows:

March	$ 50,000
April	120,000
May	120,000
June	150,000
July (estimated)	159,000
August (estimated)	180,000
September (estimated)	142,000
October (estimated)	90,000

The sales are 40 percent cash and 60 percent regular credit. Regular credit sales are collected as follows:

Month of sale	10%
Month after sale	60%
Second month after sale	20%

Third month after sale	8%	
Bad debts	2%	
Total	100%	

Interest income of $1,000 is expected in August. In September, the restaurant plans to sell some extra equipment. The chef estimates the equipment will bring $2,000; the book value of the equipment is $1,000. During September, 1,000 shares of capital stock with $1 par value are to be sold for $5 per share. Cash is to be received in September for the stock sales.

Payments for food are made one month after the sale. The food cost percentage is 35 percent. Beverages are purchased and paid for one month in advance and the beverage cost percentage is 25 percent. Beverages sales are 50 percent of food sales.

Labor is paid during the month wages are earned and represents 40 percent of total sales. Fixed expenses, except for insurance, depreciation, and property taxes, are $8,000 per month and are paid monthly.

Insurance premiums of $3,000 are paid quarterly in January, April, July, and October of each year. The property taxes of $20,000 for the year are paid in two installments of $10,000 each in July and December. Depreciation expense is $3,000 per month.

The board of directors is expected to declare a dividend per share of $0.25 in July, payable in August (20,000 shares are outstanding).

In September, the firm plans to acquire fixed assets using cash totaling $20,000. If the firm is to borrow cash to maintain the desired cash balances, it must do so in increments of $1,000. The interest rate is 12 percent, and principal and interest must be paid back in 30 days. (Assume that the funds borrowed, if any, are paid back in the following month.) Assume that a year has 365 days when calculating interest on short-term loans.

Required:

Prepare a monthly cash budget for Ziggy's Diner for July through September using the cash receipts and disbursements approach.

Problem 20

The Lakeland Diner has provided the information below for the preparation of its cash budget.

Beginning cash on July 1 is $5,000. The owner of the diner would like to maintain a minimum cash balance at the end of each month equal to one week's (seven days') disbursements for the current month, not including disbursements related to working capital loans. (Assume that disbursements are made evenly throughout a month.)

Monthly total sales are as follows:

March	$ 50,000	September (estimated)	$160,000
April	110,000	October (estimated)	150,000
May	130,000	November (estimated)	130,000
June	150,000	December (estimated)	120,000
July (estimated)	170,000	January (estimated)	100,000
August (estimated)	180,000	February (estimated)	90,000

The sales are 30 percent cash, 50 percent credit card, and 20 percent regular credit. The diner accepts only MasterCard. Cash is received from MasterCard for each day's sales, and the brokerage charge is 3 percent. Regular credit sales are collected as follows:

Month of sale	10%
Month after sale	70%
Second month after sale	10%
Third month after sale	9%
Bad debts	1%
Total	100%

Interest income of $3,000 is expected in July. In October, the firm plans to sell some extra equipment. The chef estimates the equipment will bring $5,000. The book value of the equipment is $2,000. During August, 2,000 shares of capital stock with $1 par value are to be sold for $4 per share. Cash is to be received in August for the stock sales. Investment dividends of $8,000 are expected to be received in November.

Payments for food are usually made one month after the sale, and the food cost percentage is 38 percent. Beverages are usually purchased and paid for one month in advance, and the beverage cost percent is 23 percent. Beverage sales are 75 percent of food sales. Employee wages are paid during the month they are earned and represent 35 percent of total sales. Other expenses, except insurance, depreciation, and property taxes, are $20,000 per month and are paid on a monthly basis. Insurance premiums of $5,000 are paid quarterly in January, April, July, and October of each year. The property taxes of $30,000 for the year are paid in two installments of $15,000 in July and December. Depreciation expense is $5,000 per month.

The board of directors is expected to declare a dividend/share of $0.25 in September, payable in October (24,000 shares are outstanding).

In August, the diner plans to acquire fixed assets totaling $20,000 with cash. If the diner is to borrow working capital, it must do so in increments of $1,000. The rate of interest is 12 percent, and principal and interest must be paid back in 30 days. (Assume that the funds borrowed, if any, are paid back the following month.) For the interest expense calculation, assume that a year has 365 days.

Required:

Prepare the cash budget for the Lakeland Diner for the months of July through December using the cash receipts and disbursements approach.

Problem 21

Jay Wolfe, owner of the Wolfe Lodge, needs your assistance. His lodge is a 100-room, full-service lodging operation. The cash balance in its checking account at the end of October 20X6 is $10,500. He has a quarterly mortgage reduction payment due on December 31, 20X6, of $200,000 and wonders if he will have sufficient cash. His operation has no other investments but depends on the lodge's operations to provide cash as needed.

The condensed operating budget is as follows:

	November	December
Room sales	$800,000	$750,000
Room department expenses	275,000	235,000

Undistributed operating expenses	250,000	263,000
Other expenses:		
Property taxes	-0-	40,000
Property insurance	8,000	8,000
Depreciation expense	50,000	50,000
Interest expense	30,000	30,000

The incorporated Wolfe Lodge pays 30 percent of its pretax income as income tax expenses to the federal government. All expenses are paid in the month of the expense, so there are no payables except for the income tax expense for November and December, which will need to be paid in January 20X7.

Mr. Wolfe plans to spend $80,000 to upgrade the Internet connections in late December. The sales are 40 percent cash and 60 percent on credit cards. The brokerage cost on the credit card is 3 percent and the expense is budgeted as an A&G expense and included in the budgeted figures. Credit card collections are 95 percent in the month of sales and 5 percent in the following month. October 20X6 credit card sales of $30,000 (net of the brokerage cost) are projected to be collected during November 20X6. The brokerage cost of 3 percent can be ignored for cash flow purposes.

Required:

1. What is the projected cash balance at the end of 20X6?

2. What recommendations regarding cash payment procedures can you provide to Jay Wolfe?

Problem 22

Sammi Hayes has a small, rooms-only operation (Sammi's Place). All sales are for cash and all expenses are paid for during the month incurred. The operating projections for 20X8 are as follows:

Revenues:	
Room sales	$880,000
Other	5% of total revenues
Direct expenses:	
Wages expense	22% of room sales
Other room expenses	20% of room sales
Undistributed operating expenses:	
A&G	$40,000
Marketing expenses	30,000
POM	25,000
Utilities expense	30,000
Other expenses:	
Property taxes	20,000
Insurance	15,000
Depreciation	30,000
Interest	25,000
Income tax	30% of pretax income

During August 20X8, Ms. Hayes plans to purchase $50,000 of new equipment with the operation's funds. The mortgage payment for the year is $80,000, which includes the $15,000 of interest as shown above. Ms. Hayes, the sole stockholder, plans to have the incorporated rooms operation pay her a dividend of $30,000 for the year.

Required:

1. Prepare the budgeted income statement for 20X8. (Round all figures to the nearest $1.)

2. Prepare a simplified cash flow statement showing sources and uses of cash for 20X8.

Problem 23

Lettuce Produce Company has been very diligent in its credit policy and collection. The company just learned that there is something known as the operating cycle and the cash conversion cycle, and is wondering how it is performing in these two measures. The balances of the food inventory, accounts receivable, and accounts payable are as follows; sales for 20X2 was $2 million, and the cost of sales was 35 percent:

	December 31	
	20X1	20X2
Food inventory	$50,000	$35,000
Accounts receivable	60,000	90,000
Accounts payable	25,000	35,000

Required:

1. Determine Lettuce Produce Company's operating cycle.

2. Determine Lettuce Produce Company's cash conversion cycle.

Problem 24

The Scotts own Willow Lodge, a five-room bed and breakfast place. Noting that any sort of credit card or mobile payment has a fee, and that their clients are exclusively referrals from friends or family, they only take cash and also carry out all their payment transaction in cash. For the year 20X2, the Scotts are estimating the following figures:

Revenues:	
Rooms revenue	$200,000
Other	2% of rooms revenue
Direct Expenses:	
Labor cost	25% of rooms revenue
Other rooms expenses	22% of rooms revenue
Undistributed Operating Expenses:	
Administrative and general	$8,000
Sales and marketing	3,000

Property operations and maintenance	4,000
Utilities	12,000
Other Expenses:	
Property tax	$11,500
Insurance	8,800
Depreciation	40,000
Interest	3,500
Income tax	30% tax bracket

The Scotts plan to buy three new air conditioning units and install them in April, before the summer months, at a cost of $22,500. The mortgage payment of the lodge is $25,000 for the year and includes the $3,500 of interest. The Scotts are also planning to take dividends of $7,500 at the end of the year.

Required:

1. Prepare the budgeted income statement for 20X2, and round all figures to the nearest dollar.

2. Prepare a simplified cash flow statement showing sources and uses of cash for 20X2.

Problem 25

Mochi Donuts has the following financial information:

Cash on September 1, 20X1, is $9,500. The bakery would like to maintain a minimum cash balance of $5,000 at the end of each month.

Monthly sales for August 20X1 were $115,000. Mochi expects to make $150,000 in September and $175,000 in October because the owner won a bake-off on local TV a week ago, and the projected sales have already gone up tremendously with people calling in orders to Mochi to make their signature item, a donut birthday cake.

The sales are 35 percent cash and 65 percent credit card. In order to be competitive, Mochi takes all major credit cards. Although the charges are converted to cash on the day of sale, Mochi has to pay a 3.2 percent average of sales as its credit card fees.

As business is growing, Mochi has placed an order for some bigger equipment. The old equipment will have a net book value of $500 is expected to be sold for cash. And, since it is in very good condition, Mochi expects to gain $1,000 on the sale.

All cost of sales is paid for the month following the sale and average 30 percent. Labor is paid for the last day of the month and averages 35 percent of sales. Other expenses approximate $15,750 per month and are paid for in that month. In September, $10,000 is expected to be used on new equipment, all from a bank loan.

Required:

Prepare the cash budgets for September and October 20X1.

12

INTERNAL CONTROL

needs drive good employees to produce. Focusing on employee needs puts managerial energy in the wrong areas—areas that managers can do little about.

It is the second condition, *opportunity*, upon which management can exert some influence. If management can preclude the opportunity for stealing, then it can truly prevent fraud and embezzlement. The purpose of this chapter is to discuss internal control characteristics and systems that will help eliminate the opportunity for theft. Clearly, the best way to prevent theft is to eliminate the opportunity.

The third condition, *failure of conscience*, involves conditions that allow a thief to rationalize the act of stealing. People need to rationalize theft. They need to convince themselves that they are somehow justified in taking what does not belong to them. Unlike economic and psychological needs, however, management can have some indirect influence on this need. Management can create an environment in which it is difficult to rationalize acts against the operation. This can be accomplished by applying internal control characteristics firmly but evenly throughout the organization—having the same rules for top management as for other employees. If a manager simply picks up a soft drink or pastry in a casual manner, this may cause other employees to think, "The boss takes what they want. Why shouldn't I?" However, if all managers are required to sign a check for food and drink in the same manner as any hotel guest would, this creates an environment of control and recordkeeping. Similar situations exist for such issues as steward's sales (when merchandise is sold to staff at reduced rates), searching packages at the door, and punching in at the time clocks. The rules should be applied evenly across the board, thus precluding one form of rationalization.

Again, out of all three conditions necessary for fraud and embezzlement to take place, management has the most influence on opportunity. Most of the characteristics of internal control discussed in this chapter are designed to prevent opportunities for theft.

12.2 THE HOSPITALITY INDUSTRY'S VULNERABILITY TO THEFT

Neal Geller has pointed out that hospitality businesses have general operating characteristics that render them relatively more vulnerable to theft than businesses in many other industries. These characteristics include the following:[2]

- There are many cash transactions.
- The industry provides many jobs requiring relatively low skills.
- Many hospitality positions are perceived as being of low social status.
- Items of relatively high value are commonly used in normal operations.
- Hospitality operations use many commodities that employees need and must buy for use in their own homes.

Some hotel and restaurant guests use cash to settle their accounts and to make other purchases during their stays. Even though credit and debit cards are increasingly being used, a number of transactions that involve cash occur each day. Many hotels have several profit centers that are open for much of the day (sometimes even 24 hours). These operations need cash banks. They also require several cashier shifts rather than the single shift many retail outlets can get by with.

Many hospitality positions are filled by relatively unskilled employees. These positions also tend to be low-paying jobs with little social status. These factors further combine to contribute to high turnover. All of these factors do little to help the internal control environment.

In addition to Geller's list of hospitality business characteristics, many lodging properties are small. Even large hotels are often operated like a small business. Large hotels are aggregations of many relatively small revenue outlets. In a large, full-service hotel, the rooms department may be a major revenue center, but there will be many bars, foodservice outlets, and other profit centers that individually are small operations. Thus, the critical mass or economics of scale that assist large operations with efficiency and control are often lacking. These characteristics of the hospitality industry highlight the critical need for an effective internal control system.

The club industry in its most recent uniform system of accounts (*Uniform System of Financial Reporting for Clubs*, 7th Edition) recognized the need for clubs to focus on the internal controls by including a section on accounting best practices.[3]

12.3 DEFINITION AND OBJECTIVES OF INTERNAL CONTROL

There are many definitions of internal control. One of the best known is provided by the American Institute of Certified Public Accountants (AICPA). This definition states, "Internal control comprises the plan of organization and all of the coordinate methods and measures adopted within a business to safeguard its assets, check the accuracy and reliability of its accounting data, promote operational efficiency, and encourage adherence to prescribed managerial policies."[4]

According to this definition, internal control consists of the plan of organization and the methods and measures within the operation to accomplish four major objectives. Several methods and measures used by hospitality operations will be discussed later in this chapter. At this point, it is important to realize that each hospitality operation must have a satisfactory plan of organization that should be in writing and that everyone in the operation should understand. Further, the organizational plan should provide for independence among operating, custodial, and accounting functions in order to prevent fraudulent conversion and assist in providing accurate and reliable accounting data. For example, in a restaurant operation, food should be stored and issued by custodians and requisitioned for use by preparation (operating) personnel. The accounting for the food should be accomplished by accounting personnel. Thus, the storing and issuing, preparation, and accounting functions are separate and independent of each other.

The four AICPA objectives of internal control can be defined as follows:

1. **Safeguard Assets.** A major objective of internal control is to protect company assets. This objective includes, but is not necessarily limited to (a) the protection of existing assets from loss such as theft; (b) the maintenance of resources, especially equipment, to ensure efficient utilization; and (c) the safeguarding of resources, especially inventories for resale, to prevent waste and spoilage. This objective is achieved by various control procedures and safeguards that might include the proper use of coolers and freezers for storing food, the use of locks to secure assets, the use of safes or vaults for cash, limiting personnel access to various assets, and segregating the operating, custodial, and accounting functions.

2. **Check Accuracy and Reliability of Accounting Data.** This objective consists of all the checks and balances within the accounting system to ensure the accuracy and reliability of accounting information. Accurate and reliable accounting information must be available not only for reports to owners, governmental agencies, and other outsiders, but also for management's own use in internal operations. For hospitality establishments, this objective may best be accomplished by adopting a uniform system of accounts. Because accounting information is most useful when received on a timely basis, regular reports for management's use must be prepared promptly.

3. **Promote Operational Efficiency.** Operational efficiency results from providing products and services at a minimum cost. In a hospitality establishment, training programs and proper supervision promote operational efficiency. For example, when room attendants are properly trained and supervised, the cost of cleaning rooms is lower. In addition, the use of mechanical and electronic equipment often improves operational efficiency. Point-of-sale (POS) devices in restaurant operations electronically communicate orders from server stations to preparation areas and often result in greater efficiency. POS devices in lodging operations also automatically post a restaurant sale to a guest's folio. This reduces labor and eliminates the possibility that the guest will check out before all charges have been properly posted to their account. Thus, the POS device also safeguards assets.

4. **Encourage Adherence to Prescribed Managerial Policies.** Another major objective of internal control is to ensure that employees follow managerial policies. For example, most operations have a policy that hourly employees must clock in and out themselves—one employee may not clock in another employee. Placing the time clock where managerial personnel can observe employees clocking in and out should encourage workers to adhere to the policy.

These four objectives may seem to conflict at times. For example, procedures to safeguard assets at a hotel may be so detailed that operational efficiency is reduced. Requiring four signatures to obtain a case of steaks from the storeroom may forestall theft, yet it may be so time-consuming that increased labor costs far exceed the potential losses without this elaborate control. Perfect controls, even if possible, generally would not be cost-justified. Management must weigh the cost of instituting a control against the benefit it would provide. When the proper balance of costs and benefits is achieved, management is performing efficiently.

The four objectives of internal control may be divided between the accounting and administrative functions. The first two objectives, safeguarding assets and ensuring the accuracy and reliability of accounting data, are considered **accounting controls**. The last two objectives, promoting operational efficiency and encouraging adherence to managerial policies, are considered **administrative controls**. Historically, accountants (especially independent external auditors) have focused their attention on internal accounting controls. However, more recently, hospitality establishments are closely reviewing administrative controls, which are more applicable to operations than accounting controls. This focus is necessary if hospitality operations are to achieve their overall objectives of providing appropriate guest service and thereby maximizing their profits. The review of administrative controls is often assigned to internal auditors who, in addition to checking accounting controls, are looking at administrative controls more than in the past.

Internal accounting controls are not only highly desirable, but they are also required by law. The Foreign Corrupt Practices Act (FCPA) of 1977, designed to stop illegal payments by publicly held corporations, contains the following provisions covering internal accounting control and recordkeeping:

1. Make and keep books, records, and accounts that, in reasonable detail, accurately and fairly reflect the transactions and dispositions of the assets of the company.

2. Devise and maintain a system of internal accounting control sufficient to provide reasonable assurances that:

   a. Transactions are executed in accordance with management's general and specific authorization;
   b. Transactions are recorded as necessary to (1) permit preparation of financial statements in conformity with generally accepted accounting principles or any other criteria applicable to such statements, and (2) maintain accountability of assets;
   c. Access to assets is permitted only in accordance with management's general and specific authorization; and
   d. The recorded accountability for assets is compared with the existing assets at reasonable intervals, and appropriate action is taken with respect to any differences.

The focus is on accounting controls, not administrative controls. The basic intent of the recordkeeping provision is to provide for reasonably accurate *external* financial reports, while the basic intent of the internal accounting control provision is to signal questionable or illegal payments. The FCPA pertains to those corporations subject to the Securities Acts, essentially corporations and their subsidiaries. Companies violating these provisions may be fined up to $10,000; company personnel may be fined up to $10,000 and imprisoned for up to 5 years. The Sarbanes-Oxley Act of 2002, to be discussed later in this chapter, also addressed internal control issues.

12.4 CHARACTERISTICS OF INTERNAL CONTROL

The four major objectives of internal control can only be achieved by instituting the many methods and measures of control. For example, to help safeguard assets, an operation might maintain a safe for holding cash overnight. Another procedure to safeguard cash may require that cash receipts be deposited with the bank when they total (for example) $2,000. Before discussing other methods and measures of an internal control system, we will present several general characteristics of such a system, including the following:

- Management leadership
- Organizational structure
- Sound practices
- Fixed responsibility
- Limited access

- Competent and trustworthy personnel
- Segregation of duties
- Authorization procedures
- Adequate records
- Procedure manuals
- Physical controls
- Budgets and internal reports
- Independent performance checks

These characteristics are sometimes referred to as elements or principles of internal control. They are essential to all effective internal control systems and apply to any business enterprise.

Management Leadership

Management's leadership is the key to any hospitality operation's system of internal control. The board of directors establishes the operation's highest-level policies and management communicates and enforces these policies. These policies should be clearly stated and communicated to all management levels. In addition, the various management levels are responsible for ensuring that the internal control system is adequate. The tone they set in communicating and enforcing policies may determine the degree to which employees will accept them and carry them out. Although there may be exceptions to board and top-level management policies, these exceptions should be minimized so as not to render the policies useless.

Organizational Structure

Only in the smallest hospitality operations is one person able to supervise all employees personally. In most establishments, the organizational structure is divided into the functional areas of marketing/sales, production, accounting/finance, and personnel. The organization chart represents the organizational structure of an operation. (See Exhibit 12.1 for a sample organization chart showing management positions for a full-service hotel.) Personnel must know the organization chart and follow the chain of command. Management policies usually prevent employees from circumventing the chain of command by requiring them to discuss any complaints or suggestions with their immediate supervisors or, in some cases, the human resources department. This approach not only reduces confusion but normally results in greater efficiency. Cases of management fraud constitute an exception to this general rule. In such extreme cases, employees must be able to communicate with the highest levels of management or with internal auditors.

Each position on the organization chart usually has a corresponding written job description. A job description consists of a detailed list of duties for the position. The procedure manual indicates how a job or duty should be performed.

In some hotel chains, the individual hotel controller answers directly to the area controller rather than to the hotel's general manager. Nevertheless, in this situation, the controller and general manager should work as a team, not as adversaries.

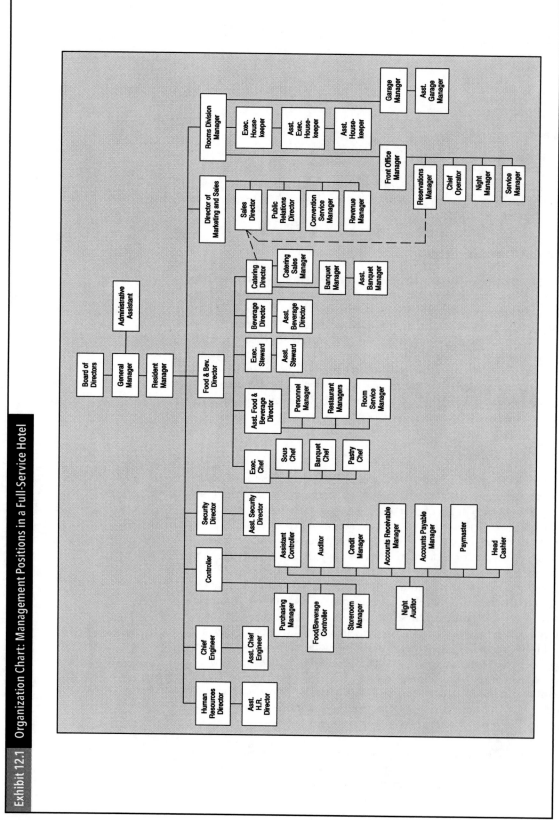

Source: Michael L. Kasavana, *Managing Front Office Operations*, Tenth Ed. (Lansing, Mich.: American Hotel & Lodging Educational Institute, 2017), p. 64.

Sound Practices

Sound practices are policy measures generally set by the board of directors to create an environment conducive to excellent internal control. Several hospitality operations have adopted the following practices:

- Bonding employees—Employees in a position of trust are covered by fidelity insurance. Some operations carry a blanket bond for minimum coverage on all employees.

- Mandatory vacation policy—Employees are required to take annual vacations. This is rigidly enforced for employees in positions of trust. Other employees then perform the absent employees' duties. If the absent employees have engaged in dishonest practices, the replacements may discover them, and management can take action.

- Code of ethics—Recently, some operations have required management personnel to follow a code of management ethics prohibiting illegal acts. Such codes are discussed later in this chapter.

Fixed Responsibility

Where practical, responsibility for a given activity should always be designated to a single individual. In that way, the person can be informed of their responsibilities, be given a set of standard operating procedures, and be expected to follow them. If the responsibility is given to one individual, then management knows where to start looking when there is a problem. This principle should also be viewed from the employees' perspective, however. The employees are held responsible for assets or actions, so they need the conditions to allow them to carry out their responsibilities. For example, a front office cashier should be solely and fully responsible for their bank; there should be no sharing of banks and no sharing of custody. It is unfair to make a person responsible for a bank and then give others access to it.[5]

Competent and Trustworthy Personnel

A key characteristic of internal control—perhaps the most important—is personnel. In the hospitality industry, the major difference between competitors is generally the quality of service, which is often a result of staff competency. For example, "service with a smile" may often be more important than the quality of the food served. Personnel must exhibit a caring attitude toward their guests in order for the operation to be successful.

An operation's system of internal control may be rendered useless if personnel are not competent and trustworthy. Perhaps just as important, failure to implement pre-employment screening procedures (such as checking the references and recommendations supplied by job applicants) may leave an employer open to litigation for negligent hiring—commonly defined as an employer's failure to exercise reasonable care in the selection of its employees. Pre-employment screening may also include checking for criminal records as well as conducting credit reference checks.

Generally, systems of internal control are not designed to prevent collusion (two or more people working together to defraud the property). Therefore, the careful selection, training, and supervision of personnel is vital. The operation must hire people with potential and train them properly in the work to be accomplished. This includes not only communicating what the jobs are and how to do them, but also following up to make sure that training has been effective. In addition, employees must understand the importance of their jobs in relation to the operation's overall objectives.

Finally, employees must be properly rewarded for work performed. This includes not only compensation, but also praise for a job well done and promotions when a person is ready and a position is available.

Segregation of Duties

The **segregation of duties** involves assigning different personnel to the functions of accounting, custody of assets, and production. Duties within the accounting function should also be segregated. The major objective of segregating duties is to prevent and detect errors and theft.

To illustrate the segregation of duties, consider the following description of a foodservice operation. A server takes a guest's order and records it on a guest check. A cook prepares the guest's food order from a copy of the guest check. The food itself was issued from storage by means of a requisition, submitted earlier in the day, based on estimated sales. The guest receives a copy of the guest check and pays the cashier. The cashier records the sale after checking the server's accuracy. In this example, the functions of order taker (sales), cook (production), storekeeper (custody of assets), and cashier (accounting) are separate. In addition to meeting the internal control objective of safeguarding assets by segregating duties, this separation promotes operational efficiency. Additional segregation of duties may further enhance operational efficiency. For example, the production area of a large restaurant may employ many people, including chefs, a Garde manger, a pastry chef, a butcher, a sous chef, and more.

Various tasks within the accounting department are divided among personnel to ensure proper checks and balances. For example, different personnel maintain the general ledger, the city ledger, and the guest ledger. Similarly, the cash reconciliation is prepared by personnel other than those accounting for cash receipts and/or disbursements.

Authorization Procedures

Management must properly authorize every business transaction. Management's authorization may be either general or specific. Management provides general authorization for employees to follow in the normal course of performing their jobs. For example, in a foodservice operation, servers are instructed to sell food and beverage items on the menu at the listed prices. No specific authorization is required to approve a sale in this case. In addition, a guest may pay for purchases with a debit or credit card. If the guest's debit or credit card is satisfactory, then the cashier may accept it and process the payment without specific authorization.

However, management may also require that certain transactions receive specific authorization. For example, suppose the purchase of fixed assets in excess of a certain amount requires the company president's approval. In this case, the transaction cannot be completed without the president's written authorization.

Adequate Records

Documents for recording transactions are essential to effective internal control. They include such forms as registration cards, folios, guest checks, payroll checks, receiving reports, purchase orders, timecards, and room out-of-order reports. Documents should be designed so that the preparer and ultimate user can understand them. Documents designed for multiple uses will minimize the number of different forms an operation needs. For example, a guest check for a foodservice operation could be a three-part form with the original copy serving as the customer's bill, the second copy used to communicate the order to production personnel, and the third copy for the server.

Documents are generally pre-numbered to facilitate control. Documents should be prepared when the transaction occurs in order to minimize errors. For example, when a hotel guest charges a meal to their room, a voucher is immediately prepared and transferred to the front office. This reduces the chance that the guest will check out without paying the foodservice charge.

Procedure Manuals

Each job within the hospitality operation can be reduced to writing. The procedure manual should list the details of each position, including how and when to perform each task. The procedure manual encourages consistent job performance, especially for relatively new employees who may be unsure about the details of their jobs. In addition, the procedure manual enables personnel to temporarily fill another position during a regular employee's absence.

Physical Controls

Physical controls are a critical element of safeguarding assets. Physical controls include security devices and measures for protecting assets, such as safes and locked storerooms. In addition, forms and accounting records need to be secured through proper storage and limited access. Mechanical and electronic equipment used to execute and record transactions also helps to safeguard assets. For example, cash registers that limit access to tapes help ensure the prompt and accurate recording of sales transactions in foodservice and beverage operations.

Budgets and Internal Reports

Budgets and other internal reports are essential elements of a system of internal control. These reports are an important part of an operation's communications system. When budgets are used for control purposes, they help to ensure that management's goals will be attained. If actual performance falls short of the goals, management is informed and able to take corrective action.

Other reports also alert management to operating performance and enable management to take corrective action as necessary. These reports include those prepared daily (daily report of operations), weekly (weekly forecasts), monthly (future bookings reports), and annually (long-range planning).

Independent Performance Checks

This characteristic of internal control is designed to ensure that the other elements of the internal control system are functioning properly. In order for a performance check to be successful, it must be independent—that is, the personnel performing the internal verification must be independent of the personnel responsible for the data being checked. In a number of hospitality operations, the independent performance check is conducted by the internal auditors. In order for the internal audit function to be successful, the auditors must be independent of both operations and accounting and must report directly to top management. (The internal audit function is discussed further in the next section of this chapter.)

Another independent performance check, especially in relation to the accounting function, is the work performed by the independent external auditors. The auditors not only verify financial statements, but also study the internal accounting control system and test it as a basis for how extensive the remaining audit will be. That is, the stronger the system of internal control is, the more reliance can be placed on it. Therefore, all other things being the same, a strong internal control system requires less extensive auditing.

Independent performance checks are the result of the segregation of duties. For example, the preparation of the bank reconciliation by personnel independent of those accounting for cash receipts and disbursements constitutes an independent check.

12.5 INTERNAL AUDITING

The internal audit function in many lodging and food service chains is a relatively recent development.[6] Some of the 100 largest lodging chains in the United States still do not have a chain-wide internal audit function, although several are in the process of establishing internal audit departments. The Institute of Internal Auditors defines **internal auditing** as "an independent appraisal activity within an organization for the review of operations as a service to management. It is a managerial control which functions by measuring and evaluating the effectiveness of other controls."[7]

In order for the internal audit function to be effective, it must be independent of the departments and functions that it audits. Since internal auditors review accounting functions, they should answer to the president of the organization or to the audit committee of the board of directors. However, in many firms, the audit function is part of the accounting department.

The above definition states that the internal audit is a "service to management." The ultimate purpose is to enhance profitability; thus, the internal auditor should be viewed as a partner seeking to assist management. The internal auditor's reports should be constructive and contain explanations and recommendations for improvements. Internal auditors often follow up to ensure that their recommendations are implemented.

The internal audit focuses on both accounting and administrative controls. Like the independent external auditor, the internal auditor is concerned with safeguarding assets and ensuring the reliability of accounting records (and thus the financial statements). However, unlike the external auditor, the internal auditor is concerned with operational efficiency. The internal auditor's review of front office procedures may reveal a more efficient and profitable way to staff the front office. In addition, the internal auditor is concerned with adherence to managerial policies. For example, the internal auditor may investigate whether advance approval of overtime was sought and received as required. The internal auditor may also investigate compliance with a mandatory vacation policy for employees who handle cash.

Exhibit 12.2 lists typical responsibilities of the internal audit department of a large business. Of course, the responsibilities of the internal audit department should be tailored to each operation's needs.

Research of the 100 largest lodging chains in the United States reveals the internal audit procedures in lodging operations. Exhibit 12.3 lists four categories of activities and examples of both financial and nonfinancial data for each. Exhibit 12.4 reveals the percentage of respondents that reported conducting these internal audit activities, a range of activity of those responding, and the average percentage for each activity.

Exhibit 12.3   Chart of Internal Audit Activities

Categories of Internal Auditing Activities	Financial Data	Nonfinancial Data
Checking compliance with internal controls and procedures	1. Reviewing the bank reconciliation	5. Determining that there is adequate separation of duties in the handling of cash transactions
Checking compliance with applicable laws and procedures	2. Determining whether the hotel corporation's tax return is in compliance with Internal Revenue Service Code	6. Determining whether the food and beverage operations are in compliance with local health department regulations
Determining whether corporate resources are being used efficiently	3. Conducting analytical reviews on receivables, fixed assets, inventory, etc.	7. Determining the efficiency of the chain's marketing effort
Determining whether corporate resources are being used effectively	4. Determining whether the return on investment for a hotel is above the hotel's hurdle rate	8. Determining the effectiveness of community service projects

Source: Raymond S. Schmidgall and James W. Damitio, "Internal Auditing Activities of the Major Chains," *Hospitality Research Journal* (1991): p. 262.

Exhibit 12.4 Internal Auditing Activity–Summary of Comparisons

Lodging Chains			
Using Financial Data	Percentage of Firms Reporting	Range of Activity	Average Percentage
Checking compliance with internal controls	100%	10–90%	42.47%
Checking compliance with laws	70%	0–30%	8.47
Checking on efficient use of resources	47%	0–10%	2.47
Checking on effective use of resources	50%	1–15%	2.97
Totals Using Financial Data			56.37%
Using Nonfinancial Data	Percentage of Firms Reporting	Range of Activity	Average Percentage
Checking compliance with internal controls	87%	0–60%	27.83%
Checking compliance with laws	70%	0–25%	6.00
Checking on efficient use of resources	60%	0–27%	4.13
Checking on effective use of resources	60%	0–35%	5.67
Totals Using Nonfinancial Data			43.63%
		Total	100.0%

Source: Raymond S. Schmidgall and James W. Damitio, "Internal Auditing Activities of the Major Chains," *Hospitality Research Journal* (1991): p. 263.

12.6 BASICS OF INTERNAL ACCOUNTING CONTROL

This section covers basic requirements of internal accounting control, including several methods of control for the various accounting functions. However, this list of methods is not exhaustive. Each hospitality operation must review these areas and determine control methods best suited to its needs.

Cash Control

Cash is the most vulnerable of all assets. It is therefore imperative to have an effective system of internal control over cash. The following list suggests commonly used cash control procedures.

1. All bank accounts and check signers must be authorized by the chief financial officer.

2. All bank accounts should be reconciled monthly, and the bank reconciliation should be reviewed by the controller.

3. The person reconciling bank accounts should receive bank statements (including canceled checks) directly from the bank. Employees who sign checks or have other accounting duties in connection with cash transactions should not reconcile the bank accounts. The reconciliation procedure should

include examination of signatures and endorsements and verification of the clerical accuracy of cash receipt and disbursement records. Exhibit 12.5 presents a sample bank reconciliation. It is important to record the journal entries for the reconciling items and not merely leave them as reconciled on the bank reconciliation.

4. The custody of cash should be the responsibility of the general cashier. Another employee should be assigned to account for cash received and to review cash transactions. This segregation of duties provides a check on the cashier's performance.

5. The general cashier must take annual vacations and their duties must be assumed by another employee.

6. House banks and petty cash funds should be counted at unannounced intervals by employees independent of the cash control function. Special attention should be given to the propriety of noncash items such as IOUs and accommodation checks (i.e., checks cashed for guests merely to provide them with cash).

7. Disbursements from petty cash funds should be supported by cash register tapes, invoices, or other documents. Such supporting data should be checked when funds are replenished and then canceled to prevent duplicate payment.

Exhibit 12.5 Bank Reconciliation–Hoosier Hotel

Bank Reconciliation
Hoosier Hotel
December 31, 20X2

Balance per bank statement—12/31/20X2		$14,622.18
Add: Deposit in Transit		3,641.18
Less: Outstanding checks		
Ck. 4315	$ 18.36	
Ck. 4422	156.14	
Ck. 4429	3,689.18	
Ck. 4440	172.47	
Ck. 4441	396.15	
Ck. 4442	100.00	
Ck. 4443	7.43	
Ck. 4444	799.18	−5,338.91
Other:		
Insufficient funds check received Dec. 31*		+324.32
Service charge—December, 20X2**		+ 15.24
Cash balance per books—12/31/20X2		$13,264.01
Prepared by _____		
Approved by _____		

* Redeposited January 1, 20X3.
** Amount recorded on books in January 20X3, since it was minor in amount.

Cash Receipts

The following procedures are commonly used for the internal control of cash receipts:

1. Accounting and physical control over cash receipts should be established when the cash is first received, whether at the front desk, at a profit center, or through the mail. For example, incoming mail receipts should be initially listed by an employee independent of both the general cashier and the accounts receivable department. This procedure establishes an independent record that later can be checked against daily bank deposits and the general ledger posting to accounts receivable. Initial control of cash received in the hotel or restaurant is accomplished with cash registers and front office accounting machines.

2. Restrictive endorsements, such as "For deposit only to Hoosier Hotel's account," should be placed on checks when first received to guard against the obstruction or illegal diversion of such cash receipts.

3. Employees in the accounts receivable department should not handle checks or currency. Postings to accounts receivable ledger cards should be based on remittance advice or listings of cash receipts.

4. Cash received should be given to the general cashier as soon as is practical. Cash receipts should be deposited daily and intact. They should not be mixed with other cash funds used to pay invoices, incidental expenses, or cash accommodation checks.

5. The general cashier and their subordinates should not be responsible for any of the following activities:
   a. Preparation or mailing of city ledger statements
   b. Posting accounts receivable records or balancing detail ledgers with general ledger control accounts
   c. Posting the general ledger
   d. Authorizing rebates, allowances, discounts, or writing off uncollectible accounts
   e. Preparing cash disbursements or reconciling bank accounts

   These activities are prohibited in order to reduce the opportunity for the general cashier and their subordinates to steal from the operation.

6. General instructions for cashiers often include the following:
   a. The cash drawer must be closed after each sale.
   b. Cashiers must circle and initial any overrings on the tape at the time of occurrence.
   c. Cash registers must be locked and keys removed when unattended.
   d. Cash sales must be rung up when they are made. Sales made on an honor system are prohibited.
   e. Cashiers may not have briefcases, handbags, purses, cosmetic bags, and so forth at cashier stations.
   f. Cashiers should immediately inform the manager if they are experiencing problems with the cash register.
   g. Cashiers should verify the amount of cash banks when they receive and sign for them and should not be allowed to count the banks after that time.
   h. When feasible (or permitted by equipment), items should be rung up separately to allow the cash register to total the sale.

Debit and Credit Cards. Many lodging establishments accept debit and credit cards in lieu of cash payments from guests. Procedures to establish control in this area include the following:

1. All guests must be required to establish credit at registration. This can be done either by presenting valid debit/credit cards or by providing proof of prior approval for direct billing status. Guests who are unable to establish such credit should be required to pay cash in advance for their period of stay.

2. When accepting debit/credit card payment, the cashier should match the guest's name with the name on the card and verify the expiration date on the card.

3. All debit and credit cards must be validated for use either by checking the card company's warning bulletin or by obtaining an approval code through an electronic terminal.

Cash Disbursements. There are several procedures that help to establish a strong system of internal control over cash disbursements.

1. Generally, all disbursements should be made by check. An exception is petty cash disbursements.

2. Checks should be pre-numbered and used in numerical sequence. In addition, it is a good idea to use a check protector (an imprinting device) to enter the amounts on the checks; this deters anyone from altering the amount.

3. Checks drawn in excess of a minimum amount (such as $50) should contain two signatures, while checks under this may require only one signature. Each check signer should carefully review supporting documents to ensure that the documentation has been properly audited and approved. Check signers should not be responsible for preparing checks and should not have custody of blank checks.

4. When a mechanical check signing device is used, only the employee authorized to use it should have the key. The operation should maintain an independent record of the number of checks processed through the device, and that number should be reconciled with the numerical sequence of the checks used.

5. Vouchers, invoices, and other documents supporting cash disbursements should be canceled by stamping them "PAID" when the check is signed. This procedure is designed to prevent duplicate payments should the document become detached from the check copy.

6. Signed checks and disbursement vouchers should not be returned to the check preparer, but instead should be given to an employee independent of this function for immediate mailing.

7. Only authorized check preparers should have access to blank checks. Voided checks should be mutilated to prevent reuse by removing the signature line.

Accounts Receivable

Accounts receivable represent promises to pay the hospitality operation. Direct billing status for individuals and organizations must be approved in advance. Generally, they complete an application for credit (similar to the one shown in Exhibit 12.6) and submit it for approval. A critical control in the accounts receivable area is the segregation of duties to prevent accounts receivable employees from pocketing cash received in payment of accounts. Control procedures for accounts receivable include the following:

1. Accounts receivable employees should not handle cash received in payment of accounts. Postings to accounts receivable for cash received should be made from remittance advice or check listings. Control totals for postings should be made independently of accounts receivable employees for posting by the general ledger clerk to the accounts receivable control account.

2. At the end of the month, the total of guest accounts should be reconciled with the independently determined balance in the general ledger control

Exhibit 12.6 Typical Credit Application Form

Application for Credit

1. NAME _____
   Individual or Organization Responsible for Payment

2. ADDRESS _____ Zip Code _____
   For Billing Purposes

3. CONTACT _____ Telephone No. _____

4. NAMES OF OFFICERS OR PERSONS AUTHORIZED TO SIGN FOR DIRECT BILLS WITH YOUR FIRM.

   _____
   Signature   Print   Title

   _____
   Signature   Print   Title

5. DATE OF EVENT _____   Approximate Value $ _____
   TERMS: CASH _____
           DIRECT BILL _____   To be paid by: _____
           PAY AT CHECKOUT _____   Credit Card Type: _____
           ADVANCE _____   Credit Card No. _____
           CREDIT CARD _____   Expiration Date: _____

6. DEPOSIT REQUIRED ☐ Yes ☐ No   How Much? _____

7. BANK REFERENCE: NAME _____ Account No. _____
                   BRANCH _____

TRADE (CREDIT) REFERENCES:

   1. NAME _____   TELE # _____
      CITY _____   DATE OF LAST EVENT ____
      REFERENCE _____

   2. NAME _____   TELE # _____
      CITY _____   DATE OF LAST EVENT ____
      REFERENCE _____

   3. NAME _____   TELE # _____
      CITY _____   DATE OF LAST EVENT ____
      REFERENCE _____

APPROVED CREDIT CARD: _____   No. _____

The aforestated information is for the purpose of obtaining an account and is warranted to be true. It is understood that all statements are due and payable upon receipt. It is agreed that a late payment charge of one-and one-half percent per month of the unpaid balance may be imposed on accounts owing after 30 days from the initial billing date. Should collection become necessary, we agree to pay all costs incurred, including a reasonable attorney's fee, whether or not suit is filed, and hold the seller harmless, pertaining thereto. We hereby authorize the Hotel to investigate the references listed above, or any other statements or data pertaining to credit and financial responsibility. We understand that the credit card number listed above may be used to settle any authorized charges for which payment is not remitted within thirty days of the performance of services and/or goods on the part of the Hotel.

_____
Signature of Corporate Officer or Owner   Title   Date

To Be Filled Out By Hotel Credit Department

8. CREDIT DECISION And Reason Therefor   APPROVED _____ DISAPPROVED _____
   _____
   _____

Booked by _____
              Hotel Employee   Accounting

account. These procedures provide protection against manipulation by the accounts receivable employees. The failure to segregate cash handling and accounts receivable may facilitate **lapping**, a common fraudulent practice. Lapping occurs when an accounts receivable clerk steals cash received on an account, then posts cash received the next day on a second account to the first account. For example, assume that Guest A pays $100 on their account and the accounts receivable clerk takes the $100. The following day, Guest B pays $150. The accounts receivable clerk takes $50 for personal use and credits Guest A's account for $100. At this point, the accounts receivable clerk has stolen $150. This fraudulent activity may continue for quite some time when there is no segregation of duties or other compensating controls.

3. Noncash entries to receivable accounts, such as writing off an account as uncollectible, should originate with employees or managers who do not handle cash and are not responsible for maintaining accounts receivable.

4. The credit manager and a member of management should resolve disputed items. Clerical employees should not routinely adjust accounts receivable.

5. A key feature of control over receivables is an adequate system of internal reporting. Periodically, the accounts receivable should be aged, and special collection efforts should be applied to delinquent accounts. The trend of accounts receivable balances in relation to credit terms should be tracked over time.

6. All collection efforts should be carefully documented, and uncollectible accounts should be written off only with the approval of the controller.[8]

Accounts Payable

There are several internal control procedures for accounts payable. These procedures include the following:

1. Vendors' invoices should be routed directly to the accounts payable department. Purchasing personnel should not handle or approve invoices.

2. Control should be established over vendors' invoices when received. This may be accomplished by the use of a voucher system (see Exhibit 12.7). The voucher system uses pre-numbered vouchers that are prepared from vendors' invoices and recorded in a voucher journal. Invoices should be reviewed for possible cash discounts, and the due dates noted to take advantage of any available discounts.

3. The terms of sale, prices, and list of goods received on vendors' invoices should be checked against purchase orders and receiving reports. All amount extensions and totals should be checked. The person auditing the vendors' invoices should initial these documents.

4. All vouchers, invoices, and supporting documents should be canceled when paid.

5. Only accounting personnel not responsible for the general ledger should maintain the accounts payable subsidiary ledger. The accounts payable subsidiary ledger should be reconciled monthly with the general ledger control account for accounts payable.

6. A monthly trial balance of accounts payable should be prepared for the controller's review. Suppliers should be paid on a timely basis in order to maintain good supplier relationships.

Exhibit 12.7 Voucher from Voucher System

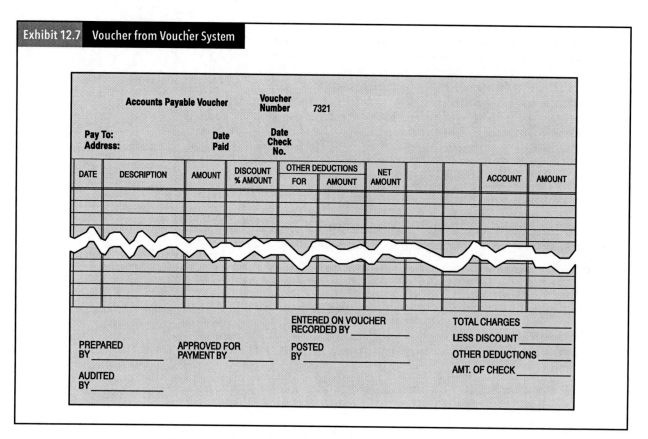

Purchasing and Receiving

This section covers only a few of the major controls of purchasing and receiving.[9] Common control procedures include the following:

1. To the extent practical, the purchasing agent should make all purchases acting upon approved purchase requisitions from department heads.

2. A written purchase order (PO) system should be used. Copies of each PO should be sent to receiving and accounting. In this way, receiving will be aware of materials ordered, while the accounts payable department can use the PO to audit the vendor's invoice.

3. A receiving department, separate from the purchasing agent, should receive all incoming goods. All materials received should be carefully checked.

4. The receiving department should prepare a receiving report for each vendor's delivery. A copy of the receiving report should be forwarded to the accounts payable department for verification against the vendor's invoice.

Payroll

Payroll is the largest expense for most hospitality operations. Therefore, controls in this area are critical if the operation is to meet its internal control objectives. Several common control procedures include:

1. Payroll functions should be segregated as follows:
   a. Authorizing employment and wage rates
   b. Reporting hours worked

c. Preparing payroll

d. Signing payroll checks

e. Distributing paychecks to employees

f. Reconciling payroll bank accounts

2. Only the human resources department or executives with hiring/terminating authority should authorize additions to, or terminations from, the staff. Generally, the human resources department carefully recruits new employees and provides the payroll department with all the relevant information on newly hired employees.

3. Procedures for reporting time worked should be clearly defined. Hourly personnel should use time clocks. Departmental supervisors should approve all hourly employees' time reports.

4. Employees should generally be paid with checks rather than cash. Separate payroll accounts should be maintained. An employee independent of the payroll department should reconcile the payroll bank account.

5. Payroll preparation procedures should include checking the clock card used for the department supervisor's approval and rechecking the hours worked.

6. Payroll sheets and net pay amounts should be checked independently.

7. Personnel independent of the payroll department should distribute paychecks. In addition, department heads should not distribute payroll checks.

8. Undelivered paychecks should be given to the controller or a person designated by the controller. This person should not be from the payroll department. The undelivered paychecks should be held until delivered or voided after a specified number of days.

Inventories

Purchasing and receiving control procedures apply to inventories also. Additional inventory control procedures include the following:

1. Accounting department employees should maintain inventory records. These employees should not have access to inventory, nor should employees with custody of inventory have access to inventory records.

2. Personnel independent of the storage function should periodically take a physical inventory. Accounting personnel should extend the physical inventory and compare it to the book inventory if a perpetual inventory record system is maintained. (*Extending* the physical inventory means listing the proper costs per unit and multiplying the counts of each item by the cost per unit.)

3. Taking physical inventory is best accomplished when:
   a. Like items are grouped together in the storeroom.
   b. Pre-printed inventory forms are used to list all inventory items.
   c. The inventory form is arranged in the same sequence as the inventory items are maintained in the storeroom.
   d. Two individuals conduct the physical inventory; one can count the items while the other records the count. (As noted earlier, the personnel should be independent of the storing function.)

4. The inventory records must be adjusted for any differences between the books and the physical inventory. The inventory adjustment must be approved by an executive such as the controller.

5. Any significant inventory overages or shortages should be investigated, the causes determined, and procedures designed to prevent recurrence of errors.

6. Other operating controls relating to inventory include the following:
   a. Control must be maintained over physical inventories. This is accomplished by storing inventory in the appropriate facilities; for example, food must be stored at proper temperatures.
   b. Daily inventories and usage rates of high-priced items should be monitored.
   c. Access to inventory should be restricted to storage employees. Limiting access is accomplished, in part, by securing inventory in locked facilities.
   d. Personnel handling inventory (storage and production personnel) should leave the facilities by an exit easily observed by management.
   e. Records of spoilage, overcooked food, and so forth should be maintained for use in reconciling the physical inventory to the book inventory and for accounting for other discrepancies in food inventory.

Fixed Assets

Fixed assets generally constitute the largest percentage of most hospitality operations' assets. These assets are not liquid; however, controls must still be established to maintain these resources for their intended use—providing services to guests. Several common control procedures are listed below.

1. The board of directors usually issues formal policies establishing which executives and committees have the authority to purchase fixed assets.

2. A work order system should be established for the orderly accumulation of property costs when facilities are acquired. Each approved project is assigned a work order number, and all expenditures are charged to this number as the work progresses.

3. Accounting records maintained under a typical work order system include the following:
   a. An expenditure authorization that defines the project scope, purpose, cost justification, and budgeted amount.
   b. Cost sheets that summarize actual expenditures for comparison to budgeted amounts.
   c. Supporting evidence of costs charged to the project account. This evidence includes vendors' invoices, material requisitions, and labor time tickets.

4. General ledger control should be established for each principal classification of property cost and each related depreciation accumulation.

5. Physical inventories of fixed assets should be taken periodically by personnel independent of the person with custody of the assets and of the person maintaining the accounting records. The physical inventory should be compared to the equipment listed in the accounting records. Any discrepancies must be resolved and action taken to prevent recurrence of similar errors.

6. The sale, retirement, or scrapping of fixed assets requires formal executive approval. Approval must be from executives not having custody of the fixed asset. Accounting department personnel must determine that retired assets are removed from the books and that proceeds received are properly accounted for.

Marketable Securities

Marketable securities include investments in stocks and bonds of other corporations. Controls over marketable securities often include the following:

1. Accounting department records should identify each marketable security owned by name and certificate number.

2. All marketable security transactions should be approved by the board of directors or a designated committee.

3. Marketable securities should be kept in a safe deposit box to which only the custodian has access.

4. Periodically, independent physical counts of marketable securities should be taken and the count compared with the accounting records.

5. Income from marketable securities recorded in accounting records should be periodically compared to what the investment should be generating. For example, a $100,000 bond at 8 percent interest should provide $8,000 of interest annually.

12.7 IMPLEMENTATION AND REVIEW OF INTERNAL CONTROLS

Top-level management is responsible for implementing and maintaining the system of internal controls. Since this system is critical to the well-being of the hospitality operation, management must regularly review it to ensure that it is adequate. The internal control system may break down periodically. New personnel may not understand procedures and thus not follow them. For example, a new employee may return disputed statements to the accounts receivable clerk for resolution, reasoning that the clerk can resolve such differences most efficiently.

The internal control system may also need restructuring due to changing business conditions and other circumstances. For example, 10 years ago, a hospitality operation may have established a policy stating that cash receipts had to be deposited when they reached $1,000. Due to inflation, the amount might now be raised to $2,000.

An operation's internal controls may be documented and reviewed by flow-charting and by using internal control questionnaires. A **flowchart** diagrams the flow of documents through an organization, indicating the origin, processing, and final deposition of each document. In addition, the flowchart shows the segregation of duties. Exhibit 12.8 is a simplified flowchart of a club operation's payroll system.[10]

Flowcharting is useful because it provides a concise overview of the internal control system. It facilitates review of the internal control system, enabling management to identify weaknesses for corrective action.

A second device for studying a hospitality operation's system of internal control is the **internal control questionnaire (ICQ)**. The ICQ uses a series of questions about controls in each accounting area to identify weaknesses. ICQs generally provide complete coverage for each accounting area. However, they do not reveal document flows as do flowcharts. From a practical viewpoint, both flowcharts and ICQs should be used in documenting and reviewing an operation's system of internal control.

Exhibit 12.8 Flowchart of a Payroll System

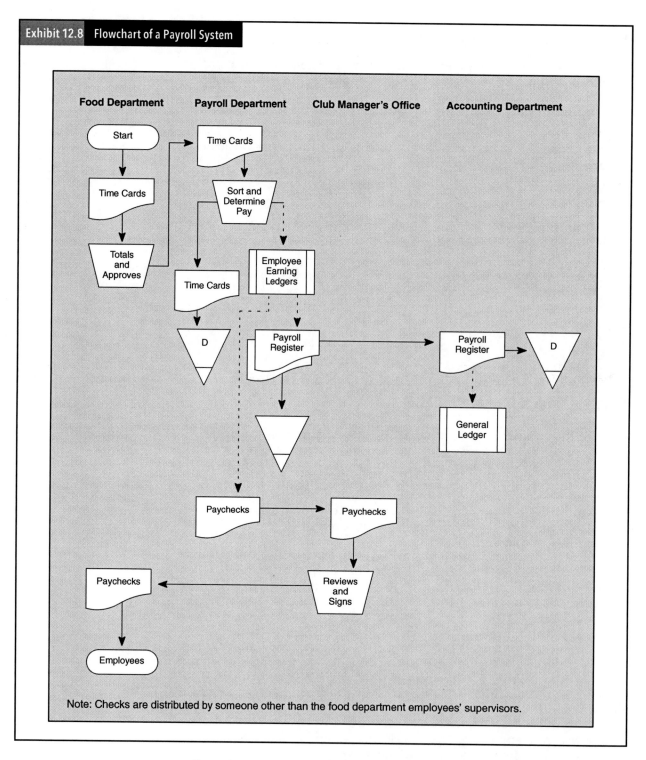

Food Department   Payroll Department   Club Manager's Office   Accounting Department

Start

Time Cards

Time Cards

Sort and Determine Pay

Totals and Approves

Time Cards

Employee Earning Ledgers

D

Payroll Register

Payroll Register

D

General Ledger

Paychecks

Paychecks

Reviews and Signs

Paychecks

Employees

Note: Checks are distributed by someone other than the food department employees' supervisors.

Once the review is completed, management must act to strengthen the internal control system. If a system is documented and reviewed without proper follow-up, then the real value of the review process is lost.

12.8 TECHNOLOGY IN INTERNAL CONTROL

Throughout this chapter, the topic of internal control has been discussed, including its definition, objectives, characteristics and principles, documentation, and methods to safeguard our assets via accounting. One item that can provide invaluable assistance in internal control is technology. In today's world, when individuals, small businesses, corporations, school and universities, and governments all rely on technology for various functions, technology plays an important role in internal control as well.

There are only two ways to bring more value to the bottom line: increase sales and decrease costs. In increasing sales, customer relationship management (CRM) technology has long been used to manage the database of guests and potential customers. With the proper information on guests, hotels can anticipate their needs and desires to create the most memorable stay experience and, at the same time, increase sales levels.

On the costs side, the prime costs of restaurants are cost of food sold and labor. The highest expense line item in a hotel is labor. Thus, any technology to help hospitality operations to keep labor and food costs in line is a plus. There are various types of restaurant accounting software that can be paired to a point-of-sale (POS) system to calculate, even by shift, both direct labor and benefits statistics as a percentage of sales to give operators, owners, and managers real-time information to make scheduling adjustments. Of course, all these hours and changes can automatically feed into a payroll system to calculate payroll and generate paychecks. Some are even linked to weather reports to help management make better scheduling decisions. There are also time clocks that can be programmed to restrict employees from clocking in or out outside their scheduled work time so as to control excess work hours. Some of these devices are equipped with biometrics capability to stop other people from clocking in for employees who are not present.

As for food costs, the control points are numerous and thus technology can be very useful. Technology exists whereby waste transaction reports can be generated through restaurant-specific accounting and operations software. With such a platform, a restaurateur can obtain on any device a snapshot of the actual versus budgeted food cost, track vendor pricing and bids, use menu engineering to make changes, and even manage the food order amounts and timing. If a comprehensive, integrated system is too costly, foodservice operations may opt for an inventory management system, which helps track all food items and ingredients by looking at the number of menu items ordered, kitchen output, and food left on the line and the storeroom at the end of a shift. Systems like these combine automation with a manual data-entry component.

Monitoring utilities is another area where technology and automation are very helpful. With the Internet of Things (IoT), everyday devices and appliances that have not typically had such capabilities are linked to the Internet, whereby they become "smart" and are able to connect, share information, and even interact with the guests. Hotels have been using this technology for years to control all guestroom thermostats at a central location; with IoT, the thermostats can now talk to each other. This can improve data collection, increase levels of automation, and allow for multiple devices to be controlled or monitored from one centralized unit, such as a computer, tablet, or mobile phone. Voice-controlled devices or voice assistants, such as Amazon's Echo, are a great example of IoT.

Technology has many other applications, including notifications of void checks at any POS terminal to a mobile device of any programmed responsible party, from the owner to the unit supervisor. And a daily report can be generated for follow-up purposes should certain employees be shown to have a record of excessive void transactions. This capability obviously will make an employee think twice before voiding any transaction.

Of course, technology also has its negative sides. When companies collect guests' information and store it in their CRMs, guest data privacy and security can become an issue. Thus, the General Data Protection Regulation (GDPR), which originated in the European Union, has been adopted as the standard in the United States with which companies need to comply and uphold. Too many incidents of ransomware and other hacks have caused concerns, and companies are aware of the implications. Many companies have implemented additional safeguards and even purchased cyber insurance to mitigate possible damages. As with all things, hospitality companies need to be cautious regarding the pros and cons of technology and use it responsibly for the benefit of guests and the company.

12.9 THE SARBANES-OXLEY ACT OF 2002

The Sarbanes-Oxley Act of 2002, also known as SOX, was passed by Congress after accounting frauds were tied to the collapse of Enron, Global Crossing, and WorldCom. This act created the Public Company Accounting Oversight Board (PCAOB) to oversee the external audit and auditors of public companies; that is, companies whose stock and/or bonds can be purchased by the public.

SOX requires management to submit to the SEC an internal control report with the company's annually filed financial statements. The external auditors are required to attest to and report on management's assessment of the company's internal control. An audit committee is required and the board of directors must assume this role if there is no separate audit committee. Finally, the act requires the CEO and CFO to certify that the financial statements are fairly presented and, in essence, that the internal controls are adequate.

The duties of the PCAOB include establishing auditing, quality control, ethics, independence, and other standards relating to the preparation of audit reports for issuers. Auditors must describe in each audit report the testing of the internal control structure and the procedures used by the hospitality company to implement these controls. The act specifically states that the audit report must present:

1. The findings of the auditor from such testing

2. An evaluation of whether such internal control structure and procedures:
   a. Include maintenance of records that, in reasonable detail, accurately and fairly reflect the transactions and dispositions of the assets of the issuer
   b. Provide reasonable assurance that transactions are recorded as necessary to permit preparation of financial statements in accordance with generally accepted accounting principles, and that receipts and expenditures of the issuer are being made only in accordance with authorizations of management and directors of the issuer

3. A description, at a minimum, of material weaknesses in such internal controls, and of any material noncompliance found on the basis of such testing

Recordkeeping requirements set out in the Foreign Corrupt Practices Act are set out in greater detail in SOX. Auditors are required to test and report on the adequacy of internal controls. Generally accepted auditing standards, which provide guidance to external auditors, include these steps but now the requirements carry the full force of federal law.

An example of an auditor's report on internal control is shown in Exhibit 12.9. This report is written by Ernst & Young, auditor of the Hilton Hotels Corporation.

SOX requires that management submit to the SEC an "internal control report." This report must do the following:

1. State the responsibility of management for establishing and maintaining an adequate internal control structure and procedures for financial reporting

2. Contain an assessment, as of the end of the most recent fiscal year of the issuer, of the effectiveness of the internal control structure and procedures of the issuer for financial reporting

---

Exhibit 12.9 **Auditor's Report on Internal Control**

Report of Independent Registered Public Accounting Firm

To the Stockholders and the Board of Directors of Hilton Worldwide Holdings Inc.

Opinion on Internal Control Over Financial Reporting

We have audited Hilton Worldwide Holdings Inc.'s internal control over financial reporting as of December 31, 2021, based on criteria established in Internal Control—Integrated Framework issued by the Committee of Sponsoring Organizations of the Treadway Commission (2013 framework) (the COSO criteria). In our opinion, Hilton Worldwide Holdings Inc. (the Company) maintained, in all material respects, effective internal control over financial reporting as of December 31, 2021, based on the COSO criteria.

We also have audited, in accordance with the standards of the Public Company Accounting Oversight Board (United States) (PCAOB), the consolidated balance sheets of the Company as of December 31, 2021 and 2020, the related consolidated statements of operations, comprehensive income (loss), cash flows and stockholders' equity (deficit), for each of the three years in the period ended December 31, 2021 and the related notes, and our report dated February 16, 2022 expressed an unqualified opinion thereon.

Basis for Opinion

The Company's management is responsible for maintaining effective internal control over financial reporting and for its assessment of the effectiveness of internal control over financial reporting included in the accompanying Management's Report on Internal Control Over Financial Reporting. Our responsibility is to express an opinion on the Company's internal control over financial reporting based on our audit. We are a public accounting firm registered with the PCAOB and are required to be independent with respect to the Company in accordance with the U.S. federal securities laws and the applicable rules and regulations of the Securities and Exchange Commission and the PCAOB.

We conducted our audit in accordance with the standards of the PCAOB. Those standards require that we plan and perform the audit to obtain reasonable assurance about whether effective internal control over financial reporting was maintained in all material respects.

Our audit included obtaining an understanding of internal control over financial reporting, assessing the risk that a material weakness exists, testing and evaluating the design and operating effectiveness of internal control based on the assessed risk, and performing such other procedures as we considered necessary in the circumstances. We believe that our audit provides a reasonable basis for our opinion.

(Continued)

Exhibit 12.9 Auditor's Report on Internal Control (*Continued*)

Definition and Limitations of Internal Control Over Financial Reporting

A company's internal control over financial reporting is a process designed to provide reasonable assurance regarding the reliability of financial reporting and the preparation of financial statements for external purposes in accordance with generally accepted accounting principles. A company's internal control over financial reporting includes those policies and procedures that (1) pertain to the maintenance of records that, in reasonable detail, accurately and fairly reflect the transactions and dispositions of the assets of the company; (2) provide reasonable assurance that transactions are recorded as necessary to permit preparation of financial statements in accordance with generally accepted accounting principles, and that receipts and expenditures of the company are being made only in accordance with authorizations of management and directors of the company; and (3) provide reasonable assurance regarding prevention or timely detection of unauthorized acquisition, use, or disposition of the company's assets that could have a material effect on the financial statements.

Because of its inherent limitations, internal control over financial reporting may not prevent or detect misstatements. Also, projections of any evaluation of effectiveness to future periods are subject to the risk that controls may become inadequate because of changes in conditions, or that the degree of compliance with the policies or procedures may deteriorate.

/s/ Ernst & Young LLP

Tysons, Virginia
February 16, 2022
Source: Hilton Worldwide Holdings Inc. 2022 Form 10-K

The external auditors are required to attest to and report on management's assessment of the company's internal controls.

SOX requires companies to have an audit committee, which is defined as follows:

1. A committee (or equivalent body) established by and among the board of directors of an issuer for the purpose of overseeing the accounting and financial reporting processes of the issuer and audits of the financial statements of the issuer

2. If no such committee exists with respect to an issuer, the entire board of directors of the issuer

At least one member of the audit committee must be a financial expert. If no member is a financial expert, the company must explain why it does not have a financial expert on the committee.

SOX effectively gives the audit committee the power to employ and dismiss external auditors. The external auditors must provide the following to the audit committee:

1. All critical accounting policies and practices to be used

2. All alternative treatments of financial information within generally accepted accounting principles that have been discussed with management officials of the issuer, ramifications of the use of such alternative disclosures and treatments, and the treatment preferred by the registered public accounting firm

3. Other material written communications between the registered public accounting firm and the management of the issuer, such as any management letter or schedule of unadjusted differences

SOX makes clear that the audit committee is not the only party responsible for the audit process and the adequacy of internal controls. Senior management, specifically the CEO and the CFO, must certify that the financial statements are fairly presented and that:

1. The signing officers:
   a. Are responsible for establishing and maintaining internal controls
   b. Have designed such internal controls to ensure that material information relating to the issuer and its consolidated subsidiaries is made known to such officers by others within those entities, particularly during the period in which the periodic reports are being prepared
   c. Have evaluated the effectiveness of the issuer's internal controls as of a date within 90 days prior to the report
   d. Have presented in the report their conclusions about the effectiveness of their internal controls based on their evaluation as of that date

2. The signing officers have disclosed to the issuer's auditors and the audit committee of the board of directors (or persons fulfilling the equivalent function):

   a. All significant deficiencies in the design or operation of internal controls that could adversely affect the issuer's ability to record, process, summarize, and report financial data and have identified for the issuer's auditors any material weaknesses in internal controls
   b. Any fraud, whether or not material, that involves management or other employees who have a significant role in the issuer's internal controls
   c. The signing officers have indicated in the report whether or not there were significant changes in internal controls or in other factors that could significantly affect internal controls subsequent to the date of their evaluation, including any corrective actions with regard to significant deficiencies and material weaknesses

Congress has clearly placed responsibility for internal controls with senior management. Hilton's evaluation of internal controls and procedures and report on internal control, included in its 10-K filed with the SEC, are shown in Exhibit 12.10. Although SOX applies to public companies, financial experts believe that it also sets the tone for corporate governance of private companies. State legislatures may well pass similar legislation covering nonpublic companies in the future. As one commentator wrote, "While the act is aimed at publicly traded corporations, certain provisions may be adopted as prudent policies by the club industry."[11]

12.10 INTERNAL CONTROL IN SMALL OPERATIONS

Although the hospitality industry has a number of giant firms with system-wide sales exceeding $1 billion, the vast majority of establishments are small. The elaborate control procedures presented thus far are not practical for operations with only a few employees because there are simply not enough people for the proper segregation of duties.

The key person in internal control of a small operation is the owner or manager. Several duties, if performed by the owner or manager, help to offset what might otherwise be weaknesses in the internal control system. These critical duties are outlined below.

Exhibit 12.10 Management's Evaluation of Internal Control

Disclosure Controls and Procedures

The Company maintains a set of disclosure controls and procedures as that term is defined in Rules 13a-15(e) and 15d-15(e) under the Exchange Act that are designed to ensure that information required to be disclosed by the company in reports that it files or submits under the Exchange Act, is recorded, processed, summarized and reported within the time periods specified in SEC rules and forms, and that such information is accumulated and communicated to the Company's management, including its Chief Executive Officer and Chief Financial Officer, as appropriate, to allow timely decisions regarding required disclosures. The design of any disclosure controls and procedures is based in part upon certain assumptions about the likelihood of future events, and there can be no assurances that any design will succeed in achieving its stated goals under all potential future conditions. Any controls and procedures, no matter how well designed and operated, can provide only reasonable, not absolute, assurance of achieving the desired control objectives. In accordance with Rule 13a-15(b) of the Exchange Act, as of the end of the period covered by this annual report, an evaluation was carried out under the supervision and with the participation of the Company's management, including its Chief Executive Officer and Chief Financial Officer, of the effectiveness of its disclosure controls and procedures. Based on that evaluation, the Company's Chief Executive Officer and Chief Financial Officer concluded that the Company's disclosure controls and procedures, as of the end of the period covered by this annual report, were effective to provide reasonable assurance that information required to be disclosed by the company in reports that it files or submits under the Exchange Act is recorded, processes, summarized and reported within the time periods specified in SEC rules and forms and is accumulated and communicated to the Company's management, including the Chief Executive Officer and Chief Financial Officer, as appropriate to allow timely decisions regarding required disclosure.

Management's Annual Report on Internal Control Over Financial Reporting

We have set forth management's report on internal control over financial reporting and the attestation report of our independent registered public accounting firm on the effectiveness of our internal control over financial reporting in Item 8 of this Annual Report on Form 10-K. Management's report on internal control over financial reporting is incorporated in this Item 9A by reference.

Changes in Internal Control

There has been no change in the Company's internal control over financial reporting during the Company's most recent fiscal quarter that has materially affected, or is reasonably likely to materially affect, the Company's internal control over financial reporting.

In May 2013, the Committee of Sponsoring Organizations of the Treadway Commission ("COSO") released an updated version of its Internal Control—Integrated Framework ("2013 Framework"). Initially issued in 1992, the original framework ("1992 Framework") provided guidance to organizations to design, implement and evaluate the effectiveness of internal control concepts, and simplify their use and application. The 2013 Framework is intended to improve upon systems of internal control over external financial reporting by formalizing the principles embedded in the 1992 Framework, incorporating business and operating environment changes, and increasing the framework's ease of use and application. The 1992 Framework was available until December 15, 2014, after which it was superseded by the 2013 Framework. We transitioned to the 2013 Framework during the fourth quarter of 2014 which resulted in no significant changes to our internal control over financial reporting.

Source: Hilton Hotels Corporation 2014 Form 10-K.

1. Cash receipts
   a. Open all mail and list cash receipts, retaining one copy of the list.
   b. Deposit all cash daily and compare the deposit with the cash receipts debit recorded by the bookkeeper.
   c. Reconcile cash receipts with cash register tapes.

2. Cash disbursements
   a. Sign all checks, carefully review documentation, and cancel all supporting documentation.
   b. Use only pre-numbered checks and account for them as checks are signed.
   c. Total check disbursements periodically and compare the total to the bookkeeper's cash credit.
   d. Prepare the bank reconciliation.

3. Sales
   a. Keep all cash registers locked and remove cash register tapes when not in use.
   b. Compare cash register tape totals with the cash debit for the day and the cash receipts deposited.

4. Payroll
   a. Examine the payroll worksheet (or payroll journal), noting employees' names, authorized gross pay, hours worked, deductions, and net pay. Add the payroll and compare the net pay with the cash credit.
   b. Distribute payroll checks.

5. Accounts receivable
   a. Review aging of accounts receivable.
   b. Compare statements with individual ledger accounts and mail statements.
   c. Resolve all disputed account balances.

6. Inventories
   a. Periodically supervise or take the physical inventory.
   b. Compare the physical inventory with the perpetual inventory on the books.
   c. Compare cost of goods sold with total sales each month, and investigate any major discrepancies in cost of goods sold percentages.

7. Purchases
   a. Randomly review price quotes for inventory items purchased.
   b. Use a purchase order system and account for all purchase orders.
   c. Randomly compare purchase orders with receiving reports, and vendors' invoices with vendors' statements.

8. General
   a. Review all general journal entries.
   b. Employ a competent, trustworthy bookkeeper.
   c. Engage an independent auditor to conduct an annual audit and to periodically conduct limited surprise audits of cash, inventory, and accounts receivable.

12.11 ADDITIONAL CLASSIFICATION OF CONTROLS

At the beginning of this chapter, internal controls were classified as either accounting or administrative controls. Controls may also be classified based on whether they take effect before or after a problem occurs. **Preventive controls** are implemented before a problem occurs. They include such things as the use of locks to safeguard assets, the separation of duties to preclude operating personnel from controlling inventories, and general and specific authorization policies. Preventive controls are less expensive to establish than detective controls. **Detective controls** are designed to discover problems and to monitor preventive controls. Detective controls include external audits, surprise internal cash audits, and bank reconciliations. Detective controls may serve in part as preventive controls; for example, if employees know that audits will be conducted, they will be less likely to take advantage of their access to cash and other assets.

12.12 CODES OF ETHICS

Many hospitality companies have adopted a formal code of ethics for their personnel to follow, codifying unacceptable behavior. Common elements appearing in codes of ethics of corporations (not limited to hospitality) include:

- Privacy of communication
- Conflict of interest
- Political contributions in the United States
- Company records
- Gifts, favors, entertainment, trips, and outings
- Use of company assets (facilities, airplane, etc.)
- Antitrust laws (fair competition)
- Relations with competitors
- Relations with suppliers
- Relations with customers
- Insider information
- Security regulations

As an example from hospitality, consider the Hilton Hotels Corporation's code of ethics. The code is strongly supported by corporate management. General managers and department heads in Hilton hotels are responsible for advising the employees under their supervision of the parts of the code that apply to them and their duties. An excerpt from Hilton's code dealing with the prohibition of substantial gifts reads as follows:

> Officers and employees shall not solicit, accept or agree to accept, at any time of the year, for themselves or on behalf of the Company, any gift which directly or indirectly benefits them, from any person or firm having or seeking a business relationship with the Company, or from any employee or agent of such a person or firm; however, this prohibition does not apply to the acceptance over a twelve-month period (from each person or firm) of gifts of small value totaling not more than $200, except that in no event shall gifts of cash ever be accepted. In addition, the prohibition does not apply to free or reduced rate hotel accommodations, meals, entertainment and other services to the extent commonly furnished in the hotel industry on a reciprocal basis, and it does not apply to meals furnished in connection with a business purpose.

The hospitality industry has many characteristics that make it relatively vulnerable to theft. In part because of these traits, an effective internal control system is critical.

Internal control is the overall system of protecting the establishment's assets, ensuring the accuracy and reliability of its accounting records, promoting efficient operations, and encouraging adherence to management policies. An operation must have an adequate internal control system in order to operate profitably in the long run.

There are four main objectives of every internal control system. The first two, checking the accuracy of accounting data and safeguarding assets, are known as accounting controls. These controls ensure that assets are recorded properly and that they are safe from loss through negligence or theft. The other two controls are administrative controls. Promoting operational efficiency means that the operation's products and/or services are produced efficiently. Adherence to managerial policies is important because established rules are only effective if they are followed.

There are several characteristics of a strong internal control system. These characteristics include the physical control of assets, the development of budgets, management leadership, and organizational structure. Competent and trustworthy personnel are necessary for operational efficiency and adequate physical control of the assets.

Management needs to examine every function of the hospitality operation and establish controls for each one. For example, the cash account must have adequate controls because it is highly vulnerable to theft. Management should consider physical controls, segregation of duties, management policies, proper authorization procedures, and adequate performance checks. These characteristics of internal control can help protect the operation's cash.

Management must consider the costs and benefits of internal control policies. There are many technology systems and applications that can assist owners and managers in this area, including biometrics. A "perfect" system—one that guarantees the safety of assets—would probably be cost-prohibitive. This is especially true for smaller operations that do not have enough personnel to completely segregate duties. In these instances, managers and managing owners must be aware of the available precautions and take an active role in the operation to ensure its success.

Many hospitality companies have adopted formal codes of ethics to spell out unacceptable behavior.

accounting controls—Controls for safeguarding assets and ensuring the accuracy and reliability of accounting data.

administrative controls—Controls for promoting operational efficiency and encouraging adherence to managerial policies.

detective controls—Controls designed to discover problems and to monitor preventive controls. Detective controls include external audits, surprise cash internal audits, and bank reconciliations.

flowchart—A visual representation of the movement of information and documents within an operation.

internal auditing—A managerial control that measures and evaluates the effectiveness of other controls and is defined by the Institute of Internal Auditors as an "independent appraisal activity within an organization for the review of operations as a service to management."

internal control questionnaire (ICQ)—A device for studying an operation's system of internal control. The ICQ uses a series of questions about controls in each accounting area to identify weaknesses.

lapping—A type of theft that occurs when an accounts receivable clerk steals cash received on an account, then posts cash received the next day on a second account to the first account.

preventive controls—Controls implemented before a problem occurs, including such things as the use of locks to safeguard assets, the separation of duties to preclude operating personnel from controlling inventories, and general and specific authorization policies.

segregation of duties—An element of internal control systems in which different personnel are assigned the different functions of accounting, custody of assets, and production; the purpose is to prevent and detect errors and theft.

1. What is internal control?

2. What are the four AICPA objectives of internal control?

3. What are four characteristics of internal control?

4. Which characteristic of internal control is most important? Why have you chosen this one?

5. Why is the control of cash important to a hospitality operation?

6. What is segregation of duties?

7. How can internal control systems be documented and reviewed?

8. How does flowcharting differ from an internal control questionnaire?

9. How can computers be used to strengthen an enterprise's internal control system?

10. What are three procedures to safeguard inventory?

Problem 1

Listed below are several control procedures used by the Fredericksburg Inn.

1. A biometric time clock is purchased for employees to clock in and out.
2. Accounting and cash activities are separated.
3. The duties of restaurant servers and busers are divided.
4. Different personnel place food orders and receive the food items.
5. The *Uniform System of Accounts for the Lodging Industry (USALI)* is used.
6. Internal auditors prepare the bank reconciliation.

Required:

Indicate the objective of internal control that each procedure most likely is directed toward.

Problem 2

The Smooth Sailing Inn has instituted several new control procedures in regard to its cash activities, as follows:

Procedure	Preventive Control	Detective Control
1. Cash receipts received through the mail are listed by the person opening the mail. The list is sent to the accounts receivable clerk and the checks are sent to the cashier.		
2. The inn installs locks for all storage areas and only authorized personnel can gain entry.		
3. The internal auditor prepares the bank reconciliation.		
4. Purchase of any noninventory item that is over $100 needs the approval of the general manager.		
5. Cash register tapes are removed during a surprise audit by the internal auditor, who also counts the cash received at the register.		

Required:

Indicate whether each control procedure is most likely a preventive or detective control.

Problem 3

The Homestyle Bar and Grill has the following service procedures:

1. Patrons seat themselves, as the FSC believes this saves money by not employing a host. During lunch several days of the week, the café operates at capacity for two hours.

2. A staff of five servers takes the food orders and forwards them to the cooks. They will also serve the food and refill any drink orders and are responsible for their own cash bank and cashing out the customers. Generally, a server covers seven tables with up to four people per table.

3. Bartenders have their own cash banks to close out their own tickets, reducing the wait time for guests making payments.

4. Busers clear tables and set up tables for new patrons. Tips are shared among the busers, servers, and the restaurant in a ratio of 1:3:1: busers receive 20 percent of the tips, servers receive 60 percent, and the restaurant receives the remaining 20 percent of the tips.

Required:

1. Critique these procedures by indicating weaknesses (including violations of the law, if you notice any).

2. Recommend changes to address any weaknesses.

Problem 4

The Lions Hotel is a 500-room property with two restaurants. Several controls currently used at the hotel are listed below:

Control	Preventive/ Detective	Accounting/ Administrative
1. The Lions Hotel uses cash registers throughout the property.	_____	_____
2. Two employee time clocks are located just outside the restaurant manager's office for all restaurant employees and outside the housekeeping manager's office for all rooms employees.	_____	_____
3. An external auditor conducts a surprise cash audit quarterly.	_____	_____
4. Only the restaurant manager may approve food sales allowances.	_____	_____
5. Each room attendant's cleaning work is inspected by a housekeeping supervisor.	_____	_____

Control	Preventive/ Detective	Accounting/ Administrative
6. Cash receipts are deposited intact and on a daily basis.		
7. The internal auditor prepares the monthly bank reconciliation.		
8. Eggs, cheese, and dairy products are stored in coolers at the proper temperatures.		
9. Supplier invoices are reconciled to the suppliers' monthly statements.		
10. All employees are to enter and leave the premises via the employee entrance.		

Required:

1. Indicate whether each control is preventive (P) or detective (D) and whether it is an accounting (AC) or administrative (AD) control.

2. If you believe a given control may be both P and D or AC and AD, provide your reasoning.

Problem 5

Several control procedures used at the Bulldog's Stop are listed below:

Procedure	Preventive/Detective	Accounting/ Administrative
1. A cash bank is assigned to each server.		
2. Guest checks are reviewed by the internal auditor.		
3. Standard recipes are followed in preparing all entrées.		
4. Payroll checks are distributed to employees by the owner.		
5. Checks written to pay bills in excess of $100 require two signatures.		
6. Written purchase orders are required for all equipment purchases.		

Procedure	Preventive/Detective	Accounting/ Administrative
7. Meat is stored in coolers at the proper temperature.	_____	_____
8. Cash is deposited nightly at the local bank using the bank's night depository service.	_____	_____

Required:

Indicate whether each control procedure is preventive (P) or detective (D), and whether it is an accounting (AC) or administrative (AD) control.

Problem 6

The Sunbelt Corporation has an internal audit department that periodically sends a team of two auditors to visit its individual hotels to check their internal controls and assist with implementing changes in procedures to improve control. It also has the firm of Goodman & Associates conduct its annual external audit. For each activity, indicate which group of auditors (internal or external) will most likely take action.

1. Evaluates the efficiency of Hotel Alphonse's sales department

2. Conducts the examination of the financial statements of Sunbelt's checking account

3. Prepares the bank reconciliation for Sunbelt's payroll checking account

4. Confirms the cash balance of Sunbelt's investment account with First National Bank

5. Engages "mystery shoppers" to evaluate the performance of Hotel Beatrice's restaurant service

6. Observes the physical inventory of food and beverages at Sunbelt's inventory warehouse in connection with the year-end financial audit

7. Conducts an examination to determine deficiencies in controls resulting in a loss of $1,000 at Hotel Clarkson

Problem 7

At the Divinity Hotel, a 150-room property, the procedure for handling checks returned by the bank marked "insufficient funds" was to carry them as part of the bank balance. That is, when the bank returned a check because payment was refused and charged it to the hotel's account, no entry was made in the books. The returned check was immediately redeposited, and the bank usually collected it. At the end of the month, those checks that had not been collected were treated as reconciling items (NSF checks) by the bookkeeper preparing the bank reconciliation. If the check was later collected, the bookkeeper made no formal entry; however, in preparing the next month's bank reconciliation, the bookkeeper reduced the amount of NSF checks. If the check was still uncollectible after three months, a journal entry was recorded charging "Bad Debt Expense" and crediting "Cash in Bank."

Required:

1. Explain any deficiencies in the Divinity Hotel's cash control system.
2. Provide the manager with suggestions for improving the system.

Problem 8

The Lodge 2000 has a $150 petty cash fund that is periodically replenished. The assistant general manager is custodian of the fund and requests the controller to replenish the fund with $125 on August 15 since only $25 of cash remains. The detailed disbursements are as follows:

Date	Item	Amount
8/2	Postage	$ 15.00
8/3	Fuel for lawn mower	10.50
8/4	Postage	8.50
8/5	Contributions to Boy Scouts	15.00
8/7	Postage due for supplies delivery	8.20
8/10	Uber (GM)	12.50
8/12	Legal pads for office use	9.34
8/12	Freight on equipment delivery	22.90
8/13	Postage	10.20
8/14	Doughnuts for office staff	10.50

Required:

1. Determine the amount the petty cash fund is over or short.
2. What do you recommend regarding your finding in part 1?
3. Prepare the journal entry to record the replenishment of the petty cash by $125.

Problem 9

The Hayden Hotel's checking account record showed a balance $9,725.29 on January 31, 20X2. The bank statement indicated a balance of $14,112.50 on the same date. Checks written before February 1, 20X2, that had not cleared the bank were as follows:

Check 1069	$ 146.81
Check 1073	3,621.00
Check 1074	450.29
Check 1075	15.92
Check 1077	1,123.46
Check 1079	998.43

The bank statement reflected service charges of $53.24, which were not recorded on the books until February 20X2. A check for $750.23 marked "insufficient funds" was returned by the bank on January 31 and was redeposited on February 2. No entry was recorded on the books when the check was returned or redeposited. On February 1, cash receipts of $1,165.23 from business on January 31 were deposited in the bank. This cash was recorded as sales during January 20X2.

Required:

Prepare the Hayden Hotel's bank reconciliation for January 20X2.

Problem 10

The Terica Café uses a standard cost approach to aid in controlling its food costs. Listed below are the sales price, standard food cost, and quantity sold for its five sandwiches for the week ended August 28.

Item	Selling Price	Standard Food Cost	Quantity Sold
Sliced Pork Tenderloin	$ 9.95	$ 3.20	50
Chipotle Chicken	9.75	3.25	100
Ultimate Burger	10.25	3.75	150
Marine Delight	12.95	4.15	80
Dijon Egg Salad	8.85	2.35	40

The actual sales for the week equaled $4,400, while the total actual food costs equaled $1,470.10.

Required:

1. Calculate the standard food cost percentage based on the information above.

2. Calculate the standard food cost percentage assuming 100 of each item are sold during a week.

3. Calculate the actual food cost percentage for the week.

Problem 11

The Buckeye Motel's books indicated that the general checking account at the end of December 20X1 contained $12,235.72. The bank statement on December 31, 20X1, showed a closing balance of $8,526. Additional information is as follows:

1. Last month's bank reconciliation showed five outstanding checks:

Check 8923	$ 200.10
Check 8936	$ 298.15
Check 8944	$ 156.21
Check 8945	$ 549.49
Check 8946	$ 337.75

2. A comparison of the canceled checks from the bank with the check register revealed five checks written in December 20X1 that had not been paid by the bank:

Check 9164	$ 484.21
Check 9173	$ 671.12
Check 9190	$ 598.01
Check 9191	$ 103.05
Check 9192	$ 88.54

3. In addition, three checks were canceled in December that had been issued in the prior month:

Check 8944	$ 156.21
Check 8945	$ 549.49
Check 8946	$ 337.75

4. Cash receipts of $1,000.75 recorded on the books on December 31, 20X1, were deposited with the bank on January 2, 20X2.

5. A check for $750.00 received from a guest was returned by the bank on December 31, 20X1, marked "insufficient funds." The check was redeposited on January 2, 20X2. No entry was recorded to reflect the returned check on December 31, 20X1.

Required:

Prepare the Buckeye Motel's December 20X1 bank reconciliation.

Problem 12

Jeremy Harris, who has been working for 25 years as the bookkeeper for a family-owned restaurant, is planning to retire. Due to his loyalty, he has been given many additional responsibilities over the years. He is now responsible for the following:

a. Handling all cash receipts, including payments received on account

b. Preparing and distributing all checks, including all checks written on the payroll and general accounts

c. Signing checks when the owner/manager is absent, which amounts to about 15 percent of the checks

d. Preparing the bank reconciliations for both checking accounts

e. Performing all of the accounting related to accounts receivable

Required:

1. You have been asked to evaluate the above responsibilities and, from an internal perspective, advise the owner on how Harris's duties could be split between two people.

2. You are asked to tell the owner/manager what responsibilities currently handled by Harris should be handled by the owner/manager.

Problem 13

Many of the front office manager's headaches are caused by the skipper—the guest who departs without paying the bill. However, a dishonest employee can cause even more problems by using this situation as a coverup. Consider the following situation. A guest checks in and is assigned to an $80 room. The clerk forgets to ask for a mailing address. The following day, the guest, hurrying to catch a flight, runs to the cashier's window, throws down $80 in cash, says "Check me out of 423," and rushes off.

The cashier looks at the bill in the file and notices that the guest left no address. The cashier reasons that the credit department will never track down the guest, so he pockets the $80 and leaves the bill in the file. The next day, room 423 is reported unoccupied. The bill by this time stands at $160 and is charged to "skippers."

Some hotels make no effort to locate skippers; at any rate, such attempts are usually without success. In this case, even finding the guest will not solve the problem; the guest has no receipt to prove their claim that the bill was paid.

Required:

What steps could be taken to adequately control cash in this situation?

Problem 14

Gerald Reeves, general manager of the 400-room Sunup Hotel, needs yard work done at his personal residence. He approaches the hotel's best maintenance worker and offers to personally pay him the same hourly wage the worker receives from the hotel to work the desired 5 hours of work per week at the general manager's house. It is understood the work would be done during the worker's day off from his hotel work.

Required:

Evaluate the ethical implications of Reeves's action and proposal.

Problem 15

At the Wolverine Inn, salaries and wages were paid semimonthly by individual checks to the order of each employee. These checks, drawn on a special payroll bank account, were signed jointly by the accountant and the payroll supervisor. Transfers for the total amount of the payroll for the period were made semimonthly to this special account by a check drawn on the regular bank account. In addition to the amounts periodically transferred, there remained a large balance from the period, representing the uncashed checks.

The Wolverine Inn's accountant had to be absent several days each month. It was her custom to leave a few signed blank checks to be used to pay employees who might quit during her absence.

With an assured minimum balance in the payroll account and the signed blank checks, the payroll supervisor saw an opportunity and seized it. He drew a check to his own order for an amount within the usual minimum balance. Since he always reconciled the monthly bank statements for this account, he was fairly safe from detection.

Required:

1. Which characteristics of internal control were violated in this situation?

2. How could this theft have been prevented?

Problem 16

Carrie Nimrod is the payroll clerk of the Sun River Hotel. Her responsibilities include rechecking the hours worked by hourly employees, preparing payroll accounts, signing the checks, and preparing the bank reconciliation for the payroll bank account. Any undelivered and payroll checks are returned to Ms. Nimrod for safekeeping. Ryan Quick, the hotel's controller, suggests she can carry out these duties very efficiently rather than involve other members of the accounting staff who are less familiar with the payroll tasks.

Required:

Critique the above assignment of tasks for Ms. Nimrod and suggest how these duties should be segregated.

Problem 17

Check-out time at the Wyman Hotel was 2 p.m. Guests checking out after that time were supposed to be charged for an extra day. However, the front office clerks did not post the extra charge on the guest folio until the money was paid. The usual procedure was to collect from those guests who failed to question the charge and then enter the amount on the folio. If the guest objected to the charge, the charge was dropped, as Wyman's management did not want unhappy guests.

One of the cashiers saw the opportunity for some personal gain in this procedure. The cashier would occasionally withhold the money paid by a hotel guest for the extra day, making no charge or credit for it on the guest's folio. The cashier did this only when the guest did not take the receipted statement. The cashier was able to add considerably to his monthly wages until, by chance, the assistant front office manager noticed his deceptive practices.

Required:

1. List weaknesses in Wyman's procedures for accounting for the extra charges.

2. What corrective action do you recommend?

Problem 18

The bookkeeper of Bella, a fine-dining restaurant, has been unable to balance the firm's checkbook on December 31, 20X3, and has requested your assistance. Information is provided below:

1. Outstanding checks as of November 30, 20X3, were as follows:

Check 2186	$ 449.00
Check 2194	$ 165.21
Check 2210	$ 648.34
Check 2211	$ 218.76
Check 2212	$ 99.81

2. Outstanding checks as of December 31, 20X3, were as follows:

Check 2186	$ 449.00
Check 2212	$ 99.81
Check 2376	$ 253.40
Check 2377	$ 155.18
Check 2378	$ 349.00

3. Cash of $2,428.28 received on December 31, 20X3, was deposited on January 2, 20X4.

4. Bank service charges for December of $22.47 have not been recorded as of December 31, 20X3.

5. Checks returned by the bank on December 31, 20X3, were as follows:
   a. James Jones for $186.21, marked "insufficient funds"
   b. Wilma Hill for $157.83, marked "account closed"
   These items have not been recorded in the books since they have been received from the bank.

6. The cash balance per the bank statement as of December 31, 20X3, was $2,134.98, while the cash balance per the books is $3,505.38.

Required:

1. Prepare the bank reconciliation for December 31, 20X3.

2. Suggest the adjusting entries based on the above information.

Problem 19

The Sundowner Café's bank reconciliation for its general checking account as of August 20X2 was as follows:

Bank balance @ 8/31/X2	$ 2,600.00	
Outstanding checks:		
Ck. 1152	$ 150.00	
Ck. 1184	317.50	
Ck. 1185	122.50	–590.00
		2010.00
Cash deposit in-transit @ 8/31/X2		$ +480.50
Book balance @ 8/31/X2		$ 2,490.50

During the month of September 20X2, only 10 checks were written, as follows:

Check#	
1186	$ 248.50
1187	519.46
1188	1258.54
1189	115.50
1190	80.00
1191	25.10

(Continued)

1192	627.90
1193	418.20
1194	500.00
1195	321.80

The bank statement for September 20X2 indicates 10 checks were canceled (paid) by the bank, as follows:

Check#	
1184	$ 317.50
1185	122.50
1186	248.50
1187	519.46
1189	115.50
1190	50.00
1191	25.10
1192	627.90
1193	418.20
1194	500.00

In addition, the bank statement revealed the following:

- A check for $135.15 received from M.J. Smith was returned due to insufficient funds (no prior accounting entry recorded).
- Service charge of $8 for September (not previously recorded).
- Cash deposit of $855.00 for September 30 recorded on Sundowner's books but not credited to Sundowner's bank account in September.
- Debit memo for cost of new general account checks for $125.50 (not previously recorded on Sundowner's books).

Required:

1. Prepare the bank reconciliation for September 20X2.
2. Prepare the adjusting entry to record relevant expenses and other items.

Problem 20

Mr. Slippery, the chief accountant of a large hotel, was in addition to his regular duties in charge of the collection of city ledger and delinquent accounts and of returned checks. Thus, he was performing most of the duties of the credit manager.

In allowing Mr. Slippery to handle collection correspondence, prepare and send out the monthly statements, and receive the checks and cash in payment, the management was violating the most important of the fundamental principles of control in the hotel operation: *The bookkeeper must never be in charge of the cash.* The hotel was never audited by public accountants; if it had been, they would undoubtedly have recommended that the duties be shifted so as to take the collection of accounts out of the chief accountant's hands. That, however, would have meant giving the unpleasant duty to an assistant manager, and since the integrity of the chief accountant was considered to be above suspicion, such a recommendation would probably not have been heeded.

Mr. Slippery was fully aware of how easy it would be for him to appropriate money in various amounts and ways, with almost 100 percent protection against discovery. Accordingly, it did not take him long to make the most of the opportunities offered.

All mail concerning collections and remittances was placed on his desk. The envelopes addressed to him personally as credit manager were not opened, but those addressed to the hotel were opened by the manager's secretary and passed on to the chief accountant. Two rules were violated by this practice:

1. All business mail, regardless of the name or the position designated on the envelope, should be opened by someone in the manager's office.

2. Whoever opens the mail should make a record in triplicate of all remittances received, keeping a copy, and then sending the original to the head cashier and a third copy to the credit department so that the credit manager must account for all checks, money orders, etc.

In the course of the collection of the numerous city ledger accounts, a great many checks and money orders were received. Mr. Slippery had little trouble in appropriating some of them to his own use. He would destroy the remittance letter, and at the end of the month would dictate a letter asking the guest for payment. This, of course, never was mailed, but a copy was kept to support the eventual charge-off. He would get one of the front office cashiers to cash the withheld check, on the explanation that a friend upstairs in his office had asked him to cash a personal check. He would pocket the cash, the check going in with the other checks of the cashier through the hotel's account at the bank, and nobody being any the wiser.

When, once in a great while, somebody paid him personally in cash, it was still easier to get away with the money. And on one occasion, the head cashier, after having twice deposited a check only to have it come back marked "insufficient funds," turned it over to the chief accountant for collection. The latter, through correspondence, obtained a new check for the amount, drawn on another bank. This he personally cashed at the front office, and in time the old one was charged off.

By these operations, carried on with practically no risk, Mr. Slippery almost doubled his salary. All the book entries were regular, as he had not made any false entries or forced any footings—he did not have to!

When, occasionally, he forgot to destroy a statement that had been paid, there would of course be a protest from the guest or former guest. This would be referred by the manager to the accountant, and he would write an apologetic letter regretting that an "error" had been made.

Mr. Slippery never took a vacation, and he was never sick; but one day he had the misfortune of being in a serious automobile accident. While he was in the hospital, the city ledger bills were mailed, and a flood of complaints immediately poured in from people who had already paid their bills. An audit and investigation by a firm of public accountants brought out the full details of the manipulations.

Required:

1. State the weaknesses in the hotel's system of internal control.

2. Indicate desired changes to overcome the weaknesses stated in #1.

Problem 21

Crepes on Wheels has five special dessert crepes on its menu. The standard food cost, selling price, and quantity sold for each for the first week of June 20X8 were as follows:

Crepe	Standard Cost	Selling Price	Quantity Sold
A	$ 1.85	$ 5.95	120
B	2.00	6.00	100
C	2.15	6.45	140
D	2.20	6.55	130
E	2.25	6.95	90

The actual cost of sales and sales for the first week of June 20X8 were $1,305 and $3,694, respectively.

Required:

a. Calculate the actual food cost percentage for the week.

b. Based on the above, what should be the standard food cost percentage?

c. Why is there a difference between your answers for required parts A and B?

Problem 22

Kenzie Walker, owner of a 130-room hotel, has successfully managed the operations of the lodging operation since she purchased it 20 years ago. She has just received the retirement notice from her trusted part-time accountant, who began working for the hotel several years prior to Ms. Walker purchasing it. The part-time accountant made all cash deposits, approved all invoices for payment, wrote all checks, maintained the general accounting records, signed all checks, and prepared the monthly bank reconciliation. Ms. Walker wonders if the internal controls could be strengthened in the areas handled by the part-time accountant.

Required:

1. What duties being conducted by the part-time accountant should be segregated?

2. Explain two tasks the owner should assume to strengthen internal control.

Problem 23

Salt & Pepper Salads is trying to perform its bank reconciliation for the month of November, and its owner, your favorite cousin, Tom, needs your help. His books show a cash balance of an even $8,000, while the bank statement he just received for this past month shows a cash balance of only $6,865.34.

Tom was paying all his bills yesterday and wrote the following checks, and did not see these checks included in the bank statement:

1. #112 in the amount of $200.99 to Energy Source for the electric bill

2. #113 in the amount of $877.26 to SYSCO for food purchased

3. #114 in the amount of $36.41 to Flyers Everyone for flyers made

4. #115 in the amount of $45.61 to Staples for office supplies

He also deposited two checks yesterday, and they have not been processed by the bank as yet:

5. A check for $988.36 from Mr. Velez, for whom Tom catered an office lunch event

6. A check of $745.00 from Ms. Shaw, for a wedding shower Tom catered for her daughter

The bank paid Tom $2.63 in interest for the month. Unfortunately, one of the checks Tom deposited from a client turned out to have nonsufficient funds, so the bank charged Tom $35 as a processing fee. That particular check was from Ms. Joyce, in the amount of $679.20. The book also collected a check for Tom in the amount of $200. Since Tom did not keep a minimum balance of $10,000, the bank also charges him a monthly fee of $50.

Required:

Prepare a bank reconciliation for the month ended November 30, 20X1.

Problem 24

Norman Stevens has been with Allegro Hotel for a number years, starting as a buser in one of the restaurant's outlets while in high school; he worked as a server in the restaurants and at banquets through college, then as a restaurant manager in the café upon graduation. He has been the purchaser for the hotel for two years. He sets the specifications for the food items with the chef, takes inventory, inputs all the data, sets the par stock levels, places the orders, receives the orders, places the food in storage most of the time with one buser's help, and processes any purchase returns and allowances. He is a well-liked team member of Allegro, and the general manager, Irene Winter, believes these tasks are properly allocated to Norman.

Required:

Critique the above assignment of tasks, and suggest how these duties should be segregated and what other means of internal control can be introduced in this scenario.

Problem 25

Paco just started his Taco Truck business with five signature items, various sodas and juices, and some Mexican pastries for dessert. His five signature tacos, along with their selling prices, standard food cost, and number of tacos sold during the month of September, are listed below:

	Selling Price	Standard Food Cost	Tacos Sold
Fish Taco	$ 3.70	$ 1.11	498
Carne Asada	$ 4.70	$ 2.65	427
Carnitas	$ 4.50	$ 1.26	456
Barbacoa	$ 4.25	$ 1.30	538
Taco Chicharron	$ 3.50	$ 0.95	391

The total sales for September were $9,556.50 and the total food cost was $3,540.88.

Required:

1. Calculate the standard food cost percentage based on the information given by Paco and that the sales quantities are the same for the five items.

2. What is the food cost percentage given the sales mix above?

3. What is the actual food cost percentage for September?

4. Is Paco doing a good job in controlling the food cost of his Taco Truck?

13

CAPITAL BUDGETING

Chapter 13 Outline

Competencies

1. Define capital expenditures and how they differ from revenue expenditures. (pp. 600–601)

2. Explain the relationship of capital budgeting to operations budgeting and identify types of capital budgeting decisions. (pp. 601–602)

3. Calculate the time value of money. (pp. 603–607)

4. Describe the relevance of cash flow to capital budgeting. (pp. 607–609)

5. Describe and apply five capital budgeting models. (pp. 611–618)

6. Explain the need for and process of capital rationing. (p. 620)

KEY TERMS

accounting rate of return (ARR)

annuity

capital rationing

discount rate

hurdle rate

incremental cash flow

internal rate of return (IRR)

net present value (NPV)

payback

profitability index (PI)

time value of money

Property and equipment constitute the majority of assets for hospitality operations, especially in the lodging segment. This sets hospitality operations apart from many manufacturing firms, where most assets are current. Capital budgeting is the process of determining how much to spend on property and equipment and which assets to purchase. Capital budgeting addresses such questions as the following:

1. What piece of equipment among several alternatives should be purchased?
2. Should old equipment be replaced with new?
3. What is meant by the time value of money?
4. How is cash flow computed from an investment?
5. How is payback computed?
6. When is the net present value method preferred to the internal rate of return method?
7. How are alternative investments with different lives considered in the capital budgeting process?
8. Which property and equipment items are purchased under capital rationing?

We will begin our consideration of the capital budget by discussing capital expenditures and summarizing the *CapEx 2018* study. We then look at the relationship between the capital budget and the operations budget. We will then focus on the concept of the time value of money and the computation of cash flow and payback from investments in property and equipment. Next, we will explain different models of capital budgets and see how they apply to choices among various kinds of projects. Finally, we will discuss capital rationing and identify special problems with capital budgeting.

13.1 CAPITAL EXPENDITURES AND *CAPEX 2018*

Capital expenditures, or CapEx, are expenditures for which the benefits are expected to be received over a period of greater than one year. For example, when a hotel is built, its owners expect to realize its benefits over many years. Expenditures for property and equipment assets are capital expenditures, as are renovations. This is in contrast to revenue expenditures, for which the benefits are expected to be received within 12 months. Revenue expenditures include repair and maintenance costs. The link between these expenditures is reasonably clear in that as buildings and equipment age, they require more repairs (revenue expenditures) until they must be renovated or replaced (capital expenditures).

The International Society of Hospitality Consultants has over the years published capital expenditure studies. Because of the close tie between repairs/maintenance and renovation/replacement, these studies include data on repair and maintenance costs as well. The most recent study, *CapEx 2018*, covers capital expenditures in the lodging industry from 2013 through 2017.[1] This study is based on responses from 902 hotels, representing 64 hotel brands in the United States. Their summary of findings disclosed the following:

■ The capital spend of all properties as a percentage of total revenues decreased by 0.7 percent, from 8.3 percent in 2014 to 7.6 percent in 2018. However, capital spend per available room grew by 31.7 percent, increasing from $3,702 in *CapEx 2014* to $4,877 in *CapEx 2018*. (See Exhibit 13.1.)

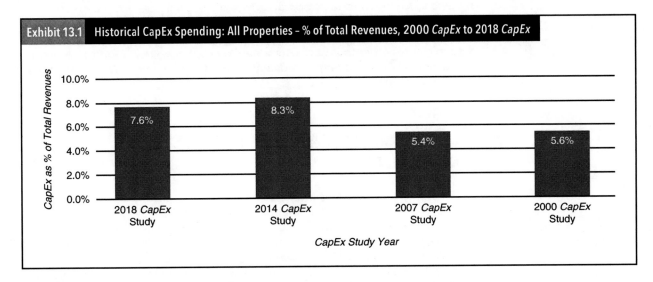

- The peak CapEx spend is typically between Years 16 to 25. In this study, the peak annual spend for all properties was just under 10 percent, and then stabilized between 8 and 9 percent of total revenues for the remaining life of the asset.

- CapEx required to maintain full-service hotels is considerably greater than for select-service hotels. For hotels with an average daily rate (ADR) less than $125, full-service hotels spent 2 percent more than select-service hotels. And, for hotels with ADRs between $125 and $200, full-service hotels outspent select-service by 4.1 percent.

- By location, airport properties spent 10.4 percent on CapEx, followed by suburban hotels at 9.5 percent. The lowest was 6.4 percent, reported by the urban hotels.

- Real estate investment trust (REIT) properties outspent non-REIT hotels in all years except 2017. REITs' average annual spend ranged from 5.6 percent in 2017 to 8.7 percent in 2015, while non-REIT hotel owners' spending ranged from 5.5 percent in 2013 to 8.0 percent in 2015 and 2017, respectively.

13.2 RELATIONSHIP OF CAPITAL BUDGET TO OPERATIONS BUDGET

Preparing the operations budget may be a prerequisite to capital budgeting for equipment. If the operations budget suggests that sales will increase beyond what present equipment is reasonably able to produce, then the present equipment has become functionally obsolete and must be replaced. For example, if a restaurant's budget is based on a realistic assumption that breakfast business could sizably increase, it may be necessary to invest in a large rotary toaster instead of continuing to use a four-piece drop-in model.

Capital budgets are prepared not only for the current year, but also are often projected for several years into the future. Construction projects undertaken by some hotel properties may take up to 30 months to complete. Even though capital budgets may be prepared for several years, they must be reviewed annually to consider the impact of changing economic conditions. The capital budget is adjusted as new information becomes available regarding changes in demand for the hospitality operation's goods and services, technological changes, and changes in the cost of providing goods and services. Evaluating past capital budgeting decisions in light of such current information is useful in determining whether those projects should be continued, expanded, reduced in scope, or possibly even terminated. Such current information may also affect the capital budgeting process itself.

13.3 TYPES OF CAPITAL BUDGETING DECISIONS

Capital budgeting decisions are made for a variety of reasons. Some are the result of meeting government requirements. For example, the Occupational Safety and Health Administration (OSHA) requires certain safety equipment and guards on meat-cutting equipment. The hospitality operation may spend several hundred or even thousands of dollars in order to upgrade equipment and meet OSHA's requirements. Regardless of the potential profit or cost savings (if any) from this upgrading of equipment, the government regulation forces the hospitality operation to make the expenditure.

A second capital budgeting decision is acquiring equipment to reduce the operation's costs. For example, a lodging operation may have leased vehicles to provide airport transportation. However, to reduce this cost, a van could be purchased.

A third capital budgeting decision is acquiring property and equipment to increase sales. For example, a lodging operation may add a wing of 100 rooms or expand a dining facility from 75 seats to 150. Another example is a lodging operation determining which franchise is most desirable. As a result of this expansion and/or franchise, both sales and expenses are increased, and, if the proper decision is made, total profits should increase to justify the capital expenditure.

A fourth capital budgeting decision is replacing existing equipment. This replacement may be required because the present equipment is functionally obsolete, or perhaps because the replacement is simply more economical.

A fifth capital budgeting decision may be the expansion in another location. Often successful entrepreneurs like to add a second location to their operations.

A sixth capital budgeting decision is brand standard. This can be of a substantial nature, as brands do not provide a cost-benefit justification for requiring these expenditures. Rather, when brand standards are not followed, one may lose the franchise.

All six kinds of capital budgeting decisions require significant expenditures resulting in property and equipment. The return on the expenditures will accrue over an extended period of time. The expenditures should generally be cost justified in the sense that the expected benefits will exceed the cost. The more sophisticated capital budgeting models require a comparison of current cost expenditures for the property and equipment against a future stream of funds. In order to compare current year expenditures to future years' income, the future years' income must be placed on an equal basis. The process of placing future years' income on an equal basis with current year expenditures in order to facilitate comparison is known as the **time value of money**.

13.4 TIME VALUE OF MONEY

The saying, "$100 today is worth more than $100 a year from now" is true, in part because $100 today could be invested to provide $100 plus the interest for one year in the future. If the $100 can be invested at 12 percent annual interest, then the $100 will be worth $112 in one year. This is determined as follows:

$$\text{Principal} + (\text{Principal} \times \text{Time} \times \text{Interest Rate}) = \text{Total}$$
$$100 + 100 \times 1 \times 0.12 = \underline{\$112}$$

Principal is the sum of dollars at the beginning of the investment period ($100 in this case). Time is expressed in years, as long as an annual interest rate is used. The interest rate is expressed in decimal form. The interest of $12 plus the principal of $100 equals the amount available one year hence.

A shorter formula for calculating a future value is as follows:

$$F = A(1 + i)^n$$
$$\text{where} \quad F = \text{Future Value}$$
$$A = \text{Present Amount}$$
$$i = \text{Interest Rate}$$
$$n = \text{Number of Years (or Interest Periods)}$$

One hundred dollars invested at 12 percent for two years will yield $125.44, determined as follows:

$$F = 100(1 + 0.12)^2$$
$$= 100(1.2544)$$
$$= \underline{\$125.44}$$

An alternative to using this formula to calculate the future value of a present amount is to use a table of future value factors, such as that found in Exhibit 13.2. The future value factors are based on present amounts at the end of each period. For example, the future amount of $100 two years from now at 15 percent interest is $132.25. This is determined by finding the number in the 15 percent column and the period 2 row (1.3225) and multiplying it by $100.

The present value of a future amount is the present amount that must be invested at x percent interest to yield the future amount. For example, what is the present value of $100 one year hence when the interest rate is 12 percent? The formula to determine the present value of the future amount is as follows:

$$P = F\frac{1}{(1 + i)^n}$$
$$\text{where} \quad P = \text{Present Amount}$$
$$F = \text{Future Amount}$$
$$i = \text{Interest Rate}$$
$$n = \text{Number of Years}$$

Therefore, the present value of $100 one year hence (assuming an interest rate of 12 percent) is $89.29, determined as follows:

$$P = 100\frac{1}{(1 + 0.12)^1}$$
$$= 100(0.8929)$$
$$= \underline{\$89.29}$$

Exhibit 13.2 — Table of Future Value Factors for a Single Cash Flow

$$FV_{n,k} = (1 + k)^n$$

INTEREST RATES

Periods	0.5%	0.67%	0.75%	1%	1.5%	2%	2.5%	3%	3.5%	4%	4.5%	5%	6%	7%	8%	9%	10%	11%	12%	13%	14%	15%	16%	18%	20%	24%	30%	36%
1	1.0050	1.0067	1.0075	1.0100	1.0150	1.0200	1.0250	1.0300	1.0350	1.0400	1.0450	1.0500	1.0600	1.0700	1.0800	1.0900	1.1000	1.1100	1.1200	1.1300	1.1400	1.1500	1.1600	1.1800	1.2000	1.2400	1.3000	1.3600
2	1.0100	1.0134	1.0151	1.0201	1.0302	1.0404	1.0506	1.0609	1.0712	1.0816	1.0920	1.1025	1.1236	1.1449	1.1664	1.1881	1.2100	1.2321	1.2544	1.2769	1.2996	1.3225	1.3456	1.3924	1.4400	1.5376	1.6900	1.8496
3	1.0151	1.0201	1.0227	1.0303	1.0457	1.0612	1.0769	1.0927	1.1087	1.1249	1.1412	1.1576	1.1910	1.2250	1.2597	1.2950	1.3310	1.3676	1.4049	1.4429	1.4815	1.5209	1.5609	1.6430	1.7280	1.9066	2.1970	2.5155
4	1.0202	1.0269	1.0303	1.0406	1.0614	1.0824	1.1038	1.1255	1.1475	1.1699	1.1925	1.2155	1.2625	1.3108	1.3605	1.4116	1.4641	1.5181	1.5735	1.6305	1.6890	1.7490	1.8106	1.9388	2.0736	2.3642	2.8561	3.4210
5	1.0253	1.0338	1.0381	1.0510	1.0773	1.1041	1.1314	1.1593	1.1877	1.2167	1.2462	1.2763	1.3382	1.4026	1.4693	1.5386	1.6105	1.6851	1.7623	1.8424	1.9254	2.0114	2.1003	2.2878	2.4883	2.9316	3.7129	4.6526
6	1.0304	1.0407	1.0459	1.0615	1.0934	1.1262	1.1597	1.1941	1.2293	1.2653	1.3023	1.3401	1.4185	1.5007	1.5869	1.6771	1.7716	1.8704	1.9738	2.0820	2.1950	2.3131	2.4364	2.6996	2.9860	3.6352	4.8268	6.3275
7	1.0355	1.0476	1.0537	1.0721	1.1098	1.1487	1.1887	1.2299	1.2723	1.3159	1.3609	1.4071	1.5036	1.6058	1.7138	1.8280	1.9487	2.0762	2.2107	2.3526	2.5023	2.6600	2.8262	3.1855	3.5832	4.5077	6.2749	8.6054
8	1.0407	1.0546	1.0616	1.0829	1.1265	1.1717	1.2184	1.2668	1.3168	1.3686	1.4221	1.4775	1.5938	1.7182	1.8509	1.9926	2.1436	2.3045	2.4760	2.6584	2.8526	3.0590	3.2784	3.7589	4.2998	5.5895	8.1573	11.7034
9	1.0459	1.0616	1.0696	1.0937	1.1434	1.1951	1.2489	1.3048	1.3629	1.4233	1.4861	1.5513	1.6895	1.8385	1.9990	2.1719	2.3579	2.5580	2.7731	3.0040	3.2519	3.5179	3.8030	4.4355	5.1598	6.9310	10.6045	15.9166
10	1.0511	1.0687	1.0776	1.1046	1.1605	1.2190	1.2801	1.3439	1.4106	1.4802	1.5530	1.6289	1.7908	1.9672	2.1589	2.3674	2.5937	2.8394	3.1058	3.3946	3.7072	4.0456	4.4114	5.2338	6.1917	8.5944	13.7858	21.6466
11	1.0564	1.0758	1.0857	1.1157	1.1779	1.2434	1.3121	1.3842	1.4600	1.5395	1.6229	1.7103	1.8983	2.1049	2.3316	2.5804	2.8531	3.1518	3.4785	3.8359	4.2262	4.6524	5.1173	6.1759	7.4301	10.6571	17.9216	29.4393
12	1.0617	1.0830	1.0938	1.1268	1.1956	1.2682	1.3449	1.4258	1.5111	1.6010	1.6959	1.7959	2.0122	2.2522	2.5182	2.8127	3.1384	3.4985	3.8960	4.3345	4.8179	5.3503	5.9360	7.2876	8.9161	13.2148	23.2981	40.0375
13	1.0670	1.0902	1.1020	1.1381	1.2136	1.2936	1.3785	1.4685	1.5640	1.6651	1.7722	1.8856	2.1329	2.4098	2.7196	3.0658	3.4523	3.8833	4.3635	4.8980	5.4924	6.1528	6.8858	8.5994	10.6993	16.3863	30.2875	54.4510
14	1.0723	1.0975	1.1103	1.1495	1.2318	1.3195	1.4130	1.5126	1.6187	1.7317	1.8519	1.9799	2.2609	2.5785	2.9372	3.3417	3.7975	4.3104	4.8871	5.5348	6.2613	7.0757	7.9875	10.1472	12.8392	20.3191	39.3738	74.0534
15	1.0777	1.1048	1.1186	1.1610	1.2502	1.3459	1.4483	1.5580	1.6753	1.8009	1.9353	2.0789	2.3966	2.7590	3.1722	3.6425	4.1772	4.7846	5.4736	6.2543	7.1379	8.1371	9.2655	11.9737	15.4070	25.1956	51.1859	100.713
16	1.0831	1.1122	1.1270	1.1726	1.2690	1.3728	1.4845	1.6047	1.7340	1.8730	2.0224	2.1829	2.5404	2.9522	3.4259	3.9703	4.5950	5.3109	6.1304	7.0673	8.1372	9.3576	10.7480	14.1290	18.4884	31.2426	66.5417	136.969
17	1.0885	1.1196	1.1354	1.1843	1.2880	1.4002	1.5216	1.6528	1.7947	1.9479	2.1134	2.2920	2.6928	3.1588	3.7000	4.3276	5.0545	5.8951	6.8660	7.9861	9.2765	10.7613	12.4677	16.6722	22.1861	38.7408	86.5042	186.278
18	1.0939	1.1270	1.1440	1.1961	1.3073	1.4282	1.5597	1.7024	1.8575	2.0258	2.2085	2.4066	2.8543	3.3799	3.9960	4.7171	5.5599	6.5436	7.6900	9.0243	10.5752	12.3755	14.4625	19.6733	26.6233	48.0386	112.455	253.338
19	1.0994	1.1346	1.1525	1.2081	1.3270	1.4568	1.5987	1.7535	1.9225	2.1068	2.3079	2.5270	3.0256	3.6165	4.3157	5.1417	6.1159	7.2633	8.6128	10.1974	12.0557	14.2318	16.7765	23.2144	31.9480	59.5679	146.192	344.540
20	1.1049	1.1421	1.1612	1.2202	1.3469	1.4859	1.6386	1.8061	1.9898	2.1911	2.4117	2.6533	3.2071	3.8697	4.6610	5.6044	6.7275	8.0623	9.6463	11.5231	13.7435	16.3665	19.4608	27.3930	38.3376	73.8641	190.050	468.574
21	1.1104	1.1497	1.1699	1.2324	1.3671	1.5157	1.6795	1.8603	2.0594	2.2788	2.5202	2.7860	3.3996	4.1406	5.0338	6.1088	7.4002	8.9492	10.8038	13.0211	15.6676	18.8215	22.5745	32.3238	46.0051	91.5915	247.065	637.261
22	1.1160	1.1574	1.1787	1.2447	1.3876	1.5460	1.7216	1.9161	2.1315	2.3699	2.6337	2.9253	3.6035	4.4304	5.4365	6.6586	8.1403	9.9336	12.1003	14.7138	17.8610	21.6447	26.1864	38.1421	55.2061	113.574	321.184	866.674
23	1.1216	1.1651	1.1875	1.2572	1.4084	1.5769	1.7646	1.9736	2.2061	2.4647	2.7522	3.0715	3.8197	4.7405	5.8715	7.2579	8.9543	11.0263	13.5523	16.6266	20.3616	24.8915	30.3762	45.0076	66.2474	140.831	417.539	1178.68
24	1.1272	1.1729	1.1964	1.2697	1.4295	1.6084	1.8087	2.0328	2.2833	2.5633	2.8760	3.2251	4.0489	5.0724	6.3412	7.9111	9.8497	12.2392	15.1786	18.7881	23.2122	28.6252	35.2364	53.1090	79.4968	174.631	542.801	1603.00
25	1.1328	1.1807	1.2054	1.2824	1.4509	1.6406	1.8539	2.0938	2.3632	2.6658	3.0054	3.3864	4.2919	5.4274	6.8485	8.6231	10.8347	13.5855	17.0001	21.2305	26.4619	32.9190	40.8742	62.6686	95.3962	216.542	705.641	2180.08
26	1.1385	1.1886	1.2144	1.2953	1.4727	1.6734	1.9003	2.1566	2.4460	2.7725	3.1407	3.5557	4.5494	5.8074	7.3964	9.3992	11.9182	15.0799	19.0401	23.9905	30.1666	37.8568	47.4141	73.9490	114.475	268.512	917.333	2964.91
27	1.1442	1.1965	1.2235	1.3082	1.4948	1.7069	1.9478	2.2213	2.5316	2.8834	3.2820	3.7335	4.8223	6.2139	7.9881	10.2451	13.1100	16.7386	21.3249	27.1093	34.3899	43.5353	55.0004	87.2598	137.371	332.955	1192.53	4032.28
28	1.1499	1.2045	1.2327	1.3213	1.5172	1.7410	1.9965	2.2879	2.6202	2.9987	3.4297	3.9201	5.1117	6.6488	8.6271	11.1671	14.4210	18.5799	23.8839	30.6335	39.2045	50.0656	63.8004	102.967	164.845	412.864	1550.29	5483.90
29	1.1556	1.2125	1.2420	1.3345	1.5400	1.7758	2.0464	2.3566	2.7119	3.1187	3.5840	4.1161	5.4184	7.1143	9.3173	12.1722	15.8631	20.6237	26.7499	34.6158	44.6931	57.5755	74.0085	121.501	197.814	511.952	2015.38	7458.10
30	1.1614	1.2208	1.2513	1.3478	1.5631	1.8114	2.0976	2.4273	2.8068	3.2434	3.7453	4.3219	5.7435	7.6123	10.0627	13.2677	17.4494	22.8923	29.9599	39.1159	50.9502	66.2118	85.8499	143.371	237.376	634.820	2620.00	10143.0
32	1.1730	1.2369	1.2701	1.3749	1.6103	1.8845	2.2038	2.5751	3.0067	3.5081	4.0900	4.7649	6.4534	8.7153	11.7371	15.7633	21.1138	28.2056	37.5817	49.9471	66.2148	87.5651	115.520	199.629	341.822	976.099	4427.79	18760.5
34	1.1848	1.2532	1.2892	1.4026	1.6590	1.9607	2.3153	2.7319	3.2209	3.7943	4.4664	5.2533	7.2510	9.9781	13.6901	18.7284	25.5477	34.7521	47.1425	63.7774	86.0528	115.805	155.443	277.964	492.224	1500.85	7482.97	34699.5
36	1.1967	1.2698	1.3086	1.4308	1.7091	2.0399	2.4325	2.8983	3.4503	4.1039	4.8774	5.7918	8.1473	11.4239	15.9682	22.2512	30.9127	42.8181	59.1356	81.4374	111.834	153.152	209.164	387.037	708.802	2307.71	12646.2	64180.1
38	1.2087	1.2872	1.3283	1.4595	1.7608	2.1223	2.5557	3.0748	3.6960	4.4388	5.3262	6.3855	9.1543	13.0793	18.6253	26.4367	37.4043	52.7362	73.9048	103.987	145.340	202.543	281.452	538.910	1020.67	3548.33	21372.1	…
40	1.2208	1.3045	1.3483	1.4889	1.8140	2.2080	2.6851	3.2620	3.9593	4.8010	5.8164	7.0400	10.2857	14.9745	21.7245	31.4094	45.2593	65.0009	93.0510	132.782	188.884	267.864	378.721	750.378	1469.77	5455.91	36118.9	…
48	1.2705	1.3757	1.4314	1.6122	2.0435	2.5871	3.2715	4.1323	5.2136	6.5705	8.2715	10.4013	16.3939	25.7289	40.2106	62.5852	97.0172	149.797	230.391	352.992	538.807	819.401	1241.61	2820.57	6319.75	30455.9	…	…
60	1.3489	1.4898	1.5657	1.8167	2.4432	3.2810	4.3998	5.8916	7.8781	10.5196	14.0274	18.6792	32.9877	57.9464	101.257	176.031	304.482	524.057	897.597	1530.05	2595.92	4384.00	7370.20	20555.1	56347.5	…	…	…
120	1.8194	2.2196	2.4514	3.3004	5.9693	10.7652	19.3581	34.7110	62.0643	110.663	196.768	348.912	1088.19	3357.79	10253.0	30987.0	92709.1	…	…	…	…	…	…	…	…	…	…	…
180	2.4541	3.3069	3.8380	5.9958	14.5844	35.3208	85.1718	204.503	488.948	1164.13	2740.23	6517.39	35896.8	…	…	…	…	…	…	…	…	…	…	…	…	…	…	…
240	3.3102	4.9268	6.0092	10.8926	35.6328	115.889	374.738	1204.85	3851.98	12246.7	38717.7	…	…	…	…	…	…	…	…	…	…	…	…	…	…	…	…	…
300	4.4650	7.3402	9.4084	19.7885	87.0588	380.235	1648.77	7098.51	30346.2	…	…	…	…	…	…	…	…	…	…	…	…	…	…	…	…	…	…	…
360	6.0226	10.9357	14.7306	35.9496	212.704	1247.56	5754.23	41821.6	…	…	…	…	…	…	…	…	…	…	…	…	…	…	…	…	…	…	…	…

$FV_{n,k} > 99{,}999$

The present value of $100 two years hence (assuming an interest rate of 12 percent) is $79.72, determined as follows:

$$P = 100\frac{1}{(1 + 0.12)^2}$$

$$= 100(0.7972)$$

$$= \underline{\$79.72}$$

An alternative to using this formula to calculate the present value of a future amount is to use a table of present value factors, such as that found in Exhibit 13.3. The present value factors in Exhibit 13.3 are based on future amounts at the end of the period. For example, the present value of $100 a year from now at 15 percent interest is $86.96. This is determined by finding the number in the 15 percent column and the period one row (0.8696) and multiplying it by $100. The present value of $100 today is simply $100.

Most capital investments provide a stream of receipts for several years. When the amounts are the same and at equal intervals, such as the end of each year, the stream is referred to as an **annuity**. Exhibit 13.4 shows the calculation of the present value of an annuity (at 15 percent) of $10,000 due at the end of each year for five years. The present value factors used in the calculation are from the present value table in Exhibit 13.3.

The present value of an annuity will vary significantly based on the interest rate (also called the **discount rate**) and the timing of the future receipts. Everything else being the same, the higher the discount rate, the lower the present value. Likewise, everything else being the same, the more distant the receipt, the smaller the present value.

An alternative to multiplying each future amount by the present value factor from the present value table in Exhibit 13.3 is to sum the present factors and make one multiplication. This is illustrated in Exhibit 13.5. Thus, the $33,522 calculated in Exhibit 13.5 equals the calculation performed in Exhibit 13.4. Rather than using the present values from Exhibit 13.3, present values for an annuity are provided in Exhibit 13.6. As a check on your understanding of the present value of an annuity table, locate the present value factor for five years and 15 percent. As you would expect, it is 3.3522. Thus, the present value for an annuity table is nothing more than a summation of present value factors from Exhibit 13.3. However, this table of present value factors for an annuity will save much time, especially when streams of receipts for several years must be calculated.

A problem that calls for the use of both present value factors (Exhibit 13.3) and present value factors for an annuity (Exhibit 13.6) is presented in Exhibit 13.7. This problem is solved by treating the stream of receipts as a $10,000 annuity and two separate payments of $5,000 and $10,000 due at the end of Years 2 and 4, respectively.

Similarly, to calculate future values of an annuity, it is simplest to refer to the table of future value factors for an annuity (Exhibit 13.8). For example, assume that a hotel company decides to invest $10,000 at the end of each year for five years at an annual interest rate of 10 percent, compounded annually. What will be the value of the investment at the end of Year 5? Using the factor for 10 percent and five periods from Exhibit 13.8, we can determine the answer as follows:

$$\$10,000 \times 6.1051 = \underline{\underline{\$61,051}}$$

Exhibit 13.3   Table of Present Value Factors for a Single Cash Flow

$$PV_{n,k} = \frac{1}{(1+k)^n}$$

INTEREST RATES

Periods	0.5%	0.67%	0.75%	1%	1.5%	2%	2.5%	3%	3.5%	4%	4.5%	5%	6%	7%	8%	9%	10%	11%	12%	13%	14%	15%	16%	18%	20%	24%	30%	36%
1	0.9950	0.9934	0.9926	0.9901	0.9852	0.9804	0.9756	0.9709	0.9662	0.9615	0.9569	0.9524	0.9434	0.9346	0.9259	0.9174	0.9091	0.9009	0.8929	0.8850	0.8772	0.8696	0.8621	0.8475	0.8333	0.8065	0.7692	0.7353
2	0.9901	0.9868	0.9852	0.9803	0.9707	0.9612	0.9518	0.9426	0.9335	0.9246	0.9157	0.9070	0.8900	0.8734	0.8573	0.8417	0.8264	0.8116	0.7972	0.7831	0.7695	0.7561	0.7432	0.7182	0.6944	0.6504	0.5917	0.5407
3	0.9851	0.9803	0.9778	0.9706	0.9563	0.9423	0.9286	0.9151	0.9019	0.8890	0.8763	0.8638	0.8396	0.8163	0.7938	0.7722	0.7513	0.7312	0.7118	0.6931	0.6750	0.6575	0.6407	0.6086	0.5787	0.5245	0.4552	0.3975
4	0.9802	0.9738	0.9706	0.9610	0.9422	0.9238	0.9060	0.8885	0.8714	0.8548	0.8386	0.8227	0.7921	0.7629	0.7350	0.7084	0.6830	0.6587	0.6355	0.6133	0.5921	0.5718	0.5523	0.5158	0.4823	0.4230	0.3501	0.2923
5	0.9754	0.9673	0.9633	0.9515	0.9283	0.9057	0.8839	0.8626	0.8420	0.8219	0.8025	0.7835	0.7473	0.7130	0.6806	0.6499	0.6209	0.5935	0.5674	0.5428	0.5194	0.4972	0.4761	0.4371	0.4019	0.3411	0.2693	0.2149
6	0.9705	0.9609	0.9562	0.9420	0.9145	0.8880	0.8623	0.8375	0.8135	0.7903	0.7679	0.7462	0.7050	0.6663	0.6302	0.5963	0.5645	0.5346	0.5066	0.4803	0.4556	0.4323	0.4104	0.3704	0.3349	0.2751	0.2072	0.1589
7	0.9657	0.9546	0.9490	0.9327	0.9010	0.8706	0.8413	0.8131	0.7860	0.7599	0.7348	0.7107	0.6651	0.6227	0.5835	0.5470	0.5132	0.4817	0.4523	0.4251	0.3996	0.3759	0.3538	0.3139	0.2791	0.2218	0.1594	0.1162
8	0.9609	0.9482	0.9420	0.9235	0.8877	0.8535	0.8207	0.7894	0.7594	0.7307	0.7032	0.6768	0.6274	0.5820	0.5403	0.5019	0.4665	0.4339	0.4039	0.3762	0.3506	0.3269	0.3050	0.2660	0.2326	0.1789	0.1226	0.0854
9	0.9561	0.9420	0.9350	0.9143	0.8746	0.8368	0.8007	0.7664	0.7337	0.7026	0.6729	0.6446	0.5919	0.5439	0.5002	0.4604	0.4241	0.3909	0.3606	0.3329	0.3075	0.2843	0.2630	0.2255	0.1938	0.1443	0.0943	0.0628
10	0.9513	0.9357	0.9280	0.9053	0.8617	0.8203	0.7812	0.7441	0.7089	0.6756	0.6439	0.6139	0.5584	0.5083	0.4632	0.4224	0.3855	0.3522	0.3220	0.2946	0.2697	0.2472	0.2267	0.1911	0.1615	0.1164	0.0725	0.0462
11	0.9466	0.9295	0.9211	0.8963	0.8489	0.8043	0.7621	0.7224	0.6849	0.6496	0.6162	0.5847	0.5268	0.4751	0.4289	0.3875	0.3505	0.3173	0.2875	0.2607	0.2366	0.2149	0.1954	0.1619	0.1346	0.0938	0.0558	0.0340
12	0.9419	0.9232	0.9142	0.8874	0.8364	0.7885	0.7436	0.7014	0.6618	0.6246	0.5897	0.5568	0.4970	0.4440	0.3971	0.3555	0.3186	0.2858	0.2567	0.2307	0.2076	0.1869	0.1685	0.1372	0.1122	0.0757	0.0429	0.0250
13	0.9372	0.9172	0.9074	0.8787	0.8240	0.7730	0.7254	0.6810	0.6394	0.6006	0.5643	0.5303	0.4688	0.4150	0.3677	0.3262	0.2897	0.2575	0.2292	0.2042	0.1821	0.1625	0.1452	0.1163	0.0935	0.0610	0.0330	0.0184
14	0.9326	0.9112	0.9007	0.8700	0.8118	0.7579	0.7077	0.6611	0.6178	0.5775	0.5400	0.5051	0.4423	0.3878	0.3405	0.2992	0.2633	0.2320	0.2046	0.1807	0.1597	0.1413	0.1252	0.0985	0.0779	0.0492	0.0254	0.0135
15	0.9279	0.9051	0.8940	0.8613	0.7999	0.7430	0.6905	0.6419	0.5969	0.5553	0.5167	0.4810	0.4173	0.3624	0.3152	0.2745	0.2394	0.2090	0.1827	0.1599	0.1401	0.1229	0.1079	0.0835	0.0649	0.0397	0.0195	0.0099
16	0.9233	0.8991	0.8873	0.8528	0.7880	0.7284	0.6736	0.6232	0.5767	0.5339	0.4945	0.4581	0.3936	0.3387	0.2919	0.2519	0.2176	0.1883	0.1631	0.1415	0.1229	0.1069	0.0930	0.0708	0.0541	0.0320	0.0150	0.0073
17	0.9187	0.8932	0.8807	0.8444	0.7764	0.7142	0.6572	0.6050	0.5572	0.5134	0.4732	0.4363	0.3714	0.3166	0.2703	0.2311	0.1978	0.1696	0.1456	0.1252	0.1078	0.0929	0.0802	0.0600	0.0451	0.0258	0.0116	0.0054
18	0.9141	0.8873	0.8742	0.8360	0.7649	0.7002	0.6412	0.5874	0.5384	0.4936	0.4528	0.4155	0.3503	0.2959	0.2502	0.2120	0.1799	0.1528	0.1300	0.1108	0.0946	0.0808	0.0691	0.0508	0.0376	0.0208	0.0089	0.0039
19	0.9096	0.8815	0.8676	0.8277	0.7536	0.6864	0.6255	0.5703	0.5202	0.4746	0.4333	0.3957	0.3305	0.2765	0.2317	0.1945	0.1635	0.1377	0.1161	0.0981	0.0829	0.0703	0.0596	0.0431	0.0313	0.0168	0.0068	0.0029
20	0.9051	0.8756	0.8612	0.8195	0.7425	0.6730	0.6103	0.5537	0.5026	0.4564	0.4146	0.3769	0.3118	0.2584	0.2145	0.1784	0.1486	0.1240	0.1037	0.0868	0.0728	0.0611	0.0514	0.0365	0.0261	0.0135	0.0053	0.0021
21	0.9006	0.8698	0.8548	0.8114	0.7315	0.6598	0.5954	0.5375	0.4856	0.4388	0.3968	0.3589	0.2942	0.2415	0.1987	0.1637	0.1351	0.1117	0.0926	0.0768	0.0638	0.0531	0.0443	0.0309	0.0217	0.0109	0.0040	0.0016
22	0.8961	0.8640	0.8484	0.8034	0.7207	0.6468	0.5809	0.5219	0.4692	0.4220	0.3797	0.3418	0.2775	0.2257	0.1839	0.1502	0.1228	0.1007	0.0826	0.0680	0.0560	0.0462	0.0382	0.0262	0.0181	0.0088	0.0031	0.0012
23	0.8916	0.8583	0.8421	0.7954	0.7100	0.6342	0.5667	0.5067	0.4533	0.4057	0.3634	0.3256	0.2618	0.2109	0.1703	0.1378	0.1117	0.0907	0.0738	0.0601	0.0491	0.0402	0.0329	0.0222	0.0151	0.0071	0.0024	0.0008
24	0.8872	0.8526	0.8358	0.7876	0.6995	0.6217	0.5529	0.4919	0.4380	0.3901	0.3477	0.3101	0.2470	0.1971	0.1577	0.1264	0.1015	0.0817	0.0659	0.0532	0.0431	0.0349	0.0284	0.0188	0.0126	0.0057	0.0018	0.0006
25	0.8828	0.8470	0.8296	0.7798	0.6892	0.6095	0.5394	0.4776	0.4231	0.3751	0.3327	0.2953	0.2330	0.1842	0.1460	0.1160	0.0923	0.0736	0.0588	0.0471	0.0378	0.0304	0.0245	0.0160	0.0105	0.0046	0.0014	0.0005
26	0.8784	0.8413	0.8234	0.7720	0.6790	0.5976	0.5262	0.4637	0.4088	0.3607	0.3184	0.2812	0.2198	0.1722	0.1352	0.1064	0.0839	0.0663	0.0525	0.0417	0.0331	0.0264	0.0211	0.0135	0.0087	0.0037	0.0011	0.0003
27	0.8740	0.8357	0.8173	0.7644	0.6690	0.5859	0.5134	0.4502	0.3950	0.3468	0.3047	0.2678	0.2074	0.1609	0.1252	0.0976	0.0763	0.0597	0.0469	0.0369	0.0291	0.0230	0.0182	0.0115	0.0073	0.0030	0.0008	0.0002
28	0.8697	0.8301	0.8112	0.7568	0.6591	0.5744	0.5009	0.4371	0.3817	0.3335	0.2916	0.2551	0.1956	0.1504	0.1159	0.0895	0.0693	0.0538	0.0419	0.0326	0.0255	0.0200	0.0157	0.0097	0.0061	0.0024	0.0006	0.0002
29	0.8653	0.8247	0.8052	0.7493	0.6494	0.5631	0.4887	0.4243	0.3687	0.3207	0.2790	0.2429	0.1846	0.1406	0.1073	0.0822	0.0630	0.0485	0.0374	0.0289	0.0224	0.0174	0.0135	0.0082	0.0051	0.0020	0.0005	0.0001
30	0.8610	0.8193	0.7992	0.7419	0.6398	0.5521	0.4767	0.4120	0.3563	0.3083	0.2670	0.2314	0.1741	0.1314	0.0994	0.0754	0.0573	0.0437	0.0334	0.0256	0.0196	0.0151	0.0116	0.0070	0.0042	0.0016	0.0004	0.0001
32	0.8525	0.8085	0.7873	0.7273	0.6210	0.5306	0.4538	0.3883	0.3326	0.2851	0.2445	0.2099	0.1550	0.1147	0.0852	0.0634	0.0474	0.0355	0.0266	0.0200	0.0151	0.0114	0.0087	0.0050	0.0029	0.0010	0.0002	0.0001
34	0.8440	0.7978	0.7757	0.7130	0.6028	0.5100	0.4319	0.3660	0.3105	0.2636	0.2239	0.1904	0.1379	0.1002	0.0730	0.0534	0.0391	0.0288	0.0212	0.0157	0.0116	0.0086	0.0064	0.0036	0.0020	0.0006	0.0001	0.0000
36	0.8356	0.7873	0.7641	0.6989	0.5851	0.4902	0.4111	0.3450	0.2898	0.2437	0.2050	0.1727	0.1227	0.0875	0.0626	0.0449	0.0323	0.0234	0.0169	0.0123	0.0089	0.0065	0.0048	0.0026	0.0014	0.0004	0.0001	0.0000
38	0.8274	0.7768	0.7528	0.6852	0.5679	0.4712	0.3913	0.3252	0.2706	0.2253	0.1879	0.1566	0.1092	0.0765	0.0537	0.0378	0.0267	0.0190	0.0135	0.0096	0.0069	0.0049	0.0036	0.0019	0.0010	0.0003	0.0000	0.0000
40	0.8191	0.7666	0.7416	0.6717	0.5513	0.4529	0.3724	0.3066	0.2526	0.2083	0.1719	0.1420	0.0972	0.0668	0.0460	0.0318	0.0221	0.0154	0.0107	0.0075	0.0053	0.0037	0.0026	0.0013	0.0007	0.0002	0.0000	0.0000
48	0.7871	0.7269	0.6986	0.6203	0.4894	0.3865	0.3057	0.2420	0.1918	0.1522	0.1209	0.0961	0.0610	0.0389	0.0249	0.0160	0.0103	0.0067	0.0043	0.0028	0.0019	0.0012	0.0008	0.0004	0.0002	0.0001	0.0000	0.0000
50	0.7793	0.7173	0.6883	0.6080	0.4750	0.3715	0.2909	0.2281	0.1727	0.1407	0.1107	0.0872	0.0543	0.0339	0.0213	0.0134	0.0085	0.0054	0.0035	0.0022	0.0014	0.0009	0.0006	0.0003	0.0001	0.0000	0.0000	0.0000
60	0.7414	0.6712	0.6387	0.5504	0.4093	0.3048	0.2273	0.1697	0.1269	0.0951	0.0713	0.0535	0.0303	0.0173	0.0099	0.0057	0.0033	0.0011	0.0004	0.0001	0.0000	0.0000	0.0000	0.0000	0.0000	0.0000	0.0000	0.0000
120	0.5496	0.4505	0.4079	0.3030	0.1675	0.0929	0.0517	0.0288	0.0161	0.0090	0.0051	0.0029	0.0009	0.0003	0.0001	0.0000	0.0000	0.0000	0.0000	0.0000	0.0000	0.0000	0.0000	0.0000	0.0000	0.0000	0.0000	0.0000
180	0.4075	0.3024	0.2605	0.1668	0.0668	0.0283	0.0117	0.0049	0.0020	0.0009	0.0004	0.0002	0.0000	0.0000	0.0000	0.0000	0.0000	0.0000	0.0000	0.0000	0.0000	0.0000	0.0000	0.0000	0.0000	0.0000	0.0000	0.0000
240	0.3021	0.2030	0.1664	0.0918	0.0281	0.0086	0.0027	0.0008	0.0003	0.0001	0.0001	0.0000	0.0000	0.0000	0.0000	0.0000	0.0000	0.0000	0.0000	0.0000	0.0000	0.0000	0.0000	0.0000	0.0000	0.0000	0.0000	0.0000
300	0.2240	0.1362	0.1063	0.0505	0.0118	0.0026	0.0006	0.0001	0.0001	0.0000	0.0000	0.0000	0.0000	0.0000	0.0000	0.0000	0.0000	0.0000	0.0000	0.0000	0.0000	0.0000	0.0000	0.0000	0.0000	0.0000	0.0000	0.0000
360	0.1660	0.0914	0.0679	0.0278	0.0050	0.0008	0.0001	0.0000	0.0000	0.0000	0.0000	0.0000	0.0000	0.0000	0.0000	0.0000	0.0000	0.0000	0.0000	0.0000	0.0000	0.0000	0.0000	0.0000	0.0000	0.0000	0.0000	0.0000

Exhibit 13.4 Present Value of a $10,000 Five-Year Annuity at 15 Percent

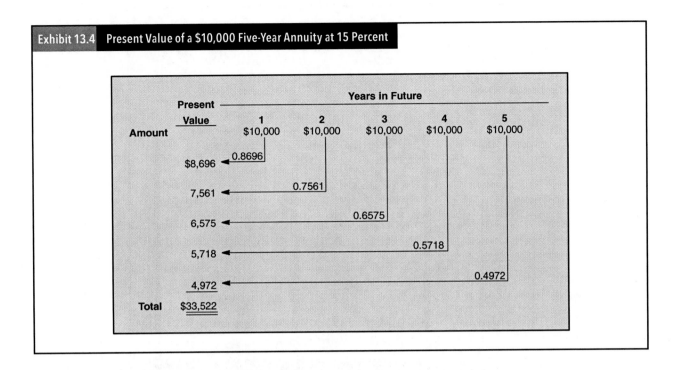

Exhibit 13.5 Shortcut Calculations of the Present Value of a $10,000 Five-Year Annuity at 15 Percent

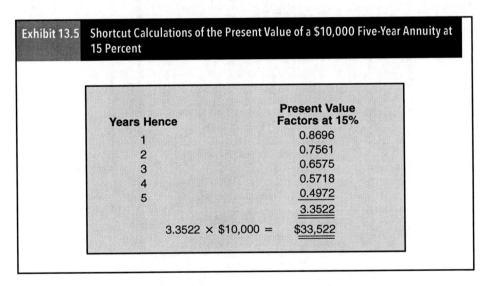

13.5 CASH FLOW IN CAPITAL BUDGETING

In most capital budgeting decisions, an investment results only when the future cash flow from the investment justifies the expenditure. Therefore, the concern is with the cash flow from the proposed investment. From the hospitality operation's perspective, the incremental cash flow is the focus rather than the operation's cash flow. **Incremental cash flow** is simply the change in the cash flow of the operation resulting from the investment. Cash flow relating to an investment includes the following:

- Investment initial cost (cash outflow)
- Investment revenues (cash inflow)

Exhibit 13.6   Table of Present Value Factors for an Annuity

$$PVA_{n,k} = \frac{1 - \left(\frac{1}{(1+k)^n}\right)}{k}$$

| | | | | | | | | | | | | | | INTEREST RATES | | | | | | | | | | | | | |
Periods	0.5%	0.67%	0.75%	1%	1.5%	2%	2.5%	3%	3.5%	4%	4.5%	5%	6%	7%	8%	9%	10%	11%	12%	13%	14%	15%	16%	18%	20%	24%	30%	36%
1	0.9950	0.9934	0.9926	0.9901	0.9852	0.9804	0.9756	0.9709	0.9662	0.9615	0.9569	0.9524	0.9434	0.9346	0.9259	0.9174	0.9091	0.9009	0.8929	0.8850	0.8772	0.8696	0.8621	0.8475	0.8333	0.8065	0.7692	0.7353
2	1.9851	1.9802	1.9777	1.9704	1.9559	1.9416	1.9274	1.9135	1.8997	1.8861	1.8727	1.8594	1.8334	1.8080	1.7833	1.7591	1.7355	1.7125	1.6901	1.6681	1.6467	1.6257	1.6052	1.5656	1.5278	1.4568	1.3609	1.2760
3	2.9702	2.9604	2.9556	2.9410	2.9122	2.8839	2.8560	2.8286	2.8016	2.7751	2.7490	2.7232	2.6730	2.6243	2.5771	2.5313	2.4869	2.4437	2.4018	2.3612	2.3216	2.2832	2.2459	2.1743	2.1065	1.9813	1.8161	1.6735
4	3.9505	3.9342	3.9261	3.9020	3.8544	3.8077	3.7620	3.7171	3.6731	3.6299	3.5875	3.5460	3.4651	3.3872	3.3121	3.2397	3.1699	3.1024	3.0373	2.9745	2.9137	2.8550	2.7982	2.6901	2.5887	2.4043	2.1662	1.9658
5	4.9259	4.9015	4.8894	4.8534	4.7826	4.7135	4.6458	4.5797	4.5151	4.4518	4.3900	4.3295	4.2124	4.1002	3.9927	3.8897	3.7908	3.6959	3.6048	3.5172	3.4331	3.3522	3.2743	3.1272	2.9906	2.7454	2.4356	2.1807
6	5.8964	5.8625	5.8456	5.7955	5.6972	5.6014	5.5081	5.4172	5.3286	5.2421	5.1579	5.0757	4.9173	4.7665	4.6229	4.4859	4.3553	4.2305	4.1114	3.9975	3.8887	3.7845	3.6847	3.4976	3.3255	3.0205	2.6427	2.3388
7	6.8621	6.8170	6.7946	6.7282	6.5982	6.4720	6.3494	6.2303	6.1145	6.0021	5.8927	5.7864	5.5824	5.3893	5.2064	5.0330	4.8684	4.7122	4.5638	4.4226	4.2883	4.1604	4.0386	3.8115	3.6046	3.2423	2.8021	2.4550
8	7.8230	7.7652	7.7366	7.6517	7.4859	7.3255	7.1701	7.0197	6.8740	6.7327	6.5959	6.4632	6.2098	5.9713	5.7466	5.5348	5.3349	5.1461	4.9676	4.7988	4.6389	4.4873	4.3436	4.0776	3.8372	3.4212	2.9247	2.5404
9	8.7791	8.7072	8.6716	8.5660	8.3605	8.1622	7.9709	7.7861	7.6077	7.4353	7.2688	7.1078	6.8017	6.5152	6.2469	5.9952	5.7590	5.5370	5.3282	5.1317	4.9464	4.7716	4.6065	4.3030	4.0310	3.5655	3.0190	2.6033
10	9.7304	9.6429	9.5996	9.4713	9.2222	8.9826	8.7521	8.5302	8.3166	8.1109	7.9127	7.7217	7.3601	7.0236	6.7101	6.4177	6.1446	5.8892	5.6502	5.4262	5.2161	5.0188	4.8332	4.4941	4.1925	3.6819	3.0915	2.6495
11	10.6770	10.5724	10.5207	10.3676	10.0711	9.7868	9.5142	9.2526	9.0016	8.7605	8.5289	8.3064	7.8869	7.4987	7.1390	6.8052	6.4951	6.2065	5.9377	5.6869	5.4527	5.2337	5.0286	4.6560	4.3271	3.7757	3.1473	2.6834
12	11.6189	11.4958	11.4349	11.2551	10.9075	10.5753	10.2578	9.9540	9.6633	9.3851	9.1186	8.8633	8.3838	7.9427	7.5361	7.1607	6.8137	6.4924	6.1944	5.9176	5.6603	5.4206	5.1971	4.7932	4.4392	3.8514	3.1903	2.7084
13	12.5562	12.4130	12.3423	12.1337	11.7315	11.3484	10.9832	10.6350	10.3027	9.9856	9.6829	9.3936	8.8527	8.3577	7.9038	7.4869	7.1034	6.7499	6.4235	6.1218	5.8424	5.5831	5.3423	4.9095	4.5327	3.9124	3.2233	2.7268
14	13.4887	13.3242	13.2430	13.0037	12.5434	12.1062	11.6909	11.2961	10.9205	10.5631	10.2228	9.8986	9.2950	8.7455	8.2442	7.7862	7.3667	6.9819	6.6282	6.3025	6.0021	5.7245	5.4675	5.0081	4.6106	3.9616	3.2487	2.7403
15	14.4166	14.2293	14.1370	13.8651	13.3432	12.8493	12.3814	11.9379	11.5174	11.1184	10.7395	10.3797	9.7122	9.1079	8.5595	8.0607	7.6061	7.1909	6.8109	6.4624	6.1422	5.8474	5.5755	5.0916	4.6755	4.0013	3.2682	2.7502
16	15.3399	15.1285	15.0243	14.7179	14.1313	13.5777	13.0550	12.5611	12.0941	11.6523	11.2340	10.8378	10.1059	9.4466	8.8514	8.3126	7.8237	7.3792	6.9740	6.6039	6.2651	5.9542	5.6685	5.1624	4.7296	4.0333	2.2832	2.7575
17	16.2586	16.0217	15.9050	15.5623	14.9076	14.2919	13.7122	13.1661	12.6513	12.1657	11.7072	11.2741	10.4773	9.7632	9.1216	8.5436	8.0216	7.5488	7.1196	6.7291	6.3729	6.0472	5.7487	5.2223	4.7746	4.0591	3.2948	2.7629
18	17.1728	16.9089	16.7792	16.3983	15.6726	14.9920	14.3534	13.7535	13.1897	12.6593	12.1600	11.6896	10.8276	10.0591	9.3719	8.7556	8.2014	7.7016	7.2497	6.8399	6.4674	6.1280	5.8178	5.2732	4.8122	4.0799	3.3037	2.7668
19	18.0824	17.7903	17.6468	17.2260	16.4262	15.6785	14.9789	14.3238	13.7098	13.1339	12.5933	12.0853	11.1581	10.3356	9.6036	8.9501	8.3649	7.8393	7.3658	6.9380	6.5504	6.1982	5.8775	5.3162	4.8435	4.0967	3.3105	2.7697
20	18.9874	18.6659	18.5080	18.0456	17.1686	16.3514	15.5892	14.8775	14.2124	13.5903	13.0079	12.4622	11.4699	10.5940	9.8181	9.1285	8.5136	7.9633	7.4694	7.0248	6.6231	6.2593	5.9288	5.3527	4.8696	4.1103	3.3158	2.7718
21	19.8880	19.5357	19.3628	18.8570	17.9001	17.0112	16.1845	15.4150	14.6980	14.0292	13.4047	12.8212	11.7641	10.8355	10.0168	9.2922	8.6487	8.0751	7.5620	7.1016	6.6870	6.3125	5.9731	5.3837	4.8913	4.1212	3.3198	2.7734
22	20.7841	20.3997	20.2112	19.6604	18.6208	17.6580	16.7654	15.9369	15.1671	14.4511	13.7844	13.1630	12.0416	11.0612	10.2007	9.4424	8.7715	8.1757	7.6446	7.1695	6.7429	6.3587	6.0113	5.4099	4.9094	4.1300	3.3230	2.7746
23	21.6757	21.2579	21.0533	20.4558	19.3309	18.2922	17.3321	16.4436	15.6204	14.8568	14.1478	13.4886	12.3034	11.2722	10.3711	9.5802	8.8832	8.2664	7.7184	7.2297	6.7921	6.3988	6.0442	5.4321	4.9245	4.1371	3.3254	2.7754
24	22.5629	22.1104	21.8891	21.2434	20.0304	18.9139	17.8850	16.9355	16.0584	15.2470	14.4955	13.7986	12.5504	11.4693	10.5288	9.7066	8.9847	8.3481	7.7843	7.2829	6.8351	6.4338	6.0726	5.4509	4.9371	4.1428	3.3272	2.7760
25	23.4456	22.9575	22.7188	22.0232	20.7196	19.5235	18.4244	17.4131	16.4815	15.6221	14.8282	14.0939	12.7834	11.6536	10.6748	9.8226	9.0770	8.4217	7.8431	7.3300	6.8729	6.4641	6.0971	5.4669	4.9476	4.1474	3.3286	2.7765
26	24.3240	23.7988	23.5422	22.7952	21.3986	20.1210	18.9506	17.8768	16.8904	15.9828	15.1466	14.3752	13.0032	11.8258	10.8100	9.9290	9.1609	8.4881	7.8957	7.3717	6.9061	6.4906	6.1182	5.4804	4.9563	4.1511	3.3297	2.7768
27	25.1980	24.5345	24.3595	23.5596	22.0676	20.7069	19.4640	18.3270	17.2854	16.3296	15.4513	14.6430	13.2105	11.9867	10.9352	10.0266	9.2372	8.5478	7.9426	7.4086	6.9352	6.5135	6.1364	5.4919	4.9636	4.1542	3.3305	2.7771
28	26.0677	25.4648	25.1707	24.3164	22.7267	21.2813	19.9649	18.7641	17.6670	16.6631	15.7429	14.8981	13.4062	12.1371	11.0511	10.1161	9.3066	8.6016	7.9844	7.4412	6.9607	6.5335	6.1520	5.5016	4.9697	4.1566	3.3312	2.7773
29	26.9330	26.2896	25.9759	25.0658	23.3761	21.8444	20.4535	19.1885	18.0358	16.9837	16.0219	15.1411	13.5907	12.2777	11.1584	10.1983	9.3696	8.6501	8.0218	7.4701	6.9830	6.5509	6.1656	5.5098	4.9747	4.1585	3.3317	2.7774
30	27.7941	27.1088	26.7751	25.8077	24.0158	22.3965	20.9303	19.6004	18.3920	17.2920	16.2889	15.3725	13.7648	12.4090	11.2578	10.2737	9.4269	8.6938	8.0552	7.4957	7.0027	6.5660	6.1772	5.5168	4.9789	4.1601	3.3321	2.7775
31	29.9033	28.2312	28.2657	27.5996	25.2671	24.4683	21.8492	20.3888	19.0689	18.7364	16.7889	15.8027	14.0840	12.6466	11.4350	10.4062	9.5284	8.7686	8.1116	7.5383	7.0350	6.5991	6.1959	5.5277	4.9854	4.1624	3.3326	2.7776
32	31.1956	29.3624	29.3628	28.7027	25.7238	25.4888	22.7238	21.1318	20.7007	18.4112	17.2468	16.1929	14.3681	12.8540	11.5869	10.5178	9.6086	8.8293	8.1566	7.5717	7.0599	6.6166	6.2098	5.5356	4.9898	4.1639	3.3329	2.7777
33	32.8710	31.3703	30.1075	30.1075	26.4488	25.4888	23.7238	21.3318	20.2905	18.6380	17.4391	16.3742	14.4982	12.9477	11.6546	10.5668	9.6442	8.8552	8.1755	7.5856	7.0700	6.6231	6.2153	5.5386	4.9915	4.1644	3.3330	2.7777
34	34.5299	33.3107	32.9581	31.4847	26.9489	26.4406	24.3486	21.8323	20.8411	18.9679	17.6660	16.5469	14.8460	13.1935	11.8289	10.6895	9.7097	8.9511	8.2438	7.5979	7.0790	6.6231	6.2201	5.5412	4.9929	4.1649	3.3331	2.7778
35	36.1722	35.0090	34.4469	32.8347	29.9158	27.3555	25.1028	23.1148	21.4872	19.7928	18.4016	16.3742	14.4982	13.3317	11.9246	10.7574	9.7446	8.9511	8.2438	7.6344	7.1050	6.6418	6.2335	5.5482	4.9966	4.1667	3.3333	2.7778
40	42.5803	40.9619	40.1848	39.7740	34.0426	30.6731	27.7732	25.2667	23.0912	21.1951	19.3556	18.0772	15.5500	13.7305	12.1891	10.9336	9.8806	9.0417	8.2972	7.7705	7.2360	6.6585	6.2450	5.5536	4.9992	4.1665	3.3326	2.7778
50	44.1428	42.4015	41.1866	39.1961	34.9997	31.4236	28.3623	25.7298	23.4556	21.4822	19.7620	18.2559	15.7619	14.0392	12.2335	11.0480	9.9148	9.0736	8.3240	7.6752	7.1327	6.6605	6.2463	5.5541	4.9995	4.1667	3.3333	2.7778
60	90.0735	82.4215	78.9417	44.7055	55.4085	45.3506	39.3807	34.7597	25.4488	20.6380	18.0291	16.1614	15.0299	14.0392	12.3766	11.0661	9.9672	9.0909	8.3333	7.6873	7.1401	6.6651	6.2492	5.5553	4.9999	4.1667	3.3333	2.7778
120	118.504	104.641	98.5934	83.3217	60.0956	48.5844	39.5304	33.1703	28.5130	24.9785	22.2142	20.0000	16.6667	14.2857	12.5000	11.1108	9.9999	9.0909	8.3333	7.6923	7.1429	6.6667	6.2500	5.5556	5.0000	4.1667	3.3333	2.7778
180	139.581	119.551	111.145	83.3217	64.7957	49.5686	39.8933	33.3057	28.5640	24.9990	22.2216	20.0000	16.6667	14.2857	12.5000	11.1111	10.0000	9.0909	8.3333	7.6923	7.1429	6.6667	6.2500	5.5556	5.0000	4.1667	3.3333	2.7778
240	139.581	119.551	111.145	90.8194	64.7957	49.5686	39.8933	33.3057	28.5640	24.9990	22.2216	20.0000	16.6667	14.2857	12.5000	11.1111	10.0000	9.0909	8.3333	7.6923	7.1429	6.6667	6.2500	5.5556	5.0000	4.1667	3.3333	2.7778
300	155.207	129.565	119.162	94.9466	65.9009	49.8685	39.9757	33.3286	28.5705	24.9998	22.2222	20.0000	16.6667	14.2857	12.5000	11.1111	10.0000	9.0909	8.3333	7.6923	7.1429	6.6667	6.2500	5.5556	5.0000	4.1667	3.3333	2.7778
360	166.792	136.283	124.282	97.2183	66.3532	49.9599	39.9945	33.3325	28.5713	25.0000	22.2222	20.0000	16.6667	14.2857	12.5000	11.1111	10.0000	9.0909	8.3333	7.6923	7.1429	6.6667	6.2500	5.5556	5.0000	4.1667	3.3333	2.7778

Exhibit 13.7 Present Value of a Stream of Unequal Future Receipts

Problem:

Determine the present value of receipts from an investment using a 15 percent discount factor that provides the following stream of income:

Years Hence	Amount
0	$10,000
1	10,000
2	15,000
3	10,000
4	20,000
5	10,000

Solution:

Years Hence	Amount	Annuity	Excess of Annuity
0	$10,000	$10,000	$ 0
1	10,000	10,000	0
2	15,000	10,000	5,000
3	10,000	10,000	0
4	20,000	10,000	10,000
5	10,000	10,000	0

Calculation:

Present value of amount due today	=	$10,000
Present value of the $10,000 annuity for 5 years		
$10,000 × 3.3522	=	33,522
Present value of $5,000 due 2 years hence		
$5,000 × 0.7561	=	3,781
Present value of $10,000 due 4 years hence		
$10,000 × 0.5718	=	5,718
Total		$53,021

- Investment expenses except depreciation (cash outflow)
- Residual value of an asset at the time of sale (cash inflow)

Depreciation expense results from writing off the cost of the investment; however, it is not a cash outflow and, therefore, does not affect the capital budgeting decision. It is used in determining the income taxes relating to the investment since the IRS allows depreciation to be deducted in computing taxable income.

Exhibit 13.9 illustrates the relevant cash flows of a proposed investment of the Hampton Hotel. The Hampton Hotel is considering installing a game room. Since space is available with only minor modifications, the focus is on the cost of machines and related future revenues and expenses. Depreciation of $7,000 per year is used only in determining the pretax income from the investment. The cash flow generated by the investment in game machines is $36,840 for three years, resulting in an incremental net cash flow of $15,840 after the cost of the machines is subtracted. The means of financing the game machines is not considered. In capital budgeting models, the discount rate includes the interest cost, if any.

Exhibit 13.8 Table of Future Value Factors for an Annuity

$$FVA_{n,k} = \frac{(1+k)^n - 1}{k}$$

INTEREST RATES

Periods	0.5%	0.67%	0.75%	1%	1.5%	2%	2.5%	3%	3.5%	4%	4.5%	5%	6%	7%	8%	9%	10%	11%	12%	13%	14%	15%	16%	18%	20%	24%	30%	36%
1	1.0000	1.0000	1.0000	1.0000	1.0000	1.0000	1.0000	1.0000	1.0000	1.0000	1.0000	1.0000	1.0000	1.0000	1.0000	1.0000	1.0000	1.0000	1.0000	1.0000	1.0000	1.0000	1.0000	1.0000	1.0000	1.0000	1.0000	1.0000
2	2.0050	2.0067	2.0075	2.0100	2.0150	2.0200	2.0250	2.0300	2.0350	2.0400	2.0450	2.0500	2.0600	2.0700	2.0800	2.0900	2.1000	2.1100	2.1200	2.1300	2.1400	2.1500	2.1600	2.1800	2.2000	2.2400	2.3000	2.3600
3	3.0150	3.0200	3.0226	3.0301	3.0452	3.0604	3.0756	3.0909	3.1062	3.1216	3.1370	3.1525	3.1836	3.2149	3.2464	3.2781	3.3100	3.3421	3.3744	3.4069	3.4396	3.4725	3.5056	3.5724	3.6400	3.7776	3.9900	4.2096
4	4.0301	4.0402	4.0452	4.0604	4.0909	4.1216	4.1525	4.1836	4.2149	4.2465	4.2782	4.3101	4.3746	4.4399	4.5061	4.5731	4.6410	4.7097	4.7793	4.8498	4.9211	4.9934	5.0665	5.2154	5.3680	5.6842	6.1870	6.7251
5	5.0503	5.0671	5.0756	5.1010	5.1523	5.2040	5.2563	5.3091	5.3625	5.4163	5.4707	5.5256	5.6371	5.7507	5.8666	5.9847	6.1051	6.2278	6.3528	6.4803	6.6101	6.7424	6.8771	7.1542	7.4416	8.0484	9.0431	10.1461
6	6.0755	6.1009	6.1136	6.1520	6.2296	6.3081	6.3877	6.4684	6.5502	6.6330	6.7169	6.8019	6.9753	7.1533	7.3359	7.5233	7.7156	7.9129	8.1152	8.3227	8.5355	8.7537	8.9775	9.4420	9.9299	10.9801	12.7560	14.7987
7	7.1059	7.1416	7.1595	7.2135	7.3230	7.4343	7.5474	7.6625	7.7794	7.8983	8.0192	8.1420	8.3938	8.6540	8.9228	9.2004	9.4872	9.7833	10.0890	10.4047	10.7305	11.0668	11.4139	12.1415	12.9159	14.6153	17.5828	21.1262
8	8.1414	8.1892	8.2132	8.2857	8.4328	8.5830	8.7361	8.8923	9.0517	9.2142	9.3800	9.5491	9.8975	10.2598	10.6366	11.0285	11.4359	11.8594	12.2997	12.7573	13.2328	13.7268	14.2401	15.3270	16.4991	19.1229	23.8577	29.7316
9	9.1821	9.2493	9.2748	9.3685	9.5593	9.7546	9.9545	10.1591	10.3685	10.5828	10.8021	11.0266	11.4913	11.9780	12.4876	13.0210	13.5795	14.1640	14.7757	15.4157	16.0853	16.7858	17.5185	19.0859	20.7989	24.7125	32.0150	41.4350
10	10.2280	10.3054	10.3443	10.4622	10.7027	10.9497	11.2034	11.4639	11.7314	12.0061	12.2882	12.5779	13.1808	13.8164	14.4866	15.1929	15.9374	16.7220	17.5487	18.4197	19.3373	20.3037	21.3215	23.5213	25.9587	31.6434	42.6195	57.3516
11	11.2792	11.3741	11.4219	11.5668	11.8633	12.1687	12.4835	12.8078	13.1420	13.4864	13.8412	14.2068	14.9716	15.7836	16.6455	17.5603	18.5312	19.5614	20.6546	21.8143	23.0445	24.3493	25.7329	28.7551	32.1504	40.2379	56.4053	78.9982
12	12.3356	12.4499	12.5076	12.6825	13.0412	13.4121	13.7956	14.1920	14.6020	15.0258	15.4640	15.9171	16.8699	17.8885	18.9771	20.1407	21.3843	22.7132	24.1331	25.6502	27.2707	29.0017	30.8502	34.9311	39.5805	50.8950	74.3270	108.437
13	13.3972	13.5329	13.6014	13.8093	14.2368	14.6803	15.1404	15.6178	16.1130	16.6268	17.1599	17.7130	18.8821	20.1406	21.4953	22.9534	24.5227	26.2116	28.0291	29.9847	32.0887	34.3519	36.7862	42.2187	48.4966	64.1097	97.6250	148.475
14	14.4642	14.6231	14.7034	14.9474	15.4504	15.9739	16.5190	17.0863	17.6770	18.2919	18.9321	19.5986	21.0151	22.5505	24.2149	26.0192	27.9750	30.0949	32.3926	34.8827	37.5811	40.5047	43.6720	50.8180	59.1959	80.4961	127.913	202.926
15	15.5365	15.7206	15.8137	16.0969	16.6821	17.2934	17.9319	18.5989	19.2957	20.0236	20.7841	21.5786	23.2760	25.1290	27.1521	29.3609	31.7725	34.4054	37.2797	40.4175	43.8424	47.5804	51.6595	60.9653	72.0351	100.815	167.286	276.979
16	16.6142	16.8254	16.9323	17.2579	17.9324	18.6393	19.3802	20.1569	20.9710	21.8245	22.7193	23.6575	25.6725	27.8881	30.3243	33.0034	35.9497	39.1899	42.7533	46.6717	50.9804	55.7175	60.9250	72.9390	87.4421	126.011	218.472	377.692
17	17.6973	17.9376	18.0593	18.4304	19.2014	20.0121	20.8647	21.7616	22.7050	23.6975	24.7417	25.8404	28.2129	30.8402	33.7502	36.9737	40.5447	44.5008	48.8837	53.7391	59.1176	65.0751	71.6730	87.0680	105.931	157.253	285.014	514.661
18	18.7858	19.0572	19.1947	19.6147	20.4894	21.4123	22.3863	23.4144	24.4997	25.6454	26.8551	28.1324	30.9057	33.9990	37.4502	41.3013	45.5992	50.3959	55.7497	61.7251	68.3941	75.8364	84.1407	103.740	128.117	195.994	371.518	700.939
19	19.8797	20.1842	20.3387	20.8109	21.7967	22.8406	23.9460	25.1169	26.3572	27.6712	29.0636	30.5390	33.7600	37.3790	41.4463	46.0185	51.1591	56.9395	63.4397	70.7494	78.9692	88.2118	98.6032	123.414	154.740	244.033	483.973	954.277
20	20.9791	21.3188	21.4912	22.0190	23.1237	24.2974	25.5447	26.8704	28.2797	29.7781	31.3714	33.0660	36.7856	40.9955	45.7620	51.1601	57.2750	64.2028	72.0524	80.9468	91.0249	102.444	115.380	146.628	186.688	303.601	630.165	1298.82
21	22.0840	22.4609	22.6524	23.2392	24.4705	25.7833	27.1833	28.6765	30.2695	31.9692	33.7831	35.7193	39.9927	44.8652	50.4229	56.7645	64.0025	72.2651	81.6987	92.4699	104.768	118.810	134.841	174.021	225.026	377.465	820.215	1767.39
22	23.1944	23.6107	23.8223	24.4716	25.8376	27.2990	28.8629	30.5368	32.3289	34.2480	36.3034	38.5052	43.3923	49.0057	55.4568	62.8733	71.4027	81.2143	92.5026	105.491	120.436	137.632	157.415	206.345	271.031	469.056	1067.28	2404.65
23	24.3104	24.7681	25.0010	25.7163	27.2251	28.8450	30.5844	32.4529	34.4604	36.6179	38.9370	41.4305	46.9958	53.4361	60.8933	69.5319	79.5430	91.1479	104.603	120.205	138.297	159.276	183.601	244.487	326.237	582.630	1388.46	3271.33
24	25.4320	25.9332	26.1885	26.9735	28.6335	30.4219	32.3490	34.4265	36.6665	39.0826	41.6892	44.5020	50.8156	58.1767	66.7648	76.7898	88.4973	102.174	118.155	136.831	158.659	184.168	213.978	289.494	392.484	723.461	1806.00	4450.00
25	26.5591	27.1061	27.3849	28.2432	30.0630	32.0303	34.1578	36.4593	38.9499	41.6459	44.5652	47.7271	54.8645	63.2490	73.1059	84.7009	98.3471	114.413	133.334	155.620	181.871	212.793	249.214	342.603	471.981	898.092	2348.80	6053.00
26	27.6919	28.2868	28.5903	29.5256	31.5140	33.6709	36.0117	38.5530	41.3131	44.3117	47.5706	51.1135	59.1564	68.6765	79.9544	93.3240	109.182	127.999	150.334	176.850	208.333	245.712	290.088	405.272	567.377	1114.63	3054.44	8233.09
27	28.8304	29.4754	29.8047	30.8209	32.9867	35.3443	37.9120	40.7096	43.7591	47.0842	50.7113	54.6691	63.7058	74.4838	87.3508	102.723	121.100	143.079	169.374	200.841	238.499	283.569	337.502	479.221	681.853	1383.15	3971.78	11198.0
28	29.9745	30.6719	31.0282	32.1291	34.4815	37.0512	39.8598	42.9309	46.2906	49.9676	53.9933	58.4026	68.5281	80.6977	95.3388	112.968	134.210	159.817	190.699	227.950	272.889	327.104	392.503	566.481	819.223	1716.10	5164.31	15230.3
29	31.1244	31.8663	32.2609	33.4504	35.9987	38.7922	41.8563	45.2189	48.9108	52.9663	58.4241	62.3227	73.6398	87.3465	103.966	124.135	148.631	178.397	214.583	258.583	312.094	377.170	456.303	669.447	984.068	2128.96	6714.60	20714.2
30	32.2800	33.0889	33.5029	34.7849	37.5387	40.5681	43.9027	47.5754	51.6227	56.0849	61.0071	66.4388	79.0582	94.4608	113.283	136.308	164.494	199.021	241.333	293.199	356.787	434.745	530.312	790.948	1181.88	2640.92	8729.99	28172.3
32	34.6086	35.5382	36.0148	37.4941	40.6883	44.2270	48.1503	52.5028	57.3345	62.7015	68.6662	75.2988	90.8898	110.218	134.214	164.037	201.138	247.324	304.848	376.516	465.820	577.100	715.747	1103.50	1704.11	4062.91	14756.0	52109.8
34	36.9606	38.0203	38.5646	40.2577	43.9331	48.0338	52.6129	57.7302	63.4532	69.8579	77.0303	85.0670	104.184	128.259	158.627	196.982	245.477	306.837	384.521	482.903	607.520	765.365	965.270	1538.69	2456.12	6249.38	24939.9	96384.6
36	39.3361	40.5355	41.1527	43.0769	47.2760	51.9944	57.3014	63.2759	70.0076	77.5983	86.1640	95.8363	119.121	148.913	187.102	236.125	299.127	380.164	484.463	618.749	791.673	1014.35	1301.03	2144.65	3539.01	9611.28	42150.7	
38	41.7388	43.0645	43.7368	45.9397	50.5199	56.1149	62.2273	69.1594	76.8841	85.9703	96.1382	107.710	135.904	172.561	220.316	282.630	364.043	470.511	609.831	792.211	1031.00	1343.62	1752.82	2988.39	5098.37	14780.5	71137.0	
40	44.1588	45.6675	46.4465	48.8862	54.2679	60.4020	67.4026	75.4013	84.5503	95.0255	107.030	120.800	154.762	199.635	259.057	337.882	442.593	581.826	767.091	1013.70	1342.03	1779.09	2360.76	4163.21	7343.86	22728.8		
48	54.0978	56.3499	57.5207	61.2226	69.5652	79.3535	90.8596	104.408	120.388	139.263	161.588	188.025	256.565	353.270	490.132	684.280	960.172	1352.70	1911.59	2707.63	3841.48	5456.00	7753.78	15664.3	31593.7			
50	56.6452	59.1104	60.3943	64.4632	73.6828	84.5794	97.4843	112.797	130.998	152.667	178.503	209.348	290.336	406.529	573.770	815.084	1163.91	1668.77	2400.02	3459.51	4994.52	7217.72	10435.6	21813.1	45497.2			
60	69.7700	73.4769	75.4241	81.6697	96.2147	114.052	135.992	163.053	196.517	237.991	289.498	353.584	533.128	813.520	1253.21	1944.79	3034.82	4755.07	7471.64	11761.9	18535.1	29220.0	46055.5					
120	163.879	182.946	193.514	230.039	331.288	488.258	734.325	1123.70	1744.09	2741.56	4350.40	6958.24	18119.8	47954.1														
180	290.819	346.038	378.406	499.580	905.625	1716.04	3366.87	6783.45	13941.4	29078.2	61314.4																	
240	462.041	589.020	667.887	989.255	2308.85	5744.44	14949.5	40028.4																				
300	692.994	951.026	1121.12	1878.85	5737.25	18961.7	65910.7																					
360	1004.52	1490.36	1830.74	3494.96	14113.6	62328.1																						

*$FVA_{n,k} \geq 100{,}000$

Exhibit 13.9   Cash Flows from Game Room–Hampton Hotel

Cost of machines	$21,000
Life of machines	3 years
Tax rate	40%
Salvage value of machines	-0-
Annual revenues	$25,000
Related annual expenses including depreciation and income taxes	$10,000
Method of depreciation	Straight-line

Cash Flow Calculation

	Years		
	1	2	3
Revenues	$25,000	$25,000	$25,000
Expenses except for depreciation and income taxes	10,000	10,000	10,000
Income taxes	2,720[1]	2,720[1]	2,720[1]
Cash flow	$12,280	$12,280	$12,280

Net cash flow is determined as follows:

Cash flows from above $12,280 × 3 =	$36,840
Cost of machines	21,000
Net Cash Flow	$15,840

[1]   Income taxes:

Pre-depreciation income	$15,000
Less: depreciation	7,000[2]
Taxable income	8,000
Taxable rate	× 0.34
Income taxes	$2,720

[2] $$\text{Annual depreciation} = \frac{\text{Cost} - \text{Salvage Value}}{\text{Life}} = \frac{\$21,000 - 0}{3} = \$7,000$$

13.6 CAPITAL BUDGETING MODELS

Managers in hospitality operations use several different models in making capital budgeting decisions. The models vary from simple to sophisticated. The simple models are accounting rate of return (ARR) and payback, while more sophisticated models, which require the discounting of future cash flows, are net present value (NPV), internal rate of return (IRR), and profitability index (PI). The advantages and disadvantages of each model are addressed and illustrated using the investment data in Exhibit 13.10.

Exhibit 13.10 Proposed Investment in Pizza Equipment–Hampton Hotel

Investment			Accept/Reject Criteria		
Cost of equipment	$48,000		ARR	=	40%
Installation costs	2,000		Payback	=	3 years
			IRR	=	15%
Total	$50,000		NPV	=	> 0
			PI	=	> 1

Depreciation Consideration		Depreciation Percentages	
Salvage value	$-0-	Year	
Life for tax purposes	5 years	1	15%
		2	22%
		3	21%
		4	21%
		5	21%

Estimated Project Revenue and Expenses

	Years				
	1	2	3	4	5
Project revenues	$100,000	$120,000	$140,000	$160,000	$180,000
Project expenses:					
Labor	25,500	26,200	33,900	37,100	40,300
Cost of product	25,000	30,000	35,000	40,000	45,000
Supplies	5,000	6,000	7,000	8,000	9,000
Utilities	4,000	4,800	5,600	6,400	7,200
Depreciation	7,500	11,000	10,500	10,500	10,500
Other operating expenses	11,000	12,000	14,000	16,000	18,000
Income taxes	11,000	15,000	17,000	21,000	25,000
Project income	$ 11,000	$ 15,000	$ 17,000	$ 21,000	$ 25,000

Total project income for years 1–5 = $89,000

Cash flow:					
Project income	$11,000	$15,000	$17,000	$21,000	$25,000
Add: Depreciation	7,500	11,000	10,500	10,500	10,500
Total	$18,500	$26,000	$27,500	$31,500	$35,500

Accounting Rate of Return

The **accounting rate of return (ARR)** model considers the average annual project income (project revenues less project expenses generated by the investment) and the average investment. The calculation of ARR is simply:

$$\text{ARR} = \frac{\text{Average Annual Project Income}}{\text{Average Investment}}$$

The average annual project income is the total project income over its life divided by the number of years. Average investment is project cost plus salvage value divided by two. The proposed investment is accepted if the ARR exceeds the minimum ARR required. For example, if the minimum acceptable ARR is 40 percent, a 52 percent ARR results in project acceptance.

The ARR model can be illustrated by using the Hampton Hotel's proposed investment in pizza equipment illustrated in Exhibit 13.10. The total project income over the five-year period is $89,000, which results in an average annual project income of $17,800. The average investment is $25,000, determined as follows:

$$\text{Average Investement} = \frac{\text{Project Cost} + \text{Salvage}}{2}$$

$$= \frac{\$50,000 + \$0}{2}$$

$$= \underline{\underline{\$25,000}}$$

The ARR of 71.2 percent is determined as follows:

$$\text{ARR} = \frac{\text{Average Annual Project Income}}{\text{Average Investment}}$$

$$= \frac{\$17,800}{\$25,000}$$

$$= \underline{\underline{71.2\%}}$$

If the Hampton Hotel were to use this capital budgeting model, management would invest in the pizza equipment since the project ARR of 71.2 percent exceeds the required minimum of 40 percent.

Some managers consider ARR to be useful because it relies on accounting income and, thus, it is easy to calculate and easy to understand. However, these advantages are more than offset by its disadvantages: ARR fails to consider cash flows or the time value of money.

Payback

The **payback** model compares annual cash flows to the project cost to determine a payback period. If the calculated payback period is equal to or less than the pay back objective, then the project is accepted.

The payback model is reasonably popular in the hospitality industry because it is conceptually simple. Management or, in some cases, the owner or a board of directors simply sets the payback period at the determined length of time required for the operation to get its money back from the project.

The payback model is often used as a screening device in conjunction with more sophisticated models, especially in high-risk situations. Some operations will not consider evaluating proposed projects using the NPV or IRR approaches unless their initial review using the payback model suggests that the proposed project is viable.

When the annual cash flows are equal, the payback period is determined as follows:

$$\text{Payback Period} = \frac{\text{Project Cost}}{\text{Annual Cash Flow}}$$

When the annual cash flows are not equal, the payback period is determined differently. First, subtract as many full-year cash flows as possible from the project cost. If the numbers do not come out evenly, divide the amount remaining after all full-year cash flows have been subtracted by the cash flow for the year directly following those full-year cash flows. The payback period equals the number of years (including fractional years if applicable) it takes for cash flows to equal project cost.

Using figures from Exhibit 13.10, the payback period for the Hampton Hotel's proposed investment in pizza equipment can be calculated as follows:

Project Cost	=	$	50,000
Less Year 1 Cash Flow			−18,500
			31,500
Less Year 2 Cash Flow			−26,000
		$	5,500
Year 3 Cash Flow	=	$	27,500
Portion of Year 3 needed to balance project cash flows with project cost		$	5,500 ÷ $27,500 = 0.2
Payback Period	=		2.2 years

Since the payback period of 2.2 years is less than the accept/reject criterion of three years as stated in Exhibit 13.10, based on the payback model, the Hampton Hotel would invest in the proposed pizza project.

Disadvantages to the payback model that require careful consideration are that it fails to consider either the time value of money or the project flows after the payback period. The latter disadvantage is readily apparent when comparing two mutually exclusive projects (A and B), as shown in Exhibit 13.11. Based on the payback method, project A would be accepted rather than project B because the payback period of 2.33 years for project A is less than 2.6 years for project B. However, the excess cash flow is $10,000 larger for project B. The calculation of the present value of all cash flows of $10,986 and $15,833 for projects A and B, respectively, is convincing. If this is not readily clear, it will be as we now turn to consider the net present value model.

Net Present Value Model

Both the **net present value (NPV)** and internal rate of return (IRR) models overcome the weaknesses of the previous models in that they consider the time value of money over the projected life of the capital project. The net present value approach discounts cash flows to their present value. The net present value is calculated by subtracting the project cost from the present value of the discounted cash flow stream. The project is accepted if the NPV is greater than zero. If the capital budgeting decision considers mutually exclusive alternatives,

Exhibit 13.11	Comparison of Two Mutually Exclusive Projects–Payback Model

			Project Cash Flows	
Years Hence			**Project A**	**Project B**
0	(cost of the projects)		$10,000	$10,000
1	(cash inflows)		5,000	3,000
2			4,000	4,000
3			3,000	5,000
4			2,000	6,000
5			1,000	7,000
Payback period			2.33 years	2.60 years
Excess cash flow: cash flow generated beyond payback period			$5,000	$15,000
Present value of all cash inflows discounted at 15%			$10,986	$15,833

Years Hence	Cash Flow	Present Value Factor (15%)	Present Value of Cash Flow
0	$(50,000)	1.0000	$(50,000)
1	18,500	0.8696	16,088
2	26,000	0.7561	19,659
3	27,500	0.6575	18,081
4	31,500	0.5718	18,012
5	35,500	0.4972	17,651
		Net Present Value	$39,491

the alternative with the highest NPV is accepted and other alternatives are rejected.

The advantage of the NPV model over the ARR and payback models is the consideration of cash flows and the time value of money. Some managers have suggested that a disadvantage of the NPV model is its complexity. This argument may have been convincing to hospitality operations in the past, but as the hospitality industry continues to mature, the best methods of capital budgeting must be used if decision-making is to be optimized.

Using the Hampton Hotel's proposed investment in pizza equipment (Exhibit 13.10) and assuming a discount rate of 15 percent, Exhibit 13.12 shows the net present value to be $39,491. Therefore, based on the NPV model, the Hampton Hotel should make the proposed investment because NPV is positive.

The NPV may be easily determined using a spreadsheet program such as Excel. The formula is simply:

$$= \text{NPK } (k,\ CF_1{:}CF_n) + C$$

where k =   Interest rate

      CF =   Cash flows resulting from the investment

      C =   Cost of the investment

The cost of the investment must be entered in a cell as a negative amount.

Exhibit 13.13 shows the use of Excel to determine the NPV for the proposed investment in pizza equipment by the Hampton Hotel. The slight difference of $3 between the NPV of $39,491 shown in Exhibit 13.12 and the $39,488 shown in Exhibit 13.13 is due to the rounding of numbers in the present value table.

Internal Rate of Return

The **internal rate of return (IRR)** model is a capital budgeting approach that considers cash flows and the time value of money and determines the rate of return earned by a proposed project. In determining IRR, the net present value of cash flows is set at zero and the discount rate is determined. The formula is as follows:

$$0 = \frac{CF_1}{1+r} + \frac{CF_2}{(1+r)^2} + \cdots + \frac{CF_n}{(1+r)^n} - PC$$

	A	B	C	D	E	F
1						
2						
3						
4						
5						
6						
7						
8		Hampton Hotel				
9						
10		$k =$		0.15		
11		Cost =		$-50,000$		
12						
13		Annual				
14		Cash				
15		Flows				
16		1		18,500		
17		2		26,000		
18		3		27,500		
19		4		31,500		
20		5		35,500		
21						
22						
23						
24		NPV =		=NPV(D10,D16:D20)+D11		
25		NPV =		$39,488		
26						
27		IRR =		=IRR(D11:D20)		
28		IRR =		41.3726%		

where CF = Cash flow

  r = Internal rate of return

  PC = Project cost

Assume that a proposed project costs $6,850 and is expected to yield a cash flow stream of $3,000 for 3 years. The internal rate of return is 15 percent, which can be demonstrated as follows:

$$0 = \frac{\$3,000}{1.15} + \frac{\$3,000}{(1.15)^2} + \frac{\$3,000}{(1.15)^3} - \$6,850$$

$$0 = \underline{\underline{0}}$$

Using the IRR model, a project is accepted if the IRR is equal to, or greater than, the established minimum IRR, which is commonly called **hurdle rate** by hospitality financial managers.

Like the NPV model, the IRR model is superior to the ARR and payback approaches because it considers the time value of money. The IRR is also superior to the ARR model because it considers cash flows. When there is a capital budgeting decision involving mutually exclusive projects, results from the IRR model may conflict with the NPV approach. This conflict may occur because of the IRR's assumption that all project cash flows are reinvested at the internal rate of return. Since operations normally invest in the most profitable projects first, one should not assume that other projects would result in the same return. This conflict will be discussed in greater detail later in this chapter.

The IRR model is illustrated using the Hampton Hotel's proposed investment in pizza equipment. Although the brief illustration of IRR above may have appeared simple, in practice, manual calculations are by trial and error. Various discount rates must be tried until the approximate net present value is found to be zero. The manual approach is illustrated in Exhibit 13.14.

The exact IRR lies between 41 and 42 percent. Interpolation would result in approximate determination of 41.4 percent. Since the IRR of 41.4 percent exceeds the target of 15 percent, using this capital budgeting model, the Hampton Hotel should invest in the proposed pizza equipment.

The IRR may be easily determined using Excel. The formula is simply $= IRR(C:CF_n)$ where:

C = Cost of the investment

CF = Cash flows resulting from the investment

Comparison of NPV and IRR Models

As discussed previously, the NPV and IRR models are preferred to the simplistic ARR and payback models. However, which is preferred, NPV or IRR? The NPV and IRR models, when applied in most situations, provide the same solution whether the situation considers a single project or mutually exclusive projects. However, in some of the latter situations, the NPV could suggest one project while the IRR model suggests a different project. This outcome results from the assumed

---

Exhibit 13.14   Illustration of IRR–Proposed Investment in Pizza Equipment by Hampton Hotel

Years Hence	Cash Flow	41%		42%	
		PV Factor[1]	PV Cash Flow	PV Factor[1]	PV Cash Flow
0	$ (50,000)	1.000	$ (50,000)	1.000	$ (50,000)
1	18,500	0.7092	13,120	0.7042	13,028
2	26,000	0.5030	13,078	0.4960	12,896
3	27,500	0.3568	9,812	0.3493	9,606
4	31,500	0.2530	7,970	0.2459	7,746
5	35,500	0.1749	6,369	0.1732	6,149
		Total	$ 349		$ (575)

[1]PV factors determined by the formula:

$$\frac{1}{(1 + r)^1} , \quad \frac{1}{(1 + r)^2} , \quad \frac{1}{(1 + r)^3} , \quad \frac{1}{(1 + r)^4} \quad \text{and} \quad \frac{1}{(1 + r)^5}$$

PV factor for 1 year at 41% is determined by dividing 1 by $(1.41)^1$ to equal 0.7092.

reinvestment rates of each model. The NPV model assumes reinvestment at the discount rate used (15 percent in the Hampton Hotel problem), while the IRR model assumes reinvestment at the computed IRR (41.4 percent in the Hampton Hotel problem). Even if the superior projects are first selected, it is doubtful that reinvestment would be at the calculated IRR. Reinvestment will likelier be at a lower rate. Therefore, when mutually exclusive projects are considered, the NPV approach is more useful.

The NPV is generally easier to compute than the IRR. However, computers and calculators have reduced the laborious calculations of the IRR model. Many industry financial managers prefer the IRR model because the results are easier to interpret.

Profitability Index

The **profitability index (PI)** is a relatively new capital budgeting technique. Like IRR, it is a variation of the NPV model. The PI compares the present value of capital projects' future cash inflows with the initial investment resulting in a ratio, as follows:

$$PI = \frac{\dfrac{CF_1}{(1+k)} + \dfrac{CF_2}{(1+k)^2} + \cdots + \dfrac{CF_n}{(1+k)^n}}{\text{Cost of Investment}}$$

where CF =   Future cash inflow or cash savings

k =   Cost of capital

n =   Life of project in years

Essentially, the PI is the ratio of the present value of cash inflows or savings to the present value of outflows (investment). NPV, on the other hand, is the difference between the present value of cash inflows and cash outflow. When the present value of the cash inflows exceed the cost of investment, the PI is greater than one. Of course, the larger the PI, the more preferable the project.

Let's use the proposed investment in pizza equipment by the hypothetical Hampton Hotel described in Exhibit 13.12 to illustrate the calculation. Based on the present value of cash inflows over the five-year period of $89,941 and the investment cost of $50,000, the PI is 1.79. Since the PI exceeds one, it suggests this capital project should be undertaken.

13.7 MUTUALLY EXCLUSIVE PROJECTS WITH DIFFERENT LIVES

To this point in our discussion, mutually exclusive projects have been assumed to have the same useful life. In reality, many mutually exclusive projects do not have equal lives. In such situations, three approaches to decision-making are as follows:

1. Assume that the shorter-lived project is followed with another project and that the combined lives of the two projects equal the life of the mutually exclusive longer-lived project.

2. Assume that the longer-lived project is disposed of at the end of the shorter-lived project's life.

3. Ignore the differences in lives of the two mutually exclusive projects.

The third approach is reasonable only if the lives are both long and the differences are inconsequential. For example, a difference of one year for proposed projects with 14- and 15-year lives may be immaterial.

The first approach is illustrated in Exhibit 13.15. In this example, a hotel is considering whether to replace its laundry washer with Machine A, which has a 10-year life and no salvage, or with Machine B, which has a five-year life and no salvage value. At the end of Machine B's life, Machine C, which will have a five-year life and no salvage, will be acquired. Thus, the life of Machine A (10 years) equals the combined lives of Machines B and C. The capital budgeting model and discount rate used are NPV and 15 percent, respectively. The results suggest that Machine B be purchased now followed by Machine C at the end of Year 5.

The second approach, that of assuming the longer-lived project is disposed of at the end of the short-lived project's life, is illustrated in Exhibit 13.16. The same situation is assumed as in Exhibit 13.15 except the comparison is only for five years, as Machine B is totally used at the end of Year 5. In addition, at the end of Year 5, Machine A is assumed to have a salvage value of $7,000. The NPV of Machines A and B are −$1,463 and $4,057, respectively. Therefore, based on the available information, Machine B would be purchased.

Exhibit 13.15	Comparison of Machine Acquisitions with Different Lives– Approach #1

	Cash Flows		
	Alternative A	Alternative B	
Years Hence	Machine A (1)	Machine B (2)	Machine C (3)
0	$(15,000)	$(6,000)	
1	3,000	3,000	
2	3,000	3,000	
3	3,000	3,000	
4	3,000	3,000	
5	3,000	3,000	$(11,000)
6	3,000		3,000
7	3,000		3,000
8	3,000		3,000
9	3,000		3,000
10	3,000		3,000

NPV—Alternative A	NPV—Alternative B
NPV = $3,000 (5.0188) − $15,000	NPV = $3,000 (5.0188) − $6,000 − $11,000 (0.4972)
NPV = $56	NPV = $3,587

(1) Machine A costs $15,000 and provides a project cash flow of $3,000 per year for its 10-year life.

(2) Machine B costs $6,000 and provides a project cash flow of $3,000 per year for its five-year life of Years 1 through 5.

(3) Machine C (purchased to replace Machine B) costs $11,000 at the end of Year 5 and provides project cash flow of $3,000 per year for its five-year life of Years 6 through 10.

Machine A costs $15,000 and provides project cash flow of $3,000 per year for 5 years and then may be sold for $7,000. Machine B costs $6,000 and provides project cash flow of $3,000 per year for 5 years. At the end of 5 years, the machine is worthless.

	Cash Flows	
Years Hence	Machine A	Machine B
0	$(15,000)	$(6,000)
1	3,000	3,000
2	3,000	3,000
3	3,000	3,000
4	3,000	3,000
5	10,000	3,000

NPV—Machine A	NPV—Machine B
NPV = $3,000 (3.3522) + $7,000 (0.4972) −$15,000	NPV = $3,000 (3.3522) − $6,000
NPV = −$1,463	NPV = $4,057

13.8 CAPITAL RATIONING

Up to this point, no limit on projects has been discussed as long as the project returns exceeded the reject criteria. In reality, there are often limited funds available. For example, a parent corporation may limit funds provided to a subsidiary corporation, or a corporation may limit funds provided to a division. This concept of limiting funds for capital purposes, regardless of the expected profitability of the projects, is called **capital rationing**. Under capital rationing, the combination of projects with the highest net present value should be selected.

Exhibit 13.17 considers five proposed projects and calculates several possible combinations and their NPVs. In this illustration, projects B and C are considered to be mutually exclusive, and only $150,000 is available for capital projects.

The optimum combination is projects A, B, and E because this yields the highest combined NPV. Other feasible combinations result in a lower NPV. In the several combinations where all funds would not be spent on projects, excess funds would be invested at the going interest rate; however, the present value of the return on the excess funds would be the amount invested, thus there would be no related NPV on these excess funds. (This assumes that the going interest rate is equal to the discount rate.)

13.9 USE OF CAPITAL BUDGETING MODELS IN THE LODGING INDUSTRY

A recent survey of the 150 largest lodging chains revealed that 74 percent of the respondents use IRR, while 66 percent, 55 percent, and 32 percent use payback, NPV, and ARR, respectively.[2] These results differ significantly from a similar survey in 1980, which showed that only 33 percent of hospitality businesses used IRR,

Exhibit 13.17   Capital Rationing–Five Proposed Projects

Project	Project Cost	NPV
A	$ 60,000	$ 30,000
B	70,000	20,000
C	50,000	15,000
D	100,000	40,000
E	20,000	10,000

Combination	Total Investment	Total NPV
A, B, & E	$ 150,000	$ 60,000
A, C, & E	130,000	55,000
A & B	130,000	50,000
A & C	110,000	45,000
C & D	150,000	55,000
D & E	120,000	50,000

while 71 percent and 36 percent used payback and NPV, respectively.[3] The more recent survey did not request reasons for the changes, but it seems likely that computer usage is a major reason. Calculations of NPV and IRR are virtually child's play for the computer.

Managers must carefully consider many necessary additions or changes in fixed assets in order to operate their businesses effectively. Projects are evaluated based on their costs and corresponding revenues. Projects that generate the most money for the firm should be accepted and the others should be rejected. This process is called capital budgeting.

Capital budgeting is appropriate in a number of decision-making processes. It can be used when purchasing equipment to meet government standards or to replace existing equipment. It is also valuable when considering the purchase of equipment that could either increase the operation's revenues or decrease its costs. In each of these cases, budgeting is performed to determine if the revenues (or cost savings) generated by the equipment are greater than the corresponding expenditures, or to decide which option is best for the operation. By using capital budgeting models, management actively works to maximize the operation's profits.

Four capital budgeting approaches were examined in this chapter: accounting rate of return (ARR), payback, net present value (NPV), and internal rate of return (IRR). ARR is defined as the average annual project income divided by the average investment. Although it is a simple method, it does have a number of deficiencies and is, therefore, not used frequently. The payback method is also simple and is used more than the ARR in the hospitality industry. It examines the cash flows generated by the equipment and determines the number of years of cash flows required to recover the investment. The NPV approach looks at the cash flows relating to the project and discounts them to their present value. A project with NPV greater than zero is accepted. The final approach discussed, IRR, examines the cash flows to determine the rate of return the investment generates. In other words, it sets the project NPV equal to zero and calculates the discount rate.

The NPV and IRR methods are more complex than the ARR and payback approaches, but they also provide more valuable results. They both examine cash flows and recognize the time value of money. The major difference between the two is that IRR somewhat unrealistically assumes that the project cash flows will be reinvested in projects that generate the same return. Thus, when mutually exclusive projects are analyzed, the NPV method is preferred over the IRR.

accounting rate of return (ARR)—An approach to evaluating capital budgeting decisions based on the average annual project income (project revenues less project expenses) divided by the average investment.

annuity—A stream of funds provided by a capital investment when the amounts provided are the same and at equal intervals (such as the end of each year).

capital rationing—An approach to capital budgeting used to evaluate combinations of projects according to their net present value (NPV).

discount rate—The term used for *k* when finding a present value.

hurdle rate—The established minimum internal rate of return that must be met or exceeded for a project to be accepted under the internal rate of return model of capital budgeting.

incremental cash flow—The change in cash flow of an operation that results from an investment.

internal rate of return (IRR)—An approach to evaluating capital budgeting decisions based on the rate of return generated by the investment.

net present value (NPV)—An approach to evaluating capital budgeting decisions based on discounting the cash flows relating to the project to their present value; calculated by subtracting the project cost from the present value of the discounted cash flow stream.

payback—An approach to evaluating capital budgeting decisions based on the number of years of annual cash flow generated by the fixed asset purchase required to recover the investment.

profitability index (PI)—An approach to evaluating capital budgeting decisions based on comparing the present value of future cash inflows to the investment cost.

time value of money—The process of placing future years' income on an equal basis with current year expenditures in order to facilitate comparison.

1. What is capital budgeting?

2. What are four situations that might require capital budgeting?

3. Why is one dollar today worth more than one dollar a year from now?

4. How is the payback method of capital budgeting performed?

5. What is project cash flow?

6. What are the disadvantages of using the payback method of capital budgeting?

7. How can two mutually exclusive projects with different lengths of lives be analyzed?

8. What role does the accept/reject criterion play in the NPV and IRR methods of capital budgeting?

9. Which method of capital budgeting is the most effective? Explain your choice.

10. What is capital rationing?

Problem 1

Phillip Dunbar, owner of the Dunbar Hotel, desires to know how much each of the following investments will grow to at the end of its life:

1. $15,000 invested today for 10 years, with annual interest of 8 percent compounded annually

2. $7,500 invested today for five years, earning annual interest of 10 percent compounded semiannually

3. $9,000 invested in 1 year for four years, earning annual interest of 12 percent compounded quarterly

Required:

Determine the future amount of each investment.

Problem 2

Susie Brannen desires to know the amount of money that must be invested today to accumulate $150,000 five years in the future. The options are as follows:

1. x amount at an annual rate of interest of 10 percent

2. x amount at a semiannual rate of interest of 5 percent

3. x amount at a quarterly rate of interest of 2 percent

Required:

Determine the amount of $x for each investment.

Problem 3

John Neston, age 18, just started college. He desires to invest $12,000 on each birthday, starting at his nineteenth birthday, for 10 years. He will let the investment accumulate interest until he is 65.

Required:

Calculate the amount his investment should equal at age 65. Use a 10 percent annual interest rate in your calculations.

Problem 4

Sheena Hintz is a 25-year-old foodservice executive. She is already thinking of investing in her retirement. She presents you with two alternatives:

1. Invest $10,000 annually, starting in 1 year, for 10 years. Then let the investment grow from age 35 to 65.

2. Wait until age 36 to invest $12,000 per year for 30 years.

For both investment alternatives, assume a 10 percent annual earnings rate.

Required:

Determine the future value at age 65 of each investment alternative.

Problem 5

Rosa Wilburn believes she will live to be 85. If she is to draw out $100,000 a year at the beginning of each year during her retirement years, she will need a large pool of funds available. Assume during her retirement years that she can earn 6 percent annually on her investment.

Required:

Determine the amount of funds Rosa must have at her retirement at age 65. Assume she will make 20 annual withdrawals at the beginning of each retirement year.

Problem 6

James Wayne, proprietor of the Wayne Country Inn, desires to know the present value of various streams of dollars. Today is the beginning of Year 1. Assume an annual discount rate of 12 percent for all alternatives. The streams are as follows:

1. $12,000 received at the beginning of each year for 10 years
2. $120,000 received at the end of the tenth year
3. $12,000 received at the end of each year for 10 years
4. $14,000 received at the beginning of each year for the first five years, and $6,000 received at the beginning of each year for the last five years

Required:

Determine the present value of each stream of dollars for the four scenarios.

Problem 7

T.M. Anderson is looking forward to his daughter, Sybil, attending a major western U.S. university to study hotel management. The dean of the school suggests annual costs beginning in 10 years will most likely be $25,000, with expected annual increases of $2,000 per year thereafter for at least four years. T.M. would like to start investing funds in the form of an annuity at the end of the year to finance Sybil's education. Assume T.M.'s investments will earn an annual return of 8 percent.

Required:

1. Determine the amount T.M. must invest at the end of each year for 10 years to finance Sybil's freshman year at college.

2. Determine the amount T.M. must invest at the end of each year (starting in one year) for 10 years to finance Sybil's second year in college. Note: $27,000 will be needed for her second year; however, T.M.'s plan is to stop investing after 10 years.

3. Determine the amount T.M. must invest each year for 10 years for Sybil's college education. Assume she is on the *five*-year plan.

Problem 8

John White is considering purchasing a mobile ice cream truck for $50,000. He plans to hire three students to operate the truck eight hours a day, five days a week, for 48 weeks of the year at Sunshine University. He believes the truck will have a five-year useful life and should be depreciated on a straight-line basis to zero, even though he believes he can sell it for $2,000 at the end of five years. He believes the annual revenues and cash expenses for five years will be as follows:

Ice cream sales	$150,000
Cost of ice cream	20%
Labor costs	40%
Supplies	5%
Maintenance	5,000
Other expenses	10%

Assume his average tax rate is 20 percent.

Required:

1. Calculate his annual net income.

2. Calculate his annual cash inflows.

3. Determine the profitability index for this proposed project. Assume a cost of capital of 8 percent.

Problem 9

Martice Smith and Associates is considering investing $5 million in a new motel and has predicted the following income stream over its 10-year life.

Year	Net Income
1	$ (245,000)
2	(115,600)
3	18,400
4	276,320
5	455,000
6	1,066,700
7	1,150,000
8	1,069,300
9	1,055,700
10	1,000,250

The motel is expected to have no salvage value at the end of its 10-year life.
Required:

1. Using the ARR method, what is the rate of return for this project?

2. If Martice Smith and Associates requires 35 percent return on its investment, should this motel be purchased?

Problem 10

Walter Adams is the manager of the Springs Café. The café has decided to add pizza to its menu. The estimated equipment costs, incremental revenues from pizza sales, and incremental cash expenses related to the sales are as follows:

1. Cost of equipment: $15,000

2. Incremental annual revenues (for five years): $80,000

3. Incremental annual expenses (for five years): $70,000

Other information:

1. Assume the estimated life of the equipment is five years and that there will be no salvage value. Further, assume the depreciation method used is straight-line.

2. Assume the relevant discount rate for NPV purposes is 8 percent.

Required:

1. Determine the ARR.

2. Determine the payback period.

3. Determine the NPV.

4. Determine the IRR.

Problem 11

Kevin Crabtree, manager of the Dallas Inn, is concerned about which industrial washer to purchase of the two he has researched. The expected life of the Apex washer is three years, while the Best washer has a life expectancy of six years. The initial cost and net cash inflows are as follows:

	Apex	Best
Cost	$11,000	$20,000
Net Cash Inflows for Years		
1	9,000	9,000
2	9,000	9,000
3	9,000	9,000
4	–	9,000
5	–	9,000
6	–	9,000

At the end of Year 3, the Apex washer could be replaced with a similar model for another three years, though the expected cost is forecast to be $12,000 at that time. Assume the cash flows will remain at $9,000 annually for Years 4–6 if an Apex replacement washer is purchased at the end of Year 3. Assume the cost of capital of the Dallas Inn is 10 percent.

Required:

Determine which washer should be purchased.

Problem 12

Carol Rollins, owner of Carollins, is considering buying an energy-efficient oven for her restaurant. However, she is concerned that the cost savings adequately offset the purchase price; she would prefer the project to have no more than a three-year payback period. She is basing her decision on the following information:

Project Cost: $25,500

Cost Savings:

| | Years | | | | |
	1	2	3	4	5
Energy	$2,500	$2,750	$3,000	3,100	$3,100
Maintenance	3,500	3,000	2,000	1,000	1,000
Total	$6,000	$5,750	$5,000	$4,100	$4,100

Required:

1. Determine if Ms. Rollins should invest in this oven.
2. If there were an estimated cash savings of $5,500 for each year, would this oven be purchased, based on the payback criterion?

Problem 13

Sandra Ramirez, owner of the Animal Kingdom, an amusement park, is contemplating purchasing a new roller coaster/water combination ride for $1.6 million. She has determined that it would increase park revenues by $400,000 a year because of its originality, but it will cost approximately $65,000 a year to operate. Assume a 15 percent discount rate and a ten-year life for the equipment.

Required:

Use the NPV model to determine if the equipment should be purchased.

Problem 14

The Lake Crest Club is considering adding pizza to its menu. However, a conveyor oven that costs $22,000 will have to be purchased. It has an estimated seven-year life, and Joseph Nguyen, the manager, has determined that the club could sell approximately $50,000 worth of pizzas each year with a food cost of 30 percent, labor cost of 32 percent, and other negligible operating costs. At the end of seven years, the conveyor oven should be able to bring $1,000 at an auction. Assume that the club requires a 15 percent return on investment.

Required:

Use the IRR method to determine if the machine should be purchased.

Problem 15

The Sakura Club is considering the addition of a game room for the children of its members. The equipment is estimated to cost $105,000. Annual expenses related to the equipment are forecast to be $18,000 and forecasted annual revenues equal $55,000. Assume the equipment is expected to have a five-year useful life and will be worthless at the end of five years. The equipment will be depreciated using the straight-line method. Assume the Sakura Club is a nonprofit club that does not pay income taxes.

Required:

1. Determine the payback period for this investment.

2. Determine the net present value. Assume a discount rate of 12 percent.

Problem 16

Sharissa Williams, the sole proprietor of the Mobile Inn, is considering either adding rooms or adding a foodservice operation to her lodging facility. The expected cost of each would be $500,000. The related net cash inflows for the first 10 years according to a feasibility study recently completed are as follows:

Years	Additional Rooms	Foodservice Operation
1	$ 80,000	$ 20,000
2	90,000	60,000
3	100,000	80,000
4	110,000	100,000
5	120,000	120,000
6	130,000	140,000
7	140,000	160,000
8	150,000	180,000
9	160,000	200,000
10	170,000	220,000

Required:

1. Using the payback approach to capital budgeting, which project has the shortest pay back?

2. What is the NPV of each project? Assume a discount rate of 10 percent. Assume a zero value for the investment at the end of 10 years.

Problem 17

The Groesbeck Golf Club (GGC) has decided to construct forward tees on its 18-hole course. The estimated construction cost is $50,000. The GGC's owner, Gayle Groesbeck, believes many more rounds of golf will be played and other profit centers will also benefit. Her estimates on an annual basis for 10 years are as follows:

a. Increased maintenance = $5,000

b. Increased green fees (2,000 rounds at $10 per round) = $20,000

c. Increased food sales (net of related costs) = $2,000

d. Increased miscellaneous sales (shirts, clubs, etc.) = $8,000

e. Increased cost of miscellaneous sales and related variable costs = $4,000

Required:

1. Determine the IRR for this investment.

2. Determine the NPV given a discount rate of 12 percent.

Problem 18

Leta O'Donnel, a wealthy Midwesterner, is considering the purchase of the Fairview Hotel for $20 million. The expected pre-depreciation earnings for Years 1–10 are as follows:

Year	Pre-Depreciation Income
1	$ (500,000)
2	(100,000)
3	400,000
4	1,000,000
5	3,000,000
6	5,000,000
7	5,000,000
8	5,000,000
9	5,000,000
10	5,000,000

Assume that the hotel can be sold at the end of Year 10 for $15 million.

For depreciation purposes, the depreciation methods and purchase cost of the Fairview Hotel are allocated as follows:

Land	10%	(no depreciation)
Equipment	20%	(double declining balance; 10 years)
Building	70%	(straight-line; $5,000,000 salvage value; 30 years)
	100%	

Further assume an average income tax rate of 30 percent and that all net operating losses are carried forward for up to five years.

Required:

1. Assuming a discount rate of 12 percent, determine the net present value of this investment.

2. Determine the IRR of this investment.

3. Explain why the Fairview Hotel should or should not be purchased.

Problem 19

The Holt Company is considering selling one of its buildings and leasing it back for the remaining five years of the building's life. The building is to be demolished in five years to make way for a new highway. The restaurant's earnings before depreciation, interest, property taxes, insurance, and income tax for each of the next five years are estimated as follows:

Year 1	Year 2	Year 3	Year 4	Year 5
$121,000	$125,000	$131,000	$133,000	$135,000

If the building is not sold and leased back, the building depreciation, property taxes, insurance, and interest expense figures for the five years would be the following:

	Year 1	Year 2	Year 3	Year 4	Year 5
Depreciation	$10,000	$8,000	$6,000	$4,000	$2,000
Interest	?	?	?	?	?
Property taxes	3,000	3,200	3,400	3,600	3,800
Insurance	3,000	3,000	3,000	3,000	3,000

The depreciation expense over the next five years will result in a zero net book value at the end of Year 5. Interest expense pertains to a mortgage of $10,000 with principal repayments of $2,000 at the end of each year. The interest rate is 10 percent. The Holt Company's average tax rate is 33 percent. The local government will pay only $20,000 for the land and building at the end of five years.

If the building is sold now, the price would be $50,000. Assume that a capital gains tax rate on gain on the sale is 25 percent and that any tax due will be paid at the time of the sale. The building could be leased back at $12,000 per year.

Required:

Use the net present value model to determine whether the building should be sold and leased back. Assume a discount rate of 12 percent.

Problem 20

Daniel David, president of the Grand Rabbits Corporation, is considering two investment projects. Only one of the two will be selected this year. Information regarding each project is as follows:

Investment Project #1: Renovate an existing motel for $1 million. After tax, cash flows are expected to be $200,000 per year for 20 years.

Investment Project #2: Build a new motel for $4 million. After tax, annual cash flows are expected as follows:

Year	Cash Flow
1	$ (200,000)
2	(50,000)
3	200,000
4	600,000
5–20	1,100,000

Assume a discount rate of 12 percent.

Required:

1. Based on the NPV model, which of the two projects should be selected?

2. Based on the IRR model, which of the two projects should be selected?

Problem 21

Tyson Fields is considering two alternative investments. The cost of each is $100,000. The annual net cash inflows for the five-year investment periods are as follows:

Alternatives

Year	A	B
1	$20,000	$10,000
2	30,000	60,000
3	40,000	60,000
4	40,000	20,000
5	30,000	10,000

Required:

a. Calculate the payback period for each alternative.

b. Using a discount rate of 10 percent, what is the NPV of each alternative?

c. What is the internal rate of return for each alternative?

d. Calculate the profitability index for each alternative.

Problem 22

The WM Motel, owned by William and Anna Roosevelt, is considering adding minibars to its guestrooms. The estimated cost is $500,000. The proprietors believe that annual sales could average $1 million. The variable costs are estimated to be as follows:

Cost of food and beverages	30%
Cost of labor	30
Cost of other cash expenses	10

The minibars would be depreciated over five years using the straight-line method. Assume a zero-salvage value. The WM Motel's marginal tax rate is 30 percent.

Required:

a. Calculate the payback period.

b. Calculate the accounting rate of return.

c. Calculate the NPV using a discount rate of 6 percent.

d. Based on the above, explain why the minibars should or should not be added to the guestrooms.

Problem 23

Hannah has always wanted to open a cyber coffee shop and has made some cash flow projections. She estimates that it will cost her $225,000 to develop the project, and the cash inflows for the next six years will be $45,000, $69,000,

$125,000, $185,000, $189,000, and $200,000 respectively. Her cost of capital is at 9.5 percent.

Required:

1. Determine the ARR.

2. Determine the payback period.

3. Determine the NPV and IRR.

Problem 24

Bernard has been approached about a hotel investment proposal by a young entrepreneur named Rick. The young man seems to have done his homework and presents Bernard with a five-year pro forma showing cash flows of $128,000, $138,900, $141,250, $142,870, and $146,780, respectively. Bernard knows he can earn an 8 percent return if he puts his money in a mutual fund. Rick is asking for $500,000.

Required:

1. Calculate the NPV of this project assuming that Bernard's cost of capital is 8 percent.

2. Should Bernard accept this project? Please explain.

3. Calculate the IRR of this project.

4. Does the investment decision of the IRR differ from your answer in #2? Please explain.

Problem 25

The 18-hole Royal Golf Course needs a new sprinkler system, which is estimated to cost $1 million. The golf course superintendent has advised the board that the current system must be replaced within the next year because it is beginning to fail. The board has known about this problem for several years but has been putting off the repair due to the cost. The members, however, have been complaining because the condition of the course is deteriorating. After looking into the matter further, the board estimates that the property has lost nearly $250,000 in incremental profits over the past year alone due to the membership terminations and lower guest fees and golf shop sales. If this problem is not solved quickly, more members will leave, and revenues will continue to decrease. The general manager of Royal has requested a loan for $1 million from a local bank. The bank has offered a loan at a 6.5 percent interest rate for a term of 10 years.

Required:

1. Calculate the payback period on the project based on the amount of revenues currently being lost by the golf operation.

2. The golf course superintendent believes that with the installation of the new sprinkler system, the club will see new members joining and golf shop revenues increasing. He estimates the club will enjoy the following incremental profits, which level off in Year 5 and will continue through Year 10:

Incremental Profits

Yr. 1	$ 150,000
Yr. 2	$ 175,000
Yr. 3	$ 200,000
Yr. 4	$ 225,000
Yr. 5	$ 250,000

Based on the incremental profits above and a discount rate of 9 percent, calculate the NPV and IRR of the irrigation project, assuming the sprinkler system has a ten-year useful life with no salvage value at the end of 10 years.

14

LEASE ACCOUNTING

Chapter 14 Outline

Competencies

1. Describe leases and explain the function of a lease agreement. (pp. 638–639)
2. Describe some of the advantages and disadvantages of leases. (pp. 639–640)
3. Identify and describe common lease provisions. (pp. 640–641)
4. Differentiate between operating and finance leases and explain how they are accounted for. (pp. 642–650)
5. Define leasehold improvements and sale and leasebacks. (pp. 650–653)
6. Explain the effect that capital leases have on financial ratios. (pp. 653–654)
7. Select and use relevant information to make buy-or-lease decisions. (pp. 654–658)

KEY TERMS

contingent rent
economic life
executory costs
fair market value
finance leases
lease
leasehold improvements
lessee
lessor
management contract
operating lease
rent
residual value
sale and leaseback
triple-net lease
variable lease

Leasing entitles someone to use equipment, land, or buildings without buying them. Leasing often provides a way to use resources when purchasing them is not possible or desirable. For example, a foodservice chain may lease space in a shopping mall because that space is not for sale. A hotel may lease equipment for a single day for a special function. This chapter will address several questions about lease accounting, including the following:

1. What are the advantages and disadvantages of leasing resources?

2. What are executory costs in relation to leases?

3. How are leases classified for accounting purposes?

4. What are the criteria for capitalizing leases?

5. How are leasehold improvements amortized?

6. What is a triple-net lease?

7. What is an incremental interest rate?

8. What is a sale and leaseback?

9. How are financial ratios affected by the accounting for leases?

10. What are several common provisions of lease agreements?

In this chapter, we will first consider the various uses of leases in the hospitality industry. We will discuss some of their advantages and disadvantages, as well as some provisions common to all leases. We will then focus on the differences between operating leases and capital leases and present guidelines for accounting for the different types of leasing arrangements. We will also investigate the effects that leases may have on a hospitality operation's financial statements and ratios. Finally, we will address the issues surrounding buy versus lease decisions.

14.1 LEASES AND THEIR USES

A **lease** is an agreement conveying the right to use resources (equipment, buildings, and/or land) for specified purposes and a limited time. From an operational perspective, the resource is available for use; operating personnel generally have little concern whether the company owns or leases it. Lease agreements govern the parties to the lease, usually the lessor and the lessee. The **lessor** owns the property and conveys the right of its use to the **lessee** in exchange for periodic cash payments called **rent**.

Leasing is popular in the United States with businesses in general and with the hospitality industry in particular. For example, restaurants may lease space in shopping malls, lodging companies may lease hotels, and gambling casinos may lease slot machines.

Historically, several hotel companies have leased many of their hotels from real estate and insurance companies. The **variable lease**, a form of leasing agreement in which rental payments are based on revenue, was a common lease arrangement used by Holiday Corporation during the 1950s and 1960s. Holiday Corporation (the lessee) paid the lessors a percentage of rooms, food, and beverage revenues. For example, a 25-5-5 lease resulted in the lessee paying the lessor 25 percent of rooms revenue, 5 percent of food revenue, and 5 percent of beverage revenue. Since these rental payments were based on revenues and

Leased Equipment	Percent of Respondents	Length of Lease		Maintenance Contract
		Range	Average	
Copiers	56.9%	1–20 years	4.2 years	97%
Mailing equipment	35.4%	1–20 years	4.1 years	86%
Vehicles	29.2%	2–10 years	3.8 years	44%
Telecommunication equipment	21.5%	1–6 years	3.5 years	92%
Fax machines	12.3%	1–20 years	5.6 years	57%
Kitchen equipment	10.8%	2–5 years	3.5 years	57%
Other*	8.0%	3–10 years	4.6 years	100%
Computers, services	6.2%	3–5 years	4 years	75%
Check verification system	1.5%	1 year	1 year	100%

*Other items include folding machines and golf carts.

Source: Lan Jiang and Raymond S. Schmidgall, "A Longitudinal Study of Equipment Leasing in the U.S. Lodging Industry," *The Journal of Hospitality Financial Management* 19:2 (2011): 63.

since the lessee corporation paid all operational expenses before generating any profits, the lessee shouldered much of the hotel property's financial risk.

The leasing of hotels is less popular today. Few hotel companies sign new property leases. Instead, they manage hotels under **management contract** arrangements. Under these contracts, the hotel owners make substantial payments from the hotel's gross revenues to the hotel management companies, much like the hotel companies used to pay lessors for leased properties.[1]

Many hotels continue to lease equipment ranging from telephone systems to computers to vehicles. Equipment leasing is widely used by lodging firms. Exhibit 14.1 shows that copiers are leased by nearly 57 percent of all respondents in a study on leasing. The types of equipment leased, length of leases, and the use of maintenance contracts for leased equipment are also shown. Many foodservice corporations lease both their buildings and equipment. In part, the extent of leasing by hospitality companies is revealed in footnotes to their annual financial statements.

Advantages and Disadvantages of Leases

The following list presents some of the advantages of leasing.

- Leasing conserves working capital because it requires little or no cash deposit; cash equal to 20 percent to 40 percent of the purchase price is required when purchasing property and equipment. Therefore, for the cash-strapped operation, leasing may be the only way to obtain the desired property or equipment.

- Leasing often involves less red tape than buying with external financing. Although a lease agreement must be prepared, it usually is less complicated than the many documents required to make a purchase, especially when financing is involved.

- Leasing allows more frequent equipment changes, especially when equipment becomes functionally obsolete. However, the lessee cannot expect this flexibility to be cost-free.

- Leasing allows the lessee to receive tax benefits that otherwise may not be available. For example, an unprofitable operation may not be able to take advantage of tax credits available to purchasers of certain equipment. However, a lessor, who can use the tax credits, may pass on part of the tax credit in the form of lower rental payments to the lessee.

- Leasing generally places less restrictive contracts on a lessee than financial institutions often place on long-term borrowers.

Therefore, in many cases, leasing may be a lower overall cost alternative for many hospitality operations. However, there are also disadvantages of leasing, such as the following:

- Any **residual value** (the estimated market value of a leased item at the end of the lease term) of the leased property benefits the lessor unless the lessee has the opportunity to acquire the leased property at the end of the lease.

- The greater the probability of technological obsolescence, the greater the lease payment (all other things being the same).

- The cost of leasing in some situations is ultimately higher than purchasing. This is especially true when there are only a limited number of less-than-competitive lessors.

- Disposal of a financial lease before the end of the lease period often results in additional costs.

The above list of advantages and disadvantages is not exhaustive.[2]

Some of the most cited reasons for leasing are (1) protection from obsolescence, (2) uniform cash flows, (3) tax advantages, and (4) lower down payment with leasing versus purchasing, (5) keep upgrading, (6) offers fixed-rate financing, and (7) better utilizes equipment.

Provisions of Lease Contracts

Each lease is a unique product of negotiations between the lessor and lessee that meets the specific needs of each party. However, certain common provisions are included in almost all lease contracts:

1. Term of lease—The term of a lease may be as short as a few hours (usually for a piece of equipment) or as long as several decades (as is common with real estate). Leases should be long enough to ensure a proper return on the investment for leasehold improvements and other costs. A new foodservice operation may desire a relatively short initial lease (say, 5 years) with several five-year renewable options. This would allow the company to escape from an undesirable situation.

2. Purpose of lease—This provision generally limits the lessee to using the property for certain purposes. For example, a restaurant lease may state,

"The lessee shall use the leased premises as a restaurant and for no other purpose without first having obtained the written consent of the lessor."

3. Rental payments—The lease specifies the amount of rental payment and when it is due. It also indicates any adjustments; for example, adjustments for inflation are often based on the consumer price index for a given city. **Contingent rent** is also specified. Contingent rent is rent based on specified variables, such as a percentage of revenues above a given amount. For example, a lease may stipulate that contingent rent equal to 3 percent of all annual food and beverage sales in excess of $700,000 is due the fifteenth day of the first month after the end of the fiscal year.

4. Renewal options—Many leases contain a clause giving the lessee the option to renew the lease. For example, a lease may provide "an option to renew this lease for an additional five-year period on the expiration of the leasing term upon giving lessor written notice 90 days before the expiration of the lease."

5. Obligations for property taxes, insurance, and maintenance—Leases, especially long-term leases, specify who shall pay the **executory costs**—that is, the property taxes, insurance, and maintenance costs—on the leased property. A lease in which the lessee is obligated to pay these costs in addition to the direct lease payments is commonly called a **triple-net lease**.

6. Other common lease provisions include:

   ■ The lessor's right to inspect the lessee's books, especially when part of the lease payment is tied to sales or some other operational figure.
   ■ The lessor's obligations to restore facilities damaged by fire, tornadoes, and similar natural phenomena.
   ■ The lessee's opportunity to sublease the property.
   ■ The lessee's opportunity to make payments for which the lessor is responsible, such as loan payments to preclude default on the lessor's financing of the leased property.
   ■ Security deposits, if any, required of the lessee.
   ■ Indemnity clauses protecting the lessor.

14.2 LEASE ACCOUNTING

Historically, leases were accounted for simply as executory contracts—that is, the rental expense was generally recognized with the passage of time. Leases were not capitalized as assets, nor were liabilities recognized for the lessee's obligations under lease contracts. However, as leases have become more sophisticated and economically similar to sale/purchase transactions, many accountants have argued for a change in lease accounting.

The Accounting Principles Board, the past accounting rule-making body, issued four opinions regarding lease accounting. The Financial Accounting Standards Board (FASB), the present rule-making body, has issued more than 10 statements relating to lease accounting. A major result of these rules is that many long-term leases are now capitalized—that is, they are recorded as fixed assets with recognition of a liability.

Most of the remainder of this chapter presents lease accounting guidelines for lessees. Lease accounting for lessors is beyond the scope of this chapter. Our discussion is meant to cover the major elements of lease accounting and is certainly not exhaustive. The student interested in further study of lease accounting should consult an intermediate accounting text and/or FASB statements.

Classification of Leases

In general, leases are classified either as operating or finance lease. **Operating leases** are normally of relatively short duration, where the lessor retains the responsibility of the executory costs, can be canceled easily, generally last less than the full economic life of the asset, and thus will have a residual value. **Finance leases** are where the lessor transfers substantially all risks and rewards of ownership of the asset to the lessee. Regardless of whether a lease is operating or finance, it is required to show a "right-of-use" (ROU) asset and an offsetting lease liability. Most hospitality companies started reporting this new adoption on their 2019 financial statements. For example, in their 2019 10K reports, Hilton, Hyatt, and Marriott all have the new line items of Operating lease right-of-use assets and Current operating lease liabilities on their consolidated balance sheets. The right-of-use asset is a balance sheet item reflecting a lessee's right to use a leased asset over the course of the lease term. ASC 842 and IFRS 16 each requires lessees to record the ROU asset for both operating and finance leases and with the corresponding lease liability representing the lessee's obligation to make payments on the lease.

According to FASB, a lease is classified as a finance lease if any one of the following criteria is met; otherwise, the lease is deemed operating:[3,4]

1. Lease transfers ownership of property by the end of the lease term.

2. Lease grants the lessee an option to purchase the asset and is reasonably certain to exercise.

3. Lease term is for a major part of the remaining economic useful life of the asset.

4. Sum of the present value of the lease payments and present value of any residual value guaranteed by the lessee equal or exceed substantially all of the fair market value of the asset.

5. Asset is of a specialized nature and is not expected to have an alternative use to the lessor at the end of the lease term.

Of the above five criteria, the last one is a new addition to the previous four. The "economic life" in criterion #3 refers to the useful life of the leased property. For criterion #4, "present value" refers to determining present value, "residual value" refers to the estimated market value of the leased item at the end of the lease term, and "fair market value" represents the amount the leased item would cost if it were purchased rather than leased. Exhibit 14.2 is a step-by-step process to determine if a lease is operating or finance.

In addition, Exhibit 14.3 also details the percentage of ROU assets as a percentage of total assets for selected hospitality companies with data from their annual reports.

Accounting for Operating Leases

As discussed, an operating lease does not transfer ownership of property by the end of the lease term. It also does not grant the lessee an option to purchase the asset. An operating lease has a lease term less than 75 percent of the economic useful life of the asset and has the sum of the present values of the lease payments and residual value guaranteed by the lessee less than the fair market value of the asset. Finally, the lease of the asset is not of a specialized nature and does have an alternative use to the lessor at the end of the lease term.

In the example below, St. Matthew Golf Club leases some golf equipment from GolfTrac at a cost of $22,497.46 on January 1, 20X1:

1. The lease is for a three-year term, non-cancelable.

2. The golf equipment has a fair market value of $80,000, economic life of five years, with a non-guaranteed residual value of $20,000 at the end of the lease.

3. The implicit rate of the lessor, GolfTrac is at 5 percent, thus St. Matthew will use the 5 percent for the lease calculation.

4. The equipment will be reverted to GolfTrac at the end of the three-year period.

5. There is no renewal clause in the lease.

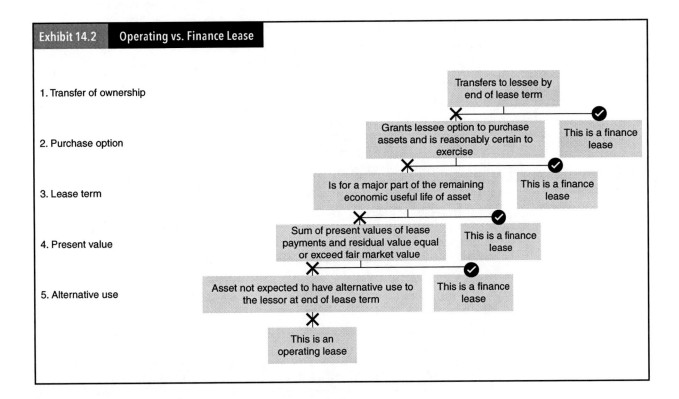

Exhibit 14.2   Operating vs. Finance Lease

1. Transfer of ownership
2. Purchase option
3. Lease term
4. Present value
5. Alternative use

Transfers to lessee by end of lease term — This is a finance lease

Grants lessee option to purchase assets and is reasonably certain to exercise — This is a finance lease

Is for a major part of the remaining economic useful life of asset — This is a finance lease

Sum of present values of lease payments and residual value equal or exceed fair market value — This is a finance lease

Asset not expected to have alternative use to the lessor at end of lease term — This is a finance lease

This is an operating lease

Exhibit 14.3   ROU Assets of Selected Hospitality Firms - 2020

Company	ROU Assets (in millions)	Total Assets (in millions)	ROU Assets as a % of Total Assets
Hilton Worldwide Holdings, Inc.	772	16,755	4.61
Hyatt Hotels Corp.	474	9,129	5.19
Marriott International, Inc.	752	24,701	3.04
Brinker International, Inc.	1,054.6	2,356	44.76
McDonalds Corp.	13,827.7	52,626.8	26.28
United Airlines	4,537	59,548	7.62
Southwest Airlines	1,892	34,588	5.47

The Analysis

Step 1 – Determine Type of Lease.

Using the five criteria stated, determine whether a lease is an operating or finance lease. In this scenario, this indeed is an operating lease because:

1. There is no transfer of ownership of property by the end of the lease term.

2. GolfTrac does not grant St. Matthew an option to purchase the asset.

3. The lease term is less than 75 percent of the economic useful life of the asset.

4. There is residual value guaranteed by the lessee.

5. The golf equipment is not of a specialized nature and GolfTrac can find an alternative use at the end of the lease term.

Step 2 – Compute Lease Payment.

As the payment is due at the beginning of the year, the calculation is an annuity due calculation. If the payment is not due until the end of the year, then this will be a regular annuity calculation. The lease payment can also be calculated using the present value interest factor of an annuity of 5 percent for three years at 2.8594, and then dividing the present value of $64,329.48 by the interest factor of 2.8594 to derive a lease payment of $22,497.54. The difference of $0.08 is due to the use of an interest factor with four decimal places versus a business calculator that uses all decimal places. Thus, the lease payment of $22,497.46 is more accurate. Exhibit 14.4 below details this calculation.

Step 3 – Journalize Entries to Record Lease and First Payment.

Using these numbers, St. Matthew can make the following entries to record the operating lease and the first payment of the lease on January 1, 20X1:

To Record Operating Lease			
Jan 1, 20X1	Right-of-Use Asset	64,329.48	
	Lease Liability		64,329.48

Exhibit 14.4	Lease Payment Calculation for St. Matthew Golf Club

Fair value of the golf equipment	$ 80,000.00
Present value of the residual value in year 5 at 5%: FV = 20,000, N = 5, I/Y = 5, Compute PV	15,670.52
Lease value (fair value – present value of residual value)	64,329.48
Lease payment Since the payment is due at the beginning of each period, this is an annuity due calculation rather than a regular annuity: PV = 64,329.48, N = 3, I/Y = 5, Compute PMT = 22,497.46	22,497.46

To Record First Payment			
Jan 1, 20X1	Lease Liability	22,497.46	
	Cash		22,497.46

Step 4 – Calculate Lease Amortization Schedule.

St. Matthew can now calculate a lease amortization and a lease expense schedule, with the implicit interest of 5 percent for the three-year period for an annuity due. As the first payment is paid at the beginning of the year, the effective balance of the lease is $41,832.02 on January 1. And, since 5 percent of the balance is the interest or $2,091.60, the principal that is being paid down is $20,405.68, leaving a balance of 21,426.16 ($41,832.02 – $20,405.86) at the beginning of Year 2. Using the same process, the entire lease amortization schedule can be completed. Due to rounding, any difference (in this example, $0.00) is added the last payment so the balance of the lease can be completely discharged.

Step 5 – Calculate Lease Expense Schedule.

The lease expense schedule is used to journalize the expenses at the end of the year on December 31, 20X1, 20X2, and 20X3. St. Matthew is using the straight-line approach, thus it is going to record equal amounts of lease expense of $22,497.46 for each of the three years, with the $0.01 adjustment, totaling $67,492.39 to GolfTrac, with a value of $64,329,48. At the end of each year, St. Matthew records part of its $22,497.46 lease payment as interest due to amortization of its ROU asset. Thus, for Year 1, of the $22,497.46 lease payment, $2,091.60 is recorded as interest and the remainder of $20,405.86 is the amount of amortization of the ROU asset. Subtracting $20,405.86 from the original value of $64,329.48, the carrying value of the ROU asset is $43,923.62 at the end of the first year.

For Year 2, of the $22,497.46 lease payment, $1,071.31 is recorded as interest and the remainder of $21,426.15 is the amount of amortization of the ROU asset. Subtracting $21,426.15 from the carrying value of $43,923.62, the new carrying value of the ROU asset is $22,497.47 at the end of the second year. Therefore, after the payment of $22,497.47 is made for the third year, the lease obligation is paid off. The $0.01 difference is being added to the last payment to totally discharge the lease. Exhibit 14.6 details the calculation.

At the end of Year 1, St. Matthew Golf Club will make the following journal entries to record the lease expense of $22,497.46 and will recognize the interest on the lease liability and also the amortization of the ROU asset.

Exhibit 14.5	Lease Amortization Schedule for St. Matthew Golf Club

St. Matthew Golf Club Lease Amortization Schedule

Date	Annual Lease Payment	Interest on Liability at 5%	Reduction of Lease Liability	Balance of Lease Liability
1/1/20X1				64,329.48
1/1/20X1	22,497.46	-0-	22,497.46	41,832.02
1/1/20X2	22,497.46	2,091.60	20,405.86	21,426.16
1/1/20X3	22,497.47	1,071.31	21,426.16	-0-
Total	67,492.39	3,162.91	64,329.48	

Lease Expense Schedule for St. Matthew Golf Club

St. Matthew Golf Club Lease Expense Schedule

Date	Lease Expense (Straight-line approach) (A)	Interest on Liability at 5% (B)	Amortization of ROU Asset (A-B)	Carrying Value of ROU Asset
1/1/20X1				64,329.48
12/31/20X1	22,497.46	2,091.60	20,405.86	43,923.62
12/31/20X2	22,497.46	1,071.31	21,426.15	22,497.47
12/31/20X3	22,497.47	-0-	22,497.47	-0-
Total	67,492.39	3,162.91	64,329.48	

To Record Lease Expense at End of Year 1			
Dec 31, 20X1	Lease Expense	22,497.46	
	Right-of-Use Asset		20,405.86
	Lease Liability		2,091.60

On January 1, 20X2, St. Matthew will again journalize the lease liability for the second payment, just like it did for the first payment.

To Record Second Payment			
Jan 1, 20X2	Lease Liability	22,479.46	
	Cash		22,479.46

And at the end of Year 2, St. Matthew will use the lease expense schedule to record the lease expense.

To Record Lease Expense at End of Year 2			
Dec 31, 20X2	Lease Expense	22,497.46	
	Right-of-Use Asset		21,426.15
	Lease Liability		1,071.31

For its last payment on January 1, 20X3, St. Matthew will record the final payment as follows:

To Record Third and Last Payment			
Jan 1, 20X3	Lease Liability	22,479.46	
	Cash		22,479.46

And the following entry reflects the recording of the lease expense for 20X3, the last year of the lease. With this last entry, the right-of-use asset is fully amortized.

To Record Lease Expense at End of Year 3			
Dec 31, 20X3	Lease Expense	22,497.47	
	Right-of-Use Asset		22,497.47

Accounting for Finance Leases

Now that you have a good understanding of an operating lease, let's look at its counterpart, the finance lease. As discussed previously, so long as one of the five criteria is met, the lease is a finance lease. In essence, if the lease has substantive characteristics of a sale of the asset, it is a finance lease.

In the example below, Chocobake, a bakery for chocolate lovers, signed a lease with BakeEquip for an oven on January 1, 20X1. The fair value of the oven at the beginning of the lease is $45,000:

1. The lease is for a five-year term, non-cancelable, and the lease period is approximately the economic life of the leased oven.

2. At the end of the lease, BakeEquip retains the ownership of the oven.

3. There is no renewal clause in the lease, but there is a purchase option that Chocobake can execute at the end of the lease. The terms are very favorable, and it is reasonably certain that Chocobake will exercise that option at the end of the five-year lease.

4. The annual payment is $10,000 per year for the 5 years.

5. The implicit rate of the lessor BakeEquip is at 5 percent, thus Chocobake will use the 5 percent for the lease calculation.

The Analysis

Step 1 – Determine Type of Lease.
   Using the five criteria stated, this scenario indeed is a finance lease because:

1. Lease transfers ownership of property by the end of the lease term – NO.

2. Lease grants the lessee an option to purchase the asset and is reasonably certain to exercise – **YES, this makes the lease a finance lease.**

3. Lease term is for a major part of the remaining economic useful life of the asset – **YES, this makes the lease a finance lease.**

4. Sum of the present value of the lease payments and present value of any residual value guaranteed by the lessee equal or exceed substantially all of the fair market value of the asset – **YES, this makes the lease a finance lease**
   (Present value of the five payments of $10,000 per year at 5 percent as an annuity due is $45,459.51, which exceeds the fair market value of $45,000.)

5. Asset is of a specialized nature and is not expected to have an alternative use to the lessor at the end of the lease term – NO.

Step 2 – Compute Lease Payment.
   Since the lease payment is given at $10,000 per year for five years, lease payment calculation is not needed. However, the value of the right-of-use asset has

to be calculated. The capitalized amount will be taking the $10,000 payment and multiplying it by the present value interest factor of an annuity due at 5 percent for five years (4.5460), which totals to $45,460. Alternatively, this can be calculated with a business calculator or a spreadsheet with the following variables for an annuity due:

Payment = $10,000, N = 5, I/Y = 5%, Compute PV, and PV = $45,459.51.

Again, with the present value interest factor of an annuity due only rounded to three decimal points, the answer from the business calculator of $45,459.51 will be more accurate.

Step 3 – Journalize Entries to Record Lease and First Payment.

Using these numbers, Chocobake can make the following entries to record the finance lease and the first payment of the lease on January 1, 20X1. The present value of the lease payments of $45,459.51 is used rather than the total lease payments of $50,000.

To Record Finance Lease			
Jan 1, 20X1	Right-of-Use Asset	45,459.51	
	Lease Liability		45,459.51

To Record First Payment			
Jan 1, 20X1	Lease Liability	10,000.00	
	Cash		10,000.00

Step 4 – Calculate Lease Amortization Schedule.

Chocobake can now calculate a lease amortization and a lease expense schedule, with the implicit interest of 5 percent for the five-year period for an annuity due to determine the annual interest expense. As the first payment is paid at the beginning of the year, the effective balance of the lease is $35,459.51 on January 1. And, since 5 percent of the balance is the interest or $1,772.98, the principal that is being paid down is $8,227.02, leaving a balance of $27,232.49 ($35,459.51 – $8,227.02) at the beginning of Year 2. Using the same process, the entire lease amortization schedule can be completed, and the $0.01 difference in the total reduction of debt and the lease itself is due to rounding and is added to the last lease payment to discharge the lease. Again, each lease payment of $10,000 includes two parts: the interest on the lease liability and the reduction of the lease liability itself. The interest is effectively the financing cost of the oven.

Step 5 – Journal Entries on the Balance Sheet and Income Statement

At the end of Year 1, Chocobake will make the following journal entries to record the interest expense of $1,772.98 as follows:

To Record Lease Expense at End of Year 1			
Dec 31, 20X1	Lease Expense	1,772.98	
	Lease Liability		1,772.98

Exhibit 14.7   Lease Amortization Schedule for Chocobake

Chocobake Lease Amortization Schedule

Date	Annual Lease Payment	Interest on Liability at 5%	Reduction of Lease Liability	Balance of Lease Liability
1/1/20X1				45,459.51
1/1/20X1	10,000.00	-0-	10,000.00	35,459.51
1/1/20X2	10,000.00	1,772.98	8,227.02	27,232.49
1/1/20X3	10,000.00	1,361.62	8,638.38	18,594.11
1/1/20X4	10,000.00	929.71	9,070.29	9,523.82
1/1/20X5	10,000.01	476.19	9,523.82	-0-
Total	50,000.01	4,540.50	45,459.51	

In addition, Chocobake will also amortize the right-of-use asset, using the straight-line method, by simply dividing the total lease liability by the lease period ($45,459.51 ÷ 5 years = $9,091.90).

To Record Amortization Expense at End of Year 1		
Dec 31, 20X1 Amortization Expense	9,091.90	
Right-of-Use Asset		9,091.90

Therefore, in the balance sheet, on December 21, 20X1, the five-year right-of-use asset and the liabilities associated with it are as follows:

Assets:	
Right-of-Use Assets ($45,459.51 − $9,091.90)	$36,367.61
Current Liabilities	
Lease Liabilities ($1,772.98 + $8,227.02)	$10,000.00
Long-Term Liabilities	
Lease Liabilities	$27,232.49

And, in the income statement, for the year ending December 31, 20X1, both the interest expense and the amortization expense will be shown:

Expenses:	
Interest Expense (lease liabilities)	$1,772.98
Amortization Expense (right-of-use assets)	$9,091.90

On January 1, 20X2, the second lease payment will be journalized as follows:

To Record Second Payment			
Jan 1, 20X2	Lease Liability (1,772.98 + $8,227.02)	10,000.00	
	Cash		10,000.00

The same entries, the interest expense and amortization expense, will need to be recorded each year as that will decrease the lease liability and also the right-of-use assets accounts in the balance sheet. At the end of the five-year lease, both the lease liability account and the right-of-use assets account will have a zero balance as the lease obligation will be discharged.

14.3 LEASEHOLD IMPROVEMENTS

Buildings that are leased for several years, such as restaurants in shopping malls, often require extensive improvements before the commencement of operations. Often, the space leased is not capitalized since none of the capitalization criteria is met. However, any improvements to the space must be capitalized as **leasehold improvements**. For example, the cost of walls, ceilings, carpeting, and lighting is an intangible asset, and the cost must be amortized against revenue over the life of the lease or the life of the leasehold improvement, whichever is shorter. For example, assume that the Chambers Hotel leased three acres of adjoining land for parking facilities and the land was improved by adding storm sewers, sidewalks, lighting, and pavement at the cost of $200,000. Further assume that the life of the improvement is 10 years, while the land was leased for 30 years. The annual amortization of the leasehold improvement would be 1/10 of the cost—$20,000 per year for 10 years. This expense is generally recognized monthly (1/12 of annual amortization) as follows:

Amortization of Leasehold Improvement	$1,666.67	
Leasehold Improvement		$1,666.67

14.4 SALE AND LEASEBACKS

Sale and leasebacks, or sometimes known as sale-leasebacks, are transactions whereby an owner of real estate agrees to sell the real estate to an investor and then lease it back. The original owner's use of the property continues without interruption. The property is sold to the investor (lessor) at market value and then leased back to the seller (lessee) for an amount equal to the investor's cost plus a reasonable return.

The major reason for sale and leaseback transactions is to raise capital that was previously tied up in the property. The investors in these transactions are usually looking for a financial return, as they have no interest in managing hospitality operations. For the lessees, they can negotiate the lease agreement to include repurchase clauses or refinancing options. As land is not a depreciable asset, if the lease has a substantive land component, then a sale-leaseback option can also lessen the tax payments.

First, one important consideration in identifying if the transaction is a true sale-leaseback or strict financing is whether there is a sale of the underlying asset. If the control is transferred from the lessee to the lessor, then it is a sale; if not, it is a simple financing transaction. The lessee should account for the lease based on the FASB's five criteria for classifying leases. If the seller (lessee) makes a profit from the sale of the now leased assets, such profit should generally be deferred and amortized over the lease term. Losses should be recognized in their entirety when the sale and leaseback agreement is signed.

Let us look at an example and the journal entries to record a sale-leaseback transaction. A very successful restaurant, Steak 77, sold all the kitchen equipment to BankOne on January 1, 20X0 for a sum of $500,000 that has a book value of $475,000, and negotiated an immediate leaseback. The terms of the lease are as follows:

1. The term of the lease is 3 years. The lease agreement is non-cancelable, requiring equal rental payments of $120,000 at the end of each year (ordinary annuity basis), beginning December 31, 20X0.

2. The lease contains no renewal or purchase options. The equipment reverts to BankOne at the termination of the lease.

3. The equipment has a fair value of $500,000 on January 1, 20X0, and an estimated remaining economic life of 5 years. The residual value (unguaranteed) at the end of the lease is $50,000.

4. The annual payments assure the lessor a 6 percent return.

The Analysis

Step 1 – Determine Type of Lease.
Using the five criteria stated, this scenario is an operating lease because:

1. Lease transfers ownership of property by the end of the lease term – NO.

2. Lease grants the lessee an option to purchase the asset and is reasonably certain to exercise – NO.

3. Lease term is for a major part of the remaining economic useful life of the asset – NO.

4. Sum of the present value of the lease payments and present value of any residual value guaranteed by the lessee equal or exceed substantially all of the fair market value of the asset – NO (320,761.43 is only 64.15 percent of the fair value of $500,000).

5. Asset is of a specialized nature and is not expected to have an alternative use to the lessor at the end of the lease term – NO.

Applying the classification tests, the leaseback of the equipment is classified as an operating lease. Since BankOne still controls the asset at the end of the lease and Steak 77 only has the right-of-use for the three years, this is a true sale. Thus, the journal entries to record this transaction are indicated as follows:

To Record Sale of Equipment and Lease			
Jan 1, 20X0	Cash	500,000.00	
	Gain on Sale		25,000.00
	Equipment		475,000.00
Jan 1, 20X0	Right-of-Use Asset	320,761.43	
	Lease Liability		320,761.43

As the sale price of equipment is higher than its book value, Steak 77 records a gain on sale of $25,000. The value of the right-of-use asset is the present value of a regular annuity of three payments of $120,000 per year payable at the end of the year. Exhibit 14.8 shows the details of the amortization schedule with the lease value being $320,761.43. Thus, this is the right-of-use asset value. Accordingly, a lease liability is also established for the same amount.

Exhibit 14.8	Lease Amortization Schedule for Steak 77

Steak 77 Lease Amortization Schedule

Date	Annual Lease Payment	Interest on Liability at 6%	Reduction of Lease Liability	Balance of Lease Liability
1/1/20X0				320,761.43
12/31/20X0	120,000.00	19,245.69	100,754.31	220,007.12
12/31/20X1	120,000.00	13,200.43	106,799.57	113,207.54*
12/31/20X2	120,000.00	6,792.45	113,207.55*	-0-
Total	360,000.00	39,238.57	320,761.43	

*difference due to rounding

At the end of the first year, the first lease payment of $120,000 is made on December 31, 20X0. As a payment is made, the lease liability is also being reduced, and so is the value of the right-of-use asset. Exhibit 14.9 shows the amortization of the ROU asset and also the reduction of the carrying value. The journal entries to record this lease payment are as follows:

To Record First Payments			
Dec 31, 20X0	Lease Expense	120,000.00	
	Lease Liability	100,754.31	
	Right-of-Use Asset		100,754.31
	Cash		120,000.00

Similar sets of entries are made at the end of Year 2 and Year 3 on December 31, 20X1 and December 31, 20X2, respectively. After the third payment is made, the lease obligation is discharged.

To Record Second and Third Payments			
Dec. 31, 20X1	Lease Expense	120,000.00	
	Lease Liability	106,799.57	
	Right-of-Use Asset		106,799.57
	Cash		120,000.00
Dec 31, 20X2	Lease Expense	120,000.00	
	Lease Liability	113,207.55	
	Right-of-Use Asset		113,207.55
	Cash		120,000.00

Exhibit 14.9	Lease Expense Schedule for Steak 77

Steak 77 Lease Expense Schedule

Date	Lease Expense (Straight-line approach) (A)	Interest on Liability at 5% (B)	Amortization of ROU Asset (A-B)	Carrying Value of ROU Asset
1/1/20X1				320,761.43
12/31/20X1	120,000.00	19,245.69	100,754.31	220,007.12
12/31/20X2	120,000.00	13,200.43	106,799.57	113,207.54*
12/31/20X3	120,000.00	6,792.45	113,207.55*	-0-
Total	360,000.00	39,238.57	320,761.43	

*difference due to rounding

Students interested in a more detailed discussion of this topic are encouraged to consult an intermediate accounting text.

14.5 LEASES AND THEIR EFFECT ON FINANCIAL RATIOS

Whether a leased item is accounted for as a finance lease or an operating lease, it has to be shown in the balance sheet as a right-of-use asset and also a lease liability. The value of these two accounts will then be amortized over the term of the lease. Therefore, several financial ratios are affected. The balance sheet disclosure of leases includes both assets and liabilities. Thus, most financial ratios involving noncurrent assets and long-term liabilities are affected by how leases are accounted for. Four financial ratios affected by capitalizing leases are shown in Exhibit 14.10. In general, leases negatively affect these ratios; that is, the ratios suggest a less desirable financial situation as both and liabilities increase with a lease.

Ratio	Ratio Formula	How Lease Affects Ratio
1. Asset Turnover	*revenue ÷ average total assets*	Leases result in increasing the average total assets, therefore reducing the asset turnover ratio
2. Return on Assets	*net income ÷ average total assets*	Increase in the average total assets will also reduce the return on assets
3. Debt-Equity Ratio	*total debt ÷ total equity*	Leases also result in increasing total debt, therefore increasing the debt-equity ratio
4. Times Interest Earned	*earnings before interest and taxes ÷ interest expense*	As interest expense increases with leases, leases therefore will reduce the times interest earned ratio

14.6 CHOOSING TO BUY OR LEASE

Should a hospitality operation lease or buy equipment? The elements to consider when answering this question include the effect of the decision on taxes and the time value of money. Each will be considered as we explore the concept of leasing versus buying.

Calculating the Options

Suppose the management of the hypothetical Michigan Resort (MR) must decide whether to buy or lease a fairway mower. To begin with, let's consider only the purchase cost of the fairway mower and the lease payments the MR would have to make for the buy and lease options. Assume that the purchase cost of the mower is $25,000, while the annual lease payments would be $6,000 at the signing of the lease for the first year and $5,565 for the next four years (paid at the end of Years 1–4). Further assume that the MR is responsible for maintenance with either option. The lease payments total $28,260; therefore, the apparent advantage to the MR of buying over leasing is $3,260.

However, we must not forget to consider the time value of money. Assume that the MR's relevant interest rate for this scenario is 10 percent. To compare the costs of buying and leasing, the present value of the cash payments for each must be determined. The cost of the mower is not discounted, since we assume the mower is paid for with cash at the beginning of the first year. The initial lease payment made at the signing of the lease is not discounted. However, the future lease payments must be discounted to recognize the present value of those payments. Cash flows covering the lease payments for the five-year period should be discounted as follows:

Present value of first payment:	$ 6,000
Present value of next four (annuity) payments:	
$5,565 (PVA $_{n\,=\,4,\,k\,=\,10}$) = $5,565 × 3.1699	$17,640
Total	$23,640

This result suggests that leasing the mower would cost $1,360 less ($25,000 −$23,640) than buying it.

However, there are yet other considerations—in particular, taxes and the salvage value of the mower at the end of the five years. Tax considerations for the purchase options involve treating the lease payment as an expense each year. Salvage value must be considered since, under the buy alternative, the salvage value provides cash.

Assume that, based on discussions with the equipment dealer, the MR's golf course superintendent estimates that the salvage value of the mower will be $6,000; that is, the mower can be sold for $6,000 at the end of year five. Further assume that the MR's tax rate is 30 percent, and that the enterprise uses the straight-line method of depreciation. Exhibit 14.11 presents the effects of considering taxes and salvage value.

This time, buying appears to be more advantageous than leasing by a mere $237. Note, however, that this is just an example based on assumptions. If the salvage value of the mower were somewhat lower, then the net result would probably favor leasing. On the other hand, a faster depreciation of the mower under the buy option might favor buying, and so on.

In addition, this example considers only the proposed lease without an option to buy the mower at a nominal price at the end of the lease period. Under many leases, especially capital leases, this option is available. When a hospitality business is not subject to income tax, the approach is simply to compare the

Exhibit 14.11	Discounted Cash Flow Payments–Considering Tax Effects and Salvage Value					

	Time Years					
	0	1	2	3	4	5
Purchase Option						
Purchase price	$ 25,000					
Salvage value						−$6,000
Depreciation tax shield[1]	-0-	− $1,140	− $1,140	− $1,140	− $1,140	− $1,140
Net purchase cost						
Annual cash flows	25,000	− 1,140	− 1,140	− 1,140	− 1,140	− 7,140
Discount factors	× 1	× .9091	× .8264	× .7513	× .6830	× .6209
Present value of cash flows	$ 25,000	$1,036	−$ 942	−$ 856	−$ 779	−$4,433
	Total present value of cash flows for purchase option = $16,954					
Lease Option						
Lease	$6,000	$5,565	$5,565	$5,565	$5,565	-0-
Lease tax shield[2,3]		− 1,800	− 1,670	− 1,670	− 1,670	− 1,670
Annual cash flow	6,000	3,765	3,895	3,895	3,895	− 1,670
Present value factors	× 1	× .9091	× .8264	× .7513	× .6830	× .6209
Present value of cash flows	$6,000	$3,423	$3,219	$2,296	$2,660	−$1,037
	Total present value of cash flows from lease option = $17,191					
	Difference—apparent advantage of buying:	$237				

[1] Depreciation expense × Tax rate = Depreciation tax shield

Depreciation expense:

$$\frac{\$25,000 - \$6,000}{5} = \$3,800$$

$3,800(0.30) = $1,140

[2] $6,000(0.30) = $1,800
[3] $5,565(0.30) = $1,670

Exhibit 14.12	Discounted Cash Flow Payments–Capital Lease vs. Purchase Options

	Time Years					
	0	**1**	**2**	**3**	**4**	**5**
Purchase Option						
Purchase price	$25,000					
Salvage value						−$6,000
Annual cash flows −6,000	25,000	−0−		−0−	−0−	−0−
Present value factors	× .1					× .6209
Present value of annual cash flow	$25,000					−$3,725

Total present value of cash flows for purchase option = $21,275

	0	**1**	**2**	**3**	**4**	**5**
Lease Option						
Lease payments	$6,000	$5,565	$5,565	$5,565	$5,565	-0-
Nominal price						$1,000
Nominal price						−$6,000
Annual cash flows	6,000	5,565	5,565	5,565	5,565	−1,670
Present value factors	× .1	× .9091	× .8264	× .7513	× .6830	× .6209
Present value of annual cash flow	$6,000	$5,059	$4,599	$4,181	$3,801	$3,105

Total present value of cash flows from lease option = $20,535
Difference—apparent advantage of buying: $740

* Taxes are not considered in this example. The assumed purchase price at the end of the lease period is a nominal amount of $1,000.

present value of the cash flows and select the alternative with the lowest cash outflow. Exhibit 14.12 depicts an example that ignores taxes and assumes a purchase price of $1,000 at the end of the lease.

These are just two examples that illustrate a systematic way of carefully comparing the alternative costs of leasing and buying equipment. Each example will result in different numbers, yet the process of evaluation is the same.

Sample Application

Exhibit 14.13 is a quote received by the ABC Golf Course (ABC) from a Deere dealer for a John Deere 3215B Fairway Mower. The acquisition alternatives available to ABC are as follows:

Purchase cost	=	$30,591
True lease—36 months	=	$705.43 per month
Lease/purchase—36 months	=	$964.23 per month

Exhibit 14.13   Sample Equipment Quote

JOHN DEERE
WEINGARTZ SUPPLY CO., INC.
GOLF and TURF

August 28, 20X1

ABC Golf Course
Joe Superintendent
123 Golf Lane
Anywhere, MI 48000
Fax: 555-GOLF

Dear Joe:

We are pleased to quote on the following equipment for your consideration.

Quan	Model #	Description	Unit Price	Total Price
1	1662M	John Deere 3215B Fairway Mower 31.5 hp Fairway Traction Unit	$30,591.00	$30,591.00
	4000	2 Wheel Drive		
	1025	(5) 7 Blade Heavy Section Cutting Units		
	2045	(5) 3" Spiral Design Self Cleaning Rollers		

List Price $36,425.00

36-Month True Lease Monthly Payment	**$705.43**
36-Month Lease/Purchase $1.00 Buyout **Monthly Payment**	**$964.23**

This quote is good for 30 days. Prices and payments do not include any applicable taxes.

Respectfully Submitted,
Joe Salesman

We will assume that the costs of maintenance are the responsibility of ABC, regardless of how the fairway mower is acquired. We also assume that the mower will have a salvage value of $10,000 at the end of three years. Further, to simplify the illustration, we assume that ABC is a not-for-profit organization, so income taxes can be ignored. In addition, the discount factor will be 12 percent on an annual basis, or 1 percent monthly.

What should Joe Superintendent of ABC do? Based on the analysis of the annual cash flows for the three options, it appears Joe should select the true lease option. Exhibit 14.14 reveals that the present value of cash flows for this option is $21,451.12 compared to $22,202.30 for the lease/purchase option and $23,473 for the purchase.

The major assumptions in this illustration are the discount rate and the salvage value. If these change significantly, the analysis will reveal a different decision.

Exhibit 14.14   Analysis of Purchase/Lease Options

Purchase Option

Cost	$ 30,591.00
Salvage Value (3 years hence)	
$10,000 × .7118[1]	(7,118.00)
Present value of cash flows	$ 23,473.00

True Lease Option

Initial monthly payment	705.43
Future lease payments (present value)	
$705.43 × 29.4086[1]	20,745.71
Present value of cash flows	$ 21,451.14

Lease/Purchase Option

Initial monthly payment	964.23
Future lease payments (present values)	
$964.23 × 29.4086[2]	28,356.65
Salvage value (present value)[3]	(7,118.00)
Present value of cash flows	$ 22,202.88

[1]Present value factor 12 percent/3 years

[2]Present value factor 1 percent/35 months

$$\text{Present value factor} = \frac{1 - \dfrac{1}{(1 + i)^n}}{i}$$

i = discount factor of 1%

n = 35 months

[3]This assumes the $1 is paid and the mower could be sold for $10,000. The $1 payment is ignored to simplify the present value calculations.

Leasing is a special type of financing used by many hospitality businesses. By entering into a lease agreement, the lessee acquires the right to use specific resources for a limited time and a specific purpose. The advantages for the lessee include the conservation of working capital, the benefits of tax deductions that might not otherwise be available, and, in some cases (when the lease is accounted for as an operating lease), a favorable effect on the balance sheet ratios. In exchange for these advantages, the lessee must make some sacrifices. In many instances, the residual value of the property remains with the lessor, there may be substantial penalties for termination of the lease contract, and the cost of leasing may be higher than purchasing the leased item. The operator contemplating a lease arrangement must weigh the advantages and disadvantages before entering into the contract.

In many cases in the hospitality industry, the lease contract proves advantageous. There are many aspects common to most leases. Provisions contained in most lease contracts include the length and purpose of the contract, the specific rent payments, any lessee obligations, and renewal options.

When deciding between leasing and purchasing an asset, many businesses consider how the agreement will affect the financial statements.

In addition to accounting for the initial lease, leasehold improvements must be recorded and subsequently amortized over either the life of the lease or the life of the improvement, whichever is shorter. Management should study all the variations of the lease agreement before signing any contract. Other establishments may value the difference between the total lease payments and the benefits of having a present cash flow.

Historically, leases have been a popular way to finance assets. The trend indicates that leases will continue as viable means of hospitality financing, especially for equipment.

contingent rent—Rent based on specified variables, such as a percentage of revenues above a given amount.

economic life—Refers to the useful life of the leased property.

executory costs—Obligations for property taxes, insurance, and maintenance of leased property.

fair market value—Represents the amount the leased item would cost if it were purchased rather than leased.

finance leases—A classification of lease agreements that are of relatively long duration, generally non-cancelable, and in which the lessee assumes responsibility for executory costs.

lease—An agreement conveying the right to use resources (equipment, buildings, and/or land) for specified purposes for limited periods of time. The lessor owns the property and conveys the right of its use to the lessee in exchange for periodic cash payments called rent.

leasehold improvements—Renovations or remodeling performed on leased buildings or space prior to the commencement of operations. For accounting purposes, all leasehold improvements are capitalized (i.e., recorded as an asset with recognition of a liability).

lessee—Party that makes periodic cash payments called rent to a lessor in exchange for the right to use property.

lessor—Party that owns property and conveys the right of its use to the lessee in exchange for periodic cash payments called rent.

management contract—Contract under which hotel owners make substantial payments from the hotel's gross revenues to hotel management companies.

operating lease—A classification of lease agreements that are usually of relatively short duration, easily cancelled, and in which the lessor retains responsibility for executory costs.

rent—Cash payments made by a lessee to a lessor.

residual value—With regard to leasing, the estimated market value of a leased item at the end of the lease term.

sale and leaseback—A transaction whereby an owner of real estate agrees with an investor to sell the real estate to the investor and simultaneously rent it back for a future period of time, allowing uninterrupted use of the property while providing the operation with capital that was previously tied up in the property.

triple-net lease—A form of lease agreement in which the lessee is obligated to pay property taxes, insurance, and maintenance on the leased property.

variable lease—A form of leasing agreement in which rental payments are based on revenues.

1. What are three major advantages to the lessee of lease financing?

2. What are some provisions common to most leases?

3. What are the FASB's five criteria for determining if a lease is a capital or an operating lease?

4. If a hotel operation enters into a finance lease agreement, what effect will it have on the debt-equity ratio?

5. What major effects do leases have on an operation's balance sheet?

6. What are leasehold improvements?

7. What is a sale and leaseback agreement?

8. What are lease executory costs and how do they influence the determination of whether a lessee should capitalize a lease?

9. What is meant by guaranteed residual value? How does it affect the present value of lease payments?

10. At what value is a capitalized lease recorded?

Problem 1

Mi Ran Kim leases the building in which her restaurant is located. For the past five years, she has paid rent of $5,000 per month. The lessor has proposed two alternative rental payment plans for the next three years as follows:

1. Monthly rent of $5,000 per month for the first year, $5,200 per month for the second year, and $5,400 per month for the third year.

2. Monthly rent of $4,000 per month and 1 percent of sales for each month for Years 1 to 3.

Mi Ran forecasts her average monthly sales as follows:

Year	Sales
1	$100,000
2	$120,000
3	$140,000

Required:

1. Calculate the total lease expense per year for each alternative.

Problem 2

Paula Anderson, owner of Anderson's Place, must renew her five-year building lease in three months. For the past five years, she has paid the lessor $4,200 per month. The lessor has suggested that Paula consider a variable lease of 5 percent of sales. Anderson's Place had total sales of $920,000 in 20X5 and expects total sales of $950,000 this year (20X6). Further, Paula expects total sales to increase by 12 percent per year beginning in 20X7. Assume Anderson's Place has a marginal tax rate of 25 percent.

Required:

1. Calculate the sales level at which the lease expense will be the same regardless of whether the lease is fixed or variable as proposed above.

2. Determine whether Paula should agree to the proposed arrangement or stay with the $4,200 per month.

3. Assume Paula makes the wrong decision. Calculate the after-tax cost of the error over the next five years.

Problem 3

Juan Perez is about to sign a lease for some golf equipment for his golf course. The previous lease, which if he chooses to continue, will be a monthly fee of $3,000 per month for the first year, with a 5 percent increase for the second year and another 5 percent the third year. If he goes with a new company, it will be $1,000 per month plus 1 percent of the golf revenue. Juan has the following average monthly projected revenue for the next three years below:

Year	Golf Revenue
1	$175,000
2	$225,000
3	$265,000

Required:

1. Calculate the total lease expense per year for each alternative.

2. Should Juan Perez continue with the current leasing company or choose the new one?

Problem 4

As Liam is opening his third restaurant, he has three locations that are very promising, but the lease payments are very different. The downtown location is asking for a fixed lease with no increase, simply $3,000 per month for the three-year lease. The uptown location offers him a lower lease in Year 1 at only $2,000 per month for the first year but will increase to $3,100 in Year 2 and $4,200 in Year 3. The suburb location is a mixed lease with a base of $1,750 per month and half a percent of the monthly sales. Liam is expecting monthly sales of $180,000 in year and that sales will increase by 15 percent per year.

Required:

1. Calculate the total lease expense per year for each alternative.

2. Which of the three options is best for Liam?

Problem 5

Kathy Waltz, owner of the new Trio Cafe, signed a building lease for three years for $1,000 per month on April 1, 20X9. This is an operating lease, and Kathy's incremental interest rate is at 5 percent.

Required:

1. Prepare the journal entry to record the operating lease.

2. Prepare the journal entry to record the first lease payment on April 1.

Problem 6

Food Truck Inc. is a business that does all the modification needed to change an ordinary truck into an all-purpose food truck. Javier Mercado is considering leasing a truck from Food Truck Inc. for his taco truck venture. The terms of the lease are as follows:

1. The truck is not of any specialized nature and at the end of the lease, Food Truck Inc. can lease the truck to another lessee.

2. The truck has an estimated useful life of 10 years.

3. The lease is for two years starting January 1, 20X8 with the first payment due at signing and the last payment to be paid on December 31, 20X9.

4. The ownership of the truck is always that of Food Truck Inc.

5. There is no option for Javier to buy the truck after the two-year period whether his business succeeds or not.

6. The lease payment is $800 per month.

7. The fair market value of the truck is $50,000.

8. The implicit interest rate for Food Truck Inc. is 12 percent and is known to Javier Mercado.

Required:

1. Using the five criteria of the FASB, is this an operating or a finance lease? Explain your answer by providing justification for each criteria to derive your decision.

Problem 7

Irene Arredondo signed a lease with Premier Equipment for the kitchen equipment she needs to open her coffee shop and bakery. The lease was signed on January 1, 20X7. The fair value of the equipment at the beginning of the lease is $100,000:

1. The lease is for a four-year term, non-cancelable.

2. At the end of the lease, Premier Equipment retains the ownership of the equipment.

3. There is no renewal clause in the lease, but there is a purchase option that Irene can execute at the end of the lease. The terms are very favorable, and it is reasonably certain that she will exercise that option at the end of the four-year lease.

4. The annual payment is $30,000 per year for the 4 years with the first payment due at signing.

5. Irene has no knowledge of this rate, and her incremental rate of debt is at 7 percent.

6. The economic life of this equipment is estimated to be eight years.

7. If Irene is not going to exercise the option, Premier Equipment can easily lease it to another restaurateur.

Required:

Using the five criteria of the FASB, is this an operating or a finance lease? Explain your answer by providing justification for each criteria to derive your decision.

Problem 8

Tao Wang is considering leasing space for five years for his Chinese Buffet food establishment. He has three lease options as follows:

1. Fixed lease options:
   a. Pay $5,000 per month for 60 months beginning on the first day of the five-year lease.
   b. Pay $55,000 per year on the first day of each year for five years.

2. Mixed lease option: Pay $25,000 on the first day of each year and 3 percent of annual sales on the last day of each year for five years. The forecasted annual sales are $1,400,000 for the first year, and sales are expected to increase by 5 percent each year.

Assume Tao's cost of capital is 10 percent.

Required:

1. Determine the annual cash rents under each option.

2. Determine the present value of the cash rents under each option.

Problem 9

Soonmi Lee is considering signing a 10-year lease for her Oriental Garden Inn. Her two best alternatives are as follows:

	Alternative #1	Alternative #2
Monthly rent	$2,100	7 percent of sales
Energy costs	Paid by lessee	Paid by lessor
Repairs to building	Paid by lessee	Paid by lessor
Building insurance	Paid by lessee	Paid by lessor

The average monthly revenues over the 10-year period are expected to start at $40,000 and increase by $1,200 per month each year. The estimated monthly costs for energy, repairs, and building insurance total $1,000 and are expected to increase by $50 per month each year.

Required:

1. Determine the annual costs of each alternative over the 10-year period.

2. Based on cost minimization, which lease do you recommend? Why?

Problem 10

Fidencio Dover, owner of Fido's Pizzeria, has just signed a finance lease for several major machines (ovens and so forth). The lease required an initial payment of $12,000 when the lease was signed and five future payments of $12,000 each at one-year intervals. The restaurant's incremental interest rate is 12 percent.

Required:

1. Determine the amount of the lease liability.

2. Prepare an amortization table for the liability related to the capitalized lease. (Use the format provided in Exhibit 14.5.)

Problem 11

The Gopher Inn is contemplating the purchase or lease of new dishwashing equipment. Ron Chewning, owner of the Gopher Inn, has asked you to examine the proposed net lease arrangement, which is as follows:

1.	Term of lease	5 years
2.	Estimated life of equipment	8 years
3.	Incremental cost of borrowing	10 percent
4.	Average cost of borrowing	9 percent
5.	Lease payments due:	
6.	First payment due at signing (January 1, 20X1)	
7.	Next four payments annually beginning January 1, 20X2	
	—Annual lease payment amounts (include $500 maintenance)	$5,000
	—First lease payment amount (includes $500 maintenance)	$4,000
8.	Fair market value	$14,000
9.	Option to buy at the end of lease	No
10.	Will the equipment be given to lessee at the end of the lease term?	No

Required:

1. Determine the present value of the lease payments.

Problem 12

Sunny Park, owner of Park Inns, has just leased two vans for guest transportation. The term of the lease is three years. The lease requires quarterly payments of $2,500 at the beginning of each quarter. Assume an incremental borrowing rate of 16 percent.

Required:

1. Determine the present value of the lease payments.

2. What will be the total lease payment over the life of the lease?

3. How much interest expense is recorded over the life of the lease?

Problem 13

The Irish Inn is contemplating the purchase or lease of a new dryer. Tip O'Reilly, owner of the Irish Inn, believes that the lease should be an operating lease. He has asked you to examine the proposed arrangement, which is as follows:

1.	Term of lease:	6 years
2.	Estimated life of dryer:	9 years
3.	Average cost of debt:	11 percent
4.	Incremental cost of debt:	12 percent
5.	Lease payments due:	
	—first payment due at signing (January 1, 20X1)	
	—next five payments annually beginning January 1, 20X2	

6. Annual lease payment: $1,000
7. First lease payment: $1,000
8. Fair market value: $4,500

There is also no option to buy at the end of lease; the dryer reverts to lessor at the end of the lease period.

Required:

1. Is the owner correct in his belief that the lease is an operating lease? Show all your work in arriving at your decision.

2. What is the present value of the lease payment stream?

3. Prepare the journal entry to record the lease if indeed it should be a finance lease.

4. What is the amount of interest for 20X1?

5. What is the amount of interest over the life of the lease (20X1–20X5)?

6. Journalize the annual amortization expense of the lease.

Problem 14

The Betonya Hotel has decided to lease its computer system from IMC Corporation. The lease is a five-year net lease commencing on January 1, 20X1. Details of the lease and other information are as follows:

1. Quarterly lease payments are $5,500.

2. The lease payments include $200 for maintenance.

3. The first lease payment is to be made on March 31, 20X1.

4. The 19 additional future quarterly payments start on June 30, 20X1.

5. The estimated life of the computer system is eight years and the computer system's estimated market value at the end of the five years is $5,000.

6. The fair market value of the computer system is $75,000 on January 1, 20X1.

7. The lessee has agreed to guarantee a residual value of $4,000. It is probable that the expected residual value zero, thus the entire guaranteed residual value should be included in computation of the lease liability.

8. The lessor's implicit interest rate is 10 percent.

9. The lessee's average and marginal interest rates are 9 percent and 11 percent, respectively.

Required:

1. Is this an operating or finance lease? Why? Please explain and be specific.

2. Provide the journal entry to record the lease on January 1, 20X1.

3. Provide the journal entry to record the second payment.

Problem 15

Alfredo Salvador is contemplating the purchase or lease of a new computer for his hotel. The proposed lease arrangement is as follows:

1.	Term of lease:	5 years
2.	Estimated life of computer:	10 years
3.	Average cost of debt:	10 percent
4.	Incremental cost of debt:	9 percent
5.	Lease payments due:	
	a. first payment due at signing (January 1, 20X1)	
	b. next four payments annually beginning January 1, 20X2	
6.	Annual lease payment:	$10,000
7.	Fair market value:	$50,000
8.	Lessee's guarantee of residual value:	$5,000

The expected residual value is estimated to be zero.

Required:

1. Determine the present value of the payment stream.

2. Prepare the journal entry to record the finance lease and the first payment of the lease.

3. Prepare the journal entry to record the second lease payment.

Problem 16

On January 1, 20X5, the Clairemount Hotel plans to sign a five-year lease for its telephone system. Provisions of the lease are as follows:

1. The lease is non-cancelable.

2. Annual payments beginning on January 1, 20X5, are $35,000 each for five years.

3. The telephone system has a fair market value of $140,000 at January 1, 20X5.

4. The estimated useful life of the system is seven years.

5. Included in the $35,000 annual payment is $5,000 for maintenance costs.

6. The Clairemount Hotel's average and incremental interest rates are 12 percent and 11 percent, respectively. The lessor's implicit interest rate is 10 percent.

7. The Clairemount Hotel agrees to guarantee a residual value of $10,000.

Required:

1. Determine the present value of the lessee's payments related to the lease.

2. Is this an operating or finance lease? Explain your position.

Problem 17

The Koelling Hotel has just signed a net lease with IRC, Inc., for a new front office system. Lease provisions and other relevant information are as follows:

1. The lease term is five years starting on January 1, 20X2.

2. Annual payments are $60,000 starting on January 1, 20X2.

3. The fair market value of the system on January 1, 20X2, is $225,000.

4. The estimated economic life of the computer is seven years.

5. The lease payments include $10,000 for maintenance and $3,000 for insurance.

6. The Koelling Hotel's incremental borrowing rate is 10 percent, while IRC's implicit rate of return on leasing the computer is 12 percent.

Assume that the lease is a finance lease.

Required:

1. Provide the journal entry to record the first lease payment and the lease.

2. Provide the journal entry to record the second payment.

3. Calculate the total interest expense over the 5 years.

Problem 18

Robert Traub, owner/manager of Traub's Place, has just signed a seven-year net lease for kitchen equipment. Details are as follows:

1. The estimated life of the equipment is 10 years.

2. Semi-annual lease payments commencing with the signing of the lease on January 1, 20X3, are $10,000.

3. Each lease payment includes executory costs of $500.

4. Traub's incremental interest rate is 10 percent, while its average interest rate is 9 percent.

5. Traub's guarantees a residual value of $10,000.

6. The fair market value of the leased equipment is $90,000.

Assume that the lease is a finance lease.

Required:

1. Record the initial lease payment and the lease.

2. Prepare an amortization schedule for the lease liability.

Problem 19

Milton Lee signed a building lease for his restaurant. The lease is for eight years, and he also needs to spend $250,000 to paint the walls, ceiling, and change out the flooring. The life of the improvement is going to be the same as the lease of eight years.

Required:

1. Calculate the amount of the monthly amortization.

2. Prepare the journal entry.

Problem 20

The King's Inn's financial situation at the end of 20X3 and 20X4 is summarized as follows:

	20X3	20X4
Total property and equipment (fixed assets)	$5,800,000	$6,850,000
Total assets	$6,500,000	$7,600,000
Interest expense (for the year)	$ 600,000	$ 725,000
Income taxes (for the year)	$ 400,000	$ 420,000
Net income (for the year)	$ 500,000	$ 550,000

On January 1, 20X4, King's Inn leased the adjoining sports facilities for its guests to use. The lease was deemed a finance lease.

Required:

1. Calculate the following ratios for King's Inn:
   a. Return on fixed assets
   b. Return on total assets
   c. Number of times interest earned

2. Based on your calculations and your knowledge of operating and finance leases, how would the results of the ratios be different if the lease were an operating lease? Why?

Problem 21

Two lodging firms, East Coast and West Bank, began operations with 120-room properties and identical balance sheets.

Three years later, both "acquired" additional 100-room properties. East Coast's acquisition was valued at $3,000,000 and was financed in its entirety with a loan at an 8 percent interest rate from New York Insurance Co. West Bank "acquired" its additional 100 rooms by leasing the rooms from Lease More for 15 years. An 8 percent return for Lease More was built into the lease.

The balance sheet for each company prior to the "acquisitions" is as follows:

Total Assets	$5,000,000
Debt	2,500,000
Equity	2,500,000
Total Claims	$5,000,000

Required:

1. Show the balance sheet for East Coast after its acquisition.

2. Assume the lease for West Bank is a finance lease and that the present value of the lease payments is $3,000,000. Show the simplified balance sheet after the lease liability is recognized.

3. Calculate the debt-equity ratio for each company after the acquisition.

4. Assume the net income for each company for the year after the "acquisition" is $800,000. Furthermore, based on the balance sheets from required parts 1 and 2 above, determine the return on assets and return on equity for each company.

Problem 22

Flora Atkins is the owner of Flora House, a successful bed and breakfast inn. She sold the property to Big Hotel on January 1, 20X8 for a sum of $2,000,000 that has a book value of $1,950,000, and negotiated an immediate leaseback with the following terms:

1. The lease is for three years. The lease agreement is non-cancelable, with equal payments of $150,000 at the end of each year (ordinary annuity basis), beginning December 31, 20X8.

2. The lease contains no renewal or purchase options. The property reverts back to Big Hotel at the termination of the lease.

3. The fair value of Flora House on the day of sale of January 1, is the same as the sale price of $2,000,000.

4. The property has an estimated economic life of 20 years.

5. The interest rate use for this lease is at 8 percent.

Required:

1. Is this a true sale and leaseback? Explain and be specific.

2. Prepare the journal entry to record the sale and the lease liability.

Problem 23

On April 1, 20X9, Isaac Ip sold the equipment of his restaurant to Yummy Foods for $45,000 and has negotiated for a leaseback agreement with a lease for three years at $10,000 per year payable at the end of the year. His marginal interest rate is 6 percent, and the book value of the equipment is at $48,000. The lease agreement is non-cancelable and has no renewal or purchase options. The equipment will be Yummy Foods' property at the termination of the lease. The equipment is quite new and has had an estimated economic life of 10 years.

Required:

1. Is this a true sale and leaseback? Explain and be specific.

2. Prepare the journal entry to record the sale and the lease liability.

Problem 24

Mary Monet finally found the perfect building to open her restaurant. She signed this lease on January 1, 20X5 for five years with the first payment due at signing. The lease amount is $10,000 per year, and the lessor's implicit rate of interest is not known to Mary, so she has to use her own marginal rate of interest at 10 percent.

Required:

1. Prepare the amortization schedule for this lease.

2. What is the total interest Mary pays on this lease?

Problem 25

Jackson and Luke Mullins have long wanted to open a hunting lodge. The brothers grew up hunting, and this is their dream. Their uncle has a nice piece of property with a few cabins so the brothers offered their uncle a three-year lease, at $9,000 per payment every quarter, and they signed the lease on July 1, 20X4. Since this is their first business venture, their marginal cost of capital is quite high at 12 percent. However, their uncle let them make their first payment at the end of the first quarter on September 30, 20X4.

Required:

1. Prepare the amortization schedule for this lease.

2. What is the total interest Jackson and Luke have to pay on this lease?

15

INCOME TAXES

Chapter 15 Outline

Competencies

1. Describe how an individual's tax is determined and the major elements of Form 1040. (pp. 678–683)

2. Describe the differences between tax avoidance and tax evasion. (p. 683–685)

3. Describe the tax advantages and disadvantages of each form of business organization. (pp. 685–689)

4. Describe the various accounting methods available and how they can be used to minimize or postpone taxes. (pp. 689–697)

5. Explain how accounting for depreciation, preopening expenses, first-year losses, and loss carryforwards affects the reporting of income and expenses for tax purposes. (pp. 697–699)

6. Identify some of the issues management should consider with respect to state and municipal taxes and property taxes. (pp. 699–700)

KEY TERMS

accumulated earnings tax

assessed valuation

C corporation

certificate of limited partnership

corporation

double taxation

general partner

income exclusions

limited liability company (LLC)

limited partner

limited partnership

modified accelerated cost recovery system (MACRS)

partnership

property taxes

S corporation

sole proprietorship

tax avoidance

tax credits

tax deductions

tax evasion

In 1789, Benjamin Franklin wrote, "But in this world nothing can be said to be certain, except death and taxes."[1] Most businesses and individuals view taxes similarly—as a necessary evil. Most also try to pay as little tax as legally possible. Hospitality managers must attempt to minimize the operation's income taxes in order to increase the owners' financial returns. Questions about taxes addressed in this chapter include the following:

1. Are taxes a major consideration when purchasing capital assets?
2. What is the difference between income exclusions and deductions?
3. How do tax deductions differ from tax credits?
4. How do tax avoidance and tax evasion differ?
5. What are the advantages of a sole proprietorship form of organization?
6. What is double taxation?
7. How can double taxation be avoided by a corporate form of organization?
8. What is a limited partnership and what are its advantages over a general partnership?
9. Which federal tax forms does each type of organization file?

This chapter begins with a discussion of the effect of taxes on business decisions. It presents a brief history and explanation of the objectives of federal income taxes. Next, tax basics for the individual taxpayer are covered. Tax avoidance and tax evasion are discussed, followed by an overview, including the tax advantages and disadvantages, of the various forms of business organization. We then discuss cash versus accrual accounting and accounting income versus taxable income. Finally, state, municipal, and property taxes are discussed briefly.

The purpose of this chapter is not to explain all of the ramifications of the various tax laws, most of which are very complex. Rather, this chapter attempts to illustrate the importance of taxes in a hospitality operation's economic decisions.

15.1 TAX CONSIDERATIONS IN ECONOMIC DECISIONS

Taxes are an important consideration in most major financial decisions. For example, the purchase of furniture and equipment may be delayed because a new tax incentive will take effect the following year. This is not to suggest that an investment in fixed assets should be delayed simply because of a tax advantage. Other business goals may indicate that the purchase should be made immediately. However, when current business objectives allow a choice of timing, management should plan acquisitions to gain tax advantages that will lower the net cost of acquiring the asset and result in greater net income. Similarly, the disposition of marketable securities, investments, fixed assets, or even an entire business should be considered with the tax effects of the proposed transaction in mind.

Because federal, state, and city taxes may consume over 50 percent of a business's earnings, management must be ever vigilant to the effect tax rules may have on business decisions. One major purpose of hospitality associations such as the American Hotel & Lodging Association and the National Restaurant Association is to lobby for tax legislation beneficial to the hospitality industry.

15.2 HISTORY AND OBJECTIVES OF FEDERAL INCOME TAXES

Although the U.S. government first used an income tax to raise revenue during the Civil War, it was not until 1913 that the Sixteenth Amendment established the constitutionality of such a tax and cleared the way for federal income tax as we know it today. Since 1913, Congress has made amendments to the original law and charged the Treasury Department with its enforcement through its Internal Revenue Service (IRS) branch.

Until the late 1960s, major tax law changes were infrequent, often seven to 10 years apart. In recent years, however, significant changes have been made to the Internal Revenue Code nearly every year. The most recent major tax law was the Tax Cut and Job Act of 2017 (TCJA), which amended the Internal Revenue Code of 1986. Major changes included reducing tax rates for individuals and business corporations. The standard deduction and family tax credits were increased, and personal exemptions eliminated. Deductions for state and local income taxes and property taxes were limited, as well as mortgage interest deductions. The alternative minimum tax (AMT) was reduced for individuals and eliminated for corporations. Many of the provisions of the TCJA expire in 2025.

The primary objective of income taxes is to raise revenue necessary for the operation of the federal government. This goal has been expanded at various times to include stimulating certain aspects of the economy and accomplishing various social goals.

Exhibit 15.1 reveals the income and outlays for the federal government for fiscal year 2020 (which began on Oct. 1, 2019, and ended on Sept. 30, 2020). Those projections called for federal income of $34 trillion and outlays of

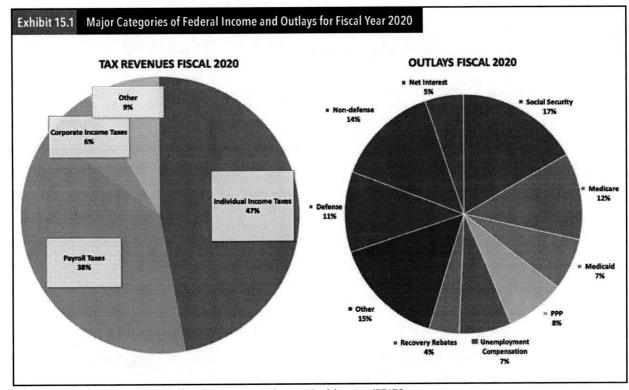

Exhibit 15.1   Major Categories of Federal Income and Outlays for Fiscal Year 2020

TAX REVENUES FISCAL 2020

- Other 9%
- Corporate Income Taxes 6%
- Individual Income Taxes 47%
- Payroll Taxes 38%

OUTLAYS FISCAL 2020

- Net Interest 5%
- Non-defense 14%
- Social Security 17%
- Medicare 12%
- Defense 11%
- Medicaid 7%
- Other 15%
- PPP 8%
- Recovery Rebates 4%
- Unemployment Compensation 7%

Source: Congressional Budget Office, https://www.cbo.gov/publication/57170.

Exhibit 15.2   Who Pays the Tax: 2012 vs. 2018

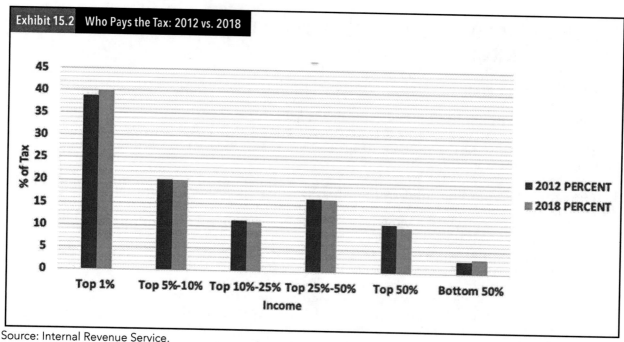

Source: Internal Revenue Service.

$6.6 trillion, leaving a deficit of $3.2 trillion, with personal income taxes making up 47 percent of the total federal government income. Who pays these taxes? Exhibit 15.2 shows a comparison of 2012 and 2018, reflecting several income percentiles, their share of adjusted gross income, and their percentage of federal income taxes.

15.3 TAX BASICS

Taxes are levied on individuals and corporations. The income of a sole proprietorship must be reported on the proprietor's individual tax return. Similarly, partnerships are not generally taxed, but their partners are. That is, partnerships must report their incomes to their partners, who must include their share of partnership income on their individual returns. The members of limited liability companies (LLCs) similarly must include their company incomes on their individual returns. Although corporations are separate legal entities in themselves, they are ultimately owned by individual investors. Therefore, corporate tax decisions are often based on the impact they may have on the individual investors. For example, the use of an accelerated method of depreciation reduces taxable income, which in turn reduces taxes and the cash paid in taxes. This allows more cash to be invested or more cash dividends to be paid to investors.

In other words, all of these forms of business organization ultimately affect individual tax returns. Thus, a brief discussion of individual income taxes is warranted.

The individual income tax return is Form 1040 (shown later in Exhibit 15.5). In 2021, individuals with gross income above a certain amount had to file Form 1040 or one of its variations, Form 1040A, Form 1040SR, Form 1040NR, or Form 1040EZ. An individual's tax is determined as follows:

	Income
Less:	Adjustments to Income
Equals:	Adjusted Gross Income (AGI)
Less:	Deductions
Less:	Qualified Business Income Deductions
Equals:	Taxable Income
Times:	Tax Rate
Equals:	Federal Income Tax
Less:	Tax Credits
Plus:	Other Federal Taxes
Equals:	Total Tax

In addition to Form 1040, several schedules must be filed, when appropriate. For example, Schedule C summarizes a sole proprietor's business for the year. Discussing all of the numerous schedules is beyond the scope of this chapter. All federal tax schedules and materials explaining these schedules are available at www.irs.gov.

The following brief discussion covers the major elements of Form 1040.

Income, Income Exclusions, and Adjustments

Income on Form 1040 includes, but is not limited to, wages, salaries, and tips (as reported on Form W-2), as well as interest and dividend income, business income or loss from a sole proprietorship, capital gains or losses, rents, royalties, partnership income or loss, and S corporation income or loss (S corporations are discussed later in the chapter).

Certain nontaxable income (such as interest from state and local government bonds), often referred to as **income exclusions**, is reported on the individual's tax return but excluded from income for tax purposes.

Gross income less adjustments to gross income (shown on Schedule 1) equals adjusted gross income (AGI). Adjustments to gross income include, but are not limited to, individual retirement account deductions and some other retirement investments.

Deductions and Taxable Income

Individual taxpayers should itemize tax deductions if their total deductions exceed the standardized deduction. Tax deductions are amounts that are deducted from AGI in accordance with prevailing tax laws. For example, in 2021, it was beneficial for married taxpayers (if neither was 65 or older or was blind) filing jointly to itemize if their deductions exceeded $25,100. Itemized deductions include medical and dental expenses in excess of 7.5 percent of AGI, other taxes (such as state and local income taxes) paid during the tax year, real estate taxes, home mortgage interest expense, contributions to charitable organizations, limited amounts for casualty and theft losses, and certain miscellaneous deductions.

Also, a qualified business income (QBI) deduction from Form 8995 or Form 8995-A may be taken if the taxpayer meets the requirements. As part of the TCJA, business owners are allowed a deduction from gross income on their tax returns related to their income from pass-through entities such as sole proprietorships, partnerships, limited liability companies, and S corporations. These will be discussed further in Section 15.5.

The qualified business income deduction (QBID) is determined by figuring the net profit for the business, which is then reduced by one-half of the self-employment (SE) tax included as an adjustment and payments for medical insurance, just to mention a couple reduction items. The net QBI is then multiplied by 20 percent to equal the amount of the reduction.

For example, assume a sole proprietorship (Schedule C) shows net profit (line 31) of $100,000. Further, assume that one-half of the SE tax is $7,065 and medical insurance paid by the business for the taxpayer is $5,000 for the year. The QBID would be calculated as follows:

Net profit from business	$100,000
Less: One-half SE tax	(7,065)
Less: cost of medical insurance	(5,000)
Net QBI	$ 87,935
	× 0.20
QBID	$ 17,587

Of course, there are limitations related to the QBID; the deduction cannot be more than 20 percent of the taxpayer's taxable income before the deduction, for example. There are also total taxable income limitations. These, as with many provisions of the Internal Revenue Code, are beyond the scope of this book.

Taxes and Credits

Income taxes are calculated on the basis of taxable income. The current tax rate system for individuals is graduated, with 2021 rates ranging from 10 percent to 37 percent. In addition, the tax code provides for minimum taxes (the *alternative minimum tax*) for certain individuals who would otherwise not have to pay income taxes. Income taxes less credits plus other applicable taxes equals the total taxes due.

In contrast to tax deductions, which are deducted from AGI to determine taxable income, **tax credits** are deducted directly from taxes due. Credits deductible from income taxes include, but are not limited to, credit for child and dependent care expenses and education credits.

Other taxes that must be added to the income taxes due include self-employment tax, commonly known as Social Security for the sole proprietor, and Social Security taxes on tip income not reported to the employer.

The tax code is quite complex, as are the many forms and schedules required to complete some individual tax returns. Individuals with complicated returns should strongly consider obtaining assistance from a tax expert.

A Tax Illustration

Warren and Mary Schmitz have one child and own Redbird Restaurant, an unincorporated business. Exhibit 15.3 presents a summary income statement of their restaurant operation, managed by Warren. Mary earns $60,000 as a part-time education specialist at the local community college. Her W-2 shows $15,000 withheld for federal income taxes. Exhibit 15.4 shows the Schmitzes' other income, adjustments to income, deductions, and other taxes. Exhibits 15.5 through 15.8 illustrate the Schmitzes' Form 1040, Schedule A, Schedule C, and Schedule 1, respectively. Schedule SE—Computation of Social Security Self-Employment Tax, and Form 4562—Depreciation must also be filed with the Schmitzes' return. These schedules are not included as exhibits here, but their results appear (as appropriate) on the exhibits; for example, the total depreciation of $102,366 from Form 4562 is shown on line 13 of Schedule C (Exhibit 15.7), and the self-employment tax of $16,197 from Schedule SE is shown on line 23 of Form 1040 Schedule 1. The self-employment tax is computed as follows:

Net profit (from Schedule C)		$ 114,634			
Reduced by 0.9235 factor		× 0.9235			
Net earnings from self-employment		$ 105,864			
			Tax Rate*		
Earnings subject to Social Security portion		$ 105,864	× 0.124 =		$13,127
Earnings subject to Medicare portion		$ 105,864	× 0.029 =		3,070
Total self-employment taxes					$16,197

Exhibit 15.3 Summary Income Statement–Redbird Restaurant

Summary Income Statement
Redbird Restaurant
For the year ended Dec. 31, 2021

Sales		$1,250,000
Cost of Sales		463,000
Gross Profit		787,000
Controllable Expenses:		
Payroll	$390,000	
Employee Benefits	40,000	
Taxes and Licenses	2,000	
Supplies	8,000	
Utilities	27,000	
Advertising	20,000	
Legal and Professional	3,000	
Office Expense	8,500	
Travel	4,500	
Repairs and Maintenance	3,000	
Other	24,000	530,000
Income before Occupation Costs		257,000
Rent		15,000
Insurance		15,000
Interest		10,000
Depreciation		102,366
Income before Taxes		$ 114,634

Exhibit 15.4 Information about the Schmitz Family Income

Other Income:
   Interest income of $5,000
Adjustments:
   A retirement plan of $15,000 (for Warren) IRA
Deductions:

Medical Expenses	$ –0–
Property taxes on house	4,500
Interest – mortgage on house	14,000
Contributions	18,000

Other Taxes:

Self-employment tax	16,197*
Federal taxes paid during year by Warren	$ 30,000

   * Per Schedule SE (not included)

* The first \$142,800 of net earnings during 2021 is subject to the Social Security tax portion of the self-employment taxes. All net earnings are subject to the Medicare portion of the self-employment taxes.

Notice that income from the restaurant, shown on Schedule C, is entered on Form 1040, line 8. The restaurant income is shown on Schedule 1 as is the deductible portion of the self-employment tax (\$16,197 × 0.50 = \$8,099). The QBI deduction (line 13 of Form 1040) is determined by multiplying the net income of \$114,634 from the restaurant less the SE deduction of \$8,099 by 20 percent (\$106,265 × 0.20 = \$21,307). Further, note the Schmitzes have a refund of \$12,786.

Exhibit 15.5   Schmitz Family Income Tax Return (Form 1040)

Form 1040   Department of the Treasury—Internal Revenue Service (99)   2021   U.S. Individual Income Tax Return   OMB No. 1545-0074   IRS Use Only—Do not write or staple in this space.

Filing Status Check only one box.
[ ] Single [X] Married filing jointly [ ] Married filing separately (MFS) [ ] Head of household (HOH) [ ] Qualifying widow(er) (QW)

If you checked the MFS box, enter the name of your spouse. If you checked the HOH or QW box, enter the child's name if the qualifying person is a child but not your dependent ▶

Your first name and middle initial	Last name	Your social security number
Warren B	Schmitz	337-38-3435

If joint return, spouse's first name and middle initial	Last name	Spouse's social security number
Mary Y	Schmitz	348-50-4359

Home address (number and street). If you have a P.O. box, see instructions.   1111 Redbird Avenue   Apt. no.

Presidential Election Campaign Check here if you, or your spouse if filing jointly, want \$3 to go to this fund. Checking a box below will not change your tax or refund.   [ ] You [ ] Spouse

City, town, or post office. If you have a foreign address, also complete spaces below.   Topeka   State KS   ZIP code 99999

Foreign country name   Foreign province/state/county   Foreign postal code

At any time during 2021, did you receive, sell, exchange, or otherwise dispose of any financial interest in any virtual currency? [ ] Yes [X] No

Standard Deduction Someone can claim: [ ] You as a dependent [ ] Your spouse as a dependent
[ ] Spouse itemizes on a separate return or you were a dual-status alien

Age/Blindness You: [ ] Were born before January 2, 1957 [ ] Are blind   Spouse: [ ] Was born before January 2, 1957 [ ] Is blind

Dependents (see instructions): If more than four dependents, see instructions and check here ▶ [ ]

(1) First name Last name	(2) Social security number	(3) Relationship to you	(4) ✔ if qualifies for (see instructions): Child tax credit	Credit for other dependents
Heidi X Schmitz	351-78-8964	Daughter	[ ]	[X]
			[ ]	[ ]
			[ ]	[ ]
			[ ]	[ ]

Attach Sch. B if required.

1	Wages, salaries, tips, etc. Attach Form(s) W-2		1	60,000.
2a	Tax-exempt interest	2a	b Taxable interest 2b	5,000.
3a	Qualified dividends	3a	b Ordinary dividends 3b	
4a	IRA distributions	4a	b Taxable amount 4b	
5a	Pensions and annuities	5a	b Taxable amount 5b	
6a	Social security benefits	6a	b Taxable amount 6b	
7	Capital gain or (loss). Attach Schedule D if required. If not required, check here ▶ [ ]		7	
8	Other income from Schedule 1, line 10		8	114,634.
9	Add lines 1, 2b, 3b, 4b, 5b, 6b, 7, and 8. This is your **total income** ▶		9	179,634.
10	Adjustments to income from Schedule 1, line 26		10	8,099.
11	Subtract line 10 from line 9. This is your **adjusted gross income** ▶		11	171,535.
12a	Standard deduction or itemized deductions (from Schedule A) 12a 36,500.			
b	Charitable contributions if you take the standard deduction (see instructions) 12b			
c	Add lines 12a and 12b		12c	36,500.
13	Qualified business income deduction from Form 8995 or Form 8995-A		13	21,307.
14	Add lines 12c and 13		14	57,807.
15	**Taxable income.** Subtract line 14 from line 11. If zero or less, enter -0-		15	113,728.

Standard Deduction for—
• Single or Married filing separately, \$12,550
• Married filing jointly or Qualifying widow(er), \$25,100
• Head of household, \$18,800
• If you checked any box under Standard Deduction, see instructions.

For Disclosure, Privacy Act, and Paperwork Reduction Act Notice, see separate instructions.   Form **1040** (2021)

16	**Tax** (see instructions). Check if any from Form(s): 1 ☐ 8814 2 ☐ 4972 3 ☐ _____			16	16,517.
17	Amount from Schedule 2, line 3			17	0.
18	Add lines 16 and 17			18	16,517.
19	Nonrefundable child tax credit or credit for other dependents from Schedule 8812			19	500.
20	Amount from Schedule 3, line 8			20	
21	Add lines 19 and 20			21	500.
22	Subtract line 21 from line 18. If zero or less, enter -0-			22	16,017.
23	Other taxes, including self-employment tax, from Schedule 2, line 21			23	16,197.
24	Add lines 22 and 23. This is your **total tax** ▶			24	32,214.
25	Federal income tax withheld from:				
a	Form(s) W-2	25a	15,000.		
b	Form(s) 1099	25b			
c	Other forms (see instructions)	25c			
d	Add lines 25a through 25c			25d	15,000.
26	2021 estimated tax payments and amount applied from 2020 return			26	30,000.
27a	Earned income credit (EIC)	27a			
	Check here if you were born after January 1, 1998, and before January 2, 2004, and you satisfy all the other requirements for taxpayers who are at least age 18, to claim the EIC. See instructions ▶ ☐				
b	Nontaxable combat pay election	27b			
c	Prior year (2019) earned income	27c			
28	Refundable child tax credit or additional child tax credit from Schedule 8812	28			
29	American opportunity credit from Form 8863, line 8	29			
30	Recovery rebate credit. See instructions	30			
31	Amount from Schedule 3, line 15	31			
32	Add lines 27a and 28 through 31. These are your **total other payments and refundable credits** ▶			32	
33	Add lines 25d, 26, and 32. These are your **total payments** ▶			33	45,000.

If you have a qualifying child, attach Sch. EIC.

No

Refund	34	If line 33 is more than line 24, subtract line 24 from line 33. This is the amount you **overpaid**		34	12,786.
	35a	Amount of line 34 you want **refunded to you**. If Form 8888 is attached, check here ▶ ☐		35a	12,786.
Direct deposit? See instructions.	▶b	Routing number X X X X X X X X X ▶c Type: ☐ Checking ☐ Savings			
	▶d	Account number X X X X X X X X X X X X X X X X X. X			
	36	Amount of line 34 you want **applied to your 2022 estimated tax** ▶	36		
Amount You Owe	37	**Amount you owe.** Subtract line 33 from line 24. For details on how to pay, see instructions ▶		37	
	38	Estimated tax penalty (see instructions) ▶	38		

Third Party Designee	Do you want to allow another person to discuss this return with the IRS? See instructions ▶ ☐ **Yes. Complete below.** ☒ **No**		
	Designee's name ▶	Phone no. ▶	Personal identification number (PIN) ▶

Sign Here

Under penalties of perjury, I declare that I have examined this return and accompanying schedules and statements, and to the best of my knowledge and belief, they are true, correct, and complete. Declaration of preparer (other than taxpayer) is based on all information of which preparer has any knowledge.

Your signature	Date	Your occupation entreprenuer	If the IRS sent you an Identity Protection PIN, enter it here (see inst.) ▶
Spouse's signature. If a joint return, **both must sign.**	Date	Spouse's occupation Education	If the IRS sent your spouse an Identity Protection PIN, enter it here (see inst.) ▶
Phone no.	Email address		

Joint return? See instructions. Keep a copy for your records.

Paid Preparer Use Only	Preparer's name	Preparer's signature	Date	PTIN	Check if: ☐ Self-employed
	Firm's name ▶ Self-Prepared			Phone no.	
	Firm's address ▶			Firm's EIN ▶	

Go to *www.irs.gov/Form1040* for instructions and the latest information.   BAA   REV 01/24/22 TTW   Form **1040** (2021)

15.4 TAX AVOIDANCE

Tax avoidance—that is, planning a transaction to mitigate the tax impact or to avoid the application of taxes completely—is entirely legal and should be aggressively pursued. Judge Learned Hand stated it well:

> Over and over again courts have said there is nothing sinister in so arranging one's affairs as to keep taxes as low as possible. Everybody does so, rich or poor; and all do right, for nobody owes any public duty to pay more than the law demands: taxes are enforced extractions, not voluntary contributions. To demand more in the name of morals is mere cant.[2]

Exhibit 15.6 The Schmitzes' Itemized Deductions

SCHEDULE A (Form 1040) Department of the Treasury Internal Revenue Service (99)	**Itemized Deductions** ▶ Go to www.irs.gov/ScheduleA for instructions and the latest information. ▶ Attach to Form 1040 or 1040-SR. **Caution:** If you are claiming a net qualified disaster loss on Form 4684, see the instructions for line 16.	OMB No. 1545-0074 20**21** Attachment Sequence No. **07**

Name(s) shown on Form 1040 or 1040-SR | Your social security number
Warren B & Mary Y Schmitz | 337-38-3435

Medical and Dental Expenses		**Caution:** Do not include expenses reimbursed or paid by others.		
	1	Medical and dental expenses (see instructions)	**1**	
	2	Enter amount from Form 1040 or 1040-SR, line 11	**2** 171,535.	
	3	Multiply line 2 by 7.5% (0.075)	**3** 12,865.	
	4	Subtract line 3 from line 1. If line 3 is more than line 1, enter -0-		**4**
Taxes You Paid	5	State and local taxes.		
	a	State and local income taxes or general sales taxes. You may include either income taxes or general sales taxes on line 5a, but not both. If you elect to include general sales taxes instead of income taxes, check this box ▶ ☐	**5a**	
	b	State and local real estate taxes (see instructions)	**5b** 4,500.	
	c	State and local personal property taxes	**5c**	
	d	Add lines 5a through 5c	**5d** 4,500.	
	e	Enter the smaller of line 5d or $10,000 ($5,000 if married filing separately)	**5e** 4,500.	
	6	Other taxes. List type and amount ▶	**6**	
	7	Add lines 5e and 6		**7** 4,500.
Interest You Paid **Caution:** Your mortgage interest deduction may be limited (see instructions).	8	Home mortgage interest and points. If you didn't use all of your home mortgage loan(s) to buy, build, or improve your home, see instructions and check this box ▶ ☐		
	a	Home mortgage interest and points reported to you on Form 1098. See instructions if limited	**8a** 14,000.	
	b	Home mortgage interest not reported to you on Form 1098. See instructions if limited. If paid to the person from whom you bought the home, see instructions and show that person's name, identifying no., and address ▶	**8b**	
	c	Points not reported to you on Form 1098. See instructions for special rules	**8c**	
	d	Mortgage insurance premiums (see instructions)	**8d**	
	e	Add lines 8a through 8d	**8e** 14,000.	
	9	Investment interest. Attach Form 4952 if required. See instructions	**9**	
	10	Add lines 8e and 9		**10** 14,000.
Gifts to Charity **Caution:** If you made a gift and got a benefit for it, see instructions.	11	Gifts by cash or check. If you made any gift of $250 or more, see instructions	**11** 18,000.	
	12	Other than by cash or check. If you made any gift of $250 or more, see instructions. You **must** attach Form 8283 if over $500.	**12**	
	13	Carryover from prior year	**13**	
	14	Add lines 11 through 13		**14** 18,000.
Casualty and Theft Losses	15	Casualty and theft loss(es) from a federally declared disaster (other than net qualified disaster losses). Attach Form 4684 and enter the amount from line 18 of that form. See instructions		**15**
Other Itemized Deductions	16	Other—from list in instructions. List type and amount ▶		**16**
Total Itemized Deductions	17	Add the amounts in the far right column for lines 4 through 16. Also, enter this amount on Form 1040 or 1040-SR, line 12a		**17** 36,500.
	18	If you elect to itemize deductions even though they are less than your standard deduction, check this box ▶ ☐		

For Paperwork Reduction Act Notice, see the Instructions for Forms 1040 and 1040-SR. **BAA** REV 09/02/21 TTW   Schedule A (Form 1040) 2021

Management can and should conduct the hospitality operation's business so as to achieve the lowest possible tax cost within the constraints of other business considerations and the prevailing tax laws and regulations. Good tax planning is simply good business management.

For example, consider the purchase or sale of a hospitality establishment. An incorporated seller must decide whether to sell the stock of the company or its assets. Assuming a gain on the transaction, the after-tax differences between these two alternatives can be dramatic. Even in a situation generating an overall loss, tax recognition of gain may be required on certain elements of the transaction if the decision was to sell assets rather than stock.

Conversely, a buyer will be reluctant to acquire the stock of a corporation if the tax basis of the corporation's assets is substantially below the selling price of the stock. In this situation, the buyer's goal is generally to acquire the assets of the corporation at their fair market value in order to preserve this higher base for future depreciation purposes. Even if the stock must be acquired, it is usually possible to effect a tax reorganization to realize a step-up in tax basis.

The point of all this is that, with proper tax planning, tax laws frequently allow both buyer and seller to realize most of their opposing goals. This fairly complex example also illustrates the need for most investors to consult tax experts in order to minimize their taxes. Recognizing these opportunities for tax planning and avoiding excessive or burdensome taxes is perfectly legal and represents a key management responsibility.

In contrast to tax avoidance, **tax evasion** is the fraudulent denial or concealment of a current or future tax liability, such as underreporting income or claiming unsubstantiated or excessive deductions. For example, a business that intentionally fails to report or underreports revenues, dividends, interest, fees, or profits from business transactions is guilty of tax evasion. Similarly, tax evasion occurs when nondeductible expenses (such as personal expenses or costs related to personal use of business property) are intentionally deducted on tax returns as business expenses. Activities of this nature are illegal and untenable for the management of any business.

15.5 FORMS OF BUSINESS ORGANIZATION

The importance of addressing tax questions early is perhaps best illustrated by looking at a new business. One of the basic decisions a businessperson must make is determining the legal form of an operation: sole proprietorship, partnership, limited liability company, corporation, or one of their hybrid forms, such as limited partnership or S corporation.

Each of these entities offers tax advantages and disadvantages. Tax considerations, however, are only one factor in such a decision. There are practical business and legal considerations, as well as governmental regulatory requirements. The following sections briefly discuss the forms of business organization and the major advantages and limitations of each. Exhibit 15.9 presents an outline of this information.

Sole Proprietorships

The **sole proprietorship** is the most common form of organization in the hospitality industry. As the name implies, the business is owned by a single individual. This form of organization is popular because it is easy to form. Establishing a sole proprietorship may only require filing an assumed business name statement with the proper authorities (such as the county government) and filing a Schedule C on the owner's federal, state, and local tax returns.

The following list indicates some advantages of the sole proprietorship form of organization:

1. Proprietorship eliminates double taxation (defined later under corporate disadvantages). Income is reported only on the owner's individual tax return.

2. Expected losses during start-up and the early years can offset the owner's other income. Losses that exceed the owner's other income may result in net operating losses that can be used to recover some or all of the owner's taxes in the future.

3. Business tax credits retain their character—that is, if they are tax credits to the business, they are tax credits to be used directly by the owner.

4. The owner maintains complete control over the business by being the sole owner.

Several disadvantages may discourage a hospitality business owner from operating as a sole proprietor. These disadvantages include the following:

1. Hospitality operations may be risky. The sole proprietor does not enjoy the limited liability available with some other organizational forms; that is, they are personally liable for the obligations of the business. However, adequate insurance can at least partially alleviate this problem.

2. Most benefits are severely limited or completely disallowed as deducted tax expenses if they are for the benefit of the sole proprietor. For example, only 60 percent of the cost of medical insurance for the sole proprietor can be included as a deductible tax expense.

3. The transfer of a portion of the ownership interest in a sole proprietorship requires a change to either partnership or corporate form. In addition, the continuity of the business is not assured at the death of the owner. By contrast, a corporation is legally separate from its owners.

4. The sole proprietor is generally unable to raise large amounts of capital, while a corporation may be able to issue stock or sell bonds.

The sole proprietorship may be an ideal form of organization if the anticipated risk is minimal and is covered by insurance, if the owner is either unable or unwilling to maintain the necessary organizational documents and tax returns of more complicated business entities, and if the business does not require extensive borrowing.

Partnerships

The **partnership** consists of two or more owners joined together but not incorporated, for the purpose of operating a business. A partnership offers most of the tax and other advantages and disadvantages of a sole proprietorship. The advantages include the following:

1. More than one owner results in greater financial strength. The added capital can provide greater resources for expansion of the business.

2. Partnership arrangements allow flexibility in the allocation of profits, losses, and certain tax benefits among the owners. Such allocations must be reasonable and justified as having economic substance in order to satisfy the IRS.

3. Profits, losses, and tax credits pass through the partnership entity to the owners' individual returns, thus preventing double taxation.

4. Control of the business resides with the partners.

Major disadvantages of the partnership include the following:

1. Partners are taxed on their share of the profits, regardless of whether the partnership actually provides a cash distribution to the partners.

2. Partners may become frustrated in sharing the decision-making process. They may hold different opinions, and, theoretically, each has an equal right to manage the business.

3. Partners generally have unlimited legal liability for the obligations of the business. This can be a significant factor when uninsurable business risks exist. This disadvantage may be partially overcome by the use of a limited partnership form of organization.

Limited Partnerships

A **limited partnership** is a partnership of two or more individuals having at least one **general partner** (a partner with unlimited liability) and at least one **limited partner** (a partner with limited liability). Unlike a general partnership agreement (which can be oral), the limited partnership agreement must be in writing, and the **certificate of limited partnership** document must be filed with the proper governmental authorities. Most states regulate the public sale of limited partnership interests. The process of filing documents with the Securities and Exchange Commission to sell limited partnership interests may result in sizable legal fees and other costs. Smaller private issues (issues not generally available to the general public) generally seek an exemption from registration.

The major distinguishing feature of limited partnerships is the limited liability afforded to limited partners: their liabilities are limited to their investments. However, limited partners cannot actively participate in controlling or managing the business. If they do, they will generally lose their limited liability status in any legal matters.

In recent years, the limited partnership has become an attractive financing vehicle for the expansion of hospitality operations. Limited partnerships have been formed for specific projects, with the hospitality establishment acting as the general partner and investors as the limited partners. The limited partnership enables the hospitality establishment to obtain needed capital and still maintain control over operations.

The basic tax advantages available to general partners are also available to limited partners. In addition to limited liability, another advantage available to limited partners (but not to general partners) is that, within certain limits, the limited partners' interests may be assigned without prior approval of the general partners.

Limited Liability Companies

A **limited liability company (LLC)** is a form of business that is relatively new in the United States. The LLC files articles of organization and is controlled by its operating agreement. It is an unincorporated organization that limits the liability of its owners (called *members*) to their investment, much as corporations do for stockholders and limited partnerships do for limited partners. In addition, the

LLC is treated like a partnership for tax purposes, so income and losses pass through to the members. This eliminates the double taxation faced by regular corporations. An LLC should be considered as the organizational format of choice for anyone who previously would have formed an S corporation, a general partnership, or a limited partnership. It offers more protection than a general partnership and is more flexible than an S corporation or a limited partnership. Unlike an S corporation, an LLC is not restricted to 100 or fewer owners; also, it can be layered with partnerships and corporations. An LLC can have different types of memberships and is not limited to one type of stock, as the S corporation is. All members of an LLC have limited liability, unlike the partners of a general partnership or the general partner(s) of a limited partnership. Furthermore, the members can have an active role in management, unlike limited partners of a limited partnership.

Yet an LLC is not for everyone. To begin with, LLCs must have at least two members, so this format is not an option for a sole proprietor. Also, because some states do not recognize the tax exemption status of LLCs, LLCs are liable to corporate income taxes in those states. In addition, an LLC does not have a perpetual life like a corporation.

Corporations

A **corporation** is a legal entity created by a state or another political authority. The corporation receives a charter or articles of incorporation and has the following general characteristics:

1. An exclusive name

2. Continued existence independent of its stockholders

3. Paid-in capital represented by transferred shares of capital stock

4. Limited liability for its owners

5. Overall control vested in its directors

While hospitality businesses organized as sole proprietorships account for the largest number of businesses, hospitality corporations account for the greatest volume in terms of sales, assets, profits, and employees. Revenues from corporate lodging businesses constitute nearly two-thirds of the total lodging revenues across the United States.[3] Several hospitality corporations, such as Hilton Hotels, Marriott International, and McDonald's Corporation, have annual sales of several billion dollars. The major advantages of the corporate form over other forms of business organization include the following:

1. Its shareholders' liability is normally limited to their investments.

2. Owners are taxed only on distributed profits.

3. Employees can be motivated by equity participation (such as stock bonus plans and stock options) and by certain tax-favored benefits.

4. Equity capital can be raised by selling capital stock to the public.

5. A corporation can use its stock to acquire other companies and thereby offer the sellers a tax-free exchange.

6. Tax rates are often lower for small corporations than for individuals.

7. There is free transferability of capital stock by owners.

8. The corporation exists independently of the owners.

As with the other forms of business organization, there are disadvantages of the corporate form. Some of these include the following:

1. Corporate profits are taxed twice. First, they are taxed on the corporation's own income. Then, any profits paid out as dividends are considered taxable income to the individual stockholders. This is known as **double taxation**. Exhibit 15.10 illustrates that the effective tax rate on the second $100,000 of corporate pretax income could be as high as 50.23 percent (based on 2021 tax rates). The calculations assume that the individual stockholder/taxpayer's marginal tax rate is 35 percent and that all after-tax profits are distributed. Thus, the corporate tax of 21 percent plus the individual tax of 29.23 percent (37 percent of 79 percent) equals 60.35 percent, the effective tax rate. If this business had been unincorporated, the maximum effective tax rate would have been only 37 percent.

2. The corporation cannot pass on tax advantages (such as operating losses and tax credits) that might be more advantageous to the owners than to the corporation.

S Corporations

Some of the tax drawbacks of the corporate form of organization can be overcome by filing as an **S corporation** (the *S* merely refers to subchapter S of the code). In essence, this filing allows the corporation to be taxed like a partnership.

The philosophy behind the S corporation provisions of the Internal Revenue Code is that a firm should be able to select its form of organization free of tax considerations. The S corporation is a hybrid form allowing limited liability for owners but avoiding the corporate "curse" of double taxation.

To qualify as an S corporation, the corporation must meet several tests, including, but not limited to (1) having 100 or fewer stockholders, (2) being a domestic corporation, and (3) having only one class of stock.

This form of organization can be very useful when corporate losses are anticipated and owners have taxable income that can absorb the losses. It can also be very useful when corporations are profitable without having uses for extra capital; since profits are passed through to stockholders, they are not taxed as accumulated earnings.

15.6 MINIMIZING TAXES

As pointed out earlier, all taxpayers wish to pay as little tax as possible. An example will illustrate how a business can accomplish this end. The owners/managers of a corporation may receive compensation in the form of benefits, salary, and dividends; this package should be structured to minimize taxes. Consider the taxability of these three compensation elements to both the corporation and the sole stockholder:

	C Corporation	Owner/Manager
Fringe benefits	Deductible	Nontaxable
Salary	Deductible	Taxable
Dividends	Nondeductible	Taxable

Certain benefits, such as health insurance, are a tax-deductible expense for a **C corporation** (the term often used in tax literature to refer to all non-S corporations) and are not taxable to the recipient, in this case the owner/manager. On the other hand, the corporation may deduct salaries in determining its federal income taxes, but the owner/manager must pay taxes on their own salary. Dividends are not a deductible expense to the corporation, and they are taxable to the owner/ manager.

To further illustrate these concepts, consider George Brown, the sole stockholder of Brown's Eatery, an incorporated restaurant business. George has invested $200,000 in the business. In 20X4, he received a salary of $100,000 and the business had taxable income of $100,000. George received no benefits or dividends.

For the purpose of simplicity, assume a corporate tax rate of 20 percent on the first $200,000 of taxable income and an individual tax rate of 25 percent on the first $100,000 of earnings. George Brown and Brown's Eatery paid taxes in 20X4 totaling $45,000, determined as follows:

Taxpayer	Taxable Income	Tax Rate	Taxes
Brown's Eatery	$100,000	20%	$20,000
George Brown	100,000	25%	25,000
		Total	$45,000

In this case, the IRS may rule that part of George Brown's salary is dividends, especially if his salary is considered unreasonably high. Assume that the IRS rules $20,000 of his salary to be dividends. The total taxes increase by $4,000 to $49,000—the salary deduction of $20,000 denied to the corporation times the corporation's tax rate of 20 percent.

The IRS considers the following factors in determining whether salaries are reasonable:

- The amounts being paid by corporations of similar size in the same industry

- The economic conditions and salary levels in the geographic region in which the corporation operates

- The nature of the shareholder/employee responsibilities and the amount of time the shareholder/employee devotes to the business

- The shareholder/employee's qualifications in terms of education and experience

The owner/manager must formally document the basis of a relatively large salary; that is, they must explain the duties and functions performed to justify the salary. The corporation's board of directors should approve the owner/manager's salary.

In this example, we initially assumed that George did not receive any benefits. Suppose that George's effective salary of $80,000 is reduced to $70,000 and he receives $10,000 in benefits (such as health and life insurance). Assume that these benefits are 100 percent deductible by the corporation and nontaxable to George. The taxes paid by George and his corporation now total $46,500, determined as follows:

Taxpayer	Taxable Income	Tax Rate	Taxes
Brown's Eatery	$120,000*	20%	$24,000
George Brown	90,000**	25%	22,500
		Total	$46,500

*Original net income	$ 100,000
Salary declared by IRS as dividends	20,000
Decrease in salary	10,000
Cost of fringe benefits	(10,000)
Total	$ 120,000
**Salary	$ 70,000
Dividends	20,000
Total	$ 90,000

The total tax bill is $2,500 less than it would be if Brown's Eatery provided George with no benefits. The $2,500 reduction is George's tax rate of 25 percent multiplied by the cost of the fringe benefits:

$$0.25 \times \$10,000 = \$2,500$$

Thus, to minimize taxes, the preferred order is benefits, salary, and dividends. However, just as the IRS is vigilant to determine that salaries are reasonable and do not include dividends, the IRS also has rules regarding benefits. Certain benefits are taxable, such as the premiums paid on life insurance policies when the insurance coverage exceeds $50,000 and the insured is the owner of the policy. The IRS treats the premium on the excess coverage as taxable income to the benefiting employee. It might appear at this point that a small C corporation is better off not declaring dividends above a required minimum that satisfies the IRS. However, if corporations accumulate earnings in order to avoid double taxation, they may be subject to an **accumulated earnings tax**. The current rate is 20 percent on accumulated earnings in excess of $250,000. Specifics of this tax are beyond the scope of this chapter; however, the tax can be avoided by showing a reasonable need for accumulating earnings (such as business expansion).

How would George Brown's taxes change if he had filed as an S corporation? This example assumes that the benefits under an S corporation would be nontaxable, as they were for the C corporation. The restaurant's taxable income of $120,000 would be passed directly to George for tax purposes. Therefore, his 20X4 taxes would have been $47,500, determined as follows:

George's salary	$ 70,000
Brown's Eatery income taxable to George	120,000
Total taxable income	190,000
George's tax rate	× 0.25
Total taxes	$ 47,500

Thus, the S corporation form of organization costs George an extra $2,500. This result is due entirely to the 5 percent difference in the restaurant's tax rate of 20 percent as a C corporation and George's tax rate of 25 percent.

The tax rates vary for C corporations and individuals. At lower taxable income levels, individual rates exceed corporate rates. Thus, based on the assumed rates used in our illustration, the C corporation is better than the S corporation for Brown's Eatery.

The 2021 U.S. federal tax rate schedules for individuals and corporations were as follows:

Individual (Married filing jointly)

Taxable Income	Tax Rate
Not more than $19,900	10% of taxable income
Over $19,900 but not more than $81,050	$1,990.00 + 12% of excess over $19,900
Over $81,050 but not more than $172,750	$9,328.00 + 22% of excess over $81,050
Over $172,750 but not more than $329,850	$29,502.00 + 24% of excess over $172,750
Over $329,850 but not more than $418,850	$67,206.00 + 32% of excess over $329,850
Over $418,850 but not more than $628,300	$95,686.00 + 35% of excess over $418,850
Over $628,300	$168,993.50 + 37% of excess over $628,300

Corporation: a flat rate of 21%

For example, $100,000 of taxable income to a married individual filing a joint return results in federal income taxes of $13,479:

	Taxable Income		Taxes
First	$ 81,050	=	$ 9,328.00
Next	18,950 × 0.22	=	4.169.00
Total	$100,000		$13,497.00

Thus, the effective average rate is 13.50 percent.

For a corporation, the income taxes on $100,000 of taxable income is $21,000. Simply, $100,000 × 0.21 = $21,000. Thus, the marginal rate average rate is 21 percent.

15.7 ACCOUNTING METHODS

There are different accounting methods available. After the legal form of operation has been chosen, management must determine which accounting method best reflects the type of business and provides optimum ability to minimize or postpone taxes. Minimizing or postponing taxes is achieved by effectively timing the recognition of income and deduction of expenses.

Cash Method versus Accrual Method

Tax laws require the taxpayer to use the method of accounting that most clearly reflects income. The accrual method of accounting is appropriate for taxpayers with significant inventories. Further, the use of the accrual method of accounting is required if the taxpayer is a corporation or a partnership with a C corporation as a partner. However, if the business is small (average annual sales of $26 million or less for 2021), the cash method of accounting may be used for tax purposes. Under this method, items of income and expense are generally reported for tax purposes when cash is actually received or paid out.

Even under the cash method, there are exceptions. For example, fixed assets must generally be depreciated over the life of the asset rather than being deducted as an expense in the year paid. Exhibit 15.7 shows that the Redbird Restaurant was accounted for on a cash basis. For tax purposes, food inventories were $0; however, there was depreciation of $102,366 for 2021.

Exhibit 15.7 The Schmitzes' Profit or Loss from Business

SCHEDULE C
(Form 1040)

Department of the Treasury
Internal Revenue Service (99)

Profit or Loss From Business
(Sole Proprietorship)

▶ Go to *www.irs.gov/ScheduleC* for instructions and the latest information.
▶ **Attach to Form 1040, 1040-SR, 1040-NR, or 1041; partnerships must generally file Form 1065.**

OMB No. 1545-0074

2021

Attachment
Sequence No. **09**

Name of proprietor	Social security number (SSN)
Warren B Schmitz	337-38-3435

A Principal business or profession, including product or service (see instructions)
restaurant

B Enter code from instructions
▶ 7 2 2 5 1 3

C Business name. If no separate business name, leave blank.

D Employer ID number (EIN) (see instr.)

E Business address (including suite or room no.) ▶ 114 State Street
City, town or post office, state, and ZIP code   Topeka, KS 99999

F Accounting method: **(1)** ☒ Cash   **(2)** ☐ Accrual   **(3)** ☐ Other (specify) ▶ _____

G Did you "materially participate" in the operation of this business during 2021? If "No," see instructions for limit on losses ☒ Yes ☐ No

H If you started or acquired this business during 2021, check here ▶ ☐

I Did you make any payments in 2021 that would require you to file Form(s) 1099? See instructions ☐ Yes ☒ No

J If "Yes," did you or will you file required Form(s) 1099? ☐ Yes ☐ No

Part I   Income

1	Gross receipts or sales. See instructions for line 1 and check the box if this income was reported to you on Form W-2 and the "Statutory employee" box on that form was checked ▶ ☐	1	1,250,000.
2	Returns and allowances	2	
3	Subtract line 2 from line 1	3	1,250,000.
4	Cost of goods sold (from line 42)	4	893,000.
5	**Gross profit.** Subtract line 4 from line 3	5	357,000.
6	Other income, including federal and state gasoline or fuel tax credit or refund (see instructions)	6	
7	**Gross income.** Add lines 5 and 6 ▶	7	357,000.

Part II   Expenses. Enter expenses for business use of your home **only** on line 30.

8	Advertising	8	20,000.	18	Office expense (see instructions)	18	8,500.
9	Car and truck expenses (see instructions)	9		19	Pension and profit-sharing plans	19	
10	Commissions and fees	10		20	Rent or lease (see instructions):		
11	Contract labor (see instructions)	11		a	Vehicles, machinery, and equipment	20a	
12	Depletion	12		b	Other business property	20b	15,000.
13	Depreciation and section 179 expense deduction (not included in Part III) (see instructions)	13	102,366.	21	Repairs and maintenance	21	3,000.
				22	Supplies (not included in Part III)	22	8,000.
				23	Taxes and licenses	23	2,000.
				24	Travel and meals:		
14	Employee benefit programs (other than on line 19)	14		a	Travel	24a	4,500.
15	Insurance (other than health)	15	15,000.	b	Deductible meals (see instructions)	24b	
16	Interest (see instructions):			25	Utilities	25	27,000.
a	Mortgage (paid to banks, etc.)	16a	10,000.	26	Wages (less employment credits)	26	
b	Other	16b		27a	Other expenses (from line 48)	27a	24,000.
17	Legal and professional services	17	3,000.	b	Reserved for future use	27b	

28	**Total expenses** before expenses for business use of home. Add lines 8 through 27a ▶	28	242,366.
29	Tentative profit or (loss). Subtract line 28 from line 7	29	114,634.
30	Expenses for business use of your home. Do not report these expenses elsewhere. Attach Form 8829 unless using the simplified method. See instructions. **Simplified method filers only:** Enter the total square footage of (a) your home: _____ and (b) the part of your home used for business: _____. Use the Simplified Method Worksheet in the instructions to figure the amount to enter on line 30	30	
31	**Net profit or (loss).** Subtract line 30 from line 29. • If a profit, enter on both **Schedule 1 (Form 1040), line 3,** and on **Schedule SE, line 2.** (If you checked the box on line 1, see instructions). Estates and trusts, enter on **Form 1041, line 3.** • If a loss, you **must** go to line 32.	31	114,634.
32	If you have a loss, check the box that describes your investment in this activity. See instructions. • If you checked 32a, enter the loss on both **Schedule 1 (Form 1040), line 3,** and on **Schedule SE, line 2.** (If you checked the box on line 1, see the line 31 instructions.) Estates and trusts, enter on **Form 1041, line 3.** • If you checked 32b, you **must** attach **Form 6198.** Your loss may be limited.	32a ☐ All investment is at risk. 32b ☐ Some investment is not at risk.	

For Paperwork Reduction Act Notice, see the separate instructions.   **BAA**   REV 01/24/22 TTW   Schedule C (Form 1040) 2021

Exhibit 15.8 Schedule 1–Additional Income and Adjustments to Income

SCHEDULE 1
(Form 1040)

Department of the Treasury
Internal Revenue Service

Additional Income and Adjustments to Income

► Attach to Form 1040, 1040-SR, or 1040-NR.
► Go to *www.irs.gov/Form1040* for instructions and the latest information.

OMB No 1545-0074

2021

Attachment
Sequence No. 01

Name(s) shown on Form 1040, 1040-SR, or 1040-NR
Warren B & Mary Y Schmitz

Your social security number
337-38-3435

Part I Additional Income

1	Taxable refunds, credits, or offsets of state and local income taxes	1	
2a	Alimony received	2a	
b	Date of original divorce or separation agreement (see instructions) ►		
3	Business income or (loss). Attach Schedule C	3	114,634.
4	Other gains or (losses). Attach Form 4797	4	
5	Rental real estate, royalties, partnerships, S corporations, trusts, etc. Attach Schedule E	5	
6	Farm income or (loss). Attach Schedule F	6	
7	Unemployment compensation	7	
8	Other income:		

a	Net operating loss	8a	( )
b	Gambling income	8b	
c	Cancellation of debt	8c	
d	Foreign earned income exclusion from Form 2555	8d	( )
e	Taxable Health Savings Account distribution	8e	
f	Alaska Permanent Fund dividends	8f	
g	Jury duty pay	8g	
h	Prizes and awards	8h	
i	Activity not engaged in for profit income	8i	
j	Stock options	8j	
k	Income from the rental of personal property if you engaged in the rental for profit but were not in the business of renting such property	8k	
l	Olympic and Paralympic medals and USOC prize money (see instructions)	8l	
m	Section 951(a) inclusion (see instructions)	8m	
n	Section 951A(a) inclusion (see instructions)	8n	
o	Section 461(l) excess business loss adjustment	8o	
p	Taxable distributions from an ABLE account (see instructions) .	8p	
z	Other income. List type and amount ►	8z	

9	Total other income. Add lines 8a through 8z	9	
10	Combine lines 1 through 7 and 9. Enter here and on Form 1040, 1040-SR, or 1040-NR, line 8	10	114,634.

For Paperwork Reduction Act Notice, see your tax return instructions.

Schedule 1 (Form 1040) 2021

Part II	Adjustments to Income		
11	Educator expenses	11	
12	Certain business expenses of reservists, performing artists, and fee-basis government officials. Attach Form 2106	12	
13	Health savings account deduction. Attach Form 8889	13	
14	Moving expenses for members of the Armed Forces. Attach Form 3903	14	
15	Deductible part of self-employment tax. Attach Schedule SE	15	8,099.
16	Self-employed SEP, SIMPLE, and qualified plans	16	
17	Self-employed health insurance deduction	17	
18	Penalty on early withdrawal of savings	18	
19a	Alimony paid	19a	
b	Recipient's SSN . . . . ▶		
c	Date of original divorce or separation agreement (see instructions) ▶		
20	IRA deduction	20	
21	Student loan interest deduction	21	
22	Reserved for future use	22	
23	Archer MSA deduction	23	
24	Other adjustments:		
a	Jury duty pay (see instructions)	24a	
b	Deductible expenses related to income reported on line 8k from the rental of personal property engaged in for profit	24b	
c	Nontaxable amount of the value of Olympic and Paralympic medals and USOC prize money reported on line 8l	24c	
d	Reforestation amortization and expenses	24d	
e	Repayment of supplemental unemployment benefits under the Trade Act of 1974	24e	
f	Contributions to section 501(c)(18)(D) pension plans	24f	
g	Contributions by certain chaplains to section 403(b) plans . .	24g	
h	Attorney fees and court costs for actions involving certain unlawful discrimination claims (see instructions)	24h	
i	Attorney fees and court costs you paid in connection with an award from the IRS for information you provided that helped the IRS detect tax law violations	24i	
j	Housing deduction from Form 2555	24j	
k	Excess deductions of section 67(e) expenses from Schedule K-1 (Form 1041)	24k	
z	Other adjustments. List type and amount ▶ _____	24z	
25	Total other adjustments. Add lines 24a through 24z	25	
26	Add lines 11 through 23 and 25. These are your **adjustments to income.** Enter here and on Form 1040 or 1040-SR, line 10, or Form 1040-NR, line 10a	26	8,099.

BAA   REV 01/24/22 TTW   Schedule 1 (Form 1040) 2021

Exhibit 15.9 Operating Forms for the Hospitality Business

	Sole Proprietorship	Partnership		Limited Liability Company	Corporation	
		General	Limited		Regular	S Corporation
Instrument of Creation	None (assumed name statement may be required	Agreement—oral or written	Certificate of limited partnership	Articles of organization	Articles of incorporation	Articles of incorporation, file election with IRS
Organizational Documents	None	Partnership agreement	Certificate of Limited partnership agreement	Operating agreement	Articles of incorporation, bylaws, minutes	Articles of incorporation, bylaws, minutes
Type of Tax Return	Schedule C for Form 1040	Form 1065	Form 1065	Form 1065	Form 1120	Form 1120S
Tax Rates	Individual	Individual	Individual	Individual	Corporate	Individual
Limited Liability	No	No	Yes—Limited Partners; No—General Partners	Yes	Yes	Yes
Recognition of Losses	Owner	Partners	Partners	Members	Corporation	Shareholders

Exhibit 15.10 Illustration of Double Taxation

	Dollars	Percentage
Corporate Pretax Income over $100,000	$100,000	100.00%
Less: Corporate Tax (39%)	39,000	39.00
Dividend Distribution	61,000	61.00
Less: Individual Income Taxes (35%)	21,350	21.35
After-Tax Benefit to Stockholder	$ 39,650	39.65%

A cash-basis taxpayer has some flexibility in reporting income and expenses. The timing of income collection, or the payment of expenses, can be controlled to some extent, particularly near year-end.

The accrual method of accounting reports income when it is earned, rather than when the cash is collected. It reflects expenses when they are incurred, rather than when they are paid. As is the case with many areas of tax law, there are exceptions to the general rule. Under the accrual method, some items of income (such as advance rentals) are taxed when collected rather than when earned. Similarly, an expense item must be fixed and determinable before it can be deducted for tax purposes. Estimated expenses, while generally acceptable for financial accounting, may not be deducted for tax reporting until all factors that affect the expense item have become fixed and determinable.

Installment Sales Method

For financial accounting purposes, when goods or property are sold on the installment method (i.e., the sales price is received in periodic payments over time), the entire sales price is recognized at the time of sale, and the entire cost of goods sold deducted as an expense of sale. Tax reporting, however, allows recognizing the profit on sales made on the installment method on a prorated basis as cash is received. This method is frequently chosen upon the sale of a business such as a hotel or restaurant.

15.8 ACCOUNTING INCOME VERSUS TAXABLE INCOME

Thus far, the importance of tax planning for a transaction at an early stage of its development has been emphasized. In addition, several options for selecting the legal entity within which to conduct a business have been presented. After the form of organization is selected, the method of accounting (cash versus accrual) most suitable for mitigating the tax costs of operation is chosen. All of these choices are made with the overall business objectives of the operation in mind.

These choices can result in differences between the amount and timing of income or expenses reported in financial statements and the amounts reported on the tax return. Other tax requirements or choices can cause further differences in the amount or timing of the reporting of income and expenses.

Accelerated Depreciation

Tax legislation in 1981 and 1982 liberalized tax depreciation rules with enactment of an Accelerated Cost Recovery System (ACRS), which provided for faster recovery (depreciation) of capital expenditures. The 1986 tax law significantly tightened the tax rules for depreciating real estate but retained the liberal rules for depreciating personal property, such as equipment and furniture. Since 1986, the depreciation rules have been based on the **modified accelerated cost recovery system (MACRS)**.

In financial accounting, a building may be depreciated over 30 years or more. MACRS currently requires, for tax purposes, recovery over 39 years. (For property placed in service before May 13, 1993, recovery may be over 31.5 years.) Similarly, furniture and equipment may be depreciated over seven to 10 years (or more) for financial accounting purposes, while the same items are depreciated for tax purposes over five years under MACRS. (Within certain limits, the first $1.05 million of equipment purchases [amount for 2021] may be expensed immediately for tax purposes, while for accounting purposes, the equipment would be depreciated as normal.) Thus, the timing of reporting net income for financial purposes can be significantly different from that for taxable income.

In the later years of an asset's life, the deduction for depreciation, especially with furniture and equipment, will be greater for financial accounting than for tax accounting. At the end of the asset's life, the deduction for depreciation will be the same in total for both financial reporting and tax accounting. The difference is in the timing of the deduction.

Exhibit 15.11 uses a purchase of $1 million worth of equipment to illustrate the difference between MACRS recovery expense and depreciation using the straight-line method. For tax purposes, MACRS allows the cost of the equipment to be recovered over five years, while for financial reporting purposes, the hospitality operation chooses to depreciate the equipment over 10 years using

Year	MACRS Recovery[1]	Straight-Line Recovery[2]	Difference
20X1	$ 200,000	$ 100,000	$ 100,000
20X2	320,000	100,000	220,000
20X3	192,000	100,000	92,000
20X4	115,200	100,000	15,200
20X5	115,200	100,000	15,200
20X6	57,600	100,000	(42,400)
20X7	0	100,000	(100,000)
20X8	0	100,000	(100,000)
20X9	0	100,000	(100,000)
20X0	0	100,000	(100,000)
Total	$ 1,000,000	$ 1,000,000	$ 0

[1] The MACRS for 5-year tax life is calculated using the double declining method and the half-year convention; that is, one-half of a year's depreciation is taken in the year of the purchase (20X1) and one-half in 20X6.

1st year	–	20.00%
2nd year	–	32.00
3rd year	–	19.20
4th year	–	11.52
5th year	–	11.52
6th year	–	5.76
Total		100.00%

[2] Assuming a zero salvage value. Annual depreciation is determined by dividing the cost ($1,000,000) by the life (10 years) to equal the annual depreciation ($100,000).

the straight-line method. In the first five years, MACRS results in $442,400 more expense (cost recovery) than the straight-line method, while the reverse results in the last five years.

Preopening Expenses

For many years, hospitality firms were able to deduct, for tax purposes, many expenses as they were incurred before formally opening a new hotel, even if such expenses were deferred for financial reporting purposes. This was especially true if the operation was not the first hotel in the business. The current tax law disallows immediate write-off and requires preopening expenses to be amortized over a five-year period beginning with the month the hotel or restaurant opens for business.

First-Year Losses

First-year losses of a hospitality operation are usually capitalized as a deferred charge and amortized over several years for financial accounting purposes. However, for tax purposes, such costs are generally deductible as incurred, so taxable income is lower than financial accounting income, improving the first-year cash flow by deferring taxes. This situation reverses after the first year. As the first-year losses are amortized for financial accounting with no offsetting amortization for tax accounting, the result is a higher taxable income than book income and a corresponding higher tax payment.

Loss Carryforwards

A final example of the differences between financial and tax accounting is the treatment of operating losses sustained by a business. Current tax laws allow a net operating loss to be carried forward for an unlimited number of years.

15.9 STATE AND MUNICIPAL TAXES

Until recently, managers paid little attention to state and local taxes because rates were low and the amounts involved did not warrant serious study. This has changed in recent years as state and local governments have been increasing tax rates and seeking new ways to generate tax revenues. Today's manager should realize that state and local taxes also require planning to reduce the overall tax burden.

The financial manager of a multistate operation should be aware that the manner in which business is conducted in a state determines whether and how the business is subject to that state's tax laws. Early tax planning is as important here as it is in all areas of tax planning.

Planning is also important in a multicorporate form of business when one corporate unit is profitable and a second is unprofitable. The manager should investigate whether state tax laws allow consolidation of operations to offset the income of one corporation with the loss of another, minimizing the total tax burden. If state laws do not permit consolidation and the mix of profit and loss is expected to continue for some time, the manager should consider whether a corporate reorganization is desirable. A reorganization that merged the losing operation into the profitable one would achieve the same tax results as filing a consolidated return. Of course, in this situation, other business objectives should also be weighed.

15.10 PROPERTY TAXES

Taxes levied on real estate and personal property such as furniture, fixtures, and equipment are commonly called **property taxes**. In recent years, property taxes for hotels have approximated 3 percent of gross revenues, which may seem insignificant. However, a 0.5 percent reduction for a hotel with $20 million in sales would save the business $100,000.

Property taxes are generally levied at the local level. The tax is a result of the assessed value of the property and the tax rate. Property taxes differ by state and locality; for example, the general property tax formula in Michigan is:

$$\text{Property Taxes} = \frac{\text{Assessed Valuation}}{1,000} \times \text{Tax Rate}$$

In this formula, the **assessed valuation** is the value the tax assessor places on the property to be taxed. The tax rate is stated in *mills*, which is tax dollars per $1,000 of assessed valuation. Assume that Rocky's Hotel had an assessed valuation of $10 million and a tax rate of 60 mills. The annual property tax would be calculated as follows:

$$\text{Property Taxes} = \frac{\$10,000,000}{1,000} \times 60$$

$$= \$600,000$$

Although property taxes are normally viewed as a fixed cost (i.e., not controllable by management), management should challenge any assessed valuation considered to be excessive. For example, in Michigan the assessed valuation is by law 50 percent of market value. Assume that Rocky's Hotel had recently been purchased for $18 million. Based on Michigan law, the assessed valuation for Rocky's Hotel should be reduced to $9 million, which is 50 percent of the market price. The $1 million assessed valuation reduction, given the tax rate of 60 mills, reduces property taxes by $60,000 annually.

Governments levy income taxes to raise the revenue they need to provide their constituents with services and to achieve a variety of social goals. Both individuals and businesses pay taxes. Most financial business decisions have tax implications. Therefore, hospitality managers must understand taxes in order to make sound decisions.

Federal income taxes are based on a self-reporting system, whereby the taxpayer prepares the appropriate tax forms. For the individual, tax considerations include income, adjustments to income, deductions, credits, other taxes, and taxes paid. Form 1040, Form 1040A, or Form 1040EZ must be filed by all qualifying taxpayers.

Tax avoidance refers to legally paying the least amount of tax. Tax evasion is the illegal attempt to pay less or no tax. Hospitality managers should strive for tax avoidance.

One major tax consideration is the form of organization a business selects. The major forms are the sole proprietorship, the partnership, the limited liability company, and the corporation, while hybrid forms include the limited partnership and the S corporation. Each form offers advantages and disadvantages. The disadvantage of individual unlimited liability can be overcome by incorporating; however, incorporation results in double taxation. Avoiding double taxation and unlimited liability can be achieved by filing as an S corporation and a limited liability company; however, S corporations are limited to one type of stock and 100 or fewer stockholders. An operation should consider the size, goals, and riskiness of its business, then select a form that minimizes the disadvantages and maximizes the advantages.

Just as there are different business forms, there are different accounting methods. Businesses must decide whether cash accounting or accrual accounting better meets their needs. There are also differences between accounting for financial purposes and accounting for tax purposes. These differences may involve the treatments of depreciation, preopening expenses, first-year losses, and loss carryforwards.

State, municipal, and property taxes all deserve the manager's attention. These taxes, which used to be negligible, have been growing. Although property taxes are thought of as fixed expenses, attentive managers may be able to successfully challenge assessed valuations and reduce the property tax burden.

accumulated earnings tax—A tax designed to prevent corporations from accumulating earnings in order to avoid double taxation. The tax can be avoided by showing a reasonable need for accumulating earnings (such as business expansion).

assessed valuation—With regard to property taxes, the value the tax assessor places on the property to be taxed.

C corporation—The term often used in tax literature to refer to all non-S corporations.

certificate of limited partnership—A document that must be filed with the proper governmental authorities. Unlike a general partnership agreement (which can be oral), the limited partnership agreement must be in writing.

corporation—A form of business organization that provides a separate legal entity apart from its owners.

double taxation—Occurs when both corporate profits and dividends paid to stockholders are taxed.

general partner—A member of a partnership with unlimited liability for the debts of the partnership.

income exclusions—Income that is reported on federal tax returns but not subject to taxation; exclusions from income shown on tax forms include amounts for dividends and a portion of long-term capital gains.

limited liability company (LLC)—A form of business organization that combines the corporate feature of limited liability with the favorable tax treatment of partnerships and sole proprietorships. May have an unlimited number of owners (who are referred to as members) and is not restricted to one class of stock.

limited partner—A member of a limited partnership having limited liability. Limited partners may not actively participate in managing the business.

limited partnership—A form of business organization consisting of a partnership between two or more individuals having at least one general partner and one limited partner in which the latter's liabilities are limited to investments.

modified accelerated cost recovery system (MACRS)—The legal basis for depreciation rules since 1986; allows for faster "recovery" (depreciation) of capital expenditures for tax purposes.

partnership—A form of business organization involving two or more owners that is not incorporated.

property taxes—Taxes levied on real estate and personal property, such as furniture, fixtures, and equipment.

S corporation—A hybrid form of organization that allows a corporation to be taxed in the same manner as a partnership.

sole proprietorship—An unincorporated business organized by one person.

tax avoidance—Planning transactions to mitigate the impact of taxes or avoid the application of taxes in such a manner as to achieve the lowest possible tax cost within the constraints of other business considerations and the prevailing tax laws and regulations.

tax credits—Amounts that are subtracted directly from income taxes calculated on taxable income in accordance with prevailing tax laws.

tax deductions—Amounts that are deducted from adjusted gross income in accordance with prevailing tax laws.

tax evasion—The fraudulent denial or concealment of a current or future tax liability, such as the underreporting of income and claiming unsubstantiated or excessive income deductions.

1. What are five types of income that must be reported on an individual's tax return?

2. How do tax deductions differ from tax credits?

3. What are the major advantages of a sole proprietorship?

4. What are the major advantages of a corporation?

5. How may the disadvantage of unlimited liability be overcome in selecting a form of organization?

6. Why are limited partnerships so useful in raising capital funds for hospitality operations?

7. How does accelerated depreciation (as opposed to straight-line depreciation) save profitable hospitality businesses tax dollars?

8. What are two limitations to S corporations?

9. What is double taxation?

10. Under what circumstances is the sole proprietorship form best?

Problem 1

Terri Bensen, a married taxpayer who files jointly with her husband, has taxable income for 20X0 of $120,000.

Required:

1. Determine Terri's federal income taxes based on the 2021 rates.

2. What are Terri's average and marginal tax rates?

Problem 2

The Olympia Inn has an assessed valuation of $18 million. The property tax rate is 60 mills.

Required:

Determine the Olympia Inn's annual property taxes.

Problem 3

Wills Corporation has a marginal tax rate (MTR) of 35 percent, while its only stockholder, Blair Wills, has an MTR of 33 percent. Wills Corporation has several hundred thousand dollars of taxable income. Assume that on its last $100,000 of taxable income, it pays taxes at its MTR and pays dividends to its only stockholder of the remaining amount ($100,000 less the taxes thereon). Further assume that Blair pays taxes at his MTR on the dividends received from Wills Corporation.

Required:

1. What is the amount of taxes paid on the $100,000 by Wills Corporation?

2. How much is paid in taxes by Blair on the dividends received from Wills Corporation?

3. What is the effective double taxation rate?

Problem 4

The Mayfair Hotel in central Michigan has had an increase in its assessed valuation for property tax purposes of $250,000 for 20X8. The new assessed valuation is $10.25 million. Phil Roehl, the owner, has asked you to assist in the appeal of the $250,000 increase. The millage tax rate is 40 mills. Assume your customary consulting fee is $200 per hour.

Required:

1. What were the annual property taxes for 20X7?

2. What will be the increase in annual property taxes for 20X8?

3. If you, as the consultant, spend 40 hours on the appeal and the appeal is successful, will the appeal be cost-justified?

Problem 5

Leslie Boyer is considering opening a franchised quick-service restaurant (QSR). He believes that in a typical year, he will gross nearly $1.2 million and net $100,000 before income taxes. Angela, his wife, is expected to have taxable income of $100,000 from her apartment rentals. Her business is not incorporated. Leslie wants to avoid double taxation but also wants to limit his liability.

Required:

1. What form of organization do you suggest? Assume that the LLC has not been approved by the state where Leslie lives.

2. How might Leslie overcome the liability problem without incorporating?

Problem 6

Based on the information in the previous problem, calculate income taxes for the Boyers (ignore exemptions and deductions) and their businesses in the following situations:

1. Assume that the Boyers' average tax rate is 25 percent and that both the QSR and the real estate business are unincorporated.

2. Assume that the Boyers' average tax rate is 25 percent, the average corporate rate is 20 percent, and the QSR is incorporated.

3. Assume the same situation as in #2 above and that the QSR pays Leslie $50,000 in dividends that are taxed at the Boyers' average tax rate.

4. Assume that the Boyers' average tax rate is 25 percent, the average corporate rate is 20 percent, and the QSR is incorporated but is treated as an S corporation for tax purposes.

Problem 7

Jacob Mark's tax information for 20X5 is as follows:

Salary	$60,000
Interest income	$ 3,000
Individual retirement account	$ 2,000
Itemized deductions	$12,000
Tax credits	$ 3,000
Federal income taxes withheld	$ 5,000

Required:

Based on the above and using the 2021 tax rates for a married individual filing jointly, determine how much Jacob must pay or will receive as a refund for 20X5. Assume a standard deduction of $25,100.

Problem 8

Sarah and James Conley have two dependent children. Their tax information for 20X8 is as follows:

Salary	$80,000
Dividend income	5,000
Interest income	2,000
401(k) investment	5,000
Deductions:	
Medical	3,000
State income taxes	4,000
Charitable contributions	10,000
Mortgage interest	10,000
House property taxes	4,000
Tax credits	5,000
Federal income taxes withheld	12,000

Required:

Based on the above and using 2021 tax rates for married individuals filing jointly, determine how much the Conleys must pay or will be refunded for 20X8. Assume dividends are taxed at 15 percent and a standard deduction of $25,100.

Problem 9

Shana Black's tax for 20X5 is as follows:

Salary	$90,000
Interest income	10,000
Sole proprietorship income	10,000
Contribution to 401(k)	3,000
Itemized deductions	20,000
Standard deduction	25,100
Tax credits	1,000
Federal income taxes withheld	15,000
Self-employment (SE) taxes	
Use reduction factor of	0.9235
Use SE rate of	15.3%

Required:

Based on the above and using the 2021 tax rates for married individuals filing jointly, determine how much Shana must pay in taxes or receive as a refund for 20X5. Ignore the qualified business income deduction.

Problem 10

A.M. Gregson, the sole stockholder of Gregson Corporation (a C corporation), has hired A. McCullum, a tax consultant, to advise her regarding tax issues and compensation. In 20X1 Gregson received $200,000 in cash and benefits from her corporation as follows:

Salary	$100,000
Dividends	$ 80,000
Benefits	$ 20,000

Assume her average tax rate is 28 percent for both 20X1 and 20X2. The tax consultant recommends her compensation for 20X2 be divided as follows:

Salary	$150,000
Dividends	$ 20,000
Benefits	$ 30,000

Required:

1. What is her tax liability for 20X1?

2. What is her tax liability for 20X2?

3. If Gregson Corporation's marginal tax rate is 35 percent for both 20X1 and 20X2, how much will the suggested change in Gregson's compensation (including dividends) save the corporation, compared to what it would have paid had her compensation (including dividends) not been changed?

Problem 11

The Biggbie Corporation earned $500,000 of taxable income in 20X7 and pays its stockholders dividends equal to 50 percent of its net income. Assume its average tax rate is 30 percent, while its stockholders will pay taxes of 20 percent of dividends received.

Required:

1. Calculate the taxes paid by Biggbie Corporation.

2. Calculate the taxes paid by Biggbie Corporation's stockholders.

3. Determine the tax savings to Biggbie and its stockholders if Biggbie Corporation filed as an S corporation. Assume the stockholders' relevant tax rate is 20 percent.

Problem 12

Nicole Bustle is earning a mint selling real estate. During the past five years, she has had average annual taxable income of $200,000. Her husband, Richie, would like to open a 100-unit motor hotel. The feasibility study conducted for the lodging facility suggests losses of $150,000, $100,000, and $50,000 for the first three years, respectively. The following three years, the motor hotel is expected to generate pretax profits of $100,000 per year. Assume that the Bustles' average tax rate is 28 percent. Further assume that the average corporate tax rate is 20 percent and that corporate tax losses can be carried forward for up to five years.

Required:

Based on the above information, how should Richie Bustle organize his motor hotel business? Note: Consider providing "tax savings" to support your answer.

Problem 13

Jerry Lupica owns and manages the Easter Hotel. He and his wife, Josie, file a joint return. Their tax situation for 20X2 is as follows:

A. Income

Income from Easter Inn	$ 50,000
Interest income	3,000
Josie's salary	60,000
Schedule E income (from rental house)	5,000

B. Adjustments to Income

IRA	$4,000
One-half of self-employment (SE) taxes	?
SE health insurance deduction	3,000

C. Itemized Deductions (Schedule A)

Medical	$ 4,000
Property taxes	5,000
State income taxes	3,000
Home mortgage interest	10,000
Charitable contributions	10,000

D. QBID
Use the Easter Hotel's income, half of the SE tax, the health insurance deduction, and a 20 percent rate to calculate the QBID.

E. Tax Rate
See the tax schedule in the chapter for 2021.
The SE tax rate is 15.3 percent on the first $142,800.
Note: Social Security taxes were properly withheld from Josie's paychecks.
Self-employment taxes must be determined for Jerry. (Remember to use the 0.9235 deduction factor shown in the chapter.)

F. Tax Payments
Josie's employer withheld $5,000 of federal income taxes during 20X2.
Jerry paid estimated federal taxes of $10,000 during 20X2.

Required:

Calculate the amount of federal taxes due from or to be refunded to the Lupicas. (Note: Follow the illustrated tax problem in the chapter.)

Problem 14

Ted Papit owns and manages the Long Road Café. He and his wife, Diana, file a joint return. Their tax situation for 20X2 is as follows:

A. Income

Income from Long Road Café	$80,000
Interest income	3,000
Diana's salary	30,000
Schedule E income (from rental house)	4,000
Gain on sale of Marriott common stock	5,000

B. Adjustments to Income

IRA	$4,000
One-half of self-employment (SE) taxes	?
SE health insurance deduction	6,000

C. Itemized Deductions (Schedule A)

Medical	$ 4,000
Property taxes	5,000
State income taxes	3,000
Home mortgage interest	10,000
Charitable contributions	8,000

D. Tax Rates
Use the tax schedule in the chapter for 2021.
The tax rate on the gain on the sale of stock is 15 percent.
Self-employment tax rate is 15.3 percent on the first $142,500.
Note: Social Security taxes were properly withheld from Diana's paychecks. Self-employment taxes must be determined for Ted. (Remember to use the 0.9235 deduction factor shown in the chapter.)

E. Tax Payment
Diana's employer withheld $4,000 of federal income taxes during 20X2. Ted paid estimated federal income taxes of $15,000 during 20X2.

Required:

Determine the amount of federal taxes due to be refunded to the Papits. Do not consider a qualified business income deduction.

Problem 15

J. Deere Restaurants Inc. must decide whether to use the cash or accrual method of accounting for tax purposes. The chairperson, John Deere, has provided you with the following information:

	Basis	
	Cash	Accrual
Sales	$1,000,000	$1,100,000
Cost of Sales	350,000	325,000
Labor	300,000	310,000
Other Expenses (excluding taxes)	200,000	190,000

John believes the approach that minimizes taxes for the first year is the preferred method. Assume that the taxes for J. Deere Restaurants Inc. will be based on the following tax structure:

Taxable Income	Tax Rate
$0–$50,000	15%
$50,000.01–$75,000	$7,500 + 25% of the amount over $50,000
$75,000.01–$100,000	$13,750 + 34% of the amount over $75,000
$100,000.01–$335,000	$22,250 + 39% of the amount over $100,000
over $335,000	$113,900 + 34% of the amount over $335,000

Required:

Determine whether J. Deere Restaurants Inc. should use the cash or accrual method of accounting.

Problem 16

Corbin Glenn is the owner of Corbin's Place, which generated $180,000. The business is a sole proprietorship, and he will prepare a Schedule C as part of his tax return. His wife earns $80,000 as a manager of another business. Corbin has asked for your assistance in determining the amount of his SE tax and also helping to determine his QBID. Additional information he provides is as follows:

1. The SE tax rate is 15.3 percent. This is divided between 12.4 percent for Social Security and 2.9 percent for Medicare.

2. His medical insurance is $10,000 for the year.

Required:

1. Determine the amount of his SE taxes.

2. Determine his QBID.

Problem 17

The Celtic Corporation has purchased $2 million worth of equipment for its hotels in the current year. The president, Fred Boston, has heard that using the MACRS recovery offers cash savings over the straight-line method. The equipment could be depreciated over five years for tax purposes using the recovery rates shown in Exhibit 15.11. It could also be depreciated over 10 years using the straight-line method and have zero salvage value. The marginal tax rate for the Celtic Corporation is 30 percent. Taxes saved due to the difference between MACRS and straight-line depreciation are invested at the end of each year at 10 percent interest compounded annually.

Required:

1. Determine the amount of the "tax savings fund" from taxes saved and interest earned over the first five years. Use the half-year convention for depreciation, as shown in Exhibit 15.11.

2. Calculate the interest earned over the 10-year period. Assume that for the sixth through tenth years the taxes paid due to excess straight-line depreciation over MACRS come at the end of each year from the "tax savings fund."

Problem 18

Jill Wiggins, a married taxpayer who is self-employed, provides you with her tax information for 20X1:

Professional earnings from self-employment:	$50,000
Dividend income:	$20,000

Assume tax rates are as follows:

Taxable Income	Tax Rate
<$20,000	15%
$20,001–$40,000	25%
>$40,000	35%

Itemized deductions total $15,000.

The SE tax rate is 15.3 percent on the first $142,800 of earned income.

Jill has paid estimated taxes of $15,000. (Remember to consider the 0.9235 reduction factor for self-employment taxes.) Ignore any qualified business income deduction.

Required:

Determine the following:

1. Self-employment taxes for 20X1.

2. Income taxes for 20X1.

3. Amount due or refund due to Jill Wiggins for 20X1.

Problem 19

M. Scott is the sole owner of an incorporated lodging chain. The chain generates net income of $250,000 each year. At the present time, assume Scott receives annual nontaxable fringe benefits of $10,000. Assume Scott's average tax rate is 40 percent. Scott receives a salary of $140,000 from the chain each year.

Scott is an excellent owner/manager but needs help with taxes. At a conference for entrepreneurs, he recently heard about S corporations, double taxation, excessive salary being labeled as dividends by the IRS, and so on. Assume corporation income tax rates as follows:

Taxable Income	Rate
0–$100,000	15%
$100,001–$200,000	25%
$200,001–$400,000	30%
Over $400,000	40%

Required (show all your calculations):

1. Based on the above, calculate the federal income taxes paid by Scott and by the incorporated lodging chain. (Ignore deductions, exemptions, etc., in calculating his personal income taxes.)

2. How would you advise Scott to minimize the taxes he and his chain pay? If the chain remains as a C corporation, dividends would have to be at least equal to $20,000, and the allowable maximum fringe benefits should be assumed to cost no more than $30,000. (Any fringe benefits in excess of $30,000 should be considered salary.)

3. How much is saved in federal taxes for both the chain and M. Scott based on your advice?

Problem 20

Zera Adams owns a very successful foodservice chain. The chain is incorporated and generates pretax income of $300,000 each year. Her salary is $40,000 per year and she receives no benefits. The foodservice chain pays her dividends equal to 40 percent of its net income each year. Zera's average tax rate is 28 percent. Assume the corporate income tax rate is a flat 21 percent.

Zera is an excellent owner/manager but does not know much about taxes. At a recent conference for entrepreneurs, she heard about S corporations, double taxation, excessive salary being considered dividends, and other related matters. She is the sole owner of her business and insists the business retain its corporate form; however, she wants to minimize taxes.

Required:

1. Based on the above information, calculate the income taxes paid by the corporation and Zera (ignore deductions in calculating her personal income taxes).

2. How would you advise Zera to minimize her taxes? Consider that the minimum dividends would have to be 12 percent of net income and the maximum salary could be $70,000. The maximum benefits would cost $20,000. Assume that these benefits are deductible to the corporation and nontaxable to Zera. She still wants to receive salary, dividends, and benefits totaling $134,800.

3. Based on your advice, what would be the tax reduction?

Problem 21

Gayle Koelling owns and manages the unincorporated Christmas Inn. She and her husband, Melvin, file a joint return. Their tax situation for 20X2 is as follows:

A. Income

Income from the Christmas Inn	$60,000
Interest income	600
Dividend income	2,000
Capital gain from sale of investment	10,000
Melvin's salary	75,000

B. Itemized Deductions (Schedule A)

Medical	$3,000
Property taxes	4,000
State income taxes	4,000
Intangibles tax	300
Home mortgage interest	6,000
Charitable contributions	8,000

C. Standard deduction is $25,000.

D. QBID—Be sure to subtract the one-half SE tax from the Christmas Inn income.

E. Tax Rate

Average federal income tax rate—25 percent.
Self-employment (SE) tax rate—15.3 percent on the first $117,000 of earned income and 2.9 percent on anything above that amount.
Note: Social Security taxes were properly withheld from Melvin's paychecks. Self-employment taxes need to be calculated for Gayle. (Remember to consider the 0.9235 reduction factor for SE taxes.)

F. Tax Payments

Melvin's employer withheld $10,000 of federal income tax during 20X2. Gayle paid estimated federal taxes of $20,000 during 20X2.

Required:

Calculate the amount of federal taxes due or to be refunded to the Koellings for 20X2. Note: Follow Schedule A (Exhibit 15.6) to determine the deductibility of the Koellings' itemized deductions in determining their taxable income.

Problem 22

Mark Reed is the sole owner of a successful lodging chain. The chain is unincorporated and generates pretax income of $300,000 each year. At the present time, he receives no tax-free benefits. Assume Mark's average tax rate is 30 percent. Mark draws $90,000 from the chain each year for his personal use and leaves the remainder in the chain to finance growth. The $90,000 has *not* been subtracted in determining the pretax income of $300,000.

Mark is an excellent owner/manager but is weak on taxation. At a conference for entrepreneurs, he recently heard about S corporations, double taxation, excessive salary being labeled as dividends by the IRS, and so forth. Assume corporation income tax rates as follows:

Taxable Income	Rate
0–$100,000	15%
$100,001–$200,000	25%
Over $200,000	35%

Required:

1. Based on the above, calculate the income taxes paid by Mark. (Ignore deductions, exemptions, etc. in calculating his personal income taxes.)

2. How would you advise him to minimize the taxes he pays? If he incorporates, dividends would have to be at least equal to $10,000 (unless the company files as an S corporation) and the allowable benefits maximum should be assumed to be no more than $15,000. Any benefits in excess of $15,000 should be considered salary. Further assume that the maximum salary allowable by the IRS (if his corporation files as a C corporation) is $75,000. He desires to continue receiving a total of $90,000 annually in cash and/or benefits.

Problem 23

Mike Miller owns a successful foodservice chain. The chain is incorporated and generates net income of $300,000 each year. His salary is $80,000 per year. At the present time, he receives benefits worth $5,000. The corporation chain pays him dividends equal to 60 percent of its net income. Assume the corporation income tax rate is a flat 21 percent.

Assume Miller's average tax rate is 25 percent.

Miller is an excellent owner/manager but is weak on taxation. At a conference for entrepreneurs, he recently heard about S corporations, double taxation, excessive salary being labeled as dividends by the IRS, and so forth. He is the sole owner of his business and insists the business retain its corporate form; however, he desires to minimize taxes.

Required:

1. Based on the corporation and by him. (Ignore deductions, exemptions, etc. in calculating his personal income taxes.)

2. How would you advise him to minimize the taxes he and his corporation pay? Assume dividends would have to be at least equal to 10 percent of net income (unless the company files as an S corporation) and the allowable benefits maximum should be assumed to cost no more than $15,000. Anything in excess of $15,000 should be considered salary. Further, assume the maximum salary allowable by the IRS (if his corporation files as a C corporation) is $100,000 in total. He desires to continue receiving $265,000 annually in benefits, salary, and dividends.

Problem 24

Randall Huffman, owner of Huffman Café, has purchased $500,000 of equipment for his café. Assume the salvage value is zero. He is undecided just how he will expense the cost of equipment for tax and financial reporting purposes.
Under MACRS, the relevant rates of depreciation by year are as follows:

1st year	20.00%
2nd year	32.00
3rd year	19.20
4th year	11.52
5th year	11.52
6th year	5.763

Assume the equipment using MACRS (for tax purposes) is depreciated over five years using the half-year convention. Use the double declining balance (DDB) method to depreciate the equipment over eight years.

Required:

1. Prepare a schedule to show the annual amounts based on MACRS cost recovery and DDB depreciation.

2. What is the difference over the eight years of the amounts written off to expense?

Problem 25

Brody Sellers, owner of Sellers in Hittle Township, wants to know the potential tax liability of his lodging operation given various levels of taxable income and the difference between a sole proprietorship and a C corporation. Assume Sellers potentially generates pretax income at three levels:

Low level	$100,000
Medium level	$300,000
High level	$500,000

Required:

1. Using the 2021 tax rate, calculate the income tax liability if Sellers is a C corporation.

2. Using the 2021 tax rates, calculate the income tax liability if Sellers is a sole proprietorship. Assume Brody would file with his wife, Landry. Ignore any deductions.

APPENDIX A

HILTON WORLDWIDE HOLDINGS, INC.
CONSOLIDATED FINANCIAL STATEMENTS

HILTON WORLDWIDE HOLDINGS INC.
CONSOLIDATED BALANCE SHEETS
(in millions, except share data)

	December 31, 2021	December 31, 2020
ASSETS		
Current Assets:		
Cash and cash equivalents	$ 1,427	$ 3,218
Restricted cash and cash equivalents	85	45
Accounts receivable, net of allowance for credit losses of $126 and $132	1,068	771
Prepaid expenses	89	70
Other	202	98
Total current assets (variable interest entities – $30 and $53)	2,871	4,202
Intangibles and Other Assets:		
Goodwill	5,071	5,095
Brands	4,883	4,904
Management and franchise contracts, net	758	653
Other intangible assets, net	194	266
Operating lease right-of-use assets	694	772
Property and equipment, net	305	346
Deferred income tax assets	213	194
Other	452	323
Total intangibles and other assets (variable interest entities – $184 and $199)	12,570	12,553
TOTAL ASSETS	$ 15,441	$ 16,755
LIABILITIES AND EQUITY (DEFICIT)		
Current Liabilities:		
Accounts payable, accrued expenses and other	$ 1,568	$ 1,302
Current maturities of long-term debt	54	56
Current portion of deferred revenues	350	370
Current portion of liability for guest loyalty program	1,047	703
Total current liabilities (variable interest entities – $50 and $57)	3,019	2,431
Long-term debt	8,712	10,431
Operating lease liabilities	870	971
Deferred revenues	896	1,004
Deferred income tax liabilities	700	649
Liability for guest loyalty program	1,317	1,766
Other	746	989
Total liabilities (variable interest entities – $212 and $248)	16,260	18,241
Commitments and contingencies – see Note 19		

(Continued)

(*Continued*)

Equity (Deficit):		
Preferred stock, $0.01 par value; 3,000,000,000 authorized shares, none issued or outstanding as of December 31, 2021 and 2020	—	—
Common stock, $0.01 par value; 10,000,000,000 authorized shares, 332,011,359 issued and 279,091,009 outstanding as of December 31, 2021 and 330,511,254 issued and 277,590,904 outstanding as of December 31, 2020	3	3
Treasury stock, at cost; 52,920,350 shares as of December 31, 2021 and December 31, 2020	(4,443)	(4,453)
Additional paid-in capital	10,720	10,552
Accumulated deficit	(6,322)	(6,732)
Accumulated other comprehensive loss	(779)	(860)
Total Hilton stockholders' deficit	(821)	(1,490)
Noncontrolling interests	2	4
Total deficit	(819)	(1,486)
TOTAL LIABILITIES AND EQUITY (DEFICIT)	$ 15,441	$ 16,755

HILTON WORLDWIDE HOLDINGS INC.
CONSOLIDATED STATEMENTS OF OPERATIONS
(in millions, except per share data)

	Year Ended December 31,		
	2021	**2020**	**2019**
Revenues			
Franchise and licensing fees	$ 1,493	$ 945	$ 1,681
Base and other management fees	176	123	332
Incentive management fees	98	38	230
Owned and leased hotels	598	421	1,422
Other revenues	79	73	101
	2,444	1,600	3,766
Other revenues from managed and franchised properties	3,344	2,707	5,686
Total revenues	5,788	4,307	9,452
Expenses			
Owned and leased hotels	679	620	1,254
Depreciation and amortization	188	331	346
General and administrative	405	311	441
Reorganization costs	—	41	—
Impairment losses	—	258	—
Other expenses	45	60	72
	1,317	1,621	2,113
Other expenses from managed and franchised properties	3,454	3,104	5,763
Total expenses	4,771	4,725	7,876
Gain (loss) on sales of assets, net	(7)	—	81
Operating income (loss)	1,010	(418)	1,657
Interest expense	(397)	(429)	(414)
Loss on foreign currency transactions	(7)	(27)	(2)
Loss on debt extinguishments	(69)	(48)	—
Other non-operating income (loss), net	23	(2)	3
Income (loss) before income taxes	560	(924)	1,244
Income tax benefit (expense)	(153)	204	(358)
Net income (loss)	407	(720)	886
Net loss (income) attributable to noncontrolling interests	3	5	(5)
Net income (loss) attributable to Hilton stockholders	$ 410	$ (715)	$ 881
Earnings (loss) per share:			
Basic	$ 1.47	$ (2.58)	$ 3.07
Diluted	$ 1.46	$ (2.58)	$ 3.04
Cash dividends declared per share	$ —	$ 0.15	$ 0.60

HILTON WORLDWIDE HOLDINGS INC.
CONSOLIDATED STATEMENTS OF CASH FLOWS
(in millions)

	Year Ended December 31,		
	2021	2020	2019
Operating Activities:			
Net income (loss)	$ 407	$ (720)	$ 886
Adjustments to reconcile net income (loss) to net cash provided by operating activities:			
Amortization of contract acquisition costs	32	29	29
Depreciation and amortization expenses	188	331	346
Impairment losses	—	258	—
Loss (gain) on sales of assets, net	7	—	(81)
Loss on foreign currency transactions	7	27	2
Loss on debt extinguishments	69	48	—
Share-based compensation expense	193	97	154
Amortization of deferred financing costs and discount	16	17	16
Deferred income taxes	(4)	(235)	(20)
Contract acquisition costs	(200)	(50)	(90)
Changes in operating assets and liabilities:			
Accounts receivable, net	(301)	488	(105)
Prepaid expenses	(22)	60	6
Other current assets	(107)	(26)	15
Accounts payable, accrued expenses and other	273	(414)	99
Change in operating lease right-of-use assets	96	94	43
Change in operating lease liabilities	(123)	(142)	(80)
Change in deferred revenues	(128)	215	(17)
Change in liability for guest loyalty program	(105)	610	191
Change in other liabilities	(111)	8	(14)
Other	(78)	13	4
Net cash provided by operating activities	109	708	1,384
Investing Activities:			
Capital expenditures for property and equipment	(35)	(46)	(81)
Proceeds from asset dispositions	6	—	120
Capitalized software costs	(44)	(46)	(124)
Other	16	(15)	(38)
Net cash used in investing activities	(57)	(107)	(123)
Financing Activities:			
Borrowings	1,510	4,590	2,200
Repayment of debt	(3,230)	(2,121)	(1,547)
Debt issuance costs and redemption premiums	(76)	(71)	(29)
Dividends paid	—	(42)	(172)
Repurchases of common stock	—	(296)	(1,538)
Share-based compensation tax withholdings	(49)	(58)	(44)
Proceeds from share-based compensation	52	31	17
Other	—	(1)	—
Net cash provided by (used in) financing activities	(1,793)	2,032	(1,113)

(Continued)

(Continued)

Effect of exchange rate changes on cash, restricted cash and cash equivalents	(10)	—	(2)
Net increase (decrease) in cash, restricted cash and cash equivalents	(1,751)	2,633	146
Cash, restricted cash and cash equivalents, beginning of period	3,263	630	484
Cash, restricted cash and cash equivalents, end of period	$ 1,512	$ 3,263	$ 630

APPENDIX B

UNIFORM SYSTEM SCHEDULES

Directly below is the income statement for the Eatonwood Hotel for the year ended 12/31/20X4. The following pages present the nine supporting schedules referenced on the income statement below.

Eatonwood Hotel
Summary Statement of Income
For the year ended December 31, 20X4

	Schedule	Net Revenue	Cost of Sales	Labor Costs & Related Expenses	Other Expenses	Profit (Loss)
Operated Departments:						
Rooms	1	$6,070,356	$ –	$ 1,068,383	$ 473,487	$4,528,486
Food and Beverage	2	2,806,899	1,057,573	885,334	250,922	613,070
Miscellaneous Income	3	188,092				188,092
Total Operated Departments		9,065,347	1,057,573	1,953,717	724,409	5,329,648
Undistributed Operating Expenses:						
Administrative and General	4			269,914	217,851	487,765
Information and Telecom. Systems	5		23,495	150,351	75,297	249,143
Sales and Marketing	6			117,190	215,456	332,646
Property Operation and Maintenance	7			200,170	161,386	361,556
Utilities	8				337,277	337,277
Total U.O.E.			23,495	737,625	1,007,267	1,768,387
Totals		9,065,347	1,081,068	2,691,342	1,731,676	
Gross Operating Profit						3,561,261
Nonoperating Expenses:						
Property Taxes						218,000
Insurance						154,000
Total Nonoperating Expenses						372,000
EBITDA						3,189,261
Interest, Depreciation, and Amortization						
Interest Expense						261,347
Depreciation						775,423
Amortization						15,421
Total Interest, Depreciation, and Amortization						1,052,191
Income before Income Taxes						2,137,070
Income Taxes						641,121
Net Income						$1,495,949

Note: This Summary Income Statement format is a modification of the Eleventh Revised Edition of the *Uniform System of Accounts for the Lodging Industry (USALI)*. Several schedules follow to show the relationship between the Summary Income Statement and the schedules. The schedules are based on the Eleventh Revised Edition of the *USALI* but do not use all line items shown on the formal schedule per the *USALI*.

Rooms—Schedule #1
Eatonwood Hotel
For the year ended December 31, 20X4

Revenue
  Transient Rooms Revenue
    Retail .... $ 4,632,841
    Discount 1,458,015
  Total Transient Rooms Revenue 6,090,856
Allowances .... (20,500)
Net Revenue 6,070,356

Expenses
  Labor and Related Expenses
    Salaries and Wages
      Management 175,000
      Nonmanagement
        Front Office 125,500
        Housekeeping 458,350
        Reservations 97,069
    Total Salaries and Wages 855,919
    Payroll-Related Expenses
      Payroll Taxes 75,422
      Employee Benefits 137,042
    Total Payroll-Related Expenses 212,464
  Total Labor Costs and Related Expenses 1,068,383

  Other Expenses
    Cleaning Supplies 20,100
    Commissions 66,775
    Complimentary Services and Gifts 2,420
    Contract Services 30,874
    Guest Relocation 1,241
    Guest Supplies 48,565
    Laundry and Dry Cleaning 42,495
    Linen 12,140
    Miscellaneous 5,100
    Operating Supplies 122,600
    Reservations 40,908
    Training 19,564
    Uniform Costs 15,705
    Uniform Laundry 45,000
  Total Other Expenses 473,487

Total Expenses 1,541,870

Departmental Profit $4,528,486

Food and Beverage—Schedule #2
Eatonwood Hotel
For the year ended December 31, 20X4

Revenue		
Food Revenue		
Venue Food Revenue	$1,600,318	
Banquet Food Revenue	374,000	
Total Food Revenue	1,974,318	
Beverage Revenue		
Venue Beverage Revenue	662,000	
Banquet Beverage Revenue	122,101	
Total Beverage Revenue	784,101	
Less: Allowances	12,482	
Total Food and Beverage Revenue	2,745,937	
Other Revenue		
Cover Charges	1,966	
Service Charges	40,467	
Miscellaneous Other Revenue	18,529	
Total Other Revenue	60,962	
Total Revenue	2,806,899	
Cost of Sales		
Cost of Food Sales	895,315	
Cost of Beverage Sales	162,258	
Total Cost of Sales	1,057,573	
Gross Profit	1,749,326	
Expenses		
Labor Costs and Related Expenses		
Salaries, Wages, and Service Charges		
Salaries and Wages		
Management		
Service	120,000	
Kitchen	80,000	
Nonmanagement		
Banquet Service	85,521	
Kitchen	103,112	
Venues	262,386	
Total Salaries and Wages	651,019	
Service Charge Distribution	40,467	
Total Salaries, Wages, and Service Charges	691,486	
Payroll-Related Expenses		
Payroll Taxes	78,150	
Employee Benefits	115,698	
Total Payroll-Related Expenses	193,848	
Total Labor Costs and Related Expenses	885,334	
Other Expenses		
China	13,870	
Contract Services	28,088	
Glassware	7,114	
Kitchen Fuel	2,345	

(Continued)

(Continued)

Laundry and Dry Cleaning	11,515
Licenses and Permits	7,675
Linen	7,800
Miscellaneous	14,459
Music and Entertainment	23,593
Operating Supplies	71,712
Paper and Plastics	9,349
Training	12,000
Uniform Costs	15,680
Uniform Laundry	8,450
Utensils	17,272
Total Other Expenses	250,922
Total Expenses	1,136,256
Departmental Profit	$ 613,070

Miscellaneous Income—Schedule #3
Eatonwood Hotel
For the Year Ended December 31, 20X4

Commissions	$ 32,471
Interest Income	83,500
Space Rentals and Concessions	68,750
Other	3,371
Total Miscellaneous Income	$188,092

Administrative and General—Schedule #4
Eatonwood Hotel
For the year ended December 31, 20X4

Expenses
    Labor Costs and Related Expenses
        Salaries and Wages

Management	$110,000
Nonmanagement	
Accounting	42,100
Human Resources	28,320
Purchasing/Receiving	25,487
Security	18,500
Total Salaries and Wages	224,407
Payroll-Related Expenses	
Payroll Taxes	18,211
Employee Benefits	27,296
Total Payroll-Related Expenses	45,507
Total Labor Costs and Related Expenses	269,914
Other Expenses	
Audit Charges	3,600
Bank Charges	2,115
Cash Overages and Shortages	816
Contract Services	1,609
Credit and Collection	15,746
Credit Card Commissions	62,906
Donations	10,000
Dues and Subscriptions	7,283
Human Resources	30,349
Loss and Damage	1,615
Miscellaneous	3,200
Operating Supplies	15,914
Postage and Overnight Delivery Charges	7,421
Professional Fees	4,619
Provision for Doubtful Accounts	22,406
Security	4,911
Training	7,500
Travel	15,841
Total Other Expenses	217,851
Total Expenses	$487,765

Information and Telecommunications Systems—Schedule #5
Eatonwood Hotel
For the year ended December 31, 20X4

Expenses
  Labor Costs and Related Expenses
    Salaries and Wages

Management	$ 60,000
Nonmanagement	
Information Technology	32,500
Telecommunications	28,750
Total Salaries and Wages	121,250
Payroll-Related Expenses	
Payroll Taxes	10,913
Employee Benefits	18,188
Total Payroll-Related Expenses	29,101
Total Labor Costs and Related Expenses	150,351
Cost of Services	
Cost of Cell Phones	1,245
Cost of Internet Services	15,468
Cost of Long-Distance Calls	6,782
Total Cost of Services	23,495
System Expenses	
Administration and General	13,459
Energy Management	7,582
Food and Beverage	8,753
Human Resources	3,588
Information Security	4,578
Information Systems	3,552
Property Operation and Maintenance	2,559
Rooms	9,877
Sales and Marketing	6,899
Telecommunications	3,981
Total System Expenses	64,828
Other Expenses	
Contract Services	1,542
Dues and Subscriptions	650
Miscellaneous	758
Operating Supplies	2,578
System Storage and Optimization	2,500
Training	985
Travel—Other	1,456
Total Other Expenses	10,469
Total Expenses	$249,143

Sales and Marketing—Schedule #6
Eatonwood Hotel
For the year ended December 31, 20X4

Expenses
  Labor Costs and Related Expenses
    Salaries and Wages

Management	$ 55,000
Nonmanagement	38,975
Total Salaries and Wages	93,975
Payroll-Related Expenses	
Payroll Taxes	9,150
Employee Benefits	14,065
Total Payroll-Related Expenses	23,215
Total Labor Costs and Related Expenses	117,190
Other Expenses	
Agency Fees	24,625
Collateral Material	15,783
Complimentary Services and Gifts	1,562
Contract Services	4,231
Direct Mail	15,782
Dues and Subscriptions	4,522
In-House Graphics	15,444
Media	75,465
Miscellaneous	1,588
Operating Supplies	5,811
Outside Services Market Research	6,522
Photography	4,578
Postage and Overnight Delivery Charges	4,500
Trade Shows	9,800
Training	3,366
Travel—Meals and Entertainment	9,877
Travel—Other	6,500
Website	5,500
Total Other Expenses	215,456
Total Expenses	$332,646

Property Operation and Maintenance—Schedule #7
Eatonwood Hotel
For the year ended December 31, 20X4

Expenses
    Labor Costs and Related Expenses
        Salaries and Wages

Management	$ 65,000
Nonmanagement	94,500
Total Salaries and Wages	159,500
Payroll-Related Expenses	
Payroll Taxes	16,390
Employee Benefits	24,280
Total Payroll-Related Expenses	40,670
Total Labor Costs and Related Expenses	200,170
Other Expenses	
Building	12,460
Contract Services	10,100
Dues and Subscriptions	1,560
Electrical and Mechanical Equipment	4,892
Elevators	10,619
Engineering Supplies	10,117
Floor Covering	12,924
Furniture and Equipment	15,141
Grounds Maintenance and Landscaping	6,152
Heating, Ventilation, and Air Conditioning Equip.	7,892
Kitchen Equipment	2,015
Laundry Equipment	1,914
Life/Safety	4,570
Light Bulbs	3,418
Miscellaneous	2,578
Operating Supplies	6,539
Painting and Wallcovering	7,822
Plumbing	9,800
Swimming Pool	7,822
Training	3,441
Uniform Costs	2,615
Uniform Laundry	5,562
Vehicle Repair	4,588
Waste Removal	6,845
Total Other Expenses	161,386
Total Expenses	$361,556

Utilities—Schedule #8
Eatonwood Hotel
For the year ended December 31, 20X4

Utilities	
Electricity	$158,302
Gas	124,689
Oil	8,500
Water/Sewer	45,786
Total Expenses	$337,277

In addition to the schedules used in the preceding example, the *Uniform System of Accounts for the Lodging Industry*, Eleventh Rev. Ed., contains several other schedules that can be used when circumstances warrant their use. Blank versions of these schedules are presented in the remainder of this Appendix.

Other Operated Departments

	PERIOD OF												
	CURRENT PERIOD						YEAR-TO-DATE						
	ACTUAL		FORECAST/ BUDGET		PRIOR YEAR		ACTUAL		FORECAST/ BUDGET		PRIOR YEAR		
	$	%	$	%	$	%	$	%	$	%	$	%	
DEPARTMENTAL REVENUE													
Other Operated Department 1													
Other Operated Department 2													
- - -													
Other Operated Department x													
Minor Operated Departments													
TOTAL DEPARTMENTAL REVENUE													
DEPARTMENTAL EXPENSES[1]													
Other Operated Department 1													
Other Operated Department 2													
- - -													
Other Operated Department x													
Minor Operated Departments													
TOTAL DEPARTMENTAL EXPENSES													
DEPARTMENTAL PROFIT													
Other Operated Department 1													
Other Operated Department 2													
- - -													
Other Operated Department x													
Minor Operated Departments													
TOTAL OTHER OPERATED DEPARTMENT PROFIT													

[1] Departmental Expenses is the sum of Cost of Sales (when applicable) and Total Expenses.

	PERIOD OF											
	CURRENT PERIOD						YEAR-TO-DATE					
	ACTUAL		FORECAST/ BUDGET		PRIOR YEAR		ACTUAL		FORECAST/ BUDGET		PRIOR YEAR	
	$	%	$	%	$	%	$	%	$	%	$	%
REVENUE												
Greens Fee Revenue												
Tournament Fee Revenue												
Golf Cart Rental Revenue												
Golf Equipment Rental Revenue												
Practice Range Fee Revenue												
Lesson Fee Revenue												
Golf Club Maintenance Revenue												
Storage Fee Revenue												
Membership Fee Revenue												
Merchandise Revenue												
Clothing Revenue												
Other Revenue												
Less: Allowances												
TOTAL GOLF COURSE AND PRO SHOP REVENUE												
COST OF SALES												
Cost of Merchandise Sales												
Cost of Clothing Sales												
TOTAL COST OF SALES												
GROSS PROFIT												
EXPENSES												
Labor Costs and Related Expenses												
Salaries, Wages, Service Charges, Contracted Labor, and Bonuses												
Salaries and Wages												
Management												
Nonmanagement												
Golf Pros/Operations												
Greens/Maintenance												
Pro Shop												
Subtotal: Salaries and Wages												
Service Charge Distribution												
Contracted, Leased, and Outsourced Labor												
Bonuses and Incentives												
Total Salaries, Wages, Service Charges, Contracted Labor, and Bonuses												
Payroll-Related Expenses												
Payroll Taxes												

(Continued)

(Continued)

	PERIOD OF					
	CURRENT PERIOD			YEAR-TO-DATE		
	ACTUAL	FORECAST/ BUDGET	PRIOR YEAR	ACTUAL	FORECAST/ BUDGET	PRIOR YEAR
	$	%	$	%	$	%	$	%	$	%	$	%
Supplemental Pay												
Employee Benefits												
Total Payroll-Related Expenses												
Total Labor Costs and Related Expenses												
Other Expenses												
Cleaning Supplies												
Cluster Services												
Complimentary Services and Gifts												
Contract Services												
Corporate Office Reimbursables												
Decorations												
Dues and Subscriptions												
Entertainment—In-House												
Equipment Rental												
Gasoline and Lubricants												
Grounds Maintenance and Landscaping												
Irrigation												
Laundry and Dry Cleaning												
Licenses and Permits												
Linen												
Management Fees												
Miscellaneous												
Operating Supplies												
Printing and Stationery												
Reservations												
Royalty Fees												
Tournament Expenses												
Training												
Transportation												
Travel—Meals and Entertainment												
Travel—Other												
Uniform Costs												
Uniform Laundry												
Vehicle Repairs and Maintenance												
Water												
Total Other Expenses												
TOTAL EXPENSES												
DEPARTMENTAL PROFIT												

	PERIOD OF											
	CURRENT PERIOD						YEAR-TO-DATE					
	ACTUAL		FORECAST/ BUDGET		PRIOR YEAR		ACTUAL		FORECAST/ BUDGET		PRIOR YEAR	
	$	%	$	%	$	%	$	%	$	%	$	%
REVENUE												
Massage and Body Treatment Revenue												
Skin Care Revenue												
Hair Care Revenue												
Nail Care Revenue												
Fitness Revenue												
Health and Wellness Revenue												
Membership Fee Revenue												
Retail Revenue												
Other Revenue												
Less: Allowances												
TOTAL HEALTH CLUB/SPA REVENUE												
COST OF SALES												
GROSS PROFIT												
EXPENSES												
Labor Costs and Related Expenses												
Salaries, Wages, Service Charges, Contracted Labor, and Bonuses												
Salaries and Wages												
Management												
Nonmanagement												
Attendant/Housekeeping												
Fitness												
Reception/Retail												
Therapists/Technicians												
Subtotal: Salaries and Wages												
Service Charge Distribution												
Contracted, Leased, and Outsourced Labor												
Bonuses and Incentives												
Total Salaries, Wages, Service Charges, Contracted Labor, and Bonuses												
Payroll-Related Expenses												
Payroll Taxes												
Supplemental Pay												

(Continued)

(Continued)

	Period Of											
	Current Period						Year-To-Date					
	Actual		Forecast/ Budget		Prior Year		Actual		Forecast/ Budget		Prior Year	
	$	%	$	%	$	%	$	%	$	%	$	%
Employee Benefits												
Total Payroll-Related Expenses												
Total Labor Costs and Related Expenses												
Other Expenses												
Ambience												
Athletic Supplies												
Cleaning Supplies												
Cluster Services												
Complimentary Services and Gifts												
Contract Services												
Corporate Office Reimbursables												
Decorations												
Dues and Subscriptions												
Entertainment—In-House												
Equipment Rental												
Health and Beauty Products												
Laundry and Dry Cleaning												
Licenses and Permits												
Linen												
Management Fees												
Miscellaneous												
Operating Supplies												
Printing and Stationery												
Reservations												
Royalty Fees												
Swimming Pool												
Training												
Travel—Meals and Entertainment												
Travel—Other												
Uniform Costs												
Uniform Laundry												
Total Other Expenses												
TOTAL EXPENSES												
DEPARTMENTAL PROFIT												

Parking

	PERIOD OF											
	CURRENT PERIOD						YEAR-TO-DATE					
	ACTUAL		FORECAST/ BUDGET		PRIOR YEAR		ACTUAL		FORECAST/ BUDGET		PRIOR YEAR	
	$	%	$	%	$	%	$	%	$	%	$	%
REVENUE												
Self-Parking Revenue												
Valet Parking Revenue												
Other Revenue												
Less: Allowances												
TOTAL PARKING REVENUE												
COST OF SALES												
GROSS PROFIT												
EXPENSES												
Labor Costs and Related Expenses												
Salaries, Wages, Service Charges, Contracted Labor, and Bonuses												
Salaries and Wages												
Management												
Nonmanagement												
Subtotal: Salaries and Wages												
Service Charge Distribution												
Contracted, Leased, and Outsourced Labor												
Bonuses and Incentives												
Total Salaries, Wages, Service Charges, Contracted Labor, and Bonuses												
Payroll-Related Expenses												
Payroll Taxes												
Supplemental Pay												
Employee Benefits												
Total Payroll-Related Expenses												
Total Labor Costs and Related Expenses												
Other Expenses												
Cleaning Supplies												
Cluster Services												
Complimentary Services and Gifts												

(Continued)

(Continued)

	PERIOD OF											
	CURRENT PERIOD						YEAR-TO-DATE					
	ACTUAL		FORECAST/ BUDGET		PRIOR YEAR		ACTUAL		FORECAST/ BUDGET		PRIOR YEAR	
	$	%	$	%	$	%	$	%	$	%	$	%
Contract Services												
Corporate Office Reimbursables												
Decorations												
Dues and Subscriptions												
Entertainment—In-House												
Equipment Rental												
Laundry and Dry Cleaning												
Licenses and Permits												
Management Fees												
Miscellaneous												
Operating Supplies												
Printing and Stationery												
Rent												
Royalty Fees												
Training												
Travel—Meals and Entertainment												
Travel—Other												
Uniform Costs												
Uniform Laundry												
Total Other Expenses												
TOTAL EXPENSES												
DEPARTMENTAL PROFIT												

	PERIOD OF											
	CURRENT PERIOD						YEAR-TO-DATE					
	ACTUAL		FORECAST/ BUDGET		PRIOR YEAR		ACTUAL		FORECAST/ BUDGET		PRIOR YEAR	
	$	%	$	%	$	%	$	%	$	%	$	%
REVENUE												
Revenue												
Less: Allowances												
TOTAL [SCHEDULE NAME] REVENUE												
COST OF SALES												
GROSS PROFIT												
EXPENSES												
Labor Costs and Related Expenses												
Salaries, Wages, Service Charges, Contracted Labor, and Bonuses												
Salaries and Wages												
Management												
Nonmanagement												
Subcategories as needed												
Subtotal: Salaries and Wages												
Service Charge Distribution												
Contracted, Leased, and Outsourced Labor												
Bonuses and Incentives												
Total Salaries, Wages, Service Charges, Contracted Labor, and Bonuses												
Payroll-Related Expenses												
Payroll Taxes												
Supplemental Pay												
Employee Benefits												
Total Payroll-Related Expenses												
Total Labor Costs and Related Expenses												
Other Expenses												
Cleaning Supplies												
Cluster Services												
Complimentary Services and Gifts												
Contract Services												
Corporate Office Reimbursables												
Decorations												
Dues and Subscriptions												
Entertainment—In-House												
Equipment Rental												

(Continued)

(Continued)

	PERIOD OF							
	CURRENT PERIOD					YEAR-TO-DATE					
	ACTUAL		FORECAST/ BUDGET		PRIOR YEAR		ACTUAL		FORECAST/ BUDGET		PRIOR YEAR	
	$	%	$	%	$	%	$	%	$	%	$	%
Laundry and Dry Cleaning												
Licenses and Permits												
Linen												
Management Fees												
Miscellaneous												
Operating Supplies												
[Other detailed expenses as warranted]												
Printing and Stationery												
Royalty Fees												
Training												
Travel—Meals and Entertainment												
Travel—Other												
Uniform Costs												
Uniform Laundry												
Total Other Expenses												
TOTAL EXPENSES												
DEPARTMENTAL PROFIT												

Minor Operated Departments

	Period Of											
	Current Period						Year-To-Date					
	Actual		Forecast/ Budget		Prior Year		Actual		Forecast/ Budget		Prior Year	
	$	%	$	%	$	%	$	%	$	%	$	%
DEPARTMENTAL REVENUE												
Minor Operated Department 1												
Minor Operated Department 2												
- - -												
Minor Operated Department x												
Less: Allowances												
TOTAL DEPARTMENTAL REVENUE												
DEPARTMENTAL EXPENSES[1]												
Minor Operated Department 1												
Minor Operated Department 2												
- - -												
Minor Operated Department x												
TOTAL MINOR OPERATED DEPARTMENTAL EXPENSES												
DEPARTMENTAL PROFIT												
Minor Operated Department 1												
Minor Operated Department 2												
- - -												
Minor Operated Department x												
TOTAL MINOR OPERATED DEPARTMENT PROFIT												

[1] Departmental Expenses is the sum of Cost of Sales (when applicable) and Total Expenses.

Miscellaneous Income

	Period Of											
	Current Period						Year-To-Date					
	Actual		Forecast/ Budget		Prior Year		Actual		Forecast/ Budget		Prior Year	
	$	%	$	%	$	%	$	%	$	%	$	%
Attrition Fees												
Cancellation Fees												
Cash Discounts Earned												
Commissions												
Guest-Related Foreign Currency Transaction Gains (Losses)												
Guest Laundry and Dry Cleaning												
Interest Income												
Net Revenue from Renting Mixed-Ownership Units												
Other Breakage												
Package Breakage												
Proceeds from Business Interruption Insurance												
Resort Fees												
Space Rental and Concessions												
Other												
Total Miscellaneous Income												

	PERIOD OF											
	CURRENT PERIOD						YEAR-TO-DATE					
	ACTUAL		FORECAST/ BUDGET		PRIOR YEAR		ACTUAL		FORECAST/ BUDGET		PRIOR YEAR	
	$	%	$	%	$	%	$	%	$	%	$	%
EXPENSES												
Labor Costs and Related Expenses												
Salaries, Wages, Service Charges, Contracted Labor, and Bonuses												
Salaries and Wages												
Management												
Nonmanagement												
Accounting												
General Support												
Human Resources												
Purchasing/Receiving												
Security												
Subtotal: Salaries and Wages												
Service Charge Distribution												
Contracted, Leased, and Outsourced Labor												
Bonuses and Incentives												
Total Salaries, Wages, Service Charges, Contracted Labor, and Bonuses												
Payroll-Related Expenses												
Payroll Taxes												
Supplemental Pay												
Employee Benefits												
Total Payroll-Related Expenses												
Total Labor Costs and Related Expenses												
Other Expenses												
Audit Charges												
Bank Charges												
Cash Overages and Shortages												
Centralized Accounting Charges												
Cluster Services												
Complimentary Services and Gifts												
Contract Services												
Corporate Office Reimbursables												
Credit and Collection												
Credit Card Commissions												
Decorations												

(Continued)

(Continued)

	Period Of					
	Current Period			Year-To-Date		
	Actual	Forecast/ Budget	Prior Year	Actual	Forecast/ Budget	Prior Year
	$	%	$	%	$	%	$	%	$	%	$	%
Donations												
Dues and Subscriptions												
Entertainment—In-House												
Equipment Rental												
Human Resources												
Legal Services												
Licenses and Permits												
Loss and Damage												
Miscellaneous												
Non-Guest-Related Foreign Currency Exchange Gains (Losses)												
Operating Supplies												
Payroll Processing												
Postage and Overnight Delivery Charges												
Professional Fees												
Provision for Doubtful Accounts												
Security												
Settlement Costs												
Staff Transportation												
Training												
Travel—Meals and Entertainment												
Travel—Other												
Uniform Costs												
Uniform Laundry												
Total Other Expenses												
TOTAL EXPENSES												

	PERIOD OF											
	CURRENT PERIOD						YEAR-TO-DATE					
	ACTUAL		FORECAST/ BUDGET		PRIOR YEAR		ACTUAL		FORECAST/ BUDGET		PRIOR YEAR	
	$	%	$	%	$	%	$	%	$	%	$	%
EXPENSES												
Labor Costs and Related Expenses												
Salaries, Wages, Service Charges, Contracted Labor, and Bonuses												
Salaries and Wages												
Management												
Nonmanagement												
Information Technology												
Telecommunications												
Subtotal: Salaries and Wages												
Service Charge Distribution												
Contracted, Leased, and Outsourced Labor												
Bonuses and Incentives												
Total Salaries, Wages, Service Charges, Contracted Labor, and Bonuses												
Payroll-Related Expenses												
Payroll Taxes												
Supplemental Pay												
Employee Benefits												
Total Payroll-Related Expenses												
Total Labor Costs and Related Expenses												
Cost of Services												
Cost of Cell Phones												
Cost of Internet Services												
Cost of Local Calls												
Cost of Long Distance Calls												
Other Cost of Services												
Total Cost of Services												
System Expenses												
Administrative and General												
Centralized Information System Charges												
Energy Management												
Food and Beverage												
Golf												
Hardware												

(Continued)

(*Continued*)

	Period Of					
	Current Period			**Year-To-Date**		
	Actual	Forecast/ Budget	Prior Year	Actual	Forecast/ Budget	Prior Year
	$ %	$ %	$ %	$ %	$ %	$ %
Health Club/Spa						
Human Resources						
Information Security						
Information Systems						
Other						
Parking						
Property Operation and Maintenance						
Rooms						
Sales and Marketing						
Telecommunications						
Total System Expenses						
Other Expenses						
Cluster Services						
Contract Services						
Corporate Office Reimbursables						
Dues and Subscriptions						
Entertainment—In-House						
Equipment Rental						
Miscellaneous						
Operating Supplies						
Other Equipment						
System Storage and Optimization						
Training						
Travel—Meals and Entertainment						
Travel—Other						
Uniform Costs						
Uniform Laundry						
Total Other Expenses						
Total Expenses						

	PERIOD OF					
	CURRENT PERIOD			YEAR-TO-DATE		
	ACTUAL	FORECAST/ BUDGET	PRIOR YEAR	ACTUAL	FORECAST/ BUDGET	PRIOR YEAR
	$ %	$ %	$ %	$ %	$ %	$ %
EXPENSES						
Labor Costs and Related Expenses						
Salaries, Wages, Service Charges, Contracted Labor, and Bonuses						
Salaries and Wages						
Management						
Nonmanagement						
Subtotal: Salaries and Wages						
Service Charge Distribution						
Contracted, Leased, and Outsourced Labor						
Bonuses and Incentives						
Total Salaries, Wages, Service Charges, Contracted Labor, and Bonuses						
Payroll-Related Expenses						
Payroll Taxes						
Supplemental Pay						
Employee Benefits						
Total Payroll-Related Expenses						
Total Labor Costs and Related Expenses						
Other Expenses						
Agency Fees						
Cluster Services						
Collateral Material						
Complimentary Services and Gifts						
Contract Services						
Corporate Office Reimbursables						
Decorations						
Direct Mail						
Dues and Subscriptions						
Entertainment—In-House						
Equipment Rental						
Familiarization Trips						
Franchise and Affiliation Marketing						

(Continued)

(Continued)

	PERIOD OF											
	CURRENT PERIOD						YEAR-TO-DATE					
	ACTUAL		FORECAST/ BUDGET		PRIOR YEAR		ACTUAL		FORECAST/ BUDGET		PRIOR YEAR	
	$	%	$	%	$	%	$	%	$	%	$	%
Franchise and Affiliation Fees—Royalties												
In-House Graphics												
Loyalty Programs												
Media												
Miscellaneous												
Operating Supplies												
Outside Sales Representation												
Outside Services Market Research												
Outside Signage												
Photography												
Postage and Overnight Delivery Charges												
Promotion												
Trade Shows												
Training												
Travel—Meals and Entertainment												
Travel—Other												
Uniform Laundry												
Website												
Total Other Expenses												
TOTAL EXPENSES												

	PERIOD OF											
	CURRENT PERIOD						YEAR-TO-DATE					
	ACTUAL		FORECAST/ BUDGET		PRIOR YEAR		ACTUAL		FORECAST/ BUDGET		PRIOR YEAR	
	$	%	$	%	$	%	$	%	$	%	$	%
EXPENSES												
Labor Costs and Related Expenses												
Salaries, Wages, Service Charges, Contracted Labor, and Bonuses												
Salaries and Wages												
Management												
Nonmanagement												
Subtotal: Salaries and Wages												
Service Charge Distribution												
Contracted, Leased, and Outsourced Labor												
Bonuses and Incentives												
Total Salaries, Wages, Service Charges, Contracted Labor, and Bonuses												
Payroll-Related Expenses												
Payroll Taxes												
Supplemental Pay												
Employee Benefits												
Total Payroll-Related Expenses												
Total Labor Costs and Related Expenses												
Other Expenses												
Building												
Cluster Services												
Contract Services												
Corporate Office Reimbursables												
Dues and Subscriptions												
Electrical and Mechanical Equipment												
Elevators and Escalators												
Engineering Supplies												
Entertainment—In-House												
Equipment Rental												
Floor Covering												
Furniture and Equipment												
Grounds Maintenance and Landscaping												

(Continued)

(Continued)

	PERIOD OF											
	CURRENT PERIOD						YEAR-TO-DATE					
	ACTUAL		FORECAST/ BUDGET		PRIOR YEAR		ACTUAL		FORECAST/ BUDGET		PRIOR YEAR	
	$	%	$	%	$	%	$	%	$	%	$	%
Heating, Ventilation, and Air-Conditioning Equipment												
Kitchen Equipment												
Laundry Equipment												
Licenses and Permits												
Life/Safety												
Light Bulbs												
Miscellaneous												
Operating Supplies												
Painting and Wallcovering												
Plumbing												
Swimming Pool												
Training												
Travel—Meals and Entertainment												
Travel—Other												
Uniform Costs												
Uniform Laundry												
Vehicle Repair												
Waste Removal												
Total Other Expenses												
TOTAL EXPENSES												

Utilities

	PERIOD OF											
	CURRENT PERIOD						YEAR-TO-DATE					
	ACTUAL		FORECAST/ BUDGET		PRIOR YEAR		ACTUAL		FORECAST/ BUDGET		PRIOR YEAR	
	$	%	$	%	$	%	$	%	$	%	$	%
UTILITIES												
Electricity												
Gas												
Oil												
Water/Sewer												
Steam												
Chilled Water												
Other Fuels												
Contract Services												
TOTAL EXPENSES												

Management Fees

	PERIOD OF											
	CURRENT PERIOD						YEAR-TO-DATE					
	ACTUAL		FORECAST/ BUDGET		PRIOR YEAR		ACTUAL		FORECAST/ BUDGET		PRIOR YEAR	
	$	%	$	%	$	%	$	%	$	%	$	%
MANAGEMENT FEES												
Base Fee												
Incentive Fees												
TOTAL MANAGEMENT FEES												

Nonoperating Income and Expenses

	PERIOD OF											
	CURRENT PERIOD						YEAR-TO-DATE					
	ACTUAL		FORECAST/ BUDGET		PRIOR YEAR		ACTUAL		FORECAST/ BUDGET		PRIOR YEAR	
	$	%	$	%	$	%	$	%	$	%	$	%
INCOME												
Cost Recovery Income												
Interest Income												
Other Income												
TOTAL INCOME												
RENT												
Land and Buildings												
Other Property and Equipment												
TOTAL RENT												
PROPERTY AND OTHER TAXES												
Business and Occupation Taxes												
Other Taxes and Assessments												
Personal Property Taxes												
Real Estate Taxes												
TOTAL PROPERTY AND OTHER TAXES												
INSURANCE												
Building and Contents												
Liability												
Deductible												
TOTAL INSURANCE												
OTHER												
Cost Recovery Expense												
Gain/Loss on Fixed Assets												
Owner Expenses												
Unrealized Foreign Exchange Gains or Losses												
TOTAL OTHER												
TOTAL NONOPERATING INCOME AND EXPENSES												

House Laundry

	PERIOD OF											
	CURRENT PERIOD						YEAR-TO-DATE					
	ACTUAL		FORECAST/ BUDGET		PRIOR YEAR		ACTUAL		FORECAST/ BUDGET		PRIOR YEAR	
	$	%	$	%	$	%	$	%	$	%	$	%
EXPENSES												
Labor Costs and Related Expenses												
Salaries, Wages, Service Charges, Contracted Labor, and Bonuses												
Salaries and Wages												
Management												
Nonmanagement												
Subtotal: Salaries and Wages												
Service Charge Distribution												
Contracted, Leased, and Outsourced Labor												
Bonuses and Incentives												
Total Salaries, Wages, Service Charges, Contracted Labor, and Bonuses												
Payroll-Related Expenses												
Payroll Taxes												
Supplemental Pay												
Employee Benefits												
Total Payroll-Related Expenses												
Total Labor Costs and Related Expenses												
Other Expenses												
Cleaning Supplies												
Complimentary Services and Gifts												
Contract Services												
Corporate Office Reimbursables												
Decorations												
Dues and Subscriptions												
Entertainment—In-House												
Equipment Rental												
Laundry and Dry Cleaning												
Laundry Supplies												
Licenses and Permits												
Miscellaneous												
Operating Supplies												
Printing and Stationery												
Training												

(Continued)

(Continued)

	PERIOD OF					
	CURRENT PERIOD			YEAR-TO-DATE		
	ACTUAL	FORECAST/ BUDGET	PRIOR YEAR	ACTUAL	FORECAST/ BUDGET	PRIOR YEAR
	$	%	$	%	$	%	$	%	$	%	$	%
Travel—Meals and Entertainment												
Travel—Other												
Uniform Costs												
Uniform Laundry												
Total Other Expenses												
TOTAL EXPENSES												
CREDITS												
Cost of Guest and Outside Laundry												
Concessionaires' Laundry												
COST OF HOUSE LAUNDRY												
ALLOCATIONS												
Allocation to Rooms												
Allocation to Food and Beverage												
Allocation to Department 1												
Allocation to Department 2												
- - -												
Allocation to Department x												
TOTAL ALLOCATIONS												
NET RECOVERY												

	PERIOD OF					
	CURRENT PERIOD			YEAR-TO-DATE		
	ACTUAL	FORECAST/ BUDGET	PRIOR YEAR	ACTUAL	FORECAST/ BUDGET	PRIOR YEAR
	$	%	$	%	$	%	$	%	$	%	$	%
EXPENSES												
Cost of Food												
Labor Costs and Related Expenses												
Salaries, Wages, Service Charges, Contracted Labor, and Bonuses												
Salaries and Wages												
Management												
Nonmanagement												
Kitchen												
Service												
Subtotal: Salaries and Wages												
Service Charge Distribution												
Contracted, Leased, and Outsourced Labor												
Bonuses and Incentives												
Total Salaries, Wages, Service Charges, Contracted Labor, and Bonuses												
Payroll-Related Expenses												
Payroll Taxes												
Supplemental Pay												
Employee Benefits												
Total Payroll-Related Expenses												
Total Labor Costs and Related Expenses												
Other Expenses												
China												
Cleaning Supplies												
Contract Services												
Corporate Office Reimbursables												
Decorations												
Dishwashing Supplies												
Dues and Subscriptions												
Entertainment—In-House												
Equipment Rental												
Flatware												
Glassware												
Ice												

(Continued)

(Continued)

| | Current Period | | | | | | Year-To-Date | | | | | |
| | Actual | | Forecast/Budget | | Prior Year | | Actual | | Forecast/Budget | | Prior Year | |
	$	%	$	%	$	%	$	%	$	%	$	%
Kitchen Fuel												
Kitchen Smallwares												
Laundry and Dry Cleaning												
Licenses and Permits												
Linen												
Miscellaneous												
Operating Supplies												
Paper and Plastics												
Printing and Stationery												
Training												
Travel—Meals and Entertainment												
Travel—Other												
Uniform Costs												
Uniform Laundry												
Utensils												
Total Other Expenses												
TOTAL EXPENSES												
NET REVENUE												
COST OF STAFF DINING												
ALLOCATIONS												
Allocation to Rooms												
Allocation to Food and Beverage												
Allocation to Department 1												
Allocation to Department 2												
- - -												
Allocation to Department x												
TOTAL ALLOCATIONS												
NET RECOVERY												

Payroll-Related Expenses

	Period Of											
	Current Period						Year-To-Date					
	Actual		Forecast/ Budget		Prior Year		Actual		Forecast/ Budget		Prior Year	
	$	%	$	%	$	%	$	%	$	%	$	%
Payroll Taxes												
National Disability Insurance												
National Medical Insurance												
National Retirement Contribution												
National Unemployment Insurance												
State Disability Insurance												
State Medical Insurance												
State Retirement Contribution												
State Unemployment Insurance												
Total Payroll Taxes												
Supplemental Pay												
Other Pay												
Personal Days												
Severance Pay												
Sick Pay												
Holiday Pay												
Vacation/Paid Time Off												
Total Supplemental Pay												
Employee Benefits												
Automobile Allowance												
Child Care												
Contributory Savings Plan												
Dental Insurance												
Disability Insurance												
Expat Benefits												
Group Life Insurance												
Health Insurance												
Housing and Educational												
Meals												
Miscellaneous												
Nonunion Insurance												
Nonunion Pension												
Profit Sharing												
Public Subsidized Transportation												
Stock Benefits												
Stock Options												

(Continued)

(Continued)

	Period Of											
	Current Period						Year-To-Date					
	Actual		Forecast/ Budget		Prior Year		Actual		Forecast/ Budget		Prior Year	
	$	%	$	%	$	%	$	%	$	%	$	%
Union Insurance												
Union Other												
Union Pension												
Workers' Compensation Insurance												
Total Employee Benefits												
Total Payroll-Related Expenses												

APPENDIX C

SHOULD OVERHEAD COSTS BE ALLOCATED?*

By A. Neal Geller and Raymond S. Schmidgall

The allocation process is fairly complex and not well understood by the lodging industry. This appendix, therefore, has two purposes:

1. to discuss the advantages and drawbacks of allocation, and

2. to illustrate cost allocation.

Cost allocation is the assignment of overhead costs to operated departments according to benefits received, responsibilities, or other logical measures of use. Overhead costs, including the general manager's salary, are spread across profit centers, such as rooms and food and beverage.

Advantages of Allocation

The major advantage of cost allocation is that it results in better decision-making by the general and departmental managers. These decisions are improved when based on fully allocated income statements:

PRICING. Pricing is best accomplished when the full costs of an operated department are known.

MARKETING. Management can best determine which services to emphasize after the full costs of each operated department are realized.

CHANGES IN CAPACITY. Expansion or reduction in the capacity of the hotel/motel operation should be based on the profit potential (net of indirect costs) of the operating departments.

STAFFING. More judicious staffing decisions are possible with the full cost of each operated department known to management. In addition, cost allocation provides department heads with more realistic assessments of overhead costs their department must cover. Without the benefit of fully allocated income statements, a rooms department manager, for example, may not understand why a 70 percent contribution from the rooms department is imperative for the firm to realize a profit.

Finally, fully allocated income statements are useful in dealing with government regulations. They provide better information for wage-and-price guidelines, government per diem rates, and general lobbying efforts.

Drawbacks of Allocation

The major drawbacks of cost allocation relate primarily to the managers of operated departments and to misunderstandings as to its use. For example:

■ Department heads may not understand the process and may resist it.

■ Department heads may defer discretionary costs such as repairs, or otherwise strive to achieve short-run profitability at the expense of the long-run profitability of the company.

■ Fully allocated department statements are not appropriate for performance evaluation.

This article first appeared in *Lodging*.
*Note: This was written prior to the revision of the *Uniform System of Accounts for Hotels (USAH)*, which resulted in the 10th edition of the *Uniform System of Accounts for the Lodging Industry (USALI)*. However, in terms of allocating expenses, the approaches suggested here have not changed with the revision of the uniform system. Therefore, it is as relevant to cost allocation as when it was first written.

The effects of these drawbacks will be minimized if top-level management will do the following:

1. Explain completely the process of cost allocation and emphasize the benefits to the hotel/motel (or company).

2. Emphasize the importance of management for the long-term rather than focusing all the attention on the current period.

3. Separate department costs in fully allocated statements between direct and indirect. Further, separate the indirect costs between "controllable by department head"—if any—and "beyond the control of the department head."

4. Stress a team approach to managing the various profit and cost centers of the hotel/motel operation.

Bases of Allocation

The *USAH* contains several suggested bases for cost allocation, as you will see in Exhibit C.1. A cost allocation base is a factor that determines how much is allocated to a cost objective (department). For example, the rent expense of a hotel may be allocated on the basis of square footage of each department. If the rent expense is $10,000 for the period and the square footage of the rooms and food departments is 18,000 and 6,000 square feet, respectively, then 75 percent ($7,500) would be allocated to the rooms department and 25 percent ($2,500) to the food department.

It is important to note that the allocation bases should be chosen separately from the allocation method used. While the rent may be allocated to operated departments as shown in the above example, or indirectly through the service center, the allocation base can be the same. (Again, note Exhibit C.1.)

Methods of Allocation

The allocation method determines the degree of directness in allocating indirect costs from their cost centers to the profit centers. The three methods listed in the *USAH* are diagrammed and discussed briefly here.

The direct method (see Exhibit C.2) results in all indirect costs flowing directly from the cost centers to the profit centers. With this approach, no portion of fixed cost is allocated to service centers. The direct method is simple and easily understood.

The step method (see Exhibit C.3) requires a two-step allocation process. First, fixed costs are allocated to the profit and service centers. Second, the costs of service centers, including the allocated fixed costs, are allocated to the profit centers. In the second step, the costs of the service centers providing the most services to the other service centers are allocated first.

Once a service center's costs are allocated, no additional costs are allocated to this service center. The step method does not consider the reciprocal provision of services among other service centers. The formula method incorporates this additional refinement. The step method is more realistic than the direct method because it recognizes services provided by some service centers to others.

The formula method also requires two steps in the allocation process (see Exhibit C.4). The first step—the allocation of fixed costs—is the same as under the step method. The second step gives full consideration for services rendered by service centers to each other. The second step is generally complex and requires mathematical computations best performed by a computer.

Illustration of Allocation

The direct and step methods of cost allocation are illustrated here by using Walters Motor Inn. The formula method is not illustrated because it is beyond the scope of this appendix.

The Walters Motor Inn is a seventy-room property with food and beverage operations. It uses the *Uniform System of Accounts for Hotels (USAH)*. To simplify the illustrations, we have included only three undistributed operating expense categories and two fixed charge categories. The Inn's income statement for March, developed in accordance with the *USAH*, is shown in Exhibit C.5. Note that the indirect expenses have not been allocated to the profit centers so that the rooms and food and beverage departmental incomes, prior to cost allocation, are $34,000 and $14,500, respectively.

Exhibit C.1   Suggested Allocation Bases

Allocated Costs	Allocation Bases
Rent	1. Percentage applicable to revenue sources 2. Square feet of area occupied (fixed rent)
Real Estate Taxes	Square feet of area occupied
Insurance—Building and Contents	1. Square feet of area occupied 2. Square feet plus investment in furniture and fixture
Interest	Same as above
Depreciation—Building	Square feet of area occupied
Depreciation—Furnishing and Equipment	1. Department asset records 2. Square feet of area occupied
Depreciation—Capital Leases	1. Department use of leased equipment 2. Square feet of area occupied
Telephone	Number of extensions
Payroll Taxes and Employee Benefits	1. Number of employees 2. Detailed payroll records 3. Salaries and wages
Administrative and General	1. Accumulated costs 2. Number of employees
Data Processing	1. Accumulated costs 2. Number of employees
Marketing	Ratio to sales
Guest Entertainment	Ratio to sales
Energy Costs	1. Sub-meters 2. Cubic feet of area occupied
Property Operation and Maintenance	1. Job orders 2. Number of employees 3. Square footage
Human Resources	Number of employees
Transportation	Number of employees

Source: *Uniform System of Accounts for Hotels*, 8th revised edition, p. 137.

Exhibit C.2   The Direct Method

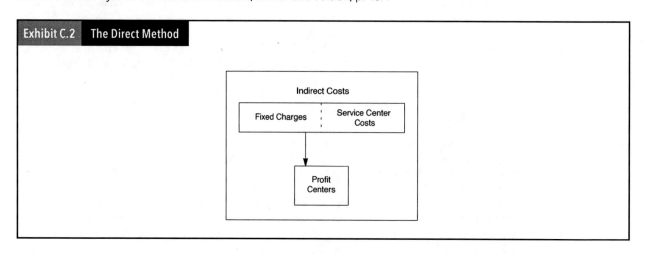

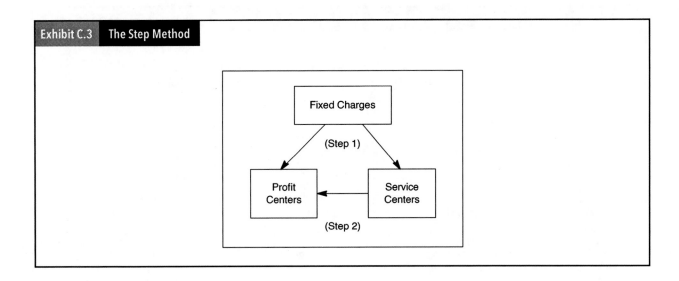

Exhibit C.3   The Step Method

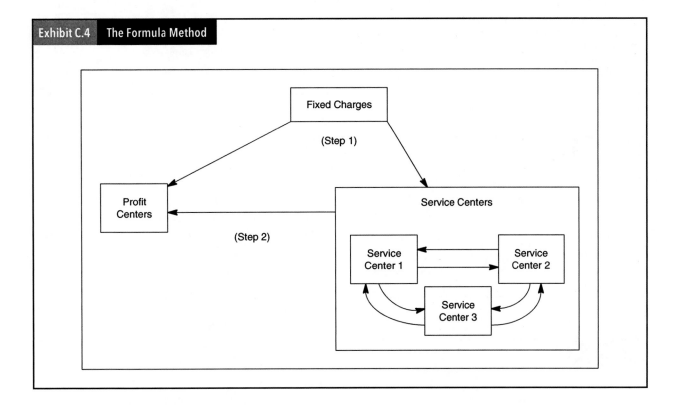

Exhibit C.4   The Formula Method

Regardless of the allocation method used, a cost allocation base must be selected for each indirect cost. The indirect expenses and the allocation bases selected for cost allocation of the Walters Motor Inn's indirect expenses are shown in Exhibit C.5-A.

The bases selected were chosen on recommendations from the *USAH*. The notable exception is Property Operation and Maintenance and Utility Costs. To simplify the illustrations, these two costs (POM and UC) were combined and allocated using one of the recommended bases for property operation and maintenance. The information required to establish the allocation bases for the Walters Motor Inn is shown in Exhibit C.5-B.

	Rooms	Food & Beverage	Total
Revenue	$50,000	$ 50,000	$100,000
Cost of Sales	-0-	18,000	18,000
Payroll and Related Expenses	12,000	13,000	25,000
Other Direct Expenses	4,000	4,500	8,500
Total Expenses	16,000	35,500	51,500
Departmental Income (Loss)	$34,000	$ 14,500	48,500

	Payroll & Related	Other	
Undistributed Operating Expenses:			
Administrative & General (A & G)	$ 10,000	$2,000	12,000
Marketing	2,000	1,000	3,000
Property Operation, Maintenance and Utility Costs (POM & UC)	2,000	4,000	6,000
Total Income after Undistributed Operating Expenses			27,500
Insurance			3,000
Depreciation			18,000
Total Insurance and Depreciation			21,000
Income before Income Taxes			6,500
Income Taxes			2,000
Net Income			$ 4,500

Exhibit C.5-A

Indirect Expenses	Bases
Insurance	Book value of fixed assets (BV-FA)
Depreciation	Square footage (SF)
POM & UC	Square footage (SF)
Marketing	Ratio to sales (RS)
A & G	Number of employees (NE)

Exhibit C.5-B

Department	Book Value of Fixed Assets	Square Footage	Number of Employees
Rooms	$900,000	40,000	14
Food & Beverage	300,000	15,000	20
A & G	50,000	2,500	4
Marketing	30,000	500	1
POM & UC	220,000	2,000	1

Illustration of Direct Method

The direct method of cost allocation is accomplished by allocating all indirect expenses to the profit centers and then preparing the fully allocated income statement. For the Walters Motor Inn, four bases of allocation are used.

The base for allocating the Inn's insurance is the book value of fixed assets of the rooms and food and beverage departments. The total book value-fixed assets for the two profit centers is $1.2 million, of which $900,000 pertains to the rooms department and $300,000 pertains to the food and beverage department. Since the book value-fixed assets of the rooms department is 75 percent of the combined book value-fixed assets for the two departments, the rooms department is allocated $2,250 of the insurance expenses (0.75 x $3,000).

The proportions of other indirect expenses and amounts allocated to the rooms and food and beverage departments were determined in similar fashion using the selected base of allocation as noted previously. Exhibit C.6 contains the indirect costs, the amount to be allocated, the allocation base, the proportions to be allocated to rooms and food and beverage, and the amounts allocated to these two departments.

Exhibit C.7 contains the fully allocated income statement. Under this method, the rooms department income after allocation is $7,853 while the food and beverage department loss after allocation is $1,353. Note that income taxes are not allocated to profit centers.

Exhibit C.6   Allocation of Costs–Direct Method

			Proportion to		Amounts Allocated to	
Expense to be Allocated	Amount to be Allocated	Allocation Base	Rooms	Food & Beverage	Rooms	Food & Beverage
Insurance	$ 3,000	BV-FA	.7500	.2500	$ 2,250	$ 750
Depreciation	18,000	SF	.7273	.2727	13,091	4,909
POM & UC	6,000	SF	.7273	.2727	4,364	1,636
Marketing	3,000	RS	.5000	.5000	1,500	1,500
A & G	12,000	NE	.4118	.5882	4,942	7,058
TOTAL	$42,000				$26,147	$15,853

Exhibit C.7   Fully Allocated Income Statement–Walters Motor Inn Direct Method–For the Month of March

	Rooms	Food & Beverage	Total
Revenue	$50,000	$50,000	$100,000
Cost of Sales	-0-	18,000	18,000
Payroll and Related Expenses	12,000	13,000	25,000
Other Direct Expenses	4,000	4,500	8,500
Total Expenses	16,000	35,500	51,500
Departmental Income	34,000	14,500	48,500
Allocated Expenses (from Exhibit C.6)	26,147	15,853	42,000
Departmental Income (Loss) after Allocation	$ 7,853	$ (1,353)	6,500
Income Taxes			2,000
Net Income			$ 4,500

Illustration of Step Method

The step method of allocation requires two steps:

1. Allocate fixed charges to service centers and profit centers, and

2. Allocate service center expenses to profit centers.

Following these steps, the fully allocated income statement is prepared.

The bases for allocating indirect expenses of the Walters Motor Inn were the same as used to illustrate allocation by the direct method. The difference under the step method is that part of the indirect expenses was first allocated to service centers. Thus, in determining the proportionate share of a base for each cost objective, one must consider both the amounts pertaining to profit centers and to service centers.

The two fixed charges to be allocated are insurance and depreciation. The ratios used to allocate these expenses were calculated as shown in Exhibit C.8. Using the ratios thus calculated, the fixed charges were allocated as shown in Exhibit C.9.

In Step 2, the service center expenses plus the fixed charges allocated to the service centers were allocated to the profit centers. A portion of these new totals was allocated directly to the profit centers with the remaining portion allocated in an established sequence to the service centers until all indirect expenses were allocated to the two profit centers.

Step 2 of the cost allocation of the Walters Motor Inn was accomplished by allocating Administrative and General expenses, Property Operation/Maintenance expenses, Utility Costs, and Marketing expenses. The order is specified on the basis of service centers serving the largest number of service centers.

The Administrative and General expenses to be allocated in Step 2 total $12,850—$12,000 from the unallocated income statement plus $850 of fixed charges allocated in Step 1. Using the number of employees as the allocation base, the $12,850 was allocated to the two remaining service centers, and two profit centers, as shown in Exhibit C.10.

Exhibit C.8

	Insurance		Depreciation	
Service and Profit Centers	BV-FA	Proportionate Share of BV-FA	Square Feet	Proportionate Share of Sq. Ft.
Rooms	$ 900,000	.6000	40,000	.6667
Food & Beverage	300,000	.2000	15,000	.2500
A & G	50,000	.0333	2,500	.0417
Marketing	30,000	.0200	500	.0083
POM & UC	220,000	.1467	2,000	.0333
TOTAL	$1,500,000	1.0000	60,000	1.0000

Exhibit C.9 Step 1: Allocation of Fixed Charges to Profit Centers and Service Centers

			Allocated to			
Fixed Charge	Total Amount	Rooms	F & B	A & G	Marketing	POM & UC
Insurance	$ 3,000	$ 1,800	$ 600	$100	$ 60	$ 440
Depreciation	18,000	12,000	4,500	750	150	600
TOTAL	$21,000	$13,800	$5,100	$850	$210	$1,040

Exhibit C.10

Department	Number of Employees	Proportioned Share of Total Employees	Amount Allocated
Rooms	14	.3889	$ 4,998
Food & Beverage	20	.5555	7,138
POM & UC	1	.0278	357
Marketing	1	.0278	357
TOTAL	36	1.0000	$ 12,850

Exhibit C.11

Department	Square Feet	Proportioned Share of Square Footage	Amount Allocated
Rooms	40,000	.7207	$ 5,331
Food & Beverage	15,000	.2703	1,999
Marketing	500	.0090	67
TOTAL	55,000	1.0000	$ 7,397

Exhibit C.12   Step 2: Allocation of Expenses from Service Centers to Profit Centers

	Service Centers			Profit Centers	
	A & G	POM & UC	Marketing	Rooms	Food & Beverage
Unallocated Service Center Costs	$ 12,000	$ 6,000	$ 3,000	$ -0-	$ -0-
Allocated per Step 1	850	1,040	210	13,800	5,100
Costs to Be Allocated	12,850	7,040	3,210		
A & G	(12,850)	357	357	4,998	7,138
	$ -0-	7,397			
POM & UC		(7,397)	67	5,331	1,999
		$ -0-	3,634		
Marketing			(3,634)	1,817	1,817
TOTAL			$ -0-	$ 25,946	$ 16,054

Property Operation/Maintenance and Utility Costs are allocated next under Step 2. The total to be allocated is $7,397. This is the sum of $6,000 from the unallocated income statement, $1,040 from Step 1, and $357 from Administrative and General. The total was allocated to the marketing department and the two profit centers on the basis of square footage. The proportionate share and amounts of Property Operation/ Maintenance and Utility Costs were calculated as shown in Exhibit C.11.

Lastly, the Marketing expense was allocated to the two profit centers on the basis of ratio to sales. Therefore, the total Marketing expense of $3,634 ($3,000 from the unallocated income statement, $210 from Step 1, $357 from Administrative and General, and $67 from Property Operation/Maintenance and Utility Costs) was allocated with $1,817 to the rooms and $1,817 to the food and beverage department. Exhibit C.12 shows the step down process (Step 2) of the step method.

Exhibit C.13   Fully Allocated Income Statement, Walters Motor Inn Step Method–For the Month of March

	Rooms	Food & Beverage	Total
Revenue	$50,000	$50,000	$100,000
Cost of Sales	-0-	18,000	18,000
Payroll and Related Expenses	12,000	13,000	25,000
Other Direct Expenses	4,000	4,500	8,500
Total Expenses	16,000	35,500	51,500
Departmental Income	34,000	14,500	48,500
Allocated Expenses (from Exhibit C.9)	25,946	16,054	42,000
Departmental Income (Loss) after Allocation	$ 8,054	$ (1,554)	6,500
Income Taxes			2,000
Net Income			$ 4.500

The fully allocated income statement under the step method of cost allocation is shown in Exhibit C.13. After cost allocation, the rooms department income is $8,054 while the food and beverage department shows a loss of $1,554.

Conclusion

The precision offered by the allocation procedures discussed and illustrated here increases from the direct to the step methods. So does the cost of preparation.

The decision to use a more sophisticated cost-allocation method must be made following a cost-benefit analysis. Hotel management must determine the value of the more precise information.

Cost allocation is an attention-getting tool. It should not lead to hasty decisions. The results raise a number of questions for management; among them:

■ What action should be taken if the departmental income after allocation is negative?

■ Should a department's services be curtailed if a loss is shown after a full allocation?

■ Should advertising for a department's services be increased if a loss is shown after full allocation?

Management decisions should be made only after careful cost-benefit analysis. Allocation of indirect costs allows management to make such decisions in a more informed and accurate manner.

ENDNOTES

CHAPTER 1

1. *Marriott 2020 Annual Report.* Retrieved from sec.gov.

2. *Trends in the Hotel Industry—USA Edition 2020* (Atlanta, GA: CBRE Hotels Research, 2020).

3. This text assumes that the reader has read an introductory accounting text or has access to one. *Hospitality Industry Financial Accounting*, 4th ed., by Raymond S. Schmidgall and James W. Damitio (Lansing, MI: American Hotel & Lodging Educational Institute, 2015) contains several chapters that provide detailed coverage of the concepts in this section. Another appropriate text is Raymond Cote's *Hotel and Restaurant Accounting*, 8th ed. (Lansing, MI: American Hotel & Lodging Educational Institute, 2019).

4. W. F. Edmonson, *A Code of Ethics: Do Corporate Executives and Employees Need It?* (Fulton, MS: Itawamba Community College Press, 1990).

5. Stephen S. J. Hall, *Ethics in Hospitality Management* (Lansing, MI: American Hotel & Lodging Educational Institute, 1992).

CHAPTER 2

1. *Uniform System of Accounts for the Lodging Industry*, 11th rev. ed. (Austin, TX: Hospitality Financial and Technology Professionals, 2014).

2. *Hilton Hotels Corporation 2020 Annual Report* and *2021 Annual Report*. Retrieved from sec.gov.

3. The detailed accounting for these items (capitalization, depreciation, amortization) is covered in Raymond S. Schmidgall and James W. Damitio, *Hospitality Industry Financial Accounting*, 4th ed. (Lansing, MI: American Hotel & Lodging Educational Institute, 2015).

CHAPTER 3

1. *Statement of Financial Accounting Standards #30, Reporting Comprehensive Income*, (Stamford, CT: FASB, 1997).

2. Uniform systems of accounts are available as follows:
Uniform System of Accounts for the Lodging Industry, 11th rev. ed. (Lansing, MI: American Hotel & Lodging Educational Institute, 2014). ©Hotel Association of New York City.
Uniform System of Financial Reporting for Clubs, 7th ed. (Washington, DC: Club Managers Association of America, 2012).
Uniform System of Accounts for Restaurants, 8th ed. (Washington, DC: National Restaurant Association, 2012).

3. *Trends in the Hotel Industry—US Edition 2020* (Atlanta: CBRE Hotels Research, 2020).

CHAPTER 5

1. This may be determined mathematically using the following formula:

$$\frac{CA - x}{CL - x} = \text{desired current ratio where } x \text{ indicates the amount of current assets that would be used to retire current liabilities. The calculation for the Grand Hotel is as follows:}$$

$$\frac{338,000 - x}{214,000 - x} = 2; \quad x = 90,000; \quad \frac{248,000}{124,000} = 2 \text{ times}$$

2. The interested student is referred to intermediate accounting texts, most of which contain a full discussion of EPS calculations in various situations.

3. Raymond S. Schmidgall, "Financial Ratios: Perceptions of Lodging Industry General Managers and Financial Executives," *FIU Hospitality Review*, Fall 1989, pp. 1–9.

4. As a note of caution, the research is based on perceptions of lodging general managers and financial controllers and does not necessarily reflect the actual views of corporate executives, owners, and bankers. Nonetheless, the great consistency of answers among all respondents suggests that this information is reliable.

CHAPTER 6

1. This basic equation is most useful for forecasting purposes and for budgeting purposes.

$$\frac{\text{Fixed Cost}}{\text{Element}} = \frac{(85,200)(58,636,800) - (26,000)(189,257,000)}{12(58,636,800) - (26,000)(26,000)}$$

$$= \$2,719.57 \text{ per month}$$

2. Garrison, R., Noreen, E., & Brewer, P. (2021). *Managerial Accounting* (17th ed.). New York: Irwin McGraw-Hill.

3. Vokurka, R., & Lummus, R. (2001). "At what overhead level does activity-based costing pay off?" *Production and Inventory Management Journal* 42(1), 40–47.

4. Raab, C., Mayer, K., & Shoemaker, S. (2010). "Menu engineering using activity-based costing: An exploratory study using a profit factor comparison approach." *Journal of Hospitality & Tourism Research* 34(2), 204–224. https://doi.org/10.1177/1096348009349823.

CHAPTER 7

1. Eisen, D., & Resco, L. (May 2020). *Analysis: At what occupancy rate can a hotel break-even?* Retrieved from https://www.hotstats.com/blog/analysis-at-what-occupancy-rate-can-a-hotel-break-even.

2. Younes, E., & Kett, R. (October 2003). *An investment driven breakeven analysis for hotels - ID.RevPAR & ID.GOPPAR: the investment driven RevPAR and GOPPAR.* Retrieved from https://www.hospitalitynet.org/news/4017398.html.

CHAPTER 8

1. Source: Chuck Day, inventory manager, Marriott International; and Jeffrey Beck, associate professor, The School of Hospitality Business, Michigan State University.

2. Based on terminology used in the *Uniform System of Accounts for Restaurants*, 8th ed. (Washington, D.C.: National Restaurant Association, 2012).

3. Michael L. Kasavana and Donald I. Smith, *Menu Engineering—A Practical Guide to Menu Analysis*, rev. ed. (Okemos, MI: Hospitality Publications Inc., 1990).

CHAPTER 9

1. *Marriott International Inc., 2020 Annual Report*, p. 4.

2. The reader interested in pursuing forecasting approaches shown in Exhibit 9.3 that are not discussed in this chapter should see Spyros G. Makridakis, Steven C. Wheelwright, and Rob J. Hyndman, *Forecasting: Methods and Applications*, 3rd ed. (New York: Wiley & Sons, 1997).

3. For more information, see Makridakis, et al.

4. Using this formula, a number between 0 and –1 is also possible. Such a result would indicate a negative relationship. In practical terms, a negative result is extremely unlikely in hospitality forecasting because the forecasting variables generally used are directly related.

5.
$$a = \frac{\sum x^2 \sum y - \sum x \sum xy}{n \sum x^2 - (\sum x)^2} \quad or \quad a = \frac{\sum y}{n} - \frac{b \sum x}{n}$$

$$b = \frac{n \sum xy - \sum x \sum y}{n \sum x^2 - (\sum x)^2}$$

6. The interested reader should see Makridakis, et al.

CHAPTER 10

1. A *service center* is a department outside the profit centers that provides services to the profit centers or the hotel as a whole—for example, the marketing department. A *cost center* is a department within a profit center for which costs are tracked—for example, housekeeping within the rooms department.

2. DeFranco, A., & Schmidgall, R. S. (2017). Cash budgets, controls, and management in clubs, *Journal of Hospitality Financial Management* 25(2), 112–122.

3. For more information on zero-base budgeting, see Peter A. Pyrrh, *Zero-Base Budgeting* (New York: Wiley & Sons, 1973), and Lee M. Kruel, "Zero-base budgeting of hotel indirect expense," *Cornell Hotel and Restaurant Administration Quarterly*, November 1978, pp. 11–14.

4. For more information on lodging feasibility studies, see William P. Andrew, James W. Damitio, and Raymond S. Schmidgall, *Financial Management for the Hospitality Industry* (Upper Saddle River, NJ: Pearson Prentice Hall, 2007), pp. 487–524.

5. Raymond S. Schmidgall and Jack D. Ninemeier, "Foodservice budgeting: How the chains do it," *Cornell Hotel and Restaurant Administration Quarterly*, February 1986, pp. 51–55; Schmidgall and Ninemeier, "Budgeting in hotel chains: Coordination and control," *Cornell Hotel and Restaurant Administration Quarterly*, May 1987, pp. 79–84.

CHAPTER 11

1. Tighe, D. (May 12, 2021). "Global e-commerce payment methods 2020 & 2024, by share of transaction volume," *Statista*. Retrieved from https://www.statista.com/statistics/1111233/payment-method-usage-transaction-volume-share-worldwide/.

2. Jones, J. (August 21, 2017). "Vegas visitors can now use their electronic wallet to pay hotel bills or buy show tickets, but not for gambling," *Los Angeles Times*. Retrieved from https://www.latimes.com/travel/deals/la-tr-las-vegas-electronic-wallet-hotels-20170817-story.html.

3. For more information, see Agnes L. DeFranco and Raymond S. Schmidgall, "Cash in hotels and clubs: 2020 and beyond," *Journal of Hospitality Financial Management* 28, no. 2: 116–127.

4. Ibid.

5. For a thorough discussion of this topic, see Ellis Knotts, "Handling the credit function at small hotels," *Lodging*, June 1979.

6. Alternatively, the effective interest rate can be calculated without using actual invoice amounts as follows:

$$\text{Effective Interest Rate} = \frac{\text{Percentage discount}}{100\% - \text{Percentage discount}} \times \frac{\text{Days in year}}{\text{Difference between end of discount period and final due day}}$$

7. Nypost.com/2014/01/26/unused-gift-cards-44b-since-2008-study/.

8. For a detailed discussion of integrated cash management systems for multiunit firms, see Laurent P. Caraux and A. Neal Geller, "Cash management: A total system approach for the hotel industry," *Cornell Hotel and Restaurant Administration Quarterly,* November 1977.

CHAPTER 12

1. *AH&LA Hotel Internal Control Guide* (Lansing, MI: American Hotel & Lodging Educational Institute, 1997).

2. A. Neal Geller, *Internal Control: A Fraud-Prevention Handbook for Hotel and Restaurant Managers* (Ithaca, NY: Cornell University Press, 1991).

3. *Uniform System of Financial Reporting for Clubs,* 7th ed. (Washington DC: Club Managers Association of America, 2012).

4. Committee on Auditing Procedure, *Internal Control—Elements of a Coordinated System and Its Importance to Management and the Independent Public Accountant* (New York: AICPA, 1949), p. 6.

5. *Hotel Internal Control Guide.*

6. For further discussion of internal auditing, see the *Hotel Internal Control Guide.*

7. "Statement of Responsibilities of the Internal Auditor," *The Internal Auditor,* September/October 1971, p. 12.

8. The reader interested in the detailed procedures of the credit function at hotels should consider an article by Ellis Knotts in *Lodging,* June 1979, titled "Handling the Credit Function at Small Hotels." This article covers credit extension, credit monitoring, and collection of hotel accounts receivable.

9. The reader interested in a detailed explanation of purchasing and receiving controls should read Chapter 6 of Jack D. Ninemeier's *Planning and Control for Food and Beverage Operations,* 8th ed. (Lansing, MI: American Hotel & Lodging Educational Institute, 2013).

10. Standardized flowcharting symbols help improve communication of details in an information system. Most flowcharting symbols were established by the United States of America Standards Institute. For information on the meaning of the different shapes used in a flowchart, see any standard flowcharting reference.

11. Thomas F. Blaney, "The Sarbanes-Oxley Act—How Does It Affect Clubs?" *The Bottomline,* April/May 2004, p. 24.

CHAPTER 13

1. *ISHC CapEx '18.* International Society of Hospitality Consultants and the Hospitality Asset Managers Association.

2. Raymond S. Schmidgall and James W. Damitio, "Hotels and Long-Term Investment," *The Bottomline,* August–September 1990.

3. James J. Eyster, Jr., and A. Neal Geller, "The Capital Investment Decision: Techniques Used in the Hospitality Industry," *The Cornell Hotel and Restaurant Administration Quarterly,* May 1981, pp. 69–73.

CHAPTER 14

1. The reader interested in studying management contracts is referred to James J. Eyster's *The Negotiation and Administration of Hotel and Restaurant Management Contracts,* 3rd ed. (Ithaca, N.Y.: School of Hotel Administration, Cornell University, 1988).

2. For more detail on this topic, see Pietrat Elgers and John J. Clark, *The Lease-Buy Decision* (New York: The Free Press, 1980) and T. M. Clarke, *Leasing* (London: McGraw-Hill, 1978).

3. FASB Financial Accounting Standard ASU 2016-02_Section A. https://www.fasb.org/page/document?pdf=ASU+2016-02_Section+A.pdf&title=Update%202016-02%E2%80%94Leases%20(Topic%20842)%20Section%20A%E2%80%94Leases:%20Amendments%20to%20the%20FASB%20Accounting%20Standards%20Codification%C2%AE. https://www.fasb.org/jsp/FASB/Document_C/DocumentPage?cid=1176167901010&acceptedDisclaimer=true.

4. Rhode, K. (2019). "Operating vs. finance leases: The impact of the new standard," *Accounting Today*. https://www.accountingtoday.com/opinion/operating-vs-finance-leases-how-businesses-are-impacted-under-the-new-standard.

CHAPTER 15

1. Letter to Jean Baptiste Le Roy, Nov. 13, 1789.

2. *Commissioner v. Newman* (CA-2), 47-1 USTC 99175, 159 Fed.(2d) 848.

3. Albert J. Gomes, *Hospitality in Transition* (New York: American Hotel & Lodging Association, 1985).

INDEX

forecasting, 371
    price elasticity of, 359–361
departmental income, 106–107
departmental profit or loss, 102
departmental statements, 92, 104–106
depreciation, 58, 104, 609
    accelerated, 58, 697–698
detective controls, 578
differential costs, 284
digital payments, 517
direct costs, 279
direct expenses, 98–99, 101–102
direct method, 146–148
disbursement float, 517
disclosure, types of, 14
discontinued operations, 93
discounting room rates, 368–370
discount rate, 605
discretionary fixed costs, 267
distribution chain, 7, 9
dividends, 26, 51, 503
double occupancy, 216–217
double taxation, 689, 696
dynamic pricing, 370–374

E

earnings, retained, 24, 58
earnings per share (EPS), 222–223
EBITDA (earnings before interest,
    taxes, depreciation, and
    amortization), 104, 218
EBITDA margin ratio, 219
EBITDA per available room, 220
econometrics, 409
economic decisions, tax
    considerations in, 676
effective cost, 503
effective interest rate, 503, 521–522
efficiency variances, 473, 474
elastic demand, 359
embezzlement, 548–549
equipment
    operating, 55, 57
    property and, 27, 56–57
equity
    owners,' 20, 52, 58–59, 61
    return on, 205, 221, 222
ethical codes, 28, 555, 578
ethics, 28
executory costs, 641
expenditures
    capital, 600–601
    revenue, 600
expenses, 93
    administrative and general,
      103
    budgeting, 454–455
    direct, 98–99, 101–102
    estimating, 454–455

interest, 104, 455–456
labor, 98, 102, 472–475, 476
nonoperating, 103–104, 218
operating, 98–99
preopening, 698
prepaid, 55
undistributed, 102–103
explicit forecasts, 404
exponential smoothing, 411–412
external auditing, 572–575
extraordinary gains and losses, 93

F

failure of conscience, in fraud and
    embezzlement, 549
fair market value, 642
FCPA. *See* Foreign Corrupt Practices
    Act
finance leases, 642, 643, 647–650
financial accounting, 19
Financial Accounting Standards Board
    (FASB), 12, 13, 14, 142, 641
financial audit, 20
financial leverage, 205, 206
financial ratios. *See* ratio(s)
financial statements
    balance sheet, 48–89
    consolidated, 63
    footnotes, 59, 62–63, 96
    income statement, 90–139
    preparation of, 24
    statement of cash flows,
      140–189
financing activities, 144, 145
    net cash flows from, 154–155
first-year losses, 698
fixed assets, 9, 13, 16
    depreciation of, 104
    internal control of, 568
    sale of, 103–104
fixed charge coverage ratio, 208
fixed charges, 455–456
fixed costs, 267–268, 315
    capacity, 267
    discretionary, 267
    vs. variable, 278–279
flexible budgets, 460–462
flex ratio, 234–235
float, 517
flowcharts, 569, 570
flow through ratio, 232–234
fluctuation explanation, 65
food cost percentage, 195, 231
food costs, 571
food sales mix, 376–378
foodservice operations, 5
footnotes, 59, 62–63, 96
forecasting, 402–444
    cases, 418–427

causal approaches, 408,
    412–414
in club industry, 418–419
data patterns, 407–408
exponential smoothing,
    411–412
in hospitality industry, 405
implicit vs. explicit, 404
labor, 420–423
method selection, 415–416
moving averages, 410–411
naïve method, 409–410
nature of, 406–407
overview of, 408–415
personnel responsible for,
    405–406
qualitative, 408, 409, 415
quantitative, 408, 409–415
regression analysis, 412–414
revenue, 452–454
short-term, 415–418
time series approaches, 408,
    409
Foreign Corrupt Practices Act (FCPA),
    552, 573
Form 1040, 678, 679, 682–683, 684,
    693–695
franchise costs, 57
fraud, 548–549
full disclosure principle, 14, 59, 62
fundamental accounting equation,
    20–21
future value, 603–607, 610

G

gains, 93
General Data Protection Regulation
    (GDPR), 572
general journal, 22
generally accepted accounting
    principles (GAAP), 12–19, 27
general partners, 26, 27, 687
gift card accounting, 522–525
gift card breakage, 523
Global Data Protection Regulation
    (GDPR), 517
going-concern principle, 13
goods used internally, 101–102
goodwill, 57
graphs, profit-volume, 327–328
gross margin, 377–378
gross operating profit (GOP), 99, 103
    margin ratio, 218–219
    per available room (GOPAR),
      219
gross profit, 376–379
gross return on assets (GROA),
    220–221

sales volume, costs in relation to, 267–272
Sarbanes-Oxley Act, 552, 572–575
scatter diagram, 274–275
SCF. *See* statement of cash flows
Schedule C, 693
Schedule I, 694–695
schedules, 104–106
S corporations, 26, 27, 689, 691, 696
seasonality, 5–7, 8
seasonal pattern, 407–408
seat turnover, 217
Securities Acts, 552
security deposits, 57
segregation of duties, 556, 558, 563
sensitivity analysis, 320–321
short distribution time, 7, 9
short-term
    debt, 526–527
    forecasting, 415–418
    investments, 54
significance criteria, 467–468
single allocation base approach (SABA), 280–281
size, 507
small operations, internal control in, 575–577
smart devices, 571
smoothing, 409, 411–412
smoothing constant, 411
sole proprietorship, 26, 27, 59, 678, 685–686, 696
solvency ratios, 196, 205–210
sound practices, for internal control, 555
SOX. *See* Sarbanes-Oxley Act
specialized journals, 22
standard costs, 287
standards
    international, 27
    ratio, 193–194
statement of cash flows (SCF), 140–189
    analysis, 163–164
    classification of cash flows, 144–146
    comprehensive illustration of, 156–163
    format of, 146
    preparation of, 148–156
    purpose of, 142–144
    in relation to other financial statements, 143–144
state taxes, 699
step costs, 269
stock
    capital, 58
    common, 58
    preferred, 58
    treasury, 58
straight-line depreciation, 58
strategic planning, 449

summary
    income statements, 94, 101–102
    operating statements, 99, 100
sunk costs, 286

T

taxable income, 679–680
    vs. accounting income, 697–699
tax accounting, 19
Tax Cut and Job Act (TCJA), 677
tax(es)
    accounting methods and, 692–697
    alternative minimum, 677, 680
    avoidance, 683, 685
    basics of, 678–683
    business organization form and, 685–689
    credits, 680
    deductions, 679–680, 684
    evasion, 685
    income, 325–327, 674–716
    minimizing, 689–692
    municipal, 699
    property, 103, 699–700
    state, 699
technology
    expenses, 103
    in internal control, 571–572
temporary accounts, 20
theft, in hospitality industry, 549–550
time, 507, 603
time series approaches, 408, 409
times interest earned, 654
time span, 7, 9
time value of money, 602–607
total capitalization, 207
total costs, 271–272
total revenue per available customer (TRevPAC), 230
total revenue per available room (TRevPAR), 229
trade credit, 521
trade payables, 521
transaction motive, 503
transient hotels, 7
treasury stock, 58
trend pattern, 407
trial-and-error pricing, 361
trial balance, 21, 23, 24
triple-net lease, 641
turnover, 195
    asset, 213
    inventory, 210–212
    property and equipment, 212–213
    seat, 217

U

undistributed operating expenses, 102–103
Uniform System of Accounts and Expense Dictionary for Small Hotels, Motels, and Motor Hotels (USASH), 96
Uniform System of Accounts for Hotels (USAH), 96
Uniform System of Accounts for Restaurants (USAR), 113–114
Uniform System of Accounts for the Lodging Industry (USALI), 96, 98, 99
Uniform System of Financial Reporting for Clubs (USFRC), 115–116
uniform systems of accounts, 11, 96–98
unit elastic, 359
unit of measurement principle, 13–14
unsecured bank loans, 526–527
utilities, 103, 571

V

vacation policy, mandatory, 555
variable costs, 268, 315
    vs. fixed, 278–279
variable labor expense, 476
variable labor variance analysis, 472–475
variable leases, 638–639
variance analysis, 468–478
    cost of goods sold, 470–472
    example, 475–477
    revenue, 468–470
    variable labor, 472–475
variances, budgetary, 463–478
vertical analysis, 65–67, 110–112
void transactions, 572
volume variances, 470, 471, 473, 474
voucher system, 566

W

web-based menus, 363
weighted average contribution margin ratio, 321–323
Wendy's, 420–423
working capital, 56
    management of, 518–519
    turnover ratio, 204–205
work orders, 568

Z

zero-based budgeting (ZBB), 455